W9-BLP-474

Reading for Thinking

Seventh Edition

Laraine Flemming

Denice Josten
St. Louis Community College
Contributing Consultant

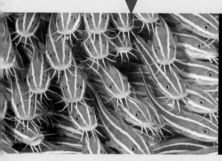 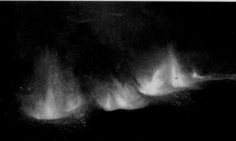 

WADSWORTH
CENGAGE Learning™

Australia • Brazil • Japan • Korea • Mexico • Singapore • Spain • United Kingdom • United States

WADSWORTH
CENGAGE Learning™

Reading for Thinking, **Seventh Edition**
Laraine Flemming

Publisher: Lyn Uhl

Director of Developmental English
and College Success: Annie Todd

Development Editor: Kathy Sands-Boehmer

Assistant Editor: Melanie Opacki

Editorial Assistant: Matt Conte

Media Editor: Amy Gibbons

Marketing Manager: Kirsten Stoller

Marketing Coordinator: Ryan Ahern

Marketing Communications Manager:
Courtney Morris

Content Project Manager: Rosemary Winfield

Art Director: Jill Ort

Print Buyer: Susan Spencer

Rights Acquisition Specialists: Katie Huha,
Jennifer Meyer Dare

Production Service: Books By Design, Inc.

Text Designer: Books By Design, Inc.

Cover Designer: Roycroft Design

Cover Image: Getty Images

Compositor: S4Carlisle Publishing Services

© 2012, 2009, 2006 Wadsworth, Cengage Learning

Title page photos: (left) Image Source/Jupiter Images; (middle)
© Arctic-Images/Corbis; (right) © Ulrich Flemming

Text credits appear on page 684, which constitutes an extension of the
copyright page.

ALL RIGHTS RESERVED. No part of this work covered by the copyright
herein may be reproduced, transmitted, stored, or used in any form or by
any means graphic, electronic, or mechanical, including but not limited to
photocopying, recording, scanning, digitizing, taping, Web distribution,
information networks, or information storage and retrieval systems, except
as permitted under Section 107 or 108 of the 1976 United States Copyright
Act, without the prior written permission of the publisher.

For product information and technology assistance, contact us at
Cengage Learning Customer & Sales Support, 1-800-354-9706.

For permission to use material from this text or product,
submit all requests online at **www.cengage.com/permissions.**
Further permissions questions can be emailed to
permissionrequest@cengage.com.

Library of Congress Control Number: 2010933764

Student Edition:
ISBN-13: 978-0-495-90639-1
ISBN-10: 0-495-90639-5

Wadsworth
20 Channel Center Street
Boston, MA 02210
USA

Cengage Learning is a leading provider of customized learning solutions with
office locations around the globe, including Singapore, the United Kingdom,
Australia, Mexico, Brazil and Japan. Locate your local office at
international.cengage.com/region.

Cengage Learning products are represented in Canada by
Nelson Education, Ltd.

For your course and learning solutions, visit **www.cengage.com.**

Purchase any of our products at your local college store or at our preferred
online store **www.cengagebrain.com.**

Printed in the United States of America
2 3 4 5 6 7 14 13 12 11

Contents

GASTON
217-719-0773

Copyright © Cengage Learning. All rights reserved.

Copyright © Cengage Learning. All rights reserved.

4 Identifying and Learning from Organizational Patterns 175

Copyright © Cengage Learning. All rights reserved.

5 Understanding, Outlining, and Summarizing Longer Readings 247

Reviewing with Longer Readings 312

Copyright © Cengage Learning. All rights reserved.

Copyright © Cengage Learning. All rights reserved.

Copyright © Cengage Learning. All rights reserved.

Copyright © Cengage Learning. All rights reserved.

Preface

Thanks to the terrific reviewers who inspired this edition of *Reading for Thinking*, I am happy to say that the Seventh Edition has many new features, all of which should benefit both teachers and students. Before describing those new features, however, I want to emphasize that several key aspects of the book remain unchanged.

The Seventh Edition of *Reading for Thinking*, the most advanced text in my three-book series, still assumes that critical reading is not something completely separate from comprehension. As in previous editions, students learn how to expand their idea of comprehension until it includes recognizing purpose; determining tone; and evaluating evidence, logic, and bias.

Unchanged as well is the book's emphasis on engaging and stimulating readings. Over one-third of the readings are new. But as before, these reading selections have been carefully chosen to fit the underlying premise of all my books: The more interesting the material, the easier it is to motivate reluctant readers.

The skills coverage in *Reading for Thinking* remains as comprehensive as ever. The book opens with the basics of focus and concentration and progresses to identifying main ideas, supporting details, and organizational patterns. By the final chapter, students are evaluating arguments and looking for evidence of excessive bias.

As in earlier editions, the Seventh Edition carefully models every thinking and reading strategy introduced while providing numerous exercises and tests for review. It also employs the same easy-to-grasp, step-by-step approach that previous users have applauded.

New Features in the Seventh Edition

Having summarized what's the same in this edition let me now point out what's brand new.

New Vocabulary Exercises and Tests in Every Chapter

Word Check is a new match-word-with-meaning exercise that reviews all the vocabulary words defined in a chapter's footnotes. *Word Check* is followed by a second new exercise called *More About Form and Meaning*, which asks students to use new words in sentences. As an added bonus, the sentences themselves were carefully constructed to reveal more about the nuances and context of each new word. With the exception of Chapter 1, **Acquiring the Keys to Academic Success**, every chapter now includes tests of new vocabulary.

Linking Vocabulary and Background Knowledge

The end-of-chapter vocabulary tests intentionally use passages focusing on famous historical figures and cultural events. Thus while students are filling in the blanks with newly learned vocabulary, they are also picking up background knowledge about topics such as Charles Darwin's theory of natural selection, the stock market crash of 1929, consumer advocate Ralph Nader's famous attack on the auto industry, and the worldwide controversy aroused by the execution of accused spies Julius and Ethel Rosenberg.

Expanded Discussion of Reading on the Web

Whether they are taking online courses or researching an idea for a term paper, students are doing more and more reading on the Web. Unfortunately, much research suggests that they haven't yet developed many strategies for managing the flood of information that comes up on the screen after they type in a search term. For that reason, this edition has expanded its original discussion of reading on the Web to cover a number of topics critical to making Web use as efficient as possible. Chapter 1, **Acquiring the Keys to Academic Success**, offers revised and expanded explanations of how to construct relevant search terms, evaluate websites, and control the distractions that come with hypertext.

New Web Exercises in Every Chapter

Every chapter includes Web-based assignments, which test students' ability to develop relevant searches. Equally important, these assignments foster sustained thought by asking students to apply or interpret what they have learned on the Web. The assignments were designed to challenge the media-driven notion that reading on the Web diminishes the ability to concentrate. On the contrary, the right assignments can encourage students to think longer thoughts and enhance their ability to concentrate.

Copyright © Cengage Learning. All rights reserved.

New Chapter on Synthesizing Sources

Synthesizing is an essential academic skill that rarely gets enough attention. In this edition of *Reading for Thinking*, however, it gets an entire chapter. Chapter 7, **Synthesizing Sources,** teaches specific strategies for analyzing and making connections among several sources that cover the same topic but not always from the same perspective. The chapter opens with short snippets, progresses to longer paragraphs, and ends with brief, multiparagraph readings. The careful step-by-step sequence encourages mastery of a reading and writing skill that can, initially at least, seem intimidating to student readers.

More Attention to Connections Between Individual Sentences

Experienced readers mentally track the chains of repetition and reference writers use to make their sentences cohere and build meaning. Readers less familiar with words in print, however, often miss the linguistic and content links writers provide. These readers need more practice tracking the connections between and among sentences. The Seventh Edition provides that practice in the ongoing feature *Taking a Closer Look.* Each box bearing this title asks questions about sentence relationships, encouraging students to think more closely about how one sentence relates to another.

More on Paraphrasing

This edition of *Reading for Thinking* covers paraphrasing in greater depth. As before, students learn the difference between reading and writing paraphrases. They also get more chances to practice both, following a revised and very concrete explanation of how to paraphrase step by step.

New Explanation and Exercises for Summarizing

Because summarizing is central to both comprehension and critical reading, the Seventh Edition offers an expanded discussion of summary writing. There are newly revised pointers on how to summarize both paragraphs and longer readings, along with more models for illustration and more exercises for practice.

Copyright © Cengage Learning. All rights reserved.

A New Format

Reading for Thinking has a new two-part structure. Chapters 1 through 5 review comprehension skills and learning strategies. Following Chapter 5, **Understanding, Outlining, and Summarizing Longer Readings**, are four multiparagraph selections, covering issues like what current research says about the effectiveness of multitasking and what happens when a town council uses eminent domain to take private property. With the help of the readings and their accompanying questions, students can review all the skills and strategies introduced in the first five chapters.

Another set of four, multiparagraph readings follows the book's final chapter, **Analyzing Arguments**. These readings cover topics like the effect of heavy technology use on human empathy and the unintended consequences of a tax rebellion. The questions accompanying the readings review both comprehension *and* critical reading skills. Each of the eight new readings also includes a writing assignment, a drawing conclusions question, and an Internet follow-up activity.

More Simplified Approach to Analyzing Arguments

In this edition, Chapter 10, **Analyzing Arguments**, offers six different models of how writers typically introduce the point of an argument. At times they start with a traditional perspective on a topic and then challenge that conventional approach, making the challenge the core of their argument. Or almost as frequently, they predict the negative consequences that will arise if some specific action isn't taken soon. This template-based explanation underscores an overarching theme of *Reading for Thinking*: Readers need to be familiar with, look for, and make predictions based on written cues.

More Follow Up with Writing

Some discussions of reading skills—explanations of how recognizing organizational patterns can improve comprehension come to mind— readily lend themselves to follow-up writing assignments. Thus this edition includes writing assignments meant to sharpen students' understanding of what reading entails. For instance, to better understand what goes into suggesting purpose and creating tone, students read a cool, strictly factual account of animal neglect and are asked to rewrite it to express a persuasive purpose, revealed mainly through their choice of tone.

Copyright © Cengage Learning. All rights reserved.

More Illustrations of Textbook Bias

Students tend to think that textbooks are devoid of any point of view or bias. But as many of the selections included in the Seventh Edition show, textbook authors are not always one hundred percent neutral about their subjects. An author's choice of detail and language frequently reflects a specific point of view on a subject or even a bias in favor of one particular position or perspective. There's nothing wrong with that. Students just need to be aware that their textbooks may offer some opinion mixed with what are otherwise factual descriptions of people and events. This edition of *Reading for Thinking* does a thorough job of raising that awareness.

Many New Reading Selections

Choosing the right reading selections is an important part of any revision. It certainly was a big part of this one. All of the readings were chosen because of their high interest level and wide range of topics. Along with many others, there are new readings on the courageous performance of dogs in wartime, the search capabilities of Google, and the alleged lack of empathy among those born after 1980.

New Allusion Alerts

The Sixth Edition already included explanations and exercises related to common allusions. The Seventh Edition continues that tradition but with a revised selection of allusions. The goal of the revision was to focus on allusions students are likely to encounter, in and out of textbooks— for example, "the Gilded Age," "meeting one's Waterloo," and "invisible hand of the market."

Additional Resources

Aplia for Reading for Thinking™: Engage, Prepare, Educate

Harness the power of Aplia's innovative, easy-to-use technology matched with the tone, language, level, and structure you'll find in *Reading for Thinking* to give your students a seamless, interactive learning experience. Aplia's developmental reading solution ensures that students stay on top of their coursework with regularly scheduled assignments and interactive learning tools. Founded by a professor to enhance his own courses, Aplia provides automatically graded coursework with detailed,

Copyright © Cengage Learning. All rights reserved.

immediate feedback on every question, as well as innovative teaching materials. Our easy-to-use system has been used by more than 1,000,000 students at over 1,200 institutions. Aplia uses a wealth of teaching tools to motivate students to become stronger readers:

- Aplia's Student Engagement Page integrates multimedia content, compelling readings, and interactive problems to heighten student interest.
- In-context vocabulary features new and challenging words with auditory reinforcement.
- Interactive assignments offer students immediate, detailed explanations for every answer.

For more information, please visit www.aplia.com/developmentalreading.

Reading CourseMate

 CourseMate

Reading for Thinking, Seventh Edition, includes Reading CourseMate, a complement to your textbook. Reading CourseMate includes

- an interactive eBook
- chapter from a history textbook with accompanying set of questions
- interactive teaching and learning tools, including:
  — quizzes
  — flash cards
  — videos tied to the chapter content
  — timed reading practice
- Engagement Tracker, a first-of-its-kind tool that monitors student engagement in the course

Go to www.cengagebrain.com to access these resources, and look for this icon ⊕, which denotes a resource available within CourseMate.

PowerLecture with ExamView

Organized around topics covered in the book, this easy-to-use tool helps you assemble, edit, and present tailored multimedia lectures. You can create a lecture from scratch, customize the provided templates, or use the ready-made Microsoft PowerPoint slides as they are. The CD-ROM also includes the Instructor's Resource Manual, and Web links.

Instructor's Resource Manual

This manual includes answer keys, a sample syllabus, additional quizzes, and more!

Copyright © Cengage Learning. All rights reserved.

New Sample E-book Chapter

The e-chapter allows for practice of all the skills introduced in Chapter 1 and is available at www.cengagebrain.com.

Chapter-Specific PowerPoints for Every Chapter

More than just a recap of key points, these PowerPoints provide instruction in concepts and skills.

Acknowledgments

As I indicated at the opening of this preface, the reviewers for this edition were extremely important, and their comments and suggestions were invaluable. Many thanks to Jesus Adame, El Paso Community College; Kathy Barker, Grays Harbor College; Frances Boffo, St. Philips College; Nora J. Dawkins, Miami Dade College, North; Lynetta L. Doye, Pulaski Technical College; Danica Hubbard, College of Dupage; Judith B. Isonhood, Hinds Community College; Denice Josten, St. Louis Community College at Forest Park; Mark Knockermus, Northeastern Technical College; Geraldine L. S. Levitre, Community College of Rhode Island; Laura McCullough, Vance Granville Community College; Myra M. Medina, Miami Dade College; Gustavo Monje, Northern Virginia Community College; Sandra Nelson, San Juan College; Bernard L. Ngovo, Pima Community College; Margaret J. Terrell, Columbus Technical College; Jenni Wessel-Fields, Black Hawk College; and Barbara Dean Wolfe, Hillyer College, University of Hartford.

And to the list of people instrumental in producing this edition, I have to add my editor Annie Todd, whose brains, warmth, and wit make her the gold standard for editors everywhere; my manuscript editor, Kathy Sands-Boehmer, who pored over the first draft with me, making numerous useful suggestions; and my marketing manager, the indefatigable Kirsten Stoller, whose unstinting support and enthusiasm for my books has left me awed and grateful. Thanks go as well to Nancy Benjamin at Books By Design, who for many years now has made sure that I always put my best foot forward in print. The same goes for my friend and editor Mary Schnabel, who reads every single word I write and catches everything I miss. And finally, to Ulrich Flemming, whose drawings and photos have long been a stellar addition to all my books. This edition of *Reading for Thinking* is no exception.

Laraine Flemming

Copyright © Cengage Learning. All rights reserved.

Acquiring the Keys to Academic Success

© Phil Schermeister/Corbis

IN THIS CHAPTER, YOU WILL LEARN

- how to use a five-step method for completing textbook assignments.
- how annotating and underlining aid both comprehension and memory.
- why paraphrasing and summarizing while reading are critical to academic success.
- how to use the World Wide Web to prepare for textbook assignments.

> *"You don't understand anything*
> *until you learn it more than one way."*
>
> —Marvin Minsky, computer scientist

By the time you finish this textbook, you'll possess all the reading and learning strategies you need to succeed in college. However, like most of us, you probably don't want to wait that long. The good news is that you can see quick results by consistently putting into practice all the learning techniques and study habits introduced in Chapter 1. Start using them now and refine them as you go along.

Make Sure You Have a Study Method for Completing Textbook Assignments

If you are reading a novel purely for your own pleasure, it's fine to just open the book and start reading. You don't need to make an effort to focus or distribute your attention selectively. But if you do the same thing with a textbook assignment, it's easy to pay too much attention to the details that don't matter and miss the ones that do. Effective textbook reading requires a method.

SQ3R Is Worth the Effort

One of the most popular and time-tested methods for study reading was created by psychology instructor Francis Robinson. The method is called SQ3R, and it reflects Robinson's understanding of the human mind. Robinson knew, for instance, that we tend to forget new information right after learning it. For that reason, SQ3R includes a recall step right after reading.

Robinson also knew that good reading comprehension relies heavily on the mind's ability to make and confirm predictions about how an author's thoughts are going to unfold. Thus, SQ3R starts by giving readers a basis for making predictions. Those predictions are then confirmed or contradicted through the actual reading of the text.

Since Robinson created SQ3R, other systems have come along, most of them quite similar and distinguished only by the acronym,[†] or the initials used to create the name. If you are familiar with one of those

---

[†]Others you might consider are PQRST (Preview, Question, Read, Summarize, Test) and REAP (Read, Encode, Annotate, Ponder). I suggest trying two or three different methods and figure out which one suits you best.

Copyright © Cengage Learning. All rights reserved.

systems and feel that it works, then, by all means, continue to use it. But if you don't already have a method for reading textbooks and tend to read textbooks the same way you might read an article in *USA Today*, then consider learning, adapting, and applying the following steps in SQ3R.

S: Survey

A quick overview orients the reader and allows him to comprehend at least partially what is to come.
—Francis Robinson, *Effective Study*[†]

To survey, or preview, a chapter, take a few minutes—ten or fifteen—to get an overview of the chapter's contents and organization. Although exactly what elements of the chapter you look at during a survey will vary with the textbook format, you should always read any portions of text titled *introduction, summary,* or *review.* Then skim the remaining pages, looking for the kinds of clues to significance listed in the following box.

Textbook Clues to Significance
◆

1. Major and minor headings
2. Marginal notes and vocabulary definitions
3. Questions appearing between or opening chapter sections
4. Pictures, cartoons, graphs, tables, and charts, including the captions
5. Words printed in boldface, colored ink, or italics
6. Icons, or symbols, used to highlight information in the text
7. Boxed statements or lists

A Note on Being a Flexible Reader

Experienced readers are flexible readers. They know, that is, that one reading strategy does not fit all texts. Thus they are always ready to try something different if their first approach doesn't produce results. This principle applies to all aspects of reading, including surveying.

For example, if you've read the introduction and summary page and glanced at all the possible clues listed above, yet still have no idea what direction the chapter will take, read the opening sentence of every paragraph. Still struggling? Then read the first and last sentence of every paragraph.

[†]All quotations attributed to Robinson in this section come from the fourth edition of Robinson's book, *Effective Study,* published by Harper and Row in 1961.

Copyright © Cengage Learning. All rights reserved.

Q: Question

The use of a question at the beginning of each section gives . . . a core idea around which to organize the material which follows.[†]
—Francis Robinson

Raising and answering questions while you read will help you stay motivated. Each time you can answer a question, you'll feel a sense of accomplishment. You are also likely to zero in more quickly on the most important elements of the chapter section. But there is an additional bonus as well.

Posing questions based on the headings, illustrations, and visual aids can help you distribute your attention while you read. That's because the purpose of headings, illustrations, and visual aids is to highlight and emphasize key information. Guided by them, you are bound to focus on what the author considered important.

Take, for instance, this picture of Thomas J. "Stonewall" Jackson, which appears in an American history book. Based on the caption, you might well ask the question: What made this man a hero?

Thomas J. "Stonewall" Jackson was widely viewed as the hero who saved the South in the Battle of Bull Run.

© The Corcoran Gallery of Art/Corbis

[†]Robinson's method, if consistently applied, can really boost your comprehension, but no one would ever claim he was a stylish writer.

Copyright © Cengage Learning. All rights reserved.

Now read to find the answer:

In the first Battle of Bull Run,[†] Union soldiers were met by a Confederate force of 22,000 under the command of General Beauregard, recently arrived from Charleston. The Union general, McDowell, attacked immediately, guessing the Confederate left flank to be the weakest point in the line. Although McDowell's troops were shocked by the ferocity of the musket fire that greeted them, they almost cracked the southern line. Had it cracked, the war might have been over in the upper South. At the critical moment, however, 9,000 Virginians commanded by Joseph E. Johnston arrived on the field after a frantic train ride from the Shenandoah Valley. A brigade under the command of Thomas J. Jackson, a 37-year-old mathematics instructor at Virginia Military, shored up the sagging Confederate left. The Union soldiers fell back and broke in hysteria, fleeing for Washington. (Adapted from Conlin, *The American Past*, p. 370.)

The caption accompanying the picture identified Jackson as a hero because he helped turn the tide in the first Battle of Bull Run. A reader not armed with a question based on the caption might have missed how important Jackson was to the South during the Civil War. In contrast, readers who had focused their attention using a question based on the caption would never have missed Jackson's importance.

R-1: Read

As soon as you start reading your assignment, see if the opening sentences give you a sense of the overall point or main idea the author intends to develop. Then read to confirm or revise your prediction. For instance, here is the opening sentence of a textbook selection about marriage. What does this sentence suggest?

In the discussion of the status and vitality of marriage, we often hear that a retreat from marriage has taken place in the United States in recent decades. (Strong et al., *The Marriage and Family Experience*, p. 324.)

The sentence suggests that the author is going to challenge what "we often hear." It suggests that interpretation because that's what writers frequently do after telling readers that some idea has been oft-repeated. The writers then go on to challenge what they just said. Here's that

[†]There were two battles at the same location, a stream known as Bull Run. In the South, the battles were called the battles of Manassas, a town in Virginia.

Copyright © Cengage Learning. All rights reserved.

opening sentence again, along with the rest of the paragraph. Note how the author switches gears by sentence 3 and fulfills the expectations created by sentence 1:

> [1]In the discussion of the status and vitality of marriage, we often hear that a retreat from marriage has taken place in the United States in recent decades [2]R. S. Oropesa and Nancy Landale (2004) describe the retreat from marriage as evident in a number of recent and ongoing trends: "historic" delays in the age at which women and men first marry, nearly "unprecedented" proportions of the population never marrying, "dramatic" increases in cohabitation and nonmarital births and continued high divorce rates. [3]Yet closer inspection indicates that the retreat from marriage has not occurred among all social groups. [4]Instead both racial and economic differences can be identified.

Note how the expectations created by the first sentence are fulfilled in sentence 3 and even more so in sentence 4.

Keep in mind, too, that your predictions can be wrong and still be useful. That's because you will be focused on the text and attuned to any statements that confirm or force you to revise your initial thoughts. Confirming or revising your predictions will give you the focused concentration that textbook reading requires.

Reading in Chunks

In addition to looking for clues that help you shape your expectations of what's to come, remember to break your assignments into manageable pieces. Don't assume you are going to read the entire chapter in a sitting. Instead plan on reading ten or fifteen pages per study session.

R-2: Recall

When Robinson first devised the SQ3R system, the second *R* meant *Recite*. Robinson's thought was that whenever students finished a chapter section, they should look away from the book and briefly recite answers to the questions they had posed initially. Robinson saw recitation as a way of monitoring, or checking, comprehension so that students couldn't trick themselves into thinking they had understood a passage they actually needed to read a second time.

Because Robinson himself was inclined to modify this step, suggesting, for instance, that students write out the answers in order to clarify

Copyright © Cengage Learning. All rights reserved.

fuzzy thinking, more modern versions of SQ3R have broadened the meaning of the second *R*, which now almost always means *Recall*.

Given the substitution of the more general term, there are a number of different ways to fulfill this step. You can look away from the text and see if you can recite the key points in the passage, as Robinson suggested. You can also write out answers to your original questions or even ask a friend or roommate to prompt you with a few key words while you respond with the ideas linked to those words. Whatever method you choose, see how much you can recall from what you've just read. If it turns out you can recall very little, then mark the chapter section for a second reading.

R-3: Review

After you finish reading the entire chapter, take a few minutes to review everything you have read. You can, for instance, list the headings and jot down a few key points about each one. You can also ask a friend or your roommate to pose questions based on the heading and then you can answer the questions. Consider as well making a concept map or an informal outline. On the following page, for example, is a concept map based on the reading that appears on pages 9–12.[†]

CHECK YOUR UNDERSTANDING

Monitor your comprehension of this chapter section by answering the following questions.

1. *True* or *False*. The Survey step in SQ3R requires you to skim the entire chapter from beginning to end.

2. *True* or *False*. The questions you pose as part of SQ3R should all be brief ones that require only a yes or no answer.

3. *True* or *False*. Textbook reading assignments should usually be completed in one sitting.

4. *True* or *False*. The only way to complete the second *R* in SQ3R is to recite aloud the key points of each chapter section.

5. *True* or *False*. There is no set way to review a chapter once you complete it. The method of review changes with the student and the material.

[†]Thanks for the concept map go to Professor Pat Domenico from Community College of Rhode Island.

Copyright © Cengage Learning. All rights reserved.

SQ3R Review—Concept Map

```
                        ┌─────────────────────┐
                        │   Nisei and Issei   │
                        └─────────────────────┘
              ┌──────────────────────┴───────────────────────┐
      ┌───────────────┐                              ┌───────────────┐
      │     Nisei     │                              │     Issei     │
      └───────────────┘                              └───────────────┘
              │                                              │
┌─────────────────────────┐                  ┌─────────────────────────┐
│ Second-generation        │                  │  Immigrants from Japan. │
│ Japanese, born in        │                  └─────────────────────────┘
│ Hawaii, U.S. citizens.   │                              │
└─────────────────────────┘                  ┌─────────────────────────┐
              │                                │  Strong desire to       │
┌─────────────────────────┐                  │  prove loyalty to U.S.  │
│ Largest ethnic group:    │                  └─────────────────────────┘
│ 1/3 of population.       │
└─────────────────────────┘
              │
┌─────────────────────────┐
│ Attack on Pearl Harbor   │
│ raised fear of sabotage  │
│ and espionage by         │
│ Hawaiians of             │
│ Japanese descent.        │
└─────────────────────────┘
              │
┌─────────────────────────┐
│ But official military    │
│ and administrative       │
│ policy maintained        │
│ traditional interracial  │
│ harmony.                 │
└─────────────────────────┘
              │
┌─────────────────────────┐
│   No internment.         │
└─────────────────────────┘
```

Nisei branch:
- Second-generation Japanese, born in Hawaii, U.S. citizens.
- Largest ethnic group: 1/3 of population.
- Attack on Pearl Harbor raised fear of sabotage and espionage by Hawaiians of Japanese descent.
- But official military and administrative policy maintained traditional interracial harmony.
- No internment.

Issei branch:
- Immigrants from Japan.
- Strong desire to prove loyalty to U.S.
  - Destroyed old books, photographs of relatives and *obi*.
  - Encouraged their children (AJAs[†]) to become "superpatriots."
    - AJAs contributed war bonds, sponsored campaigns against Tokyo, converted Japanese religious & educational facilities into factories producing items needed for the war.
    - AJAs served in military campaigns as translators and interpreters.
      - Contributions gave new sense of self-worth and expectation of equal opportunity and treatment.

[†]American-born Japanese Americans.

**An online chapter for practicing SQ3R skills can be found at www.cengagebrain.com.

Copyright © Cengage Learning. All rights reserved.

◆ EXERCISE 1   Surveying Reading Selections

DIRECTIONS   Survey the following selection using the steps listed in the box below. When you finish, answer the questions at the end of the selection.

Survey Steps
◆

1. Read the title and ask yourself, "What does the author want to tell readers about wartime Hawaii?"
2. Read the first paragraph and ask yourself, "What point does the author want to make in the reading?"
3. Read the headings and turn them into questions.
4. Read the first sentence of every paragraph.
5. Read the last paragraph.
6. Ask yourself whether you already know anything about wartime Hawaii that might enhance your understanding of this reading.

Wartime Hawaii

1 Much as the war came to the United States initially and most dramatically at Pearl Harbor, the outlines of an increasingly multicultural United States emerging from World War II could be seen first and most clearly in Hawaii. The nearly one million soldiers, sailors, and marines stopping in Hawaii on their way to the battlefront, as well as the more than one hundred thousand men and women who left the mainland to find war work on the islands, expected the Hollywood image of a simple Pacific paradise: blue sky, green sea, and white sand; palm trees and tropical sunsets; exotic women with flowers in their hair. They found instead a complex multiracial and multiethnic society. The experience would change them, as they in turn would change the islands.

Hawaii's Multiracial Society

2 Before December 7, 1941, few Americans knew where Pearl Harbor was or even that Hawaii was a part of their country, a colonial possession, a territory annexed by the U.S. government in 1898. Few realized that Honolulu, a tiny fishing village when Captain James Cook sailed by the difficult entrance to its harbor in 1778, had subsequently become the major maritime center of a kingdom, the seat of a territorial government, and a gritty port city that would serve as the major staging

Copyright © Cengage Learning. All rights reserved.

ground for the war to be waged in the Pacific. And few knew that this American outpost, as a result of successive waves of immigration beginning in the 1870s by Chinese, Portuguese, Japanese, and Filipinos, had a population in 1940 in which native Hawaiians and white Americans (called *haoles*, which in Hawaiian means "strangers") each constituted only 15 percent of the islands' inhabitants.

The Nisei and Issei

3   The approximately 160,000 Hawaiians of Japanese ancestry—including some 100,000 second-generation Japanese, or Nisei, who had been born in Hawaii and were therefore U.S. citizens—composed Hawaii's largest ethnic group, more than a third of the population. Japan's attack on Pearl Harbor immediately raised fears of sabotage or espionage by Hawaiians of Japanese descent. Rumors flew of arrow-shaped signs cut into the sugarcane fields to direct Japanese planes to military targets and of Nisei women waving kimonos to signal Japanese pilots.

4   But in stark contrast to the wholesale incarceration, or imprisonment, of the Japanese in the Pacific coast states, where the dangers of spying activities were slight compared to Hawaii, official military and administrative policy in the islands was to maintain traditional interracial harmony throughout the war, and to treat all law-abiding inhabitants of Japanese ancestry justly and humanely. "This is America and we must do things the American way," announced Hawaii's military governor. "We must distinguish between loyalty and disloyalty among our people." There was no mass internment of the Nisei and Issei (those who emigrated from Japan) as there was on the mainland.

5   For the Issei, loyalty to the United States had become an obligation, a matter of honor. To eliminate potential associations with the enemy, they destroyed old books, photographs of relatives, and brocaded *obi* (kimono sashes) and replaced portraits of the Japanese emperor with pictures of President Roosevelt. A burning desire to prove that they were true Americans prompted many of their Hawaiian-born children, often referred to as AJAs (Americans of Japanese ancestry), to become "superpatriots."

6   AJAs contributed heavily to war-bond drives and sponsored their own "Bombs on Tokyo" campaign. They cleared areas for new military camps and converted the halls of Buddhist temples, Shinto[†] shrines and Japanese-language schools (all closed for the duration and reopened after the war) into manufactories of bandages, knit socks, sweaters, and hospital gowns (the gowns sewn for the Red Cross and Office of Civil Defense).

[†]Shinto: a religion native to Japan characterized by worship of nature and ancestors.

Copyright © Cengage Learning. All rights reserved.

Copyright © Cengage Learning. All rights reserved.

7   Their newly expanded contact with other Hawaiians, including *haoles*, hastened their assimilation, or absorption, into the larger Hawaiian society. In addition, AJAs served in the military campaigns in the Pacific as interpreters. They cracked and translated enemy codes. They also fought in Europe with the all-Nisei 442d Regimental Combat Team, the most highly decorated organization in the U.S. Army. These contributions gave the Japanese in Hawaii, as it did other ethnic groups, a new sense of their worth and dignity. The war experience aroused expectations of equal opportunity and treatment, of full participation in island politics, of no longer accepting a subordinate status to *haoles*.

Changing Attitudes Toward *Haoles*

8   In addition, the attitudes of many Hawaiians toward *haoles* changed as native islanders witnessed a large number of whites doing manual labor for the first time. Their view that whites would always hold superior positions in society—as bosses, plantation owners, business leaders, and politicians—was turned topsy-turvy by the flood of Caucasian mainland war workers. The hordes of white servicemen crowding into Honolulu's Hotel Street vice district for liquor, for tattoos, for posed pictures with hula girls in grass skirts, for three-dollar sex at the many brothels,[†] and then for treatment at prophylaxis[†] stations to ward off venereal diseases also tarnished traditional notions of white superiority.

The Majority Becomes a Minority

9   Most of the whites who had come to Hawaii had never lived where whites did not constitute a majority and where they were the ones who were different. Most had never before encountered or conversed with those of African or Asian ancestry. Suddenly, they were in the midst of a mixture of ethnic and racial groups unmatched anywhere in the United States, in the midst of a society of people of diverse cultures working together for a common cause. So also were the nearly thirty thousand African-American servicemen and workers who arrived in the islands before the war's end. Having experienced nothing like the fluid and relaxed racial relations of Hawaii's multiethnic society, blacks discovered an alternative to the racist America they knew. Some chose never to go back to the mainland. Others returned home to the states to press for the rights and freedoms they had first tasted in Hawaii. In so many ways, wartime Hawaii, termed "the first strange place" by historians

---

†brothels: houses of prostitution.
†prophylaxis: preventive treatment for diseases.

Beth Bailey and David Farber, would anticipate the "strangeness" of U.S. society today. (Adapted from Boyer et al., *Enduring Vision*, pp. 779a–b.)

1. The soldiers and wartime workers who came to Hawaii expected to find _____. Instead, they found

   _____.

2. Who composed Hawaii's largest ethnic group? _____

   _____.

3. *True* or *False*. Unlike the mainland, Hawaii maintained interracial harmony throughout the war.

4. In wartime Hawaii, whites who lived there suddenly discovered what it was like to be _____.

5. In wartime Hawaii, African Americans discovered _____

   _____.

◆ Mark Pages While You Read

The desire to leave textbooks without a mark on them is understandable. You probably want to sell them at the end of the semester. Unfortunately, that short-term goal may well interfere with your long-term goal of leaving college a more informed and professionally prepared person. Although the research varies as to what kinds of marks on a text are most valuable,[†] I don't know of any studies suggesting that marking pages doesn't help both comprehension and remembering—as long as you do it consciously and selectively.

Mindless highlighting appears to do absolutely nothing for your comprehension or your memory. Similarly, underlining without thinking about why you are marking a particular sentence or phrase is not going to improve your comprehension. Likewise, marginal comments like *Boring, Whatever,* and *Who Cares* are not going to advance your college career. What will advance it is applying the following pointers for thoughtful annotation and selective marking of pages.

[†]Some studies suggest underlining works; others come out on the side of diagramming, while very few support the most popular method—highlighting with a colored marker.

Copyright © Cengage Learning. All rights reserved.

Annotating and Marking Textbook Pages

◆

1. Underline (or highlight) sparingly, <u>marking</u> <u>only</u> those <u>words</u> and <u>phrases</u> <u>essential</u> to the author's <u>meaning</u>.

2. If an entire sentence seems important, don't underline the whole sentence. Paraphrase it in the margins—i.e., use your own words to express the author's ideas. (More on paraphrasing on pages 16–20.)

3. Make mini-diagrams in the margins of your textbook. For instance, draw arrows to show connections between cause and effect, generalization, and example, or claim and proof. Use chains of boxes or circles to describe a sequence or chain of events; e.g., Heavy tax collection 1786 → Shays' Rebellion 1787

4. Paraphrase the main, or central, points of chapter sections, along with one or two examples, details, studies, or statistics used to explain the key points; e.g., "Amphibia suggest environmental threat; e.g., three-legged frogs."

5. Identify possible test questions; e.g., T. Q: "Explain the purpose of the Federalist Papers."

6. Record ideas for term papers; e.g., T. P: "In a very short period of time, J. Robert Oppenheimer went from hero to outcast."

7. Make marginal notes, synthesizing, or combining, what you learned from lectures and outside readings with what you are discovering from the chapter; e.g., "Baylin is like Zinn in his emphasis on the economic basis for the colonists' rebellion against the British." (More on synthesizing in Chapter 7.)

8. Compare and contrast the author's point of view with those of writers who agree or disagree.

9. Circle vocabulary words that seem central to the subject under discussion, jotting down brief definitions in the margin. You can also double underline the actual textbook definitions.

10. Make personal connections to movies you might have seen or novels you might have read dealing with the same or similar subjects; e.g., "Movie *Bad Day at Black Rock* good example of author's thinking."

11. Check your underlining at the end of each chapter section to see if reading just the underlined words and phrases makes enough sense for you.

12. If you are reading a particularly difficult chapter, it's a good idea to underline in pencil first. Use pen only on the second reading.

Copyright © Cengage Learning. All rights reserved.

13. Create your own personal index. Every time you see a word or an idea that you think is central to the author's explanation, list it along with the page number on a blank page or inside cover. When you are through reading, go back and add definitions.

14. Use the top margins of the page to create general categories or headings that sum up portions of the text; e.g., "Causes of the Revolutionary War"; "Characteristics of Minerals"; "Effects of Acid Rain."

Symbols for Underlining and Annotating

The following chart lists symbols for underlining and annotating pages. Feel free to adapt the symbols listed here to better suit your particular needs. You can even make up your own symbols. Whichever symbols you choose, though, be sure to use them consistently. That way you will remember what they represent.

Symbols for Marking Textbook Pages ◆		
Arrows to identify cause and effect relationships		
Boxes to highlight names you need to remember	Charles Darwin	
Cause and effect diagrams to indicate relationships	Coercive Acts ——→ Revolutionary War	
Circles to highlight key points, specialized vocabulary, key terms, statistics, dates, and unfamiliar words	(1830)	
Colon to signal the simpler or more specific restatement of a complex or general thought.	: By 1960, parts of Great Lakes polluted: contamination by bacteria and industrial chemicals.	
Cross-reference notes to compare closely related statements in the text	See p. 27 *or* Compare p. 27	
Double underlining to highlight the main idea of the entire reading	= = =	

Copyright © Cengage Learning. All rights reserved.

Equals sign to signal a definition	=
Exclamation points to indicate your surprise at the author's statements	!
Mini-outlines to indicate relationships	*Issei* want to prove loyalty buy war bonds
Numbers to itemize and separate a series of statistics, studies, reasons, etc.	1, 2, 3, 4
Question marks to indicate confusion	?
Quotation marks to remind about quotes that might be effective in term papers	" "
Star to identify a crucial piece of information	★
Single underlining to highlight key ideas in paragraphs	—— —— ——
Initials to identify ideas for term papers, possible sources of test questions, or passages in need of a second reading	TP, TQ, RR
Vertical lines to emphasize key passages longer than a sentence or two	‖

To illustrate what the pages of your textbook should look like when you finish underlining and annotating, here's an excerpt from the reading on pages 9–12:

The *Nisei* and *Issei*

= born in U.S.— second generation

The approximately 160,000 Hawaiians of Japanese ancestry—including some 100,000 second-generation Japanese, or [*Nisei*], who had been born in Hawaii and were therefore U.S. citizens—composed Hawaii's largest

Copyright © Cengage Learning. All rights reserved.

Pearl
Harbor → breeds
fear of
sabotage

ethnic group, more than a third of the population. Japan's attack on <u>Pearl</u> <u>Harbor immediately raised fears of sabotage or espionage by Hawaiians</u> <u>of Japanese descent.</u> Rumors flew of arrow-shaped signs cut in the sugarcane fields to direct Japanese planes to military targets and of *Nisei* women waving kimonos to signal Japanese pilots.

Contrast to
internment camps
in Pacific coast states

But in stark contrast to the wholesale incarceration, or imprisonment, of the <u>Japanese in the Pacific coast states,</u> where the dangers of subversive activities <u>were slight in comparison to Hawaii, official military and administrative policy</u> <u>in the islands was to maintain traditional interracial harmony</u> throughout the war, and to treat all law-abiding inhabitants of Japanese ancestry justly and humanely. "This is America and we must do things the American way," announced Hawaii's military governor. "We must distinguish between loyalty and disloyalty among our people." There was no mass internment of the *Nisei* and *Issei* (those who emigrated from Japan) as there was on the mainland.

★ ★
use quotes in paper?

Issei emigrated
from Japan

Ways *Issei* tried
to show loyalty

For the *Issei*, <u>loyalty to the United States</u> had become an <u>obligation,</u> a ① matter of honor. To eliminate potential associations with the enemy, they ② 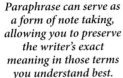 destroyed old books, photographs of relatives, and brocaded *obi* (kimono sashes), and replaced portraits of the Japanese emperor with pictures of President Roosevelt. A burning desire to prove that they were true Americans prompted many of their Hawaiian-born children, often referred to as <u>AJAs (Americans of Japanese ancestry)</u>, to become "superpatriots." ③ ④ AJAs contributed heavily to war-bond drives and sponsored their own "Bombs on Tokyo" campaign.

Paraphrase to Monitor Comprehension and Encourage Remembering

Paraphrase can serve as a form of note taking, allowing you to preserve the writer's exact meaning in those terms you understand best.
—Charles Bazerman,
The Informed Writer

The term *paraphrasing* is probably familiar to you from writing courses. You know, for instance, that if you want to sum up an author's ideas in a term paper, you have to paraphrase them, using your words to make or explain the same point. If you don't paraphrase, you can easily end up with several pages of tacked-together quotations—the last thing you want to hand in to your instructor.

Paraphrasing while reading, though, is different from paraphrasing for a term paper. A reading paraphrase certainly requires you to be accurate. However, it doesn't require you to be quite so complete. Compare, for instance, two different paraphrases of the original text shown below. The first paraphrase is for a paper. The second is a reading paraphrase, created solely for the purposes of monitoring comprehension or taking marginal notes.

Copyright © Cengage Learning. All rights reserved.

Original
◆

The word *irony* derives from "Eiron," one of the core characters in classical Greek drama. Eiron is a trickster who likes making fun of boastful, self-important people. By pretending he is ignorant and asking naïve questions, Eiron provokes the overly proud into revealing their ignorance. Eiron's technique, however, was not confined to the stage. In his lectures to students, the Greek philosopher Socrates used a similar strategy: He would pretend complete ignorance when asking a question such as "What is truth?" His goal was to provoke the person answering into revealing ignorance or lack of depth. This technique is known as "Socratic irony."

Paraphrase for a Paper
◆

Eiron was one of the staple characters in early Greek drama. He was a trickster, who acted as if he knew nothing while encouraging others to give explanations that revealed their ignorance. The Greek philosopher Socrates used a similar device. He would pose seemingly naïve questions like "What is truth?" and pretend he didn't know the answer. When the person questioned responded, Socrates would make it clear that the other person's answer was poorly thought out. This pretense of ignorance in order to uncover a lack of knowledge or depth is called "Socratic irony."

Reading Paraphrase
◆

Word irony comes from Eiron, trickster in Greek plays, who asked dumb questions to reveal ignorance. "Socratic irony" uses similar method, pretending ignorance to uncover superficial thinking.

Copyright © Cengage Learning. All rights reserved.

As the above example shows, paraphrasing to check reading comprehension or take notes doesn't require recalling every detail of the original. You just need to answer two questions: (1) What does the author say about some person, practice, idea, place, or event? (2) How did the author clarify, illustrate, or prove that point?

Be aware, though, that more difficult or unfamiliar material may require you to ask additional and more specific questions. If the text revolves around events happening over time, ask "What chain of events is the author describing, and why?" "What do they lead to or result from?"

If the passage points out similarities and differences between two topics, ask yourself what the point of the comparisons is. Whatever the questions, the goal is always the same: to uncover the core elements of the passage.

Paraphrase in Marginal Notes

For another illustration of a reading paraphrase, study the passage and marginal notes that follow. The passage is the original text; the notes are the reader's paraphrase of that text.

Many students cope with stress by asking for pets in the classroom.

Across the country, a growing number of students are seeking permission to bring "psychiatric service" animals into college classrooms and dormitories. The students say the animals, which range from cats and dogs to snakes, rats, and even tarantulas, help them cope with the stress of college life. But the law is unclear on whether colleges must accommodate such animals, and many colleges have struggled with how to distinguish a student with a true need from one who simply does not want to be separated from Fluffy or Spot.

Officials unsure when pets medical necessity.

As they should, the marginal notes identify the author's general point: Students are asking to bring pets into classrooms in order to alleviate stress. Notice, too, that the first marginal note tells you not just who's doing what but also why they are doing it: Students want to bring animals into the classroom because they want help coping with stress.

The second marginal note answers the question, What are the consequences or results? Apparently college administrators are unsure as to where they should draw the line when it comes to allowing animals in the classroom.

These two brief notes, one of them not even a grammatically correct sentence, are all a reader would need to paraphrase for a comprehension check and memory aid. As the examples show, paraphrasing while reading doesn't require the same precision or completeness paraphrasing for a paper does. Each kind of paraphrasing has a different purpose.

Pointers on Paraphrasing While Reading

The more you get into the habit of paraphrasing while you read, the better you will be at it. Here are some pointers to get you started.

Copyright © Cengage Learning. All rights reserved.

1. **Find substitutes for key words.** If you have trouble getting started paraphrasing, ask yourself what words or phrases in the passage are consistently referred to or repeated. Then see if you can find substitutes for some or all of those words. For instance, if the passage repeatedly refers to "an increase in cell-phone use over landlines," change the wording of that phrase to "cell phones starting to take a back seat to landlines." Finding replacements for *cell phones* and *landlines* would be difficult. However, you can find other ways to talk about the increased use of cell phones over landlines.

2. **Paraphrase only the basics.** When you paraphrase to check your comprehension or jot some marginal notes, your goal is to sum up in your own words the main idea or point of the paragraph along with one or two details used to explain or prove it. Abbreviations of all kinds are allowed in this context or situation. After all, you are the only one reading the paraphrase. Just don't abbreviate so much that later on you don't know what the note means.

3. **Look up from the page while paraphrasing.** If you look at the paragraph while you paraphrase it, you are likely to think you have understood the material better than you do. You'll be inclined to use the author's words and forget about finding your own. That defeats the purpose of paraphrasing.

4. **Use questions to focus your paraphrase.** If you finish a chapter section and have only a foggy notion of what the author wanted to say, don't get discouraged and give up. Force yourself to figure out answers for questions like these: What words or phrases are repeatedly referred to in this passage? What comment does the author make about those words? How does he or she prove or clarify that point?

   For more complicated readings, make your questions more specific; for example, What events does the author describe? What were the circumstances of those events? Who did what and why did they do it?

5. **Be ready to re-read.** If you pose any of the questions above and ponder them a minute or two without getting an answer, mark the passage you were trying to paraphrase for a second reading. Good readers know that difficult texts sometimes require a second, even a third reading.

Copyright © Cengage Learning. All rights reserved.

6. **Make the end the beginning.** Sometimes, if you are having trouble paraphrasing, it helps to reverse the order of the ideas. For instance, you might turn this sentence "Asperger syndrome is a form of autism, but people who suffer from it do not lack linguistic skills" into this paraphrase: "Although lack of linguistic skill is not a symptom, Asperger syndrome is still a type of autism."

CHECK YOUR UNDERSTANDING

In your own words, why should you paraphrase while reading?

_____

_____

◆ **EXERCISE 2**   **Thinking About Paraphrasing**

DIRECTIONS   Read each passage. Then select the letter of the best reading paraphrase.

Original 1. Erik Erikson's theory of developmental tasks appropriate to different stages of life has profoundly influenced the way many psychologists think. Yet because research on Erikson's stages of development would require extensive and costly long-range studies, his ideas have not been scientifically proven. (Adapted from Engler, *Personality Theories*, p. 1266.)

Reading Paraphrase   a. Theory of stages and tasks very influential but no longitudinal studies to prove it.

b. Erik Erikson's theory of developmental stages and tasks very influential despite lack of long-term studies as proof.

c. Erikson has had a big influence on how we describe ourselves and our lives. No longitudinal studies have been done. Too expensive.

Original 2. Coal is the single biggest air polluter in coal-burning nations, and burning coal accounts for at least one-fourth of the world's annual CO_2 emissions. To a growing number of scientists and economists, the burning of coal is one of the most serious environmental problems of the twenty-first century. (Miller and Spoolman. *Sustaining the Earth*, p. 200.)

Reading Paraphrase   a. Big coal-burning power plants have major impact on environment in industrialized countries.

Copyright © Cengage Learning. All rights reserved.

    b. Coal among biggest social problems of coal-burning nations.

    c. Many scientists think burning coal a huge environmental threat due to CO_2 produced.

Get into the Habit of Using Summaries for Note-Taking

I couldn't imagine a more crucial skill than summarizing; we can't manage information, make connections, or rebut arguments without it.
—Mike Rose, *Lives on the Boundary*

Like paraphrasing, only in a more extended form, summarizing is a way of monitoring your understanding. It can tell you if you have really mastered the difficult chapter section you just read. While you clearly can't jot summaries in the margins of your texts—well, maybe very brief ones—you can jot them into the pages of a notebook. Summarizing a chapter section will tell you how well you have understood both the author's general point and the specific details used to explain it.

The Goal of Summarizing

The goal of a summary is to reduce the original text to about one-quarter of its original length while retaining the most important information presented in the passage or reading. Good summaries reduce the original text to a bare bones version that (1) identifies the overall message or main idea along with (2) a few absolutely essential details that explain or prove the author's point.

Any time you struggle to summarize a chapter section you think you have understood perfectly, it's a strong clue that your comprehension is not complete. Either you haven't understood the main idea or haven't grasped a key relationship. When this happens, don't keep struggling to write the summary. Instead, mark the passage for another reading.

Summarize Selectively

Summarizing what you read isn't something you can or should do for an entire chapter assignment. Rather, it's the kind of review you should save for special passages or sections—the ones you think might be the basis for an exam question or might prove useful for a term paper. Summarize as well material you found difficult to understand but now think you have

Copyright © Cengage Learning. All rights reserved.

understood. (Summarizing will tell you if you are correct.) Sorting out the main idea and the most essential details will force you to really dig into the material. In turn, digging deeper into the text will help you understand it better. Summarizing will also help you remember what you've read.

Summaries Are an Essential Part of College Coursework

In addition to being a comprehension strategy and a way of anchoring information in memory, summarizing is an essential skill to master if you want to succeed in college. Instructors assign summaries for homework and use them as the basis for essay exams. Although Chapter 5 will treat summarizing in more depth, you should start now to learn the basics of summary writing. Practice on shorter textbook passages and you'll be prepared for the longer texts to come.

Pointers for Summary Writing

To get you off to a good start, here are some tips. The first seven apply to all kinds of summaries, whether they are written for your own personal use or for an instructor's assignment. The last two apply mainly to summaries written for other people to read.

1. **Mark your text before you summarize.** To make sure you have thoroughly mastered the author's ideas before you try to summarize them, underline, mark, and annotate the page, indicating what's important and what's not. As you learned earlier in this chapter, marking your text can help solidify your understanding of the material.

   Thoroughly marking up the material you plan on summarizing is also a good way of deciding which sentences or passages are essential and which ones are not. Some people prepare for summary writing by penciling a line through any sentences they consider nonessential.

2. **Paraphrase the key point of each paragraph.** Generally, how you annotate pages should vary with the material. But if you are annotating and underlining in preparation for writing a summary, then you should identify the key point of every paragraph and note the main idea in the margins. When you are finished, go through your marginal list and put an asterisk or checkmark next to the ideas essential to your summary.

Copyright © Cengage Learning. All rights reserved.

Copyright © Cengage Learning. All rights reserved.

3. **Use the author's main idea to guide your selection of details.** If the main idea, or central point, of the paragraph or chapter section you are summarizing identifies a set number of theories, stages, studies, and so on—for example, "Erik Erikson described four stages of psychosocial development"—then your summary needs to include one of each theory, stage, or study. Skip one and you haven't fully explained the overall main idea. Where you can abbreviate is in the amount of time you spend describing each stage. Although the author might have given each stage three sentences of description apiece, you might describe each one in a sentence.

   However, if the central point is something like "Adolescence is an especially turbulent time of life" and the rest of the chapter section describes four or five ways in which adolescence is a time of conflict and change, then it's probably safe to include only two or three of the illustrations given. After all, what makes adolescence so turbulent is, to some degree, general knowledge, even common sense. You don't need lots of examples to explain the point.

4. **Look for underlying relationships.** As you read, try to determine how the author connects ideas as he or she moves from sentence to sentence. Is the author identifying the specific causes of one event or comparing and contrasting opposing points of view on the same subject? Does he trace a series of dates and events that preceded some major social change, or is she listing the various solutions experts have proposed for a pressing problem?

5. **Maintain relationships in your summary.** If the author compares and contrasts Thomas Jefferson and Andrew Jackson to illustrate how differently each president viewed the issue of government intervention in state politics, your summary should make the same overall point: When it came to intervening in state politics, the two presidents differed.

   Your summary should not treat each man individually as if two separate portraits of two famous presidents had been the author's original purpose, or intention. If the material you are reading is organized by a comparison and contrast relationship, your summary should rely on the same organizational pattern. (For more on common organizational patterns, see Chapter 4.)

6. **Get right to the point.** Although textbook writers are more inclined than most to open with the central, or key, point of a chapter

section, they, too, frequently start with an introductory sentence or two. Here's an example:

Original

President Theodore Roosevelt was not alone in his concern that American companies were becoming monopolies[†] that undermined competition. Progressive[†] politicians had been saying for years that big industry was controlling the economic market, instead of letting it regulate itself through supply and demand. Roosevelt, however, was the first president who decided to do something about the growing power of monopolies. It was Roosevelt's attack on big business that earned him his reputation as a "trustbuster."

In this paragraph, the author leads up to the point of the passage by telling readers how others before Roosevelt were concerned about monopolies' growing influence. But that information is purely introductory. The real focus of the passage is on what Roosevelt actually did about the problem. Thus, a summary of a passage like the one above would eliminate the introductory material. Instead, it would start with the key point about Roosevelt taking action to bust up monopolies:

Sample Summary

Theodore Roosevelt was the first president to attack the growing power of monopolies. That's what earned him the nickname "trustbuster."

7. **Leave out any opinions of your own.** Whether you are summarizing for research or for an assignment, your goal is to create an accurate version of the original material. That means you shouldn't distort the original by adding a value judgment. A summary should be a miniature version of the author's ideas and express only the author's thoughts.

8. **If the writing gets choppy, connect sentences with transitions that identify relationships.** Summaries require you to **synthesize** information—to pull ideas from different sentences or paragraphs and link them together into a new and original whole. (More on this subject in Chapter 5.) The pulling together of ideas from different parts of a reading can produce a summary with an

---

[†]monopolies: companies that gain complete control over the production of a product and are not subject to competition in the marketplace.
[†]progressive: person committed to social change.

Copyright © Cengage Learning. All rights reserved.

awkward, choppy style. While summaries used as chapter notes don't necessarily have to flow smoothly, it's still true that, even at a glance, you should be able to determine *why* one sentence follows another.

The quickest way to achieve such clarity is to use transitions like the ones listed in the box below. **Transitions** are words, phrases, even sentences that signal the relationship between sentences.

Common Transitional Signals and the Messages They Convey ◆	*Transition*	*Author's Message*
	For instance, As illustration, For example, To be more precise	"An example or illustration is on the way."
	Consequently, Thus, Therefore, As a result, In response	"Having identified causes, I'm now listing effects."
	Afterward, In the next step, At the next stage, In the following year, At this point	"I'm trying to show readers how events occur or occurred in real time."
	Similarly, Likewise, In the same vein	"I want readers to notice how these two people or ideas resemble one another."
	In contrast, However, In opposition, Whereas	"I want readers to focus on how two people, ideas, or events don't resemble one another."
	Moreover, In addition, Then, too	"I want readers to recognize that I am still following the same train of thought."

9. **Tell your instructor what you are summarizing.** If you are writing a summary as part of an assignment, include the author and title of the article, weaving it as gracefully as possible into the opening sentence; for instance, "Dexter Filkins in his *New York Times* appraisal of David Halberstam's career, 'A Skeptical Vietnam Voice Still Echoes in the Fog of Iraq,' points out that Halberstam refused to uncritically accept and print what the government said about success or failure in Vietnam. Along with journalists like

Copyright © Cengage Learning. All rights reserved.

Neil Sheehan and Malcolm Brown, Halberstam reflected a skepticism that was, until the Vietnam War, unheard of in the American press." When you are assigned to write a summary, check with your instructor about how to include the source and author of the original text.

◆ **EXERCISE 3   Recognizing Effective Summaries**

DIRECTIONS   Read each passage. Then circle the letter of the best summary.

1. **The Controversy Over the Death Penalty**

Original 1

Obviously, a great deal of controversy continues to surround the issue of executing criminals. Researchers generally agree that if punishment is to discourage future criminal behavior, it must be swift and certain. Neither of these conditions is met by the death penalty in the United States, and few reasonable and informed people today argue that capital punishment acts as a deterrent, except in the specific case of the individual who is executed. Studies comparing homicide rates between states with and without death penalties either find no significant difference or disclose that states with capital punishment actually have higher rates of homicide.

2   Also disturbing is the fact that personal characteristics of judges influence their decisions. Republicans are much more likely to vote for the death penalty, as are older judges and those with previous experience as a prosecutor. In this sense, the death penalty resembles a lottery. Application of the death penalty can also be shocking, in more ways than one. Florida's "Old Sparky" overheated in 1997, causing flames and smoke to erupt from a leather mask worn by the unfortunate murderer, Pedro Medina. (This gruesome scene helped to convince Florida officials to replace the chair with lethal injection in January 2000.) Perhaps most distressful of all aspects of the death penalty is the possibility that an innocent party may be executed. (Excerpted from Bowman and Kearney, *State and Local Government*, p. 463.)

Summary

a. In the United States, the death penalty is extremely controversial, and many people oppose its use because they believe it to be ineffective, unfair, and cruel. However, death-penalty opponents tend to exaggerate these so-called flaws. They also ignore the fact that execution has been a just form of punishment for hundreds of evildoers who deserved to pay the ultimate price for taking a life and, in some cases, lives.

Copyright © Cengage Learning. All rights reserved.

b. The death penalty is a flawed form of punishment that studies show does not affect the homicide rate. Not only does it fail to deter people from committing murder, it is also applied inconsistently, because judges differ in their readiness to exact the death penalty. In addition, as the 1997 Florida execution of Pedro Medina illustrates, the application of the death penalty can cause inhumane suffering to those being executed.

c. The case of Pedro Medina is a perfect illustration of why Americans should follow the Europeans and abolish the death penalty. Medina was executed in an electric chair so ancient it was nicknamed "Old Sparky." After officials pulled the switch on Medina, the machine overheated and flames erupted from the executed murderer's head. Is it any wonder Florida officials replaced the electric chair with lethal injection?

2. The Pony Express

Original 1 The Pony Express lasted only eighteen months, from April 1860 to the fall of 1861. It was never intended to be more than a temporary means of communication while telegraph lines were strung from Missouri to California. The Pony Express cut twelve days off the time it had taken for Washington to communicate with Sacramento via steamships.

© Phil Schermeister/Corbis

2 Pony Express riding was a genuinely romantic adventure: lone riders walking, trotting, now and then sprinting their ponies across half a continent to carry a few pounds of government dispatches and some very expensive private letters. But being a Pony Express rider was also dangerous. According to the company's Help Wanted assignment, what was wanted were "young, skinny, wiry fellows, not over eighteen." However, they also had to be "expert riders willing to risk death daily . . . orphans preferred."

3 Pony Express riders maintained a demanding schedule. They were based at large stations 75 to 100 miles apart. At each relay station, which was little more than a shack and a stable, they changed their sweating ponies for fresh mounts that were saddled and ready to go. The riders made 308 cross-continent runs for a total of 606,000 miles. Riders carried almost 35,000 pieces of mail. In the eighteen months the Pony Express was in existence, only one mail pouch was lost. (Adapted from Conlin, *The American Past*, p. 497.)

Summary a. Often risking their lives, the riders of the Pony Express significantly reduced the amount of time needed for transcontinental mail delivery. Working in relays, the horsemen would bring mail to stations set

Copyright © Cengage Learning. All rights reserved.

at regular intervals along the Pony Express route, changing mounts and exchanging mail pouches at each station. Operating from 1860 to 1861, the Pony Express ended when telegraph service began. By that time, it had carried almost 35,000 pieces of mail, losing only one pouch in the process.

b. Pony Express riders were among the most courageous heroes of the American West. Riding the vast, uninhabited areas of the western states from 1860 to 1861, these men pioneered swift, regular mail service. Not only were they skilled horsemen able to ride long distances at a full gallop, they were also fearless in the face of danger. Thanks to their brave service, communication between easterners and westerners greatly improved.

c. From 1860 to 1861, the men who rode for the Pony Express delivered the mail. At each new station, the riders would switch to a fresh horse. Using this system, one rider was able to cover 75 to 100 miles of the 1,966-mile route before another rider took his mail pouch and continued on. As they moved across deserted parts of Missouri, Kansas, Nebraska, Wyoming, Utah, Nevada, and California, Pony Express riders faced hazards like robbers and blizzards.

TAKING A CLOSER LOOK

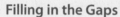

Filling in the Gaps

In the excerpt about the Pony Express, why does the author include an excerpt from a Help Wanted ad?

_____

_____

Why do you think the ad asks for orphans?

_____

_____

---

www

INTERNET FOLLOW-UP: Learning More About the Pony Express

Use the Web to find out what role William F. Cody played during the Pony Express's brief run.

_____

_____

Copyright © Cengage Learning. All rights reserved.

◆ **EXERCISE 4**   **Writing Effective Summaries**

DIRECTIONS   After you finish reading each chapter section, summarize it in the blanks that follow.

EXAMPLE

Going West

1   In nineteenth-century America, many people were convinced that moving West would give them a better life. Railroad expansion had made remote farming regions accessible, and the construction of grain elevators eased problems of shipping and storage. As a result of population growth, the demand for farm products had grown rapidly, and the prospects for commercial agriculture—growing crops for profit—seemed more favorable than ever.

2   Life on the farm, however, was much harder than the advertisements and railroad agents suggested. The newly arrived Easterners often encountered shortages of essentials they had once taken for granted. The open prairies contained little lumber for housing and fuel. Pioneer families were forced to build houses of sod and to burn manure for heat. Water was sometimes as scarce as timber. Few families were lucky or wealthy enough to buy land near a stream that did not dry up in summer and freeze in winter. Machinery for drilling wells was scarce until the 1880s, and even then it was very expensive.

3   The weather was seldom predictable. In summer, weeks of intense heat and parching winds often gave way to violent storms that washed away crops and property. In winter, the wind and cold from blizzards piled up mountainous snowdrifts that halted all outdoor movement. (Adapted from Norton et al., *A People and a Nation*, pp. 492–493.)

Summary   During the nineteenth century, scores of men and women moved to the West believing that farming was a way to improve their lot in life. But farm life proved to be much harder than most expected. Essentials like lumber and water were hard to come by, while the weather was harsh and unpredictable. In summer, the intense heat could be followed by storms that wiped out crops. In winter, blizzards could trap everyone indoors.

Copyright © Cengage Learning. All rights reserved.

1. An Environmental Success Story

1 The cleanup of Ohio's Cuyahoga River is one of the most significant successes in environmental history. In the nineteen sixties, the river was so polluted it caught fire several times. In 1969, photographs were taken of the flaming river flowing through the city of Cleveland. Highly publicized, the photos of the burning river ignited public outrage. That outrage forced elected officials to enact laws limiting the discharge of industrial wastes into river and sewage systems. City officials also allotted funds to upgrade sewage treatment facilities.

2 Today the river is cleaner, no longer flammable, and widely used by boaters and anglers. This accomplishment illustrates the power of bottom-up pressure by citizens, who prodded elected officials to transform a dangerously polluted river into a valuable public resource.

(Adapted from Miller and Spoolman, *Sustaining the Earth*, p. 176.)

Summary _____

_____

_____

_____

_____

_____

2. Toxic Agents

1 There are three major types of potentially toxic agents. *Mutagens* are chemicals or forms of radiation that cause or increase the frequency of mutations, or changes, in the DNA molecules found in cells. Most mutations cause no harm but some can lead to cancers and other disorders. For example, nitrous acid, formed by the digestion of nitrite preservatives in foods, can cause mutations linked to increases in stomach cancer in people who consume large amounts of processed foods.

2 *Teratogens* are chemicals that cause harm or birth defects to a fetus or an embryo. Ethyl alcohol is a teratogen. Drinking during pregnancy can lead to offspring with low birth weight and a number of physical, developmental, behavioral, and mental problems. Other teratogens are arsenic, benzene, chlorine, chloroform, chromium, DDT, lead, mercury, PCBs, thalidomide, and vinyl chloride.

Copyright © Cengage Learning. All rights reserved.

3   *Carcinogens* are chemicals or types of radiation that can cause or promote cancer—a disease in which malignant cells multiply uncontrollably and create tumors that can damage the body and often lead to death. Examples of carcinogens are arsenic, benzene, vinyl chloride, chromium, PCBs, and various chemicals in tobacco smoke.

(Adapted from Miller and Spoolman, *Living in the Environment*, p. 426.)

Summary   _____

_____

_____

_____

_____

_____

_____

_____

TAKING A CLOSER LOOK

Making Connections Between Sentences and Paragraphs
In the second paragraph of reading 1 in this exercise, what does the phrase "this accomplishment" refer to?

_____

_____

In your own words, how does "this accomplishment" illustrate "bottom-up pressure" (paragraph 2) by citizens?

_____

_____

What's the function of the italics used in the second selection on toxic agents?

_____

Copyright © Cengage Learning. All rights reserved.

Use the World Wide Web to Build Background Knowledge

One of the Internet's strengths is its ability to help consumers find the right needle in a digital haystack.
—Jared Sandberg, journalist

For more than three decades now, research on reading has consistently come to the same conclusion: The more background knowledge you have about the topic under discussion, the easier it is to follow the writer's train of thought. On tests of reading comprehension, the people with the most background about the topic consistently get the highest scores.

When evidence for the importance of background knowledge began to emerge, it was hardly cause for joy among college students. After all, if you were a student trying to master a chapter on the theory of continental drift,† background knowledge on the subject was not especially easy to acquire. The Internet, however, has changed all that. Now you can get the background knowledge you need by logging on to the World Wide Web.

Looking for Background Knowledge on the Web

Imagine that you are reading a chapter titled "Making Marine History." (See an excerpt from a chapter with this title on pages 44–45.) Imagine as well that during your survey of the chapter both the headings and the visual aids mentioned "Polynesian† Exploration." While that phrase may mean a lot to someone versed in marine history, many readers would have no personal knowledge about this subject.

Two decades ago, those readers would have had to scurry around looking for reference books explaining Polynesian exploration. Today, however, they would only need to type the phrase into a search-engine box. In response to that search term, a search engine, in this case, Google, would come up with a list like this:

---

†continental drift: theory that explains how the continents were once combined and split apart due to the movement of plates that cover the Earth's surface.
†Polynesian: related to Polynesia, which consists of hundreds of islands that stretch across the Pacific Ocean from Hawaii to New Zealand.

Copyright © Cengage Learning. All rights reserved.

Web Images Maps News Shopping Gmail more ▼   Sign in

Google | Polynesian Exploration | (Search) Advanced Search
                                               Preferences

Web ⊞ Show options...

1. **Polynesian** culture - Wikipedia, the free encyclopedia ☆
   Jump to Origins, **exploration** and settlement (c. 1800 BC - c. 700 AD): Recent maternal
   mitochondrial DNA analysis suggests that **Polynesians**, ...
   en.wikipedia.org/wiki/**Polynesian**_culture - Cached - Similar

2. Wayfinders : **Polynesian** History and Origin ☆
   Not until the late eighteenth century with the coming of Europe's second Age of **Exploration**
   did a reasonable hypothesis about where the **Polynesians** came ...
   www.pbs.org/wayfinders/**polynesian**3.html - Cached - Similar

3. **Exploration** & Settlement ☆
   Polynesian explorers are known to have made the long sea voyage from the ... **Exploration**
   revealed numerous land and sea birds, including a very large ...
   homepages.ihug.co.nz/~tonyf/explore/explore.html - Cached - Similar

4. **Polynesian** explorers - **exploration** of New Zealand | NZHistory.net ... ☆
   Mar 2, 2007 ... The origins of Maori have been debated since Westerners first entered the
   Pacific Ocean. During his explorations of **Polynesia**, ...
   www.nzhistory.net.nz > ... > Pre-1840 contact > Early explorers - Cached - Similar

5. Discoverers Web: Non-Western Explorers ☆
   The Polynesian Voyaging Society - **Polynesian exploration** - Polynesian voyaging traditions
   - Exploration and settlement of Polynesia - Ru and Hina explore ...
   www.win.tue.nl/~engels/discovery/nonwest.html - Cached - Similar

6. On the Road of the Winds (Patrick Vinton Kirch) - review ☆
   Many of the details are still debated: the exact sequence and timing of settlements in Eastern
   Polynesia, the nature of **Polynesian exploration** and voyaging, ...
   dannyreviews.com/h/Road_Winds.html - Cached - Similar

7. **Polynesian** Navigators: Their **Exploration** and Settlement of the Pacific ☆
   by E Best - 1918 - Cited by 5 - Related articles
   We have much evidence to show that, in former times, the **Polynesians** made many voyages
   of **exploration**, during which many islands were settled and ...
   www.jstor.org/stable/207638

8. Natural Disaster and Political Crisis in a **Polynesian** Society: An ... ☆
   Natural Disaster and Political Crisis in a **Polynesian** Society. An **Exploration** of Operational
   Research I. James Spillius. References ...
   hum.sagepub.com/cgi/content/refs/10/1/3

9. The Discovery and Settlement of **Polynesia** ☆
   Irwin suggests that those who settled **Polynesia** may have used a deliberate strategy of
   exploration that allowed them to find islands without an inordinate ...
   www2.hawaii.edu/~dennisk/voyagingchiefs/discovery.html - Cached - Similar

10. Enlightenment - The Experience Festival ☆
    Because of the paucity of mineral or gemological resources, the **exploration** of **Polynesia** by
    European navigators (whose primary interest was economic), ...
    www.experiencefestival.com/**polynesian**_culture_-_origins_**exploration**_and_
    settlement_c_1800_bc_-_c_700_ad - Cached

Copyright © Cengage Learning. All rights reserved.

www.google.com

One or more of these sites is likely to give you precisely the background knowledge you will need. The question is, of course, which one do you choose?

Selecting the Right Site

Although the Web is a great resource for locating information, it can also be intimidating. Your search engine, particularly if the search term is too general (see the pointers for creating search terms, pages 38–39) can give you more information than you can handle efficiently. And even when you use a narrow enough search term, you still have to *think before hitting your first link*. Since you don't want to spend a lot of time finding the website you need, you should have some strategies in mind to help identify the most promising sites.

Website Captions Are Critical

In determining which link to hit first, pay close attention to the caption and ask yourself a question like this: How many words in the website caption are related to the reading assignment? In this case, we're looking for a website that would help with a chapter from an oceanography textbook. That means websites mentioning ocean or water exploration are promising. Because the search term we used comes from a chapter titled "Making Marine *History*," we should probably also look for sites that emphasize the Polynesians of the past rather than the present.

Don't Automatically Go to Wikipedia

Because the open-source site Wikipedia is so popular, you might be tempted to immediately go to that link first, particularly since it tops the list. But look again at the caption. It begins with the words "Recent maternal mitochondrial DNA analysis." That language is very technical. It strongly suggests that, in this case, Wikipedia won't give you the general background knowledge you need. Sites 2 and 3 seem more promising since both captions suggest the sites focus on Polynesian history. Also the brief caption descriptions don't introduce technical terms.

In this case, it would be wise to go to the third link on the list since the caption seems more closely related to your reading assignment, which addresses early Polynesian exploration in the context of oceanography.

Copyright © Cengage Learning. All rights reserved.

Here's what you would find on site 3:

EXPLORATION & SETTLEMENT

The early voyages of discovery.

by Anthony G. Flude. © 2001.

Polynesian explorers are known to have made the long sea voyage from the Marquesas islands to the Hawaiian islands, some 5000 kilometres to the northwest, in the year 400 A.D. Far away into the southwest, lay the two islands of New Zealand, empty and isolated, occupied only by birds and coastal mammals and as yet, unsettled and un-peopled.

Hawaii lies within the zone of the trade winds, which blow steadily for six months of the year in the southern Pacific Ocean, beyond which lies the Tasman Sea, with its unpredictable weather and storms.

It is difficult to get a balance of the historical events as far back as these early times in New Zealand, since there is no documentary evidence. Some Maori lay claim that their people are the 'indigenous' people of New Zealand, yet there is now sufficient scientific carbon dating evidence, to show that there were other human races here, on these islands, many years before their arrival.

Other explorers of the Pacific Ocean, of Melanesian background from the Society or Marquesas Islands, had, many years before, been swept into the Australian currents and stormy Tasman Seas where after weeks they had been finally been cast ashore onto the Taranaki coast some time before A.D. 750. These people had the name Mai-oriori, often shortened to Moriori and were referred to as the tangata-whenua," in Maori legend, suggesting that these people were here before the arrival of The Fleet.

The Moriori people were known to be the inhabitants of the coastal lands north of Taranaki and the Bay of Plenty and none had settled the South Island. They were peaceful tribes and their menfolk unskilled as fighting warriors.

Under the command of the Maori explorer Kupe, a well provisioned Polynesian catamaran (foulua) from the Cook Islands or Uvea, made landfall on the northeast coast of the North Island of New Zealand, around A.D. 950, nearly a thousand years ago.

The women aboard this giant catamaran brought with them plants to sow in their new found land. New seedlings of coconuts, gourd, taro, yam, and sweet potatoes had been carefully stored aboard away from the salt sea air. The temperate New Zealand climate did not support the first two, but they found that the clams and sweet potatoes flourished well in the rich soil in the northern summer climate.

These new settlers had to make major changes to their lives. The cool open sided dwellings of their tropical islands had to be replaced with more substantial dwellings with walls and roof to keep out the cold winds and rain. Their bark cloth garments were not warm or weatherproof and became quickly replaced with hand-woven flax fibre.

As their numbers increased over the next thirty years with the arrival of two more fleets of canoes, they began to explore further afield. The third fleet of Maori, brought to New Zealand by Kupe, carried a warlike band of fierce fighting warriors. These new arrivals brought cannibalism to New Zealand and the Moriori, easily beaten in warfare by the Maori as they advanced southwards, were slaughtered, enslaved or eaten.

This site is perfectly fine *if* you have a lot of time to spend on the topic. But for your purposes, to get a general understanding of Polynesian exploration, you should probably close this window and click on another site. You want a website where the information is presented in easy-to-digest chunks of information that won't take you long to absorb. Hit the link for website 2, and you'll find the kind of background information that is more appropriate to your purpose:

Copyright © Cengage Learning. All rights reserved.

WAYFINDERS
A PACIFIC ODYSSEY

Pacific Islanders in communications

POLYNESIAN HISTORY & ORIGIN

European Explorers | **Polynesians: An Oceanic People | Linguistic Evidence/Oral Traditions | Heyerdahl and Sharp | The Archaeological Response | Experimental Voyaging | Hokulea: The Rediscovery | Introduction**

The early European explorers who first encountered the Polynesians could not believe that a Stone Age people, with only simple sailing canoes and no navigational instruments, could themselves have discovered and settled the mid-Pacific islands. Accordingly, they dreamed up elaborate theories that explained the presence of the Polynesians in the middle of the Pacific, while denying to them the ability of having reached there through their own sailing abilities. For example, in 1595 the Spanish explorer Quiros imagined a great "Southern Continent" stretching from Asia far into the Pacific across which their ancestors walked to a point from

Early explorers visiting Polynesia.

which, by a short canoe crossing, they could reach the Marquesas. Other early explorers invoked sunken continents, transport by the first Spanish voyagers, and even special creation of the islands to explain the presence of Polynesians in the middle of the Pacific.

Not until the late eighteenth century with the coming of Europe's second Age of Exploration did a reasonable hypothesis about where the Polynesians came from, and how they managed to discover and settle their island world, begin to emerge. Whereas explorers of the previous European age of exploration were primarily searching for new routes to the riches of Asia, those of this second age sailed the seas primarily, in Braudel's words, "to obtain new information about geography, the natural world, and the mores of different peoples." In the Pacific, the leaders of this new approach to oceanic exploration criss-crossed the ocean, finding and mapping the locations of islands, cataloguing the plants and animals found there, and investigating the islanders, their language, and customs. Only then was the true extent of Polynesia realized, and was credence given to the idea that the ancestors of the Polynesians could have intentionally sailed into this great ocean to find and settle so many scattered islands.

Captain James Cook
Captain James Cook, who is considered by many to have been the greatest of the explorers in this second age of European global expansion, was the first to realize and document that a vast region of the Pacific was occupied by people who shared a common cultural base.

© World History Archive/Alamy

© North Wind Picture Archives/Alamy

Copyright © Cengage Learning. All rights reserved.

Read only the first sentence of this website, and you've already taken a big step toward understanding why the Polynesians would appear in an oceanography text: Using the most primitive boats, they sailed long distances to settle numerous islands in the middle of the Pacific Ocean. That accomplishment alone makes them a memorable addition to marine history.

Also, the list of navigation links at the top of the screen gives you an immediate overview of the site's contents. The navigation links tell you the site is not focused solely on Polynesian explorations. That means you don't really need to read anything beyond the opening page.

Note, too, that subheadings are used within the text. The subheading "Captain James Cook" is a tip that you can stop reading for background knowledge when you reach this heading. You can stop because the author is now explaining things in more detail than you might need for your assignment. Here again, keeping the purpose of your search in mind is important. It will help you decide when you have learned what you need to know before tackling your assignment.

A Strategy for Reading Hypertext

Neither of the sample sites shown on the previous pages includes much **hypertext**, or links to other websites containing related content. But this won't always be the case.

Often when you are searching online, you will land on pages that are loaded with hypertext (Wikipedia is a good example of a website full of hypertext). When this happens, be selective about the links you hit. Links to other sites can give you valuable information about the topic you are researching. However, they can also distract you from your search if you begin leapfrogging from one site to another.

To make effective use of websites heavy with hypertext, try this strategy. Read the content through once without clicking on any links. Then scan the material you just read and see if there are any portions of the text where you have no idea what the writer wanted to say. If there are and those passages contain hypertext, click on the first link and see if it gives you the background knowledge you need to understand the material. If it does, then you probably don't need to click on any other links.

If the first link doesn't give you the information you need and a second one is present, try that link next. As soon as you feel you understand what had confused you at first, you don't need to click more links just because they are there on the page.

Copyright © Cengage Learning. All rights reserved.

When working with hypertext, you shouldn't click links at random (unless, of course, you are just amusing yourself). Instead, have a purpose in mind. For example, you want to understand a particular word or term. If you aren't goal-directed when you hit hypertext, you may well end up surfing the Web without getting the background knowledge you need for your reading assignment.

Use Navigation Links Sparingly

If you think the site looks interesting and you want to pursue its contents further, bookmark it and return to it at a later date. At this stage of your reading—when your purpose is to get background knowledge for a specific assignment—you really shouldn't let yourself drift off into other pages on the site without knowing for sure that they are relevant to your search.

Navigation links at the top or to the left on a website are important tools but only when you have the time to explore the site for your own pleasure. When your goal is getting background knowledge for a reading assignment, avoid clicking the navigation links *unless* they seem directly related to your search.

Creating Effective Search Terms ◆	1. **Brief phrases are usually better than single words.** If, for instance, you are writing a paper on Harry Truman's use of loyalty oaths† to evaluate people for government jobs, it would be a mistake to type just "Truman" or even just "loyalty oath" into the search-engine box. Instead create a phrase like "Truman's loyalty oath." Phrases such as this one help narrow the number of websites a search engine brings up, and that's all to the good.
	2. **Don't stick with search terms that fail to get results.** Much of the time, your textbook headings can be used as search terms. However, if a heading doesn't get you the information you need, change the wording to make the search term more specific. If the heading of the chapter section is "César Chávez," and the list of sites that comes up in response to Chávez's name is both long and not obviously useful, modify your search term to make it "César Chávez's leadership United Farm Workers."

---

†The Democrats were being attacked for being "soft" on communism. To prove that they weren't, Truman, a Democrat, made loyalty oaths a requirement for federal employees, who had to swear loyalty to the United States and disavow any connections to groups critical of the government. No oath meant no job.

Copyright © Cengage Learning. All rights reserved.

3. **Consider using the word *AND* to focus your search term.** If you are researching the effect poverty has on psychological depression and can't use any of the headings in your textbook and no specific phrase comes to mind, try linking the two words together using "AND." Typing "depression AND poverty" into your search box will call up documents that contain both the word *poverty* and the word *depression.* In addition, the search engine will provide more focused and fewer results.

4. **Pay particular attention to sites with a URL, or Web address, ending in .edu.** This indicates that the site is related to an educational institution and the information on it is probably accurate because it's likely to have been double-checked by an editor. That's not to rule out personal or organizational websites ending in .com, but with these, you should check the information against two, even three other websites to authenticate the website's accuracy.

   Like blogs, personal websites can be terrific sources of information, hosted by people deeply interested in a particular subject and more than willing to share their knowledge. But they can also be hosted by prejudiced crackpots, who spout nonsense about, to take just one example, NASA's faking of the moon landing. Guard against gathering such misinformation by always cross-checking at least two different sites dealing with the same subject.

5. **If the order of the words is important, put quotation marks around the search term.** Sometimes the words in your search term require a specific order. When word order is important, put quotation marks around the term to indicate the exact phrase you want the search engine to bring up, for instance "adjustable rate mortgages." That tells the search engine to return only those websites which maintain the wording and order used in your search term.

Pointers for Picking a Website
◆

1. **Don't always start at the top.** The first website that comes up on your screen is not necessarily the one most appropriate to your needs. Hold off looking at any one website until you have looked over the entire first page of offerings.

2. **Keep your purpose in mind.** If your goal is to get some overall background knowledge, then you don't need to look at websites that suggest the author is focusing on some specific aspect of your

Copyright © Cengage Learning. All rights reserved.

topic. If you are reading a chapter passage on the Pony Express, and either the name or caption of a website focuses on Louise "Lou" McCloud, a female Pony Express rider who managed to disguise her gender and get a job galloping cross country, you should probably hold off and read about Lou some other time. For your purpose, a website with more general information is what's needed.

3. **Read the caption carefully.** The caption briefly describing a website's contents can help you determine what's actually on the site. If the caption seems off target from what you need to know, the website probably is too, so don't click on it.

4. **Get to know the names associated with limited-access websites.** Some websites related to your topic won't let you have access unless you pay a fee or belong to a specific organization. These are called "limited-access websites." Your search engine will bring them up repeatedly. Learn the names of some of the most common so that you avoid wasting time on them—e.g., JSTOR, Sage, Project MUSE, HighBeam, and SpringerLink. If you are writing a paper, it might be worth your while to find out if, for instance, your school library has access to some of these sites. But if you are simply getting background knowledge for a reading assignment, you are better off ignoring the limited-access sites.

A Note on Wikipedia

If you are inclined to turn to Wikipedia for background knowledge, keep in mind that it is an open-source site, meaning volunteers write and edit the entries, using a source code to post, revise, or add information. Initially, the entries on Wikipedia were only as good as the volunteers who created them, because there was no second layer of supervisory editors to make sure the information posted was accurate. But after the site made some big factual blunders, site administrators instituted an additional checking process in 2009 to avoid disseminating, or distributing, misinformation to users.

Many of Wikipedia's pages are now overseen by senior editors, who double-check both fact and interpretation. This move toward a stricter editorial policy angered some of Wikipedia's early supporters, who believed that group editing could automatically weed out errors. It was cheered, however, by those who thought the online encyclopedia was a valuable source of background knowledge, if only more efforts were made to eliminate errors.

Copyright © Cengage Learning. All rights reserved.

As one of those people encouraged by Wikipedia's stricter editing policies, I'd encourage your using a Wikipedia site when the caption suggests it fits your needs. For giving you an overview of the people and events related to a topic, Wikipedia is generally a useful online resource that continues to improve its procedures for collecting and posting information. Plus Wikipedia entries usually list sources of information. Often the sources are provided in the form of links. You can hit some of those links if you think you need more information than what the entry offers.

Fact-Checking Websites

The Web, useful as it is, also has some drawbacks. One of those drawbacks is illustrated by the following pie charts, which identify how publishers of print and online content responded when queried about how much fact-checking and editing they do.[†]

Compare the "slices" of the pie chart and you will see that a stunning 48 percent of those polled said that copyediting was less rigorous online. Even more important, 27 percent said that online content is fact-checked less rigorously than print content.

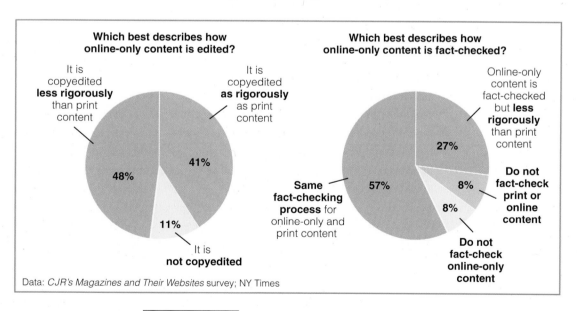

Data: *CJR's Magazines and Their Websites* survey; NY Times

[†]The study on which the charts are based was done by the *Columbia Journalism Review*. Three thousand consumer magazines and their websites were polled. Of these, 665 completed a survey consisting of 34 questions. The study was conducted between August 3 and October 1, 2009. A copy of the report is available at http://cjrarchive.org /img/posts/CJR_Mag_Web_Report.pdf.

Copyright © Cengage Learning. All rights reserved.

When your goal is to get background knowledge in preparation for reading a textbook chapter, it's probably not terribly important if the website content has not been rigorously fact-checked. After all, you are not looking for specific facts. You are looking for a general sense of what's usually covered by headings like the ones included in your chapter.

But if you are writing a term paper and need to know, for instance, exactly when the Salk vaccine used to fight the polio epidemic came on the market, then you should always double-check the facts you find on the Web. Again, don't rely on one site for specific facts. Cross-check what you learn from one site by looking at two other sites that cover the same subject.

Avoid Websites Expressing a Strong Bias

Expressing a **bias**, or personal leaning in favor of or against some person or idea, is hard to avoid. Even when we don't mean to, we often reveal, through our choice of words or selection of details, how we feel about someone or something. Thus, it should come as no surprise that websites often express a bias. As long as the writer's bias doesn't distort the facts, there's nothing wrong with that.

However, if you are just getting acquainted with a new topic or issue, you may not know when the author is distorting the facts. For that reason, avoid websites that express a strong bias for or against some person or idea. In general, stay away from websites that would make you say yes to any of the questions in the following checklist.

Website Evaluation Checklist ◆	If your answer is *yes* to any of the following questions, look elsewhere for background knowledge.
	☐ **1.** Does the website site repeatedly tell you that "studies show" without ever citing a single study?
	☐ **2.** Does the website author make statements that generalize about large numbers of people without citing at least a few representative individuals, groups, or institutions by name? "The Left has always claimed that the Rosenbergs[†] were not guilty, even in the face of overwhelming evidence that they were not."

[†]Ethel and Julius Rosenberg were executed as spies in 1953.

Copyright © Cengage Learning. All rights reserved.

☐ **3.** Is the website author fond of rhetorical questions that assume your agreement and thereby avoid the pesky need for evidence?

Before playing in the series, Shoeless Joe Jackson told the team's owner, Charles Comiskey, that a fix was in play and asked to be benched. Does that sound like a man who is guilty of cheating and should therefore be banned from Baseball's Hall of Fame? Now that you know the facts, please write the Commissioner of Baseball and ask that Joe Jackson be admitted to the Hall of Fame.

☐ **4.** Does the website author claim that no evidence is somehow proof of his or her claim?

The government, however, does not want to make the populace aware of the possible tragedy that awaits them. For that reason, there is no mention of how the predictions of Nostradamus and the Mayan calendar coincide to make 2012 the year of the apocalypse.[†] No government-affiliated scientific organization even mentions this looming catastrophe because a conspiracy of silence is in place.

☐ **5.** Is there little or no verifiable explanation of the website author's credentials or source of expertise?

Who Are We? Several of us are astronomers, employed in various fields, and some are still in school. Some of us are fairly young, and some of us are retired. Some of us are not astronomers, but have an interest in astronomy and space. Some of us are professionals in the sciences: astrophysics, chemistry, etc. Some of us are teachers. We come from all over the world: the U.S., the U.K., Australia, Germany. A few of us contribute directly to the site. Many of us contribute by proofreading or giving feedback, or by contributing to one of the main authors by e-mail. None of us are part of any vast conspiracy to hide anything. (http://www.2012hoax.org/)

☐ **6.** When you check the websites linked to the site you are thinking of using, do the linked sites consist mainly of claims that lack specific sources of information you can double-check for accuracy?

☐ **7.** Are the website author's claims backed by links that go to other articles by the same author as opposed to outside sources that verify what he or she says on the website?

[†]apocalypse: total devastation, an earth-shattering disaster.

Copyright © Cengage Learning. All rights reserved.

DIGGING Great Moments in Marine History:
DEEPER Oceanic Seafarers Colonized Distant Islands

Looking Here's the reading about the colonizing Polynesians referred to on
Ahead page 52. The Polynesian islanders were among the world's great navigators. Forced to leave an island home when resources grew scarce or
religious conflict threatened, the Polynesians simply headed out to sea
to find a new island and a new home.

1   In the history of human migration, no voyaging saga is more inspiring
than that of the Polynesian colonizations, the peopling of the central and
eastern Pacific islands. They required a profound knowledge of the sea
for these voyages, and the story of the Polynesians is a high point in our
chronology of marine science applied to travel by sea.

2   The Polynesians are one of four cultures that inhabited some 10,000 islands
 scattered across nearly 26 million square kilometers (10 million square miles)
of open Pacific Ocean. The Southeast Asian ancestors of the Oceanian peoples,
as these cultures are collectively called, spread eastward in the distant past.
Although experts differ in their estimates, there is some consensus that by
30,000 years ago New Guinea was populated by these wanderers and that
by 20,000 years ago the Philippines were occupied. By between 900 and
800 B.C.E. the so-called cradle of Polynesia—Tonga, Samoa, the Marquesas,
and the Society Islands—was settled. Oceanian navigators may already
have been using shells attached to bamboo grids to represent the
positions of their islands.

3   For a long and evidently prosperous period, the Polynesians spread
from island to island until the easily accessible islands had been
colonized. Eventually, however, overpopulation and depletion of
resources became a problem. Politics, intertribal tensions, and religious
strife shook their society. Groups of people scattered in all directions
from some of the "cradle" islands during a period of explosive dispersion.
Between A.D. 300 and 600, Polynesians successfully colonized nearly every
inhabitable island within a vast area. Easter Island was found against
prevailing winds and currents, and the remote islands of Hawaii were
discovered and occupied. These were among the last places on Earth to
be populated.

4   How did these risky voyages into unexplored territory come about?
Religious warfare may have been the strongest stimulus to colonization.
If the losers of a religious war were banished from the home islands under

Copyright © Cengage Learning. All rights reserved.

penalty of death, their only hope for survival was to reach a distant and hospitable new land.

5   Seafaring had been a long tradition in the home islands, but such trips called for radical new technology. Ocean-bound groups designed and built great dual-hulled sailing ships, some capable of transporting up to 100 people. They perfected new navigation techniques that depended on the positions of stars barely visible to the north. Polynesians devised new ways to store food, water, and seeds. Whole populations left their home islands in fleets designed especially for long-distance discovery. In some cases, fire was nurtured on board in case of landfall on an island that lacked volcanic flame. But a new island was only a possibility, a dream. Their gods may have promised the voyagers safe deliverance to new lands, but how many fleets set out from their troubled homelands only to fall victim to storms, thirst, or other dangers?

6   Yet in that anxious time, the Polynesians practiced and perfected their seafaring knowledge. To a skilled navigator, a change in the rhythmic set of waves against the hull could indicate an island out of sight over the horizon. The flight tracks of birds at dusk could suggest the direction of land. The positions of the stars told stories, as did distant clouds over an unseen island. The smell of the water, or its temperature, or salinity, or color, conveyed information—as did the direction of the wind relative to the sun, and the type of marine life clustering near the boat. The sunrise colors, the sunset colors, hue of the moon—every nuance had meaning; every detail had been passed in ritual from father to son. The greatest Polynesian minds were navigators, and reaching Hawaii was their greatest achievement.

7   Of all the islands colonized by the Polynesians, Hawaii is farthest away, across an ocean whose guide stars were completely unknown to the southern navigators. The Hawaiian Islands are isolated in the northern Pacific. There are no islands of any significance for more than 2,000 miles to the south. Moreover, Hawaii lies beyond the equatorial doldrums, a hot and often windless stretch across which these pioneers must somehow have paddled. And yet some fortunate and knowledgeable people colonized Hawaii sometime between A.D. 450 and 600. Try to imagine their feelings of relief and justification upon reaching a promised paradise under a new night sky. (Garrison, *Essentials of Oceanography*, p. 27.)

Copyright © Cengage Learning. All rights reserved.

Sharpening Your Skills

DIRECTIONS Answer the following questions by filling in the blanks or circling the letter of the correct answer.

1. In the second sentence of paragraph 1, what does "They" refer to?

    Polenesian Colonizations

2. In your own words, what does "depletion" mean in the following sentence: "Eventually, however, overpopulation and depletion of resources became a problem" (paragraph 3)?

    emptiness

3. In your own words, how does the author answer the question he poses in paragraph 4: "How did these risky voyages into unexplored territory come about?"

    Religious warefare pushed the loser to leave the island hoping to find hospitable new lanos.

4. The last sentence of paragraph 5 poses a question: "Their gods may have promised the voyagers safe deliverance to new lands, but how many fleets set out from their troubled homelands only to fall victim to storms, thirst, or other dangers?" What does the author imply or suggest about the promises of the gods?

    Author need to tell us how they face the bad weather during the trips. They had to perfect the new navigation

5. In paragraph 7, the author refers to the "equatorial doldrums" to make which point:

    a. The Polynesians knew how to survive long stretches without food or water.

    b. Even when there was no wind to propel them, the Polynesians found a way to reach Hawaii.

    c. The Polynesians were ready to risk extraordinary danger in order to get to Hawaii.

Copyright © Cengage Learning. All rights reserved.

▶ **TEST 1** **Using SQ3R**

DIRECTIONS Survey the following selection using the steps listed below. When you finish, answer the questions in Part A on page 49. Then go back and read the selection from beginning to end. When you are done, answer the questions in Part B on page 50.

Survey Steps:

1. Read the first and last paragraphs.

2. Use the title to pose a question.

3. Read the headings and the marginal note.

4. Read the first sentence of every paragraph.

5. Read through the questions on pages 49–50.

How the Need for Achievement Spurs Motivation

need achievement
A motive for action influenced by the degree to which a person establishes specific goals, cares about meeting those goals, and experiences feelings of satisfaction by doing so.

1 Many athletes who hold world records still train intensely; many people who have built multimillion-dollar businesses still work fourteen-hour days. What motivates these people? A possible answer is a motive called **need achievement** (H. A. Murray, 1938). People with a high need for achievement seek to master tasks—such as sports, business ventures, intellectual puzzles, or artistic creations—and feel intense satisfaction from doing so. They work hard at striving for excellence, enjoy themselves in the process, take great pride in achieving at a high level, and often experience success.

2 **Individual Differences** How do people with strong achievement motivation differ from others? To find out, researchers gave children a test to measure their need for achievement and then asked them to play a ring-toss game. Children scoring low on the need-for-achievement test usually stood so close or so far away from the ring-toss target that they either could not fail or could not succeed. In contrast, children scoring high on the need-for-achievement test stood at a moderate distance from the target, making the game challenging but not impossible (McLelland, 1985).

3 Experiments with adults and children suggest that people with high achievement needs tend to set challenging, but realistic, goals. They actively seek success, take risks as needed, and are intensely satisfied

Copyright © Cengage Learning. All rights reserved.

with success. Yet if they feel they have tried their best, people with high achievement motivation are not too upset by failure. Those with low achievement motivation also like to succeed, but success tends to bring them not joy but relief at having avoided failure (Winter, 1996).

4   People with strong achievement motivation tend to be preoccupied with their performance and level of ability (Harackiewicz & Elliot, 1993). They select tasks with clear outcomes, and they prefer feedback from a harsh but competent critic rather than from one who is friendlier but less competent (Klich & Feldman, 1992). They like to struggle with a problem rather than get help. They can wait for delayed rewards, and they make careful plans for the future (F. S. Mayer & Sutton, 1996). In contrast, people who are less motivated to achieve are less likely to seek or enjoy feedback, and they tend to quit in response to failure (Graham & Weiner, 1996).

5   **Development of Achievement Motivation** Achievement motivation tends to be learned in early childhood, especially from parents. For example, in one study young boys were given a very hard task, at which they were sure to fail. Fathers whose sons scored low on achievement motivation tests often became annoyed as they watched their boys work on the task, discouraged them from continuing, and interfered or even completed the task themselves (B. C. Rosen & D'Andrade, 1959). A different pattern of behavior emerged among parents of children who scored high on tests of achievement motivation. Those parents tended to (1) encourage the child to try difficult tasks, especially new ones; (2) give praise and other rewards for success; (3) encourage the child to find ways to succeed rather than merely complaining about failure; and (4) prompt the child to go on to the next, more difficult challenge (McClelland, 1985).

6   Cultural influences also affect achievement motivation. Subtle messages about a culture's view of the importance of achievement often appear in the books children read and the stories they hear. Does the story's main character work hard and overcome obstacles, thus creating expectations of a payoff for persistence? Or does the main character loaf around and then win the lottery, suggesting that rewards come randomly, regardless of effort? And if the main character succeeds, is it the result of personal initiative, as is typical of stories in individualist cultures? Or is success based on ties to a cooperative and supportive group, as is typical of stories in collectivist cultures? Such themes appear to act as blueprints for reaching one's goals. It is not surprising, then, that ideas about achievement motivation differ from culture to culture. In one study, individuals from Saudi Arabia and from the United States were asked to comment on short

Copyright © Cengage Learning. All rights reserved.

stories describing people succeeding at various tasks. Saudis tended to see the people in the stories as having succeeded because of the help they got from others, whereas Americans tended to attribute success to the internal characteristics of each story's main character (Zahrani & Kaplowitz, 1993).

7   Achievement motivation can be increased in people whose cultural training did not encourage it in childhood (McClelland, 1985). For example, high school and college students with low achievement motivation were helped to develop fantasies about their own success. They imagined setting goals that were difficult but not impossible. Then they imagined themselves concentrating on breaking a complex problem into small, manageable steps. They fantasized about working hard, failing but not being discouraged, continuing to work, and finally feeling great about achieving success. Afterward, the students' grades and academic success improved, suggesting an increase in their achievement motivation (McClelland, 1985). In short, achievement motivation is strongly influenced by social and cultural learning experiences and by the beliefs about oneself that these experiences help to create. People who come to believe in their ability to achieve are more likely to do so than those who expect to fail (Butler, 1998; Dweck, 1998; Wigfield & Eccles, 2000). (Bernstein and Nash, *Essentials of Psychology*, pp. 274–76.)

Part A: Surveying

DIRECTIONS   Answer the following questions by filling in the blanks or circling the correct response.

1. Throughout the reading, what questions is the author trying to answer?

    _____

    _____

2. *True* or *False*. People with high achievement needs tend to set themselves impossible goals.

3. *True* or *False*. Achievement motivation is learned during adolescence.

4. *True* or *False*. Culture affects achievement motivation.

5. *True* or *False*. Once established, a person's level or degree of achievement motivation cannot be changed or altered in any way.

Copyright © Cengage Learning. All rights reserved.

Part B: Reading

DIRECTIONS Answer the following questions by filling in the blanks or circling the letter of the correct response.

6. How do people with high achievement motivation respond to failure?
   a. They get outraged and give up.
   b. They criticize the person in charge for causing their failure.
   c. If they've tried their best, they don't get too upset by failure.
   d. They refuse to quit even when everything is against them.

7. Which of the following does *not* characterize people with high achievement motivation?
   a. They prefer to get feedback from someone who won't hurt their feelings.
   b. They like to struggle with a problem.
   c. They tend to make careful plans for the future.
   d. They select tasks with clear outcomes.

8. What was the difference when individuals from Saudi Arabia and the United States were asked to comment about people in stories succeeding at various tasks?

   _____

   _____

9. Which of the following does not characterize the parents of children with high achievement motivation?
   a. The parents encourage their children to try difficult tasks, especially new ones.
   b. Even if their children perform a task poorly, the parents give high praise in an effort to bolster their children's self-esteem.
   c. The parents encourage their children to find ways to succeed rather than merely complaining about failure.
   d. Once their children succeed at a task, the parents encourage them to go on to the next, more difficult challenge.

10. *True* or *False*. People who believe in their ability to achieve are more likely to succeed than people who expect to fail.

Copyright © Cengage Learning. All rights reserved.

▶ **TEST 2**   **Recognizing an Accurate Paraphrase**

DIRECTIONS   Circle the letter of the most accurate paraphrase. *Note*: Because this is a test, the answers are more like the formal paraphrases you would use for writing.

1. A *dialect* is language—including vocabulary, grammar, and pronunciation—unique to a particular group or region. Audiences sometimes make negative judgments about a speaker based on his or her dialect. Such negative judgments are called *vocal stereotypes*. (Adapted from Gronbeck et al., *Principles of Speech Communication*, p. 100.)

Paraphrase

    a. A *dialect* is a particular way of speaking. Unfortunately, people sometimes judge others based on the way they speak. Southerners, for example, complain about being stereotyped because of their accent.

    b. The term *vocal stereotypes* refers to the negative judgments people make based on dialect. A *dialect* is speech unique to a group or region, and includes vocabulary, grammar, and pronunciation.

    c. A *vocal stereotype* is a type of dialect. People who speak a particular dialect are critical of those who speak other dialects.

2. Professional nursing associations, like the National Federation of Licensed Practical Nurses, develop their own codes of ethics for nurses by means of consensus, or group agreement. These codes outline a nurse's obligation to clients and to society at large. The codes provide broad principles for determining and evaluating nursing care. (Adapted from Roe, *Clinical Nursing Skills and Concepts*, p. 6.)

Paraphrase

    a. The National Federation of Licensed Practical Nurses has created its own code of ethics to define the behavior of nurses. The code explains the relationship between doctors and nurses and defines the responsibility of each.

    b. The National Federation of Licensed Practical Nurses uses an ethical code to evaluate the nursing care of its membership. This is a practice that other nursing associations should imitate.

    c. Professional nursing associations create ethics codes based on standards agreed on by the group. The purpose of the codes is to define how nurses are supposed to act toward patients and toward society. Thus the codes can be used to judge nursing care.

Copyright © Cengage Learning. All rights reserved.

3. During World War II, movies about Japan made little effort to develop a Japanese character or explain what Japan hoped to accomplish in the war. The Japanese remained nameless, faceless, and almost totally speechless. No attempt was made to show a Japanese soldier trapped by circumstances beyond his control or a family man longing for home or an officer who despised the slaughter even if he supported the military campaign. (Adapted from Koppes and Black, *Hollywood Goes to War*, p. 254.)

Paraphrase

a. During World War II, Hollywood filmmakers were applauded for engaging in racist propaganda. The 1942 film *Wake Island*, for example, with the story of 377 Marines resisting a Japanese invasion, was a smash hit despite its racial stereotypes of Japanese soldiers. Today, such movies, even during wartime, would be sharply criticized.

b. Hollywood films made during World War II portrayed Japanese soldiers like robots, who followed government orders without question. Such films suggested that Japanese soldiers never experienced emotional conflict, unlike German soldiers who were shown disagreeing with their government's inhumane course of action. In the movies, Japanese soldiers always fulfilled their duty to Japan.

c. During World War II, Hollywood filmmakers made propaganda movies that failed to distinguish between the Japanese government's war machine and the Japanese soldier caught in that machine.

4. During the nineteenth and early twentieth centuries, the South American countries of Argentina, Uruguay, and Brazil had their own homegrown cowboys called *gauchos*. Derived from the Quechua[†] word *wáhcha*, the word *gaucho* usually referred to cowhands or horse handlers, but it could also refer to horse thieves and mercenaries, or soldiers for hire.

Paraphrase

a. In Argentina, Uruguay, and Brazil, *gauchos* were considered romantic figures. Like America's cowboys, *gauchos* were the heroes of movies and novels. The most famous novel based on the life of the gaucho was *The Four Horsemen of the Apocalypse*, which also became a movie.

———————————

[†]Quechua: language spoken by people belonging to the Incan Empire.

Copyright © Cengage Learning. All rights reserved.

b. During the nineteenth and beginning of the twentieth centuries, American-like cowboys, called *gauchos*, worked the ranches of Uruguay, Argentina, and Brazil. The term *gaucho*, originating from the Quechua word *wáhcha*, means "cowhand" or "horse handler"; the word can also refer to horse thieves and soldiers of fortune.

c. *Gauchos*, the nineteenth- and early twentieth-century horsemen of Argentina, Uruguay, and Brazil, tended to be lawless robbers and guns-for-hire. When their American counterparts were wreaking havoc in the Old West, these South American cowboys were causing trouble in their homeland.

Copyright © Cengage Learning. All rights reserved.

◗ **TEST 3**   **Recognizing an Accurate Paraphrase**

DIRECTIONS   Circle the letter of the most accurate paraphrase. *Note*: Because this is a test, these are the kinds of paraphrases you would use when writing term papers.

Original

1. In 1960, researcher Jane Goodall went to Africa's Gombe Stream National Park to study chimpanzees. No one before her had attempted to observe the animals in their natural habitat and, initially, the chimps ran from her. However, when Goodall didn't give up, the animals gradually became used to her, letting her watch them for hours. In time, Goodall's pioneering fieldwork revolutionized primate[†] research: She was the first to observe that chimps eat meat, use tools, and engage in warfare.

Paraphrase

a. Jane Goodall, who studied chimpanzees in 1960 in Africa's Gombe Stream National Park, was a better researcher than anyone who had previously studied the shy animals. Unlike earlier researchers, she got the chimps to accept her. Their acceptance gave her the opportunity to observe them in the wild for long periods of time. As a result, she found out that chimps live like humans: They eat meat, use tools, and wage war.

b. In 1960, Jane Goodall became the first person to study chimpanzees in their natural habitat of Africa's Gombe Stream National Park. After patiently overcoming the chimps' initial resistance to her presence, Goodall significantly influenced primate research by witnessing and reporting on chimpanzee behaviors such as meat eating, tool use, and warfare, none of which had been documented before.

c. If Jane Goodall hadn't gone to Africa's Gombe Stream National Park in 1960, it's unlikely that we would know today that chimpanzees are meat eaters, use tools, and occasionally engage in cannibalism. Jane Goodall had a special talent for working with the animals and could communicate to them that they had nothing to fear. The chimps allowed her to get close enough to make some astonishing discoveries.

_____

[†]primates: refers to animals characterized by refined development of hands and feet; includes apes and humans among others.

Copyright © Cengage Learning. All rights reserved.

d. When Jane Goodall went to Africa's Gombe Stream National Park in 1960, she did not know how difficult it would be to study chimpanzees in their natural surroundings. Initially the animals would not let her approach. Goodall didn't give up, though. She kept trying, and eventually the chimps permitted her to watch them for long periods of time.

Original

2. People can successfully perform two different activities simultaneously. However, one of the two activities has to be performed automatically and require little or no attention. For example, we can drive a car and talk at the same time because we can steer, brake, accelerate, and so on, without close attention to each individual action. The actions necessary to driving are practically automatic and require little thought once they have been thoroughly learned. We can also do two things at the same time if the tasks or activities involved require different kinds of attention. It's possible to read music and play the piano simultaneously because each activity requires a separate mode of concentration. (Source of information: Bernstein et al., *Psychology,* p. 177.)

Paraphrase

a. It is possible to do two different things at the same time. But one of those two things has to require little or no thought. It must be almost completely automatic. For instance, many people can drive while they talk because the motions of driving—steering, accelerating, braking, etc.—are automatic, so they don't require close concentration. We can also do two things at the same time if the two tasks are quite different and thus require different types of concentration. We can, for example, read music at the same time that our fingers play the piano keys.

b. To perform two activities at the same time, one of them has to be automatic. Driving, for example, is automatic, so we can usually drive while talking. When playing the piano, pressing the keys is an automatic response to reading the music. However, we cannot talk and read at the same time because we have to pay attention to both of these tasks. Neither one can be performed without thinking.

c. If two tasks require different kinds of attention, then they can be performed at the same time. For example, you don't really have to pay attention when you drive a car, which leaves you free to talk to your passengers. Plus, you don't have to think about how

Copyright © Cengage Learning. All rights reserved.

your fingers are moving over the keyboard, so you can read music while playing a piano. But reading and talking both force you to pay attention to what you're doing. Therefore, they cannot be performed simultaneously.

d. Because the human brain allows us to divide our attention, we can often do two things at the same time. For example, we can drive and talk at the same time because one of the tasks (driving) is automatic. Also, we can read music while playing the piano because each task requires the same kind of attention.

Original
3. Local television news directors have long known that their primary goal is to attract audiences for their advertisers. However, thanks to a large increase in media choices, competition for viewers has become fiercer. Because it's difficult to write catchy stories about politics and government, many news directors have given up trying to cover that kind of news. Instead, they concentrate on TV news programs that mix action stories—short clips about murders, robberies, rapes, fires, and car accidents—with weather, sports, human interest stories, and friendly banter between the anchors.

Paraphrase
a. Television news programmers know they have to draw big audiences to please their advertisers. Because audiences have many programs to choose from, local TV news directors try to attract viewers with action-oriented shows featuring stories about crimes, accidents, and natural disasters with news about sports and weather and the chipper chatter of the newscasters. Because it's hard to write snappy stories about government and politics, most news programs feature very little information about these topics.

b. Local TV directors know that viewers won't watch dull news programs. They also know they must attract lots of viewers to please their advertisers. For those two reasons, today's local news programs rarely include much information about boring subjects like government and politics. Instead, they tend to focus mostly on violent action. Tune in to a local TV news broadcast, and you're likely to see attractive and smiling anchormen and anchorwomen introducing videotape of mangled cars, raging fires, and storm damage, all accompanied by interviews with teary victims.

Copyright © Cengage Learning. All rights reserved.

Copyright © Cengage Learning. All rights reserved.

c. Local TV news directors know they have to create action-packed shows to draw in advertisers. Consequently, they have stopped covering politics and government. Most people would rather see video footage of crimes, accidents, weather forecasts, and sports events, particularly if it is interspersed with friendly conversation between the newscasters. News directors can't really be blamed for giving people what they want.

d. Local TV news directors know that advertisers prefer to place their ads in action-oriented shows with large audiences. They have given up trying to make subjects like government and politics interesting, and they put together shows filled with reports of murders, robberies, accidents, sports highlights, and weather information. They know people are interested in those subjects.

Original

4. A *class-action suit* is a case brought into a court of law by a person who wishes to sue an organization not only for himself or herself but also on behalf of everyone who has been wronged in the same way by that organization. One of the most famous class-action suits was brought in 1954 by the National Association for the Advancement of Colored People (NAACP), which sued on behalf of Linda Brown, a black girl from Topeka, Kansas, who was denied admission to a white elementary school, as well as all other children who were forced to attend segregated schools. The resulting Supreme Court decision, *Brown v. Board of Education*, led to the desegregation of public schools.

Paraphrase

a. Class-action suits are brought by people who want to sue an institution not only on their own behalf but also on behalf of anyone who might have been unfairly treated by the same institution. Perhaps the most famous class-action suit was brought by the NAACP, which sued in the name of Linda Brown, an African-American girl denied entry to an all-white elementary school. The suit also included the names of all other children excluded by the practice of segregation in the schools. This class-action suit, which the NAACP won, was the first step in the desegregation of all public schools.

b. The term *class-action suit* is applied to those cases where a group of people are suing one institution. The lawsuit that led to the desegregation of schools, *Brown v. Board of Education*, was a class-action suit filed by the NAACP.

c. The first and most famous class-action suit ever brought into court was *Brown v. Board of Education*, which was the first step in the desegregation of all public schools. The NAACP, fearing it could not win its case in the name of a single child, decided to sue on behalf of all the children who had ever been denied access to a local school because of the practice of segregation.

d. A class-action suit is brought by someone who wants to sue an institution not only in the name of himself or herself but also in the names of any others who might have been wrongly treated by the same institution. The famous lawsuit *Brown v. Board of Education*, which paved the way for desegregation, is probably the best example of a class-action suit that had important consequences not just for a single person but also for a host of people. This is typical of class-action suits brought by the NAACP.

Copyright © Cengage Learning. All rights reserved.

▶ **TEST 4**   **Paraphrasing with Accuracy**

DIRECTIONS   Paraphrase each of the following statements. *Note*: Because this is a test, please paraphrase as if you were writing a term paper.

Original

1. During the New Deal of the 1930s, Native Americans found two strong supporters in Secretary of the Interior Harold Ickes and Commissioner of Indian Affairs John Collier. Both opposed the existing Indian policies that since 1887 had sought to destroy the reservation system. Together they helped pass the Indian Reorganization Act of 1934, which returned land and community control to tribal organization. (Adapted from Berkin et al., *Making America*, p. 744.)

Paraphrase

_____

_____

_____

_____

_____

Original

2. In the late 1950s, union leaders Walter Reuther and George Meany battled over how to define American labor's role in the world. The liberal Reuther wanted unions to think of themselves as part of an international labor movement. The more conservative Meany insisted that American union members should concentrate on their own interests and let workers in other countries take care of themselves.

Paraphrase

_____

_____

_____

_____

_____

Copyright © Cengage Learning. All rights reserved.

Original

3. It seems that Valentine's Day is hard on relationships. Researchers Katherine Morse and Steven Neuberg have shown that the overall odds of breaking up one week before or one week after Valentine's Day are higher than normal, 5.49 times higher than normal to be exact. Morse and Neuberg further determined that the negative effect of the holiday occurred mainly in couples whose relationship was already deteriorating. The holiday had no effect on breakups among high quality or improving relationships. (Adapted from Strong, DeVault, and Cohen, *The Marriage and Family Experience*, p. 300.)

Paraphrase

_____

_____

_____

_____

_____

Original

4. Geographic information systems (GISs) play a big role in the land-based policies and operations of state and local governments. The California Department of Fish and Game uses GISs to track and monitor endangered species of plants and animals. The Georgia Department of Natural Resources uses GISs to survey wetlands and land cover in order to make environmental management decisions. Police in Denver, Colorado, use it to track neighborhood crime trends throughout the city. (Adapted from Bowman and Kearney, *State and Local Government*, p. 224.)

Paraphrase

_____

_____

_____

_____

_____

Copyright © Cengage Learning. All rights reserved.

▶ **TEST 5**   **Recognizing the Better Summary**

DIRECTIONS   Read each textbook selection. Then decide which of the two summaries does a better job reducing the excerpt, clearly and accurately, to its most essential elements.

1. **Kennedy and Vietnam**

1 At the start of John F. Kennedy's presidency in 1960, South Vietnam represented one of the most challenging issues Kennedy faced. Like Eisenhower, Kennedy saw Vietnam as a place where the United States' flexible response could stem communism and develop a strong democratic nation. But by 1961, the president of Vietnam, Ngo Dinh Diem, was losing control of the country.

2 South Vietnamese Communist rebels, called the Viet Cong, controlled a large portion of the countryside, having battled Diem's troops, the Army of the Republic of Vietnam (ARVN), to a standstill. In response, U.S. military advisers argued that the use of American troops was necessary to turn the tide.

3 Kennedy was more cautious. "The troops will march in, the bands will play," he said privately, "the crowds will cheer; and in four days everyone will have forgotten. Then we will be told we have to send in more troops. It's like taking a drink. The effect wears off and you have to take another."

4 But Kennedy gave in. The South Vietnamese forces would have to continue to do the fighting, but the president agreed to send more "advisers." By November 1963, the United States had sent $185 million in military aid and had committed sixteen thousand advisers to Vietnam—compared with only a few hundred in 1961. (Berkin et al., *Making America*, p. 858.)

Summary   a. When President John F. Kennedy came into office in 1960, he was faced with the challenge of Vietnam. Believing that Vietnam should become a democracy, he wanted to stop the communists from taking over. Yet the man Kennedy supported, Ngo Dinh Diem, was fast losing control of his country. More in control were the Viet Cong, the South Vietnamese Communist rebels. Correctly evaluating the situation, military advisers argued that the president had to send more troops. While Kennedy was cautious, he basically agreed with that evaluation. He gave in and sent more troops, while insisting that the South Vietnamese forces had to do the bulk of the fighting. By 1963, the U.S. had committed 16,000 troops to Vietnam, compared to just a few hundred in 1961.

Copyright © Cengage Learning. All rights reserved.

b. Arriving in office in 1960, President John F. Kennedy was faced with a deteriorating situation in Vietnam. The man the U.S. supported, Ngo Dinh Diem, was losing control of the country and the communists were gaining ground. In response to the situation, U.S. military advisers were saying the president should send in more troops. Kennedy, however, wasn't sure that was the right idea. Still, he gave in, and by 1963 the U.S had committed 16,000 troops to the region, a huge increase over the few hundred sent there in 1961.

2. Hispanic and Latino Power

1   By the late 1960s, many Hispanic- and Latino-Americans felt that their interests and needs were not being served by either their state or local governments. In response to this neglect, they grew both visible and vocal in their protests.

2   In November 1968, for instance, Mexican-American students walked out of their high school in the small South Texas school district of Edcouch-Elsa. The activists demanded dignity, respect, and an end to "blatant discrimination," including corporal punishment—paddling—for speaking Spanish outside Spanish class.

3   The school board blamed the walkout on outside agitators and suspended more than 150 students. But as in other school districts, the protests brought results. The Edcouch-Elsa school district implemented Mexican-American studies and bilingual programs, hired more Mexican-American teachers and counselors, and created programs to meet the unique needs of migrant farm children, who moved from one school to another during the picking season.

4   In the urban Northeast, the Puerto Rican population had increased while job opportunities had decreased. In response, the National Puerto Rican Forum lobbied the federal government for more jobs and job training. In Chicago and New York, the more militant Young Lords began organizing the younger members of the Puerto Rican population. The Young Lords, however, had a different emphasis. They wanted to make young people proud of their heritage. Thus their focus was on Puerto Rico's island culture and Hispanic past. (Adapted from Berkin et al., *Making America*, p. 929.)

Summary   a. By the late sixties, many Latino- and Hispanic-Americans felt their interests were being ignored by both state and local governments. In response, students who had been forbidden to speak Spanish staged a walkout from their schools and won the right to use their own

Copyright © Cengage Learning. All rights reserved.

language. In the Northeast, the National Puerto Rican Forum began organizing to get more jobs and funds from the government. In more urban areas, the Young Lords were organizing young people. They had a different focus. Their goal was to make young Puerto Ricans proud of their heritage.

b. By the late sixties, many Latino- and Hispanic-Americans felt that state and local governments were not addressing their interests. Angry over the situation, both groups began organizing to change it. At a school in South Texas students staged a walkout to protest what they considered an injustice: being punished for speaking their own language. Like similar protests in other districts, this one brought results with more attention being paid to the needs of Mexican-American students. In the urban Northeast, Puerto Rican groups like the National Puerto Rican Forum and the Young Lords began organizing to win jobs and promote ethnic pride.

Copyright © Cengage Learning. All rights reserved.

Vocabulary Building for College Reading

2

© Car Culture/Corbis

IN THIS CHAPTER, YOU WILL LEARN

- how to recognize words essential to your coursework.

- how context clues reveal word meaning.

- how knowing some common word parts can help you recall word meanings.

- how understanding a writer's allusions, or references, can improve your comprehension.

> *Words are power, and pleasure. They are the individual cells that make up the body of language.*
>
> —Ben Macintyre, journalist

This chapter tells you more about how to develop the kind of academic vocabulary that will help you read your textbook assignments. The chapter also introduces the topic of *allusions*—references to people, places, and events that writers employ to explain their ideas. By the time you finish Chapter 2, you will have noticeably enlarged your vocabulary and taken a giant leap forward on the road to academic achievement.

Master the Specialized Vocabulary in Your Courses

Some of your college courses will undoubtedly require you to master **specialized vocabulary**. A specialized vocabulary consists of words and phrases that rarely appear in ordinary conversation. They are, however, essential to mastering specific academic subjects.

For instance, you couldn't complete a biology text without seeing the word *respiration*, the process by which cells are supplied with oxygen. Similarly, reading a psychology text without finding the word *cognition*, the mental activity involved in thinking, is all but impossible.

Courses in business, biology, criminology, nursing, engineering, and astronomy, to name just a few, all use numerous specialized vocabulary words. To do well in these courses, you must master their specialized vocabulary. That means you need to identify specialized vocabulary words when they first appear in your textbooks.

But recognizing specialized vocabulary is only the first step. You also have to note and record the definitions (online or in note cards).[†] Then you have to review both words and meanings until you know them as well as you know the meanings of words like *dog* and *house*.

Look for Words That Get Extra Attention

Textbook authors are careful to highlight the words readers need to know and equally careful about supplying explicit definitions. Look, for instance, at the following excerpt from a psychology text. The author, Jeffrey Nevid, realizes that you probably don't spend much

---

[†]With the arrival of cloud technology, there are many online formats that allow you to make and store your notes. I like EverNote, but there are certainly others you can explore. You can also use online flash cards.

Copyright © Cengage Learning. All rights reserved.

time discussing the structure of the brain when you are chatting with friends or sitting around the family dinner table. He knows that the words used in the passage to describe parts of the brain are unlikely to be familiar.

To make sure that readers become familiar with words that describe the brain, Nevid uses boldface to make the words stand out, supplies definitions within the passage, and then repeats both words and definitions in the margins.

medulla A structure in the hindbrain involved in regulating basic life functions, such as heartbeat and respiration.

pons A structure in the hindbrain involved in regulating states of wakefulness and sleep.

brainstem The "stalk" in the lower part of the brain that connects the spinal cord to higher regions of the brain.

The Hindbrain

The lowest part of the brain, the hindbrain, is also the oldest part in evolutionary terms. The hindbrain includes the *medulla, pons,* and *cerebellum*. These structures control such basic life-support functions as breathing and heart rate.

The **medulla** and **pons** contain sensory neurons that transmit information from the spinal cord to the forebrain. The medulla is the section of the hindbrain that lies closest to the spinal cord. It forms the marrow, or core, of the **brainstem**, the "stem" or "stalk" that connects the spinal cord to the higher regions of the brain (see Figure 2.6).

(Nevid, *Psychology: Concepts and Applications,* p. 55.)

Any time you see words that are not only highlighted in the text but also annotated in the margins, you can be sure that you are looking at specialized vocabulary crucial to understanding the subject matter. Readers who know the meanings of such specialized vocabulary, automatically, without even thinking about them, have a huge advantage in reading their textbooks.

Look for Ordinary Words That Double as Specialized Vocabulary

Some words used in ordinary conversation take on a specialized meaning within the context of a particular subject. In biology, for instance, the word *producers* will not be used to refer to the people who back Hollywood movies or Broadway plays. In the context of a biology textbook, "producers" refers to a category of organisms, or living things, that acquire energy and raw materials from environmental sources and

Copyright © Cengage Learning. All rights reserved.

make their own food. Similarly, the word *consumers* in the context of biology doesn't refer to shoppers. It refers to organisms that cannot produce their own food and must feed off the tissue and waste of other organisms.

Ordinary words that take on a specialized meaning when appearing in textbooks are just as important as those specialized vocabulary words that almost never pop up in ordinary speech. Make an effort to learn both.

Use the Glossary for Troublesome Definitions

If you have any trouble understanding a specialized word or term an author has highlighted, check the glossary at the end of your textbook. This is where you can usually find brief definitions for all the words in your text.

Use Online Dictionaries

If your textbook glossary offers a definition you still find hard to understand, type the word into a search engine specifying that you need a definition for a particular subject, for instance, "definition consumers biology." That phrase tells the search engine you want a definition for the word *consumers* within the context of biology.

Much of the time, what will come up at the top of a list is an online dictionary definition simpler than the one that's in your textbook. Here, for example, is an online definition for *consumers* when it's used in the context of biology:

> An organism that generally obtains food by feeding on other organisms or organic matter due to lack of the ability to manufacture own food. (www.biology-online.org/dictionary/Consumer.)

Usually, reading the online definition followed by the textbook definition will clarify any confusion about the word's meaning. But because online definitions can occasionally be too simplified—remember Chapter 1's discussion of fact-checking online—you don't want to rely solely on online definitions. Combining your textbook definition with that of an online source is the better approach.

Copyright © Cengage Learning. All rights reserved.

◆ EXERCISE 1   Identifying Specialized Vocabulary

DIRECTIONS   Make a list of the subjects you are currently taking. Underneath each subject heading, identify at least three specialized vocabulary words, along with their definitions. Keep adding to this list so that you learn the words essential to the subject. Included is an example to show you how to get started. *Note*: The definitions and the words are separated so that you can review by covering one or the other and then recalling either the definition or the word from memory.

EXAMPLE

Biology

1. DNA
   the initials for deoxyribonucleic acid, the hereditary material for all living organisms and some viruses

2. receptor
   a molecule or cellular structure that responds to a specific form of stimulation

3. mutations
   slight changes in DNA

_____

_____

_____

_____

_____

◆ Build Up Your General Academic Vocabulary

History, government, and sociology textbooks also highlight specialized vocabulary. In this excerpt from a government textbook, the word *filibuster* appears as a heading, reappears in boldface in the text, is accompanied by a marginal note, and is followed by an explicit definition:

Copyright © Cengage Learning. All rights reserved.

Filibuster A filibuster is a last-ditch attempt to defeat a measure or bill by talking for so long that supporters give up on passing it because they want to get on with the Senate's business.

Filibuster

A **filibuster** is a prolonged speech, or series of speeches, made to delay action in a legislative assembly. It had become a common—and unpopular—feature of Senate life by the end of the nineteenth century. It was used by liberals and conservatives alike for lofty as well as self-serving purposes. The first serious effort to restrict the filibuster came in 1917, after an important foreign-policy measure submitted by President Wilson had been talked to death by, as Wilson put it, "eleven willful men." (Adapted from Wilson and Dilulio, *American Government*, p. 324.)

Here again, any time you spot a word or phrase getting this much attention from the author, you can be sure this is a word or phrase you need to know without hesitation.

However, you also need to realize that courses like history, sociology, and government don't necessarily rely as much on a specialized vocabulary as some other courses do. In these courses, there is more of an overlap and many of the words will belong to a **general academic vocabulary** appropriate to reading, speaking, and writing in classroom lectures, scholarly journals, and textbooks or reference works. But these words aren't restricted to a specific kind of knowledge or context. They are just typical of the kind of language used in an academic setting.

Pay Attention to Any Words Followed by Definitions

Subjects like government, history, and sociology don't have as many specialized vocabulary words as, say, biology, psychology, or oceanography does. Thus the texts in these subjects don't necessarily use visual aids to draw readers' attention to must-know words.

What they do instead is follow words central to the discussion with brief definitions. To illustrate, here's an example from an American history book. Note how the authors define the word *gerrymandering*:

The Court's rejection of statewide gerrymandering, or redrawing of voting districts so as to favor one party, was less controversial but equally lasting in importance. (Berkin et al., *Making America*, p. 216.)

As with boldface and definitions repeated in the margins, explicit definitions following a word, even if the word is *not* printed in bold or italic, are a signal of significance. Those definitions say to readers, the meaning of this word is important; make sure you learn it.

Copyright © Cengage Learning. All rights reserved.

Notice Word Repetition

If you are going to master an academic vocabulary, you'll also need to be attentive to words or phrases that make a repeated appearance. Do the words *exempt* and *exemption* appear frequently in your government textbook's discussion of taxes? If they do, then make sure you know that both refer to being freed of some obligation which others must fulfill.

Have you noticed that your psychology and sociology texts repeatedly use the word *marital* to mean "related to marriage" and *prevalence* to indicate frequency of occurrence? If you have, then you need to learn these words even if they don't appear in the glossary. They might not be specialized vocabulary, but they are definitely part of the academic vocabulary that authors use when talking about these subjects.

Building an Academic Vocabulary

Here, to get you started developing your academic vocabulary, are two lists of words. The first list includes words often used in discussions of politics, government, and history; the second focuses on words essential to the study of psychology and sociology.

Words Common to Politics, Government, and History ◆	**1. Legitimacy** Being lawful or in accordance with accepted standards or laws. *Sample sentence*: The United States has questioned the *legitimacy* of Iranian president Ahmadinejad. **2. Partisan** Devoted to or strongly in favor of a particular position, theory, cause, or approach; also a dedicated supporter. *Sample sentence*: *Partisan* bickering has held up the legislation protecting consumers. **3. Commercial** Related to commerce, or the buying and selling of goods, with profit as the chief aim. *Sample sentence*: After the Revolutionary War (1776–1783), those in the *commercial* sector found their fortunes on the rise. **4. Federal** Related to a form of government in which individual states recognize a central authority. In the eighteenth and nineteenth centuries, a partisan of this approach was called a *Federalist*.

Copyright © Cengage Learning. All rights reserved.

Sample sentence: In the years following the Revolutionary War, *Federalists* consistently clashed with partisans of states' rights.

5. **Ratify**   To give formal approval.

Sample sentence: Changes in early America's Articles of Confederation could only be made if the revision was *ratified* by all of the thirteen original states.

6. **Constituents**   Members of a party or group, parts of a whole. (In addition to *constituents, constituency* can be considered the plural form.)

Sample sentence: When Connecticut senator Joe Lieberman lost touch with his Democratic *constituents*, they tried to vote him out of office. But after being defeated in the primary, Lieberman won his Senate seat as an Independent.

7. **Elite**   Belonging to the upper class; wealthy; having special privileges or abilities. People who are part of the upper class are sometimes called *elites*, or *the elite*.

Sample sentence: Alexander Hamilton made it clear that members of the *elite* were meant to govern, while ordinary people were meant to put their faith in their leaders.

8. **Embargo**   A government order prohibiting the movement of ships or trade.

Sample sentence: The U.S. *embargo* on trade with Cuba is one of the most enduring *embargoes* in modern history.

9. **Amend**   To modify, change, or fix, often involving a legal document. An *amendment* can refer to the process of revision or to the final product or statement produced.

Sample sentences: The singer demanded that the lawyer *amend* the contract while she waited in his office.

Any *amendment* to the contract or to the final product will take time.

The Nineteenth *Amendment* to the U.S. Constitution gave women the right to vote.

10. **Expenditures**   Outlays of money.

Sample sentence: Military *expenditures* for the Revolutionary War left the United States heavily in debt.

Copyright © Cengage Learning. All rights reserved.

◆ **EXERCISE 2** **Putting Words into Sentences**

DIRECTIONS Fill in the blanks with one of the words from the list below.

constituents	amendments	elites	partisan	commercial
expenditures	Federalist	legitimacy	ratified	embargo

1. Although America's _____ recovery was well under-way by the 1780s, merchants were, nevertheless, hungry to develop new markets. (Adapted from Gillon and Matson, *The American Experiment*, p. 339.)

2. In 1790, the _____ of the new American government was still being questioned.

3. Founded in 1787, the _____ Party favored a strong central government and the establishment of a constitution.

4. Politicians pay too much attention to polls and not enough to the needs of their _____.

5. Prior to the revolution of 1776, many ordinary colonists, not just the _____, clung to the notion that evil British min-isters rather than the king himself were forcing unfair measures upon them. (Adapted from Boyer et al., *The Enduring Vision*, p. 153.)

6. President Thomas Jefferson's 1807 _____ on exports effectively ended what had been a boom time for merchants; smug-glers, however, made a fortune.

7. The legislation was stalled in Congress due to _____ bickering and the refusal of both sides to compromise.

Copyright © Cengage Learning. All rights reserved.

8. The consolidated Federal Funds Report covers government _____ for grants, salaries, wages, loans, and insurance.

9. Constitutional _____ one through ten make up the Bill of Rights.

10. The Equal Rights Amendment[†] has never been _____.

This next list of words can help you develop an academic vocabulary common to subjects such as psychology and sociology.

Words Common to Psychology and Sociology
◆

1. **Dynamics**   The social, intellectual, or moral forces that produce an event, an effect, or a change.

   Sample sentence: The underlying social *dynamics* of online relationships have not received the attention they deserve.

2. **Norms**   Standards of behavior considered typical; unwritten but understood rules of society.

   Sample sentence: As with so many aspects of group dynamics, the *norms* that develop in a group can play a crucial role in its effectiveness. (Brehm and Kassin, *Social Psychology*, p. 289.)

3. **Assertive**   Willing to put forth one's opinions and wishes.

   Sample sentence: Many people find it difficult to be *assertive* in social situations. (Brehm and Kassin, *Social Psychology*, p. 248.)

4. **Stimulus**   Motive or cause of action.

   Sample sentence: The *stimulus* for the study was the appearance of an unusual virus that did not behave in typical fashion.

5. **Physiology**   The branch of biology dealing with how physical organisms function.

[†]Equal Rights Amendment: amendment to the Constitution that would have guaranteed equal rights for both sexes.

Copyright © Cengage Learning. All rights reserved.

Sample sentence: She withdrew books from the Carnegie Library and studied *physiology* and hygiene, and learned a myriad* of things about herself and the ways of women's health. (Jack London, *The Valley of the Moon*.)

6. **Longitudinal**   Extending over a long period of time.

   Sample sentence: To prove or disprove Erik Erikson's theory about developmental stages spanning a lifetime, researchers need to do *longitudinal* studies of large sample populations.

7. **Genetic**   Due to heredity; inheritable; transmissible.

   Sample sentence: There may well be a *genetic* factor in the development of schizophrenia.

8. **Cognitive**   Related to thought rather than being a purely emotional response.

   Sample sentence: His *cognitive* skills were way ahead of his age, but on an emotional level, he was more child than teenager.

9. **Therapeutic**   Having to do with the treatment of disease and producing a beneficial effect.

   Sample sentence: The *therapeutic* effects of psychoanalysis have never been scientifically tested.

10. **Correlation**   Connection; relationship.

    Sample sentence: There seems to be a high *correlation* between active learning and long-term remembering.

◆ **EXERCISE 3**   **Putting Words into Sentences**

DIRECTIONS   Fill in the blanks with one of the words in the list below.

norms	longitudinal	genetic	cognitive	dynamics
assertive	stimulus	therapeutic	physiology	correlation

1. *The War Hotel* is the title of a book written by Arlene Audergon; it deals with the psychological _____ underlying human conflict.

————————————

*myriad: great number.

Copyright © Cengage Learning. All rights reserved.

2. In a(n) _____ setting, patients or clients should feel free to say things they are normally fearful of expressing.

3. Aware of the penalties they might pay, even the most independent and rebellious spirits have a difficult time ignoring society's _____.

4. A 35-year-long study showed a high _____ between consistent physical exercise and a healthy old age.

5. An environmental _____ like the smell of cookies baking in the oven can trigger powerful memories.

6. The study of animal _____ has produced enormous health benefits for humans and sometimes for animals as well.

7. _____ studies strongly suggest that personality may be as much a product of the genes as the environment.

8. It's a mistake to assume that the words _____ and *aggressive* are synonyms: The first describes a person who is not shy about expressing an opinion, the second a person who insists on making his or her opinion everyone else's as well.

9. _____ therapies generally rely less on medication and more on changing thought patterns.

10. It was once believed that an extra *y* chromosome caused a _____ disposition to criminal behavior.

Learn New Words by Creating Your Own Recall Cues

As you work on building your academic vocabulary, you'll need to keep this key learning principle in mind: The human brain has difficulty learning isolated bits of unfamiliar or unconnected information.

Copyright © Cengage Learning. All rights reserved.

The more you can link new information to something you already know, the more likely you are to remember what you've just read. The link to what you already know is the **recall cue**. It helps you call up or remember definitions you are trying to incorporate into your long-term memory.

For instance, to learn the word *expenditures*, you might link it to the word *spend*, which you hear in the second syllable. If you prefer, you could also create a different recall cue by composing a sentence like this: "When we make expenditures, we are often spending money that we shouldn't."

After a few reviews, you'll learn the meaning of the word and be able to recall it automatically. But when you are trying to first learn the meaning, thinking of that sentence will help you remember that expenditures are outlays of money or examples of spending.

Linking Words to Images Also Helps

You can also use images as recall cues. Say you are trying to remember that the word *elite* refers to those who are privileged or who have special privileges that others don't. You could go to Google images or browse online for pictures that you can copy into a vocabulary file or print out and paste onto the note card of the word you want to learn. Here, for instance, is the drawing of a snooty lion that you could use for the word *elite*.

© Ulrich Flemming

Copyright © Cengage Learning. All rights reserved.

Use Antonyms as Recall Cues

You can also remember new word meanings by making use of **antonyms**, or words opposite in meaning. For instance, if you want to remember that a *partisan* is strongly in favor of someone or something, then, in addition to its definition, link the word to its antonym as shown here.

Partisan	person strongly in favor of a theory or cause; a partisan or person who is partisan takes the part of someone else; means the opposite of critic or detractor.

◆ **EXERCISE 4** **Using Recall Cues**

DIRECTIONS Next to each word below, write down one or more recall cues that you can use to remember the word and meaning.

1. norms: _____

2. genetic: _____

3. stimulus: _____

4. embargo: _____

5. elite: _____

Use Context Clues for General Vocabulary

Textbook writers usually explicitly define the specialized vocabulary of their academic disciplines, or subjects. Still, they can't define every potentially unfamiliar word in a textbook. Readers sometimes have to use the **context**, or setting, of the word to infer, or figure out, an **approximate meaning**, one that doesn't match the dictionary definition but comes close enough to let readers continue without looking the

Copyright © Cengage Learning. All rights reserved.

word up. Based on the context, for example, what do you think *ideology* means in this excerpt?

> In English-speaking countries, the period from about 1850 to 1901 is known as the Victorian Age. The expression refers not only to the reign of England's Queen Victoria (1837–1901) but also to an *ideology* surrounding the family and governing the relations between men and women. According to the ideology that ruled the Victorian era, men were meant, by nature, to be strong and courageous, women to be nurturing and cautious. (Adapted from Bulliet et al., *The Earth and Its Peoples*, p. 730.)

Because the passage illustrates how Victorian ideology functioned—it governed relations between men and women—you might suspect that ideology is a "particular way of thinking." To understand the point of the passage, this approximate definition for *ideology* would be adequate even though the dictionary formally defines *ideology* as "the set of beliefs that forms the basis for political, economic, or social systems."

Turning to the dictionary every time you encounter an unfamiliar word can disrupt your concentration. Before looking a word up, see if context can provide an approximate definition. Four of the most common context clues are contrast, restatement, example, and general knowledge. You should become familiar with all four of them.

Contrast Clues

Sentences containing contrast clues tell you what an unfamiliar word does *not* mean, often in the form of antonyms. For instance, suppose you were asked what *ostentatious* means. You might not be able to define it. After all, the word doesn't turn up that often in everyday conversation. Now suppose as well that word had a context, or setting, like the following:

> Contrary to what many of us assume, the very rich are seldom *ostentatious* in their dress; they do not need to wear showy clothes to impress others. Secure in their wealth, they can afford to look plain and unimpressive.

In this case, the context for the word *ostentatious* offers contrast clues to its meaning. The words *plain* and *unimpressive* are antonyms for *ostentatious*. Using the contrast clues, you could **infer**, or read between the lines and determine, that *ostentatious* means "being showy" or "trying to impress."

Copyright © Cengage Learning. All rights reserved.

Restatement Clues

For clarity and emphasis, writers, particularly of textbooks, sometimes deliberately say the same thing two different ways. Look, for example, at this sentence:

> In addition to being a member of humanity, each of us also belongs to a particular social group, where we find our *peers*—like-minded people often close to us in age—with whom we can identify and relate.

Here the author tells us that in addition to being a member of the human race we all have other, more specific groups to which we belong. Among those groups are our *peers*, "like-minded people often close to us in age." Note how the author defines the word to make sure readers know what it means.

Example Clues

Be alert to passages in which the author supplies an example or illustration of an unfamiliar word. Examples of the behavior associated with a word can often give you enough information to determine an approximate definition.

> *Personification* in writing is an effective device only if it is used sparingly. Unfortunately, if the tables are always groaning, the wind is always howling, and the lights are always winking, then the technique becomes tiresome.

You could correctly infer from the examples in this passage that *personification* means talking about things or events as if they were people.

General Knowledge Clues

Although contrast, restatement, and example are common context clues, not all context clues are so obvious. Sometimes you have to base your inference solely on your familiarity with the experience or situation described in the text, as in the following example:

> With only the most primitive equipment to guide their journey, the explorers ended up taking a very *circuitous* route to India.

Copyright © Cengage Learning. All rights reserved.

This passage does not contain any contrasts, restatements, or examples. But you can still figure out that *circuitous* means "indirect or roundabout," given that people are inclined to get lost or take a long time if they are guided by primitive equipment.

CHECK YOUR UNDERSTANDING

For each sentence, define the italicized word and identify the type of context clue.

1. General George Patton demanded that his soldiers remain *stalwart*, no matter what threats they faced; Patton is famous for slapping two soldiers he considered cowardly, a gesture that ended his promising career.

   Context clue: _____

   Meaning: _____

2. Many voters believe that a candidate's marital status is *relevant*, or related to, his or her political performance.

   Context clue: _____

   Meaning: _____

3. The scientist's long, *abstruse* explanation left her audience speechless with incomprehension.

   Context clue: _____

   Meaning: _____

4. If you want to travel into the Grand Canyon, you have two choices of *conveyance*: your feet or a mule.

   Context clue: _____

   Meaning: _____

Copyright © Cengage Learning. All rights reserved.

◆ **EXERCISE 5**   **Making Use of Context Clues**

DIRECTIONS   Use context to identify an approximate definition for each italicized word.

1. By the seventeenth century, nutmeg was a favorite spice in Europe because of its flavor and *aroma*.
   a. taste
   b. appearance
   c. smell
   d. ingredient

2. *Proponents* of states' rights argued that letting the federal government interfere in state affairs was like asking for a return of the monarchy.
   a. critics
   b. supporters
   c. creators
   d. challengers

3. The music had a *cathartic* effect on the young man: Listening to the songs of his childhood, feelings long suppressed welled up to the surface and he started to weep.
   a. emotional
   b. angry
   c. bland
   d. comic

4. Angry at the *inequitable* distribution of luxuries so obvious in the city's commercial district, the teenagers robbed the well-heeled tourists and distributed the money to friends and family.
   a. luxurious
   b. usual
   c. unequal
   d. changing

Copyright © Cengage Learning. All rights reserved.

5. Most scholars consider the *Oxford English Dictionary* to be the most comprehensive dictionary available, and they turn to it for definitions of brand-new words as well as *obsolete* words or meanings no longer included in other dictionaries.

   a. up-to-date

   b. out-of-date

   c. improperly used

   d. grammatically correct

6. In the late nineteenth century, boxer John L. Sullivan *vanquished* all his opponents until "Gentleman Jim" Corbett demonstrated that speed and technique could subdue Sullivan's brute strength.

   a. conquered

   b. irritated

   c. challenged

   d. delayed

7. The story of the homeless woman's life did not make for a pleasing or happy *narrative*.

   a. sound

   a. joke

   c. description

   d. tale

8. Tabloid newspapers generally avoid serious news about government policy and international affairs; their focus is on more *titillating* stories about celebrity divorces, violent crime, and financial scandals.

   a. personally disinterested

   b. completely untrue

   c. exciting, stimulating

   d. casually described

9. The American writer Gertrude Stein claimed that when she took a final exam with the philosopher William James, she wrote a note saying, "I am so sorry, but I really do not feel a bit like an examination paper in philosophy today." According to Stein, James replied, "I understand perfectly how you feel; I often feel like that myself"

Copyright © Cengage Learning. All rights reserved.

and gave her the highest grade in the class. Stein, however, was known to *embellish* reality for the sake of a good story.

a. enjoy

b. exaggerate

c. celebrate

d. emphasize

10. The rule of the generals was meant to be *provisional*, but they ended up staying in power for more than a decade.

a. rebellious

b. strong

c. failing

d. temporary

 ## Learn Common Word Parts

Knowing something about the parts of words can help you remember new word meanings. Trying, for instance, to learn the meaning of *primordial*, "existing first or very early in time," you could use the meaning of *prim* ("first") to remember the definition. Just tell yourself that something *primordial* has to be one of the *first* creatures or plants in history.

Then during reviews, you could use the word part *prim* to jog your memory and recall the word's meaning. That means, however, that you need to have a working knowledge of common word parts and their definitions. This section will help you develop that knowledge. However, it will be up to you to do regular reviews of the word parts and meanings shown below.

Prefixes† ♦	*Prefix*	*Meaning*	*Examples*
	a, ab, de	away, away from	asexual, absent, dethrone
	a, an	not	anonymous, amoral
	in, im, il, ir, non	not	incorrect, immoral, illegal, irregular, nonstop

---

†prefixes: a letter or letters at the beginning of a word that modify or change the core meaning, e.g., *in*spect and *re*spect.

Copyright © Cengage Learning. All rights reserved.

ad, as	to, toward	adhere, associate
ante	before	anteroom
anti	against	antidote
circum	around	circumference
com, con, syn	with, together	complete, construct, synchronize
contra	against	contradict
de, dis	down from, away	decline, distance
ex, e	out of	exclude, evade
in, im, il	into	incline, immerse, illuminate
inter	between	interstate
mono	one, alone	monarch
para	beside, beyond	paraphrase
phil	love	philanthropist
plut	wealth	plutocrat
poly	many	polygamy
post	after	postpone
pre, pro	before, forward, in place of	prepare, prophet, pronoun
re	back	refer, retreat
sub, suc, suf, sup, sus	under	submerge, succumb, suffer, support, suspend
super	above, over	superwise
trans	across, beyond	transmit

Roots†	*Root*	*Meaning*	*Examples*
◆	*anthrop*	human	anthropology, philanthropy
	arch	chief	monarch, architect, archangel
	bibl	book	bibliography, Bible
	cap	head	capital, captain, decapitate
	ceed	move, yield	exceed, proceed, succeed

†roots: the parts of words that contain the central or core meaning, e.g., in*spect* and re*spect*.

Copyright © Cengage Learning. All rights reserved.

chron	time	chronology, chronicle
civ	city	civic, civilize
dic	speak	dictate, diction, dictator
equ	equal	equalize
fid	faith	confide
fin	end, finished	final
flor	flower	florist
flu, fluc, flux	flow	influence, fluctuate
gam	marriage	bigamist
gram, graph	write, written	grammar, graphic
hetero	different	heterosexual
homo	same	homosexual
lingua, lingu	tongue, language	bilingual
loc	place	location, local, allocate
log, ology	speech, study	dialogue, geology, biology
loqu	speech	loquacious
memor	memory	memorial, memorize
mit	send	admit, commit, permit
mo	set in motion	move, remove, mobile
ord	order	ordinary, ordain
path	feeling, suffering	pathetic, sympathy
phil, phile	love	philosopher
physic, physio	nature	physical, physiology
pon	place, put	postpone, opponent
popul	people	popular, population
port	carry	portable, porter, deportment
reg, rect	straighten, rule	regular, regal, rectangle
sequ, secu	follow	sequence, persecute
spec	look	specimen, spectacle, spectator
the	god	theology
ven	come	prevent
vid, vis	see	vision, visualize, video

Copyright © Cengage Learning. All rights reserved.

◆ **EXERCISE 6**   **Putting Words into Sentences**

DIRECTIONS   Fill in the blanks left in each word with one of the word parts† listed in the following box.

circum	around
merit	deserve, achieve, earn
pend	hang
homo	same
plut	wealth
phil	love
super	above
loqu, locu	speech

1. The awards, diplomas, and trophies in the lawyer's office had been placed there intentionally to show that she had accomplished and completed many tasks _____ing public approval.

2. Some people claim that what we have in the United States is not a democracy but a _____ocracy, or rule by the wealthy.

3. A _____atelist is a person passionate about stamp collecting.

4. Some philosophers have argued that we would all be better off if we were led by a _____ocracy.

5. The heavy, _____ulous leaves of the plant were covered in a dark, slimy mold.

6. The members of the group were extremely _____geneous, which may be why everyone got along so well.

7. Because an important trial was _____ing, the district attorney couldn't concentrate on the renovation of her office.

8. The cafeteria col_____y between the student and her professor looked too intense to be interrupted.

——————————
†Not all the word parts in the exercises appear on the list on pages 83–85.

Copyright © Cengage Learning. All rights reserved.

9. The crown prince had a _____cilious manner that made it clear he thought of himself as a very important man.

10. Once he had measured the garden's _____ference, he had a better idea of how many trees he needed to go around the border.

◆ **EXERCISE 7**   **Using Context and Word Analysis**

DIRECTIONS   Use context and the list of word parts on pages 83–85 to create approximate meanings for the italicized words in the following sentences.

1. Although he was a brilliant man, his *linguistic* skills did not match his cognitive abilities: He had a really hard time expressing himself.

   Linguistic means _____.

2. Although his days as a great athlete were long gone, he liked looking at the *memorabilia* from his glory days.

   Memorabilia means _____.

3. The new city *ordinance* exacted huge fines from dog owners who let their dogs off the leash.

   Ordinance means _____.

4. Henry VIII used trumped-up charges of *infidelity* to win a divorce from his wife Ann Boleyn, whom he promptly had beheaded when she could not give him a son.

   Infidelity means _____.

5. If the bird flu virus becomes capable of human-to-human transmission, it will spread like a wildfire among the *populace*.

   Populace means _____.

6. Fearful of criticism, the new *regime* took power and immediately clamped down on freedom of the press.

   Regime means _____.

Copyright © Cengage Learning. All rights reserved.

7. The man's *diction* suggested that he was British rather than American.

   Diction means _____.

8. In India, the yearly *per capita* income is rising as more and more technology companies are outsourcing to India instead of hiring workers at home.

   Per capita means _____.

9. The two government officials tried to appear friendly, but their *antipathy* was obvious.

   Antipathy means _____.

10. Bear and bare, mite and might, there and their, are all *homonyms*.

    Homonyms means _____.

◆ Make Allusions Part of Your Vocabulary Building

© Car Culture/Corbis

Allusions are references writers and speakers make to people, places, and events that, while not being directly related to the topic or issue under discussion, still contribute to the overall meaning conveyed. Take, for instance, the example below, in which the author discusses the Hubble telescope and includes an allusion to the Edsel, an extremely unsuccessful car model introduced by the Ford Motor Company in 1957. Launched with much fanfare, the Edsel was one of the biggest failures in automotive history. The question you have to answer is this: Why does the author of the following excerpt, Peter N. Spotts, allude to the Edsel in a discussion of the Hubble telescope?

> The latest findings cap "a spectacular year" for the repaired Hubble, and to think astronomers were once concerned that the instrument might become the orbiting *Edsel* of observatories.

Read the above excerpt without comprehending the Edsel allusion and you will only get part of the author's point: The Hubble had a good year. Without knowing what a flop the Edsel was, you won't get the rest

Copyright © Cengage Learning. All rights reserved.

Copyright © Cengage Learning. All rights reserved.

of the author's thought: Initially, astronomers were worried that the Hubble was going to be a huge failure like the Edsel.

Allusions and Common Knowledge

While some allusions come and go with current fashions or trends, others have made their way into the English language and are considered **common knowledge**. Writers use these allusions without explaining them to readers. They just assume that readers are familiar with the allusions. Edsel is an allusion considered to be common knowledge. Lady Macbeth from Shakespeare's play *Macbeth* is another, for example:

> As the playwright saw the character, she was a modern-day Lady Macbeth, whose relentless determination to see her husband succeed had disastrous results.

If the reader does not know that Shakespeare's Lady Macbeth drives her husband mercilessly to become king and ends up deeply regretting the bloodshed that achievement requires, then the meaning of the above sentence won't come through. A reader who understands the allusion, in contrast, will have no problem getting the point: As the playwright portrays the character, she is a woman like Lady Macbeth: Her hunger for power drives her husband to do evil deeds that have disastrous consequences.

Learning Common Allusions

What follows are some explanations of common allusions. They will help you get started on increasing the number of common cultural allusions you automatically know. As you complete the chapters in this textbook, note as well the boxes labeled "**Allusion Alert**." They all introduce some frequently used allusions, which should be part of the background knowledge you bring to a text.

Allusions, like all new words and phrases, are easier to remember when placed in a larger context. Rather than trying to memorize just the meaning of the allusion, learn the story of its origin. Once you understand how these allusions came into being, you will automatically remember what they mean.

Allusions Common to History, Politics, and Government
◆

1. **Waterloo** In 1814, the French Emperor Napoleon Bonaparte was forced into exile on the island of Elba. However, in 1815 he escaped from Elba and returned to France, where he reestablished his rule. To get the jump on his enemies, he then marched into Belgium and defeated the forces arrayed against him until he entered the battle of Waterloo. Facing British forces, Napoleon waited too long to attack. With that mistake, he gave the Germans time to reinforce the British troops and was brutally defeated. Forced into exile again, Napoleon died in 1821. As a result of Napoleon's humiliating defeat, the allusion to Waterloo has come to mean a decisive failure, for instance: "Elected by a landslide in 1964, Lyndon Baines Johnson met his Waterloo when he committed the country to waging war in Vietnam."

2. **The Gilded Age** *The Gilded Age* is the title of a late-nineteenth-century novel depicting the greed and corruption that plagued post–Civil War America. Industrialists, nicknamed robber-barons, were making huge fortunes, often by bribing political officials and intimidating employees. Although few people have read the novel, the title has stayed with us. Allusions to it suggest a time when money seems to be the only measure of value and ethics are in short supply, for example: "In his book *The Politics of Globalization and Polarization*, Maurice Mullard describes the years following the 1980s as a return to the Gilded Age."

3. **Iron Curtain** No one knows for sure who invented the phrase *iron curtain*. What is known is that the phrase referred to the veil of secrecy that dropped down over the Soviet Union and the countries it controlled following World War II. Threatened by the rising power of the United States and consumed by personal paranoia, the Russian leader Josef Stalin wanted to make sure that no information exchange could take place between capitalist and Communist countries. While the phrase *iron curtain* still refers to the barrier that existed between East and West after the war, it's also used to generally describe situations in which a barrier is erected to maintain strictest secrecy; for example, "The department has put up an iron curtain between us and the undercover cops on assignment" (From the TV drama *The Shield*).

Copyright © Cengage Learning. All rights reserved.

4. **Cold War** From roughly the late 1940s to the early 1990s, the Soviet Union and the United States did everything possible, short of all-out war, to undermine each other's power and influence. Although the term *cold war* mainly refers to this particular period and these two countries, it can also refer to other similarly "cool" conflicts that don't turn into "hot" and open warfare, for instance: "When it came to the Chinese, the secretary of state had a cold war mentality that refused to acknowledge any evidence challenging her point of view."

5. **McCarthyism** This allusion originates with Wisconsin senator Joseph R. McCarthy. In the 1950s, in an attempt to increase his own political power, McCarthy aggressively accused, without any evidence, hundreds of people of being Communists or Communist sympathizers. While McCarthy's initial attacks successfully focused on members of the State Department, he eventually went too far and ended up being censured by the Senate. From then on, he was in disgrace, and he died a broken and forgotten man. When not used in reference to McCarthy's actual attacks, *McCarthyism* generally describes an atmosphere filled with unfounded accusations and suspicion; for example, "The new administration made it clear that McCarthyism, which had dominated the previous administration, was now a thing of the past."

INTERNET FOLLOW-UP: McCarthy's Waterloo
Use the Web to find the information that would correctly complete this sentence: "Although Joseph McCarthy was initially successful beyond his wildest dreams, when he launched his anti-Communist crusade, he

destroyed his career and met his Waterloo after he _____

_____."

www

Copyright © Cengage Learning. All rights reserved.

◆ **EXERCISE 8**   **Putting Allusions into Sentences**

DIRECTIONS   Fill in the blanks with the correct allusion.

> cold war   Waterloo   Gilded Age   McCarthyism   iron curtain

1. North Korean leader Kim Jong Il has maintained a(n) _____ between his country and the rest of the world. By keeping citizens isolated from western nations in particular, Kim Jong Il keeps strict control over the populace, while keeping other nations guessing about his motives and goals.

2. After the terrorist attacks of September 11, 2001, there were warnings against a return to _____ when the U.S. government arrested and questioned possible terrorists at home and abroad. No one argued with the idea that rounding up the terrorists was a legitimate aim, but some wanted to make sure that there was sufficient evidence to take this step.

3. Titling his 2006 column "A(n) _____ Brewing Between the Press and White House Over Iran?" journalist Vaughn Ververs suggested that the press had become more ready to criticize presidential claims about nuclear threats than it had been prior to the Iraq war. If Ververs is correct, that may be why the White House, for its part, responded by harshly criticizing the media.

4. For years it looked as if Napoleon admirer and high finance superhero Conrad Black could always come back from seeming defeat. But as British journalist Jacquie McNish reported in *The Globe and Mail,* Black met his _____ in 2004, when a judge found him guilty and publicly criticized Black's business ethics.

5. Reports of multimillion dollar bonuses going to chief executive officers while the rest of the country struggles to make ends meet suggest that twenty-first century Americans may be re-living the _____.

TAKING A CLOSER LOOK

Linguistic Partners

Based on the examples you've seen so far, what verb accompanies allusions to Waterloo? _____

Copyright © Cengage Learning. All rights reserved.

Copyright © Cengage Learning. All rights reserved.

Allusions Common to Finance and Economics

◆

Here are some allusions common to the study of finance and economics. If you do any reading in either of these subjects, you are bound to run into these allusions, which have become part of our shared cultural background.

1. **Invisible hand of the market**   The phrase "invisible hand" comes from the book *The Wealth of Nations* (1776) written by the Scottish economist Adam Smith. The rest of the phrase was added over time. Smith viewed self-interest as the "invisible hand" that would automatically create a balance between supply and demand, making any other kind of regulation or control unnecessary. Smith only uses the phrase once in his book and was never a total believer in the concept. However, the phrase survives to this day. It's used whenever anyone wants to argue for or against the notion that those in business can do without outside regulations or interference. "Like many in corporate management, she was opposed to government regulation, believing instead in the invisible hand of the market."

2. **Milton Friedman and Friedmanites**   Economist and Nobel Prize–winner Milton Friedman is best known as a staunch defender of the free market economy. Even more than Adam Smith, who had doubts, Friedman believed that the invisible hand of competitive self-interest would ultimately regulate markets, making regulation totally unnecessary. Friedman taught for many years at the University of Chicago and influenced many student economists who went forth to influence the economies of the world. Friedman's followers were often called Friedmanites,[†] and Friedman's name has become a shorthand way of referring to those who believe markets can regulate themselves without any outside help, for example, "*Friedmanites* still wield enormous power at the University of Chicago."

3. **Laissez-faire**   In the seventeenth century, the French minister of finance is said to have asked a wine merchant how he could be of assistance. The wine merchant answered, "Let us alone." The story and the phrase were widely circulated, and the phrase *laissez-faire* became a way of referring to an economy or approach

---

[†]Friedman's followers were also known as "Chicago Boys."

that functioned without interference. The phrase has its widest use in the context of economics, but it can also be used to describe theories and behaviors unrelated to economics, for instance, "When it came to education, the philosopher Jean-Jacques Rousseau took a *laissez-faire* approach. He believed that the children would instinctively learn what they needed to know."

4. **John Maynard Keynes and Keynesian economics** Keynes's book *The General Theory of Employment, Interest and Money* (1936) revolutionized economic thought in a number of ways. However, when allusions are made to Keynes or Keynesian thinking, most people have one thought in mind: his belief that the government should play a role in the economy and hire the unemployed when unemployment figures rose too high. Although Keynes, like Friedman, supported the notion of self-interest playing a role in the marketplace, he believed that during times of high unemployment, the government had to step in and create jobs. When allusions to Keynes are used, the role of government intervention in the economy is almost always what the writer or speaker has in mind, for example, "Keynesian myths persist today largely because of the mistaken belief that economic slowdowns are a result of flaws in the free-market system."

5. **Main Street** Published in 1929, Sinclair Lewis's novel *Main Street* described the author's Minnesota hometown Sauk Centre, a place he thoroughly despised. Calling the fictional version of his hometown Gopher Prairie, Lewis painted its citizens as nosy and small-minded. For that reason, allusions to Main Street were once used to describe people who were close-minded and prejudiced. However, over time, the meaning of the allusion has changed. Allusions to Main Street suggest plain, hard-working Americans, for example, "When he was running for president in 1988, Michael Dukakis repeatedly insisted that he wanted to help Main Street rather than Wall Street."

Copyright © Cengage Learning. All rights reserved.

◆ **EXERCISE 9** **Putting Allusions into Sentences**

DIRECTIONS Fill in the blanks with the correct allusion.

> Main Street   Milton Friedman   Keynes   laissez-faire
> invisible hand of the market

1. Although the candidate was remarkably popular with members of the financial community, he didn't have the same appeal for those living on _____.

2. The newly installed Chilean government was advised by members of the _____ school of economics; not surprisingly, government regulations did not play a significant role in the recovery plan.

3. Even Adam Smith did not fully believe in a totally _____ economy. He thought some of those who sold their goods might occasionally cheat their customers. Thus he recommended keeping a sharp eye on transactions.

4. In the midst of the worst unemployment in decades, some people were optimistic. They believed that, in time, the _____ would bring about the right balance between supply and demand.

5. When the president filled many of his financial posts with _____ supporters, believers in an unregulated free market shook their heads in disgust.

Copyright © Cengage Learning. All rights reserved.

DIGGING DEEPER

Mad for Words

Looking Ahead

As you read the following selection, pay close attention to the italicized words. When you finish, answer the questions about context clues and word parts.

1   Prior to the completion of the *Oxford English Dictionary* (*OED*) in 1928, the most *acclaimed* dictionary in the English language was Samuel Johnson's *A Dictionary of the English Language*, published in 1755. Yet extraordinary as Johnson's achievement was, it paled by comparison to the multivolumed *OED*. Unlike the highly respected Dr. Johnson, who had included only the words he personally considered good, useful, or worthy, the makers of the *OED* made no such *distinctions* among words. Under the leadership of clergyman and scholar Richard Trench, *scores* of volunteers labored to include all of the words in the English language, along with sample sentences that illustrated changes in meaning over time.

2   Enthusiastic as Trench was, he didn't possess the organizational skills necessary to the *daunting* task at hand. It wasn't until the Scotsman and self-taught *linguist* James Murray signed on as editor, sometime in the mid-1870s, that the dreamed-of dictionary showed signs of becoming a reality. Murray created a *meticulous* system for the volunteers engaged on the project to follow. Murray's system was ordered right down to the way volunteers should organize the slips of paper they sent to his central office. Even then, of course, Murray discovered that some volunteers couldn't—or wouldn't—follow directions. Many entries were flat-out *illegible*, so hastily scribbled that neither Murray nor his staff could read them.

3   Fortunately for Murray and, above all, for the project, there were a few volunteers who got everything right, creating entries that were well-organized, thorough, and completely legible. One volunteer in particular, William C. Minor, an American living in England, earned Murray's heartfelt admiration. Month after month, Minor showered the editor with neatly written scraps of paper, each one identifying a key meaning in the history of a specific word. Also included were a sample sentence and the date of the word's first appearance. Minor's contribution was so great that Murray set out to meet the man face to face, only to make an astonishing discovery: William Minor was an American physician and convicted murderer, *incarcerated* in the Broadmoor Asylum for the Criminally Insane and condemned to stay there for the rest of his natural life.

4   Eight years before becoming Murray's favorite volunteer, Minor had murdered a man in cold blood, convinced that his victim—a complete

Copyright © Cengage Learning. All rights reserved.

stranger—intended to kill him. At the time of the murder, and indeed throughout his life, Minor was given to wild delusions about enemies sneaking into his room at night intent on doing him bodily harm. Work on the dictionary, however, seemed to quiet his *hallucinations*. It also helped relieve the misery and *tedium* of his day-to-day life.

5   Horrified by Minor's violent past and obvious madness, Murray was, nevertheless, drawn by the lonely man's passion for words. Minor, in turn, was grateful that Murray respected his contribution, and he worked even more *diligently* in order to *retain* his new friend's admiration. That hard work did not go unrewarded. In 1899, Murray publicly announced his admiration for the man who was spending his life behind bars: "So enormous have been Dr. Minor's contributions during the past seventeen or eighteen years, that we could easily illustrate the last four centuries from his quotations alone."

6   But Murray's friendship and respect could not *stave off* the rising tide of madness that continued to *engulf* Minor during his thirty-year stay at Broadmoor. By 1902, even work on the dictionary could not calm Minor's mad fantasies. When Minor started to do himself physical harm, Murray helped get him returned to America, where the unfortunate man quickly declined into complete madness, giving up all work on the *OED*. Minor died in 1920, eight years before the *Oxford English Dictionary*—seventy years in the making—was published to great acclaim. What few knew, however, was the role a madman had played in its creation. (Information for this reading drawn from Simon Winchester, *The Professor and the Madman*. New York: Harper Perennial, 1999.)

Sharpening Your Skills

DIRECTIONS   Answer the following questions by filling in the blanks.

1.   What's a good approximate definition for *acclaimed* in paragraph 1?

    _____

2.   What's a good approximate definition for *distinctions* in paragraph 1?

    _____

3.   What's a good approximate definition for *scores* in paragraph 1?

    _____

Copyright © Cengage Learning. All rights reserved.

4. What's a good approximate definition for *daunting* in paragraph 2?

   _____

5. *Lingua* is a Latin root meaning "language," and *ist* is a Greek suffix indicating "a person who performs a specific action." Put the two word parts together and you get the word *linguist* in paragraph 2. Based on context and word parts, what is a good approximate definition for *linguist*?

   _____

6. What kind of context clue does the author provide for the word *meticulous* in paragraph 2?

   _____

   What is a good approximate definition for *meticulous*?

   _____

7. In paragraph 2, what's a good approximate definition for *illegible*?

   _____

   Based on that definition, what does the prefix *il* mean?

   _____

8. What word in paragraph 3 is an antonym for *illegible*?

   _____

9. In paragraph 3, what's a good approximate definition for *incarcerated*?

   _____

10. What's a good approximate definition for *hallucinations* in paragraph 4?

    _____

    What word in paragraph 4 is a synonym for *hallucinations*?

    _____

Copyright © Cengage Learning. All rights reserved.

11. What's a good approximate definition for *tedium* in paragraph 4?

    _____

12. What's a good approximate definition for *diligently* in paragraph 5?

    _____

13. What's a good approximate definition for *retain* in paragraph 5?

    _____

    Which of the two meanings you learned for the prefix *re* fits this definition?

    _____

14. What's a good approximate definition for *stave off* in paragraph 6?

    _____

15. What's a good approximate definition for *engulf* in paragraph 6?

    _____

Copyright © Cengage Learning. All rights reserved.

▶ **TEST 1**   **Learning the Language of Government**

DIRECTIONS   Fill in the blanks with one of the following words.

> amendment   commercial   ratify   elite   federal
> embargo   constituents legitimacy expenditures   partisan

1. The U.S. Congress belongs to the legislative branch of the _____ government.

2. The Nineteenth _____ to the Constitution, which guaranteed women the right to vote, was decided by a newly elected, 24-year-old Tennessee legislator named Harry Burn, who switched from "no" to "yes" in response to a letter from his mother saying, "Hurrah, and vote for suffrage!"

3. Russia's lower house of parliament has finally voted to _____ the international treaty on climate change.

4. The senator was in favor of sex education in the schools but fearful of how his _____ might react.

5. No _____ trade should be allowed in protected wilderness areas.

6. Claiming the vote had been rigged, the rebels immediately challenged the _____ of the newly elected government.

7. During the Revolutionary War, the Minutemen were a small but _____ force, which was highly mobile and quick to assemble.

8. As a(n) _____ of no political party, the judge seemed a good choice for the Supreme Court.

9. The _____ Act of 1807 forbade all international trade to and from American ports.

10. In 2003, health care _____ in the United States were over $2.3 trillion.

Copyright © Cengage Learning. All rights reserved.

▶ TEST 2   **Learning the Vocabulary of Psychology**

DIRECTIONS   Fill in the blanks with one of the following words.

dynamics	physiology	therapeutic	longitudinal	norms
genetic	assertiveness	cognitive	stimulus	correlation

1. For some people, society's _____ exist only to be ignored or challenged.

2. No one really understands the underlying _____ of physical attraction.

3. _____ therapy focuses on changing the patient's thought patterns.

4. _____ studies of twins over the course of their lifetime suggest that, despite differences in environment, twins develop a similar behavior and temperament.

5. There is a positive _____ between smoking and lung cancer.

6. Trained to associate food with the sound of a bell, Pavlov's dogs responded to the _____ by salivating.

7. Oddly enough, when he took the anti-anxiety medication, his _____ increased, although normally, he had difficulty expressing his opinions.

8. Research consistently shows a(n) _____ component to both temperament and attitude.

9. The sports foundation was advertising for someone with a knowledge of anatomy and _____.

10. Studies have undermined the belief that the herb St. John's Wort has a(n) _____ effect on depression.

Copyright © Cengage Learning. All rights reserved.

▶ **TEST 3**　　　**Using Context Clues**

DIRECTIONS　　Use the sentences or passages to determine approximate definitions for the italicized words.

1. Currently, honeybees are disappearing and no one knows why. What scientists realize, however, is that the *ramifications* of the disappearance will be widespread. It won't just be harder to raise flowers, it will also be more difficult to produce a food supply rich in fruits and vegetables.

   Ramifications means _____.

2. The lawyer was turning into a *perennial* candidate, always running but never winning.

   Perennial means _____.

3. When the author stood at the podium to speak, there were no signs of her previous *trepidation*. In contrast to her earlier mood, she was remarkably relaxed and calm. Her voice did not break; her hands did not shake, and she seemed totally in command of the situation.

   Trepidation means _____.

4. That kind of *vituperation* has no place in a political campaign; the candidate should be explaining positions, not spewing insults.

   Vituperation means _____.

5. When it comes to publicity, the *incumbent* president obviously has more access to the press than other candidates. As the person already holding the office, the president has automatic press coverage.

   Incumbent means _____.

6. He had come from an extremely *affluent* home where money was no object. But he gave it all up to live a life of poverty and serve those needier than he.

   Affluent means _____.

Copyright © Cengage Learning. All rights reserved.

7. Although she wanted to, she could not *mitigate* the harshness of her criticism.

   Mitigate means _____.

8. The bulldog was remarkably *tenacious*. He wouldn't let go of the robber's leg even when the man rained blows down on his head. The dog only let go after his master yelled, "Stop!"

   Tenacious means _____.

9. Books on time management are popular mainly because *procrastination* is so common. After all, how many of us can honestly say we have never put off or postponed something we didn't want to do—washing the dog, writing a paper, cleaning the house—until the very last possible minute?

   Procrastination means _____.

10. After saving his mother from drowning, the twelve-year-old boy was *inundated* with letters praising him for his heroism.

    Inundated means _____.

Copyright © Cengage Learning. All rights reserved.

▶ **TEST 4** **Understanding Common Cultural Allusions**

DIRECTIONS In the blanks following every passage, explain what the italicized allusion is supposed to suggest.

1. In 2002, after American Civil Liberties Union president Nadine Strossen claimed that the word *terrorism* was "taking on the same kind of characteristics as the term *communism* in the 1950s," many civil rights and free-speech activists began publicly worrying about a possible return of *McCarthyism*.

   The allusion to *McCarthyism* implies that _____

   _____

   _____.

2. The Hundred Years' War between England and France began in 1337 and finally ended in 1453. Despite the conflict's name, however, fighting was not actually continuous for 116 years. Fighting was interspersed with extended periods of *cold war* and even periods of peace.

   The allusion to *cold war* implies that _____

   _____

   _____.

3. When it came to leadership, the administrator took a *laissez-faire* approach that left those working for her feeling confused about their responsibilities.

   The allusion to *laissez-faire* implies that _____

   _____

   _____.

4. A firm believer in *Keynesian* economics, *New York Times* columnist and Nobel-prize winner Paul Krugman would also undoubtedly support government efforts to fund job-training programs for young people.

Copyright © Cengage Learning. All rights reserved.

The allusion to *Keynes* implies that _____

_____

_____ .

5. When it comes to letting bloggers have free access to the Internet, China has apparently lowered an *iron curtain*, making it difficult to find out what's really going on in the country.

The allusion to the *iron curtain* implies that _____

_____

_____ .

6. Recent statistics confirm that income inequality in the United States has returned to *Gilded Age* levels. (Paul Krugman, *New York Review of Books*, November 20, 2003.)

The allusion to the *Gilded Age* implies that _____

_____

_____ .

7. Writing in the *Wall Street Journal* in 2010, Brett Stephens argued that the earthquake that rocked Chile in March of that year could have caused a lot more damage if the country had not been protected by the ghost of *Milton Friedman*. According to Stephens, Chile's leaders had been following Friedman's advice for thirty years and the country had become wealthy in the process.

The allusion to *Milton Friedman* implies that _____

_____

_____ .

8. Even if he or she came from a wealthy family, a candidate hoping to win an election has to stay focused on *Main Street*.

The allusion to *Main Street* implies that _____

_____

_____ .

Copyright © Cengage Learning. All rights reserved.

9. There is no doubt that the *invisible hand of the market* can out-perform the heavy hand of regulation. (Christine Todd Whitman, former governor of New Jersey and administrator of the Environmental Protection Agency.)

   The allusion to the *invisible hand of the market* implies that _____

   _____

   _____.

10. The World Champion met his *Waterloo* when he decided to fight an up-and-coming boxer ten years younger than himself.

    The allusion to *Waterloo* implies that _____

    _____

    _____.

Copyright © Cengage Learning. All rights reserved.

Reviewing Paragraph Essentials

© Arctic-Images/Corbis

IN THIS CHAPTER, YOU WILL LEARN

- how to zero in on the essential elements of a paragraph: the topic, main idea, and supporting details.

- how transitions help direct readers to topic sentences and supporting details.

- how supporting details further explain or prove topic sentences.

*There is creative reading as well
as creative writing.*

—Ralph Waldo Emerson,
American philosopher and poet

There will certainly be times in your reading when the point of the paragraph seems to jump off the page. In these moments, your grasp of the author's message is immediate. You don't have to consciously think about it. At other times, however, the topic will be so unfamiliar or the writer's style so complicated that you'll have to think your way through the paragraph almost sentence by sentence. The explanation that follows was written for precisely those kinds of paragraphs.

Start with the Topic

To find the topic of a paragraph, ask yourself this question: "Which person, event, practice, or idea is most frequently mentioned or referred to in the paragraph?" To illustrate, let's use the following paragraph:

> The use of animals in scientific research is a controversial subject that provokes strong emotions on both sides. The most radical animal rights activists define animals as sentient* beings, who can think, feel, and suffer. Activists insist, therefore, that the rights of research animals be acknowledged and respected. They also insist that all experiments requiring animal subjects should be banned. For the more conservative animal rights activists, the use of animals in research is acceptable. However, the health and well being of research animals must be strictly monitored. In response to these objections, research scientists who experiment on animals have made efforts to take better care of research animals. Most scientists argue, though, that research on animals is ethical and necessary because it saves human lives and alleviates* human suffering.

What is the topic of this paragraph? Is it "animal rights activists" or the "use of animals in research"? If you chose the "use of animals in research," you are correct. That is the topic.

It's the topic because the author repeatedly returns to it through a chain of repetition and reference, such as "use of animals in research," "research using animals," "research animals," and "scientists who experiment on animals." Although the phrase "animal rights activists" is mentioned or referred to several times, it doesn't come up as frequently as

---

*sentient: conscious, capable of feeling.
*alleviates: improves, makes better.

Copyright © Cengage Learning. All rights reserved.

words and phrases related to "using animals in research." The frequency with which an author repeats or refers to a word or phrase is a deciding factor in determining the topic of a reading.

Phrasing the Topic

Notice the number of words expressing the previous topic—five, to be exact. Occasionally, the topic of a paragraph can be expressed in a single word. However, you'll usually need a longer phrase to sum up the **precise topic**, that is, the one that leads you most directly to the author's **main idea**, or key point.

Look, for instance, at the following paragraph. What's the topic here?

Although the fighting took place far from the United States, the Vietnam War[†] deeply affected the way Americans lived their lives. Military service became an important, life-changing experience for more than two million Americans. In the typical tour of duty, soldiers encountered racial tensions, boredom, drugs, and a widespread brutality against the Vietnamese. Even those Americans who did not fight were changed by the war. Millions of young men spent a substantial part of their late adolescence or young adulthood wondering whether they would be drafted or seeking ways to avoid participation in the fighting. Far more men did not go to Vietnam than went, but the war created deep divisions among people of an entire generation. Those who fought in the war often resented those who did not. By the same token, some people who never went to Vietnam sometimes treated those who did with pity or condescension.[*] (Adapted from Schaller, Scharf, and Schulzinger, *Present Tense*, p. 301.)

Here again, no single word could effectively sum up the topic. The word *Americans* won't do. Nor will the phrase "Vietnam War." To express the focus of the paragraph, we need phrases like "the effect of the Vietnam War on American life" or "the Vietnam War's effect on Americans."

Note, too, that the words in these topics don't appear next to each other in the paragraph. Both topics were created by *synthesizing*, or combining, words from different parts of the paragraph. Notice as well that the word *life* doesn't appear anywhere in the paragraph. That's not

---

[†]Vietnam War: a long civil war in Vietnam (1954–1975) that involved both France and the United States.
[*]condescension: behaving as if one were superior in some way.

Copyright © Cengage Learning. All rights reserved.

unusual. Expressing a paragraph's topic often requires readers to supply some or even all of the necessary words.

◆ **EXERCISE 1** **Identifying Topics**

DIRECTIONS Read each paragraph. Then circle the letter of the correct topic.

1. Researchers are trying to develop new anti-malarial drugs and vaccines for Anopheles mosquitoes, which cause the deadly disease malaria. However, there are other ways to fight the disease. One is to provide poor people in malarial regions with long-lasting insecticide-treated bed nets and window screens for their dwellings. Another is to use zinc and vitamin A supplements to boost resistance to malaria in children. The number of malaria cases can also be greatly reduced by spraying the insides of homes with low concentrations of the pesticide DDT twice a year at a cost of about $10. Unfortunately, under an international treaty enacted in 2002, DDT and five similar pesticides are being phased out in developing countries. However, in 2006, the World Health Organization supported the use of DDT for malaria control. (Adapted from Miller and Spoolman, *Sustaining the Earth*, p. 240.)

Topic

    a. fighting malaria

    b. using DDT to fight malaria

    c. malarial regions

2. Conjoined twins are usually classified into three basic categories, depending on where their bodies connect. Twins of the first type are conjoined in a way that never involves the heart or the midline of the body. For example, about 2 percent of all conjoined twins are attached at the head only. About 19 percent are joined at the buttocks. Twins of the second type are always joined in a way that involves the midline of the body. Many twins joined at the midline share a heart. Around 35 percent are fused at the upper half of the trunk. Another 30 percent are joined at the lower half of their bodies. The third major type of conjoined twins includes very rare forms of physical connection. In this category are those in which one twin is smaller, less formed, and dependent on the other, as well

Copyright © Cengage Learning. All rights reserved.

as cases in which one twin is born completely within the body of his or her sibling.

Topic

a. twins sharing a heart
b. twins
c. conjoined twins

3. The ideas of Russian psychologist Lev Vygotsky have had a powerful influence on American education. Among the most important of those ideas is Vygotsky's theory that a *zone of proximal development* exists for most skills. When applied to specific mental or physical activities, the zone of proximal development refers to the point at which a child cannot solve a problem alone but can find a solution in the company of an adult or a peer who possesses the appropriate expertise. For instance, a child who doesn't know how to construct a bookshelf from looking at the directions but who can construct one with guidance from a more experienced friend is functioning in the zone of proximal development. Once children have entered the zone of proximal development, the goal is for them to mimic the more expert pattern of thought or action until mastery has been achieved. Mastery means that the children can repeat the action or the thought process without outside help or guidance.

Topic

a. Lev Vygotsky
b. zone of proximal development
c. problem solving in early childhood

4. Constructing a representative sample is essential to the use of surveys for research. A representative sample includes the same proportion of men, women, young, old, professionals, blue-collar workers, Republicans, Democrats, whites, blacks, Latinos, Asians, and so on, as are found in the population as a whole. Ultimately, a representative sample tries to mirror the makeup of the entire population. Then, during the survey, those in the representative sample are asked a series of carefully worded questions. By drawing conclusions based on the representative sample's answers, researchers think that they can draw conclusions about the larger group without polling each person. (Adapted from Coon, *Essentials of Psychology*, p. 34.)

Copyright © Cengage Learning. All rights reserved.

Topic

    a. drawing conclusions

    b. survey characteristics

    c. representative samples

Use the Topic to Discover the Main Idea

Once you know the topic of a paragraph, the next logical step is to determine the **main idea**. The main idea is the key point or central message of the paragraph. It's what unites, or ties together, all the sentences in the paragraph. Most paragraphs lacking a main idea end up being little more than collections of unrelated thoughts.

The one exception to that rule would be scientific description paragraphs, which are meant to give readers the key characteristics of a theory, a thing, or an event. But for the most part, paragraphs, even in science textbooks, will revolve around one key thought or main idea.

To discover the main idea of a paragraph, you need to ask two questions: (1) What does the author want to say *about* the topic? and (2) What one idea is developed sentence by sentence throughout the paragraph?

Let's use the passage below as an example. The subject, or topic, is "diet." Note how that word appears or is referred to in every sentence. But knowing the topic only gives us the author's subject matter. We need the author's point or message as well. We need to determine what the author is *saying* about the topic.

[1]It's highly likely that diet contributes to overeating. [2]Placing animals on a "supermarket" diet, for instance, can lead to gross obesity. [3]In one experiment, rats were given meals of chocolate chip cookies, salami, cheese, bananas, marshmallows, milk, chocolate, peanut butter, and fat.[4]Rats on this diet gained almost three times as much weight as animals that ate standard laboratory rat "chow." [5]It wasn't just that they consumed more calories. [6]Rats on the cookie and salami menu also consumed food in much greater quantities. [7]The study suggests that foods high in sweetness, fat, and variety encourage the desire to eat more. (Adapted from Coon, *Essentials of Psychology*, p. 405.)

Go through the previous paragraph sentence by sentence and you'll notice that each one further develops the opening point about diet contributing to overeating. Sentence 2 makes that point more specifically by citing a specific kind of diet, which leads to obesity. Sentences 3

Copyright © Cengage Learning. All rights reserved.

through 6 then describe a study supporting the idea introduced in sentence 1. Finally, sentence 7 restates the opening point in more specific terms, but the message is the same: A certain kind of diet can encourage overeating.

Given that every sentence further develops the point made in the opening sentence, we can safely say that the first sentence of the paragraph is also the **topic sentence**. The topic sentence is the general sentence that introduces the main idea or central message of the paragraph. It's the sentence that most effectively sums up the paragraph's contents.

Learn How Textbooks Introduce Topic Sentences

Although you can find discussions of reading comprehension suggesting that the main idea always appears in the first sentence—this is particularly true of reading instruction on the Web—don't be fooled. While textbook authors frequently make the first sentence the topic sentence, they often delay the introduction of the main idea in order to provide background or stimulate reader interest. They start, that is, with an **introductory sentence** offering some background knowledge about the topic sentence.

[1]When they hear the word *desert*, most people think of a vast expanse of sun-scorched earth. [2]Some deserts, however, are actually mild in climate, even cold. [3]There are, for instance, the deserts near cold ocean currents, like South America's Atacama Desert and Africa's Kalahari Desert. [4]Both are cooled by cold, dry ocean air. [5]Then, too, there are the dry, frozen, polar deserts found in places like northern Greenland, Arctic Canada, and Northern Alaska, where temperatures can dip well below zero. (Adapted from Chernicoff et al., *Earth: Geologic Principles and History*, p. 311.)

In this case, the introductory sentence identifies what "most people" imagine to be true about deserts. The phrase "most people" is important. It's a strong signal that the authors might be ready to challenge what most people think. And indeed they do.

By sentence 2, which is the topic sentence, the author introduces an alternative image of the desert. It's not always hot. Such delayed introductions of the topic sentence are common in textbook discussions. For that matter, they are common in all kinds of writing and are worthy of extra attention.

Copyright © Cengage Learning. All rights reserved.

Challenging Traditional Opinion

The paragraph on deserts illustrates an especially popular way of constructing textbook passages. Authors start by expressing a traditional point of view, or what most people think about the topic. Then they challenge or revise that traditional viewpoint by offering a different position or perspective.

With this kind of paragraph, the topic sentence frequently turns up as the second sentence as it did in the paragraph on deserts. However, it can also turn up in the middle, as it does in the paragraph that follows:

Topic Sentence

[1]In the discussion of the status and vitality of marriage, we often hear that a retreat from marriage has taken place in the United States in recent decades. [2]R. S. Oropesa and Nancy Landale (2004) describe the retreat from marriage as evident in a number of recent and ongoing trends: "historic" delays in the age at which women and men first marry, nearly "unprecedented" proportions of the population never marrying, "dramatic" increases in cohabitation and nonmarital births, and continued high divorce rates. [3]Yet closer inspection indicates that the retreat from marriage has not occurred among all social groups. [4]Instead, both racial and economic differences can be identified. [5]For many ethnic groups in the United States, marriage remains a powerful institution. [6]It's worth noting, for instance, that between 1970 and 2000, the percentage of Chinese-American men and women who were married actually increased as did the percentage of Japanese-American men. (Strong et al., *The Marriage and Family Experience*, p. 230.)

Waiting Until the End

Although it happens less frequently in textbooks and more commonly in literary essays, even writers of textbooks will sometimes delay the topic sentence until the very end of a paragraph. In this next paragraph, the author identifies a number of specific examples and then arrives at a more general conclusion based on the examples already provided:

[1]In China, blogger Shi Tao was sentenced to ten years in prison after his blog posted details of how the government planned to handle the fifteenth anniversary of the Tiananmen Square massacre, during which protestors were killed or imprisoned because of their public

Copyright © Cengage Learning. All rights reserved.

demands for a more democratic government. [2]According to Reporters Without Borders, Yahoo, the Internet service provider for Shi's email, helped the government link Shi's account to the offending messages. [3]In Iran, Kianoosh Sanjari was arrested for using his blog to provide details about the arrest of dissidents* by the Iranian government. [4]Amnesty International claims that after Tunisian lawyer Mohammed Abbou posted two articles denouncing the government's torture of political prisoners, he was arrested and sentenced to four years in prison. [5]Similar incidents have taken place in Vietnam. [6]When Nguyen Vu Binh wrote a series of articles demanding more political and economic freedom for Vietnamese citizens, he found himself sentenced to seven years in prison. [7]In the United States, bloggers are sometimes harshly criticized for their outspoken, even insulting expressions of opinion concerning political figures and government policies; however, countries that don't have the same respect for freedom of expression go a lot further in their determination to make bloggers toe the line.

Topic Sentence

◆ **EXERCISE 2**   **Identifying Topics and Topic Sentences**

DIRECTIONS   Read the following paragraphs. Circle the letter of the topic and write the number of the topic sentence in the blank.

EXAMPLE   [1]People have many different reasons for wanting children. [2]Some really like children and want an opportunity to be involved with their care. [3]Some women strongly desire the experience of pregnancy and childbirth while some men are excited about becoming fathers. [4]Many young adults see parenthood as a way to demonstrate their adult status. [5]For people coming from happy families, having children is a means of reliving their earlier happiness. [6]For those from unhappy families, it can be a means of doing better than their parents did. [7]Some people have children simply because it's expected of them. [8]Because society places so much emphasis on the fulfillment motherhood is supposed to bring, some women who are unsure of what they want to do with their lives use having a child as a way to create an identity. (Seifert et al., *Lifespan Development*, p. 484.)

―――――――――――

*dissidents: people who openly disagree with the policies of their government.

Copyright © Cengage Learning. All rights reserved.

Topic   a. childhood

             ⓑ. reasons people have children

             c. parenting and past childhood experience

Topic Sentence   _1_

EXPLANATION   If you analyze the sentences in the paragraph, you'll see that each one deals with the "reasons people have children." Look for an idea developed in both general and specific terms and you'll see that the first sentence expresses an idea further elaborated in every single sentence. Sentence 1 tells readers there are many different reasons people have children. Then the rest of the sentences identify those reasons.

1. [1]Most people know the name of César Chávez, the deservedly famous founder of the United Farm Workers (UFW)[†] union. [2]Not so many people, however, know the name of Dolores Huerta (1930–), the woman who helped Chávez start the UFW. [3]Yet Huerta was a key figure in the union's early achievements, and both she and her role in the union are worthy of more recognition than they have so far received. [4]Huerta's father had been a migrant worker, a union activist, and, ultimately, a member of the New Mexico state

Dolores Huerta is third from the left.

© Scott Sommerdorf/San Francisco Chronicle/Corbis

Copyright © Cengage Learning. All rights reserved.

[†]UFW: The United Farm Workers union organized migrant workers

legislature, so it's not surprising that his daughter would be drawn to union activity and political activism. [5]By the time she had reached her twenties, Huerta was working with the Agricultural Workers Organizing Committee, which is what brought her together with Chávez. [6]Highly effective as an organizer, Huerta was Chávez's second-in-command, and she played a crucial role in the 1968–1969 grape boycott, which brought the once arrogant grape farm owners to their knees, establishing the UFW as a force to be reckoned with. [7]Throughout the 1970s, Huerta was involved in the political arm of the UFW and played a critical role lobbying for farm-worker legislative protections. [8]She remained active in the cause of migrant workers throughout the 1980s and 1990s, despite being critically injured by police during a 1988 political demonstration.

Topic

a. Dolores Huerta's relationship to her father

b. Dolores Huerta's relationship to César Chávez

c. Dolores Huerta's role in the UFW

Topic Sentence _____

2. [1]The zoo industry insists that elephants in zoos throughout the country are well taken care of. [2]The industry assures the public that there is no cause to be alarmed about the well-being of these magnificent creatures. [3]Animal rights activists, however, challenge the zoo industry's claims, and there is an angry debate brewing about the health of elephants confined in zoos, with the federal government deciding to review the animals' situation in confinement. [4]According to Elliot Katz, a veterinarian and president of the California-based organization In Defense of Animals, "the state of elephant health in the U.S. is appallingly poor." [5]Katz claims that experts in the field believe elephants should not be walking back and forth on concrete floors. [6]Their feet are designed to walk miles on soil, but not back and forth on cold concrete. [7]Katz would seem to know whereof he speaks because in 2006 a number of zoo-held elephants died from complications brought on by sore feet. [8]Members of the zoo industry, however, consider the deaths exceptions. [9]Willie Theisseon, head elephant keeper at the Pittsburgh Zoo, argues that elephants dying of foot complications are probably older animals—elephants can live into their sixties—and probably came from facilities where their

Copyright © Cengage Learning. All rights reserved.

feet were injured. [10]He insists, though, that almost all such facilities have been upgraded so that the problem no longer exists. (Source of claims: www.idausa.org/.)

Topic
a. the treatment of animals by zoos
b. elephants in the wild versus elephants in zoos
c. zoo industry's treatment of elephants

Topic Sentence   _____

3. [1]Many people think that talking about *lifestyles*—tastes, preferences, and ways of living—is a trivial pursuit at best. [2]However, studying lifestyle differences reveals a lot about the differences in social classes. [3]Upper- and middle-class people think it important to be active outside their homes—in parent-teacher associations, charitable organizations, and any number of community activities. [4]They are also likely to make friends with colleagues and business associates, inviting them into their homes. [5]Usually, their spouses help cultivate these relationships. [6]In contrast, members of the working class are less likely to be involved in organizations not directly related to their family. [7]They are also less inclined to entertain their coworkers at home, although outings after work for drinks or dinner are common. (Adapted from Thio, *Society: Myths and Realities*, p. 211.)

Topic
a. lifestyles of the middle class
b. talking about lifestyles
c. lifestyle differences

Topic Sentence   _____

4. [1]When it comes to displays of formality or informality in language, large cultural differences exist. [2]The informal approach that characterizes conversations in countries like the United States, Canada, Australia, and the Scandinavian countries is quite different from the concern shown for using proper speech in many parts of Asia and Africa, where formality in language defines social position. [3]In Korea, for example, the language reveals a system of relational hierarchies.*

---

*hierarchies: levels or rankings of people based on authority or importance.

Copyright © Cengage Learning. All rights reserved.

[4]Koreans have a special vocabulary for different sexes, levels of social status, degrees of intimacy, and types of social occasions. [5]There are even different degrees of formality for speaking with old friends, acquaintances, and complete strangers. [6]One sign of being a learned person in Korea is the ability to use the language in a way that recognizes these relational distinctions. [7]When you contrast these sorts of distinctions with the casual friendliness that Americans display even when talking to strangers, it's easy to see how a Korean might find an American boorish* in conversation while an American might consider a Korean stiff and unfriendly. (Adler and Proctor, *Looking Out, Looking In*, p. 187.)

Topic   a. Koreans in conversation with Americans
               b. formality and informality in language
               c. informality in language

Topic Sentence   _____

TAKING A CLOSER LOOK

Repetition and Reference
In paragraph 4 of Exercise 2, sentence 4 serves to define what word or phrase from the previous sentence? _____

Note How Introductory Sentences Team Up with Reversal Transitions

Reversal transitions are words and phrases like *however, yet*, and *in contrast*, plus sentences like "That's not how events unfolded." Whether a word phrase, or sentence, reversal transitions serve the same function: They tell readers that the author is about to revise, challenge, or contradict what's just been said.

Not surprisingly, reversal transitions frequently follow introductory sentences. Notice, for example, how the reversal transition "yet" prepares the reader for the topic sentence in the following paragraph. The transition says to the reader, "Get ready for a change in direction. The paragraph is *not* going to follow the lead of the opening sentence."

---

*boorish: crude, disrespectful of others, vulgar.

Copyright © Cengage Learning. All rights reserved.

Topic Sentence

If you miss a few hours of sleep, you may feel a little groggy for the next day but still believe that you can muddle through without difficulty. Yet, perhaps not surprisingly, sleep deprivation is among the most common causes of motor-vehicle accidents. Such accidents are most likely to occur in the early morning hours when drivers are typically at their sleepiest. This makes sense because sleep deprivation slows reaction times and impairs concentration, memory, and problem-solving ability. Thus the effects of sleep deprivation make it more difficult to be a careful driver. (Adapted from Nevid, *Essentials of Psychology*, p. 135.)

If you look at sentence 2 in the paragraph on lifestyles on page 118 and then at the paragraph above on sleep deprivation, you'll notice that both topic sentences open with reversal transitions. These reversal transitions are an important signal. They tell readers, "There's a shift coming up. The next sentence you read is going to challenge, oppose, or modify what you just learned from the previous sentence." In the above paragraph, for instance, "yet" signals that whatever we may believe about losing sleep, the facts don't necessarily support our belief.

A reversal transition in the second (or third) sentence of a paragraph is a strong clue that the topic sentence is coming up and going to challenge the author's opening point. Thus it's in your interest to learn the most common reversal transitions. Be on the lookout for them when you read.

Reversal Transitions ◆		
	Actually	Nonetheless
	But	On the contrary
	Contrary to	On the other hand
	Conversely	Still
	Despite the fact	Unfortunately
	Even so	While this might seem true [sensible, correct, right, etc.]
	However	
	In contradiction	Yet
	In contrast	Yet in fact
	In opposition	Yet, in point of fact,
	Ironically	Yet in reality
	Just the opposite	

Copyright © Cengage Learning. All rights reserved.

CHECK YOUR UNDERSTANDING

1. What should you do to determine the topic of a paragraph?

_____

2. Once you know the topic, what's the next logical step?

_____

3. What is the function of an introductory sentence?

_____

_____

◆ **EXERCISE 3   Recognizing Topic Sentences**

> **DIRECTIONS**   Read the following paragraphs. Write the number of the topic sentence in the blank. If the paragraph contains a reversal transition that introduces the topic sentence, circle it. *Note*: Reversal transitions don't always introduce topic sentences. It's only when they appear near the beginning of a paragraph that they are likely to perform that function.

1. ¹In the 1930s, two anthropologists, Edward Sapir and Benjamin Whorf, became intrigued when they noticed that the Hopi Indians of the southwestern United States had no word to distinguish among the past, the present, and the future. ²English—as well as French, Spanish, Swahili, and other languages—distinguishes carefully among these three time frames. ³From this observation, Sapir and Whorf began to think that words might be more than labels people attach to things. ⁴Eventually they concluded that language has embedded within it specific ways of looking at the world. ⁵In other words, language not only expresses our thoughts and perceptions but also shapes the way we think and perceive. (Henslin, *Sociology*, p. 48.)

Topic Sentence   _____

2. ¹These days eating is not a movable feast, nor even a picnic. ²Rather foods are looking more and more like astronaut fare—concentrated,

Copyright © Cengage Learning. All rights reserved.

minimalized, single-serve. [3]We buy crustless, frozen peanut butter and jelly sandwiches, and dinner kits come in their own bowls. ([4]The side dish is going the way of the cloth napkin.) [5]Just 47 percent of in-home meals include a "fresh" item such as a vegetable, compared with 56 percent two decades ago. [6]Liquid meals, once the preserve of hospital patients, are in vogue. [7]"Food is functional. [8]It's a bar you eat and you've got your meal," says Kevin Elliott, vice-president of merchandising at 7-Eleven.

Topic Sentence _____

3. [1]If you ever decide to visit another world, Mars may be your best choice. [2]Mars is much friendlier than the moon, Mercury, or Venus. [3]The nights on Mars are deadly cold, but a hot summer day would be comfortable. [4]Mars also has weather, complex terrain, and signs that water once flowed over its surface. [5]Spacecraft have been visiting Mars for almost 40 years, and the pace has picked up even more recently. [6]Spacecraft have gone into orbit around Mars to photograph and analyze its surface, and six spacecraft have landed. (Adapted from Seeds and Backman, *Foundations of Astronomy*, p. 481.)

Topic Sentence _____

4. [1]Genetic screening tests blood and tissue to detect evidence of genetic, or inherited, disorders. [2]Genetic screening provides information on the reproductive risks potential mothers and fathers run by giving birth. [3]It can also predict the potential occurrence of diseases like breast cancer and Huntington's disease.[†] [4]Hospitals also routinely do genetic screening on newborns. [5]Most newborns, for instance, are routinely tested for PKU, a genetic disorder that, if left untreated, can cause seizures and intellectual disability. [6]Because affected infants are now routinely discovered through screening, we see fewer individuals with symptoms of the disorder. [7]There are, however, psychological risks associated with genetic screening. [8]How would you feel if you knew you had the potential to pass a disease on to your child or were at high risk for breast cancer? (Adapted from Starr et al., *Biology: The Unity and Diversity of Life*, p. 199.)

Topic Sentence _____

[†]Huntington's disease: an inherited illness that destroys brain cells and grows progressively worse with time.

Copyright © Cengage Learning. All rights reserved.

5. [1]As many modern media watchers have complained, today's newspapers are all too often governed by "pack journalism," and reporters are not encouraged to search out unique stories or points of view. [2]In the nineteenth century, however, reporters went all out competing for stories because the paper with the most readers sold the most ads and made the most money. [3]In 1889 Elizabeth Cochran, who wrote under her pen name "Nellie Bly," came up with a circulation booster that may have been the first "manufactured news story." [4]Jules Verne's *Around the World in Eighty Days*, a story about a British gentleman who won a bet by circling the globe in eighty days, had been a best seller. [5]Nellie thought she could beat the record. [6]She studied train and steamship timetables for connections and told the editors of Joseph Pulitzer's New York *World* that she could make the circuit in seventy-five days. [7]Bly insisted that the adventure would sell lots of papers. [8]The editors liked the idea but said they would send a man to do it. [9]However they changed their mind when Bly told them, "Send the man and I'll start the same day for some other newspaper and beat him." [10]She left on November 14, 1889, and returned to her point of departure on January 25, 1890. [11]Her trip took seventy-two days, and the *World*, thanks to Nellie Bly's exclusive story, raked in the advertising dollars.

Topic Sentence   _____

TAKING A CLOSER LOOK

Filling in the Gaps

In paragraph 4, sentence 7 tells readers that there are psychological risks associated with genetic testing. But the sentence that follows does not describe a risk. Instead, it poses a question: How would you feel if you knew you had the potential to pass a disease on to your child or were at high risk for breast cancer? How does that question relate to the "psychological risks" mentioned in the previous sentence?

_____

_____

_____

_____

Copyright © Cengage Learning. All rights reserved.

INTERNET FOLLOW-UP: What Was the Pulitzer Formula?
Paragraph 5 in the previous exercise refers to Joseph Pulitzer, the man who turned the bankrupt *World* into the country's best-selling newspaper. Search the Web to discover what kinds of stories and writing style Pulitzer relied on—called the "Pulitzer formula"—to sell newspapers.

_____

_____

_____

_____

Find a newspaper article, in print or on the Web, and rewrite it using the Pulitzer formula.

Question-and-Answer Topic Sentences

If paragraphs with the topic sentence appearing in first or second position are common in textbooks, so too are paragraphs that open with questions.

> What is genetics? In its simplest form, genetics is the study of heredity, and it explains how certain characteristics are passed on from parents to children. Much of what we know about genetics was discovered by the monk Gregor Mendel in the nineteenth century. Since then, the field of genetics has vastly expanded. As scientists study the workings of genetics, they've developed new ways of manipulating genes. For example, scientists have isolated the gene that makes insulin, a human hormone, and now use bacteria to make quantities of it.
> (Magliore, *Cracking the AP Biology Exam*, p. 105.)

Using an opening question to draw the reader's attention to the topic sentence is a very popular strategy with writers in all fields. In textbooks, however, the author is just as likely to pose the question in the paragraph's heading. When that's the case, the answer doesn't necessarily follow right on the heels of the question, although it can.

Look, for instance, at this next paragraph. Where's the answer to the question that appears in the heading?

Copyright © Cengage Learning. All rights reserved.

Question: How much intelligence does a newborn have?

Child psychologist Jerome Bruner believed that babies are smarter than most people think. To prove his point, Bruner cited an experiment in which 3- to 8-week-old babies showed signs of understanding that a person's voice and body are connected. If babies heard their mother's voice coming from where she was standing, they remained calm. If her voice came from a loud speaker several feet away, the babies became agitated* and began to cry. Experiments like this one suggest that Bruner may be right: the human mind is active from birth onward. (Adapted from Coon, *Essentials of Psychology*, p. 84.)

In this case, the answer to the question, or as much of an answer as anyone can supply, comes not at the beginning but at the end of the paragraph.

It doesn't matter if the question is posed in the heading or as the first sentence in the paragraph, it's up to the reader to locate or infer an answer. Answering questions posed in the headings or at the beginnings of paragraphs is important because the answer is very likely to be the main idea.

◆ **EXERCISE 4**   **Recognizing Topic Sentences and Reversal Transitions**

DIRECTIONS   Read each paragraph and then write the number of the topic sentence in the blank. Circle any reversal transitions introducing the topic sentences.

1. [1]Compared with a corporate executive or a military officer, a teacher may not appear to have a great deal of power. [2]But teachers have a special type of power. [3]Henry Adams† caught the sense of the teacher's long-term power in the words "A teacher affects eternity: No one can tell where his influence stops." [4]The teacher's powerful influence arises from the fact that he or she has an impact on people when they are still at a very impressionable stage. [5]Teachers take "a piece of living clay and gently form it, day by day." [6]Many careers are open to you, but few offer such truly inspiring power. (Adapted from Ryan and Cooper, *Those Who Can, Teach*, p. 148.)

Topic Sentence   _____

---

*agitated: upset.
†Henry Adams: American historian (1838–1918).

Copyright © Cengage Learning. All rights reserved.

2. [1]Before the collapse of the Communist Party in Eastern Europe, the East German secret police, the *Staatssicherheit* (or Stasi), was an enormous bureaucracy* that snooped into every part of society. [2]It had 85,000 full-time employees, including 6,000 people whose sole task was to listen in on telephone conversations. [3]Another 2,000 steamed open mail, read it, resealed the letters, and sent them on to the intended recipients. [4]The Stasi also employed 150,000 active informers and hundreds of thousands of part-time snitches. [5]Files were kept on an estimated 4 to 5 million people in a country that had a total population, including children, of just 17 million. [6]Although East Germany had a large standing army, the Stasi kept its own arsenal of 250,000 weapons. (Adapted from Janda et al., *The Challenge of Democracy*, p. 452.)

Topic Sentence _____

3. [1]What causes plants to bloom? [2]Although you may think that plants flower based on the amount of sunlight they receive, they actually bloom according to the amount of uninterrupted darkness; this principle of plant bloom is called *photoperiodism*. [3]Plants that bloom in late summer and fall, like asters and sedum, are called short-day plants. [4]They require long periods of darkness and only short periods of light. [5]Plants that flower in late spring and early summer, such as daisies and poppies, are called long-day plants. [6]They need only short periods of darkness to blossom.

Topic Sentence _____

4. [1]On May 28, 1934, Elzire Dionne gave birth to five daughters who became famous as the Dionne Quintuplets. [2]Their birth made immediate headlines and was celebrated as a medical miracle. [3]Unfortunately, the little girls' fame was their downfall; almost from the moment of birth, they were exploited by everyone around them. [4]The parents of the quintuplets were poor and didn't know how to support their family, which already included six children. [5]Confused and desperate, they agreed to put their five daughters on display at

---

*bureaucracy: a large organization divided into numerous offices or bureaus, each with its own staff.

Copyright © Cengage Learning. All rights reserved.

the Chicago World's Fair. [6]For a brief moment, it seemed as if the girls were saved from a miserable fate when the family physician, Dr. Allan Roy Dafoe, stepped in and insisted the girls were too frail to be on exhibit. [7]But after Dafoe took control of the girls' lives, he made himself rich by displaying the quintuplets to tourists and collecting fees for product endorsements.

Topic Sentence   _____

5. [1]George W. Bush is only the second man, after John Quincy Adams, to follow in the footsteps of his father and serve as president of the United States. [2]John Quincy Adams, America's sixth president, was the son of second president John Adams. [3]The elder George Bush even calls his son "Quincy." [4]George W. Bush and John Quincy Adams share other similarities, too. [5]Both men are their fathers' oldest sons. [6]Both men held public office before being elected president. [7]Adams was a U.S. senator and served as secretary of state, while Bush was governor of Texas. [8]Both men were in their fifties when they successfully ran for president. [9]Both men also achieved the presidency in a contested election because neither of them had won the popular vote.

Topic Sentence   _____

6. [1]On the surface, effective listening might seem to require little more than an acute sense of hearing. [2]But, in fact, there's a big difference between hearing and listening. [3]*Hearing* occurs when sound waves travel through the air, enter your ears, and are transmitted by the auditory nerve to your brain. [4]As long as neither your brain nor your ears are impaired, hearing is involuntary. [5]It occurs spontaneously with little conscious effort on your part. [6]*Listening*, in contrast, is a voluntary act that includes attending to, understanding, and evaluating the words or sounds you hear. [7]If you sit through a lecture without making an effort to listen, there's a good chance that the speaker's words will become just so much background noise. (Flemming and Leet, *Becoming a Successful Student*, p. 93.)

Topic Sentence   _____

Copyright © Cengage Learning. All rights reserved.

7. [1]When we are extremely fearful or angry, our heartbeat speeds up, our pulse races, and our breathing rate increases. [2]The body's metabolism* accelerates, burning up sugar in the bloodstream and fats in the tissues at a faster rate. [3]The salivary glands become less active, making the mouth feel dry. [4]The sweat glands may overreact, producing a dripping forehead, clammy hands, and "cold sweat." [5]Finally, the pupils may enlarge, producing the wide-eyed look that is characteristic of both terror and rage. [6]In effect, strong emotions are not without consequences; they bring about powerful changes in our bodies. (Rubin et al., *Psychology*, p. 370.)

Topic Sentence   _____

8. [1]Scientists believe that the probable maximum human life span is about 150 years, with the record for the oldest person to date belonging to Shigechiyo Izumi (1865–1986) of Japan, who lived to be 120 years and 237 days. [2]What is unknown is why people die. [3]There are, however, two theories about why all living things grow old and die. [4]The *free-radical theory* states that free radicals, certain chemicals produced as a by-product of biological activity, are particularly harmful to healthy cells. [5]As a person ages, free radicals gradually destroy cells until they can no longer function properly, causing the entire body (especially whole organ systems such as the kidneys or heart) to break down and die. [6]The *programmed senescence theory* suggests that the rate at which we age is predetermined, and that our genetic makeup controls the aging and death of the cells. [7]When enough of the cells die, as dictated by our genes, the organs cease to function and death occurs. (Barnes-Svarney, "Theories on Aging," *New York Public Library Science Desk Reference*, p. 161.)

Topic Sentence   _____

9. [1]In 1919, President Woodrow Wilson was serving his second term in office. [2]Suddenly, without warning, in September of that year, he suffered a near-fatal stroke that left him partially paralyzed and nearly blind. [3]When the president's doctors told Wilson's wife Edith that her husband would recover faster if he stayed in office

---

*metabolism: a complex combination of physical and chemical processes in the body that maintain life.

Copyright © Cengage Learning. All rights reserved.

rather than resigning, she made a decision. [4]For more than six months, Edith Wilson concealed the seriousness of her husband's condition by running the country for him, thereby earning her nickname as "the secret president." [5]Edith read all of the documents sent to her husband for his signature and made the decision about which ones would be brought to his attention and which not. [6]When the president seemed too ill to concentrate, she took charge and made decisions for him, communicating those decisions to his staff. [7]Wilson never fully recovered and, in 1921, at the end of his presidential term, Woodrow and Edith retired. [8]In 1924, after living three more years in virtual seclusion, President Woodrow Wilson died. [9]Edith lived to be eighty-nine years old and died in 1961.

Topic Sentence   _____

10. [1]Many people know that Joan of Arc was burned at the stake because she was suspected of being a witch. [2] However, St. Joan was convicted of another crime as well—that of dressing as a man. [3]This was a serious offense in 1481, based on the Biblical injunction*: "The woman shall not wear that which pertaineth unto a man, neither shall a man put on a woman's garment." [4]What was Joan wearing that contributed to her death at the stake? [5]On the battlefield she wore armor, but in camp, eyewitnesses claimed that she wore a long gray tunic, or blouse, over closely fitted hose or tights. [6]Unlike today, women of the fifteenth century did not wear tights. [7]They wore long dresses. [8]During her trial, Joan, in a plea for mercy, did put on a dress. [9]But she didn't wear it for long. [10]It was less than a day before she once again donned tights, claiming that without them she feared rape at the hands of her guards. [11]Her captors considered her clothing change to be an act of defiance, and Joan of Arc lost all chance for mercy at their hands. (Adapted from Zacks, *An Underground Education,* p. 153.)

Topic Sentence   _____

---

*injunction: law or rule forbidding certain actions or behavior.

Copyright © Cengage Learning. All rights reserved.

WORD CHECK I

The following words were introduced and defined in pages 108–29. See how well you can match the words with the meanings. When you finish, make sure to check the meanings of any words you missed because the same words will turn up in tests at the end of the chapter.

1. sentient _____
2. alleviates _____
3. condescension _____
4. dissidents _____
5. hierarchies _____
6. boorish _____
7. agitated _____
8. bureaucracy _____
9. metabolism _____
10. injunction _____

a. conscious, capable of feeling
b. levels or rankings of people based on authority or importance
c. rule or law forbidding some action or behavior
d. upset, stirred up
e. people who openly disagree with their government
f. behaving as if one were superior in some way
g. a large organization divided into numerous offices or bureaus, each with its own staff
h. improves, makes better, diminishes negative effects
i. crude, disrespectful of others, vulgar
j. complex of physical and chemical processes in the body that maintain life

♦ **EXERCISE 5** **More About Form and Meaning**

DIRECTIONS Fill in the blanks with one of the words below.

| bureaucratic | hierarchically | metabolism | injunction | alleviates |
| dissidents | agitated | boorish | condescension | sentient |

1. A person whose behavior is _____ would probably be better off hosting a wrestling match than a formal dinner.

2. People who overeat and gain weight often claim that their weight problem is caused by a slow _____.

3. No union wants a court to issue a(n) _____ forbidding a strike; if that happens, the union's hands are tied.

Copyright © Cengage Learning. All rights reserved.

4. Big companies are always organized _____.

5. People of royal birth may well find it difficult not to show _____ when they meet ordinary folks.

6. If you catch poison ivy, you are likely to want a medication that _____ the itch.

7. In hospitals, people with heart conditions are often not allowed to watch the World Series if they are baseball fans; doctors worry that if a patient's team loses, he or she will get too _____, causing blood pressure to rise.

8. Although some people insist that animals are _____ beings, no one would make that claim about furniture, pottery, or cupcakes.

9. Health insurance companies are famous for making clients go through a seemingly endless _____ maze before agreeing to pay for new medical procedures that don't have an established track record.

10. Henry David Thoreau, the nineteenth-century author who wrote the classic *Walden*, was one of America's first political _____. In protest against the country's war with Mexico, he refused to pay his town taxes.

Concentrate on Paraphrasing Topic Sentences

Chapter 1 introduced you to the basics of reading paraphrases. At this point, we'll focus solely on paraphrasing topic sentences that for one reason or another might be difficult to put into your own words.

Consider the Core Elements First

To paraphrase a topic sentence like the following, you would need to establish the topic or subject of the sentence first: "Despite studies suggesting that happiness has a genetic basis, some psychologists insist that

Copyright © Cengage Learning. All rights reserved.

we ourselves have the power to make ourselves happy." In this case, the topic or subject of the sentence is *happiness*.

What's the author's comment about happiness? We can create our own. Paraphrasing those core elements—the topic and a comment about the topic—would result in a reworded sentence like this one: "Some psychologists believe we can create our own happiness."

Now that paraphrase might be fine as a marginal note. But if you wanted to paraphrase for a paper, you'd have to deal with the sentence opening, which tells us that some studies suggest being happy or unhappy is a product of our genetic code. This point challenges what the rest of the sentence says, and the author indicates that relationship by using the word "despite." That opening word is the author's way of saying that he acknowledges what other studies have said *but* still thinks that happiness can be personally generated.

Opening clauses like the one above are sometimes called "orienters."[†] They orient, or familiarize, readers by helping them connect the beginnings and endings of sentences. Orienters tell readers, among other things, the time, place, manner, and situation in which the events of the sentence occur.

When creating a formal paraphrase for a paper, you need to take orienters into account. However, that's often easier to do *after* you determine the core elements. Once you have the core elements, you need only rephrase the opening. In this case, we could turn the opening "Despite studies suggesting that happiness has a genetic basis" into this paraphrase: "Even in the face of studies suggesting that happiness is in our genes." Put the paraphrased sentence opening and the core elements together and you have a statement like the following: "Even in the face of studies suggesting happiness is in our genes, some psychologists believe that we create our own happiness."

Reducing a topic sentence to its core elements is a good way of starting a paraphrase. Once you have those two elements you can figure out how to reword the other parts of the sentences that expand or refine the sentence's core meaning.

◆ **EXERCISE 6**   **Looking for Openings**

DIRECTIONS   For one week, keep an eye open for orienters, or opening words or phrases that identify the two kinds of relationships shown on the charts that follow: (1) establishing a point of view and (2) identifying

———————————
[†]Joseph Williams uses this term in *Style: Ten Lessons in Clarity and Grace*. It is useful to explain the purpose of what he also calls "message-bearing adverbials."

Copyright © Cengage Learning. All rights reserved.

the conditions under which an event occurs. See if you can fill in all the remaining blank spaces left in the charts.

Establishing a Point of View

Fortunately	Unfortunately	Allegedly
Supposedly	Critically significant	Relevant to this argument
From a social standpoint	For the very young	According to Ralph Nader

Identifying Conditions Under Which Something Occurs

Given the current financial situation	Under these circumstances
Under the terms of this agreement, contract	When the temperatures are high enough
In the context of this discussion	According to this code of ethics
If done correctly	Based on this new research
In almost all social situations	

◆ **EXERCISE 7**   **Practicing Paraphrasing**

DIRECTIONS   Read the paragraph and look closely at the underlined topic sentence. Then circle the letter of the best paraphrase.

1. [1]In 2009, a new treatment center called reSTART opened in Fall City, Washington. [2]The center's goal is to treat what the owners believe is a growing population of "Web addicts," people who find it almost impossible to stay away from their computers for any length of time. [3]For around a thousand dollars a day, the five-acre center currently only handles about six patients at a time, but the managers of the center believe their space will enlarge to meet ever-growing

Copyright © Cengage Learning. All rights reserved.

numbers of people. ⁴Although Internet addiction is not recognized as a disorder by the American Psychiatric Association and treatment is not covered by insurance, Cosette Dawna Rae, one of the center's owners, believes that centers like reSTART are going to proliferate* over time. ⁵Such centers for video addicts are, in fact, already commonplace in China, South Korea, and Taiwan. ⁶At reSTART, the treatment methods are much like the conventional* ones used for alcohol and drug addiction.⁷The patient goes cold turkey and is cut off from access to the Internet. ⁸Instead, he or she spends the days in a variety of activities that include chores, exercise, and therapy sessions.

Paraphrase

   a. Therapy centers designed to treat Internet addiction are springing up around the country with reSTART in Fall City, Washington, being a good example of what such treatment centers have to offer.

   b. Like other treatment centers for addiction, reSTART in Fall City, Washington, takes a cold-turkey approach to addiction and patients are not allowed any access to the Internet.

   c. The owners of reSTART in Fall City, Washington, believe that their facility will turn out to be the first of many as more and more people find it almost impossible to stay off the Internet.

   d. Due to the growing number of people who seem addicted to playing video games, the owners of reSTART think that their new facility will be the first of many.

2. ¹If you have ever lived in the country, you are probably familiar with the croaking sound frogs make in the night. ²For many country dwellers, it's a soothing, tranquil* sound. ³But unless strong action is taken immediately, the croaking of frogs might not be a sound anyone hears ten years from now. ⁴All the evidence suggests that frogs and others in the class known as *amphibia*—for example, salamanders and toads—are threatened with extinction. ⁵There are already reports that two-thirds of several amphibian species in Central and South America have vanished. ⁶The twin causes of the amphibians' demise are pollution and humans invading their natural habitats. ⁷Among the amphibians, though, frogs—the most populous group in the class—are under special attack. ⁸For years now, the chytrid fungus

---

*proliferate: grow in number, multiply.
*conventional: traditional, standard.
*tranquil: peaceful, calming.

Copyright © Cengage Learning. All rights reserved.

has been spreading around the world leaving dead frogs in its path. [9]The fungus coats the frogs' skin, closing off their pores. [10]As a result, the frogs have trouble breathing and absorbing water. [11]Ultimately, they die of dehydration* and suffocation. [12]In an effort to save frogs and other amphibians, conservationists have founded Amphibian Ark, a project that contacts zoos around the globe and asks them to adopt and care for at least 500 members of the amphibian class.
(Source of statistics: http://science.howstuffworks.com/bye-bye-kermie.htm.)

Paraphrase

   a. The comforting sound of frogs croaking in the night is a familiar sound to anyone who has lived in the country.

   b. The class of animals known as *amphibia* is under the threat of extinction.

   c. The class of animals known as *amphibia* includes salamanders.

   d. Many different species are currently under threat of extinction.

◆ EXERCISE 8 Practicing Paraphrasing

DIRECTIONS Read each paragraph and underline the topic sentence. Then paraphrase it in the blanks that follow. *Note*: For the purposes of this exercise, paraphrase in complete sentences as if you were paraphrasing for a term paper.

EXAMPLE [1]In an attempt to solve the problem, a number of elementary and middle schools around the country are making a strong effort to find a solution to bullying behavior in the schools. [2]At the administrative level, supervisors and principals are sending out questionnaires, asking students if they have ever been bullied. [3]The goal of the questionnaire is to determine the incidence* of bullying behavior in a particular school. [4]Administrators are also increasing student supervision in places like the playground and the cafeteria, where trouble is likely to occur. [5]They are also requesting that teachers actively patrol the halls and be alert to signs of bullying. [6]In classrooms, teachers are discussing the subject with students and asking them to write about what causes some students to bully others.

Paraphrase Nationwide, elementary and middle-school administrators are introducing strong

measures to combat bullying among students.

---

*dehydration: fluid loss.
*incidence: extent or frequency of occurrence.

Copyright © Cengage Learning. All rights reserved.

EXPLANATION Every sentence following the first one refers to bullying in the schools. Each sentence offers more specific information about the attempts that have been made to solve the problem. Thus sentence 1 is the topic sentence. Like the topic sentence, the paraphrase must indicate the two kinds of schools and the action they are taking against bullying.

1. [1]Travel and tourism are big business. [2]According to the U.S. Department of Commerce, spending by travelers reached $554.5 billion in 2003, generating 7.2 million jobs and contributing $94.7 in tax revenue. [3]To attract big-spending tourists, states spend big—and some states spend really big. [4]Wisconsin promotes its "Travel Green with Wisconsin" program in several of its regions, whereas Tennessee and Nebraska host agritourism conferences to acquaint farmers with the benefits of attracting city slickers to their farms. [5]At the local level, convention and visitors' bureaus, which are frequently the joint ventures of the chamber of commerce and city government, have been created to promote individual communities and their assets. (Bowman and Kearney, *State and Local Government*, p. 381.)

Paraphrase

_____

_____

2. [1]Between January and May 2007, beekeepers lost one-quarter of their colonies, which is a lot of bees. [2]Anyone inclined to ho-hum at this information should think again because honeybees are not important just to gardeners, who need bees to pollinate[†] their flowers; on the contrary, the disappearance of honeybees could have much wider significance. [3]The truth is the disappearance of honeybees, also known as "Colony Collapse Disorder," could cause a food crisis. [4]Honeybees pollinate nuts, avocados, apples, celery, squash, cucumbers, cherries, and blueberries. [5]And that's not even a complete list. [6]Experts estimate that about a third of the human diet is insect-pollinated, and 80 percent of the time, the honeybee is the pollinator of choice. [7]Honeybees are also part of the cycle that brings meat to the table. [8]Cattle feed on alfalfa, and alfalfa crops need bees as pollinators. [9]If scientists can't figure out why honeybees

_____

[†]pollinate: fertilize by bringing pollen from one flower to another.

Copyright © Cengage Learning. All rights reserved.

are disappearing, meat eaters might be forced to turn vegetarian precisely at the time when even vegetables are in short supply.

Paraphrase
_____

_____

TAKING A CLOSER LOOK

Reading Between the Lines

In sentence 2 of paragraph 2, the author warns "anyone inclined to ho-hum" to think again. What does she imply with that phrase?

_____

_____

WWW

INTERNET FOLLOW-UP: Do Cell Phones Have Anything to Do with Bees Disappearing?

Use the Web to find out *why* some people think cell phones are contributing to the disappearance of honeybees.

_____

_____

_____

How much hard evidence is there supporting a connection between cell phones and Colony Collapse Disorder?

_____

_____

Based on the evidence, would you consider giving up your cell phone to save the honeybees?

_____

_____

_____

Copyright © Cengage Learning. All rights reserved.

The Function of Supporting Details

In addition to topic sentences expressing main ideas, paragraphs also include major and minor supporting details. **Major supporting details** are the examples, reasons, studies, statistics, facts, and figures that explain, develop, or prove an author's main idea. **Minor supporting details** further explain major details. They supply an interesting fact, tell a story, or add repetition for emphasis.

Because topic sentences are general sentences that sum up or interpret a variety of events, facts, examples, or experiences, they are subject to misunderstanding. Writers, therefore, use supporting details to avoid being misinterpreted or misunderstood. Supporting details are the writer's way of saying to readers, "I mean this, not that."

For an illustration of supporting details at work, look at the following sentence: "Most people who have survived near-fatal automobile accidents tend to behave in the same fashion." Given only this one sentence, could you be sure you understood the author's message? After all, that sentence could mean different things to different people. Perhaps survivors have nightmares or fears about their health. But then again maybe they just become very slow drivers.

Look now at the following paragraph. Note how the supporting details clarify the author's meaning.

> Most people who have survived near-fatal automobile accidents tend to behave in the same fashion. They agonize about driving even a mile or two over the speed limit and flatly refuse to go faster than the law allows. If they are not at the wheel, their terror increases. As passengers, they are inclined to be anxious and are prone to offering advice about how to take a curve or when to stop for a light.

In this instance, the supporting details illustrate the three types of behavior that the author has in mind. Those illustrations are the author's way of answering questions such as "What does 'behave in the same fashion' mean?"

Types of Supporting Details

Supporting details can range from reasons and examples to statistics and definitions. The form they take depends on the main idea they serve. Look, for example, at the following paragraph. Here the writer wants to

Copyright © Cengage Learning. All rights reserved.

convince readers that a book defending the right to be fat is very much worth reading.

> [1]Marilyn Wann's book *Fat! So?* deserves a large and appreciative audience, one that does not consist solely of those who are overweight. [2]For starters, Wann is refreshingly unembarrassed about being fat (she tips the scales at 270), and that takes courage in a culture as obsessed as ours is with being thin. [3]If anything, the author encourages her readers—in the chapter titled "You, Too, Can Be Flabulous"—to embrace the word *fat* and use it in favorable contexts, such as "You're getting fat; you look great." [4]Yet, despite her lively, and often humorous, style, Wann is good at describing the real misery society inflicts on fat people. [5]Her chapters on the suffering endured by overweight teenagers are particularly moving; and they make a strong case for the need to attack, and attack hard, the tendency to treat the overweight as second-class citizens. [6]The book is also filled with sound advice about healthy eating habits. [7]Clearly, the author is not encouraging her readers to go out and gorge themselves on pizza and beer. [8]What she is suggesting is that they eat right to get fit, rather than thin. [9]Insisting that some people can, because of heredity, never be anything but overweight, Wann argues that these people should not suffer for the genetic hand they've been dealt. [10]On the contrary, they should learn how to flaunt* their excess poundage and make society accept them as they are.

In this paragraph, the major details all give reasons why Marilyn Wann's book deserves a wide audience. The minor details, in turn, flesh out and emphasize the major ones. Note, too, that at least two of the minor details are as important as the major detail they develop. In sentence 6, the author suggests that Wann's book is good because it offers sound advice about healthy eating. But without the presence of the minor details that follow, it would be hard to understand how a book celebrating fat could also provide tips on healthy eating. Minor details in sentences 7 and 8 help explain this seeming contradiction.

Minor Details Can Be Meaningful

Don't be fooled by the labels *major* and *minor*. Sometimes minor details can be as meaningful as major ones. Therefore, you need to judge them in terms of what they contribute to the major details they modify.

---

*flaunt: show off.

Copyright © Cengage Learning. All rights reserved.

If a minor detail simply adds a personal note or provides emphasis, you don't need to think about it much. You certainly don't need to include it in your notes. But if a major detail doesn't make much sense without the minor one that follows, then both details are equally important.

ALLUSION ALERT

Pygmalion

According to myth, Pygmalion, the king of Cyprus, carved and then fell in love with the statue of a woman who was transformed into a human being. The phrase *Pygmalion effect* reflects the myth's suggestion that wishing or believing something can make it happen. However, the allusion is usually used without the word "effect" in statements like these: "Many of the popular stories and movies about vampires are a variation on the myth of Pygmalion, with the love of a good woman transforming an evil vampire into a loving caretaker, albeit* one with fangs."

♦ **EXERCISE 9**   **Recognizing Topic Sentences and Supporting Details**

DIRECTIONS   Read each paragraph and write the number or numbers of the topic sentence in the first blank. Then answer the questions that follow by circling the correct response or filling in the blanks.

EXAMPLE   ¹What makes an effective leader? ²To be sure, no one characteristic or trait defines an effective leader. ³It is true, however, that effective leaders get the most out of employees or group members by holding them to very high standards or expectations. ⁴Setting high standards increases productivity because people tend to live up to the expectations set for them by superiors. ⁵This is an example of the Pygmalion effect, which works in a subtle, often unconscious way. ⁶When a managerial leader believes that a group member will succeed, the manager communicates this belief without realizing that he or she is doing so. ⁷Conversely, when a leader expects a group member to fail, that person will not usually disappoint the manager. ⁸The manager's expectation of success or failure becomes a self-fulfilling prophecy. ⁹Thus it pays for a manager to expect the best from employees. (Adapted from DuBrin, *Leadership*, p. 85.)

---

*albeit: even though, notwithstanding.

Copyright © Cengage Learning. All rights reserved.

a. Topic sentence: __3__

b. The major details help answer what question or questions about the topic sentence? <u>Why do effective leaders set such high standards?</u>

c. *True or* *False.* Sentence 5 is a major supporting detail. Explain your answer. <u>This supporting detail further explains the previous one, making it a minor</u> <u>but far from unimportant detail.</u>

d. *True or* *False.* Sentence 6 is also a major supporting detail. Explain your answer. <u>The point made in sentence 6 clarifies how the Pygmalion effect</u> <u>functions in a "subtle, almost unconscious way."</u>

EXPLANATION   Sentence 3 answers the opening question and most effectively sums up the paragraph. Explanations for the *true* and *false* answers already appear in the blanks above.

1. ¹Despite its rapid spread, Islam is not a religion for those who are casual about regulations; on the contrary, adhering to its rules takes effort and discipline. ²One must rise before dawn to observe the first of five prayers required daily, none of which can take place without first ritually* cleansing oneself. ³Sleep, work, and recreational activities take second place to prayer. ⁴Fasting for the month of Ramadan,† undertaking the pilgrimage to Mecca at least once in a lifetime, paying tax for relief of the Muslim poor, and accepting Islam's creed require a serious and an energetic commitment. ⁵On the whole, the vast majority of Muslims worldwide do observe those tenets.* (Adapted from Goodwin, *Price of Honor*, p. 29.)

a. Topic sentence: _____

b. The major details help answer what question or questions about the topic sentence? _____

_____

---

*ritually: according to a prescribed order, in the form of a ceremony.
†Ramadan: Muslim holy month.
*tenets: rules, principles, or beliefs held to be true by a person or an organization.

Copyright © Cengage Learning. All rights reserved.

    c. *True* or *False.* Sentence 3 is a major supporting detail. Explain

       your answer. _____

       _____

    d. *True* or *False.* Sentence 4 is also a major supporting detail.

       Explain your answer. _____

       _____

2. ¹Those cuddly toys known as teddy bears seem to have been around forever. ²But actually the first teddy bears came into being when President Theodore "Teddy" Roosevelt showed himself too much of a sportsman to shoot a staked bear cub. ³In 1902, Roosevelt visited Mississippi to settle a border dispute. In Roosevelt's honor, his hosts organized a hunting expedition. ⁴To make sure that the president would bag a trophy, they staked a bear cub to the ground so that Roosevelt's shot couldn't miss. ⁵To his credit, Roosevelt refused to shoot the bear. ⁶When the incident was publicized, largely through political cartoons, a Russian candy store owner named Morris Mitchom made a toy bear out of soft, fuzzy cloth and placed it in his shop window with a sign reading "Teddy's Bear." ⁷The bear was a hit with passersby, and teddy-bear mania spread rapidly throughout the country.

    a. Topic sentence: _____

    b. The major details help answer what question or questions about

       the topic sentence? _____

       _____

    c. *True* or *False.* Sentence 4 is a minor detail. Explain your answer.

       _____

       _____

    d. *True* or *False.* Sentence 6 is a major detail. Explain your answer.

       _____

       _____

Copyright © Cengage Learning. All rights reserved.

3. [1]"Drop dead, you creep!" is hardly the thing someone would want to say when trying to resolve a disagreement in a dating relationship. [2]But it may be an important clue as to whether such a couple should marry. [3]Many couples who communicate poorly before marriage are likely to communicate the same way after marriage, and the result can be disastrous for future marital happiness. [4]Researchers have found that how well a couple communicates before marriage can be an important predictor of later marital satisfaction (Cate and Lloyd, 1992). [5]In one study, researchers found that those premarital couples who responded more to each other's positive communications than to each other's negative communications were more satisfied four years after marriage than those who focused mainly on negative messages. [6]If communication is poor before marriage, it is not likely to significantly improve after marriage. (Adapted from Strong et al., *The Marriage and Family Experience*, p. 245.)

a. Topic sentence: _____

b. The major details help answer what question or questions about

the topic sentence? _____

_____

c. *True* or *False*. Sentence 4 is a minor detail. Explain your answer.

_____

_____

d. *True* or *False*. Sentence 5 is a major detail. Explain your answer.

_____

_____

4. [1]Many people don't know the difference between a patent and a trademark; but there is a difference. [2]Usually granted for seventeen years, a patent protects both the name of a product and its method of manufacture. [3]In 1928, for example, Jacob Schick invented and then patented the electric razor in an effort to maintain complete control of his creation. [4]Similarly, between 1895 and 1912, no one but the Shredded Wheat company was allowed to make shredded wheat because the company had the patent. [5]A trademark is a name, symbol, or other device that identifies a product and makes it

Copyright © Cengage Learning. All rights reserved.

memorable in the minds of consumers. [6]Kleenex, Jell-O, and Xerox are all examples of trademarks. [7]Aware of the power that trademarks possess, companies fight to protect them and do not allow anyone else to use one without permission. [8]Occasionally, though, a company gets careless and loses control of a trademark. [9]Aspirin, for example, is no longer considered a trademark, and any company can call a pain-reducing tablet an aspirin.

a. Topic sentence: _____

b. The major details help answer what question or questions about

   the topic sentence? _____

   _____

c. *True* or *False*. Sentence 3 is a minor detail. Explain your answer.

   _____

   _____

d. *True* or *False*. Sentence 5 is a major detail. Explain your answer.

   _____

   _____

WWW

INTERNET FOLLOW-UP: What Can Become a Trademark?
In addition to names, what other kinds of things can be trademarked?

   _____

   _____

✔ **CHECK YOUR UNDERSTANDING Through Writing**

Using the Web for your research, write a paragraph in which the topic sentence identifies at least three different kinds of trademarks. Describe the trademarks with both major and minor details, marking the major detail with an uppercase *M* and the minor detail with a lowercase *m*.

Copyright © Cengage Learning. All rights reserved.

Key Words and Supporting Details

As you differentiate between major and minor details to decide what to remember or what to include in your notes, check the topic sentence for words like *studies, groups, causes, reasons, characteristics,* and *tenets.* Topic sentences containing these general and countable category words are almost always followed by major supporting details used to identify the individual *studies, groups, causes, theories,* and so on.

In the following paragraph, the topic sentence tells readers that in 1950 U.S. agriculture underwent some "profound changes." But unless you know what those changes were, the sentence doesn't tell you much. It's up to the major details to identify which changes the author had in mind.

Read the paragraph to identify the sentences that introduce specific examples of changes. When you finish, write the number of major details on the blank at the end of the paragraph.

¹Around 1950, agriculture in the United States underwent a number of profound changes. ²For one thing, agriculture became energy intensive.* ³In 1950, an amount of energy equal to less than half a barrel of oil was used to produce a ton of grain. ⁴By 1985, the amount of energy needed to produce a ton of grain had more than doubled. ⁵Searching for ways to increase the yield of the lands already in use, farmers also began to rely heavily on inputs of water, chemical fertilizers and pesticides (many of which are petroleum-derived products), and high-yield strains of crops. ⁶In some areas, especially the drier regions of the Southwest, irrigation projects allowed dry lands to be cultivated. ⁷In contrast to past agricultural practices, farmers also began to concentrate on producing only one or two profitable crops as opposed to a variety of crops. (Adapted from Kaufman and Franz, *Biosphere 2000,* p. 182.)

_____

If you wrote a 3 in the blank, then you effectively used the key phrase "profound changes" to identify major details. Although the paragraph has seven sentences, only sentences 2, 5, and 7 introduce one of the profound changes mentioned in the topic sentence.

_____

*intensive: characterized by great power, strength, or force.

Copyright © Cengage Learning. All rights reserved.

Transitional Clues to Major Details

You already know about reversal transitions. However, it's time to talk more about addition or continuation transitions, two examples of which (*for one thing* and *also*) appear in sentences 2, 5, and 7 in the previous example paragraph. **Addition transitions** at the beginning or in the middle of sentences tell you that the author is continuing to develop an idea already introduced. They also tell you that the upcoming sentences won't contradict what's come before. Instead, the sentences will continue the same train of thought with *new* content. Addition transitions are the author's way of saying, "Here is more new information or evidence supporting the main idea I've introduced."

Here's an example of a paragraph that contains two clues to major details: (1) a topic sentence with a general word that can be more specifically individualized and (2) addition transitions that signal more support for an idea already introduced. The key phrase in the topic sentence and the addition transitions are italicized.

 [1]Emotional intelligence is a difficult term to define precisely; however, the term can be generally described using *five main characteristics*. [2]*The first key characteristic* of emotional intelligence is self-awareness, or knowing one's own feelings. [3]This characteristic may, in fact, be the most important component of emotional intelligence. [4]*Another key characteristic* is the ability to manage one's emotions. [5]Emotionally intelligent people can soothe themselves in difficult times and bounce back quickly from disappointments. [6]People with high levels of emotional intelligence can *also* use their emotions in service of their goals. [7]Faced with a challenge, they can summon the enthusiasm and confidence necessary to pursue their desires. [8]*In addition to these three characteristics*, emotionally intelligent people are *also* likely to have empathy. [9]They are, that is, able to recognize and identify the feelings of others. [10]They possess what are commonly called "people skills." [11]*The fifth and final characteristic* of emotional intelligence is the ability to help others deal with their feelings. [12]This characteristic is an important factor in maintaining meaningful relationships. (Adapted from Bernstein and Nash, *Essentials of Psychology*, p. 288.)

In this paragraph, the authors use the major details to nail down that opening phrase "five main characteristics." Each time they introduce

Copyright © Cengage Learning. All rights reserved.

a new characteristic—as opposed to further describing one already mentioned—they use a transitional device that signals to the reader, "Here's another characteristic from those five I previously mentioned."

Expanding the Definition of Transitions

What follows is a list of addition transitions. It is important to note, however, that experienced readers recognize that such lists have limitations. Writers know how important transitional devices are to readers, and good writers try hard to provide them. But they don't limit themselves solely to transitional words or phrases. They also use repetition of a key word (*characteristics* in the sample paragraph) or some reference to the previous sentence to help readers move smoothly from thought to thought. (More on this chain of references in Chapter 6)

That's why, for example, the entire phrase "The fifth and final characteristic" is italicized in the passage above, rather than just the word "final," which appears in the list below. In addition to being the subject of the entire sentence, that phrase is also a transitional device designed to tell readers, "Here's the last of those five characteristics I mentioned in the opening of the paragraph."

Addition or Continuation Transitions ◆		
	Along the same lines	In other words
	Also	In the same vein
	An additional	More precisely
	Even better	Moreover
	Even more	More to the point
	Even worse	One; two; three
	Final; finally	Then, too
	First; second; third	Too
	In addition	Yet another
	In more specific terms	

Copyright © Cengage Learning. All rights reserved.

◆ EXERCISE 10 Identifying Major and Minor Details

DIRECTIONS   Identify major and minor details by writing the appropriate sentence numbers in the boxes of the accompanying diagram.

EXAMPLE   ¹Twins can be either identical or fraternal. ²Identical twins are formed from one fertilized egg that splits in two, resulting in two children of the same sex who look very much alike. ³One-third of all twins born are identical. ⁴Fraternal twins are formed from two different fertilized eggs; these twins can be of different sexes and look quite different from one another. ⁵Two-thirds of all twins are fraternal.

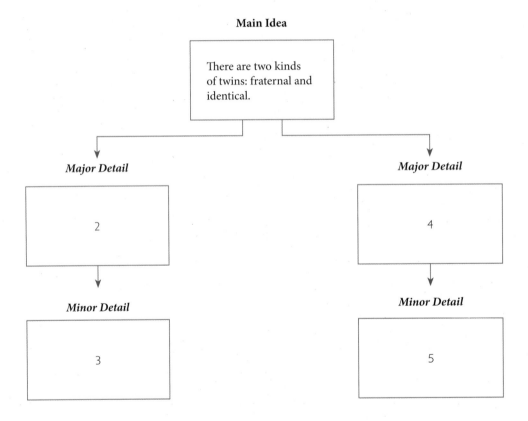

Main Idea

There are two kinds of twins: fraternal and identical.

Major Detail

2

Major Detail

4

Minor Detail

3

Minor Detail

5

EXPLANATION   In this example, each major detail fleshes out the two terms introduced in the topic sentence: *identical* and *fraternal*. Both details are followed by minor ones that give readers additional information about the different kinds of twins. *Note:* Although this paragraph neatly balances major and minor details, this is not the case in every paragraph and major details may or may not be followed by minor ones. It's also possible for one major detail to be followed by two minor ones.

Copyright © Cengage Learning. All rights reserved.

1. [1]Nightclub acts that use lions and tigers may be entertaining, but they are, for a number of reasons, bad for both the animals and their trainers. [2]Making these animals learn tricks forces them to ignore their natural instincts. [3]Even worse, using lions and tigers for entertainment means that these proud creatures spend most of their lives in cages rather than roaming free in their natural habitat. [4]Club performances that feature lions and tigers are also bad because they are unsafe for both handlers and spectators. [5]These powerful beasts are fundamentally wild, and no amount of training can guarantee they will not, without warning, turn and attack. [6]The horrific attack that took place on trainer Roy Horn of the famed duo Siegfried and Roy is a tragic illustration of that fact. [7]Horn had thirty years of training performing tigers behind him, but all that experience did not prevent him from being attacked and severely injured by a tiger.

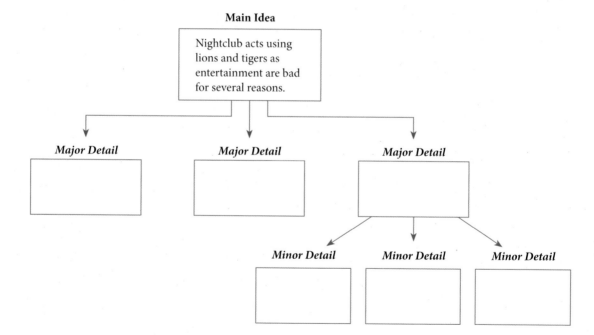

Main Idea

Nightclub acts using lions and tigers as entertainment are bad for several reasons.

Major Detail

Major Detail

Major Detail

Minor Detail

Minor Detail

Minor Detail

Copyright © Cengage Learning. All rights reserved.

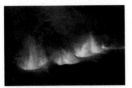

© Arctic-Images/Corbis

2. ¹Volcanic eruptions and their aftereffects are among the Earth's most destructive natural events. ²But whether a volcano poses an imminent threat to human life and property depends its status as an *active*, a *dormant*, or an *extinct* volcano. ³An active volcano is one that is currently erupting or has erupted recently. ⁴Certain active volcanoes, such as Kilauea on Hawaii or Stromboli in the eastern Mediterranean, erupt almost continuously. ⁵Active volcanoes can be found on all continents except Australia and on the floors of all major ocean basins. ⁶Indonesia, Japan, and the United States are the world's most volcanically active nations. ⁷A dormant volcano is one that has not erupted recently but is considered likely to do so in the future. ⁸The presence of relatively fresh volcanic rocks in a volcano's vicinity is an indication that it is still capable of erupting. ⁹The presence of hot water springs or small earthquakes occurring near a volcano may also indicate that the volcano is stirring to wakefulness. ¹⁰A volcano is considered extinct if it has not erupted for a very long time (perhaps tens of thousands of years) and is considered unlikely to do so in the future. ¹¹A truly extinct volcano is no longer fueled by a magma[†] source and, thus, no longer capable of erupting. ¹²Volcanoes, however, can surprise us. ¹³Residents of the Icelandic island of Heimaey believed that their volcano Helgafjell was extinct, until it erupted in 1973. (Adapted from Chernicoff and Fox, *Essentials of Geology*, p. 73.)

Main Idea

How dangerous a volcano is depends on its being *active, dormant,* or *extinct.*

Major Detail

Major Detail

Major Detail

Minor Detail

Minor Detail

Minor Detail

Minor Detail

Minor Detail

Minor Detail

Minor Detail

Minor Detail

[†]magma: heated rock material underneath the earth's crust.

Copyright © Cengage Learning. All rights reserved.

WORD CHECK II

The following words were introduced and defined in pages 134–45. See how well you can match the words with the meanings. When you finish, make sure to check the meanings of any words you missed because the same words will turn up in tests at the end of the chapter.

1. proliferate   _____
2. conventional   _____
3. tranquil   _____
4. dehydration   _____
5. incidence   _____
6. flaunt   _____
7. albeit   _____
8. ritually   _____
9. tenets   _____
10. intensive   _____

a. show off, display
b. according to a prescribed order, in the form of a ceremony
c. rules, principles, or beliefs held to be true by a person or an organization
d. characterized by great power, strength, or force
e. grow in number, multiply, increase
f. traditional, standard, long-established
g. peaceful, calming
h. fluid loss
i. extent or frequency of occurrence
j. even though, notwithstanding

◆ **EXERCISE 11   More About Form and Meaning**

DIRECTIONS   Fill in the blanks with one of the words listed below. *Note:* You will have to use one of the ten words twice in the same sentence.

conventional	proliferate	dehydration	tranquility	incidence
flaunting	intensive	rituals	albeit	tenet

1. All of the following are things we don't want to see

   _____: disease-causing bacteria, domestic violence, dog fights, and tooth loss.

2. Dizziness, dry mouth, fast pulse, and mental confusion are all signs

   of severe _____.

Copyright © Cengage Learning. All rights reserved.

3. If you are looking for more _____ in your life, you probably need to avoid traffic jams, crowded subways, and being an accountant at tax time.

4. "Never lend money to friends" is a good example of what's called _____ wisdom.

5. Belief in the gift of tongues is a(n) _____ of the Mormon faith; "the gift of tongues" means that someone who is translating the word of the Holy Spirit will suddenly have the ability to speak in a strange and unfamiliar language.

6. Marriage ceremonies, baptisms, and celebrations of the entry into adulthood are all examples of _____.

7. The word _____ comes in handy if you want to qualify a statement, as in "He turned out to be a wonderful compan- ion, _____ a bit moody."

8. Anyone who wants to speak a foreign language within six months better be prepared to make a(n) _____ effort.

9. It's impossible to discover the actual _____ of domestic violence because so many cases go unreported.

10. People who like wearing designer labels, piles of gold chains, and multiple rings set with precious stones are definitely given to _____ their wealth.

Copyright © Cengage Learning. All rights reserved.

DIGGING Peter Singer and His Fight for Animal Rights
DEEPER

Looking   Perhaps no other figure in the United States is more closely associated
Ahead   with the animal rights movement (p. 108) than philosopher Peter Singer.
Currently a professor at Princeton, Singer's positions on the equality of
human and animal concerns made him a controversial figure, as Ronald
Bailey, the author of the following reading, points out.

1   The *New Yorker* calls him "the most influential living philosopher." His
critics call him "the most dangerous man in the world." Peter Singer, the
Ira W. DeCamp Professor of Bioethics at Princeton University's Center for
Human Values, is most widely and controversially known for his view that
animals have the same moral status as humans. He is the author of many
books, including *Practical Ethics* (1979), *Rethinking Life and Death* (1995),
and *Animal Liberation* (1975), which has sold more than 450,000 copies. In
2007, he published *Writings on an Ethical Life* (Ecco Press) and *A Darwinian
Left: Politics, Evolution, and Cooperation* (Yale University Press).

2   Singer is perhaps the most thoroughgoing philosophical utilitarian† since
Jeremy Bentham.† As such, he believes animals have rights because the relevant
moral consideration is not whether a being can reason or talk but whether it can
suffer. Jettisoning the traditional distinction between humans and nonhumans,
Singer distinguishes instead between persons and nonpersons. Persons are
beings that feel, reason, have self-awareness, and look forward to a future. Thus,
fetuses and some very impaired human beings are not persons in his view and
have a lesser moral status than, say, adult gorillas and chimpanzees.

3   Given such views, it was no surprise that anti-abortion activists and
disability rights advocates loudly decried the Australian-born Singer's
appointment at Princeton. . . . Indeed, his language regarding the
treatment of disabled human beings is at times appallingly similar to the
eugenic arguments† used by Nazi theorists concerning "life unworthy of
life." Singer, however, believes that only parents, not the state, should have
the power to make decisions about the fates of disabled infants.

---

†A utilitarian believes society should be organized to maximize happiness for the greatest number of beings.
†Jeremy Bentham: a famous utilitarian philosopher, who argued that what is good is
that which brings the greatest happiness to the greatest number of people.
†eugenic arguments: Arguments that emerged in the nineteenth century to claim that
those with disabilities not be allowed to reproduce so that the human race would be
protected from harm. Adolf Hitler took these arguments a step further to bring about
the Holocaust.

Copyright © Cengage Learning. All rights reserved.

4   Singer has made similarly controversial plunges into social policy. In a recent *New York Times Magazine* essay, he argued that the affluent in developed countries are killing people by not giving away to the poor all of their wealth in excess of their needs. How did he come to this conclusion? "If . . . allowing someone to die is not intrinsically different from killing someone, it would seem that we are all murderers," he explains in *Practical Ethics*. He calculates that the average American household needs $30,000 per year; to avoid murder, anything over that should be given away to the poor. "So a household making $100,000 could cut a yearly check for $70,000," he wrote in the *Times*.

5   Rigorous adherence to a single principle has a way of hoisting one by one's own petard.† Singer's mother† suffers from severe Alzheimer's disease, and so she no longer qualifies as a person by his own standards, yet he spends considerable sums on her care. This apparent contradiction of his principles has not gone unnoticed by the media. When I asked him about it during our interview at his Manhattan apartment in late July, he sighed and explained that he is not the only person who is involved in making decisions about his mother (he has a sister). He did say that if he were solely responsible, his mother might not be alive today.

6   Singer's proclamation* about income has also come back to haunt him. To all appearances, he lives on far more than $30,000 a year. Aside from the Manhattan apartment—he asked me not to give the address or describe it as a condition of granting an interview—he and his wife Renata, to whom he has been married for some three decades, have a house in Princeton. The average salary of a full professor at Princeton runs around $100,000 per year; Singer also draws income from a trust fund that his father set up and from the sales of his books. He says he gives away 20 percent of his income to famine relief organizations, but he is certainly living on a sum far beyond $30,000. When asked about this, he forthrightly admitted that he was not living up to his own standards. He insisted that he was doing far more than most and hinted that he would increase his giving when everybody else started contributing similar amounts of their incomes.

7   There is some question as to how seriously one should take the dictates of a person who himself cannot live up to them. If he finds it impossible to follow his own rules, perhaps that means that he should reconsider his conclusions. Singer would no doubt respond that his personal failings hardly invalidate his ideas.

---

†hoisted by one's own petard: to be judged or injured by something that you intended to use on or apply only to others.
†Singer's mother died in 2009.
*proclamation: announcement.

Copyright © Cengage Learning. All rights reserved.

8   In his mid-fifties, Singer is a rail-thin, quietly genial man who seems very comfortable with himself. At one point, I asked him, "If it resulted in an overall increase in the happiness of morally significant beings, whoever they may be, would you favor the slow, painful torture of professional philosophers, including ethicists?" His reply was good-natured: "I find it fortunately hard to imagine the circumstances in which that would occur, but if I were absolutely persuaded that this was the only way to do it, I guess I would have to."

Sharpening Your Skills

DIRECTIONS   Answer the following questions by circling the letter of the correct response or filling in the blanks.

1. In paragraph 3, the author writes that Singer's "language regarding the treatment of disabled human beings is at times *appallingly* similar to the eugenic arguments used by Nazi theorists concerning 'life unworthy of life.'" Based on the context, what is a good approximate definition for *appallingly*?

   a. charmingly
   b. wittingly
   c. carefully
   d. horrifyingly

2. In paragraph 7, the author writes, "Singer would no doubt respond that his personal failings hardly *invalidate* his ideas." Based on the context, what's a good approximate definition for *invalidate*?

   a. challenge
   b. improve
   c. disprove
   d. enhance

3. In your own words, what are the "views" referred to in the first line of paragraph 3 that evoked such outrage from anti-abortion and disability rights activists?

   _____

   _____

Copyright © Cengage Learning. All rights reserved.

_____

_____

4. In paragraph 4, the topic sentence is

   a. sentence 1.

   b. sentence 2.

   c. sentence 3.

5. In paragraph 4, why is the figure $30,000 significant?

   _____

   _____

6. The writer mentions Singer's mother in paragraph 5 as a way of illustrating

   a. how Singer seems to contradict his own principles.

   b. Singer's adherence to a single principle.

   c. why Singer is so disliked.

   d. that he is a warmer person than he first appears to be.

7. What does Singer suggest when he says, at least according to the author, "that if he were solely responsible, his mother might not be alive today" (paragraph 5)?

   _____

   _____

   _____

8. Which sentence best expresses the main idea of paragraph 6?

   a. Peter Singer is fearful of being attacked were his address to become known.

   b. Peter Singer can't escape the fact that he doesn't appear to practice what he preaches.

   c. Peter Singer has a huge fortune, which makes it easy for him to give money away.

Copyright © Cengage Learning. All rights reserved.

9. In paragraph 6, the addition transition is _____; the reversal transition is _____.

10. What is the point of the author's question in the last paragraph of the reading? Why does he ask such a question since there is no chance such a situation might occur?

_____

_____

_____

_____

Copyright © Cengage Learning. All rights reserved.

Copyright © Cengage Learning. All rights reserved.

▶ **TEST 1**　　　　**Reviewing New Vocabulary**

DIRECTIONS　　Fill in the blanks with one of the words listed below.

> sentient　　hierarchical　　ritual　　　　dissidents　　boorish
> agitated　　tenets　　　　conventional　　proliferate　　tranquility

1. The Chinese Communist Party, which has ruled China since 1949, has always been an intensely _____, top-down organization with all decisions and party _____ being under the control of the party's leaders.

2. The famous French writers Simone de Beauvoir and Jean-Paul Sartre did not have a(n) _____ relationship. Together for decades, they never bothered with the _____ of marriage. They didn't even live in the same house but occupied adjoining apartments. Sartre seems to have liked things that way. De Beauvoir, who was madly jealous, had more mixed emotions.

3. When he assumed the post of General Secretary of the Communist Party in 1985, Russian leader Mikhail Gorbachev made it clear that he was ushering in a new and more open era. As a result, political _____ were emboldened by Gorbachev's words, and demonstrations in favor of more democratic freedom began to _____ in Communist-controlled countries like Hungary and East Germany.

4. If Gorbachev charmed leaders of foreign countries, his successor Boris Yeltsin had the opposite effect. Frequently loud and _____, Yeltsin often embarrassed himself in public by drinking until he was barely _____. At one point, on a visit to the United States he was mistaken for an intruder when

secret service agents discovered him stumbling drunkenly around the White House clad only in his underwear.

5. Samuel Johnson's writing is so precise, clear, and logical, it's hard to imagine that the man who wrote the English-speaking world's first real dictionary could have spent much of his life in a violent, _____ state. But Johnson, in addition to probably being plagued by Tourette's syndrome, with its uncontrollable twitches, spasms, and outbursts, worried constantly about his sanity and feared that he might go mad. Whatever his prose suggests about his peace of mind, Johnson actually had very little _____ in his life.

Copyright © Cengage Learning. All rights reserved.

▶ **TEST 2**   **Reviewing New Vocabulary**

DIRECTIONS   Fill in the blanks with one of the words listed below.

metabolism	bureaucracy	flaunting	condescending	alleviate
dehydration	intensive	incidence	injunctions	albeit

1. In the United States, the _____ of malaria is quite low. There are fewer than 2,000 cases per year, making it a rare disease. The opposite is true in other parts of the world, particularly in Africa. In Africa, malaria is the number-one killer of children under five years of age. Although _____ efforts have been made to treat malaria, few African countries are financially able to fund large-scale prevention programs. Those that can, unfortunately, often spend too much time and money creating a(n) _____ to deal with the problem and not enough time controlling and treating the disease.

2. When cyclist Floyd Landis failed a drug test and lost his crown as winner of bicycling's Tour de France, he blamed his body's fast _____ and resulting _____ as the twin sources of his test failure. When the body's physical processes speed up, water loss does occur more quickly, but exactly how that could affect the results of a drug test was anyone's guess.

3. In an attempt at using the courts to stop drug dealing, some attorneys have applied for _____ that would legally forbid alleged gang members from entering a specific neighborhood believed to be the scene of drug dealing. Police are then free to search the area specified in the court order and arrest any individuals named.

Copyright © Cengage Learning. All rights reserved.

4. Being environmentally conscious is a good thing and people who take care of the planet should be applauded. But environmentalists who want to win others to their cause should beware of _____ their green lifestyle—remember, not everyone can afford a Prius—and being _____ to people who aren't yet carrying reusable grocery bags or drinking from reusable, aluminum water bottles is not the way to win people to your cause.

5. True, sleeping pills can definitely help _____ insomnia, _____ at a price. In addition to the typical side effects, such as dry mouth, forgetfulness, and the threat of addiction, taking sleeping pills for an extended period of time can also cause *rebound insomnia*. Once you stop the medication, the insomnia can become worse than before.

Copyright © Cengage Learning. All rights reserved.

▶ TEST 3   **Recognizing Topics and Topic Sentences**

DIRECTIONS   Read each paragraph and circle the letter of the correct topic. Then write the number of the topic sentence in the blank.

1. ¹A major cause of excessive water use and waste is the underpricing of this precious resource. ²Many water authorities charge a flat fee for water use and some charge even less for the largest users of water. ³For example, about one-fifth of all U.S. public water systems do not have water meters and charge a single low rate for almost unlimited use of high-quality water. ⁴Also, many apartment dwellers have little incentive to conserve water because water use is included in their rent. ⁵When Boulder, Colorado, introduced water meters, water use per person dropped by 40 percent. ⁶Researchers have found that each 10 percent increase in water prices cuts domestic water use by 3–7 percent. (Adapted from Miller, *Living in the Environment*, p. 328.)

Topic

    a. Boulder, Colorado's use of water meters

    b. use of water meters

    c. underpricing of water

    d. flat fees for water use

Topic Sentence   _____

2. ¹On May 7, 1915, the British luxury liner *Lusitania* was sunk by a German submarine. ²Because the ship contained 123 Americans, all of whom died when the ship sank, the *Lusitania*'s shocking tragedy helped propel the United States into World War I. ³When the ship departed from Liverpool, England, on May 1, everyone on board knew there was a measure of risk in sailing. ⁴The Germans had already targeted and sunk several ships. ⁵Thus there was a very good chance that they would go after more, and the *Lusitania*, too, could fall victim to enemy fire. ⁶The *Lusitania*, though, was a fast ship. ⁷The general hope was that the ship could outrun any possible attacks. ⁸But on May 7, the captain slowed the ship down due to fog. ⁹He also made the decision to sail in waters close to shore, where German subs were known to lurk. ¹⁰At 2:10 in the afternoon, the boat took a direct hit and sank beneath three hundred feet of water in only eighteen minutes. ¹¹The speed with which it sank was due mainly to a secondary explosion, which some have since claimed

Copyright © Cengage Learning. All rights reserved.

was the result of arms that were secretly hidden on board. [12]Because the ship sank so fast and because there weren't enough crew members to man the forty-eight lifeboats, panic reigned and hundreds of people died—1,195 to be exact. [13]Furious at the tragic loss of life, the American public, which, until then, had been dead set against joining the war, became more willing to take up the battle against Germany.

Topic

a. the sinking of the *Lusitania*
b. German aggression in World War I
c. propaganda lies in World War I
d. U.S. refusal to enter World War I

Topic Sentence   _____

3. [1]In 1987, Brazilian labor leader and environmentalist Francisco "Chico" Mendes was awarded the United Nations Global 500 Prize, along with a medal from the Society for a Better World. [2]Sadly, medals couldn't save Chico Mendes's life when he took on a group of cattle ranchers in Acre, Brazil. [3]Determined to drive out rubber workers like the ones Mendes represented, the ranchers used threats and violence. [4]Mendes, who had both a reputation for courage and the respect of his fellow workers, was a special thorn in the ranchers' side, and they threatened his life. [5]To be sure, Mendes took their death threats seriously but refused to abandon his labor activities. [6]On December 15, 1988, he told a friend, "I don't think I'm going to live." [7]One week later, Mendes was shot in the chest as he stepped out of his house.

Topic

a. famous labor leaders
b. the murder of Chico Mendes
c. labor conditions in Brazil
d. honors given to Chico Mendes

Topic Sentence   _____

4. [1]The Underground Railroad was an informal network of routes traveled by American slaves escaping to freedom between 1840 and 1860. [2]These routes included paths through woods and fields;

Copyright © Cengage Learning. All rights reserved.

transportation such as boats, trains, and wagons; and homes where runaways hid from slave owners and law-enforcement officials. [3]In keeping with the idea of a railroad, slaves were referred to as "passengers," while homes that gave them shelter were "stations." [4]The people who assisted the slaves in flight were known as "conductors." [5]The conductors were abolitionists, who defied fugitive slave laws to shelter and feed runaways and guide them along the safest routes out of the South to free states in the North. [6]Harriet Tubman, for example, liberated at least 300 slaves after she herself had used the Underground Railroad to escape the chains of slavery. [7]If it hadn't been for the Underground Railroad, hundreds of slaves, including Tubman, would never have escaped slavery's cruel bondage.

Topic

   a. Harriet Tubman

   b. the Underground Railroad

   c. role of Quakers in the abolitionist movement

   d. rules of the Underground Railroad

Topic Sentence   _____

Copyright © Cengage Learning. All rights reserved.

Copyright © Cengage Learning. All rights reserved.

▶ **TEST 4**   **Recognizing Topic Sentences and Accurate Paraphrases**

DIRECTIONS   Read each paragraph and write the number of the topic sentence in the blank. Then circle the letter of the statement that best paraphrases the topic sentence.

1. [1]In the past, young adults who went off to college would earn their degrees, get jobs, and move into their own homes or apartments. [2]However, twenty-something college graduates are now more likely to return home for an extended period of time. [3]In fact, one informal poll of college seniors revealed that 63 percent of them planned to move back home after graduation. [4]This nationwide "back-to-the-nest" trend is the result of several factors. [5]Because of the unstable economy, jobs are scarce, so recent graduates are often unemployed. [6]Even those lucky enough to find jobs are concerned about keeping them. [7]Plus, young people with entry-level salaries are finding it difficult to afford their own place to live. [8]In high-cost-of-living cities, such as New York, Boston, and San Francisco in particular, recent college graduates often do not make enough money to pay the exorbitant rents. [9]Even in lower-rent areas, young people in their twenties who have student loans to repay or who plan to attend graduate school cannot afford to pay their bills and live on their own.

Topic Sentence   _____

Paraphrase

a. An unstable economy is changing U.S. society in a number of ways.

b. Many twenty-somethings are moving back home because they cannot handle financial responsibility.

c. Today's young people know far more about handling money than their counterparts in a previous generation did.

d. For a variety of financial reasons, many college graduates are going back to their parents' home to live.

2. [1]What is the difference between a computer virus and a computer worm? [2]Both can infect and damage computer systems. [3]Computer viruses and computer worms, however, differ in the way they

damage the computer systems they invade. [4]A virus, which is short for "vital information resources under siege," is a program or code that secretly enters a computer by piggybacking on email messages, files, or programs shared between two different computer systems. [5]Then the virus infects its new host by attaching itself to the files within that computer and deleting or changing them or even over-writing entire programs. [6]Just like a biological virus in the human body, a computer virus replicates itself so that it will continue to be contagious when data is shared with another computer system. [7]In 2000, for example, the famous "Love Bug" virus, which traveled via email messages, destroyed files in computers all over the world. [8]Worms, too, are malicious programs that reproduce and spread. [9]But unlike viruses, they do not need to attach themselves to other files. [10]They are programs that run independently and spread on their own through computer networks. [11]Thus they do not require human intervention to make their way from one computer to another. [12]The famous Internet worm of 1988, for example, copied itself across the Internet, destroying many computer systems as it went. [13]The more recent Sasser worm disabled computers in Britain, South Africa, and Taiwan.

Topic Sentence _____

Paraphrase

a. Both computer viruses and computer worms are programs that damage computer systems.

b. Although computer viruses and computer worms can both do significant damage to computers, they replicate and spread in different ways.

c. Computer worms are far worse than computer viruses because they do not require human participation to spread.

d. Computer viruses must reproduce themselves to be a significant threat.

3. [1]In 1949, the decision was made to use Cape Canaveral in Florida as a testing site for missiles. [2]The Cape Canaveral location was so perfectly adapted to the job of missile launching that it became the site of the Kennedy Space Center, where not just missiles but also rockets and space shuttles are launched. [3]The site was right for the space center because Cape Canaveral is a remote area. [4]However, it is still

Copyright © Cengage Learning. All rights reserved.

accessible by roads and highways. [5]That meant it could be used as a place to build and launch missiles without endangering people living nearby. [6]Although over the years the Kennedy Space Center has expanded to cover 140,000 acres, it remains remote enough to ensure the safety of nearby communities.

Topic Sentence   _____

Paraphrase

a. Cape Canaveral became the site of the Kennedy Space Center because it turned out to be the perfect place for testing and launching missiles, rockets, and space shuttles.

b. Cape Canaveral was the only site in the United States where missiles, rockets, and space shuttles could safely be launched.

c. Cape Canaveral's remoteness led to its selection as America's missile and rocket launch site.

d. Cape Canaveral now covers 140,000 acres.

4. [1]Members of living history clubs are deeply passionate about history, so much so that they are not content to simply read about a particular era. [2]Instead, members of living history clubs seek to recreate life as it was lived in their favorite time period. [3]The 24,000 members of the Society for Creative Anachronism,[†] for example, study the European Middle Ages and Renaissance by re-creating the arts and skills of those eras. [4]Each participant makes and wears clothing from the period and creates a "persona," a person whom he or she would have liked to have been. [5]When the club's members gather at meetings, which may take the form of feasts or tournaments, they reenact the behaviors of those who lived during that era. [6]They might, for instance, practice sword fighting or learn a craft like brewing, weaving, or candle making. [7]Similarly, hundreds of Civil War buffs frequently dress as soldiers and reenact whole battles, often while a crowd of spectators looks on. [8]The reenactors spend weekends camping in canvas tents, eating foods that were available to their historical counterparts, and trying to capture what it was like to have lived during the nineteenth century. [9]Other living

[†]anachronism: something that is out of its proper or appropriate order in time. For example, a play about ancient Rome would never have an actor looking at a watch because the watch is an anachronism.

Copyright © Cengage Learning. All rights reserved.

history groups around the country focus on re-creating the Roman Empire, the pirate era, or the Wild West.

Topic Sentence _____

Paraphrase

   a. Many people are fascinated by a certain period of history.

   b. The Society for Creative Anachronism is a group that reenacts the Middle Ages and Renaissance.

   c. Historical reenactments of important events are often marred by clothing, furniture, or speech that does not fit the time period.

   d. Members of living history clubs enjoy re-creating a particular historical era.

Copyright © Cengage Learning. All rights reserved.

▶ TEST 5   **Recognizing and Paraphrasing Topic Sentences**

DIRECTIONS   Read each paragraph and write the number of the topic sentence in the blank. Then paraphrase the topic sentence on the lines that follow. *Note*: Please paraphrase using complete sentences.

1. [1]In addition to using their senses, predators have a variety of methods that help them capture prey. [2]Herbivores[†] can simply walk, swim, or fly up to the plants they feed on. [3]Carnivores[†] feeding on mobile prey have two main options: pursuit and ambush. [4]Some, such as the cheetah, pursue and catch their prey by running fast; others, such as the American bald eagle, have keen eyesight and can fly; still others, such as wolves and African lions, cooperate to capture their prey by hunting in packs. [5]Other predators use camouflage to hide in plain sight and ambush their prey. [6]For example, praying mantises sit in flowers of a similar color and ambush visiting insects. [7]White ermines and snowy owls are the perfect color to hunt in snow-covered areas. [8]Some predators use chemical warfare to attack their prey. [9]For example, spiders and poisonous snakes use venom to paralyze their prey and to deter their predators. (Adapted from Miller, *Living in the Environment*, p. 152.)

Topic Sentence   _____

Paraphrase   _____

        _____

2. [1]In 1976 in an effort to combat the possible widespread outbreak of swine flu, President Gerald Ford directed the Centers for Disease Control (CDC) to launch a project called the National Influenza Immunization Program (NIIP). [2]In response, four manufacturers set out to make 200 million doses of swine flu vaccine because the CDC wanted every person in the United States to be vaccinated. [3]The CDC also developed a plan to take jet immunization guns into schools, factories, shopping centers, nursing homes, and health departments. [4]However, complications soon began to arise. [5]The vaccine, for instance, could not be produced as fast as initially

_____

[†]herbivores: plant-eating organisms, such as deer, sheep, and grasshoppers.
[†]carnivores: flesh-eating animals, such as lions and tigers.

Copyright © Cengage Learning. All rights reserved.

planned. [6]This setback, along with legal issues, drastically disrupted the production timetable and delayed the beginning of the program by three months. [7]At the same time, the NIIP was suffering from public relations problems. [8]Although the program received widespread support at first, the media began to criticize it when no new cases of swine flu occurred. [9]Then when three elderly people died after being vaccinated, the press connected their deaths to the swine flu immunizations, despite a lack of evidence. [10]However, in time, a connection was established between the swine flu vaccination and a nervous system disease called Guillain-Barré syndrome (GBS). [11]The vaccine was thought to have caused 500 people to develop this complication, resulting in death for 25 of the victims and paralysis for many others. [12]When the NIIP was finally cancelled on December 16, 1976, only 24 percent of the population had been vaccinated, and the immunizations had killed more people than swine flu had. [13]When it was finally over, the 1976 National Influenza Immunization Program turned out to have been one of the greatest public health disasters of all time. (Source of dates and statistics: Joel Warner, "The Sky Is Falling: An Analysis of the Swine Flu Affair of 1976," Haverford College, March 9, 1999, www.haverford.edu/biology/edwards/disease/viral_essays/warnervirus.htm.)

Topic Sentence _____

Paraphrase _____

_____

3. [1]Coral reefs perform many useful functions for the environment; above all, they provide a habitat for organisms that cannot survive elsewhere. [2]Yet coral reefs all over the world are being threatened by human activities. [3]Logging near the waters of Bascuit Bay in the Philippines has destroyed 5 percent of the coral reefs in the bay. [4]Dynamite fishing around the world has not only killed large numbers of fish, it has also blown apart a significant number of coral reefs in Kenya, Tanzania, and Mauritania. [5]Coral reefs have also fallen victim to the tourist industry. [6]Coral and shells are hot tourist commodities, and they have been collected in large quantities for sale to souvenir-hungry tourists. [7]Undoubtedly, the

Copyright © Cengage Learning. All rights reserved.

Copyright © Cengage Learning. All rights reserved.

most violent assault on the reefs has come from nuclear testing. [8]France, for example, has exploded more than 100 nuclear devices in Polynesian waters once rich with coral reefs that are rapidly disappearing.

Topic Sentence   _____

Paraphrase   _____

    _____

4. [1]Officials in countries such as Egypt, Afghanistan, and Greece are pressing European and American museums to return ancient art objects illegally taken from them long ago. [2]However, the museums that display these antiquities argue that they have good reasons for not returning them to their original owners. [3]Museums fear, for instance, that returning treasures to their place of origin would result in the dismantling of their collections and loss of revenue from museum visitors. [4]Museum officials also insist that many of the antiquities are too fragile to move. [5]London's British Museum, for example, says that sculptures sawed off the Parthenon in 1801 are too delicate to transport from England to Greece. [6]Museum officials argue, too, that they are better equipped to preserve such priceless treasures and accuse some countries of not taking proper care of precious artifacts. [7]Those on the side of the museums point out that in unstable or war-torn countries like Afghanistan, where the looting and destruction of museums is still a very real possibility, antiquities are at great risk. [8]Plus, returning works of art to their place of origin often significantly reduces public access to them. [9]Russia's Hermitage Museum, for example, reluctantly returned a rare copper bowl to Kazakhstan, and now the bowl is kept in a mosque where few visitors are allowed to go.

Topic Sentence   _____

Paraphrase   _____

    _____

▶ **TEST 6** **Taking Stock**

DIRECTIONS This selection from Jeffrey Nevid's *Psychology: Concepts and Applications* explains how a method of learning called "classical conditioning" came to be understood. Read it carefully and answer the questions that follow by circling the letter of the correct response or filling in the blanks.

Classical Conditioning: Learning Through Association

1 Do your muscles tighten at the sound of a dentist's drill? Do you suddenly begin to salivate when you drive by your favorite bakery? You weren't born with these responses—you learned them. But how does this kind of learning occur?

2 To understand how responses are learned, we need to consider the work of the Russian physiologist Ivan Pavlov (1849–1936). Pavlov discovered the form of learning we call *classical conditioning*. Although Pavlov's discovery is among the most important in psychology, it occurred by accident. Pavlov was studying the digestive system in dogs when he noticed that the animals would salivate to sounds associated with the delivery of food, such as the clanging of metal food carts being wheeled into his laboratory. He believed the salivation reflex was triggered in the brain by stimuli associated with feeding. He called this phenomenon a "conditional reflex." We now call it a "conditioned response" (conditioned meaning "acquired" or "learned"). Pavlov spent the rest of his career studying this form of learning, now called *classical conditioning*.

3 You might think of classical conditioning as learning by association. If you associate the sound of a dentist's drill with pain because of past experiences, the sound alone may cause you to respond with muscle tension. The tension is the body's natural reflex to pain, which it already starts to expect at the drill's sound.

4 For instance, if you associate a certain bakery with a particularly tasty treat, you may find yourself salivating as you pass by the bakery. These responses are learned through experiences in which one stimulus is paired with another that automatically elicits such natural reactions. Although classical conditioning is a relatively simple form of learning, it plays an important role in our lives. (Adapted from Nevid, *Psychology: Concepts and Applications*, p. 176.)

Copyright © Cengage Learning. All rights reserved.

1. Which of the following statements best defines classical conditioning?

    a. Classical conditioning occurs when things associated with positive or negative experiences start to produce the same responses as those actual experiences.

    b. Classical conditioning occurs when the same experiences are repeated several times and the responses become equally automatic.

    c. Classical conditioning occurs when something happens that repeatedly causes us pain, so much so that at the first hint of the experience being repeated, our muscles tense with anxiety.

2. Based on the context (paragraph 4), what you do you think a stimulus is?

    _____

3. In paragraph 2, what is the function of the following sentence: "To understand how responses are learned, we need to consider the work of the Russian physiologist Ivan Pavlov (1849–1936)"?

    a. an introductory sentence

    b. a topic sentence

    c. a major supporting detail

    d. a transitional sentence

4. In paragraph 2, what is the function of the following sentence: "Pavlov was studying the digestive system in dogs when he noticed that the animals would salivate to sounds associated with the delivery of food, such as the clanging of metal food carts being wheeled into his laboratory"?

    a. a topic sentence

    b. a major supporting detail

    c. a minor supporting detail

    d. a transitional sentence

Copyright © Cengage Learning. All rights reserved.

5. Why does the reading open and close with a reference to a dental drill and a bakery?

_____

_____

_____

_____

ALLUSION ALERT

Pavlov and His Dog

Pavlov's name has become a common allusion in English, and you will see references to people responding like Pavlov's dogs or making a Pavlovian response. For example, here's writer Colbert King reminiscing about his father: "At five sharp, my father's whistle pierced the air for blocks. The King kids, in a response that would have made Pavlov proud, could be seen abandoning marbles, cards, third base—everything—to make a beeline for home." What point is King making about the reaction he and his siblings had to the sound of his father's whistle?

_____

_____

_____

Copyright © Cengage Learning. All rights reserved.

Identifying and Learning from Organizational Patterns

IN THIS CHAPTER, YOU WILL LEARN

- how to identify the most common patterns of organization in paragraphs.
- how recognizing the patterns can focus your attention while reading and help improve both remembering and note-taking.
- how to determine the importance of mixed organizational patterns.

Image Source/Jupiter Images

Making mental connections is our most crucial learning tool, the essence of human intelligence; to forge links; to go beyond the given; to see patterns, relationships, context.

—Marilyn Ferguson, writer

Although no single rule exists for structuring information in writing, there are several organizational patterns that make frequent appearances, especially in textbooks. This chapter introduces seven of those patterns and offers some tips on how to recognize the **primary,** or most important, pattern in a paragraph.

Pattern 1: Definition

Leaf through any textbook and, more often than not, you'll notice numerous definitions. In fact, textbook authors frequently devote whole paragraphs to defining terms essential to their subject matter.

The definition pattern usually opens with the word or term being explained. That word is usually highlighted in some way, through boldface, colored type, or italics. The meaning then follows right on the heels of the highlighted word. The remainder of the paragraph expands on the definition in one or more of the following ways: (1) gives an example of the word in context, (2) describes problems associated with the definition, (3) traces the history of the word, or (4) compares it to a word with a similar meaning.

Here to illustrate is a paragraph organized by the definition pattern. Note how the paragraph has been underlined and annotated to highlight both word and meaning.

Free association means you say *anything that comes into your head.*

TQ: What role did free association play in psychoanalysis?

Free Association. In **free association,** the client is instructed to say anything that crosses his or her mind, no matter how trivial or irrelevant it may seem. The father of psychoanalysis, Sigmund Freud, who first used free association as therapy, believed these free associations would eventually work their way toward uncovering deep-seated wishes and desires that reflect underlying conflicts. In classical psychoanalysis, the client lies on a couch with the analyst sitting off to the side, out of the client's direct view and saying little. By remaining detached, the analyst hopes to create an atmosphere that encourages the client to free associate. (Nevid, *Psychology: Concepts and Applications,* p. 357.)

In this case, the author wants readers to understand the meaning of the phrase "free association." To that end, he gives the phrase special emphasis. The phrase gets a paragraph and an italicized title all to itself. Next the author uses boldface to highlight the term again, right before

Copyright © Cengage Learning. All rights reserved.

defining it. Thanks to these visual clues, the reader knows the phrase is important and is on the alert for its meaning.

Typically for the definition pattern, the author follows the word and meaning with a description of the context in which the word is used—a therapeutic setting. He also tells readers a little about the history: Sigmund Freud was the first to use free association in a therapeutic setting.

TAKING A CLOSER LOOK

Looking at Sentence Openings

Look at sentences 1, 3, and 4 in the paragraph on free association. What is the function of those opening phrases or orienters? How do they guide the reader?

_____

_____

Typical Topic Sentences

Sentences like the following are strong contenders for a definition pattern of development.

---

1. Over the past forty years, journalists and advocacy organizations have persuaded many states to pass **sunshine laws**— regulations that ensure government meetings and reports are made available to the press. (Turow, *Media Today*, p. 44.)

2. A file-management utility lets you view, rename, copy, move, and delete files and folders. (Beekman and Quinn, *Computer Confluence*, p. 163.)

3. The phrase "identification with the aggressor" refers to the tendency of victims to become dependent on those who hurt or oppress them.

Copyright © Cengage Learning. All rights reserved.

> **PATTERN POINTER** To fully understand and remember a key definition, consider making a concept map like the one shown here.
>
> client says anything that comes to mind ——— **Free Association** ——— first used by Freud
>
> no censorship allowed

Multiple-Definition Paragraphs

Multiple-definition paragraphs are also common in textbooks. Because paragraphs do not usually extend beyond ten or twelve sentences, space is limited, and this version of the definition pattern usually includes little more than the words or terms followed by their definitions. Textbook authors often use the multiple-definition pattern when they are dealing with related terms. Here's an example:

> There are many different kinds of personality disorders. People with a **narcissistic personality disorder** have an inflated or grandiose* sense of themselves, while those suffering from a **paranoid personality disorder** show a high degree of suspiciousness or mistrust. Those with a **schizoid personality disorder** have little if any interest in social relationships, display a limited range of emotional expression, and are perceived as distant and aloof. Those with a **borderline personality disorder** tend to have stormy relationships with others, dramatic mood swings, and an unstable self-image. In total, the *Diagnostic and Statistical Manual of Mental Disorders*, a handbook for mental-health professionals, identifies ten different personality disorders. The most widely studied of these is the **antisocial personality disorder (APD)**. This disorder is characterized by a complete disregard for all social conventions or rules. In the United States, personality disorders affect 10 to 15 percent of the population.

---

*grandiose: having an exaggerated sense of one's importance or influence.

Copyright © Cengage Learning. All rights reserved.

Tables

Keep in mind, too, that multiple-definition paragraphs are often accompanied by tables such as the one below. When it comes time for exam review, these tables are handy. That's because they neatly itemize individual terms, names, or events on the left and give the meaning on the right. A table is a ready-made study aid, which you can use to review what you've learned from your textbook assignment.

Schizoid personality disorder	Aloof and distant from others, with shallow or blunted emotions
Antisocial personality disorder	A pattern of antisocial and irresponsible behavior, callous treatment of others, and lack of remorse for wrongdoing
Borderline personality disorder	A failure to develop a stable self-image, together with a pattern of tumultuous moods and stormy relationships with others and lack of impulse control
Paranoid personality disorder	Persistent belief that other people are planning to do one harm
Avoidant personality disorder	Pattern of avoiding social relationships out of fear of relationships

PATTERN POINTER When you are dealing with multiple definitions, consider making your own visual aids. If the author doesn't include a table like the one above, drawing your own table is a great way to make your mind process not just the meanings of the different terms but also their relationship to one another.

◆ **EXERCISE 1** **Understanding the Definition Patterns**

DIRECTIONS   Read each passage and identify the term being defined. Paraphrase the definition. Then identify the method or methods the author uses to define the key term.

Copyright © Cengage Learning. All rights reserved.

EXAMPLE   **Corporate crime** is defined as a criminal act committed by one or more employees of a corporation while being attributed* to the organization itself. Between 1984 and 1990, 2,000 corporations were convicted in federal courts for offenses ranging from tax-law violations to environmental crimes. One problem with the term *corporate crime* is definitional. In 1989, the supertanker *Exxon Valdez* ran aground in Prince William Sound, Alaska, spilling 11 million gallons of crude oil. The spill was a major ecological disaster. Prosecutors were interested in determining the guilt or innocence of the captain, his officers, and his crew. But there were additional and far-reaching questions. Did the Exxon Corporation sacrifice the environment by putting profit above safety? If so, was this a corporate crime?[†] (Adapted from Adler, Mueller, and Laufer, *Criminology,* p. 38.)

The paragraph defines the following term or terms: <u>corporate crime</u>

Restate the definition or definitions in your own words.

<u>Corporate crime refers to a criminal action taken by a corporate employee but</u>

<u>blamed on the corporation itself.</u>

Which of the following methods does the author use to help define the key term or terms?

✓ The author gives an example of behavior or events that fit the definition.

_____ The author supplies a history of the word's development.

✓ The author describes a problem associated with applying the definition.

_____ The author compares the word defined to a word similar in meaning.

EXPLANATION   The author defines the term *corporate crime* and gives an example of behavior associated with it, for example, tax violations and environmental crimes. The author also shows that it's not always easy to know what instances, experiences, or events fit the definition.

---

*attributed: related to a particular source or cause.
[†]At the writing of this text, these same questions are being asked about the April 2010 oil spill in the Gulf of Mexico.

Copyright © Cengage Learning. All rights reserved.

1. **Branding**, or the creation of a specific name to advertise a product, such as Quaker Oats for oatmeal or Coca Cola for a soft drink, started to grow in importance in the late nineteenth century. Prior to that time, manufacturers of flour and other basic products like candy, sugar, and beans sold merchandise in sacks without any names. But over time manufacturers tried to distinguish their products from the products of others. Henry Parson Cromwell, for example, created the name *Quaker Oats* and launched an advertising campaign to extol the virtues of his product. *Quaker Oats* was followed by a host of products with specific brand names, such as *Heinz ketchup, Borden's milk,* and *Pillsbury flour.* (Adapted from Harper, *The New Mass Media,* p. 231.)

The paragraph defines the following term or terms: _Branding_

Restate the definition or definitions in your own words.

Branding refers to the action used by factories to show the name of the product on the wrapper to distinguish between 2 similar

Which of the following methods does the author use to help define _products_ the key term or terms?

✓ ____ The author gives an example of behavior or events that fit the definition.

____ The author supplies a history of the word's development.

____ The author describes a problem associated with applying the definition.

✓ ____ The author compares the word defined to a word similar in meaning.

2. Created by the Constitution, the **Supreme Court** is the highest court in the land. Although the original Supreme Court consisted of a chief justice and five associates, nine judges currently sit on the Supreme Court, and its decisions, once made, are irrevocable, or irreversible. However, defendants displeased with a decision made by a lower court can appeal that ruling to the Supreme Court in the hopes of having it overturned. In 2006, for instance, the Circuit Court of Appeals of New York found in favor of Evelyn Coke, a seventy-three-year-old employee in the home-care industry, who sued her employers for back payment of overtime compensation, which had been denied her based on a 1930s Department of Labor regulation created

Copyright © Cengage Learning. All rights reserved.

when home-care for the elderly did not yet exist. The court ruled that Coke deserved to be appropriately compensated for her overtime hours. Coke's employers, Long Island Care at Home, appealed the decision to the Supreme Court in the hopes of having it reversed. In 2007, the Supreme Court overruled the lower court's decision. (Source of case description: http://www.msnbc.msn.com/id/19173596.)

The paragraph defines the following term or terms: _Supreme Court_

Restate the definition or definitions in your own words.

The Supreme Court is the final juridical institution which decisions are irrevocable or irreversible.

Which of the following methods does the author use to help define the key term or terms?

_____ The author gives an example of behavior or events that fit the definition.

_____ The author supplies a history of the word's development.

_____ The author describes a problem associated with applying the definition.

_____ The author compares the word defined to a word similar in meaning.

Pattern 2: Process

The process pattern orders events according to when they occurred in real time and identifies the steps or stages necessary to explaining how something functions or works. Here to illustrate is a paragraph describing the digestion process. Once again, the passage is marked to highlight both the steps in the process and the kind of test question (TQ) such material might generate.

Digestive system prepares food to be turned into energy.

TQ: Explain the process of digestion.

In the human body, the digestive system breaks down food so that it can be used for energy. As [1]food enters the mouth, chewing, along with enzymes in the saliva, break it down into small pieces. [2]Next, the esophagus contracts and pushes the food into the stomach, where muscles, enzymes, and digestive acids turn the food into a thick liquid. That [3]liquid is emptied into the small intestine, where most of its

Copyright © Cengage Learning. All rights reserved.

nutrients are absorbed. [4]What remains travels to the large intestine, where water is removed from digested food and turned into waste.

(Adapted from Barnes-Svarney, *The New York Public Library Science Desk Reference,* p. 166.)

TAKING A CLOSER LOOK

Looking at Sentence Openings
Re-read the phrases that open the first two sentences in the previous paragraph. What function do they serve?

organisation and location

Verbal Clues to the Pattern

Words such as *steps, stages, phases, procedures,* and *process* are all signs that you are dealing with a process pattern. So too are the transitions in the following list.

Transitions Identifying a Sequence of Steps ♦		
	Afterward	In the final stage
	At this point	In this stage
	By the time	Next
	Finally	Then
	First; second; third	Toward the end

Typical Topic Sentences

Sentences like the ones shown below are typical of the process pattern:

1. People who grieve for the loss of a loved one frequently pass through three stages of grief.
2. The bestowing of sainthood is an extremely complex process.
3. Storing information in long-term memory requires several steps.

Copyright © Cengage Learning. All rights reserved.

Flow Charts

Paragraphs organized according to the process pattern are often accompanied by flow charts. These are diagrams that use boxes or circles connected by arrows to map a sequence of steps, stages, or operations. Here, for example, is one kind of flow chart. For another, see pages 185–86.

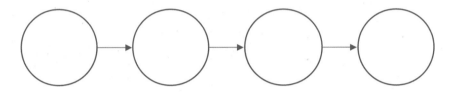

Whatever kind of flow chart the author uses, its presence is a good indicator that the author is also relying on the process pattern.

PATTERN POINTERS

1. Never get so caught up in the individual steps or stages that you lose sight of the larger process or sequence they describe. Keep thinking what each step contributes to the whole.

2. If the process pattern seems hard to grasp, draw your own diagram or make a flow chart like the one shown above.

3. During exam review, see if you can summarize, from memory, all the steps in a process, without missing a single one. Better still, see if you can draw your own flow chart.

◆ **EXERCISE 2** **Understanding Process Patterns**

DIRECTIONS Read each paragraph. Then draw a flow chart that identifies the steps in the proper order. The first box of the first flow chart has been done for you.

1. **Luminol and Bloodstains**

Tune in to television shows like the popular *CSI*, and you'll see plenty of crime-solving tools that are nothing but products of the writers'

Copyright © Cengage Learning. All rights reserved.

imaginations. Luminol, however, isn't one of them. Forensics specialists regularly use luminol to detect invisible bloodstains at crime scenes.
First, they close the curtains and turn off the lights. Then they spray
Luminol onto carpets, floors, walls, or furniture. When the chemicals in
Luminol combine with the iron in blood, the bloodstains glow greenish-
blue. Even minuscule amounts of blood will light up when the Luminol
reacts to blood cells clinging to surfaces that have been washed with
heavy-duty cleaning chemicals. Investigators photograph or videotape
the glowing patches, recording any sign of a pattern. Finally, they collect samples and run additional tests to be completely sure that the
substance causing the glow was indeed blood since Luminol can also
produce a glow when the substance comes in contact with some plant
matter and cleaning products.

Main Idea   Forensic specialists use Luminol to detect bloodstains at a crime scene.

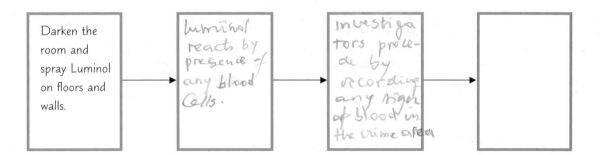

| Darken the room and spray Luminol on floors and walls. | luminol reacts by presence of any blood cells. | investigators procede by recording any sign of blood in the crime area | |

2. The Heimlich Maneuver

You can save the life of a choking victim by performing the Heimlich
maneuver. If a person suddenly cannot breathe, cough, or speak, the
person's airway is probably blocked by something that needs to be
removed. To perform the Heimlich maneuver, stand behind the victim
and make a fist with one hand. Then reach your arms around the person from behind. Place your fist against the person's belly just above the
belly button and below the rib cage. Next, cover your fist with your other
hand and press into the belly with a quick, upward thrust. If the object
in the person's throat doesn't come flying out, perform another thrust.
Repeat thrusts over and over until you dislodge the object. At the same
time, yell for help and tell someone to call 911.

Main Idea   The Heimlich maneuver can save the life of a person who is choking.

Copyright © Cengage Learning. All rights reserved.

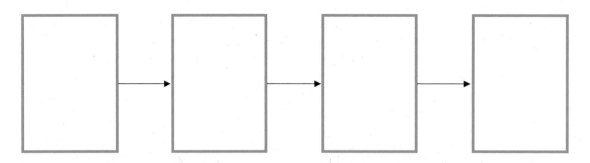

CHECK YOUR UNDERSTANDING

Fill in the blanks in the following sentences.

1. The definition pattern usually opens _____.

2. In the definition pattern, the word or term being defined is _____

   _____

   _____.

3. The process pattern orders events _____.

   The object of the process pattern is _____

   _____.

4. When you are reading a passage organized according to the process pattern, you

   should never _____

   _____.

5. While you are reading a paragraph organized according to the process pattern,

   keep thinking about _____.

Pattern 3: Sequence of Dates and Events

Authors who write about history and government frequently use a sequence of dates and events to explain or argue their claims. The dates and events are presented according to the order in which they occurred in real time. Here's an example.

Copyright © Cengage Learning. All rights reserved.

TQ: What are the dates of the Mexican-American War?

TQ: What event helped to encourage a war with Mexico?

TQ: What treaty ended the Mexican-American War?

The Democrat James Polk became president of the United States in 1844. From the very beginning of his presidency, Polk made it clear that he intended to expand the boundaries of the United States. By 1846, he had ordered General Zachary Taylor to take troops into Mexican territory. On April 24 of the same year, the Mexican military fired on Taylor's troops, and war between the United States and Mexico began, even though Congress had not yet officially declared it. By 1847, U.S. troops had arrived in Mexico City and were claiming victory. (The opening phrase in the Marines' anthem—"From the Halls of Montezuma"—is a reference to the arrival of those troops in Mexico's capital.) In 1848, Mexico and the United States signed the Treaty of Guadalupe Hidalgo, which ceded a portion of Mexican land that today includes Arizona, Utah, Nevada, and New Mexico to the United States. Polk had his wish: He had expanded and redefined U.S. borders. But in an effort to assuage* the war's critics—and there were many who considered the war with Mexico unjust—the U.S. government paid the Mexican government $15 million.

Notice how many sentences in this paragraph open with dates. That's a sure sign that the author is using the sequence of dates and events pattern to organize information.

Transition Clues

Sequence of dates and events paragraphs are likely to use time-order transitions like those listed in the following box.

Time-Order Transitions ◆	After	Between _____† and _____
	During the period between	On _____ of that year
	By the end of	_____ year(s) later
	At the end of	When _____ ended
	In the years that followed	

_____

*assuage: calm or soothe.

Copyright © Cengage Learning. All rights reserved.

Typical Topic Sentences

Along with numerous dates and events, the time-order transitions listed above are clues to this pattern. So, too, are topic sentences like those you see here.

1. From 1753 to 1815, Native Americans cooperated and fought with or tried to avoid the Spanish, French, British, and Anglo-Americans who had intruded on their homelands. (Boyer et al., *The Enduring Vision*, p. 168.)

2. British children's writer Frances Hodgson Burnett started her career in 1853 at the age of four by telling stories to her siblings; by the time she died in 1924, she had written fifty-two books and thirteen plays.

3. The young Latina singer Selena had a brief but enormously influential career.

PATTERN POINTERS

1. Never lose sight of the overall main idea or key point the dates and events are there to explain. Use the main idea to determine if all the dates and events are equal in importance.

2. If you think the paragraph is hard to understand and the sequence of dates and events difficult to follow, try making a timeline like the one shown here.

1844	Polk becomes president
	Wants to expand U.S. borders
1846	Orders Taylor into Mexican territory
April 24	Mexican troops fire on Taylor's troops
	War unofficially began
1847	U.S. troops in Mexico City claiming victory
1848	Mexico and U.S. sign Treaty of Guadalupe
	Hidalgo, ceding huge portion of Mexican land to U.S.

---

†Blanks indicate where dates, years, or numbers would go.

Copyright © Cengage Learning. All rights reserved.

INTERNET FOLLOW-UP: Polk and Manifest Destiny

What does the term "manifest destiny" mean?

_____

_____

_____

What does the term have to do with Polk's decision to go to war?

_____

ALLUSION ALERT

The Garden of Eden

In the Bible, the Garden of Eden is the lush paradise where Adam and Eve are free to wander until they fall victim to Satan's trickery. Thus references to the garden of Eden or Eden have come to suggest a place that is lush and beautiful—for instance, "With the passage of the Homestead Act, many Americans went West expecting a Garden of Eden, but what they found was dry, sandy desert."

◆ **EXERCISE 3**   **Responding to Sequence of Dates and Events Patterns**

DIRECTIONS   Read each paragraph. Underline the topic sentence. Then paraphrase it and list the supporting details, making sure to use chronological order for the crucial dates and events. Abbreviate and paraphrase as much as possible without losing the original meaning. *Note*: Your paraphrasing here should be informal, as it would be for your reading notes.

EXAMPLE   Break dancing first came to public attention in 1969 when singer James Brown performed the song "Get on the Good Foot," while doing wildly energetic and athletic dance moves that drew applause and admiration. Amazingly, after more than forty years, break dancing is still a popular dance form. Throughout the 1970s, the new style continued to develop as African-American and Latino young people incorporated movements from the martial arts, gymnastics, and acrobatics into their dancing. At the end of the 1970s, break dancing became a feature

Copyright © Cengage Learning. All rights reserved.

of urban block parties in the Bronx, New York. In the 1980s, films like *Beat Street, Breakin'*, and *Flashdance* led to break dancing's entry into mainstream popular culture. Because the media lost interest in the craze by the late 1980s, much of America assumed that the fad was over. In the late twentieth and early twenty-first centuries, though, break dancers doing moves even more powerful and complex than before re-emerged in television commercials as well as in music videos and competitions. Now a new generation of young break dancers is spinning, kicking, and back-flipping to the beat. The annual Battle of the Year international break-dancing competition is still held, and it attracts thousands of young fans, not to speak of hits on YouTube.

Main Idea

Break dancing is still popular after close to fifty years.

Supporting Details

1. 1969: James Brown's song "Get on the Good Foot" encourages wild dance moves.

2. 1970s: African Americans and Latinos incorporate moves from different sources, e.g., martial arts, gymnastics.

3. 1980s: Movies like Beat Street popularize break dancing.

4. Late 80s: Break dancing seems to fade but made a comeback and now there's a new generation.

EXPLANATION   As they should, the notes paraphrase the topic sentence and include the dates and events needed to illustrate break dancing's long and continued popularity. *Note*: In this case, the introductory sentence also provides support for the main idea, so it appears as a supporting detail.

1. Watergate,† the scandal that rocked the nation and brought down President Richard M. Nixon, began on June 17, 1972, when five men were caught trying to burglarize the offices of the Democratic

---

†Watergate: The offices of the Democratic National Committee were in the Watergate Hotel, Washington, D.C.

Copyright © Cengage Learning. All rights reserved.

National Committee. Their arrest led to an investigation that uncovered a White House plan of systematic espionage* against political opponents. Deeply involved in that plan were the two top aides to President Nixon, John Ehrlichman and H. R. Haldeman. On May 17, 1973, the Senate Committee on Presidential Activities opened hearings to investigate the scope of the espionage. Then, two days later, Attorney General Elliot Richardson appointed a special prosecutor, Harvard Law School professor Archibald Cox, to conduct a full-scale investigation of the break-in. On July 13, in the course of the investigation, White House aide Alexander Butterfield mentioned that President Nixon had taped all of the conversations that occurred in his office. When the committee asked for the tapes, Nixon refused to turn them over. Determined to fight, Nixon ordered the dismissal of prosecutor Cox on October 20. After the resulting storm of public protest, Nixon finally agreed to turn over the tapes in June 1974. Once members of the committee had examined the tapes, they discovered that eighteen-and-one-half minutes had been mysteriously erased. By July 30, the House Judiciary Committee had approved three articles of impeachment. Rather than face almost certain disgrace, Richard Milhous Nixon resigned on August 9, 1974.

Main Idea

_____

_____

Supporting Details

_____

_____

_____

_____

_____

_____

_____

_____

---

*espionage: spying or using spies to obtain secret information.

Copyright © Cengage Learning. All rights reserved.

_____

_____

_____

_____

_____

2. In 1584, an English fort and settlement with more than one hundred men was established on an island off the coast of present-day North Carolina. The British settlers named the island Roanoke, describing it as an American Eden. However, they abandoned it within a year because of bad relations with the Native Americans already living there. In 1587, another group of British colonists arrived on the island and, within a month, one of the women on the island gave birth to the first child born in the New World, naming her Virginia Dare. Only a week after the birth, the baby's grandfather, Captain John White, returned to England for supplies. Due to conflicts with Spain, White did not return to Roanoke until 1590. But upon his return, to his horror and shock, there was nothing left of the former colony. The only signs of human presence were the letters "CRO" and "CROATAN" carved on two trees. To this day, no one knows what happened to the colonists White left behind on Roanoke Island.

Main Idea _____

_____

Supporting Details _____

_____

_____

_____

_____

_____

_____

Copyright © Cengage Learning. All rights reserved.

CHECK YOUR UNDERSTANDING Through Writing

Write a paragraph organized according to the order of events. Although you can certainly choose your own topics, the following are three possible chains of events to explore: (1) how Joan of Arc went from being a warrior to a condemned prisoner, (2) the events leading up to and including the Triangle Shirtwaist Factory fire, (3) the bombing of Pearl Harbor and America's entry into World War II. Make sure you use sentence openings or orienters that help your reader understand how events unfolded over time.

ALLUSION ALERT

 Watergate
The scandal surrounding the break-in at the Watergate Hotel was so enormous it brought down a president. Not surprisingly, allusions to Watergate have become an abbreviated way of saying that something is or is not a major scandal that will have devastating consequences—e.g., "While many Americans considered President Clinton's affair with Monica Lewinsky to be stupid and immoral, they generally rejected the press's claim that it was Clinton's Watergate."

Pattern 4: Simple Listing

In passages using the process or sequence of dates and events patterns, the order of events and steps is extremely important. The writer who describes a process is not about to put the last step first or vice versa. The same is true for the sequence of dates and events pattern. No writer of a history text tracing the events in the Civil War is going to describe the battle of Antietam (1862) after the Battle of Gettysburg (1863).

In the simple listing pattern, however, all the major details are equally important and can be switched around to suit the writer. A writer who uses the simple listing pattern mainly wants to identify certain skills, factors, studies, reasons, and so on, related to a particular topic or issue—making the order in which they appear irrelevant. Look, for

Copyright © Cengage Learning. All rights reserved.

example, at the two paragraphs that follow. The content of each is the same. The order is not.

Paragraph 1

Victims of eating disorders display several distinct symptoms. They are preoccupied* with their weight or their physical appearance and often exhibit signs of low self-esteem. They are inclined to suffer from anxiety, moodiness, or depression and may also diet obsessively or avoid eating altogether. Or just the opposite, they may overeat, purge, and then start eating again. In either case, the victims exhibit rapid weight loss or pronounced weight changes. Those suffering from eating disorders may also exhibit compulsive* behaviors such as hoarding food or eating specific foods only on certain days. They are likely to wear baggy clothes to hide their bodies and withdraw from others, avoiding social situations that include food. Some victims even isolate themselves completely. Those in the grip of an eating disorder are likely to experience faintness, dizziness, and an inability to concentrate. Problems such as constipation or diarrhea are also common.

In Paragraph 1, the author announces that eating disorders have several symptoms. Knowing full well that most readers are going to ask, "What are they?" the author describes each symptom. Nothing in the paragraph, however, suggests that any one symptom is more important than the others or precedes the others in time. Thus, the author is free to list them in any way she thinks appropriate. Note how easily the order can be changed without changing the paragraph's meaning.

Paragraph 2

Victims of eating disorders are likely to experience faintness, dizziness, concentration difficulties, and bowel problems like constipation or diarrhea. They are inclined to wear baggy clothes to hide their bodies and tend to withdraw from others, avoiding in particular any social situation involving food. Some completely isolate themselves and may exhibit obsessive behaviors such as hoarding food or eating specific foods only on certain days. They may diet obsessively and avoid eating, or just the opposite, they may overeat and purge; in either case, they exhibit rapid weight loss or pronounced weight changes. Often suffering from

---

*preoccupied: overly concerned with something, also absorbed in thought.
*compulsive: involuntary, uncontrollable.

Copyright © Cengage Learning. All rights reserved.

anxiety, moodiness, or depression, they are preoccupied with their weight and physical appearance and are likely to exhibit signs of low self-esteem. Although there are other less common symptoms, the ones listed here are the typical signs of an eating disorder.) *disorder*

As you can see, unlike any of the patterns you've studied so far, simple listing has a loose and readily reorganized structure.

Typical Topic Sentences

Topic sentences typical of the simple listing pattern *almost* always (note the qualifier *almost*) contain some general words like those listed here.

cases	efforts	parts	roles
changes	examples	policies	studies
characteristics	illustrations	principles	symptoms
decisions	inventions	qualities	traits

As you know from Chapter 3, when these words appear in a topic sentence, they also help identify major details.

The following topic sentences are typical of those likely to appear in the simple listing pattern.

1. These are just a few of the numerous inventions that Dean Kamen has patented in the last two decades. (Note the wording, which is typical of simple listing topic sentences appearing at the very end of a paragraph.)
2. Before global warming threatened the very existence of polar bears, several characteristics helped the bears survive and even thrive in the Arctic.
3. In places like China, Vietnam, Egypt, and Algeria, efforts are being made to censor, even silence, bloggers who speak out against repressive governments.

Copyright © Cengage Learning. All rights reserved.

PATTERN POINTERS

1. If the topic sentence contains a general word that needs to be specifically itemized to be meaningful—for example, *statistics, studies, reasons*—use that word to guide your selection of major details. Any sentence that introduces a new case, characteristic, etc., is worth remembering and/or recording in your notes. Any sentence that doesn't is probably not especially significant.

2. The information in the simple listing pattern is often so loosely connected, the different details can be hard to remember. To help remember the details listed in this pattern, think about including a visual aid in your notes, perhaps making a concept map like the one shown below.

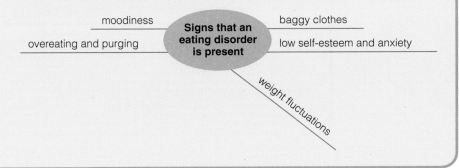

◆ **EXERCISE 4** **Learning from Simple Listing Patterns**

DIRECTIONS Read each paragraph. Then identify the topic sentence and the best paraphrase of that sentence by circling the appropriate letters. Write the crucial word or phrase from the topic sentence in the blanks and list the qualities, traits, etc., that clarify it.

1. ¹New words are added to the English language all the time, and several have been added just this year. ²For instance, the word *fanboy,* used to indicate a passionate fan of something, has officially taken up residence in Merriam-Webster's Collegiate Dictionary. ³The word *mondegreen* is also there; it refers to the misunderstanding and continued misstatement of words or phrases that are repeatedly said or sung. ⁴Kids, for example, often think that the sentence "I pledge allegiance to the flag" is "I led the pigeons to the flag." ⁵The *webinar,* or online conference, has also made it to the pages of many standard dictionaries. ⁶In dictionaries trying hard to be cutting

Copyright © Cengage Learning. All rights reserved.

edge, you'll also now find phrases like *Christmas bogus,* used to sarcastically identify the lack of a bonus from an employer, along with *virtual Friday,* used to identify the last day of school or work thanks to an extended weekend.

1. The topic sentence is

   a. sentence 1.

   b. sentence 2.

   c. sentence 3.

2. The best paraphrase of that topic sentence is

   a. English is always adopting new words and dropping old ones.

   b. The Merriam-Webster dictionary tries hard to be cutting edge and adopts all of the latest slang expressions.

   c. New words are always being coined and adopted into English.

   d. What makes the English language great is its ability to absorb new words.

3. The crucial word or phrase in the topic sentence is _____.

4. The following supporting details help clarify and explain that word or phrase.

   _____

   _____

   _____

   _____

   _____

2. ¹During World War II, the Nazis forced Jewish art dealers and collectors to sell their belongings for prices that amounted to theft. ²After the war many of the artworks illegally taken by the Nazis were sold to museums, which are now being pressured to return them to their rightful owners. ³Although far too many museums are dragging their feet, others have made it a point to give back what is, in effect, stolen artwork. ⁴The Israel Museum of Jerusalem transferred the title of one of its most prized paintings, *Boulevard*

Copyright © Cengage Learning. All rights reserved.

Montmartre: Spring by Camille Pissarro to the family of Max Silberberg. [5]Silberberg was an art collector who died in a concentration camp and whose paintings had been sold in one of the Nazis' notorious "Jewish auctions." [6]A similar decision to transfer ownership was made by the North Carolina Museum of Art in Raleigh, which conceded that a sixteenth-century painting by Lucas Cranach belonged to the family of Dr. Philipp von Gomperz. [7]After a nine-year battle with the rightful owners, the Dutch government, in 2006, removed close to 200 pieces of art from the walls of Holland's museums so that the artworks could be returned to the family of Jacques Goudstikker, who had been forced to sell the Nazis his art collection for a fraction of its worth. [8]Even Austria, which at first had flatly ignored claims that several works by famed Viennese artist Gustav Klimt really belonged to victims of Nazi persecution, has relented and returned several Klimt paintings to the original owner's family.

1. The topic sentence is

    a. sentence 1.

    b. sentence 2.

    c. sentence 3.

2. The best paraphrase of that topic sentence is

    a. The families of Holocaust victims have just begun to receive reparations for what relatives suffered during World War II.

    b. Art museums have fought hard to retain ownership of artwork confiscated from victims of Nazi persecution.

    c. Although some museums are refusing, others are returning to the rightful owners artwork that was confiscated by the Nazis.

    d. Museums are embarrassed by revelations that they benefited from the Holocaust.

3. The crucial word or phrase in the topic sentence is _____.

4. The following supporting details clarify and explain that word or phrase.

    _____

    _____

Copyright © Cengage Learning. All rights reserved.

_____

_____

_____

_____

_____

_____

✔ CHECK YOUR UNDERSTANDING Through Writing

Use the simple listing pattern to describe any of the following (again, feel free to choose your own topic): (1) mistakes you should never make at an office party, (2) ways you can build or break a friendship, or (3) abbreviations common to texting. Whichever topic you choose, remember that you need an opening or closing sentence that sums up the *mistakes, ways, abbreviations,* and so on, that you individualize in your supporting details.

◆ Pattern 5: Classification

In the classification pattern, too, the order in which information is presented is unimportant. The significant difference between simple listing and classification is that paragraphs using the classification pattern always make the same point: They tell readers how some larger group can be broken down into smaller subgroups, or classes, each with its own set of specific characteristics. Here's an illustration. *humours*

Hippocrates classified people according to the four fluids in their body.

TQ: Explain Hippocrates' system of classification.

Like other doctors of his time, the Greek physician Hippocrates believed that the human body consisted of four *humours,* or fluids: black bile, yellow bile, blood, and phlegm. Hippocrates' contribution was to classify human beings according to the predominant fluid in their bodies. Persons with an excess of black bile were labeled [1]*melancholic* and were presumed to be depressed and pessimistic. The [2]*choleric,* possessing excess yellow bile, were considered quick-tempered and irritable. Persons with a predominance of blood were classified as [3]*sanguine.* They were expected to be cheerful and optimistic. The [4]*phlegmatic,* possessing excess phlegm, were thought to be

Copyright © Cengage Learning. All rights reserved.

unemotional and uninvolved with the world at large. While the theory of the four humours has long since been discarded, the terms used to describe personality persist.

Although most classification paragraphs have a topic sentence that names the number of categories, this is not always the case. Sometimes the author just describes the subgroups of a larger category and leaves it to readers to total up the number of categories.

In addition to bills, members of Congress also pass three different kinds of resolutions. A *simple resolution* is used for matters such as establishing the rules under which the Senate or the House will operate. A *concurrent resolution* settles housekeeping and procedural matters that affect both the House and the Senate. Simple and concurrent resolutions are not signed by the president and do not have the force of law. A *joint resolution* requires the approval of both houses. It also requires the signature of the president and is the same as law. A joint resolution is necessary to propose a constitutional amendment and, in this case, the resolution must be approved by a two-thirds vote of both houses. (Adapted from Wilson and Dilulio, *American Government*, p. 351.)

In this paragraph, the main idea is suggested or implied: Congress passes three kinds of resolutions.

Typical Topic Sentences

Topic sentences like those that follow are clues to the classification pattern. Note the presence of verb phrases such as "are classified" and "can be divided," which are typical of this pattern. Note as well that the first topic sentence identifies the method or means of categorization—degree of severity—while the two others identify only the number of groups described.

1. Burns are classified into three different types based on degree of severity.
2. The earth is divided into three layers, each with its own composition and temperature.
3. There are five different kinds of listening.

Copyright © Cengage Learning. All rights reserved.

PATTERN POINTERS

1. Classification patterns can be quite lengthy. Don't, however, let the length intimidate you. Just look for the larger group being divided and the number and names of categories along with their key characteristics. (*Note*: Categories don't always get names.) If the author explains how the categories are created—for example, "Burns are classified into three different types based on degree of severity"—make sure you remember and/or record the method of classification as well as the categories that are the end result.

2. If you are having difficulty sorting out the categories in a paragraph using the classification pattern, try making a chart like the one that follows:

Three different kinds of burns based on severity		
First-degree burns 1. Burns are red and sensitive. 2. Burns affect the outer layer of skin and cause pain and swelling. 3. The skin may peel or appear whitish; it can also become clammy, as in sunburn.	Second-degree burns 1. Burns affect the epidermis and underlying dermis. 2. Burns cause redness, swelling, and blisters. 3. Burns often affect sweat glands and hair follicles.	Third-degree burns 1. Burns affect the epidermis, dermis, and hypodermis. 2. Visible burn areas may be numb, but the victim may still complain of pain. 3. Healing is slow and scarring present.

CHECK YOUR UNDERSTANDING

Explain how the simple listing and the classification pattern are both similar and different.

_____

_____

_____

_____

Copyright © Cengage Learning. All rights reserved.

◆ **EXERCISE 5** **Understanding Classification Patterns**

DIRECTIONS Read each paragraph. Then fill in the blanks and list the subgroups along with brief descriptions of each one. Paraphrase as much as possible.

1. [1]According to one theory, there are nine different personality types that describe human behavior. [2]The *reformer* likes to create order and believes that he or she knows the right way of doing things. [3]For the *reformer*, the world is an imperfect place desperately in need of fixing. [4]The *helper* feels a strong sense of personal responsibility for others and is fulfilled when lending a hand to those in need. [5]The *motivator* places the highest value on the kind of success that can be recognized and acknowledged by others in the world. [6]The *romantic* sees him- or herself as different from the rest of society and longs to be recognized as unique. [7]The *thinker* could not care less about being recognized. [8]What matters is being alone to think deep thoughts. [9]The *skeptic* questions authority even when it gets him or her into trouble, and it usually does. [10]The *enthusiast* considers the world a constant source of wonder and looks for pleasure in life. [11]The *leader* is convinced the world is heading toward ruin and needs better guidance. [12]Naturally, the leader is ready to provide that guidance. [13]The *peacemaker* believes passionately in harmony and is committed to resolving conflict; even when involved with people who enjoy a good fight, the peacemaker looks for a compromise. (Source of information: www.9types.com.)

    1. _____ is the larger group being subdivided

       into _____ smaller subgroups.

    2. Does the author explain the basis for the classification? _____ If

       so, what is the basis for the classification?_____

    3. List and describe the subgroups in your own words.

       _____

       _____

       _____

       _____

       _____

Copyright © Cengage Learning. All rights reserved.

_____

_____

_____

_____

_____

2.

Image Source/Jupiter Images

[1]Fish are vertebrates[†] that live in water and breathe with gills. [2]Based on their skeletons, the 25,000 species of fish can be broken down into three main groups. [3]The *agnatha* class are the most "primitive." [4]They lack both a jaw and a bony skeleton. [5]Examples would be lamprey eels and hagfish. [6]Lacking true bones, fish in this group are extraordinarily flexible. [7]The hagfish, for instance, can tie itself into a knot. [8]Although their ancestors had real bones, the *chondrichthyes* have a skeleton made of cartilage. [9]These fish—sharks, skates, rays, and ratfish—have loosely attached lower jaws with big and very noticeable teeth. [10]The *osteichthyes* are called bony fish because their skeletons are made of calcium. [11]Catfish and trout belong to this group. [12]Like all bony fish, they are fast-moving and able to maneuver with ease. [13]Highly adaptable creatures, they often have very specialized mouths, which help them to explore underwater resources with great efficiency.

1. _____ is the larger group being subdivided into _____ smaller subgroups.

2. Does the author explain the basis for the classification? _____ If so, what is the basis for the classification? _____

3. List and describe the subgroups in your own words.

_____

_____

_____

_____

_____

_____

_____

_____

[†]vertebrates: creatures with a backbone.

Copyright © Cengage Learning. All rights reserved.

Pattern 6: Comparison and Contrast

In all kinds of textbooks, authors are likely to compare (discuss similarities) and/or contrast (cite differences). Sometimes, in fact, writers devote an entire chapter section to pointing out the similarities and differences between two topics, but more often the comparison and contrast pattern is confined to organizing a single paragraph, for example:

TQ: Explain difference between assertive and aggressive behavior with examples.

Uncle Ralph assertive not aggressive.

Assertive behavior involves standing up for your rights and expressing your thoughts and feelings in a direct, appropriate way that does not violate the rights of others. It is a matter of getting the other person to understand your viewpoint. People who exhibit assertive behavior skills are able to handle conflict situations with ease and assurance while maintaining good interpersonal relations. In contrast, aggressive behavior involves expressing your thoughts and feelings and defending your rights in a way that openly violates the rights of others. Those exhibiting aggressive behavior seem to believe that the rights of others must be subservient to theirs. Thus they have a difficult time maintaining good interpersonal relations. They are likely to interrupt, talk fast, ignore others, and use sarcasm or other forms of verbal abuse to maintain control.

(Adapted from Reece and Brandt, *Effective Human Relations in Organizations*, pp. 350–53.)

A paragraph like this one with its two topics—assertive and aggressive behavior—and its emphasis on the difference between them has comparison and contrast written all over it. It all but cries out for you to predict a test question asking for a description of how the two topics are similar and/or different.

TAKING A CLOSER LOOK

Methods of Comparison and Contrast

Writers who use the comparison and contrast method usually employ it in one of two ways. They compare and contrast two topics sentence by sentence or they address each topic separately, using the first half of the paragraph for the first topic and the next half for the second. Which method does the author of the paragraph on assertion and aggression use?

_____

What about the paragraph about social drinkers and alcoholics on page 207?

_____

Copyright © Cengage Learning. All rights reserved.

Typical Topic Sentences

Sentences like the ones that follow are also clues to the comparison and contrast pattern. Note the consistent presence of two topics (see underscores).

> 1. In the Wild West, the life of a cowboy was not all that different from that of a cowgirl, as the life of Calamity Jane well illustrates.
> 2. The ancient Aztec civilization of Mexico and the early Incan civilization of Peru, both of which flourished in the sixteenth century, had much in common.
> 3. Unlike Secretary of State Henry Kissinger (1973–1977), Secretary of State Colin Powell (2001–2005) did not have much influence over the president.

Transitions

In addition to topic sentences like those above, the following transitions are also clues to the comparison and contrast pattern.

Transitions That Introduce Similarity ◆	Along the same lines	Just as
	By the same token	Just like
	In like manner	Likewise
	In much the same vein	Similarly
	In the same manner	

Transitions That Signal a Difference ◆	And yet	In opposition	On the other hand
	But	In reality	Still
	Conversely	Nevertheless	Unfortunately
	Despite that fact	Nonetheless	Whereas
	However	On the contrary	
	In contrast	On the one hand	

Copyright © Cengage Learning. All rights reserved.

PATTERN POINTERS

1. The presence of two topics, each described in some detail, is the major clue to recognizing the comparison and contrast pattern. However, the trick to reading the pattern is to stay focused on this question: What main idea do these similarities and differences illustrate or prove?

2. If you are struggling to understand a particularly difficult comparison and contrast paragraph or reading, try a split diagram like the one below:

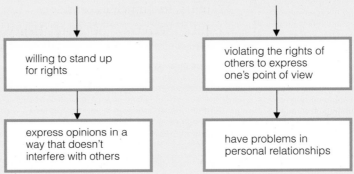

Main Idea: Assertive behavior is not the same as aggressive behavior.

| willing to stand up for rights | violating the rights of others to express one's point of view |
| express opinions in a way that doesn't interfere with others | have problems in personal relationships |

CHECK YOUR UNDERSTANDING Through Writing

Write a comparison and contrast paragraph on any one of the following topics:

1. the comedy of George Lopez and Dane Cook

2. the talents of Beyoncé and Rihanna

3. the music of Nelly Furtado and Kelly Clarkson

4. the value of Twitter versus Facebook

5. the pluses and/or minuses of e-books and print books

◆ **EXERCISE 6** **Analyzing Comparison and Contrast Patterns**

DIRECTIONS Read each paragraph. Identify the two topics. Then paraphrase the topic sentence along with the similarities and/or differences between the topics.

Copyright © Cengage Learning. All rights reserved.

1. Social drinking differs significantly from alcoholism. Social drinkers control their drinking and consume alcohol in limited amounts. Alcoholics, in contrast, can't control their drinking and consume alcohol in ever-increasing amounts. They often drink until they pass out. While social drinkers sip, alcoholics gulp. Social drinkers drink to have more fun at social gatherings; alcoholics drink alone as a way of reducing stress or avoiding problems. Social drinkers don't usually think or talk about drinking; alcoholics are preoccupied with how and when they will drink again. Finally, social drinkers do not experience physical, psychological, or job-related problems caused by their drinking. Alcoholics, however, often let drinking damage their health, ruin their relationships, and destroy their careers. (Adapted from Bernstein et al., *Psychology*, p. 597.)

Topic 1 _____

Topic 2 _____

Main Idea _____

_____

Similarities _____

_____

_____

_____

Differences _____

_____

_____

_____

2. Although chimpanzees can't talk, they are remarkably similar to humans. For example, the physical proportions for the body parts of both humans and chimpanzees are relatively close. Both species also have similar hands, feet, legs, and facial features. In fact, the DNA of humans and chimpanzees is 98.4 percent identical. In addition to these physical similarities, chimpanzee societies are like human ones in a variety of ways. Human beings establish political systems and

Copyright © Cengage Learning. All rights reserved.

fight wars. Likewise, groups of chimpanzees form hierarchies with high-ranking and low-ranking chimps, and they too engage in warfare against other groups. Moreover, observation of chimps in the wild has confirmed that chimpanzees display emotions similar to those humans experience. Humans grieve for lost loved ones, and chimps do the same. In one case, a healthy young chimp seemed to fall into a severe depression after his mother's death. He eventually stopped eating and died. Research on the brain suggests that emotions like grief arise from ancient parts of the brain found in both species.

Topic 1   _____

Topic 2   _____

Main Idea   _____

_____

Similarities   _____

_____

_____

_____

Differences   _____

_____

_____

_____

✔ CHECK YOUR UNDERSTANDING

What key question do readers need to pose when they recognize the comparison and contrast pattern at work in a paragraph?

_____

Copyright © Cengage Learning. All rights reserved.

Pattern 7: Cause and Effect

Because connecting cause to effect is so basic to our thinking, you'll find cause and effect paragraphs in every type of textbook. No matter what the subject matter, at some point authors need to explain how one event (the cause) produces another event (the effect).

TQ: What are the effects of ultraviolet radiation?

①The ultraviolet (UV) radiation from the sun that reaches the Earth's surface is a health threat. ②At the very least, exposure to the sun's rays causes aging and wrinkling of the skin. ③At the very worst, it is responsible for cataracts, sunburn, snowblindness, and skin cancer, which claims around 15,000 lives each year in the United States alone. ④Exposure to UV radiation also suppresses the immune system, enabling cancers to become established and grow. ⑤In addition, radiation slows plant growth, delays seed germination, and interferes with photosynthesis.† (Adapted from Kaufman and Franz, *Biosphere 2000*, p. 266.)

Cause and effect paragraphs are a likely source of test questions. When you encounter them in your reading, make sure you can (1) clearly identify both cause (or causes) and effect (or effects) and (2) explain how one led to or produced the other.

Typical Topic Sentences

Topic sentences like those listed here are typical of the cause and effect pattern.

> 1. The invention of air-conditioning transformed the Southern way of life.
> 2. Teacher and writer Paulo Freire (1921–1997) knew full well that poverty damages not just the body but the mind as well.
> 3. Whatever its benefit to individuals, the Homestead Act had a profound effect on the development of the American West.

---

†photosynthesis: process by which plants use sunlight to create food.

Copyright © Cengage Learning. All rights reserved.

Common Transitions and Verbs

Along with topic sentences like those listed above, the transitions and verbs listed below are likely to make their way into paragraphs organized by cause and effect.

Transitions That Signal Cause and Effect ♦	As a result	In reaction
	Consequently	In response
	Hence	Therefore
	In the aftermath	Thus

Verbs That Connect Cause and Effect ♦	brings about	initiates
	causes	leads to
	creates	produces
	engenders	results in; results from
	evokes	sets off
	fosters	stems
	generates	stimulates
	induces	triggers

Common Connectives†

Connectives are linking words that function as transitions. They tie parts of sentences or whole sentences together by identifying their relationship. In paragraphs dealing with cause and effect, you are likely to see connectives such as *because*, *as*, and *since* used to introduce a cause (or causes). The connective *so* introduces an effect (or effects).

Be on the lookout for these words and phrases because they signal how you should respond to the information being offered: You need to identify the cause and effect relationship under discussion.

---

†In previous editions, I used the word *conjunction*, but I am following the lead of people like Max Morenberg and Jeff Sommers in *The Writer's Options*. They use a term that more directly states its purpose.

Copyright © Cengage Learning. All rights reserved.

Additional Connectives That Signal Cause and Effect ◆	thanks to due to following	as a result of stemming from resulting from	as a consequence of accordingly in retaliation for in defiance of

Chains of Cause and Effect

Be alert to cause and effect paragraphs involving *chains of causes and effects* in which the effect of one event becomes the cause of another. Note in the following paragraph how the introduction of rabbits—the effect produced by one situation—becomes the cause of another.

> Thomas Austin was a dedicated British sportsman who had been an avid rabbit hunter while living in Britain. After moving to Australia, Austin was disappointed to learn that there were no wild rabbits to hunt. Determined to pursue his hobby, he ordered from England twenty-four rabbits to release into the wild and become prey for him and his hunter friends. The rabbits, however, had no natural predators and an extraordinary ability to reproduce. It wasn't long before the wild rabbit population exploded, leaving Austin with more rabbits than he had bargained for. By 1867, Austin said he had killed almost 15,000 rabbits on his property alone. Thanks to Austin's desire to pursue his hobby, vast tracts of land had also been devastated by rabbits, with Australia losing not just vegetation but entire species, thanks to millions of rabbits living off the land.

Diagrammed, the cause and effect relationship in this passage would look something like this:

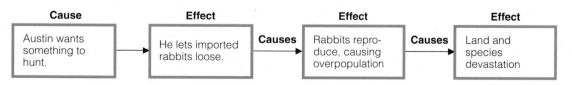

In this case, effects turn into causes of other effects. This is precisely what happens in chains of causes and effect.

Copyright © Cengage Learning. All rights reserved.

TAKING A CLOSER LOOK

Sentences Combining Cause and Effect
In the paragraph on rabbits run wild, where does the reader get a complete statement of the cause and effects?

_____

_____

▶▶ **PATTERN POINTER**   If you feel that the cause and effect relationship under discussion is not completely clear, draw a diagram that highlights the relationship between the two.

◆ **EXERCISE 7**   **Responding to Cause and Effect Patterns**

DIRECTIONS   Read each paragraph. Then fill in the blanks and circle the letter of the statement that best describes the role of the supporting details.

1. Instinctive behavior is caused by specific signals from the environment called _releasers_. For example, stalking behavior in cats may be "released" by the sight of prey. Among male ring doves, the sight of an adult female triggers, or releases, the bowing associated with courtship. Similarly, fighting behavior in territorial male European robins is released not only by the sight of another male invading their territories but also by the sight of red feathers located at a certain height. This behavior is released because red feathers appear on the breasts of competitors. Thus the sight of the feathers sends a message that a rival is nearby. (Adapted from Wallace, _Biology_, p. 450.)

   1. In this paragraph, the author describes how _____

      cause(s) or lead(s) to _____.

   2. The supporting details
      a. focus on the cause or causes.
      b. focus on the effect or effects.
      c. focus on both cause and effect.

Copyright © Cengage Learning. All rights reserved.

2. During the Civil War, the South had fewer men than the North to send to war. Thus a larger proportion of southern families were left to the care of women. Some women worked farms and herded livestock to support their families. Others found themselves worse off: They and their families were left in poverty as the war turned the country-side black and dry. Because of their dire straits, some women tried to persuade their husbands to desert. However, the vast majority of women on the domestic front fully supported the war despite the misery it caused them. (Adapted from Berkin et al., *Making America*, p. 102.)

1. In this paragraph, the author describes how _____
_____ cause(s) or lead(s) to _____ .

2. The supporting details

   a. focus on the cause or causes.

   b. focus on the effect or effects.

   c. focus on both cause and effect.

◆ **EXERCISE 8**   **Recognizing Primary Patterns**

DIRECTIONS   Circle the appropriate letter to identify the primary, or most significant, pattern of the paragraph.

1. Between 1970 and 1990, the number of cross-cultural marriages steadily increased. But that trend changed starting in late 1990 when the number of Hispanics and Asians married to whites began to decline. What's the cause of that drop? Researchers believe that the sheer number of immigrants arriving in the last decade makes it more likely for them to marry among themselves. Zhenchao Qion, professor of sociology at Ohio State University, believes the decline is likely to continue because immigrants are still arriving in the United Sates in large numbers. Thus it's more likely that the new arrivals will marry someone of the same ethnic heritage. (Source of data: Haya El Nasser, "Cross-Cultural Marriage Rates Falling," www.usatoday.com /news/nation/2007-02-15-cross-cultural-marriages_x.htm?csp=1.)

   a. process

   b. classification

   c. comparison and contrast

   d. cause and effect

Copyright © Cengage Learning. All rights reserved.

2. All of the gasoline now pumped into automobile and airplane tanks began as crude oil formed millions of years ago beneath ocean floors. In ancient seas, when tiny aquatic plants and animals died, they sank to the bottom. Sand and mud settled over them. This process was repeated over and over, each time burying large quantities of organic* material and pushing it deeper and deeper into the earth as new layers accumulated on top. The heavy weight of the layers created pressure and temperatures above 150° Fahrenheit so that the subterranean* organic matter began to "cook." Over time, the heat transformed it into a liquid hydrogen and carbon substance. This crude oil, lighter than both water and rock, drifted upward through tiny cracks in the rock until it was stopped by a layer of dense rock and forced to collect. Today, oil companies drill down into these reservoirs to extract this energy-rich petroleum and send it to oil refineries to be converted into fuel for vehicles.

a. definition

b. process

c. sequence of dates and events

d. simple listing

3. American house forms have changed over time as new building materials became available and living styles changed, but in the early days of America's history, there were essentially three types of houses. Among the earliest and most common house types was the Cape Cod. The typical Cape was two rooms deep with a huge central chimney and a roof that started just above the windows. Because it had low ceilings and few rooms, a Cape was one of the easiest houses to heat, a big advantage when a fireplace was the main source of warmth. Another early house type, the Classic Cottage, had a slightly higher front wall than the Cape and this allowed for a second tier of windows. In the Classic Cottage, the chimney could be in the middle of the house or at the end. The big advantage of the Cottage style was the increased amount of space it offered. The Colonial house was a one-and-one-half to two-story rectangle. Its façade* had a front door

---

*organic: related to living matter.
*subterranean: beneath the earth.
*façade: the face or front of a building; also a pretense or disguise.

Copyright © Cengage Learning. All rights reserved.

dividing up nine symmetrically* placed windows, sometimes referred to as "five-over-four and a door." Colonial houses were typically made of wood or brick and had columns or pediments† at the front-door entry. The Colonial style house was associated with people of some wealth, who could afford to consider comfort as well as shelter.

a. sequence of dates and events

b. simple listing

c. classification

d. comparison and contrast

4. Because students don't all learn in the exact same way, it's hard to define what makes a good, never mind a great, teacher. There are, however, several traits that good teachers do seem to share. Good teachers generally have a gift for explaining things. They know how to vary or modify an explanation based on student response. Good teachers also keep their cool. Even when students are acting out, successful teachers don't get angry or sarcastic. They find other ways to control the situation and get students back on track. Research also suggests that good teachers have a lively sense of humor. They know that mixing a joke into a discussion is an excellent way to hold students' interest. Teachers who excel at their job also have a thorough command of the subjects they teach. Elementary school teachers, for instance, have a wide general knowledge of many different fields and enough depth in each area to provide clear explanations and to effectively answer questions. For their part, high school teachers have an in-depth command of one or two specific content areas. (Source of traits: R. J. Kizlik, "Tips on Becoming a Teacher," www.adprima.com/tipson.htm.)

a. simple listing

b. classification

c. comparison and contrast

d. cause and effect

5. The legal term *due process* identifies an established course of action that must be followed during judicial* proceedings. The basis for due

---

*symmetrically: being almost exactly the same in appearance or location.
†pediments: triangular elements over a door or attached to a roof.
*judicial: related to the courts.

Copyright © Cengage Learning. All rights reserved.

process can be found in the Fifth Amendment of the Constitution, which says: "No person shall be deprived of life, liberty, or property without due process of law." Due process reflects the Constitution's guarantee that criminal legal proceedings will be fair. Because the courts must abide by due process, every individual tried by a court has to be notified that the proceedings are taking place. Every person called to court for the prosecution of a crime must have an opportunity to defend himself or herself prior to any punishment which might involve the taking of life, liberty, or property. In addition to the Fifth Amendment, the Fourteenth Amendment requires that the states, as opposed to the federal government, honor an individual's right to due process.

a. definition

b. process

c. sequence of dates and events

d. simple listing

6. Dogs have been companions to humans for some 14,000 years, and the relationship probably began because dogs could be trained to help humans hunt for food. Cats, in contrast, have been paired with humans for only one-third of that time. Once cats teamed up with humans, though, they played a role very different from that of dogs. In the past, and until fairly recently, dogs were usually considered the servants of humans. They performed as guards, guides, and protectors in activities ranging from hunting to farming. Cats, however, couldn't be trained to do anything they didn't want to do, which is perhaps why they were worshipped as gods in some societies. The cat was held in such high esteem by the Egyptians, for instance, that there were laws protecting them from injury or death. While many early cultures treated dogs with affection—the greyhound, for instance, appears in many Egyptian tomb carvings—there is little evidence that they ever achieved the status of a deity.*

a. simple listing

b. classification

c. comparison and contrast

d. cause and effect

---

*deity: god.

Copyright © Cengage Learning. All rights reserved.

7. Thanks to his talent for duplicity* and deception, the double agent and traitor Harold Adrian Russell "Kim" Philby (1912–1988) avoided detection for more than thirty years. From 1929 to 1933, while attending Cambridge University, Philby went to work for the former Soviet Union's feared intelligence agency, the KGB.† Throughout the 1930s, under cover as a journalist, Philby continued to serve as a Soviet spy. In 1940, Philby's activities as a journalist attracted the attention of the British Secret Intelligence Service (SIS), and he was offered a position as a British intelligence officer. Philby seized this opportunity as a way of gaining access to information about British and American military strategy and, most important, atomic bomb production. Yet even as he betrayed his native country by passing information on to his Soviet colleagues, Philby performed his duties so well that he rose rapidly to become head of the counterespionage division in 1944. Then in 1949, he was appointed to be the liaison* between the British Embassy and the U.S. Central Intelligence Agency (CIA). However, in 1951, his double life came close to unravelling when he alerted two fellow KGB agents that they were under surveillance,* giving them time to avoid arrest and escape to Moscow. Philby's British colleagues rightly suspected him of tipping off the two spies and asked him to resign. But in 1955, after Philby had endured years of SIS interrogation* without cracking and admitting the truth, he was reemployed as an SIS officer. In 1962, a captured Russian spy revealed Philby's double agent status and Philby fled to the Soviet Union.

   a. definition

   b. process

   c. sequence of dates and events

   d. simple listing

8. *Habeas corpus petitions* are frequently filed by individuals serving prison sentences. Usually the petitions are written to show that the court ordering the imprisonment made an error of some sort, making the imprisonment illegal. Habeas corpus petitions are also

---

*duplicity: double-dealing, deliberate dishonesty in behavior or speech.
†KGB: the Russian initials for what was, in fact, an agency of espionage and repression, the Committee for State Security.
*liaison: go-between.
*surveillance: observation.
*interrogation: formal questioning conducted by persons in authority.

Copyright © Cengage Learning. All rights reserved.

filed in family court by parents who have been denied custody of a child. In *Brown v. Vasquez*, the Supreme Court ruled that "the writ of habeas corpus is the fundamental instrument for safeguarding individual freedom against arbitrary* and lawless state action." In Latin, *habeas corpus* means "you have the body."

a. definition

b. process

c. classification

d. comparison and contrast

9. Although the Indian caste, or class, system was officially outlawed in 1949 by the Indian Constitution, it persists to this day in one form or another and remains a source of political discontent. India's caste system divides the population into four basic groups. The *Brahmin* class includes priests and scholars. Members of this class are not characterized by wealth or possessions, but its members are the object of regard and respect because of their spiritual and intellectual gifts. Next come the *Kshatriyas*, whose members are rulers, warriors, and large property owners. This class is likely to be characterized by the possession of great wealth. Next in the hierarchy is the *Vaishyas* caste, which includes merchants and traders. Those in this group may or may not have great wealth, but they are all engaged in some form of commercial transaction. The *Shudra* caste includes those who wait on and serve members of the other three classes. Those belonging to this group are servants and chauffeurs. Outside the caste system entirely are the *harijans*, once known as the "untouchables." Untouchables perform the jobs no one else wants to do, such as garbage collecting and leather dying. Although the caste system has weakened with the passage of time, it still exists, but more in the country than in the city. In some Indian regions, the caste system is mainly a state of mind, with some individuals believing themselves worthy of being treated as Brahmins while others feel as if the name "untouchable" still applies.

a. simple listing

b. classification

c. comparison and contrast

d. cause and effect

---

*arbitrary: lacking any fixed rule or consistency; based on personal whim.

Copyright © Cengage Learning. All rights reserved.

10. As it turns out, David (Bruce) Reimer's life was a tragic and unintentional experiment that shed light on the complexity of gender identity. After the boy's genitals were badly burned during circumcision, his parents took him to the renowned* psychologist and sexual identity expert John Money. Money advised them to raise the boy as a girl. Bruce was then named Brenda and started life as a female. Although in 1972 Money reported that the boy had developed a female identity—which fit Money's claim that sexual identity could be reshaped through surgery and training—independent follow-ups of the case have suggested a much different view. By 1979, at the age of fourteen, Bruce, despite two years of estrogen therapy, was still fantasizing about being a boy rather than a girl. Plagued by these dreams, he refused to continue his life as a female. It was at this point that his parents informed the boy of his medical history. Reimer responded by taking the name David and assuming the life of a man. Although he married, and adopted his wife's children, he was plagued by depression and rage. In May 2004, David Reimer took his own life. (Adapted from Freberg, *Discovering Biological Psychology*, p. 284.)

   a. definition
   b. process
   c. sequence of dates and events
   d. classification

Be Alert to Mixed Patterns of Equal Importance

In many paragraphs, there may be more than one organizational pattern. Yet often it's still clear that one pattern is primary, or the one most essential to developing the main idea. However, sometimes the patterns will seem equal in importance, and it may be difficult to tell which one predominates. For an illustration, see the following paragraph.

In 1859, the United States was the first nation to produce oil. But oil is an exhaustible resource and by 1974 America had used up more than half of its once abundant oil supply. The halfway production point of

---

*renowned: famous, respected.

Copyright © Cengage Learning. All rights reserved.

Copyright © Cengage Learning. All rights reserved.

TQ: What is "The Hubbert Peak"?

an oil field is called "The Hubbert Peak," named after M. King Hubbert, a geologist* with the U.S. Geological Survey. He predicted in 1956 that oil production in the United States would peak in 1970. At that time the United States was the world's largest oil producer. So nobody believed him, and oil company executives ridiculed him. Hubbert, however, was correct in his prediction. According to geologists, U.S. oil production peaked in 1974—just four years after Hubbert predicted—and has declined since then. Most geologists project that domestic oil production will reach the 80 percent depletion point by 2055. Already the United States produces most of its dwindling supply of oil at a high cost, about $7.50 to $10 per barrel compared to $1 to $2 per barrel in

TQ: Explain the effects of a dwindling oil supply.

Saudi Arabia. As the oil supplies continue to decrease, we will become more dependent on foreign countries for oil, which is a far cry from our situation in the mid-nineteenth century. M. King Hubbert was right after all; oil is an exhaustible resource, and we may all soon discover the consequences of that simple fact. (Adapted from Miller, *Living in the Environment*, p. 362.)

In this paragraph, the author combines two patterns—sequence of dates and events with cause and effect—to make his point. Both are equally important to the paragraph's meaning, which means your notes should take both patterns into account. You would need to record the dates and events indicating how oil supplies have diminished and describe how, over time, Hubbert's prediction came true. But you'd also need to describe the effects caused by the country's dwindling oil supply.

Combined Patterns Aren't Always Equal

Based on the previous example, you shouldn't assume, though, that combined patterns are always equally important. Look, for example, at the following paragraph. From the first sentence, it looks like the author uses the comparison and contrast pattern. But is that true for the entire paragraph?

Compared to small towns and rural communities, huge metropolitan areas like Los Angeles and New York are typically plagued by higher crime rates, more pollution, and high costs of living. But another major problem—traffic-choked highways—is quickly rising to the top of the

---

*geologist: scientist who studies the past and present makeup of the earth.

list for many major cities. With drivers in some large cities now spending the equivalent of more than two workweeks per year stuck in traffic, gridlock is starting to stunt economic growth as businesses and young professionals choose not to move to metropolitan areas with chronically congested roads. To combat this problem, many political and business leaders are advocating the widening of existing highways into "superhighways" of nine or more lanes in each direction. Phoenix, Arizona, for example, plans to expand a 12-mile stretch of Interstate 10 from 14 lanes to an average of 22 lanes. Atlanta, Georgia, may widen a stretch of Interstate 75 to 23 lanes. Building bigger roads, city planners and engineers hope, will put an end to bottlenecks. (Source of figures: Larry Copeland, "Cities Afraid of Death by Congestion," *USA Today*, March 1, 2007.)

As you can see, the comparison and contrast pattern governs only one sentence. By sentence 2, the writer is more concerned with a cause and effect relationship: Because of gridlocked traffic (cause) some cities are advocating enlarging highways (effect).

In this case, your notes could ignore the comparison and contrast pattern altogether because the main idea—"Gridlocked traffic has become a major concern of big cities"—requires no comparison and contrast development. What it requires is a more detailed explanation of the cause and the effect mentioned in sentence 2, the topic sentence.

Evaluate the Importance of Each Organizational Pattern

When an author combines two or more patterns in a reading, it's up to the reader to decide the value of each pattern. If the main idea doesn't require any help from a pattern that's present in the paragraph, then the pattern probably does little more than organize the introduction or a few minor details. In other words, it's not especially crucial to your notes.

Common Combinations ♦	Process with Cause and Effect and/or Definition
	Classification with Comparison and Contrast
	Sequence of Dates and Events with Cause and Effect
	Cause and Effect with Simple Listing

Copyright © Cengage Learning. All rights reserved.

◆ EXERCISE 9   Evaluating Combined Patterns

DIRECTIONS   Read each paragraph and identify the pattern or patterns used in the paragraph by circling the appropriate letter or letters. If there is more than one pattern used, indicate if the patterns used are equally important. *Note:* If there is only one pattern, leave the line following the paragraph blank.

1. There are four major kinds of exercise, and each one offers different benefits to the body. The first type of exercise includes those that are *aerobic.* Aerobic means "with oxygen"; this kind of exercise—activities like jogging, walking, bicycling, and swimming—requires the lungs and heart to provide a steady supply of oxygen. Aerobic exercises strengthen the cardiovascular system, which in turn lowers the risk of heart disease. Aerobic exercise also helps reduce body fat and can relieve stress and feelings of depression. The second type of exercise is *anaerobic,* meaning "without oxygen." The exercises in this group draw on energy already stored in the body's muscles, so engaging in them does not require additional oxygen. Anaerobic activities, such as sprinting and lifting heavy weights, require short bursts of power that improve speed and muscle strength, so they tend to boost athletic performance. Lifting or resisting the force of lighter weights falls into the third category of exercise, *strength training.* Exercises in this category include working out on weight machines or performing calisthenics, such as push-ups and sit-ups, to tone and strengthen muscles. The final type, *flexibility exercise,* lengthens the muscles and increases the range of motion. This category includes exercises like yoga and Pilates, both of which improve posture, maintain mobility, prevent injury, and encourage mental and physical relaxation.

    a. definition
    b. cause and effect
    c. simple listing
    d. classification

    If you circled two or more letters, are the patterns equally important to an explanation of the main idea? _____

2. Although everyone thinks it won't happen to them, house fires are one of the most common causes of deadly accidents, and no one is

Copyright © Cengage Learning. All rights reserved.

immune to the threat of a house fire. Still, there are several precautions people can take to make sure they survive a house fire. The most obvious is to install smoke detectors. If you are renting, make sure the landlord installs smoke detectors, and be sure to check the batteries. Get a fire extinguisher and have someone from the local fire station show you how to use it. Keep an evacuation kit on hand. The evacuation kit should include copies of identification; insurance cards or tags, including those for pets; and any essential medical supplies, such as insulin or blood-pressure medication. Have an escape route and know where you plan to exit the house or apartment in case of a fire. If you are living in a multi-story apartment building with a fire escape, make sure it is usable. If it isn't, tell the landlord and make sure that he or she makes the proper repairs. Know where the doors to the stairs are and take the stairs every once in a while to make sure you can negotiate them without difficulty.

a. process

b. sequence of dates and events

c. simple listing

d. cause and effect

If you circled two or more letters, are the patterns equally important to an explanation of the main idea? _____

3. On April 26, 1986, the worst accident in the history of nuclear power took place at the Chernobyl plant about 110 km north of Kiev in Ukraine.[†] At the Chernobyl plant, the uranium was contained in fuel rods surrounded by graphite bricks, which served to moderate the nuclear reaction. The accident occurred when engineers turned off most of the reactor's automatic safety and warning systems to keep them from interfering with an unauthorized safety experiment. At this point, cooling water was one of the safety systems turned off. Unfortunately, the remaining water in the reactor then turned to steam, and the steam reacted with the nuclear fuel and the graphite bricks. An explosive mixture of gases formed and ignited. The reactor was destroyed, the roof blew off the building, and the graphite bricks caught fire. Officials in the former Soviet Union claimed the fire was

[†]Ukraine: a republic on the border of the Black Sea in southeastern Europe. Kiev is the country's capital and largest city.

Copyright © Cengage Learning. All rights reserved.

extinguished on April 29. According to Soviet reports, 500 people were hospitalized and the acknowledged death count stood at 31. The incidence of thyroid cancer, leukemia, and other radiation-related illnesses is high among people who were living near the power plant. More ominously,* the radioactive particles produced by the explosion were dispersed all over the planet by the natural circulation of air. It will be years before all of the effects of the Chernobyl disaster can be assessed. (Adapted from Sherman et al., *Basic Concepts of Chemistry*, p. 484.)

a. definition

b. process

c. comparison and contrast

d. cause and effect

If you circled two or more letters, are the patterns equally important to the explanation of the main idea? _____

4. Two small lakes in a remote part of Cameroon, a small country in central Africa, made international news in the mid-1980s when deadly clouds of carbon dioxide (CO_2) gas from deep beneath the surface of the lakes escaped into the surrounding atmosphere, killing animal and human populations far downwind. The first gas discharge, which occurred at Lake Monoun in 1984, killed thirty-seven people. The second, which occurred at Lake Nyos in 1986, released a highly concentrated cloud of CO_2 that killed more than 1,700 people. The two events had similarities other than location: Both occurred at night during the rainy season, both involved volcanic crater lakes, and both are likely to recur unless some method is found to prohibit a recurrence.

a. simple listing

b. classification

c. comparison and contrast

d. cause and effect

If you circled two or more letters, are the patterns equally important to an explanation of the main idea? _____

————————————

*ominously: dangerously, threateningly.

Copyright © Cengage Learning. All rights reserved.

5. In 1862, Congress passed the **Homestead Act**. This measure offered 160 acres of land free to any American citizen who was a family head and over twenty-one years old. The only conditions were that the settler live on the land for five years and make improvements to it. In the well-watered East, 160 acres was a sizable farm. Yet in the semi-arid West, it was barely enough to support a family. To prosper, a farmer needed at least twice that amount. Despite these risks, the Homestead Act produced an explosion of settlement. Within a half century after passage of the Homestead Act, all western territories had gained enough settlers—at least 60,000—to become states. As a result of the Homestead Act, most western areas experienced enormous population growth. (DiBacco et al., *History of the United States*, p. 315.)

a. definition

b. cause and effect

c. classification

d. comparison and contrast

If you circled two or more letters, are the patterns equally important for the main idea? _____

CHECK YOUR UNDERSTANDING

What should readers do when they realize that the writer has used more than one organizational pattern?

_____

_____

Copyright © Cengage Learning. All rights reserved.

WORD CHECK

The following words were introduced and defined in pages 178–224. See how well you can match the words with the meanings. When you finish, make sure to check the meanings of any words you missed because the same words will turn up in tests at the end of the chapter.

1. grandiose _____	a. a scientist who studies the past and present makeup of the earth
2. attributed _____	
3. assuage _____	b. calm or soothe
4. espionage _____	c. related to the courts
5. preoccupied _____	d. god
6. compulsive _____	e. double-dealing, deliberate dishonesty
7. organic _____	f. having an exaggerated sense of one's importance or influence
8. subterranean _____	
9. façade _____	g. the face or front of a building; also a pretense or disguise
10. symmetrically _____	
11. judicial _____	h. observation of a person or situation
12. deity _____	i. lacking any fixed rule or consistency
13. duplicity _____	j. go-between
14. liaison _____	k. formal questioning by persons in authority
15. surveillance _____	l. being almost exactly the same in appearance and location
16. interrogation _____	
17. arbitrary _____	m. dangerously, threateningly
18. renowned _____	n. famous, respected
19. geologist _____	o. related to living matter
20. ominously _____	p. involuntary, uncontrollable
	q. overly concerned with something, also absorbed in thought
	r. related or connected to a particular source, event, or person
	s. beneath the earth
	t. spying or using spies to obtain secret information

Copyright © Cengage Learning. All rights reserved.

◆ **EXERCISE 10   More About Form and Meaning**

DIRECTIONS   Fill in the blanks with one of the words listed below.

geologist	judicial	espionage	liaison	symmetrical
interrogation	grandiose	renowned	façade	arbitrary
attribution	compulsive	subterranean	organic	ominous
assuage	surveillance	duplicity	deities	preoccupied

1. For those who like _____ adventures, cave diving is a thrill.

2. The habit of speeding is likely to make you well-acquainted with our _____ system.

3. The last thing anyone would want to be is a(n) _____ between two feuding partners.

4. A child who likes to collect rocks might well grow up to be a(n) _____.

5. Vishnu, Aphrodite, and Jesus are all considered to be _____.

6. Most people don't notice it, but both sides of their face are seldom. _____.

7. When crowds of people attend an event, there are usually numerous _____ cameras present.

8. Some individuals don't feel comfortable until they have closed doors or drawers a prescribed number of times; these people are exhibiting _____ behavior.

9. The man who is always smiling and cracking jokes while feeling devastated by the loss of his job is putting up a good _____.

Copyright © Cengage Learning. All rights reserved.

10. The screech of brakes, the clap of thunder, and the shriek of an owl at night are all _____ sounds.

11. Being famous can be the result of little more than publicity; being _____ takes a good deal more talent and work.

12. If you had a(n) _____ sense of your own importance, you would very likely be inclined to monopolize conversations and start every other sentence with the pronoun *I*.

13. It follows automatically that famous spies have engaged in some form of _____.

14. For card sharks, who make their living by cheating at cards, _____ is nothing to be ashamed of.

15. Like bad luck, good luck is _____, and you can't plan ahead for it.

16. If you use someone else's ideas or words in a term paper, make sure you provide _____.

17. It's all but impossible to watch a crime drama like *Law & Order* and not see a(n) _____.

18. Because it's not _____, plastic won't disintegrate over time, which is one of the reasons that trash dumps are overrun with it.

19. Initially, grief over the loss of a loved one is impossible to _____.

20. It's not a good idea to be _____ with text messaging while driving.

Copyright © Cengage Learning. All rights reserved.

DIGGING DEEPER   Oliver Wendell Holmes and Freedom of Speech

Looking Ahead   On pages 181–82, you read a paragraph describing the Supreme Court. In this reading, you'll learn more about one of the best-known and most esteemed members of that court, Oliver Wendell Holmes, whose judicial decisions helped strengthen the Constitutional protections for freedom of speech.

1   Until 1919, the notion of freedom of speech was honored more in theory than in practice. True, free speech was guaranteed by the Bill of Rights and the First Amendment. But that didn't mean free speech couldn't land a person in jail. In fact, in 1918, Socialist leader Eugene V. Debs was sentenced to ten years for an anti-war speech given before only 1,200 people. In the early part of the twentieth century, the First Amendment guaranteed little more than what Supreme Court Justice Oliver Wendell Holmes called the right to "say what you choose if you don't shock me."

2   Like Debs before him, jail time was what Jacob Schenck got in 1919 for preaching draft resistance. When Schenck's case came before the Supreme Court, the justices, Holmes included, unanimously upheld his conviction. Yet writing the opinion on the case, Holmes seemed determined to distinguish between unpopular speech and harmful speech. In the mind of Holmes, the circumstances or context of the words mattered and they mattered a lot: "The question in every case is whether the words are used in such circumstances and are of such a nature as to create a clear and present danger that they will bring about the substantive evils that the United States Congress has a right to prevent." In an effort to further clarify the circumstances he had in mind, Holmes used a practical example that was to make legal history: "After all, the most stringent protection of free speech would not protect a man falsely shouting fire in a theater and causing panic."

3   Holmes was taken by surprise when the Court's decision and his role in it caused a storm of criticism. He was particularly stung by the comment from Professor Ernst Freund at the University of Chicago, who argued that "tolerance of opinion is not a matter of generosity but of political prudence."* A man of great ego and even greater integrity, Holmes needed to understand the furious objections of his peers. For that reason, he

----

*prudence: wisdom.

Copyright © Cengage Learning. All rights reserved.

agreed to talk to legal expert and free-speech advocate Zechariah Chafee from Harvard Law School. Chafee convinced Holmes that free speech served the public good and set the stage for the dissenting opinion that Holmes was to write in the case known as *Abrams v. United States.*

4   Jakob Abrams and several others had been convicted of distributing pamphlets criticizing President Woodrow Wilson for sending troops to Russia to defend the Czar in the summer of 1918. Found guilty of hindering the war effort, Abrams and his cohorts appealed the guilty verdict all the way to the Supreme Court. The Court, however, was taken with Holmes's "clear and present danger" test and used it to sustain Abrams's conviction. The justices must have been surprised when Holmes, who seems to have disserved his nickname "The Great Dissenter," did not agree with their decision. Instead, he joined with Supreme Court Justice Louis Brandeis to write yet another opinion that profoundly influenced all future discussions of freedom of expression.

5   Calling the defendants in the case "puny anonymities," Holmes insisted that their pamphlets might well express sentiments that were loathsome but that didn't make their words a serious threat. Clearly, Holmes had had a change of heart between the *Schenck* and *Abrams* cases because the opinion he wrote on *Abrams* returns again and again to the notion of immediacy, suggesting that if the court couldn't see an *imminent* emergency, it had no business tampering with the First Amendment: "Only the emergency that makes it immediately dangerous to leave the correction of evil counsels to time warrants making any exception to the sweeping command, 'Congress shall make no law . . . abridging the freedom of speech.'" With that dissent, Holmes laid the groundwork for the legal system's current interpretation of free speech and its willingness to allow, in Holmes's words, "the expressions of opinions we loathe," as long as they do not offer an immediate threat to the well-being of others.

Sharpening Your Skills

DIRECTIONS   Answer the following questions by circling the letter of the correct response or filling in the blanks.

1. Based on the context, how would you define *stringent* in paragraph 2?
    a. careless
    b. open
    c. strict
    d. colorful

Copyright © Cengage Learning. All rights reserved.

2. Based on context, how would you define *cohorts* in paragraph 4?

_____

_____

3. What's the overall main idea of the entire reading?
   a. Oliver Wendell Holmes tended to confuse and annoy his colleagues on the Supreme Court because they were never sure which side he would take on freedom of speech.
   b. Oliver Wendell Holmes was instrumental in developing the legal standards for judging freedom of speech.
   c. Oliver Wendell Holmes was the greatest justice in the history of the Supreme Court.
   d. Oliver Wendell Holmes was inclined to be contradictory by nature and would often disagree with positions he had once supported.

4. Which sentence correctly paraphrases the first sentence of this reading?
   a. Before 1919, there was no legal protection for freedom of speech.
   b. Before 1919, freedom of speech was not strongly protected despite the guarantee in the Bill of Rights.
   c. After 1919, freedom of speech was valued in theory but not in reality.

5. The *Schenck* case is mentioned to
   a. illustrate Holmes's readiness to disagree with his colleagues.
   b. illustrate how Holmes's attitude toward free speech evolved.
   c. illustrate how much anti-war sentiment existed at the time.

6. Why does Holmes claim that the right of freedom of speech does not protect someone shouting "fire" in a theater?

_____

_____

_____

7. On what basis did Holmes dissent in the *Abrams* case?

_____

_____

Copyright © Cengage Learning. All rights reserved.

8. What two reversal transitions appear in paragraph 4?

_____

9. Why is it significant in Holmes's eyes that the defendants in the *Abrams* case are "puny anonymities" (paragraph 5)?

_____

_____

10. Based on what you know about Oliver Wendell Holmes, which quote do you think is his and why?

   a. The character of every act depends upon the circumstances in which it is done.

   b. Do not go where the path may lead; go instead where there is no path and leave a trail.

   Please explain what in the reading led you to this conclusion:

   _____

   _____

   _____

Copyright © Cengage Learning. All rights reserved.

▶ **TEST 1**   **Reviewing New Vocabulary**

DIRECTIONS   Fill in the blanks with one of the words listed below.

judicial	espionage	ominous	façades	renowned
organic	duplicitous	subterranean	attributing	grandiose

1. On June 19, 1953, a middle-class, middle-aged couple, Ethel and Julius Rosenberg were executed for committing acts of _____. They had been convicted in 1951 for passing secrets to the Soviet Union and, at their sentencing, the judge in the case, Irving Kaufman, issued an angry statement, _____ any number of negative consequences, including the start of the Korean War, to their unpatriotic and _____ activities. Following the conviction, there were public demonstrations of protest because many people believed the evidence against the Rosenbergs was insufficient to prove their guilt. The Rosenbergs' lawyers repeatedly applied for a(n) _____ review of the case, going as high as the Supreme Court. But they failed in their efforts and both Julius and Ethel were executed.[†]

2. As their name implies, desert _____ termites live in the ground, and they can and do survive on _____ matter like decayed cactus. That does not mean, however, that their presence is not a(n) _____ sign for homeowners. These termites do come above ground to search for food and, when they do, they can severely damage any wooden _____ within their reach. Because these termites normally live in moist, dark earth, the heat of the sun could kill them. The termites have

---

[†]Later revelations have indicated that Julius was indeed a spy. Ethel, however, was not.

Copyright © Cengage Learning. All rights reserved.

adapted to this danger by building mud tubes that allow them to tunnel above ground while remaining protected from the heat and light.

3. It appears that fame can provoke some _____ fantasies. Otherwise, it's impossible to explain how celebrities like Madonna, Tom Cruise, and Suzanne Somers[†] can publicly lay claim to knowledge about medical and scientific issues totally outside their expertise. Being _____ as entertainers does not mean they will be respected when they express their opinions on issues unrelated to their training or experience.

[†]Madonna has claimed to have a fluid that can combat radioactivity; Cruise has proclaimed his knowledge of psychiatry; and Suzanne Somers promotes the use of specially formulated hormones that are, from her perspective, not dangerous to women's health.

Copyright © Cengage Learning. All rights reserved.

▶ **TEST 2**   **Reviewing New Vocabulary**

DIRECTIONS   Fill in the blanks with one of the words listed below.

interrogate	arbitrary	preoccupied	surveillance	assuage
deity	liaison	geologist	symmetrical	compulsively

1. Children suffering from autism, a mysterious and complex disorder that makes it hard for them to interact with others, are easily upset by changes in their ordinary routine. Oddly enough, arranging blocks, cards, or other objects in _____ order can often _____ their distress. Autistic children who have been kept under close _____ by doctors or parents also consistently display other typical and unusual behaviors. They are likely to become passionately attached to objects, show no fear of serious danger, and are given to rocking themselves or spinning objects for long periods of time.

2. If school officials are forced to summon police to school in order to deal with violence on the part of a student, administrators must carefully follow all the appropriate procedures. For instance, should police need to _____ a student on school grounds, the principal must notify the parents that such an interview is taking place. If at all possible, the parent or parents should be present during questioning. The interview should also be conducted by a(n) _____ officer who has experience working with both police and educators.

3. **Charles Darwin and Alfred Wallace**

   Opening the mail one day in June 1858, Charles Darwin, the famous naturalist and eventual author of *On the Origin of Species*, a book that changed scientific thinking forever, was, as usual,

Copyright © Cengage Learning. All rights reserved.

_____. For more than twenty years, he had been _____ pondering the discoveries he made on his voyage to the Galapagos Islands. Darwin believed he had discovered the _____ but powerful mechanism, "natural selection," which could account for developmental change in all species, including humans. Cautious to a fault, though, Darwin was worried that his theory, if made public, would unleash a flood of criticism and controversy, largely because it suggested that the development of humanity was not under the control of a higher _____.

The package that came in the mail that day in June, however, shocked Darwin into focused attention. Alfred Wallace, a younger and much more daring colleague, had sent Darwin a paper outlining, in different language, the very theory that Darwin had long been thinking about publishing. That paper was all Darwin needed to end his indecision. With the help of _____ Charles Lyell and biologist Joseph Hooker, Darwin went public with his theory and by 1859 his book was in print.

Copyright © Cengage Learning. All rights reserved.

▶ **TEST 3**   **Recognizing Organizational Patterns**

DIRECTIONS   Circle the letter or letters that identify the organizational pattern or patterns used in each paragraph.

1. A **cartel** is an organization of independent firms whose purpose is to control and limit production and maintain or increase prices and profits. A cartel can result from either formal or informal agreement among members. Cartels are illegal in the United States but exist in other countries. The cartel most people are familiar with is the Organization of the Petroleum Exporting Countries (OPEC), a group of nations rather than a group of independent firms. During the 1970s, OPEC was able to coordinate oil production in such a way that it drove the market price of crude oil from $1.10 to $32.00 a barrel. For nearly eight years, each member of OPEC agreed to produce a certain limited amount of crude oil as designated by the OPEC production committee. Then in the early 1980s, the cartel began to fall apart as individual members began to cheat on the agreement. Members began to produce more than their allocation in an attempt to increase profits. As each member of the cartel did this, the price of oil fell, reaching $12 per barrel in 1988. Oil prices rose again in 1990 when Iraq invaded Kuwait, causing widespread damage to Kuwait's oil fields. But as repairs have been made to Kuwait's oil wells, Kuwait has increased production and oil prices have dropped. (Adapted from Boyes and Melvin, *Fundamentals of Economics*, p. 109.)

    a. definition
    b. classification
    c. process
    d. sequence of dates and events
    e. cause and effect

2. The Bermuda Triangle is, without a doubt, a strange and mysterious area of the Atlantic Ocean. During the last century, more than one hundred ships, boats, and airplanes vanished while traveling through this area. For example, the USS *Cyclops*, a Navy ship with 306 people aboard, disappeared there in 1918. Also lost without a trace was an entire squadron of five Navy torpedo bombers that

Copyright © Cengage Learning. All rights reserved.

took off from Fort Lauderdale, Florida, in 1945. In 1947, a United States C-54 bomber disappeared near Bermuda and was never seen again. One year later, the same thing happened to the British airliner *Star Tiger*. And in 1968, the *Scorpion*, a nuclear submarine, vanished only to be found after a long search. It was finally located in the waters on the fringes of the Triangle, but none of its crew members were on board.

a. definition

b. classification

c. simple listing

d. process

e. sequence of dates and events

3. Eighteenth-century assemblies bore little resemblance to twentieth-century state legislatures. Much of assembly business would today be termed administrative; only on rare occasions did assemblies formulate new policies or pass laws of real importance. Members of the assemblies also saw their roles differently from those of modern legislators. Instead of believing that they should act positively to improve the lives of their constituents, eighteenth-century assemblymen saw themselves as acting defensively to prevent encroachments on the people's rights. In their minds, their primary function was, for example, to stop the governors or councils from enacting oppressive taxes, rather than to pass laws that would actively benefit their constituents. (Adapted from Norton et al., *A People and a Nation*, p. 111.)

a. simple listing

b. process

c. sequence of dates and events

d. comparison and contrast

e. cause and effect

4. Numerous studies suggest that people who consider themselves happy have four key traits in common. For instance, happy people generally have high self-esteem. They have a good self-image and believe that they are intelligent, healthy, ethical, and personable. A second trait common to happy people is a sense of personal control.

Copyright © Cengage Learning. All rights reserved.

People who describe themselves as happy believe that they can make decisions which affect the course of their lives. Another characteristic of happy people is an optimistic outlook. Happy people are inclined to focus on positive experiences rather than negative ones. The fourth trait associated with happiness is an outgoing personality. Most happy people are extroverted and have a solid circle of friends and family that they can rely on for warmth and emotional support. (Source of characteristics: David G. Meyers and Ed Diener, "The Pursuit of Happiness," *Scientific American*, 1997 Special Issue: The Mind, pp. 44–47.)

a. definition
b. classification
c. simple listing
d. process
e. sequence of dates and events

5. In the second century B.C., the Chinese developed a method of converting cast iron into steel by melting the iron and then blowing air on it, thereby reducing the carbon content. But it wasn't until 1845 that American inventor William Kelly brought four Chinese steel experts to Kentucky, mastered the Chinese process, refined it, and then took out a patent. Kelly, however, went bankrupt in the financial panic that gripped the country in 1857 and had to sign ownership over to Henry Bessemer, who had been working on a similar process of steel production. By 1858, Bessemer had developed the first method of mass-producing steel. He then set up the first steelworks in Sheffield, England. Three years after Bessemer's triumph, the German-born inventors William and Frederick Siemens introduced the Open-Hearth furnace, capable of sustaining the high temperatures needed to make "Bessemer's process" work efficiently. Once the Siemens's furnace was improved on by Pierre Émile Martin of France, the stage was set for a revolutionary change in industrial production of all kinds.

a. definition
b. classification
c. simple listing
d. sequence of dates and events
e. cause and effect

Copyright © Cengage Learning. All rights reserved.

▶ **TEST 4**   **Recognizing Organizational Patterns**

DIRECTIONS   Circle the letter or letters that identify the organizational pattern or patterns used in each paragraph.

1. In general, people use three different methods of learning, and most rely more heavily on one method than another. **Visual learners** absorb new information best when they can see it represented in physical form. Thus they are likely to take detailed notes with many diagrams and symbols. If visual learners have a choice between learning by reading or listening, they are inclined to choose reading. **Auditory learners** rely most on their sense of hearing to learn new material, preferring to learn from lectures, discussions, and tours. At museums, they are the first to sign up for guided tours or make use of guides on tape by purchasing headphones. **Kinesthetic learners** are at their best when they are physically active. Thus they are likely to gesture while reviewing new information, and they like to use learning techniques that require movement. For example, kinesthetic learners might jot notes on sticky pads and attach the notes to the pages of a textbook because this method allows for maximum physical involvement. In the same vein, they are also likely to build models and take things apart to see how they work. (Source of information: "Three Different Learning Styles," University of South Dakota, www.usd.edu/trio/tut/ts/styleres.html.)

   a. classification

   b. simple listing

   c. process

   d. sequence of dates and events

   e. comparison and contrast

   f. cause and effect

2. XML (Extensible Markup Language) and HTML (Hypertext Markup Language) are coding languages, or instructions to the computer, used for the design of web pages. HTML was the brainchild of Tim Berners-Lee, a British physicist who wanted to find a way for researchers to share information over the Internet. It was formally introduced in 1993. XML is a cousin† to HTML and was

---

†Some might liken them to brother and sister since both are offshoots of SGML (Standard Generalized Markup Language).

Copyright © Cengage Learning. All rights reserved.

introduced by the World Wide Web Consortium (W3C) in 1998. HTML uses preexisting labels or "tags" to classify text and only text whereas XML allows users to create their own tags, which can be applied to all kinds of data, including images. For those who like their web pages with lots of bells and whistles, XML is the preferred markup language. But HTML still has plenty of defenders who say that XML is not a replacement for HTML because the two have different goals and can complement one another. In the words of Joe Burns, whose website www.htmlgoodies.com offers tutorials in both languages, "HTML is not dead, nor is it breathing funny. . . . I believe I will be able to write HTML and post web pages as long as I live using HTML alone. They just might not be as fancy as other pages."

a. classification

b. simple listing

c. process

d. sequence of dates and events

e. comparison and contrast

f. cause and effect

3. Bats and dolphins gather information about their surroundings by bouncing sound waves off objects in a three-step process. First, both animals send sound waves into the atmosphere. Bats make high-pitched sounds by moving air past their vocal chords, and dolphins transmit clicking sounds from nasal sacs in their foreheads. Next, these sounds hit an object in the animal's vicinity, bounce off the object, and return in the form of echoes. In the third step, the animal hears and interprets the echoes. Its brain processes the information, assessing the object's size and shape to form a mental image of it. It is even possible for bats and dolphins to determine how far away the object is based on how long it takes the echo to return.

a. classification

b. simple listing

c. process

d. sequence of dates and events

e. comparison and contrast

f. cause and effect

Copyright © Cengage Learning. All rights reserved.

4. Dean Kamen is a self-taught physicist and highly successful inventor-entrepreneur with numerous inventions to his credit. Kamen invented the first portable infusion pump capable of delivering drugs like insulin to patients who otherwise would have spent their time in hospitals rather than at home. Kamen also invented the first book-sized dialysis machine, allowing patients with kidney failure to receive treatment at home instead of in a hospital. Then, after watching a man trying to negotiate a curb in his wheelchair, Kamen created the IBOT Transporter, a six-wheeled chair that can climb stairs and rocky terrain. Moving away from the medical field, Kamen is currently at work on a machine that would generate power for industry and home use while simultaneously serving as a water purification system.

   a. definition
   b. classification
   c. simple listing
   d. process
   e. sequence of dates and events
   f. comparison and contrast

5. In February and March 2007, thousands of pets, mostly cats, died as a result of eating food contaminated by melamine, a chemical used in making plastics. While the outrage and grief over the loss of so many pets has fueled investigation into the safety of pet food, it needs to have an even more wide-ranging effect. Consumers need to be aware that globalization,† with its opening up of foreign markets, may have endangered the food supply for humans as well. Currently, not enough inspectors are available to see that all the food coming into the United States is safe. General inspectors examine mainly "at-risk" foods, those foods, such as meat, that are subject to contamination. Fruits and vegetables arrive in the market with hardly any inspection at all. This situation needs to be changed, and the pet food recall of 2007 is an alarm that we need to heed.

---

†globalization: term used to describe the interconnectedness of international markets and businesses.

Copyright © Cengage Learning. All rights reserved.

a. definition
b. classification
c. simple listing
d. process
e. sequence of dates and events
f. cause and effect

**TAKING A
CLOSER LOOK**

Pronoun Reference
In line 4 of the previous paragraph, what does the pronoun *it* refer to?

_____

_____

_____

_____

Copyright © Cengage Learning. All rights reserved.

▶ **TEST 5**   **Taking Stock**

DIRECTIONS   Read each paragraph. Then answer the following questions by circling the letter of the correct response or filling in the blanks.

1. [1]Global positioning system (GPS) technology has been around since 1978 and put to a number of good uses, from tracing tanks on the battlefield to finding hikers lost in a snowstorm. [2]Now, however, parents of teenagers have discovered a brand-new use for GPS technology: helping them keep in touch with their kids so that they know, for instance, exactly where their children are and how fast they are driving. [3]Not surprisingly, this use of GPS technology has sparked an intense debate with the parents expressing the pros in the argument while teenagers just as intensely point to the cons. [4]Advocates of using the GPS devices in this way say they help reduce risky behavior and may even save lives. [5]More specifically, they argue that teenagers won't speed if they know their parents will be alerted—some GPS systems send an email to parents if kids go over the speed limit—and that teenagers driving at or below the speed limit might help reduce the number of kids who die in car crashes. [6]According to the National Highway Traffic Safety Administration, motor vehicle crashes are the leading cause of death among 15- to 20-year-olds. [7]Jack Church, spokesman for Teen Arrive Alive, a Florida company that offers GPS-enabled cell phones, made exactly this point in a 2006 *San Francisco Gate* article: "This is about parents being given tools to better protect their kids. That's not Big Brother. That's parenting." (Source of quotations: www.pbs.org/newshour/extra/features/jan-june07/gps_2–19.html.)

   1. What is the topic? _____

   2. The topic sentence is sentence _____.

   3. How would you paraphrase the topic sentence?

      _____

      _____

   4. The supporting details develop what word or phrase in the topic sentence?

      _____

Copyright © Cengage Learning. All rights reserved.

5. Which pattern or patterns do you see at work in the paragraph?

a. definition

b. process

c. sequence of dates and events

d. classification

e. simple listing

f. comparison and contrast

g. cause and effect

2. [1]The National Security Act of 1947 was signed into law by Harry S. Truman on July 26, 1947. [2]Its purpose was to realign and reorganize the country's military forces—ground, sea, and air—all of which had operated autonomously during World War II. [3]The National Security Act also called for a Secretary of Defense, whose job it would be to unify the military's training procedures and goals. [4]James V. Forrestal got the job because he had served as Secretary of the Navy for almost three years. [5]On the face of it, Forrestal, bright, ambitious, and knowledgeable, seemed a perfect choice; however, he would be gone in less than two years and would leave in disgrace. [6]A staunch cold warrior, Forrestal was inclined to see Communist threats everywhere. [7]He even coined the term "semiwar" to support his belief that the country needed to remain permanently on high alert. [8]In addition to feeling constantly under siege by the Communists, Forrestal was deeply wounded on his home turf when, in 1948, columnists Drew Pearson and Walter Winchell accused him of everything from tax evasion to collaborating with the Nazis. [9]Things only got worse for Forrestal when he learned that Truman was ready to fire him because he was not fully supportive of the new plan for founding the country of Israel. [10]Rather than be publicly dismissed, Forrestal resigned on March 28, 1949. [11]Upon leaving office, Forrestal seemed so distraught, he was sent to Florida for a rest, but when his behavior became increasingly erratic, he was rushed to a military hospital in Bethesda, Maryland. [12]On May 22, 1949, Forrestal jumped out a sixteenth-story window, the sash of his bathrobe wrapped tightly around his neck.

1. What is the topic? _____

2. The topic sentence is sentence _____.

Copyright © Cengage Learning. All rights reserved.

3. How would you paraphrase the topic sentence?

_____

_____

4. The supporting details develop what word or phrase in the topic sentence?

_____

5. Which pattern or patterns do you see at work in the paragraph?
   a. definition
   b. process
   c. sequence of dates and events
   d. classification
   e. simple listing
   f. comparison and contrast
   g. cause and effect

Copyright © Cengage Learning. All rights reserved.

Understanding, Outlining, and Summarizing Longer Readings

© Corbis

IN THIS CHAPTER, YOU WILL LEARN

- how to adapt what you know about paragraphs to longer readings.
- how to create informal outlines.
- how to summarize longer readings.

*Summarization is one of the most underused . . .
techniques we have today, yet research has
shown that it yields some of the greatest leaps
in comprehension and long-term retention
of information.*

—Rick Wormeli, writer and teacher

In Chapter 5 you'll use some of the same skills introduced in previous chapters. However, you'll apply those skills, with a few modifications, to readings longer than a paragraph. In addition, you'll learn how to use outlines for note-taking and how to revise those outlines as you get closer to exams. You'll also get some pointers for summarizing longer, multi-paragraph readings.

Understanding Longer Readings

To thoroughly understand a paragraph, you need to answer three questions: (1) What's the topic? (2) What's the main idea? and (3) Which supporting details are central to understanding that main idea? Fortunately, the same questions apply to readings longer than a single paragraph. However, there are several crucial differences between reading a single paragraph and reading longer selections, and you need to take those differences into account.

The Main Idea Controls More Than a Paragraph

In longer readings, one main idea unifies not just a single paragraph but all or most of the paragraphs in the selection. Because it controls the content of the other paragraphs, you can think of this main idea as the "controlling main idea." In other words, it controls the content of the paragraphs that precede and follow it. These introductory and supporting paragraphs exist in order to present, explain, clarify, or argue the controlling main idea. (For a diagram illustrating this point, see page 251.)

Several Sentences May Be Needed to Express the Main Idea

The main idea of an entire reading can often be summed up in a single sentence. But the full expression of the controlling main idea often requires several sentences, maybe even a paragraph. For that reason, composition textbooks frequently use the term *thesis statement* to refer to the stated main idea of a research paper or an essay. Following that tradition, we'll use that term throughout the remaining chapters to emphasize that the main idea of a multi-paragraph reading cannot always be summed up in one sentence.

Copyright © Cengage Learning. All rights reserved.

Introductions Can Grow Longer

In paragraphs, introductions are usually limited to only a sentence or two. However, in longer readings, introducing the main idea may require several paragraphs. Although textbook authors often present readers with the main idea in the first or second paragraph, there certainly can be exceptions.

You should also be prepared for the fact that journal articles, literary essays, and newspaper editorials do not strictly adhere to any one rule for the placement of the main idea. In these kinds of texts, writers sometimes include lengthy introductions to provide background or stimulate reader interest. Depending on the length of the article or essay, there might be one introductory paragraph or several preceding the thesis statement expressing the main idea.

Thesis Statements Don't Wait Until the End to Appear

Topic sentences can appear anywhere in a paragraph—at the beginning, in the middle, or at the end. Even with the presence of a lengthy introduction, thesis statements are somewhat more fixed in location. Although writers occasionally build up to the main idea and conclude a multi-paragraph reading with the thesis statement, that's not typical, particularly not in textbook or journal readings. It's far more likely for a thesis statement to appear at the beginning of a reading, even if it does follow a multi-paragraph introduction. That means the opening paragraphs in an essay, an article, or a chapter section deserve particularly close attention.

If you are reading a multi-paragraph text and there is no hint of the thesis statement by the middle of the reading, it's possible that the author has decided to conclude with it. However, what's more likely is that the main idea is not stated. Instead, it has to be inferred, or created, based on clues provided by the author. (More on inferences in Chapter 6.)

One Supporting Detail Can Take Up Several Paragraphs

In longer readings, explaining one major supporting detail essential to the main idea can take up a paragraph or more. For that reason, multi-paragraph readings require you to do a good deal more sifting and sorting of information in order to decide which details are essential to

Copyright © Cengage Learning. All rights reserved.

your understanding of the overall main idea and which sentences or paragraphs are essential to your understanding of a major detail.

A Minor Detail Can Occupy an Entire Paragraph

As they do in paragraphs, minor details in longer readings further explain major ones. They also add colorful facts or supply repetition for emphasis. And like major details in longer readings, one minor detail can take up an entire paragraph. This means it's especially important for readers to determine which minor details add truly relevant information and which ones do not.

Remember: Main Ideas Aren't All Equal

In longer selections, readers have to mentally move back and forth between the controlling main idea and the main ideas in the rest of the selection. With each new paragraph, the reader has to connect a new main idea to the overall, or controlling, main idea of the entire selection.

For an illustration of why determining the relationship among main ideas is important, look at the following reading and the accompanying diagram. The diagram provides a picture of the reading's underlying structure.

Research on Leadership

Thesis Statement

1   In business, managers have to be leaders. Thus it comes as no surprise that researchers have been studying the nature of leadership in business. At the University of Michigan, researchers have found that leadership behavior among managers can be divided into two categories—job-centered and employee-centered.

Topic Sentence   2   Job-centered leaders closely supervise their employees in an effort to monitor and control their performance. They are primarily concerned with getting a job done. They are far less concerned with the feelings or attitudes of their employees—unless those attitudes and feelings affect the task at hand. In general, they don't encourage employees to express opinions on how best to accomplish a task.

Topic Sentence   3   In contrast, employee-centered leaders focus on reaching goals by building a sense of team spirit. It follows then that employee-centered leaders are concerned with subordinates' job satisfaction and group unity.

Copyright © Cengage Learning. All rights reserved.

Employee-centered leaders are also more willing to let employees have a voice in how they do their jobs.

Topic Sentence   4   The Michigan researchers also investigated which kind of leadership is more effective. They concluded that managers whose leadership was employee-centered were generally more effective than managers who were primarily job-centered. That is, their employees performed at higher levels and were more satisfied. (Adapted from Van Fleet and Peterson, *Contemporary Management*, p. 332.)

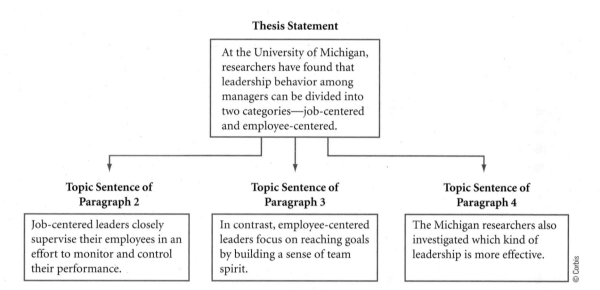

Thesis Statement

At the University of Michigan, researchers have found that leadership behavior among managers can be divided into two categories—job-centered and employee-centered.

Topic Sentence of Paragraph 2	**Topic Sentence of Paragraph 3**	**Topic Sentence of Paragraph 4**
Job-centered leaders closely supervise their employees in an effort to monitor and control their performance.	In contrast, employee-centered leaders focus on reaching goals by building a sense of team spirit.	The Michigan researchers also investigated which kind of leadership is more effective.

© Corbis

The above diagram illustrates how thesis statements and topic sentences work together. The thesis statement introduces the reading's overall main idea. Then the topic sentences of the remaining paragraphs unite to expand and clarify that point.

Within each supporting paragraph, the major details clarify the topic sentence of that particular paragraph. However, some of those major details do double duty: They also help develop the controlling main idea of the entire reading. Keep in mind, though, that some major details in a single paragraph can become minor details when viewed in the context of the reading as a whole. That's a point we can discuss in more depth when we get to the subject of note-taking.

Copyright © Cengage Learning. All rights reserved.

CHECK YOUR UNDERSTANDING

Without looking back at the text, describe how longer readings differ from single paragraphs. When you finish, compare your list to the original explanation.

1. _____

_____

2. _____

_____

3. _____

_____

4. _____

_____

5. _____

_____

6. _____

_____

◆ **EXERCISE 1   Identifying Thesis Statements**

DIRECTIONS   Read each of the following selections and underline the thesis statement. *Note*: Remember that the thesis statement does not always open the reading, and it can consist of more than one sentence.

EXAMPLE

The Death Penalty Through the Ages

1   In the United States today, the federal government and 35 states have statutes allowing the death penalty for certain crimes. Still, the death penalty, or capital punishment, is reserved almost exclusively for those who commit murder. Nationwide fewer than 100 criminals are executed every year. Between 1976—the year the death penalty was reintroduced

Copyright © Cengage Learning. All rights reserved.

as punishment—and 2010, there were 1,202 executions, all of them for the crime of homicide.

2   In times past, though, the death penalty was much more widely imposed. Often the death penalty was used to punish offenses that were rather trivial by modern standards. In ancient Babylon, for example, the Code of King Hammurabi allowed the death penalty for twenty-five different crimes. None of them involved the taking of a life. The Egyptians even imposed the death penalty for killing a cat, an animal considered sacred. In the seventh century b.c., the Draconian† Code of Athens prescribed death as the punishment for every crime committed. In the fifth century b.c., the Romans punished with death anyone who sang insulting songs, burned a stack of corn too close to a house, committed perjury, or disturbed a city's peace during the night. In 438, the Code of Theodosius designated more than eighty different crimes as deserving of the death penalty.

3   During the Middle Ages, the death penalty was used for a number of major as well as minor crimes. In Britain, people were put to death for everything from stealing a loaf of bread to sacrilege* or treason. From 1509 to 1547, during the reign of Henry VIII, as many as 72,000 people were executed for various offenses. By the 1700s, the list of crimes punishable by death increased to 220 offenses. These offenses included stealing, cutting down trees, sending threatening letters, and producing counterfeit money.

4   English settlers in America initially brought with them to the New World the idea of severe punishments for crimes both large and small. In addition to executing murderers, the Capital Laws of New England, in effect from 1636 to 1647, punished with death anyone convicted of witchcraft, adultery, assault, blasphemy, and perjury. In 1665, the New York colony imposed capital punishment on anyone found guilty of challenging the king's rights or striking a parent. Although these laws were relaxed for fear of discouraging new colonists, by 1780 the Commonwealth of Massachusetts was still executing those convicted of crimes such as burglary, homosexuality, and arson. As late as 1837, North Carolina

---

†Draconian: The word exists today and means harsh or severe. It derives from Draco, a Greek politician who codified the country's laws and in the process made them as severe as possible.
*sacrilege: treating holy objects with disrespect, stealing holy objects; also used to suggest a lack of respect for widely accepted ideas and traditions.

Copyright © Cengage Learning. All rights reserved.

required death for the crimes of assisting with arson, engaging in bigamy, encouraging slaves to riot, and hiding slaves with the intention of freeing them. (Sources of figures: U.S. Department of Justice, Office of Justice Programs, Bureau of Justice Statistics, "Capital Punishment Statistics," www.ojp.usdoj.gov/bjs/cp.htm; Michael H. Reggio.)

EXPLANATION   Tempting as it might be to assume that the first paragraph of this reading contains the thesis statement, that thought would lead you astray. None of the sentences in paragraph 1 is further developed. That means the first paragraph does not introduce the thesis statement.

Because the point made in the opening sentences of paragraph 2—in times past, the death penalty was widely imposed and often for trivial offenses—is picked up and developed beyond paragraph 2, we can correctly call that sentence not just the topic sentence of the paragraph but the thesis statement of the entire selection.

1. Is Your Home Clean?

1   Surveys show that, overall, Americans scrub and wipe down their homes fairly often. A Bounty Home Care Council survey, for example, revealed that bathrooms are cleaned an average of five times a month, and that 42 percent of people clean their bathrooms twice a week or more. However, environmental biologist Dr. Charles Gerba of the University of Arizona has shown that many clean homes just look clean. In reality, they tend to be breeding grounds for bacteria. Indeed, the homes that seem the cleanest are often the ones teeming with the most disease-causing germs. The cleanest houses are often home to the most bacteria because cleaning tools are not always properly handled and, consequently, they spread germs during cleaning.

2   Dr. Gerba's research has shown that a clean bathroom is often smeared with millions of harmful microorganisms. This is because about half the population uses sponges and rags to clean. Yet only 24 percent of those Americans disinfect the rags and sponges after each use. About 40 percent rinse them only with water, and 16 percent just put the sponges and rags away after using them. Consequently, bathroom sponges and rags are filled with germs. The more the sponges and rags are used, the more germs are spread.

Copyright © Cengage Learning. All rights reserved.

3   Clean kitchens, too, often harbor more dangerous bacteria than messy kitchens. As a matter of fact, research has shown that even in the most spotless of homes, bacteria associated with fecal matter,[†] such as *E. coli*, are regularly found in the sink and on countertops. These germs are spread by unwashed hands; raw meat; and the sponges, dishrags, and dish towels used to clean up. For example, a kitchen sponge that has been used for only two or three days is filled with bacteria. The more it's used to wipe surfaces, the more germs it spreads.

4   Dr. Gerba's research has also shown that freshly laundered clothes are not truly clean either. In one study, he swabbed the inside of 100 household washing machines in Florida and Arizona and found that more than 60 percent tested positive for coliform bacteria, which comes from fecal matter. Another 20 percent tested positive for staphylococcus, a major cause of food-borne illness. Swabs of dryers showed that even high heat settings don't kill salmonella and another bacteria (mycobacterium fortuitum) that causes skin infections. Thus every time a new load of clothes or towels goes into either the washer or the dryer, these harmful germs get into the fabrics.

5   However, Dr. Gerba and other experts say that changing to different tools and techniques will help kill and stop the spread of germs. They recommend cleaning with sturdy paper towels and then throwing them away. They also suggest using bleach on surfaces and in the laundry, as well as putting rags, towels, and sponges in the microwave for at least one minute after each use. (Sources of statistics: Amanda Hesser, "Squeaky Clean? Not Even Close," *New York Times*, January 28, 2004, p. F1; "Paper Towels Help Wipe Out Harmful Bathroom Germs," PR Newswire, November 2, 2000.)

2. Gender and Listening

1   Men and women learn different styles of listening just as they learn different styles for using verbal and nonverbal messages. Not surprisingly, these different styles can create major difficulties in opposite-sex interpersonal communication. According to Deborah Tannen, author of *You Just Don't Understand: Women and Men in Conversation*, women see conversation as a way of establishing a close relationship, and listening helps them to achieve that goal. Men don't

---

[†]fecal matter: waste eliminated from the bowels.

Copyright © Cengage Learning. All rights reserved.

share that view. They see conversation as a way of communicating information. Thus they are more likely to display their expertise and dominate a conversation. In other words, they talk more than listen. Women, in contrast, play down their expertise when in conversation and are more interested in communicating supportiveness. They show their support by listening,

2   Men and women also show that they're listening in different ways. In conversation, a woman is more apt to give lots of listening cues such as saying "Yeah" or "Uh-uh," nodding in agreement, and smiling. A man is more likely to listen without providing extensive feedback or, for that matter, any feedback at all. Perhaps that's the reason why analysis of calls to a crisis center in Finland revealed that calls received by a female counselor were significantly longer for both male and female callers (Salminen and Glad, 1992). It's likely that the greater number of listening cues given by the women encouraged the callers to keep talking. This same study also found that male callers claimed that they were helped by "just listening." Female callers said they were helped by "empathic understanding."

3   Tannen also says that men listen less to women than women listen to men. The reason, says Tannen, is that listening is considered an inferior position, whereas speaking places a person in a superior position. Men seem to assume a more argumentative posture while listening, as if getting ready to argue. They also ask questions that are more argumentative or that seek to puncture holes in the other speaker's position as a way to play up their own expertise. Women are more likely to ask supportive questions and perhaps offer criticism that is more positive than men's. Women let the speaker see that they're listening. Men use fewer listening cues in conversation. Men and women act this way to both men and women; their customary ways of talking don't seem to change depending on whether the listener is male or female.

4   There is no evidence indicating that these differences represent any negative motives on the part of men to prove themselves superior or of women to ingratiate* themselves. Rather, these differences in listening seem largely the result of the way men and women have been socialized.

(Adapted from DeVito, *The Interpersonal Communication Book*, p. 122.)

---

*ingratiate: to get oneself into the good graces of another.

Copyright © Cengage Learning. All rights reserved.

Copyright © Cengage Learning. All rights reserved.

TAKING A
CLOSER LOOK

Looking for a Pattern
Do you detect a pattern in how the author of the reading "Gender and Listening" presents material? Do the majority of the paragraphs in this reading open with a general statement followed by specific details, or do they start with specific details that build up to a general point?

_____

_____

Thinking About Purpose

Almost everything you read as a student will have been written either to inform or to persuade. Writers intent on informing will explain an idea, event, or issue without taking a stand on it or expecting readers to take one. Writers whose intent is to persuade will evaluate a particular idea, issue, or event and try to get readers to share their position.

When you are dealing with a single paragraph, it's hard to identify the author's purpose in writing, unless the language is particularly emotional in its tone. But when you have an entire reading available, you can usually determine the author's **primary**, or main, purpose by considering both the content and style of the writing.

The following reading, for instance, was written to inform. Note how the author's thesis statement does not suggest any evaluation of the issue discussed. Nor does the language try to engage the reader emotionally. These are two hallmarks of informative writing.

Sleeping Scared

1   Sleep researchers say that nightmares are a universal experience, and people from all cultures report the experience of being jolted out of sleep by a terrifying dream that seemed all too real. In sleep research labs where people are periodically woken out of rapid eye movement (REM) sleep, three-quarters of those wakened report being in the middle of a bad dream. In other words, nightmares are a common occurrence, more common than many of us realize. Ask someone to

recall how many bad dreams they had over the course of the year and the person will report one or two. But tell them to keep a dream diary and the picture changes with the diarist reporting nightmares once or twice a month.

Thesis Statement 2   While bad dreams may be common across cultures, researchers say that they do vary according to age and gender. Preschoolers, for instance, report very few nightmares. But that changes with their arrival in kindergarten, at which point bad dreams become more common. Around a quarter of all children between the ages of five and twelve report having nightmares.

3   Nightmare rates really start to climb in adolescence. They peak in young adulthood and then begin dropping. The average fifty-five-year-old has far fewer nightmares than the average twenty-five-year-old.

4   At nearly every age, females report having more nightmares than males do. They are also more likely to be awakened by the intensity of their nightmares, which, in one study at least, focused heavily on the dreamer being chased and having her life threatened. Men's bad dreams were slightly different in that they were more concerned with the dreamer being trapped in an unpleasant situation and forced to fight his way free.

(Source of study: www.asdreams.org/journal/articles/4-2levin.htm.)

Did you notice how the writer made a point of repeatedly attributing claims made in the reading to researchers? That's typical of informative writing, in which the author makes a point of not revealing his or her point of view. Notice as well that the writer keeps the language fairly **denotative**, or factual. There's no discussion of women's "horrifyingly realistic" nightmares. Instead, there's just a quick reference to the typical topics of those nightmares.

Persuasive Writing

In contrast to informative writing, persuasive writing openly acknowledges that the opinions expressed in a reading belong to the author. Writers intent on persuasion also use words, allusions, and imagery designed to engage readers and encourage them to share the writer's point of view.

Usually the writer who has a persuasive intent will create a **tone** that reveals his or her attitude toward or feeling about the material. Running the gamut from outraged to enthusiastic, tone in writing is one of the key

Copyright © Cengage Learning. All rights reserved.

indicators of purpose. The following selection fits that general rule. The author's irritated, sarcastic tone reveals the writer's persuasive purpose.

The Moon Landing and the Conspiracy Theorists

Thesis Statement

© Corbis

1 Despite all evidence to the contrary, there are people who seriously believe that NASA's Apollo space program never really landed men on the moon. These people claim that the moon landings were nothing more than a huge conspiracy, perpetuated by a government desperately in competition with the Russians and fearful of losing face.

2 These conspiracy theorists claim that the United States knew it couldn't compete with the Russians in the space race and was therefore forced to fake a series of successful moon landings. Advocates* of a conspiracy cite several pieces of what they consider evidence. Crucial to their case is the claim that astronauts never could have safely passed through the Van Allen belt, a region of radiation trapped in Earth's magnetic field. If the astronauts had truly gone through the belt, say conspiracy theorists, they would have died.

3 Yet those scientists who don't doubt the reality of the Apollo's successful mission have a two-fold answer for this alleged* evidence. They point to the fact that the metal hulls of the spaceship were designed to block radiation. They also say that the spacecraft passed so quickly through the Van Allen belt, there wasn't time for the astronauts to feel the effects of radiation. As might be expected, conspiracy theorists remain unconvinced by this straightforward and, at least for rational people, seemingly logical explanation.

4 Proponents of the "moon landing was faked" school also want to know why the U.S. flag planted on the moon is rippling when it should be still because there is no air on the moon. Here again, they simply refuse to listen to any reasonable explanation, which, it turns out, reputable* scientists can provide. The flag shown rippling in photographs only did so because an astronaut was adjusting the flag's rod at the time the picture was taken. But that, of course, is too simple an explanation for those who insist on believing, despite all evidence to the contrary, that the moon landing was faked. Zealously* committed to their beliefs, they treat factual

---

*advocates: supporters, believers.
*alleged: claimed but not yet proven beyond a doubt.
*reputable: having a good reputation.
*zealously: enthusiastically, often excessively so.

Copyright © Cengage Learning. All rights reserved.

explanations that explain away their "evidence" as little more than irritating distractions. In other words, no amount of logical counter-argument or evidence can change their mind.

As you can see, the writer of this selection has a definite opinion and works hard to make readers share it. She strongly suggests that the evidence provided by those believing the moon landing was faked does not merit much respectful attention.

In later chapters, you'll hear more about purpose in writing. But for now look over the two brief lists that follow. They will give you a general sense of how the two kinds of writing differ.

Writers Whose Primary Intent Is to Inform ◆	1. choose titles that don't evaluate the topic—for example, "Multitasking in the Car Is Now the Norm."
	2. avoid revealing their personal point of view often by attributing what they say to another person or group—for instance, "The Harvard Business School Study suggests that people on social networks spend 70 percent of their time looking at photos and profiles."
	3. employ a tone that is neutral rather than expressive of any emotion or attitude—for example, "The second Iraq war began in the spring of 2003."

Writers Whose Primary Intent Is to Persuade ◆	1. often use titles that take a stand—for instance, "Multitasking and Driving Do NOT Mix."
	2. reveal a personal opinion—for example, "As an employer, let me say out loud that I don't find arguments about social networks improving productivity especially convincing."
	3. use emotionally charged language that conveys a feeling or attitude—for example, "Kathryn Bigelow's harrowing film about the daily horrors soldiers endured on duty in Iraq allegedly takes no position on the war itself, but in its devastating scenes of violent destruction, it is a profoundly anti-war movie."

Copyright © Cengage Learning. All rights reserved.

TAKING A CLOSER LOOK

Punctuation

Why does the author of the reading about the moon landing put the word "evidence" into quotation marks? What do the quotation marks suggest?

_____

_____

_____

_____

INTERNET FOLLOW-UP: How to Respond to Conspiracy Theorists

Over the years, numerous websites have sprung up in response to the claims that the moon landings never happened. Locate one you think can be trusted, and explain why the lack of stars in the background of photos taken during the landing is *not* proof the landing was a fake.

www

_____

_____

_____

_____

_____

_____

◆ **EXERCISE 2** **Identifying Purpose**

DIRECTIONS Read each of the following selections and underline the thesis statement. Then put an *I* or a *P* in the blank to indicate if you think the author's purpose is primarily informative or persuasive.

1. **Our Oldest Enemy: The Locust**

1 In 2009, Australian farmlands were invaded by vast armies bent on nothing less than total destruction. The enemy had entered the country on foot, creeping along at just a mile an hour at first. But in time it took

Copyright © Cengage Learning. All rights reserved.

to the air, swooping in from the skies to plunder all vegetation. Covering hundreds of miles a day, this flying menace obliterated everything in its path.

2   In response to the long-awaited attack, emergency teams went into action. Aircraft roared into the skies, flying just above the ground to battle the enemy at close quarters, using deadly chemicals. Allies also took flight to help increase Australia's already airborne forces. The initial battle went on for close to a week. Then there were a series of brief encounters to finish off the last of the invaders. At war's end, the enemy dead numbered in the billions.

3   It had been no human invasion but a far more fearsome and rapacious* threat that attacked Australia's fields: The enemy was a plague of locusts. Responding to the attack with chemicals sprayed from aircraft and employing thousands of locust-eating birds, human warriors eventually wreaked havoc* on these enormously destructive pests. Nevertheless, throughout most of history, the reverse has been true. When a plague of locusts arrived, it was almost always humans who suffered more than insects.

4   The earliest written record of a locust plague is probably in the Book of Exodus, which describes an attack that took place in Egypt in about 3500 BC: "They covered the face of the whole land, so that the land was darkened . . . ; not a green thing remained, neither tree nor plant of the field, through all the land of Egypt" (Exodus 10:12–15). Another biblical account, in the Book of Job, describes trees "made white" as locusts stripped even the bark from the branches.

5   Locusts have always spelled disaster. In a single day, a typical large swarm (about 40 million insects) can eat 80,000 tons of corn, devouring a city's food supply for an entire year in just hours. In 125 B.C., locusts destroyed the grain crop in northern Africa. More than 80,000 people died of starvation. In A.D. 591, a plague of locusts in Italy caused the death of more than a million people and animals. In 1613, disaster struck the French region of La Camargue when locusts ate in a single day enough grass to feed 4,000 cattle for a year, leaving the people and animals in the region to die of starvation.

---

*rapacious: greedy and destructive.
*havoc: widespread destruction, often used with the verb *wreak* meaning "inflict" and rhyming with *week*.

Copyright © Cengage Learning. All rights reserved.

6   Between 1873 and 1877, locusts blackened the skies of the American West from California to Missouri, causing $200 million in crop damage. At the time, the U.S. government pronounced the locust to be "the most serious impediment to the settlement of the West." In 1889, the Nile valley of Egypt suffered a similar disaster when locusts so thoroughly destroyed crops over an estimated 2,000-square-mile area that even the mice starved in their wake. But make no mistake, swarms of locusts and the damage they can do are not restricted to the pages of history books. Between 1949 and 2004, locust swarms in Africa were a major cause of starvation, resulting from the insects sweeping in and devouring fields of crops. In November 2008, Australia was hit hard by a plague of locusts that measured 3.7 miles long and ate all the vegetation in its path.

------

2. A Three-Part Theory of Love

1   What is love? No one knows for sure. However, researcher R. J. Sternberg has a theory. According to Sternberg, love consists of three separate ingredients. Each one is crucial to falling in love or staying in love.

2   Passion is a feeling of heightened sexual arousal, and it's usually accompanied by a strong, romantic attraction. In the throes* of passion, a lover feels that life is hardly worth living unless the beloved is present. Unfortunately, passionate feelings almost always diminish over time, although they remain essential to the beginning of a loving relationship. Luckily, if there's a strong sense of intimacy between the partners, the loss or decrease of passion can be accepted and the love maintained.

3   Within the framework of Sternberg's theory, intimacy—feelings of closeness, sharing, and affection—is essential to staying in love. Both partners need to feel that they view the world in similar ways so that they can turn to one another in times of great sadness or joy. If the one you love is not the one you feel particularly intimate with, or close to, over time, love may not last. Typically in a relationship, intimacy grows steadily at first and then levels off.

------

*throes: experience of intense excitement.

Copyright © Cengage Learning. All rights reserved.

4   Commitment is the third ingredient of Sternberg's three-part framework. As he sees it, this ingredient is the hardest to develop and maintain. More conscious and logical than the other two, commitment requires a decision to stay with a relationship even when things are not going smoothly. While passion requires no effort, it comes spontaneously, and intimacy tends to develop naturally through shared experience and activities, commitment depends on the individual's conscious decision to stick with the relationship. It depends on the willingness of a person to say, "This relationship matters to me. I'm going to hold onto it no matter what."

———

**TAKING A
CLOSER LOOK**

Clues to Purpose
In the reading about love, what phrases in the selection give away the purpose?

_____

_____

Does the tone match the purpose?

_____

◆ Outlining Longer Readings

With longer readings that cover fairly familiar or uncomplicated material, you can probably prepare for class discussions and exams just by reviewing your underlining and marginal notes. However, if the material is unfamiliar and complicated, you should probably take notes using an informal outline.

Like a formal outline, an informal outline identifies relationships by aligning or indenting sentences, words, or phrases. With informal

Copyright © Cengage Learning. All rights reserved.

outlines, though, you needn't worry about using all sentences or all phrases, and you don't have to fuss over consistency of capital or lowercase letters. You can use whatever symbols seem appropriate to the material. You can combine letters, numbers, abbreviations, dashes, and so on, as you need them. In other words, informal outlines are not governed by a rigid set of rules.

The main thing to keep in mind is the goal of your informal outline. Your goal is to create a clear blueprint of the author's ideas and their relationship to one another. The following pointers should help you achieve that goal.

Start with the Title

The title of an essay, an article, or a chapter section usually identifies the topic being discussed. Sometimes it even identifies the main idea of the entire reading. When it does, your outline should open with the title.

Follow with the Thesis Statement

After the title should come a paraphrase of the thesis statement or a statement of the implied main idea. Because indenting to show relationships is crucial to outlining, your paraphrase should be aligned with the left-most margin.

Use Key Words in the Thesis Statement to Select Details

The thesis statement often provides a clue to what should be included in your outline. For instance, if the thesis statement is something like "Three major studies indicate that working memory can be improved through training," then you know immediately that your outline should paraphrase the results of three studies. By the same token, if the main idea is something like "In the last decade, hurricanes have gotten bigger and more destructive," your outline has to identify precisely how much bigger and more destructive hurricanes have become.

Copyright © Cengage Learning. All rights reserved.

Streamline the Major Details

In longer readings, you may find that an entire paragraph is devoted to explaining one major detail. When this is the case, you have to decide how much of the paragraph is essential to your understanding of that one detail. What's essential goes into your outline.

Include Any Crucial Minor Details

Minor details in a paragraph should be included in your outline only if they are essential to an understanding of the major ones. If you can't explain a major detail without the help of a minor one, then the minor detail should be in your outline. Outlining, like underlining, requires conscious and consistent selectivity. When you outline, the key question to answer is always, "How important is this information to my understanding of the controlling main idea?"

Indent to Reveal Relationships

Remember that outlines are blueprints. Even a quick look at yours should tell you how the ideas in a reading relate. While the symbols you use to identify different ideas help show relationships, the real signifier of a relationship is how your sentences and phrases have been indented. Ideas that line up are equal in importance. But if one sentence or phrase is indented beneath another, then the indented item is not equal to the statement above it. Instead it's in the outline to explain or prove the previous point. That means it's subordinate, or dependent on something else for its significance.

Be Consistent

Letters, numbers, dashes (—), or asterisks (**) can help you separate major and minor details. Whichever symbols you use, be sure to use them consistently within the outline. Don't switch back and forth, sometimes using numbers for major details and then switching to letters. In the long run, this kind of inconsistency will only confuse you when you get ready to use your outline for exam preparation.

Copyright © Cengage Learning. All rights reserved.

◆ **EXERCISE 3**   **Outlining Longer Readings**

DIRECTIONS   Read each selection. Then complete the following outlines.

EXAMPLE

Inducing Compliance: Turning No into Yes

1 Although it would be nice if they did, other people don't always do what we wish them to, at least not at first. Over the years, however, social scientists interested in determining how people can be made to comply without the use of force have identified a number of strategies that are effective in inducing compliance, or agreement.

2   One way of encouraging compliance is to use the foot-in-the-door strategy. The name comes from a technique used in the days when salespeople went door to door selling their products. As the saying went at the time, "If you can get your foot in the door, the sale is almost a sure thing." In psychological terms, the foot-in-the-door strategy means that if a person is willing to comply with some small request, he or she may also be willing to comply with a much larger demand.

3   For example, if the committee to re-elect your local mayor wants you to put a huge sign in your front window promoting her candidacy, members of the committee might first ask you to display a bumper sticker. Once you agree to display the bumper sticker, they might ask you to wear a button. Once you've agreed to those two smaller requests, you just might be ready to put that sign in your window.

4   Psychologists suspect that the foot-in-the-door strategy works because we are inclined to observe our own behavior. Recognizing that we have agreed to a small request, we convince ourselves that the next, larger demand isn't all that different. At that point, we are ready to comply.

5   The door-in-the-face strategy—the name was coined by psychologist Robert Cialdini—is a variation on foot-in-the-door, and it works like this: If you have flatly said no to a large and inconvenient request ("slammed the door in someone's face"), you're more likely to agree to a smaller bid for help. Say, for example, your neighbor comes by and asks you to pick up his daughter at school for the next week while he is working overtime. You might well say no because fulfilling the request takes up too much time. But if your neighbor comes back the next day and says he got a

Copyright © Cengage Learning. All rights reserved.

friend to handle Monday, Wednesday, and Friday, you are likely to agree to take over on Tuesday and Thursday.

6   This strategy works because it seems as if the person making the request is being reasonable and making a concession.* For that reason, the person doing the favor feels that it is only fair to comply with the smaller request.

7   If you or someone you know has ever purchased a car, you will recognize the low-ball technique of encouraging compliance. In the context of car-buying, the salesperson offers a "low-ball" price that is significantly less than that of the competition. Once the customer seems interested, the salesperson begins to bump up the price. In other words, the low-ball technique gets you to comply with a request that seems to cost little or nothing. Once you say yes, the person starts tacking on additional items in the hopes that you will keep agreeing.

8   For example, your roommate asks for a ride to the local ticket office, where she hopes to get tickets for an Alicia Keys concert. Because the ticket office is only five minutes away by car, you say, "Sure, no problem." It's at that point that your roommate tells you she has to be there by 5:00 in the morning because that's when the line starts forming. If you agree, you've just succumbed to the low-ball technique.

Title   Inducing Compliance

Main Idea   There are three major ways to induce compliance in people who are reluctant to agree to a request.

Supporting Details   1. Foot-in-the-door approach comes from days when salespeople went house to house and literally put their foot in the door to make a sale.

      a. get people to agree to a small request and they will agree to a bigger one.

         ex: if they put a bumper sticker on the car, they might put a lawn sign, too.

    2. Door-in-the-face strategy works after you have flatly said no to a big request at which point you might well say yes to a smaller one.

———————————

*concession: admission of agreement or defeat; also to concede.

Copyright © Cengage Learning. All rights reserved.

    a.   friend asks you to pick up his daughter at school for the entire week and you say no but if he comes back and asks for only two days, you say yes.

3. Low-ball strategy makes a request that costs so little it's hard to refuse, but once you agree the demands keep increasing.

    a.   typical ploy of car salespeople

    b.   having already said yes, a person is more inclined to keep agreeing.

EXPLANATION   In this outline, what needed to be added were the descriptions of the three strategies for compliance and the details that illustrate and explain them.

1. The Five Languages of Love

1   According to relationship expert Dr. Gary Chapman, author of *The Five Love Languages*, people express love in different ways. Chapman believes that every individual best expresses love—and prefers to receive love—through one of five different communication styles. He calls these styles "love languages."

2   Some people feel that love is best expressed through quality time spent as a couple. Quality time, according to Dr. Chapman, does not mean simply being in the same room together. Spending quality time involves doing things as a couple and devoting attention to one another. People who view the spending of quality time as an expression of affection feel loved when their partners set aside time for them, even if it's just to chat for a few moments.

3   Other people, however, prefer words of affirmation as a way of giving or receiving love. These individuals like to be told that they are loved. They expect to hear "I love you" or "I appreciate you" often. They like compliments, encouragement, and praise. They like to hear statements such as "That dress looks great on you" or "You have a wonderful smile."

4   Gifts are yet another love language. People who use this language see presents as much more than material objects. For them gifts are symbols of love and signs of affection. In their mind, no presents equals no love.

Copyright © Cengage Learning. All rights reserved.

5   People who express love through acts of service, however, aren't impressed by gifts. They believe that helping others is the best expression of love. Voluntary acts of service are what makes them happy. Cooking, doing chores, changing the baby's diaper, and walking the dog are ways to make members of this group feel cared for and supported.

6   According to Chapman, physical touch is the fifth kind of love expression. People using this form of communication prefer to communicate their feelings for their partners by holding hands, kissing, hugging, or having sex. They feel secure and loved when they can touch and be touched in return.

7   Chapman believes that problems arise when two people involved in a romantic relationship have different styles of expression. If each person expresses him- or herself in a language the partner doesn't really understand or recognize, then expressions of affection may go unnoticed and undermine the relationship. For example, people who prefer expressing love through sharing quality time may doubt their partner's affection if the partner doesn't want to engage in activities as a couple. Likewise, people who need to hear words of affection will feel rejected if their partners don't tell them how much they care. But while it's true that speaking different love languages can lead to misunderstanding, there is hope. If couples become aware of their different love languages and learn to give and receive affection in a partner's preferred style, they can enhance, even revitalize, a romantic relationship. (Sources of language description: www.fivelovelanguages.com/thefivelovelanguages/index.html; Family First, "The Five Love Languages.")

Title   The Five Languages of Love
_____

Main Idea   According to author Gary Chapman, there are at least five different
_____

languages, or ways, to express love.
_____

Supporting Details   _____

_____

_____

_____

_____

Copyright © Cengage Learning. All rights reserved.

_____

_____

_____

_____

_____

_____

_____

_____

_____

_____

_____

_____

2. The Roman Circus

1   Although nowadays we think of the circus as an amusing entertainment for kids, originally it was not quite such a harmless event. To be sure, the first circus, like its modern counterpart, included death-defying events. But there was one big difference. In the early Roman circus, death was a frequent visitor, and circus spectators were accustomed to—and expected—bloodshed.

2   The Roman "Circus Maximus" began under the rule of emperor Julius Caesar, and it specialized in two big events—brutal fights between gladiators (or between gladiators and animals) and equally bloody chariot races. In most cases, both events ended in the death of either a person or an animal. If nobody died, the audience was disappointed. Even worse, the emperor was displeased.

3   Not surprisingly, the circus event that was in fashion usually reflected the taste of the man in power. Julius Caesar, for example, favored aggressive chariot races. Because the charioteers were usually slaves racing frantically for their freedom, the horses pulling the chariots were driven unmercifully and tragic accidents were an exciting possibility that kept audience members on the edge of their seats. In the hope of surviving the event, the charioteers wore helmets and wrapped

Copyright © Cengage Learning. All rights reserved.

the chariot reins around their bodies. They also carried knives to cut themselves free if they became entangled. Spills occurred more often than not. When they did, the charioteers would be thrown from the chariot and dragged around the ring by runaway horses. Knives and helmets notwithstanding, most did not survive this kind of horrible mishap, not that the screaming crowd cared. For the audience, death was part of the thrill.

4   During the reign of Augustus, from 27 B.C. to A.D. 14, a fight to the death between man and beast was the most popular circus event, and more than 3,500 lions and tigers perished in the circus arena, taking hundreds of gladiators with them. Under the half-mad Emperor Nero, who ruled during the first century A.D., the most popular circus spectacle was lion versus Christian, with the Christians the guaranteed losers. Fortunately for both Christians and the slaves who followed in their wake, this savage circus practice was outlawed in A.D. 326 by the Emperor Constantine.

5   Although the pitting of Christians against lions was staged in a special arena, most of the circus events that took place in Rome were staged in the largest arena of them all—the Colosseum. The capacity of this great stadium, completed in A.D. 79, was enormous. It seated close to 50,000 people. In one Colosseum season alone, 2,000 gladiators went to their deaths, all in the name of circus fun. (Sources of dates and figures: Charles Panati, *Browser's Book of Beginnings*, pp. 262–64.)

Title   The Roman Circus _____

Main Idea   The circus began in ancient Rome, but it was much bloodier than the

circus we know today. _____

Supporting Details   1. The first circus, Circus Maximus, originated under Julius Caesar.

_____

_____

_____

_____

_____

_____

Copyright © Cengage Learning. All rights reserved.

_____

_____

_____

_____

_____

_____

_____

_____

ALLUSION ALERT

Bread and Circuses

With the discussion of circuses still in mind, it's a good time to introduce the allusion "bread and circuses." This allusion originates with the ancient Roman writer Juvenal, who wrote, "Two things only the people anxiously desire—bread and circuses." Juvenal's point was that every time the people of Rome were discontented, they could be easily distracted by food and entertainment. Juvenal's comment has survived in an allusion implying that when problems seem large, difficult, or unpleasant, we—or those in power—opt for distractions rather than a solution. Based on that explanation of the allusion, how would you interpret the following sentence: "Evita Perón knew how to distract the people of Argentina from her extravagant spending habits: If complaints about her free-spending ways began to surface, the people could always count on Evita for a rich diet of bread and circuses."

_____

_____

_____

Copyright © Cengage Learning. All rights reserved.

INTERNET FOLLOW-UP: How Does Compliance Relate to Social Impact Theory?

www

Look up "social impact theory" on Wikipedia. How does the Wikipedia entry relate to what you have read about compliance on pages 267–68? How does it add to your knowledge of compliance strategies? Does it confirm what you learned in the reading or suggest you should revise what you learned?

_____

_____

_____

_____

WORD CHECK I

The following words were introduced and defined in pages 253–68. See how well you can match the words with the meanings. When you finish, make sure to check the meanings of any words you missed because the same words will turn up in tests at the end of the chapter.

1. sacrilege _____

2. ingratiate _____

3. advocates _____

4. alleged _____

5. reputable _____

6. zealously _____

7. rapacious _____

8. havoc _____

9. throes _____

10. concession _____

a. supporters, believers

b. admission of agreement or defeat

c. trustworthy, respected, having a good reputation

d. to put oneself in a favorable light for others

e. claimed but not yet proven true

f. caught up in or in the midst of intense excitement

g. wide-ranging destruction

h. full of enthusiasm that is often excessive

i. treating religious objects with disrespect, expressing contempt or disrespect for objects or ideas sacred to others

j. greedy and destructive

Copyright © Cengage Learning. All rights reserved.

◆ **EXERCISE 4**   **More About Form and Meaning**

DIRECTIONS   Fill in the blanks with one of the words listed below.

sacrilege	ingratiate	allegedly	zealous	throes
havoc	advocate	reputable	rapacious	concessions

1. Someone who enters a religious shrine and smashes all the objects inside is guilty of committing _____.

2. Unfortunately, lawyers who advertise on television are not always _____.

3. People who have just recently taken up an exercise program are often extremely _____ for about a month before losing interest.

4. Cuddly and cute as they are, it seems wrong to use the word _____ to describe koala bears, but the adjective fits: The bears eat 2.5 pounds of eucalyptus leaves per day. Between the koala bears' appetite and global warming, supplies of the leaves are dwindling.

5. Showing up late for an interview without even offering a reason is no way to _____ yourself with a prospective employer.

6. The loss of electricity for almost twenty-four hours wreaked _____ with the schedule.

7. A willingness to make _____ is a key part of negotiating.

8. If a journalist reports that a person has just been arrested for a robbery but not yet proven guilty, then the person arrested is only _____ guilty.

9. It's appropriate to describe a person newly in love as being in the _____ of passion.

Copyright © Cengage Learning. All rights reserved.

10. A policy that blocks social networking sites in the workplace probably won't have many _____ under the age of thirty.

Summarizing Longer Readings

You already learned about summarizing in Chapter 1. Everything you learned from that chapter certainly still applies. However, if you are writing a summary for an assignment rather than reading notes, consider making a scratch list[†] of the reading's main ideas as your first step in summarizing. Once you have a list of all the main ideas, you can better determine the reading's underlying structure and decide what supporting details are essential to making the main ideas clear not just to you but also to another reader.

Making a Scratch List

For an illustration of how a scratch list, which is just a quickly jotted list of points, can help in summarizing, read the following selection. Then spend a few minutes studying the scratch list that follows.

The Disappearance of Carolyn Keene

1   When Judge Sonia Sotomayor was nominated to the Supreme Court in 2009, she was widely quoted for a number of reasons. Not the least among them was her reference to reading Nancy Drew mystery stories as a source of inspiration while growing up in New York City. The fictional Nancy Drew, who first appeared in print in 1930, encouraged the young Sotomayor, already struggling with juvenile diabetes and her father's early death, to think she could survive and overcome any emotional mishap or physical obstacle. As it turns out, this was a lesson Nancy Drew taught more than one famous woman. Writer and feminist Gloria Steinem has cited Nancy Drew as a role model; so, too, have the successful mystery writer Nevada Barr and Secretary of State Hillary Clinton.

2   Surprisingly, for such an old fictional character, Nancy's influence has continued. Nancy Drew books are still in print. They even appear

---

[†] The term *scratch list* means the list need not be grammatically correct. A scratch list is just a rough list of your ideas or someone else's ideas.

Copyright © Cengage Learning. All rights reserved.

in Apple's iTunes store. There are also Nancy Drew digital games. Like the books before them, the games have found a devoted female audience.

3   Given the intrepid* Nancy Drew's amazing longevity* and enduring popularity among teenage girls, one has to wonder about the author, Carolyn Keene. Was her success with the Nancy Drew series just luck or was Keene an especially astute creator of adolescent fiction, an author remarkably perceptive about the longings of the young female mind? Certainly Keene's fans seemed to think so: At the height of the series' popularity, fan letters for Carolyn Keene arrived by the carton full. What those young letter writers didn't know—and what the series' publisher, the Stratemeyer Syndicate, didn't tell them—was that Carolyn Keene didn't exist. Nancy Drew—and that may well be the secret of her ageless appeal—was the product of a three-person collaboration that began with the owner of the publishing company, Edward Stratemeyer. Stratemeyer, who had earned great success publishing books for adolescent boys, correctly understood that a new kind of woman was emerging in the late 1920s and young girls wanted and needed a new kind of fictional heroine. A remarkably astute businessman, Stratemeyer detected a fictional void* in the market, and he filled it with Nancy Drew, girl detective.

4   Always a man with a gift for spotting the current cultural trend, Stratemeyer took note when the roles of women began changing dramatically in the twenties, and young girls, looking for role models, wanted an active, assertive,* and determined heroine, who knew her own mind. As Stratemeyer first envisioned her in 1929, Nancy Drew was the perfect transitional figure for the historical moment when women were redefining themselves yet still anxious about the consequences of abandoning traditional notions of femininity. Nancy was a risk taker with a taste for adventure. However, she was also a traditional young girl with a desire for pretty clothes.

5   That, at least, was the broad general outline Stratemeyer created for Nancy's character. The details were to be worked out by a young ghost writer from Iowa, Mildred Wirt Benson, whom Stratemeyer had hired to write the series under his direction. Independent and free-spirited, Benson

---

*intrepid: brave, fearless.
*longevity: long life; length or duration of life.
*void: empty space; state of emptiness.
*assertive: outspoken, willing to speak one's mind.

Copyright © Cengage Learning. All rights reserved.

had been writing stories since she was fourteen years old and had paid for much of her college education by publishing short stories and news articles. In 1927, she became the first woman to receive a master's degree in journalism at the University of Iowa. In many ways, Benson—who got a commercial pilot's license in her mid-sixties—was the role model for Nancy Drew: She was smart, strong-willed, and adventurous. In her capacity as ghostwriter she bestowed those same characteristics on her heroine.

6   Benson wrote twenty-three of the first thirty Nancy Drew books, and practically from the start Nancy Drew outsold all of Stratemeyer's other successful adolescent series. As it so often is, conventional wisdom had been turned on its head. Adolescent fiction featuring girls could sell, and it could sell big.

7   But if Mildred Benson created a character that could grip a young girl's imagination, it was Stratemeyer's daughter Harriet who saw to it that Nancy Drew lived on into the present day. Like her father, Harriet was attentive to market trends, to what sold and what didn't. Along with her sister, who was largely a silent partner, Harriet had inherited her father's company after his death. It was Harriet who told Benson, early on, to stay away from the topic of Nancy getting married because readers would be outraged. However, by the forties, she was directing Benson to give Nancy more overt romance. Harriet thought the times were changing, and "modern" young girls wanted to see the relationship between Nancy and Ned Nickerson, her beau, heat up even if their romance didn't lead to the altar.

8   Harriet also made sure that the series didn't become dated. In the 1950s, she had the books reviewed and revised. She made sure that the newly modernized Nancy drove around in a convertible rather than a "roadster" and wore dresses instead of "frocks." Eliminated, too, were the offensive stereotypes about minorities, which were no longer acceptable to the modern reading public. In 1959, the newly updated Nancy Drew mysteries rolled off the assembly line, ready for the changing times right up to the present day.

Sample Scratch List ◆	Paragraph 1:	Numerous famous women have cited fictional heroine Nancy Drew as an influential role model.
	Paragraph 2:	New generation of young girls feel the same way.
	Paragraph 3:	Carolyn Keene didn't exist; Nancy was the product of collaboration.

Copyright © Cengage Learning. All rights reserved.

Paragraph 4:	Edward Stratemeyer recognized that times have changed and girls were looking for new role models.
Paragraph 5:	Using herself as a model, Mildred Wirt Benson gave Nancy an adventurous character.
Paragraph 6:	Nancy Drew's success proved adolescent fiction featuring girls could find a big market.
Paragraph 7:	Stratemeyer's daughter Harriet saw to it that Nancy reflected current trends and survived the passage of time.
Paragraph 8:	Harriet Stratemeyer made sure that the series was more up-to-date and free from stereotypes.

Analyzing the Scratch List

In this case, the scratch list highlights the fact that the first two paragraphs introduce related but quite different ideas. The list reveals, in other words, that the second paragraph doesn't develop the first—a clear indication that the first paragraph doesn't include the thesis statement.

In fact, it's only after paragraph 3 that the same thread of thought continues as the author adds details about what turns out to be the overall main idea of the reading: Nancy Drew was a three-person creation. The four paragraphs that follow the third pick up on that one main idea and describe each person's contribution to the Nancy Drew series.

For further proof that the main idea in paragraph 3 controls the entire reading, note how it helps explain the title. Notice, too, that it fits the reading's proportions. The other ideas listed get one or two paragraphs of explanation. The main idea in paragraph 3, in contrast, gets four paragraphs of development. That alone identifies it as the controlling main idea.

Once you have a clear sense of the overall main idea, you are in a better position to determine relationships among the remaining paragraphs. For instance, paragraphs 1 and 2 are mainly introductory. We don't hear any more about famous women who read Nancy Drew or digital games based on her character after the first two paragraphs. That means the material in paragraphs 1 and 2 doesn't have to appear in your summary unless, of course, you would like an introductory sentence

Copyright © Cengage Learning. All rights reserved.

or two, which would be your decision as a writer. Just make sure that the introduction doesn't take up too much space in your summary. By definition, a summary has to be shorter than the original. Overall, your focus should be on identifying the three creators of Nancy Drew and explaining what each one added to her character.

TAKING A CLOSER LOOK

Inferences and Examples

What does the author imply with the sentence in the last paragraph of the Nancy Drew reading when she talks about Harriet's making sure that the books referred to "a convertible rather than a 'roadster'" and "wore dresses instead of 'frocks'"?

_____

_____

Evaluating Details

The scratch list can also help you figure out what kinds of details your summary needs. Just take the main ideas in the supporting paragraphs one by one and ask yourself what crucial words or phrases need to be expanded in order to be generally understood by a reader unfamiliar with the original. Take, for instance, this main idea from paragraph 5: "Using herself as a model, Mildred Wirt Benson gave Nancy an adventurous character."

Imagining yourself as the reader of the summary, one who hasn't read the original selection, it's clear that you need an answer to this question: "What kind of model was Mildred Wirt Benson?" The phrase "adventurous character" provides some information, but you would need more specifics, maybe one or two sentences like the following: "Benson was a pioneer in journalism and had a spunky, independent nature. She managed to bestow that same spirit onto the fictional character of Nancy Drew."

Going through a scratch list in order to make decisions about what to include or leave out of your summary can be a huge help as long as you *remember that your imagined audience is not you.* It's the instructor who assigned the summary, and your instructor has probably not read

Copyright © Cengage Learning. All rights reserved.

the original article. Keeping your audience in mind will help you choose the most telling, or revealing, details. Those are the ones you want in a summary. Here to illustrate is an example:

Sample Summary: The Mystery of Carolyn Keene

Although it might still surprise some of her most devoted fans, Carolyn Keene, the alleged creator of the Nancy Drew series, which got its start in 1930, never existed. The figure of Nancy Drew that young girls have admired for generations was the fictional creation of three different minds: Edward Stratemeyer; Mildred Wirt Benson; and Harriet Stratemeyer, Edward's daughter.

Noting the changes in how women viewed themselves, Stratemeyer, a successful publisher of adolescent fiction, decided to launch a series about a girl detective. He made a detailed outline of the first plot but left the rest to a smart, young ghostwriter named Mildred Wirt Benson. Benson had a journalism degree and a spunky, independent nature. She seems to have bestowed her lively, adventurous spirit on the fictional Nancy Drew, who became a role model for young girls living in changing times.

But the decisions made by Harriet Stratemeyer, Edward's daughter, were also part of the reason the Nancy Drew series has survived. Harriet, like her father, noted the changing times and instructed Mildred to keep up with them. Harriet suggested that Nancy had to stay single yet still have a romance. She also had the books revised to get rid of dated expressions like "frock" and "roadster." More important, she eliminated the minority stereotypes, which, by the fifties, were acknowledged as offensive. Harriet Stratemeyer's revisions are one of the main reasons Nancy Drew has survived the march of time.

CHECK YOUR UNDERSTANDING

What purposes does a scratch list serve?

_____

_____

Copyright © Cengage Learning. All rights reserved.

♦ **EXERCISE 5**   **Identifying Thesis Statements and Writing Summaries**

DIRECTIONS   Read each selection. Underline the thesis statement and then summarize the reading in the blanks that follow.

1. **The Gains and Losses of Beauty**

1   No doubt about it, extremely good-looking people have a social advantage. They are less lonely; less socially anxious (especially about interactions with the opposite sex); more popular; more sexually experienced; and . . . more socially skilled (Feingold, 1992b). The social rewards for physical attractiveness appear to get off to an early start. Mothers of highly attractive newborns engage in more affectionate interactions with their babies than do mothers of less attractive infants (Langlois et al., 1995). Given such benefits, one would expect that the beautiful would also have a significant psychological advantage. But they don't. Physical attractiveness (as rated by objective judges) has little if any association with self-esteem, mental health, personality traits, or intelligence (Feingold, 1992b).

2   One possible reason why beauty doesn't affect psychological well-being is that actual physical attractiveness, as evaluated by others, may have less impact than self-perceived physical attractiveness. People who view themselves as physically attractive do report higher self-esteem and better mental health than those who believe they are unattractive (Feingold, 1992b). But other people's ratings of physical attractiveness are only modestly related to self-perceived attractiveness. When real beauties do not see themselves as beautiful, their appearance may not be psychologically valuable.

3   Physically attractive individuals may also fail to benefit from the social bias for beauty because of pressures they experience to maintain their appearance. In contemporary* American society, such pressures are particularly strong in regard to the body. Although both facial and bodily appearance contribute to perceived attractiveness, an unattractive body appears to be a greater liability* than an unattractive face (Alicke et al., 1986). Such a "body bias" can produce a healthy emphasis on nutrition and exercise. But it can sometimes lead to distinctly unhealthy consequences. For example, men may pop steroids to build up impressive muscles. Among women, the desire for a beautiful body often takes a different form.

---

*contemporary: modern, current; also a person living in the same age or era.
*liability: drawback. handicap.

Copyright © Cengage Learning. All rights reserved.

4   Women are more likely than men to suffer from what researcher Janet Polivy and her colleagues (1986) call the "modern mania for slenderness." This desire for thinness is promoted by the mass media. Popular female characters in TV shows are more likely than popular male characters to be exceedingly thin; women's magazines stress the need to maintain a slender body more than do men's magazines (Silverstein et al., 1986b). Thus some good-looking women suffer, despite their good looks, because they don't feel their body is thin enough. (Adapted from Brehm and Kassim, *Social Psychology*, p. 180.)

Summary

_____

_____

_____

_____

_____

_____

_____

_____

2. But If It's Natural, It Must Be Good for You

1   Depending on who's doing the estimating, Americans spend between $5 and $10 billion per year on herbal supplements with funny-sounding names like echinacea, ginseng, and golden seal. The production, marketing, and selling of herbal supplements is a lucrative* business with countless people consuming a variety of herbal medicines in an effort to cure both minor and major health problems. Yet herbal medicines are not regulated by the Food and Drug Administration. In fact, few scientific studies are available to prove their curative powers. There are even fewer to detect the possibility that some herbal medications might cause harm.

2   Amazingly, American consumers don't seem to care that there is so little empirical* evidence backing up claims for herbal medicines. Generally, consumers don't even seem worried about the ill effects of ingesting herbs.

_____

*lucrative: profitable.
*empirical: based on experiment, observation, and fact.
*assumption: widely held belief that is left unstated and rarely questioned.

Copyright © Cengage Learning. All rights reserved.

The reigning assumption* is that herbs are natural and anything natural can't hurt you. However, that assumption is misguided, even dangerous—just try ingesting a leaf of "natural" poison ivy. If they really want to take care of their health, consumers should demand more proof that herbal supplements can do what their makers claim. More to the point, consumers should wonder about the side effects of taking supplements that have not undergone much, if any, rigorous testing.

3   The herb widely known as comfrey, for example, is sold as a gel or an ointment for treating minor cuts and burns. To be sure, comfrey does contain allantoin, a chemical that aids in skin repair. However, comfrey is also sold as a treatment for ulcers and stomach upsets, even though there is no compelling evidence that it can help either condition. On the contrary, some evidence shows that it can destroy liver cells, so ingesting it might be extremely dangerous. Still, you are unlikely to find any warning label on a bottle of comfrey tablets, and the herb is a popular item in natural food stores.

4   It's been widely claimed that another herbal supplement, ginseng, can improve memory and mood while also boosting energy. In Germany, where there is a formal body that regulates the sale of herbal medicine, ginseng has undergone repeated testing, and the herb seems to live up to claims about its benefits. The problem with ginseng is less that the claims are exaggerated and more that authentic ginseng is hard to find and extremely expensive. Thus a bottle of tablets or powder labeled as ginseng may have very little of the herb but quite a few additives, or fillers, and some of those additives might not be altogether harmless.

5   Anyone who thinks of herbs as "all natural" and therefore harmless should also recall what happened several years ago to some of those who took an alleged weight-loss herb known as ephedra or ma hung. Ephedra contains ephedrine, a substance that acts as a stimulant to the body and seems to encourage weight loss. But the amount of ephedrine in each plant varies according to the conditions under which the herb was grown. If a particular batch of the herb contains extremely high levels of ephedrine, then ingesting the herb can cause both blood pressure and heart rate to soar.

6   No wonder then that ephedra caused at least 800 people to have problems such as fluctuating* blood pressure, dizziness, and heart rhythm irregularities. When ephedra was being marketed as one of the components of "herbal phen-fen," an allegedly miraculous, "all natural"

_____

*fluctuating: changing, going up and down.

Copyright © Cengage Learning. All rights reserved.

diet drug, scores of people who used it suffered permanent heart valve damage. At least a dozen people died as a result of taking the dietary supplement, which is more proof that the label "all natural" does not equal safe for human consumption. (Source of statistics: Christian Millman, "Remedies: Natural Disasters," *Men's Health* (14), April 1, 1999, pp. 90, 92, 94.)

Summary

_____

_____

_____

_____

_____

_____

_____

_____

_____

_____

_____

_____

_____

_____

_____

TAKING A CLOSER LOOK

Implied Questions
Paragraph 2 of the reading on beauty begins to answer what implied question?

_____

CHECK YOUR UNDERSTANDING

What's the difference between a scratch list of the main ideas in a reading and an outline of them?

_____

Copyright © Cengage Learning. All rights reserved.

WORD CHECK II

The following words were introduced and defined in pages 277–84. See how well you can match the words with the meanings. When you finish, make sure to check the meanings of any words you missed because the same words will turn up in tests at the end of the chapter.

1. intrepid	_____	a.	changing; going up and down
2. longevity	_____	b.	widely held belief that is left unstated and rarely questioned
3. void	_____		
4. assertive	_____	c.	based on observation, fact, and experiment
5. contemporary	_____	d.	profitable
6. liability	_____	e.	modern, current; also a person living in the same age or era
7. lucrative	_____		
8. empirical	_____	f.	empty space or opening; state of emptiness
9. assumption	_____	g.	long life; length or duration of life
10. fluctuating	_____	h.	handicap, drawback
		i.	brave, fearless
		j.	outspoken, willing to speak one's mind

◆ **EXERCISE 6** **More About Form and Meaning**

DIRECTIONS   Fill in the blanks with one of the words listed below.

> longevity   empiricist   fluctuations   intrepid   lucrative
> assertiveness   contemporary   liability   assumptions   void

1. Who among the following could not be called a(n) _____ president: Bill Clinton, George W. Bush, Jimmy Carter, or Thomas Jefferson?

2. The word _____ is used to describe gains and losses in stocks, weight, and price.

3. For a young girl determined to play professional basketball, being average height would be considered a(n) _____.

Copyright © Cengage Learning. All rights reserved.

4. Action heroes in movies are expected to be _____;
   if they aren't, audiences want their money back.

5. In analyzing other people's arguments, we are quick to challenge
   their underlying _____; what's harder to do is recognize and examine our own.

6. Most people dream of making _____ investments;
   except to save on taxes, not too many people search out those that
   have low earnings.

7. In Shakespeare's play *Othello*, the villain Iago tells Othello that his
   wife has been unfaithful and Othello responds by saying that he
   wants "ocular proof," or evidence that can be seen with the eye.
   That makes Othello a(n) _____.

8. If your best friend, whom you saw almost every day at both school
   and work, suddenly moved far away, there would probably be
   a(n) _____ in your life.

9. In January 2010, the world's oldest living dog, according to
   the *Guinness Book of World Records* at least, was put to sleep.
   Otto was twenty years and eleven months, which is remarkable
   _____ for a dog.

10. Someone who speaks out and states an opinion while knowing
    that everyone else in the room disagrees probably doesn't need any
    _____ training.

ALLUSION ALERT

Impressionism

The reading that follows will compare remembering to an impressionist painting. To make sense of that allusion, you need to know that the
impressionist painters belonged to a nineteenth-century movement that
turned away from realistic-looking paintings in favor of putting their
personal impressions of the world on canvas, often using brushstrokes
that made the world seem composed of tiny pieces like a mosaic.†

---

†mosaic: picture composed out of colored stones.

Copyright © Cengage Learning. All rights reserved.

DIGGING DEEPER Can We Trust Our Memories?

Looking Ahead Chapter 1 described how paraphrasing and note-taking could act as memory aids. The following reading tells you more about the workings of memory. The more you know about memory, the better equipped you are to make use of techniques that enhance your ability to remember what you read.

1 Although we'd like to think that our memories accurately reflect events we've witnessed or experienced, our recollections may not be as reliable as we believe them to be. Contemporary memory researchers reject the view that long-term memory works like a video camera that records exact copies of experience. Their view, generally called **constructionist theory**, holds that memory is a reconstructive process. What we recall from memory is not a replica of the past but a re-creation, or *reconstruction*, of the past. We stitch together bits and pieces of information stored in long-term memory to form a coherent, or unified, account of past experiences and events. Reconstruction, however, can lead to distorted memories of events and experiences.

2 According to constructionist theory, memories are not carbon copies of reality. From this vantage point, it is not surprising that people who witness the same event or read the same material may have very different memories of the event or of the passage they read. Nor would it be surprising if recollections of your childhood are not verbatim records of what actually occurred but rather reconstructions based on pieces of information from many sources—from old photographs, from what your mother told you about the time you fell from the tree when you were ten, and so on.

3 Constructionist theory leads us to expect that memories may be distorted. These distortions can range from simplifications, to omissions of details, to outright fabrications or lies (Koriat & Goldsmith, 1996). Even so, we shouldn't presume that all memories are distorted. Some may be more or less accurate reflections of events. Others, perhaps most, can be likened more to impressionist paintings than to mental snapshots of experiences.

Recovery of Repressed Memories

4 Controversy has swirled around the issue of whether long-repressed memories of childhood experiences that suddenly surface in adulthood are credible. In most cases, such memories come to light during hypnosis

Copyright © Cengage Learning. All rights reserved.

or psychotherapy. On the basis of recovered memories of sexual trauma in childhood, authorities have brought charges of sexual abuse against hundreds of people. A number of these cases have resulted in convictions and long jail sentences, even in the absence of corroborating, or supporting, evidence. But should recovered memories be taken at face value?

5   A total lack of memory of traumatic childhood events is rare, although it is possible that such memories may be lost in some cases (Bradley & Follingstad, 2001; Wakefield & Underwager, 1996). We also know that false memories can be induced in many subjects in experimental studies (Loftus, 1997; Zoellner, Foa, Brigidi, & Przeworski, 2000). Entire events that never happened can enter a subject's memory and seem just as real and accurate as memories of events that really did occur. However, evidence of false memory creation in experimental studies does not prove that recovered memories in actual cases are, in fact, false.

6   In sum, many investigators believe that some recovered memories may be genuine and that others are undoubtedly false (L. S. Brown, 1997; L. J. Rubin, 1996; Scheflin & Brown, 1996). The problem is that in the absence of corroborating evidence, we simply lack the tools to differentiate between true memories and false ones (American Psychological Association, 1995; Loftus, 1993a; Loftus & Ketcham, 1994).

7   From a constructionist standpoint, we should not be surprised that memories may be distorted, even when the person believes them to be true. The use of suggestive interviewing or therapeutic techniques or hypnosis can heighten suggestibility to false memories. Psychologists and other mental health professionals need to be cautious about assuming the veracity of recovered memories and vigilant about monitoring their own roles so that they don't contribute to the construction of false memories.

(Adapted from Nevid, *Psychology: Concepts and Applications*, pp. 229–33.)

Sharpening Your Skills

DIRECTIONS   Answer the following questions by circling the letter of the correct response or filling in the blanks.

1. Based on the context, how would you define the word *replica* in the following sentence? "What we recall from memory is not a *replica* of the past but a re-creation, or *reconstruction*, of the past" (paragraph 1).

   a. copy

   b. remainder

   c. memory

   d. thought

Copyright © Cengage Learning. All rights reserved.

2. In paragraph 2, which two phrases restate the word *replica* in paragraph 1?

   _____

3. Based on the context, how would you define the word *corroborating* in the following sentence? "The problem is that in the absence of *corroborating* evidence, we simply lack the tools to differentiate between true memories and false ones" (paragraph 6).

   a. irrelevant

   b. challenging

   c. supporting

   d. distracting

4. What is the topic of the reading?

   _____

5. Which of the following sentences best expresses the main idea of the entire reading?

   a. Memory researchers believe that with enough effort, we can avoid distorting our memories of past events. However, to avoid distorting, or mis-remembering, the past, we have to pay attention to what happens in the present.

   b. Recovered memories, despite the controversy surrounding them, are authentic.

   c. Memory researchers now believe that when we remember, we combine bits of information stored in long-term memory in order to re-create some version of past experience that makes sense.

   d. In contrast to the constructionist theory of memory, new research suggests that we store exact copies of our experiences in long-term memory.

6. Which paragraph introduces the thesis statement?

   a. paragraph 1

   b. paragraph 2

   c. paragraph 3

Copyright © Cengage Learning. All rights reserved.

7. What two reversal or contrast transitions appear in paragraph 1?

   _____

8. What is the primary pattern of organization in paragraph 1?
   a. simple listing
   b. definition
   c. comparison and contrast
   d. classification

9. What is the author's answer to the question posed in the title? _____
   Please explain.

   _____

   _____

   _____

10. What is the author's purpose?
    a. to inform
    b. to persuade

What Do You Think? Based on what you have read here, do you think the authors would consider fair a guilty verdict based solely on testimony from a witness who had recovered his or her repressed memory of rape? Please explain.

   _____

   _____

   _____

   _____

Copyright © Cengage Learning. All rights reserved.

▶ **TEST 1**   **Reviewing New Vocabulary**

DIRECTIONS   Fill in the blanks with one of the words below.

assumption	fluctuations	zealous	rapacious	longevity
lucrative	ingratiate	void	advocates	contemporary
alleged	liability	havoc	throes	assertive
empirical	intrepid	sacrilegious	concede	reputable

1. **Boom and Bust in the 1920s Stock Market**

1   Throughout the 1920s, the stock market experienced an
unprecedented boom. While historically the American economy

had experienced intense, boom-and-bust _____ ,
most of those investing in the stock market during the twenties
seemed to be undergoing a bout of amnesia. Among investors, the

_____ was that the boom would go on forever. Pouring

money into the market, the most _____ investors
assured one another that stock-market crashes were a thing of the
past. Financial depressions and crashes belonged to the country's

history but would play no part in _____ life, they
insisted. To disagree with that optimistic prediction was considered

_____ , so convinced were investors that they could

keep on making the _____ investments that had
amassed huge fortunes over the last decade.

2   But then came 1929 and Black Tuesday. Suddenly the country

plunged into the _____ of a financial depression,
the like of which had not been seen since the 1870s. Even the most

_____ and _____ of investors backed
away from the market. However, it was too late. Not just the stock market
but the entire country seemed to be plunging into a bottomless

_____ of misery. With even the richest Americans feeling
the financial pinch, the poorest wondered how they were going to get
enough to eat. By 1933, stocks had hit rock bottom, and the most devoted

fan of stock-market investment had to _____ that the
risks had been much greater than anticipated. Stocks were now worth
only 20 percent of their original value.

Copyright © Cengage Learning. All rights reserved.

3   By the time Franklin D. Roosevelt was inaugurated in 1933, the entire banking system had ceased to function. Checks, even those written on accounts of very _____ banks, were worthless as payment because no one knew for sure if the banks had the funds to make the checks good. In response to this liquidity crisis,[†] the government set up the Federal Deposit Insurance Corporation (FDIC) to eliminate bank "runs," where investors lined up to get their money and banks ran out of cash. The federal government also banned commercial banks from investing depositors' money in stocks so that banks could no longer lose that money in the market.[†] It took time and a good deal of federal money, but the country eventually emerged from its devastating financial collapse.

2. General Motors and the Fate of the Corvair

1   In the early 1950s, U.S. automakers seemed to believe that Americans would buy only big cars. However, automakers realized their mistake when compact imports like Germany's Volkswagen Beetle began winning a substantial share of the U.S. market. In response to the European threat, General Motors introduced the Corvair, a car meant to compete with the Beetle. With an engine made almost entirely of aluminum, the car was both lightweight and durable.

2   Initially the Corvair was a hit. *Motor Trend* magazine named it Car of the Year in 1960, and GM's new compact car looked like it might have serious _____ as a market favorite. However, it wasn't long before rumors began to surface. It was _____ that the car had handling problems and skidded on curves. Aware that such rumors could prove a serious _____ to success in the marketplace, General Motors completely redesigned the car, focusing particularly on the rear suspension in order to make the Corvair more stable. In 1964, GM debuted the 1965 second-generation Corvair. Once again the car appeared to have a bright future.

3   But then disaster struck. A(n) _____, young lawyer named Ralph Nader published *Unsafe at Any Speed*, an attack on the auto industry's safety record. To GM's dismay, the entire first chapter was devoted to the Corvair's handling problems. And Nader wasn't just repeating rumors. He had _____ proof in the form of a GM

[†]A liquidity crisis means there is no cash available.
[†]Most of the safeguards instituted by the Roosevelt administration were eventually eliminated, and some people think that's one reason for the financial crash of 2008.

Copyright © Cengage Learning. All rights reserved.

whistle-blower named George Caramagna, an engineer at the company, who had documented the Corvair's handling problems and fought with management about changing the design. In the end, it didn't matter that GM had changed the design and that the Corvair suspension Nader described was on the older models, not the newer ones. The book wreaked

_____ with the Corvair's sales. They dropped by half. By 1969 the car was no longer on the market.

4   The Corvair may be gone, but it's never quite been forgotten. It still has

passionate _____, who love the car and sing its praises. Some have gone to extreme lengths to prove their devotion. Rose Martin so loved her Corvair, she was buried in it in 1998. Needless to say, Ralph

Nader did not _____ himself with the car's fans when he wrote a book that forever tarnished the Corvair's reputation. (Source of decline in sales: www.conceptcarz.com/vehicle/z7043/chevrolet-corvair.aspx.)

Copyright © Cengage Learning. All rights reserved.

▶ **TEST 2**

Identifying the Controlling Main Idea and Author's Purpose

DIRECTIONS Circle the appropriate letter to identify the main idea of each selection. Then identify the reading's primary purpose by writing an *I* (inform) or a *P* (persuade) in the blank at the end of the paragraph.

1. Marital Satisfaction in New Families

1 Almost all studies that measure marital satisfaction before and after the birth of the first child have found that the birth of a child is a mixed marital blessing (Cowan & Cowan, 1988). Jay Belsky and Michael Rovine (1990) found that couples who were least satisfied with their marriages before the birth were most likely to report a decline in satisfaction after. Problems that existed before were likely to have been magnified by the additional stresses brought on by the birth.

2 Babies, however, do not appear to create severe marital distress where none existed before; nor do they bring couples with distressed marriages closer together. Rather, the early postpartum months bring on a period of disorganization and change. The leading conflict in these first months of parenthood is division of labor in the family. Couples may regain their sense of equilibrium in marriage by successfully negotiating how they will divide the new responsibilities. Husbands' participation in child and home care seems to be positively related to marital satisfaction after the birth. One study found that the more the men shared in doing family tasks, the more satisfied were the wives at six and eighteen months postpartum and the husbands at eighteen months postpartum (Cowan & Cowan, 1988).

3 While many couples experience a difficult transition to parenthood, they also find parenthood rewarding. Children affect parents in ways that lead to personal growth; allow for the reworking of childhood conflicts; build flexibility and empathy; and provide intimate, loving human connections. They also provide a lot of pleasure. In follow-up interviews of new parents when their children were eighteen months old, Philip Cowan and Carolyn Cowan (1988) found that almost every man and woman spoke of the delight they felt from knowing their child and watching him or her develop. They reported feeling pride for and closeness to their spouses, more adult with their own parents, and a renewed sense of purpose at work. (Adapted from Seifert et al., *Lifespan Development*, p. 488.) _____

a. Studies of marital happiness suggest that children are the key to a happy marriage.

Copyright © Cengage Learning. All rights reserved.

b. While the birth of a first child is a plus for a marriage, more than one child can be a strain.

c. Studies of marital happiness suggest that a baby can unite an unhappy couple.

d. Studies of marital satisfaction suggest that the birth of a child has both positive and negative effects.

2. **A Subprime Glossary for the Mortgage Scandal**

1   "Subprime" was voted the word of the year in 2008 by the American Dialect Society in recognition of the mortgage scandal and crisis that . . . enveloped housing and real estate around the country. But that umbrella term describing cheap—often suspiciously cheap—mortgages, encompasses a whole glossary of often-colorful expressions that could be described as *sub subprime*. They reflect the deceit, cynicism, and scandalous exploitation that is taking the homes of many thousands, perhaps millions of families.

2   Some other words, words that betoken possible rescue and relief, are also finally entering the vocabulary. Meanwhile, people everywhere—a widow in the Bronx who needs money for a new roof or a young couple in San Diego looking for their first home—confront an array of bewildering, often deceptive practices described by subprime words like the following.

3   *Exploding ARM* sounds violent and is for many families. It describes an adjustable-rate mortgage for which the interest rate goes up so fast that borrowers who could afford the monthly payments for the original mortgage are driven out of their homes. For example, a typical $100,000 loan at 4.5 percent would call for a monthly payment of $500. The same loan at 7.5 percent would cost $700.

4   *Foreclosure rescue* sounds benevolent but it's not, says Sarah Ludwig, director of the Neighborhood Economic Development Advocacy Project in New York. On the contrary, "Typically, it's a scam to steal a home," in which the owner is gulled into signing over title to the house in exchange for promises to pay off the arrears [unpaid mortgage debt].

5   *Jingle mail* is the answer. What's the question? Listen to Gretchen Morgenson of *The [New York] Times*, who has written scathingly about the subprime scandal since it first surfaced: What do banks call it when troubled borrowers abandon their homes? Sending them the keys.

6   *Liars' loans* describes one form of come-on to potential home buyers. Joe Nocera, *The [New York] Times* business columnist, describes these

Copyright © Cengage Learning. All rights reserved.

loans offered by banks that have "practically begged borrowers to fib about their income."

7   *Ninja loans,* short for No Income, No Job or Assets, is the sardonic* way people in the business describe poorly documented loans that were blithely made to high-risk borrowers.

8   *No-docs loans* and *low-docs loans* are variations on the same theme, mortgage loans made by lenders hungry to get in on the action during the real-estate boom years. Another variation: *stated-income loans,* for which lenders simply took borrowers' claims at face value and did not even pretend to ask for documentation of their ability to pay. (Rosenthal, "No Docs," *The New York Times Magazine,* August 17, 2008, p. 18.) _____

a. The mortgage crisis which gripped America starting in 2008 generated a host of new words that have entered the English language.

b. The mortgage crisis which gripped America starting in 2008 spawned a number of new terms, all of them suggesting the corruption at the heart of the crisis.

c. Most people believe that banks require strict documentation for all mortgage claims; however, that's not always been the case in the past.

d. The words generated by the mortgage crisis that began in 2008 all sound as if they represent good things, but, in fact, the opposite is true.

---

*sardonic: mocking, scornful, ironic.

Copyright © Cengage Learning. All rights reserved.

▶ **TEST 3**   **Recognizing Thesis Statements and Supporting Details**

DIRECTIONS   Underline the thesis statement. Then answer the questions by filling in the blanks or circling the letter of the correct response. *Note*: To decide if a detail is major or minor, you will probably need to look at the sentences in the context of the paragraphs where they appear. The numbers in parentheses identify the paragraph where each detail appears.

1. **Feminist Objections to Pornography**

1   Beginning around 1978, some—though not all—feminists became very critical of pornography and many remain so to this day. Although many younger feminists do not share the early generation's strong objections to pornographic literature and films, those who are opposed are vehement in their sense that pornography is a direct threat to the lives of women. In support of their claim, they offer four basic objections to the idea that pornography does no harm.

2   First, they argue that pornography debases women. Even milder, softcore pornography portrays women as sex objects, whose breasts, legs, and buttocks can be purchased for the viewing entertainment of men. Those who object to the sale of pornographic films argue that watching naked women for entertainment encourages disrespect for women in general.

3   The second objection revolves around the way pornography associates sex with violence toward women. As such, some feminists argue, it contributes to rape and other forms of violence against women and girls. Long-time feminist Robin Morgan says bluntly, "Pornography is the theory and rape is the practice" (1980, p. 139).

4   According to the third objection, pornography glamorizes unequal power relationships between women and men. A common theme in pornography is that of men forcing women to have sex. Thus the power of men and subordination of women is emphasized. Consistent with this point, feminists do not object to sexual materials that portray women and men sharing a balance of power.

5   Feminists also argue that pornography may serve to perpetuate traditional gender roles. By seeing or reading about dominant males and obedient dehumanized females, men are encouraged to devalue women. Even worse for future generations, adolescent boys are being encouraged to think of themselves as the controlling figure in sexual relationships.

(Adapted from Hyde, *Understanding Human Sexuality*, p. 524.)

Copyright © Cengage Learning. All rights reserved.

1. Based on the title, what question should you use to guide your reading?

   _____

2. In your own words, what is the main idea of the reading?

   _____

   _____

3. What clue in the thesis statement should you use to identify the major details?

   _____

4. Which of the following is *not* a major detail?
   a. Pornography associates sex with violence toward women (3).
   b. Robin Morgan put it bluntly: "Pornography is the theory and rape is the practice" (3).

5. Which of the following is a minor detail?
   a. Feminists argue that pornography debases women (2).
   b. Pornography glamorizes unequal power relationships (4).
   c. A common theme in pornography is that of men forcing women to have sex (4).

2. The Meaning of Touch

1   Touching and being touched is an essential part of being human. However, the amount and meaning of touch change with age, purpose, and location. Infants and their parents, for example, engage in extensive touching behavior, but this decreases during adolescence. The amount of touching behavior increases after adolescence as young people begin to establish romantic relationships. No matter how much we are touched, however, most of us want to be touched more than we are.

2   In general, the meaning of touch varies with the situation, and there are five basic categories of meaning. *Positive affective touches* transmit messages of support, appreciation, affection, or sexual intent. *Playful touches* help calm and lighten our interactions with others. *Control touches*

Copyright © Cengage Learning. All rights reserved.

are used to get other people's attention and to gain their compliance. *Ritualistic touches* are those we use during everyday rituals such as greeting others and saying goodbye. *Task-related touches* are those that are necessary for us to complete tasks on which we are working, like shaking hands after coming to an agreement. Touches also can fit into more than one category at a time.

3   Age, sex, and location also influence the amount people touch. To illustrate, people between eighteen and twenty-five and between thirty and forty report the most touching, while old people report the least. Women find touching more pleasant than men do, as long as the other person is not a stranger. Finally, people who live in the South touch more than people who live in the North.

4   The United States is generally a non-contact culture. There are, however, situations in which people are likely to touch. People are more likely to touch, for example, when giving information or advice than they are when receiving it. People are more likely to touch others when giving orders than when receiving orders, when asking for a favor than when granting a favor, or when trying to persuade others than when being persuaded. (Adapted from Gudykunst et al., *Building Bridges*, pp. 319–20.)

1. Based on the title, what question would you use to guide your reading?

   _____

   _____

2. In your own words, what is the main idea of the reading?

   _____

   _____

3. Which of the following is a major detail?
   a. People who live in the South touch more than do people who live in the North (3).
   b. Age, sex, and region influence the amount people touch (3).
   c. People are more likely to touch, for example, when giving information or advice (4).

Copyright © Cengage Learning. All rights reserved.

4. Which of the following is a major detail?

    a. In general, the meaning of touch varies with the situation, and there are five basic categories of meaning (2).

    b. We can, for example, touch others as part of a ritual to express positive affection (2).

    c. People between eighteen and twenty-five and between thirty and forty report the most touching (3).

5. Which of the following is a minor detail?

    a. Women find touching more pleasant than men do, as long as the other person is not a stranger (3).

    b. The amount and meaning of touch change with age, purpose, and location (1).

    c. Age, sex, and location also influence the amount people touch (3).

Copyright © Cengage Learning. All rights reserved.

⬥ TEST 4   Identifying Thesis Statements and Creating Informal Outlines

DIRECTIONS   Read each selection and underline the thesis statement. In the blanks that follow, create an informal outline of the reading.

1. World War II: Interning Japanese Americans

1   Compared with previous wars, the nation's wartime civil liberties record during World War II showed some improvement, particularly where African Americans and women were concerned. But there was one enormous exception: the treatment of 120,000 Japanese Americans. The internment of Japanese Americans in isolated camps was not based on any evidence of treason; their crime was solely their race—the fact that they were of Japanese descent.

2   Popular racial stereotypes used to fuel the war effort held that Japanese people abroad and at home were sneaky and evil, and the American people generally regarded Japan as the chief enemy of the United States. Moreover, the feeling was widespread that the Japanese had to be repaid for the bombing of Pearl Harbor. Thus, with a few notable exceptions, there was no public outcry over the relocation and internment of Japanese Americans.

3   Yet there were two obvious reasons why the imprisonment of Japanese Americans was completely unnecessary. First and foremost, there was absolutely no evidence of any attempt by Japanese Americans to hinder the American war effort. The government's own studies proved that fact beyond question. Thus, it's not surprising that in places where racism was not a factor—in Hawaii, for example—the public outcry for internment was much more muted.

4   Second, Japanese-American soldiers fought valiantly for the United States. The all Japanese-American 442nd Regimental Combat Team—heavily recruited from young men in internment camps—was the most decorated unit of its size in the armed forces. Suffering heavy casualties in Italy and France, members of the 442nd were awarded a Congressional Medal of Honor, several Distinguished Service Crosses, 350 Silver Stars, and more than 3,600 Purple Hearts. (Adapted from Norton et al., *A People and a Nation*, p. 795.)

Main Idea   _____

_____

Supporting Details   _____

_____

Copyright © Cengage Learning. All rights reserved.

_____

_____

_____

_____

_____

_____

_____

_____

_____

2. Phobias Can Be Crippling

1   *Phobias* are intense and irrational fears of everything from spiders to open spaces. Some of the more common phobias are fear of heights, blood, flying, dogs, and enclosed spaces. The key element distinguishing a phobia from a normal fear is irrationality. Simply put, phobias are not based on reason. For instance, someone who is phobic about spiders would be just as terrified by a harmless daddy longlegs as by a deadly tarantula. In the United States, phobias are the most prevalent of the anxiety disorders. They affect 7 to 10 percent of adults and children (Kessler et al., 1994; Robins et al., 1984; U.S. Surgeon General, 1999).

2   Perhaps the most disabling phobia is agoraphobia. Agoraphobia is an intense fear of going too far from a safe place like one's home; of being away from a familiar person, such as a spouse or close friend; or of being in a place from which departure might be difficult or help unavailable. For those who suffer from agoraphobia, leaving home causes extreme anxiety. Agoraphobics are often severely housebound. Theaters, shopping malls, public transportation, and other potentially crowded places are especially threatening. Most individuals who suffer from agoraphobia also have a history of panic attacks. In fact, their intense fear of public places starts partly because they don't want to go where they have to endure the embarassment of a panic attack while other people are around.

3   Social phobias revolve around the fear of being negatively evaluated by others or acting in a way that is embarrassing or humiliating. This anxiety is so intense and persistent that it impairs the person's normal functioning. *Common social phobias* are fear of public speaking or performance ("stage fright"), fear of eating in front of others, and fear of using public restrooms

Copyright © Cengage Learning. All rights reserved.

(Kleinknecht, 2000). A *generalized social phobia* is a more severe form in that victims experience fear in virtually all social situations (Mannuzzi et al., 1995). Sociocultural factors can alter the form of social phobias. For example, in Japan, where cultural training emphasizes group-oriented values and goals, a common social phobia is *taijin kyofusho*—fear of embarrassing those around you (Kleinknecht, 1994). (Adapted from Bernstein et al., *Psychology*, pp. 566–67.)

Main Idea

_____

_____

Supporting Details

_____

_____

_____

_____

_____

_____

_____

_____

_____

_____

_____

_____

_____

Copyright © Cengage Learning. All rights reserved.

▶ **TEST 5**   **Creating Scratch Lists of Main Ideas**

> **DIRECTIONS**   Read each excerpt and complete the scratch list that
> follows.

1. Taking a Conversational Turn

1   Have you ever conversed with another person who wouldn't stop talking?
If so, you may have wondered whether that person was clueless, obnoxious,
or just playing by a different set of cultural rules. Whatever the reason for
such behavior, lopsided conversations usually remind us that turn-taking
is a fundamental part of the give-and-take we expect from others in our
everyday interactions. Because most people don't verbalize intentions
to speak or listen, learning to navigate conversational twists and turns
can be a real challenge. The signals we use to regulate the flow of speech
consist largely of verbal cues and gestures.

2   When we are speaking and want to continue speaking, we use signals
that communicate our intention to listeners. These signals prevent unwanted
interruptions. They include raising the volume of our voice, uttering *um*'s and
ah's, continuing to gesture, gazing away from the listener, and so on.

3   However, if we don't want to continue speaking, we can relinquish our
turn by dropping the volume and pitch of our voice, slowing the tempo of
our speech, pausing, not gesturing, making eye contact with a listener, or
raising our eyebrows. These are turn-yielding signals. Some research shows
that those in conversation are more inclined to take turns when speakers
use these signals (Duncan, 1972).

4   As listeners, we also employ turn-taking signals. To express a desire to
stop listening and speak, we employ various turn-requesting signals. These
signals include an open mouth, audible inhalations, a raised index finger
or hand, leaning forward, making eye contact, quickened or exaggerated
head nods, and simultaneous speech (i.e., listener's speech overlaps the
speaker's). (Adapted from Remland, *Nonverbal Communication in Everyday Life*, pp. 255–56.)

Scratch List

Paragraph 1   _____

_____

Paragraph 2   _____

_____

Copyright © Cengage Learning. All rights reserved.

Paragraph 3 _____

_____

Paragraph 4 _____

_____

2. Suntans: Are They Worth It?

1 Every year millions of fair-skinned people spend millions of hours trying to acquire a tan. A gold, glowing tan is highly prized and much admired. It makes the teeth appear whiter, the eyes seem brighter, and the complexion smoother. Troubled skin is also likely to improve with a tan, probably because the sun's drying effect reduces the number of microorganisms on the skin. . . . For that matter, just getting a tan can be a relaxing and pleasant experience if tanning takes place on a vacation beach rather than in the backyard. But while tanning may be beneficial to the psyche, the notion that a suntan is a sign of good health is false. On the contrary, tanning can irreparably affect the appearance of the skin and set the stage for the development of skin cancer.

2 Even if a person doesn't get an annual "terrific tan," there is a visible difference in the appearance of the skin on the face, head, neck, arms, and hands that has always been exposed to the sun in comparison to the skin on the abdomen, which rarely sees the light of day. Skin that has always been protected by clothing is still "baby skin"—softer, smoother, and finer textured. If this is the normal difference between covered and uncovered skin, imagine what will happen to the skin of sun worshippers after years of ritual tanning. Getting a gorgeous tan in one's twenties can result in premature wrinkled, leathery looking skin in one's forties.

3 The relationship between ultraviolet radiation and skin cancer is well-established. Eighty to 90 percent of basal- and squamous-cell cancers occur on the parts of the body that are exposed to the sun. The incidence of skin malignancies in this country has increased, and it is no coincidence that so too has the number of tennis players, joggers, golfers, swimmers, and sunbathers, along with the time spent in outdoor sports and activities. It's also not surprising that more cases of the disease occur in southern areas of the country, where there is more sun and greater exposure.

4 Obviously, other factors besides ultraviolet radiation are involved in skin cancer. The disease sometimes occurs on areas of the body not exposed to the sun, and there are devoted sunbathers who never get the disease. As

Copyright © Cengage Learning. All rights reserved.

with all cancers, there are probably genetic or environmental factors that combine with the damaging effects of ultraviolet rays. Although there is no way of predicting whether frequent sunburns during youth will result in skin cancer in the later years, there is evidence that even several short exposures to hot sun can cause a malignancy. (Adapted from Sloane, *Biology of Women*, p. 530.)

Scratch List

Paragraph 1 _____

_____

Paragraph 2 _____

_____

Paragraph 3 _____

_____

Paragraph 4 _____

_____

Copyright © Cengage Learning. All rights reserved.

▶ **TEST 6**   **Writing Summaries**

DIRECTIONS   Study your scratch lists from the previous readings to determine which sentence is the controlling or overall main idea. Then summarize each reading on the lines below.

Summary   1. _____

_____

_____

_____

_____

_____

_____

_____

Summary   2. _____

_____

_____

_____

_____

_____

_____

_____

Copyright © Cengage Learning. All rights reserved.

◗ **TEST 7**   **Taking Stock**

DIRECTIONS   Read the following selection. Then answer the questions by circling the letter(s) of the correct response(s).

The Benefits of Sleep

1   In our modern society, it's difficult to get enough sleep. We lead busy, overworked lives and often have to forgo sleep to get everything done. Round-the-clock television shows tempt us to stay up late. And if we do manage to get a full night's sleep or grab a nap, we risk being labeled "unmotivated" or "lazy" by the go-getters around us. Yet research suggests that those who insist on getting their rest are the wisest of all. Sufficient sleep is as important to health as regular exercise and a nutritious diet. It may even make us smarter.

2   First, adequate sleep is essential to warding off disease. Research has shown that when the body is sleep-deprived, the immune system does not fight infection as effectively. One University of Chicago study, for example, focused on volunteers who slept only four hours a night for six days in a row. The participants' metabolism and hormone production were not functioning efficiently after the six days. This effect led researchers to conclude that a chronic lack of sleep leaves the body vulnerable to serious diseases, from high blood pressure to obesity. Another study indicated that lack of sleep actually increases the risk of heart attack.

3   Getting sufficient sleep also seems good for our brains. Studies show that during sleep the brain develops, checks, and expands its network of cell connections. Thus sleep gives the brain a chance to strengthen itself, leading to clearer thinking when we're awake. This explains why babies and children sleep so much: Their brains are still developing. Thus they need a lot of sleep to improve the brain's cellular network. Sleep may also be necessary to purge the brain of sensation overload. During the day, our minds are bombarded with stimulation in the form of sensory experiences, thoughts, and feelings. Sleep gives the brain time to sift through all of this information and either store it or delete it. Without time to evaluate and reorganize, the brain could become overwhelmed and unable to remember anything.

4   Indeed, numerous studies reveal that sleep has a significant effect on memory. When people are deprived of sleep, they don't learn as well as when they have enough sleep. In one study, two groups of students listened to a story. That night one group was deprived of sleep and the

Copyright © Cengage Learning. All rights reserved.

other was allowed to sleep normally. The next day each group was asked to recall some details about the story. The sleep-deprived group exhibited much poorer recall of the story than the group that had slept. Researchers therefore concluded that sleep deprivation reduces the ability to retain information.

5   Other studies support this conclusion. At Harvard University, for example, researchers found that people can improve their scores on memory tests simply by sleeping soundly for a minimum of six hours the first night after learning new information. In another study, Canadian researchers taught research subjects a game in the afternoon and then served some of them liquor before bedtime. The alcohol interfered with sleep, and the participants did not get adequate rest. The next day the sleep-deprived participants performed 40 percent worse than those who remained sober and got enough sleep. Additional studies at the University of California have shown that sleep-deprived people also have trouble learning new skills.

6   Clearly, we need to stop viewing a good night's rest as an unnecessary luxury. Sleep is crucial to good health and mental functioning. Instead of skimping on sleep, we should be finding ways to get more of it. (Source of studies: Robert A. Stickgold et al., "You Will Start to Feel Very Sleepy . . . ," *Newsweek*, January 19, 2004, pp. 58–60.)

1. Which statement best paraphrases the thesis statement?
   a. The numbers of hours we sleep has steadily decreased over the last century.
   b. Adequate sleep is crucial to good health.
   c. Getting enough sleep improves both health and learning.
   d. Many researchers are studying why we sleep.

2. Which statement best paraphrases the topic sentence of paragraph 3?
   a. The brain adjusts its network of nerve cells while we sleep.
   b. Babies and children need more sleep than adults do.
   c. Sleep prevents the brain from becoming overloaded by too much information.
   d. Sleep has positive effects on the brain.

3. Within the paragraph, is this sentence in paragraph 3 a major or minor detail? "During the day, our minds are bombarded with

Copyright © Cengage Learning. All rights reserved.

stimulation in the form of sensory experiences, thoughts, and feelings."

a. major detail

b. minor detail

4. What pattern or patterns do you see at work in the reading?
   a. definition
   b. cause and effect
   c. comparison and contrast
   d. simple listing

5. Which of the following paragraphs best summarizes the reading?
   a. According to the latest research, sleep benefits us both physically and mentally. Recent studies indicate that adequate sleep enhances the functioning of the immune system, helping the body fight off major diseases and even heart attacks. In addition, sleep helps the brain function more effectively. Getting sufficient sleep gives the brain time to improve cell connections and sort through all the thoughts and sensations it has processed during the day. Studies also indicate that sleep is important to building memory and aiding the learning process.

   b. The latest scientific research indicates that sleeping a lot is good for us. People often criticize those who insist on getting eight or nine hours of sleep every night. Heavy sleepers are looked down upon for not having enough drive or ambition. However, those who like to get a lot of sleep can now assure their critics that they do it to improve their brain. For example, studies have shown that people learn better when they get plenty of sleep. Numerous experiments indicate that information-recall suffers when people do not get sufficient sleep while trying to learn new information or a new skill. Sleep is an essential component of clear thinking.

   c. Studies are proving that sleep is essential to good health. Adequate sleep boosts the immune system, helping the body protect itself from all kinds of serious illnesses. It also protects us against heart disease. Research at Harvard University indicates that sleep helps us remember things better, too. Clearly, we have to stop working so much and watching so many late-night TV programs because these activities are interfering with our ability to get the rest we need.

Copyright © Cengage Learning. All rights reserved.

Reviewing with Longer Readings

© Ulrich Flemming

The readings that follow give you a chance to review everything you have learned up to this point. However, they also ask you to form your own opinion about the topics discussed. As the remaining chapters of this textbook strongly emphasize, figuring out what and how other people think is certainly important. But you can't stop there. Understanding other people's ideas should be the first step toward sharpening and refining your own.

◆ **READING 1** Heredity or Environment: What Can Identical Twins Tell Us?

Jim Henslin

Looking Ahead This reading from a sociology textbook focuses on identical twins and uses them to explore a question that has been discussed for decades: Which plays a bigger role in who we are and what we become, our experience or our genes?

Getting Focused Read the first and last paragraph to get a better understanding of the question posed by the title. Once you understand the question, read to see how the author answers it.

1   Identical twins share exactly the same genetic heredity. One fertilized egg divides to produce two embryos. If heredity determines personality—or attitudes, temperament, skills, and intelligence—then identical twins should be identical not only in their looks but also in these characteristics.

2   The fascinating case of Jack and Oskar helps us unravel the mystery of which affects us more, our heredity or our environment. From their experience, we can see the far-reaching effects of the environment—how social experience takes precedence over biology.

3   Jack Yufe and Oskar Stohr are identical twins born in 1932 to a Jewish father and a Catholic mother. They were separated as babies after their parents divorced. Oskar was reared in Czechoslovakia by his mother's mother, who was a strict Catholic. When Oskar was a toddler, Hitler annexed this area of Czechoslovakia, and Oskar learned to love Hitler and to hate Jews. He joined the Hitler Youth, a sort of Boy Scout organization, except that this one was designed to instill the "virtues" of patriotism, loyalty, obedience—and hatred.

4   Jack's upbringing was a mirror image of Oskar's. Reared in Trinidad by his father, he learned loyalty to Jews and hatred of Hitler and the Nazis. After the war, Jack and his father moved to Israel. When he was 17, Jack joined a kibbutz,[†] and later, served in the Israeli army.

5   In 1954, the two brothers met. It was a short meeting and Jack had been warned not to tell Oskar that they were Jews. Twenty-five years later, in 1979, when they were 47 years old, social scientists brought them together again. These researchers figured that because Jack and Oskar had the same

---

[†]kibbutz: a group living arrangement.

Copyright © Cengage Learning. All rights reserved.

genes, any differences they showed would have to be the result of their environment—their different social experiences.

6   Not only did Oskar and Jack hold different attitudes toward the war, Hitler, and Jews, but also their basic orientations to life were different. In their politics, Oskar was conservative while Jack was more liberal. Oskar enjoyed leisure, while Jack was a workaholic. And as you can predict, Jack was very proud of being a Jew. Oskar, who by this time knew he was a Jew, wouldn't even mention it.

7   That would seem to settle the matter. But there was another side. The researchers also found that Oskar and Jack had both excelled at sports as children, but had difficulty with math. They also had the same rate of speech and both liked sweet liqueur and spicy foods. Strangely, both flushed the toilet both before and after using it and enjoyed startling people by sneezing in crowded elevators. (Henslin, *Sociology*, p. 66.)

TAKING A CLOSER LOOK

Confirming Predictions

Based on what the author says in paragraph 2, which side of the debate between nature and nurture, or genes and experience, would you predict the author is going to advocate?

_____

Does the final paragraph of the reading confirm your original prediction?

_____

_____

_____

_____

Reviewing Concepts and Skills

DIRECTIONS   Answer the following questions by filling in the blanks or circling the letter of the correct response.

Making Predictions

1. What does the title suggest about identical twins?

_____

_____

Copyright © Cengage Learning. All rights reserved.

Topic   **2.** What's the topic of the reading?

    a. heredity

    b. identical twins

    c. the identical twins Jack and Oskar

Main Idea   **3.** Which sentence is the thesis statement?

    a. Identical twins share exactly the same genetic heredity.

    b. The experience of identical twins Jack and Oskar helps us unravel the mystery of which affects us more, our heredity or our environment.

    c. Jack Yufe and Oskar Stohr are identical twins born in 1932 to a Jewish father and a Catholic mother.

Context   **4.** Based on the context, what does "mirror image" mean in the following sentence: "Jack's upbringing was a mirror image of Oskar's" (paragraph 4)?

    _____

5. In paragraph 7, when the author says, "That would seem to settle the matter," what matter does he have in mind?

    _____

    _____

Sentence Functions   **6.** In paragraph 7, what function does the following sentence fulfill: "But there was another side"?

    a. topic sentence

    b. major detail

    c. reversal transition

Making Predictions   **7.** What prediction are we likely to make based on that sentence?

    _____

    _____

Copyright © Cengage Learning. All rights reserved.

Organizational
Patterns

8. What three patterns are at work in the reading?

    a. definition

    b. classification

    c. comparison and contrast

    d. cause and effect

    e. sequence of dates and events

Are they all equally important? _____

Inference
and Purpose

9. What point does the author want to make when he tells readers the following about the two men: "They also had the same rate of speech and both liked sweet liqueur and spicy foods. Strangely, both flushed the toilet both before and after using it and enjoyed startling people by sneezing in crowded elevators" (paragraph 7)?

_____

_____

_____

10. What would you say is the author's purpose?

_____

_____

www

INTERNET FOLLOW-UP: Twins Apart and Together

Use the Web to find out more about Paula Bernstein and Elyse Schein. How do they fit into a discussion of what's called nature versus nurture or experience versus genetic inheritance?

_____

_____

_____

_____

_____

_____

_____

Copyright © Cengage Learning. All rights reserved.

What Do You Think? Do you think that experience or genes play a more significant role in deciding who we are? Or do you think it's a combination of both? Whichever you believe, can you state your position and explain what made you develop that point of view?

Thinking Through Writing Write a paragraph in which you describe an early experience or a relationship that you believe influenced who you are as a person. For instance, do you tend to stick with things even when they become difficult because your mom always told you, "When the going gets tough, the tough get going"?

Structure the paragraph by opening with a statement about the characteristic you are going to trace back to childhood, e.g., "It's hard for me to give up on a task, even when I want to. I tend to stick with a job until it's finished." Then describe the origin of that characteristic.

_____

_____

_____

_____

_____

Reading Further A chapter from the twins' book *Identical Strangers* is available at www .npr.org.

Copyright © Cengage Learning. All rights reserved.

◆ **READING 2**   Media Multitaskers Pay a Mental Price

Adam Gorlick

Looking Ahead   For more than a decade, many people believed that technology had allowed us to be more productive by multitasking. We could simultaneously talk on our cell phone, read a text message, or check out Twitter. The theory was that we could accomplish more in less time than ever before. This reading by science writer Adam Gorlick suggests the reality may be somewhat different.

Getting Focused   The title says that multitaskers pay a mental price. Read to get a clear understanding of what that price is.

1   Attention, multitaskers (if you can pay attention, that is): Your brain may be in trouble. People who are regularly bombarded with several streams of electronic information do not pay attention, control their memory or switch from one job to another as well as those who prefer to complete one task at a time, a group of Stanford researchers has found.

2   High tech jugglers are everywhere—keeping up several e-mail and instant message conversations at once, text messaging while watching television and jumping from one website to another while plowing through homework assignments. But after putting about 100 students through a series of three tests, the researchers realized those media multitaskers are paying a mental price.

3   "They're suckers for irrelevancy," said communications Professor Clifford Nass, whose findings are published in the August 24 edition of the *Proceedings of the National Academy of Sciences*. "Everything distracts them."

4   Social scientists have long assumed that it's impossible to process more than one string of information at a time. The brain just can't do it. But many researchers have guessed that people who appear to multitask must have superb control over what they think about and what they pay attention to.

Is There a Gift?

5   So Nass and his colleagues, Eyal Ophir and Anthony Wagner, set out to learn what gives multitaskers their edge. What is their gift? "We kept looking for what they're better at, and we didn't find it," said Ophir, the study's lead author and a researcher in Stanford's Communication Between Humans and Interactive Media.

Copyright © Cengage Learning. All rights reserved.

6   In each of their tests, the researchers split their subjects into two groups: those who regularly do a lot of media multitasking and those who don't. In one experiment, the groups were shown sets of two red rectangles alone or surrounded by two, four, or six blue rectangles. Each configuration was flashed twice, and the participants had to determine whether the two red rectangles in the second frame were in a different position than in the first frame. They were also told to ignore the blue rectangles. The low multitaskers had no problem doing that, but the high multitaskers were constantly distracted by the irrelevant blue images. Their performance was horrible.

7   Because the high multitaskers showed they couldn't ignore things, the researchers figured they were better at storing and organizing information. Maybe they had better memories. The second test proved that theory wrong too. After being shown sequences of alphabetical letters, the multitaskers did a terrible job remembering when a letter was making a repeat appearance. "The low multitaskers did great," Ophir said. "The high multitaskers were doing worse and worse the further they went along because they kept seeing more letters and had difficulty keeping them sorted in their brains."

Still Puzzled

8 Puzzled but not yet stumped on why the heavy multitaskers weren't performing well, the researchers conducted a third test. If the heavy multitaskers couldn't filter out irrelevant information or organize their memories, perhaps they excelled at switching from one thing to another faster and better than anyone else.

9   Wrong again, the study found. The test subjects were shown images of letters and numbers at the same time and instructed what to focus on. When they were told to pay attention to numbers, they had to determine if the digits were even or odd. When told to concentrate on letters, they had to say whether they were vowels or consonants. Again, the heavy multitaskers underperformed the light multitaskers. "They couldn't help thinking about the task they weren't doing," Ophir said. "The high multitaskers are always drawing from all the information in front of them. They can't keep things separate in their minds."

10   The researchers are still studying whether chronic media multitaskers are born with an inability to concentrate or are damaging their cognitive control by willingly taking in so much at once. But today they're convinced the minds of multitaskers are not working as well as they could. "When they're in situations where there are multiple sources of information

Copyright © Cengage Learning. All rights reserved.

coming from the external world or emerging out of memory, they're not able to filter out what's not relevant to their current goal," said Wagner, an associate professor of psychology. "That failure to filter means they're slowed down by that irrelevant information."

11   So maybe its time to stop e-mailing if you're following the game on TV, and rethink singing along with the radio if you're reading the latest news online. By doing less, you accomplish more.

TAKING A CLOSER LOOK

The Function of Quotations

The quotation that opens paragraph 3 defines what word or phrase in paragraph 2?

_____

Reviewing Concepts and Skills

DIRECTIONS   Answer the following questions by filling in the blanks or circling the letter of the correct response.

Making Predictions   1. What does the title suggest to you about the reading?

_____

_____

Main Idea   2. In what paragraph did you find the thesis statement of the reading? _____ In your own words, what is the main idea?

_____

_____

_____

Context   3. Based on the context, how would you define *configuration* (paragraph 6)?

_____

Supporting Details   4. In paragraph 7, the quotation from one of the researchers would be considered a

a. major detail.

b. minor detail.

Copyright © Cengage Learning. All rights reserved.

5. In paragraph 9, the quotation from one of the researchers is a
   a. major detail.
   b. minor detail.

Organizational
Patterns

6. What are the two patterns that organize the reading?
   a. definition
   b. classification
   c. cause and effect
   d. comparison and contrast

7. The patterns organizing the reading are
   a. of equal importance.
   b. unequal in importance.

Summarizing

8. Which passage better summarizes the reading?
   a. When researchers at Stanford University set out to discover the special abilities that multitaskers possess, they found that those who multitask don't seem to have any special abilities. Their brains just don't filter out irrelevant details, and that allows them to do several things at one time. The researchers used a series of different tests, but each one produced the same result.
   b. Researchers at Stanford University set out to discover what special abilities made it possible for multitaskers to do several things at one time. But what they discovered is that multitaskers don't have any special abilities. On the contrary, in a series of different tests, they performed less well than did people who prefer to complete one task at a time.

Paraphrasing

9. In your own words, what are researchers still trying to find out?

_____

_____

10. In paragraph 10, the researchers claim that the minds of multitaskers are not working as well as they should. In your own words, what does the paragraph say the problem is?

_____

_____

Copyright © Cengage Learning. All rights reserved.

INTERNET FOLLOW-UP: Researching the Research
Use the Web to answer this question: Have other studies confirmed or contradicted the results of the study described here?

_____

_____

_____

What Do You Think? Do you think people in general will read about this research or similar studies and give up multitasking? Please explain the basis for your opinion.

_____

_____

_____

_____

_____

_____

Thinking Through Writing The Stanford study has been widely popularized, and it has made many people re-think their attitude toward multitasking. However, some people insist they are the exception and can, for example, text message and check Facebook periodically while listening to their instructor lecture. Write a paragraph or two in which you describe any one of the following positions: (1) why you were never a multitasker to begin with; (2) why, despite the researchers' conclusions, you think multitasking works well for you; or (3) why you believe the researchers are correct, but you are nevertheless addicted to multitasking. Please be sure to briefly summarize the study before you explain your position.

_____

_____

Copyright © Cengage Learning. All rights reserved.

_____

_____

_____

_____

_____

_____

Copyright © Cengage Learning. All rights reserved.

◆ **READING 3**   Property Rights: A Matter of Power

Ann O'M. Bowman and Richard C. Kearney

Looking Ahead   At the end of Chapter 3, you read about Peter Singer and the utilitarian philosophy he espoused: making decisions to produce the greatest good for the greatest number. In a very real way, that is the basis for a legal principle called "eminent domain," discussed in this reading drawn from a textbook on state and local government.

Getting Focused   The title and the preview suggest that "eminent domain" affects property rights. Read for a definition of eminent domain and how it affects property ownership.

1   The issue of property rights raises interesting questions about the exercise of power. You may have heard someone say, "I own this land; therefore, I can do anything I want with it," but that would be far from accurate. Through zoning and other regulations, government can limit what you can do with your property. Moreover, government can actually take that property away from you for a public purpose. All it has to do is follow proper procedures and compensate you, that is, pay fair market value, for the taking.

2   Suppose you own a half-acre vacant lot near the central business district of your city. The city may be eyeing your lot as the site for the new library it plans to construct. If you are not willing to sell the land, the city can use its power of eminent domain, that is, it can take your property. You can haggle over the value of the lot, perhaps demand an administrative hearing, and maybe even file a lawsuit to try to stop the city, but in the end, if the taking is for a public purpose, the city has the power to do so.

3   Where the issue gets a little dicey is over the notion of "public purpose." Obviously a library is a public purpose, but can the city use its eminent domain power to take that same lot and sell it to a developer so that he can construct an office building? The answer may surprise you.

4   The city council of New London, Connecticut, had voted in 2000 to take 90 acres of land for a redevelopment project. The city's development corporation would redevelop the area with a hotel, marina, and upscale residences that would generate much-needed jobs and tax revenue for the financially stressed city. Most of the property owners sold their land to the city, but a small group refused and, instead, filed suit claiming that the action represented an illegal taking.

Copyright © Cengage Learning. All rights reserved.

5   The plaintiffs argued that the city's plans for the land would destroy an established neighborhood to benefit private developers. In essence, they contended that the city had violated the public purpose requirement of a taking. The case, *Kelo v. City of New London*, went all the way to the U.S. Supreme Court, which, in a 5 to 4 decision in 2005, ruled in favor of the city. The reasoning went like this: New London wanted to use the land to promote economic development, which is a traditional function of government; therefore, the city's plan fulfilled a public purpose.

6   Property rights advocates deplored the Court's decision, arguing that working-class residents and small business owners were being displaced so that the city could pursue a more productive use of the land. They had an advocate in Justice Sandra Day O'Connor, who dissented, saying, "The beneficiaries [of the Court's ruling] are likely to be those citizens with disproportionate influence and power in the political process, including large corporations and developing firms."

7   Localities,[†] not surprisingly, welcomed the decision, claiming that eminent domain was an essential tool in their efforts to regain and maintain economic vitality. They pointed to other examples of the use of eminent domain to benefit private firms, particularly a Nissan automobile facility in Canton, Mississippi, and a speedway in Kansas City, Kansas.

8   The Court did invite states to place restrictions on localities' use of eminent domain if they so desired, and, as of 2009, forty-three states had done so either by legislative action or by citizen initiative. Clearly the exercise of eminent domain is costly, not only in dollars but in terms of good will. A poll conducted in New Hampshire found that 93 percent of Granite State residents opposed governmental taking of private land for economic development. This sentiment is one of the reasons why Washington, D.C., as it acquired land for the construction of a new stadium for the Washington Nationals baseball team, explicitly refused to take property. But by the same token, New York City was not reluctant to condemn property and take it for a new basketball arena for the New Jersey Nets. The definition of public purpose is likely to continue to unleash a power struggle in many communities. (Adapted from Bowman and Kearney, *State and Local Government*, p. 308.)

---

†localities: another way of referring to towns.

Copyright © Cengage Learning. All rights reserved.

TAKING A
CLOSER LOOK

How Readers Fill in the Gaps
Paragraph 1 says that the reading raises some "interesting questions" about power. What are some of the interesting questions about power that the author seems to be raising?

_____

_____

_____

Reviewing Concepts and Skills

DIRECTIONS   Answer the following questions by filling in the blanks or circling the letter of the correct response.

Topic

1. What word or phrase best expresses the topic of this reading?
   a. property rights
   b. *Kelo v. City of New London*
   c. controversy over eminent domain

Main Idea

2. Which sentence functions as the thesis statement of the reading?
   a. The issue of property rights raises interesting questions about the exercise of power.
   b. Suppose you own a half-acre vacant lot near the central business district of your city.
   c. Where the issue gets a little dicey is over the notion of "public purpose."

Context

3. Based on the context, what is the meaning of "dicey" in the following sentence:

   "Where the issue gets a little dicey is over the notion of 'public purpose'" (paragraph 3)?

   _____

   _____

Copyright © Cengage Learning. All rights reserved.

What does the meaning suggest to you about the word's relation to the game of dice?

_____

_____

_____

Making Predictions 4. In paragraph 3, the word *obviously* and the phrase "The answer may surprise you" encourage which prediction on the part of the reader?

a. The city can't actually use eminent domain in order to build a library.

b. The city can use eminent domain to let a developer build an office building.

Organizational Patterns 5. Does the reading use the definition pattern of organization to define *eminent domain*? _____

Based on the reading, please explain the principle of eminent domain.

_____

_____

Summarizing 6. Which of the following passages better summarizes paragraphs 4, 5, and 6?

a. After the New London city council used eminent domain to take over 90 acres of land for redevelopment, owners who did not want to sell argued in court that the city was not using the land for a public purpose and that it was destroying an established neighborhood. The Supreme Court sided with the city and agreed in *Kelo v. City of New London* that the city council was promoting economic development and therefore serving a public purpose.

b. In *Kelo v. City of New London*, the Supreme Court agreed that the city council of New London had acted fairly. The decision pitted five judges against four. One of the dissenters was Judge Sandra

Copyright © Cengage Learning. All rights reserved.

Day O'Connor, who argued that the decision would benefit the wealthy over ordinary persons.

What made one summary better than the other?

_____

_____

_____

_____

Paraphrasing 7. Using mostly your own words, complete the following statement by paraphrasing Sandra Day O'Connor's response to the Supreme Court's decision in *Kelo v. City of New London*. "The beneficiaries [of the Court's ruling] are likely to be those citizens with disproportionate influence and power in the political process, including large corporations and developing firms."

In her dissenting opinion, Sandra Day O'Connor argued that ___

_____

_____

_____

Supporting Details 8. How does paragraph 7 support or contradict what Justice O'Connor claimed?

_____

_____

Organizational 9. Paragraph 8 contrasts Washington, D.C., and New York City. What
Patterns is the point of the contrast?

_____

_____

Making Connections 10. What does this sentence suggest to you about the public's reaction to the use of eminent domain by towns and cities: "The court did invite states to place restrictions on localities' use of

Copyright © Cengage Learning. All rights reserved.

eminent domain if they so desired and, as of 2009, forty-three states had done so either by legislative action or by citizen initiative[†]" (paragraph 8)?

_____

_____

_____

INTERNET FOLLOW-UP: Equal Opportunity and Eminent Domain
After the _Kelo v. City of New London_ decision, what did some people hope would happen to Justice David Souter?

www

_____

_____

_____

_____

_____

What Do You Think? Do you think the Supreme Court made the right decision in _Kelo v. City of New London_? Explain.

_____

_____

_____

_____

Reading Further The eight-part series "Underfoot, Out of Reach" won journalist Daniel Gilbert the Pulitzer Prize (see page 125) in 2010. In the series, Gilbert explains how homeowners may or may not get paid for the extraction of minerals on their property. Once again eminent domain plays a key role. If you type the title into a search engine, you can find and read the series on the Web.

_____

[†]With a citizen initiative, a petition is circulated. If the petition gets a specific number of signatures from registered voters, the petition can force a vote, an action, or a discussion.

Copyright © Cengage Learning. All rights reserved.

◆ **READING 4**   ## Dealing with Conflict

Roy Berko, Andrew D. Wolvin, and Darlyn R. Wolvin

Looking Ahead   In Chapter 4, you learned about the difference between aggressive and assertive behavior. In response to a conflict or disagreement, some people are aggressive, i.e., they get angry and counterattack. Others are assertive; they state their position and hold their ground but don't escalate the emotional tension. These two responses, however, do not cover all the possible ways people react to conflict. As this reading explains, there are a variety of responses possible.

Getting Focused   The title, preview, and headings suggest that responses to conflict fall into several basic categories. Read to identify each category, along with the authors' description of the pros and cons associated with each one.

1   Most of us use a primary style for confronting conflict. Knowing your style and its ramifications can be helpful in determining whether you are satisfied with your conflict style. If you are not, you may need to acquire the skills to make a change in your habitual pattern. The basic styles of conflict management are (1) avoidance, (2) accommodation/smoothing-over, (3) compromise, (4) competition/aggression, and (5) integration with making an apology a possible component of all but competition and aggression.

Avoidance

2   Some people choose to confront conflict by engaging in conflict avoidance: They sidestep, postpone, or ignore the issue. They simply put up with the status quo no matter how unpleasant. While seemingly unproductive, avoidance may actually be a good style if the situation is a short-term one or of minor importance. If, however, the problem is really bothering you or is persistent, then it should be dealt with. Avoiding the issue often uses up a great deal of energy without resolving the aggravating situation. Very seldom do avoiders feel that they have been in a win-win situation. Avoiders usually lose a chunk of their self-respect since they so clearly downplay their own concerns in favor of the other person's. Avoiders frequently were brought up in environments in which they were told to be nice and not to argue, and eventually bad things would go away. Or they were brought up in homes where verbal or physical abuse was present, and to avoid these types of reactions, they hid from conflict.

Copyright © Cengage Learning. All rights reserved.

Accommodation/Smoothing-Over

3 Accommodators meet the needs of others and don't assert their own. In this situation, the accommodator often feels like the "good person" for having given the other person his own way. This is perfectly acceptable if the other person's needs really are more important. But unfortunately, accommodators tend to follow the pattern no matter what the situation. Thus, they often are taken advantage of, and they seldom get their needs met. Accommodators commonly come from backgrounds where they were exposed to a martyr who gave and gave and got little but still put on a happy face. They also tend to be people who have little self-respect and try to earn praise by being nice to everyone.

4   A form of accommodation known as conflict smoothing-over seeks above all else to preserve the image that everything is okay. Through smoothing-over, people sometimes get what they want, but just as often they do not. Usually they feel they have more to say and have not totally satisfied themselves.

5   As with avoidance and accommodation, smoothing-over occasionally can be useful. If, for example, the relationship between two people is more important than the subject they happen to be disagreeing about, then smoothing-over may be the best approach. Keep in mind, however, that smoothing-over does not solve the conflict; it just pushes it aside. It may very well recur in the future.

6   Those who use this technique as their normal means of confronting conflict often come from backgrounds in which the idea was stressed that being nice was the best way to be liked and popular. And being liked and popular was more important than satisfying their needs.

Compromise

7 Conflict compromise brings concerns into the open in an attempt to satisfy the needs of both parties. It usually means "trading some of what you want for some of what I want. It's meeting each other halfway." The definition of the word "compromise," however, indicates the potential weakness of this approach, for it means that both individuals give in at least to some degree to reach a solution. As a result, neither usually completely achieves what she or he wants. This is not to say that compromise is automatically a poor method of conflict management. It is not, but it can lead to frustration unless both participants are willing to continue to work until both of their needs are being met. Those who are effective compromisers normally have had experience with

Copyright © Cengage Learning. All rights reserved.

negotiations and know that you have to give to get, but you don't have to give until it hurts. Those who tend to be weak in working toward a fair and equitable compromise believe that getting something is better than getting nothing at all. Therefore, they are willing to settle for anything, no matter how little.

Competition/Aggression

8   The main element in conflict competition is power. Its purpose is to "get another person to comply with or accept your point of view, or to do something that person may not want to do." Someone has to win, and someone has to lose. This forcing mode, unfortunately, has been the European-American way of operation in many situations—in athletic events, business deals, and interpersonal relations. Indeed, many people do not seem to be happy unless they are clear winners. Realize that if someone wins, someone else must lose. The overaggressive driver must force the other car off the road.

9   The value of winning at all costs is debatable. Sometimes, even though we win, we lose in the long run. The hatred of a child for a parent as a result of continuous losing, or the negative work environment resulting from a supervisor who must always be on top, may be much worse than the occasional loss of a battle. In dealing with persons from other cultures, European Americans sometimes are perceived as being pushy and aggressive. Many sales, friendships, and relationships have been lost based on the win-at-all costs philosophy. Many of the aggressive behaviors in the personal lives of professional athletes are directly credited to their not being able to leave their win-at-all-costs attitude on the athletic field.

Integration

10   Communicators who handle their conflicts through conflict integration are concerned about their own needs as well as those of the other person. But unlike compromisers, they will not settle for only a partially satisfying solution. Integrators keep in mind that both parties can participate in a win-win resolution and are willing to collaborate. Thus, the most important aspect of integration is the realization that the relationship, the value of self-worth, and the issue are important. For this reason, integrative solutions often take a good deal of time and energy.

11   People who are competitive, who are communication-apprehensive, or who are nonassertive find it nearly impossible to use an integrative style of negotiation. They feel that they must win, or that they cannot stand up for their rights, or that they have no right to negotiate. In contrast, people

Copyright © Cengage Learning. All rights reserved.

who tend to have assertiveness skills and value the nature of relationships usually attempt to work toward integration.

12   Avoidance, accommodation, and smoothing-over are all nonassertive acts; the person's needs are not met. Competition is an aggressive act in that the person gets his needs met at the expense of another person. Integration is assertive since the objective is to get one's needs met without taking away the rights of someone else. Compromise, depending on how it is acted out, can be either nonassertive or assertive.

13   **Apologizing** Have you ever angrily said something to another person? Have you offended someone by being sarcastic or joking around when your remark was perceived to be serious and not funny? Have you ever acted inappropriately toward someone whom you really like? If the answer to any of these is "yes," the question is, what did you do about it?

14   We all have said or done something we know has hurt or offended a personal friend, a significant other, or even a stranger. For many people brought up in the culture of the United States, one key to getting along with people is knowing when and how to apologize, to say you are sorry. How we react to having offended someone has a great deal to do with our background. If you've been brought up to fight for being right, not to give in, or to hold a grudge, you are not likely to consider apologizing. If you've been brought up to believe that the feelings of others supersede your own feelings, then making an apology is probably an automatic reaction.

15   Questions arise as to when it is appropriate to apologize and how to do it. For many people it is both hard to know when to apologize and difficult to apologize. You may be ashamed of your negative actions or have too much pride to admit to another that you did something wrong. Sometimes, even though you may want to apologize, you just may not know how. But remember that apologizing often solves the small problems and keeps them from getting bigger.

16   Traditionally, an apology basically has three stages. First, the person who has done the wrong should state exactly what he or she did. For example, the person could say, "I yelled at you after you told me that the idea I had presented at the meeting was wrong." Second, the perpetrator explains why he or she took the action. For example, the person could say, "I spent a lot of time on that solution, and I felt I had to defend myself." Third, a statement of remorse is made. For instance, the person could say, "I was upset, but I shouldn't have yelled. It didn't do anything to help deal with the task on which we were working." The reason the second step is optional is that you may not know why you took the action, or an explanation may

Copyright © Cengage Learning. All rights reserved.

incite further anxiety. If either of these situations is the case, it may be wise to skip that part of the process.

17 Does the process sound too formulaic or unnatural? It may well be, especially if you aren't in the habit of apologizing, but it lays out a pattern for verbalization that can and does work. Once you adopt the style, you may make adjustments to fit your own personality and situations, but at least you now have a format for the apology process.

18 The person who has been wronged may reject your apology. That is not your problem. If you offer an apology, and the apology is sincerely worded and felt, then whether the other person accepts or rejects the action is not the issue. You have fulfilled your obligation. You have recognized that what you did or said was wrong and have taken an action to let the other person know that you are remorseful. You can only be responsible for one person's actions, your own. You cannot make the other person act as you would like him or her to act. Therefore, acceptance of the apology is out of your hands. Don't go into the process of apologizing to receive forgiveness. Go in accepting that you are doing the right thing and that's your purpose.

19 Here are some additional tips that may make it easier to say you're sorry.

20 **Take Responsibility** The starting point of any change of behavior is self-admission. Admit to yourself that you have offended someone. You may know this right away, the other person's reaction may let you know you have done something hurtful, someone else might alert you to the situation, or you may realize it yourself at a later time. However you find out, you must admit that you have done wrong and accept responsibility for your actions or you won't be prone to take action.

21 **Explain** Recognize that your actions caused a problem for the other person. If you can do so, and it is appropriate, explain why you acted as you did. For example, if you were angry and blurted out something, you might say, "I was really having a bad day, and what I said wasn't really aimed at you. I was mad at myself, and I took my anger out on you. I'm sorry."

22 **Show Your Regret** The other person needs to see that you are aware that what you did was wrong. That is, if you think you were wrong, say that you are sorry or ashamed with a statement such as "I felt bad the minute I told your secret. You trusted me, and I betrayed your trust. I shouldn't have done that." This, of course, is only appropriate if you are regretful. If not, the apology will sound phony and may cause a bigger conflict.

23 **Repair the Damage** To be complete, an apology should attempt to correct the injury. If you damaged someone's property, offer to fix it. If

Copyright © Cengage Learning. All rights reserved.

the damage is emotional, you might ask, "I'm really sorry. What can I do to make it up to you?" There may be nothing concrete you can do, but the offer is usually enough and shows your sincerity. You might follow up by saying something appropriate, such as "I'll try to keep my mouth shut in the future. In the meantime, let me buy you a cup of coffee."

24 **Speak Face-to Face** A face-to-face apology is often best because you can display your honesty. It can be a humbling experience as you must see the other person's expressions, show yours, and probably hear a verbal reply. As one expert states, it is worth the anxiety since "you will be respected by the person [whom] you are addressing as well as by yourself more if you are able and willing to make your apology in this manner [face to face]. Smiles, laughter, hugs, handshakes, and other displays of appreciation and affection are added benefits for both parties that are all possible when apologizing this way!"

25 *It's not about who "won" or who "lost."* Remember, life is not a war unless you or the other person makes it a war. Stubborn pride often leads to a loss of friends and can result in physical confrontations. "An apology is a tool to affirm the primacy of our connection with others." (Berko, Wolvin, and Wolvin, *Communicating,* pp. 185–92.)

TAKING A CLOSER LOOK

Supporting Details
What's the difference between the authors' handling of "integration" as a method of conflict resolution and their handling of the other four responses?

_____

_____

What does this suggest about the authors' attitude toward using integration as a way of handling conflict?

_____

_____

Copyright © Cengage Learning. All rights reserved.

Reviewing Concepts and Skills

DIRECTIONS Answer the following questions by filling in the blanks or circling the letter of the correct response.

Making Predictions
1. The title of the reading should immediately raise what question?

_____

Main Idea
2. Where does the thesis statement appear?
   a. paragraph 1
   b. paragraph 2
   c. paragraph 3
   d. paragraph 4

Context
3. Based on the context, how would you define the word *equitable* in this sentence: "Those who tend to be weak in working toward a fair and *equitable* compromise believe that getting something is better than getting nothing at all" (paragraph 7)?

_____

Paraphrasing
4. Paraphrase the authors' explanation of conflict avoidance.

_____

_____

5. In your own words, what's the drawback commonly associated with compromise as a response to conflict?

_____

Supporting Details
6. Would you call the detail about professional athletes (paragraph 9) a major or minor detail? _____ Explain your answer:

_____

_____

Copyright © Cengage Learning. All rights reserved.

Sentence Functions and Organizational Patterns

7. In paragraph 16, the authors provide an explicit clue to the pattern of organization used. What is the clue?

_____

What is the pattern? _____

8. What is the purpose of paragraph 19? _____

What pattern of organization does it suggest will follow? _____

Do the remaining paragraphs confirm that prediction? _____
Please explain.

_____

Applying What You Learned

9. Frank and Evelyn are arguing over Frank's failure to complete his part of their shared research paper. Frank is insisting that his share of the paper was much greater than Evelyn's and therefore he shouldn't be blamed for not getting it done on time. Evelyn listens to his explanation and says, "I know I yelled at you and I shouldn't have, but I was anxious about the paper and your behavior seemed irresponsible. Perhaps I overreacted, but I'll lose my scholarship if I don't get an A on this paper." Frank responds by saying, "You shouldn't have yelled at me. I am overworked as it is and I'm doing

more than my fair share." Frank is engaging in _____

behavior while Evelyn is trying to _____.

Purpose

10. What is the authors' purpose?
a. to inform
b. to persuade

INTERNET FOLLOW-UP: Who Were Thomas and Kilmann?
Why do people who study conflict resolution know the names Kenneth Thomas and Ralph Kilmann?

_____

_____

_____

Copyright © Cengage Learning. All rights reserved.

What Do You Think? How would you describe your own style of dealing with conflict? How does your style match the authors' descriptions? Does it fit right in, or do you need a new category?

_____

_____

_____

_____

Thinking Through Writing Write a paragraph that opens by paraphrasing the authors' definition of conflict accommodation, introduced in paragraph 3. Follow the definition with a specific example that illustrates the meaning of the term in a concrete way. In moving from the definition to the example, see if you can come up with a transitional word, phrase, or sentence that gets the reader from one point to the other.

_____

_____

_____

_____

_____

_____

_____

_____

_____

Copyright © Cengage Learning. All rights reserved.

The Role of Inferences in Comprehension and Critical Reading

Roger Ressmeyer/Corbis

IN THIS CHAPTER, YOU WILL LEARN

- how inferences are essential to helping readers identify which words are central to the author's discussion.

- how to infer main ideas that are implied but not stated in paragraphs.

- how to infer the connections between supporting details.

- how to draw logical conclusions that might not have been intended by the author but are still implied by the text.

Language does not carry meaning in sentences,
but rather triggers or releases meaning ... in the
mind of the reader.

—Walter B. Weimer and David S. Palermo, in
Cognition and the Symbolic Process

This chapter shows you how to put into words what the author suggests but doesn't say outright. In short, it teaches you more about the art of drawing inferences. Essential to understanding an author's meaning, drawing appropriate inferences also lies at the heart of both comprehension and critical reading.

Drawing Inferences to Make Connections

You already know from Chapter 3 that writers sometimes expect readers to infer a topic that is implied rather than explicitly stated. This chapter will elaborate on that point and talk about paragraphs in which the reader infers not just the topic but also the main idea of a paragraph.

Drawing inferences, however, is already crucial at the level of individual sentences. As the following examples demonstrate, writers create **chains of repetition and reference**, which readers are expected to use as a way of determining how an author's thinking develops with the addition of each new sentence.

Nouns and Pronouns

One way writers create a chain of repetition and reference is to introduce a noun† and then refer to it with pronouns. It is then up to readers to infer the connections between pronouns and antecedents, or the nouns to which pronouns refer. Here's a fairly straightforward illustration:

Edward Thorndike (1874–1949) is a famous figure in educational theory. He conducted several experiments in order to gain further understanding of the learning process. He also formulated many important laws of learning. (Adapted from Engler, *Personality Theories*, p. 209.)

The pronoun *he* in the second sentence is the author's way of saying, "I am still talking about Edward Thorndike, but I can't always call him by name, so I'm using the pronoun *he*." Notice, though, that the author expects readers to keep track of the topic, in this case Edward Thorndike, by inferring the relationship between pronoun and antecedent.

---

†noun: The grammatical term *noun* refers to people, places, ideas, and objects— e.g., *president, country, socialism,* and *house* are all nouns.

Copyright © Cengage Learning. All rights reserved.

Tricky Pronouns and Antecedents

The example about Edward Thorndike might make it seem as if inferring relationships between pronouns and antecedents is so easy the subject is not worth mentioning. But connecting the two can get tricky, particularly if there is more than one pronoun and antecedent relationship or if the noun is followed by a pronoun clause[†] rather than a single word.

Staying on the trail of pronouns and their antecedents can also become more difficult when the nouns to which the pronouns refer are far away. In the following passage, the pronouns are italicized. When you finish reading the excerpt, fill in the blanks in parentheses with the nouns each pronoun represents, or stands in for.

[1]One problem with court-assigned counsel for the poor concerns degree of effort. [2]Although most attorneys assigned by the court to defend *those who cannot afford counsel* (_____) probably take *their* (_____) job seriously, some feel only a loose commitment to *their* (_____) clients. [3]Paying clients, in *their* (_____) eyes, deserve better service and are apt to get *it* (_____). (Schmalleger, *Criminal Justice Today*, p. 41.)

In this case, the first pronoun represents the clients who cannot afford to pay. The next string of pronouns represents the attorneys, with the last pronoun *it* referring not to a person but to better service, or a good defense. In every instance, it's up to readers to infer the relationship between pronoun and antecedent based on clues in the text and the reader's knowledge of English.

Looking at *This* and *That*

Writers sometimes use *this* or *that* to refer to an entire idea rather than a single noun. Look, for example, at the following pair of sentences:

[1]No public figure wants to be crucified for having concealed warnings of terrorist attacks if the attacks actually occur because the warnings

---

[†]Pronoun clauses consist of the pronoun and verb—e.g., "The man *who would be king* must have a strong stomach for criticism."

Copyright © Cengage Learning. All rights reserved.

would almost certainly be revealed. [2]On the simplest level, this is why we've had two warnings from the administration against unspecified terrorist threats. (Adapted from Samuelson, "Unwitting Accomplice," *Perspectives on Terrorism*, p. 19.)

In this case, "this" doesn't refer to a single word. It refers to an entire thought: Public officials fear that if they get a warning of a terrorist attack but don't reveal it and the warning then becomes a reality, they will be harshly criticized by the public and the media. That entire thought is packed into the pronoun *this*. As you can see, it is the reader's job to unpack the pronoun by drawing the right inference.

In the next example, you need to connect two *that* pronouns to their antecedents. Read the passage and explain what the two italicized pronouns represent.

[1]Scholars who comment on the history of mass communication research are carrying out important work. [2]Their intent is to explore the concerns and beliefs *that* have guided professors of media journalism over the decades, as well as the assumptions about individuals and society *that* are reflected in their conclusions. (Turow, *Media Today*, p. 128.)

The first *that* in sentence 2 refers to "concerns and beliefs." These two nouns have to be the antecedent. "Scholars" couldn't be the antecedent because the scholars are the ones studying the professor's work.

The second *that* in sentence 2 follows hard on the heels of "assumptions about individuals and society." Thus, you could infer first that "assumptions about individuals and society" is the antecedent for the second *that*.

Happily, your first guess would be correct. However, in general, if the noun closest to the pronoun doesn't make sense as an antecedent, make sure you always look farther back in the passage until you find a noun that fits, that is, makes sense in the context.

It's worth noting, too, that the pronoun *their* at the end of sentence 2 refers to professors of journalism, not to the scholars described in sentence 1. Read the second sentence again, and you'll see that the scholars are exploring the concerns and beliefs of journalism professors along with, or in addition to, "the assumptions" reflected in the professors' conclusions.

Copyright © Cengage Learning. All rights reserved.

Keep an Eye on *Which*

Like *this* and *that*, the pronoun *which* can also refer to a thought larger than a single word or phrase. Consider this example:

> Power is an ingredient in almost every relationship, but the role of power, or who has more of *it*, is seldom discussed, *which* may be the reason why relationships can get rocky.

In this excerpt, the pronoun *it* refers to, or stands in for, one single word, "power." But the pronoun *which* represents a whole string of words: "the role of power, or who has more of it, is seldom discussed." Here then is another illustration of why pronouns like *this*, *that*, and *which* need your close attention. Pass them over too quickly and you might connect them to a single word instead of the broader idea they really represent.

General Category Substitutes

Instead of a pronoun, writers can also use a more general term that can include and, therefore, refer to the person, event, or idea they want to focus on throughout the passage. For instance, in the excerpt that follows, the word *document* is a more general stand-in for "the Constitution."

> [1]Once the states received copies of the Constitution, Americans began an intense discussion about whether to ratify the changes it proposed. [2]They expressed a great spectrum of opinions about different provisions within the *document*, and they used the press, the pulpit, and public podiums to spread their views on *it* to every layer of society.
>
> (Adapted from Gillon and Matson, *The American Experiment*, p. 266.)

In this example, the author uses *document*, a general word stand-in, along with the pronoun *it*, to keep readers' attention focused on the Constitution, which is the topic of the discussion.

Substitute by Association

Writers sometimes build a chain of repetition and reference by using words associated with the key word already introduced. In the following passage, for instance, the author starts out using pronouns to refer to the dogs in the bomb squad, "*their* behavior." But by the end of the second

Copyright © Cengage Learning. All rights reserved.

sentence, she uses a phrase associated with dogs to tell readers, "I'm still talking about dogs."

> ¹The dogs in the bomb squad had been carefully trained to stay at attention until the whistle blew. ²But once it did, their behavior changed dramatically, and there was much wild yipping and tail wagging.

In this example, the author uses the phrase "yipping and tail wagging" as a signal to readers that dogs are still the topic being discussed. It's not unusual for writers to use associated words to represent the topic, for example, a passage describing the reign of King George III might use "the crown" for a repeat reference to the king while a passage talking about cats might use "meowing and hissing" to indicate to readers that cats are still the subject.

◆ **EXERCISE 1**   **Filling in the Gaps with Inferences**

DIRECTIONS   Read each passage. Then answer the questions by filling in the blanks.

 EXAMPLE   ¹Early in the twentieth century, U.S. engineer Frederick Taylor (1911) published the first systematic presentation of what was soon called scientific management. ²Taylor assumed that the primary goal of an organization was to maximize efficiency. ³For a manufacturing company, *this* means getting maximum productivity. (Thio, *Society: Myths and Realities*, p. 145.)

In sentence 3, the author uses the pronoun *this* to refer to maximizing efficiency.

EXPLANATION   In the third sentence, the author uses the pronoun *this* in combination with the verb "means" to tell readers that he is about to define "maximize efficiency" from sentence 2.

 1. ¹It is possible to speak of *social character types or orientations** that are frequently shared by the people of a particular culture. ²The psychologist Erich Fromm identified five personalities that are common in Western societies. (Adapted from Engler, *Personality Theories*, p. 138.)

In sentence 2, the author uses _____ to refer to the "social character types or orientations" introduced in sentence 1.

―――――――――
*orientations: leanings, tendencies, inclinations.

Copyright © Cengage Learning. All rights reserved.

2. [1]When Julieta Venegas released her much-anticipated third *album* in November 2003, her fans were understandably shocked. [2]Titled *Sí*, the collection found the formerly introspective* entertainer from Tijuana singing about being happily in love. (Adapted from Lechner, *Rock en Español*, p. 110.)

In sentence 2, the author uses _____ to refer to the word *album* introduced in sentence 1.

3. [1]Sir Isaac Newton's *book Mathematical Principles of Natural Philosophy* was published in Latin in 1687, when he was forty-five. [2]*It* is considered by many to be the most important publication in the history of physics.

In sentence 2, the author uses the pronoun *it* and _____ to refer to the word *book* introduced in sentence 1.

4. [1]Poor environment, poor people, and poor public services are problems in *rural America* as well as in the cities. [2]There are rural slums and rural poor, less visible only because they are less concentrated. [3]Many farmers do not have enough land for profitable operation and many rural workers lack the skills needed to make a living in the cities. (Sampson et al., *The American Economy: Analysis, Issues, Principles,* p. 459.)

In sentence 3, the authors use the word _____ to refer to the phrase *rural America* introduced in sentence 1.

5. [1]Publishers are well aware that not every *book* will top the bestseller list. [2]In fact, most sell no more than a few thousand copies, leading wary publishers to carefully weed through submitted manuscripts looking for appealing titles.

In sentence 2, the author uses _____ and _____ to refer to the word *book* introduced in sentence 1.

6. [1]The colonists who chose to protest taxation by the British government in 1765 and 1767 did not think of themselves as rebels or

_____

*introspective: inward-looking, thoughtful.

Copyright © Cengage Learning. All rights reserved.

revolutionaries. [2]Indeed, most of *them* would have been shocked at the suggestion that *they* were no longer British patriots.

In sentence 2, the author uses *them* and *they* to refer to the word _____ introduced in sentence 1.

7. [1]In the late 1960s, many celebrities, including the Beatles and the Beach Boys, followed the Indian guru* *Maharishi Mahesh Yogi*. [2]But when the Beatles went to India to spend three months studying under the *Maharishi, Ringo Starr* returned home *with his wife, Maureen*. [3]The couple was apparently unhappy with the great sage's accommodations. (Adapted from Kurlansky, *1968*, p. 130.)

In sentence 3, the author uses _____ to refer to Ringo Starr and his wife from sentence 2 and _____ to refer to the Maharishi Mahesh Yogi introduced in sentence 1 and mentioned in sentence 2.

8. [1]Robert Kennedy loved children. [2]Where other politicians would smile with babies or strike a vote-getting pose with children, Bobby always looked as though he wanted to run off and play with them. [3]Children could sense *this* and were happy and uninhibited around him. (Kurlansky, *1968*, p. 138.)

In sentence 3, the pronoun *this* refers to _____

_____.

9. [1]In South Carolina, cotton growers believed that the tariff on their crop was paying the country's bills and underwriting industrial development in the North. [2]They had a *point*. (Conlin, *The American Past*, p. 267.)

In sentence 2, the word *point* refers to _____

_____.

10. [1]*Dr. Andrew Ellicott Douglass and his assistants*, who had turned up in virtually all the pueblos of the Southwest with their drills, had aroused the suspicion of the Indians. [2]The scientists tried to win

_____
*guru: wise person.

Copyright © Cengage Learning. All rights reserved.

them over by living with them for a time. ³They made efforts to learn the Indians' language and complicated code of courtesy. (Cream, *The First Americans*, p. 168.)

In sentences 2 and 3, the author uses _____ and

_____ to refer to Dr. Andrew Ellicott Douglass and *his assistants* introduced in sentence 1.

 ## Inferring Main Ideas

Now that we've looked at some of the inferences needed to connect sentences, it's time to take the next step. We need to look at how sentences can also combine to suggest an overall main idea that is implied, or strongly suggested, but never stated in a topic sentence.

Here's the first example in which the author doesn't include a topic sentence yet still manages to suggest a main idea that ties all the sentences together.

> The philosopher Arthur Schopenhauer lived most of his life completely alone. Separated from his family and distrustful of women, he had neither wife nor children. Irrationally* afraid of thieves, he kept his belongings carefully locked away and was said to keep loaded pistols near him while he slept. His sole companion was a poodle named Atma (a word that means "world soul"). However, even Atma occasionally disturbed his peace of mind. Whenever she was bothersome or barked too much, her master would grow irritated and call her *mensch*, which is German for "human being."

In this paragraph, the author supplies a number of specific details about Schopenhauer's character and behavior: (1) he lived most of his life alone, (2) he distrusted women, (3) he always thought he was going to be robbed, (4) his only companion was a dog, and (5) he called his dog a "human being" if she irritated him. However, none of those statements sums up the point of the paragraph.

This is a case where the author leaves it to the reader to infer a main idea that can sum up all the specific details in the same way a topic sentence might. In this instance, a main idea like the following would fit the bill: Schopenhauer had little use for his fellow human beings. That

_____

*irrationally: without reason or logic, not based on reason.

Copyright © Cengage Learning. All rights reserved.

idea follows logically from the details presented in the paragraph, and it's expressed in a general sentence that could sum up the paragraph's supporting details. In other words, it could easily function as a topic sentence.

The Difference Between Logical and Illogical Inferences

When readers can't find a general sentence to sum up the paragraph, they infer one that fits or follows from the details the author included. However, they are careful to make their inference logical. They base it solidly, that is, on the author's statements.

Recognizing the Difference

For an illustration of the difference between a logical and an illogical inference, imagine that we had come up with this implied main idea for the paragraph about Schopenhauer: "Schopenhauer's miserable childhood made it impossible for him to have healthy relationships with other people." Although the paragraph offers plenty of evidence that Schopenhauer did not have healthy relationships with people, it doesn't discuss his childhood.

While common sense suggests that an adult who doesn't like people may have had a troubled childhood, readers cannot rely too much on common sense to draw inferences about implied main ideas. To be useful, inferences must rely most heavily on what the author explicitly, or directly, says. Inferences based more on the reader's experience than the author's actual statements can cause a communication breakdown between reader and writer.

Evaluating Inferences

To evaluate your ability to distinguish between logical and illogical inferences, read the next paragraph. When you finish, look at the two implied main ideas that follow and decide which one fits the paragraph and which one does not.

> In the West, the Middle Eastern country of Kuwait has a reputation for being more liberal than other Middle Eastern countries, at least

Copyright © Cengage Learning. All rights reserved.

where women's rights are concerned. Yet the majority of Kuwait's female students are not permitted to study abroad, no matter how good their grades. Similarly, females almost never receive funding for international athletic competitions. Although the Kuwaiti government promised to give women the right to vote once the Persian Gulf War of 1990–1991 was over, it took the government fourteen years to make good on its promise. Even today, women are still routinely denied professional advancement. Female lawyers, for instance, are not allowed to become judges. Still, Kuwaiti feminists remain hopeful about future victories.

Based on the above paragraph, which implied main idea makes more sense?

1. It's clear that the government of Kuwait will never allow women full equality.

2. Despite Kuwait's liberal reputation, women are not treated as the equals of men in many key areas.

If you chose implied main idea 2, you've grasped the difference between logical and illogical inferences. This implied main idea is solidly backed by what the author actually says. The specific details supplied by the author support the claim that Kuwaiti women lack equality in key areas. The second implied main idea is also not contradicted by anything said in the paragraph. That's important. If you infer a main idea that is undermined or contradicted by any of the author's statements, you need to draw a different inference.

Unlike implied main idea 2, implied main idea 1 is contradicted by the paragraph's last sentence. If Kuwaiti feminists still have hope, there's no reason to infer that the Kuwaiti government will never change.

While your personal experience and background knowledge always contribute to the author's meaning, it's important that you never let your personal experience or thoughts overwhelm the actual statements supplied by the author. When it comes to interpreting the author's meaning, the actual words on the page should carry more weight than your thoughts on the topic.

Copyright © Cengage Learning. All rights reserved.

Logical Inferences
♦

1. are solidly grounded in, or based on, specific statements in the passage.
2. are not contradicted by any statements made in the passage.
3. rely more heavily on the author's words than on the reader's background knowledge or common sense.

Illogical Inferences
♦

1. do not follow from the author's actual statements.
2. are contradicted by the author.
3. rely too heavily on the reader's personal experience or general knowledge rather than on the author's words.

ALLUSION ALERT

The Fountain of Youth

The fountain of youth turns up in ancient legends, which claim that bathing in a mysterious fountain can make the old young again. In 1512 the Spanish explorer Juan Ponce de León set off to find the fountain that could erase the signs of aging. Eventually he landed in Florida, which he settled even though he had not been successful in his search. Nowadays, an allusion to the fountain of youth, with or without any reference to Ponce de León, suggests that some behavior, lotion, or activity restores or tries to restore youth—for example: "For some people exercise does seem to be a fountain of youth, and in his seventies, exercise guru Joseph Pilates had the body of a much younger man."

♦ **EXERCISE 2   Implied Main Ideas**

DIRECTIONS   Read each passage. Then circle the letter of the implied main idea.

EXAMPLE   Over the years, countless numbers of men and women have paid large sums of money for a treatment commonly known as *cell therapy*. Their reason was simple: They believed lamb-cell injections could help them maintain their youth. Such people apparently don't know that animal cells, when injected into the human body, are

Copyright © Cengage Learning. All rights reserved.

destroyed by the immune system. Others in a similar pursuit of youth have tried *chelation therapy*, which is supposed to pull heavy metals like lead and mercury from the body. Proponents claim that the treatments improve cell function, inhibit the aging process, and prevent heart disease, all by eliminating poisons from the body, yet research shows no such effect. In fact, critics question the idea of there being poisons in the body to begin with, suggesting that the therapy has nothing to treat. Other seekers of the fountain of youth use human growth hormone (HGH) tablets or sprays. These sprays and tablets can allegedly accomplish everything from eliminating wrinkles to improving memory and concentration. Yet such treatments have no research backing up these claims. There is, however, evidence that HGH in any form may produce side effects like an increased risk of cancer and cardiovascular disease.

Implied Main Idea

a. Therapies designed to keep people young are generally worthless.
b. Therapies for staying younger should be available for everyone, not just for those rich enough to afford them.
c. Treatments designed to help people maintain youth invariably do more harm than good.

EXPLANATION Nothing in the paragraph suggests that therapies to maintain youth should be made available to everyone. Nor does the paragraph suggest that all the treatments could cause harm. Most of the statements suggest that these therapies are useless against aging, making inference *a* the best choice for an implied main idea.

1. The founding fathers based the Constitution of the United States on republican rather than democratic principles. In other words, laws were to be made by the representatives of citizens, not by the citizens directly. Yet whatever the intentions of the founding fathers may have been, eighteen U.S. states provide for legislation by initiative. As it turned out, voters can place legislative measures (and sometimes constitutional amendments) directly on the ballot as long as they get the required number of signatures on a petition. In addition, forty-nine states allow for *referendums*, a procedure that lets voters reject a measure adopted by the state legislature. Fifteen states permit *recalls*. If enough signatures can be collected, an elected official has to go before the voters, who may well vote him or her out of office. This

Copyright © Cengage Learning. All rights reserved.

is precisely what happened to Governor Gray Davis of California in 2003—a recall election propelled him out of office. The election took place because many of the same citizens who had elected Davis were unhappy with his performance and wanted him gone.

Implied Main Idea

a. Whatever the founding fathers had in mind, there are still a number of ways in which the United States is governed by democratic rather than republican principles.

b. The founding fathers were fearful of a democracy in which the majority ruled.

c. Over the last ten years, U.S. citizens have consistently challenged the legality of the Constitution through initiatives, recalls, and referendums.

 2. On the one hand (if you can forgive the pun*), left-handers have often demonstrated special talents. Left-handers have been great painters (Leonardo da Vinci, Pablo Picasso), outstanding performers (Marilyn Monroe, Jimi Hendrix), and even presidents (Ronald Reagan, George H. W. Bush). (As these examples suggest, left-handedness is considerably more common among males than among females.) And left-handedness has been reported to be twice as common among children who are mathematical geniuses as it is in the overall population. On the other hand, left-handers have often been viewed as clumsy and accident-prone. They "flounder about like seals out of water," wrote one British psychologist. The very word for "left-handed" in French—*gauche*—also means "clumsy." Because of such negative attitudes toward left-handedness, in previous decades parents and teachers often encouraged children who showed signs of being left-handed to write with their right hands. (Adapted from Rubin et al., *Psychology*, p. 59.)

Implied Main Idea

a. Left-handed people tend to be more creative than right-handed people; nevertheless, the world has been organized to suit right-handers rather than left-handers.

b. Although some very gifted people have been left-handers, left-handed people have a reputation for being clumsy or awkward.

c. With the exception of baseball players, very few great athletes have been left-handers.

---

*pun: a humorous play on words, "I do it for the pun of it."

Copyright © Cengage Learning. All rights reserved.

Copyright © Cengage Learning. All rights reserved.

3. When Google started storing data back in 2001, it ran some 8,000 of its own computers, all actively responding to user requests for information. By 2003, that number had jumped to over 100,000. Currently, estimates suggest that Google has upward of 1,000,000 computer servers in twenty-five or more secret locations around the world. The computers handle billions of information requests each day. And despite the legal hurdles involved, Google has not dropped the plan to provide access to all the world's books. As the Google website explains the project: "Our ultimate goal is to work with publishers and libraries to create a comprehensive, searchable, virtual card catalog of all books in all languages that helps users discover new books and publishers discover new readers."

Implied Main Idea

a. Google's plan to create a virtual card catalog seems to have too many legal problems to be successful, but management refuses to give up the idea.

b. In a very brief amount of time, Google completely swamped its other search-engine rivals.

c. In a very short amount of time, Google has hugely expanded its operations, and there are signs that the company has even bigger plans for the future.

4. As most of us know from experience, if we concentrate too intensively on a tough problem, we can get stuck in a mental rut. Our thinking narrows, and we struggle vainly to come up with new ideas. But if we let the problem sit unattended for a time—if we "sleep on it"—we often return to it with a fresh perspective and a burst of creativity. Research by Ap Dijksterhuis, a Dutch psychologist who heads the Unconscious Lab at Radboud University in Nijmegen, indicates that such breaks in our attention give our unconscious mind time to grapple with a problem, bringing to bear information and cognitive processes unavailable to conscious deliberation. But Dijksterhuis's work also shows that our unconscious thought processes don't engage with a problem until we've clearly and consciously defined the problem. If we don't have a particular intellectual goal in mind, Dijksterhuis writes "unconscious thought does not occur." (Carr, *The Shallows*, p. 119.)

Implied Main Idea

a. Sleeping after studying is the key to thoroughly understanding new information.

b. Working on the same mathematical problem or mental task for a long period of time is an ineffective way of learning.

c. If we are working on a difficult task but know what we want to achieve, then taking a break from that task can often give us the answer we are searching for.

d. According to research done by the Dutch psychologist Ap Dijksterhuis, we can study while we are sleeping if we think about the issue or problem at hand right before going to bed.

TAKING A CLOSER LOOK

Implied Background Knowledge

In paragraph 3 of Exercise 2, what two-word phrase concerning Google's original function is implied but never stated?

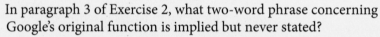

_____

Why does the author think the phrase need not be mentioned?

_____

_____

◆ **EXERCISE 3** **Inferring Main Ideas**

DIRECTIONS Read each passage. Then circle the letter of the implied main idea.

1. The widely acclaimed singer and guitarist Buddy Holly died in a 1959 plane crash at age 22. Famed singer Otis Redding was only 26 when he was killed in a plane crash in 1967. At age 27, legendary rock guitarist Jimi Hendrix died from suffocation in 1970 after swallowing a mix of liquor and pills. Jim Morrison, lead singer of the popular rock band The Doors, was also only 27 when he died of mysterious causes in 1971. Just two weeks after Hendrix's death, rock-and-roll idol Janis Joplin died of a heroin overdose, also at the age of 27. In 1979, Sid Vicious, the 21-year-old bass player of the influential Sex Pistols punk-rock band, took his own life. In 1994, Kurt Cobain, world-renowned lead singer for the band Nirvana, committed suicide; he was also only 27 years old. Rapper Tupac Shakur was only 25 years old when he was shot four times after watching Mike Tyson fight in Las Vegas. The rapper died of his wounds six days later. Christopher George Wallace, popularly known as Biggie Smalls, or The Notorious BIG, was only 24 when he

Copyright © Cengage Learning. All rights reserved.

was killed in a drive-by shooting in Los Angeles on March 9, 1997. The rap musician and music producer Disco D was only 27 when he committed suicide in 2008, after suffering from a long bout with depression.

Implied Main Idea

a. Plane crashes have taken the lives of many of rock's biggest stars.
b. Many celebrities have died when they were at the peak of their fame.
c. Many of rock and hip-hop's biggest stars died young.
d. Like hip-hop, the world of rock music was plagued by violence.

2. A Harris poll indicated that Americans, on average, believe that there is a 50 percent chance that they will be seriously hurt in a car accident. In reality, the chance of this is about 5 percent. The average woman believes that she has a 40 percent chance of getting breast cancer. However, the chance of this happening is actually only one in ten, or 10 percent. Women also believe that they have a 50 percent chance of having a heart attack, but the actual risk is just one in ten. The average man believes that he has about a 40 percent chance of getting prostate cancer, yet in reality the risk is also only one in ten. Although most people estimate their chance of getting HIV/AIDS to be about one in ten, the risk is actually about one in twenty, or 5 percent. (Source of statistics: Humphrey Taylor, "The Harris Poll #7: Perceptions of Risks," HarrisInteractive, January 27, 1999.)

Implied Main Idea

a. Most people underestimate their chances of developing many diseases or being hurt in an accident.
b. In general, people are inclined to worry about things that never happen.
c. Most people accurately estimate their chances of developing many diseases or being hurt in an accident.
d. Most people overestimate their chances of developing cancer.

3. Cleveland child psychologist Sylvia Rimm interviewed 5,400 children in eighteen states about their worries, fears, relationships, and self-confidence. She also talked with another 300 children in focus groups. She discovered that overweight children feel less intelligent and less confident than their normal-weight peers. Overweight children also worry more than their slimmer peers. Rimm discovered as well that heavier children are lonelier and sadder than other kids, describing family relationships more negatively than average-weight children describe theirs. Unfortunately, most overweight kids are

Copyright © Cengage Learning. All rights reserved.

forced to endure their peers' hurtful taunts and ridicule much more frequently than normal-weight kids do. (Source of study: Nanci Hellmich, "Heavy Kids Battle Sadness Along with Weight," *USA Today*, March 28, 2004, p. 8D.)

Implied Main Idea

a. According to Sylvia Rimm, average-weight children are very cruel to overweight children.

b. Sylvia Rimm's research indicates that negative emotions and problems lead children to overeat and become overweight.

c. Sylvia Rimm's survey indicates that overweight children suffer more than their average-weight peers do.

d. Childhood obesity is a growing problem in the United States.

4. In June 1840, Lucretia Mott and Elizabeth Cady Stanton attended the World Anti-Slavery Convention in London. Although both were activists in the cause of abolition, Mott was an actual delegate to the convention as were several other American women. Mott, though, never took her convention seat. It was denied her after several male delegates, among them Stanton's husband, vehemently expressed their disapproval of women abolitionists participating in the convention on an equal footing with men. Although there were strong protests to the exclusion of women from the proceedings, those opposed to the female delegates carried the day, and all the women attending were restricted to sitting in the balcony of the meeting hall and assuming the role of onlookers rather than participants. Still, it was in the balcony that Mott struck up a friendship with Elizabeth Cady Stanton. The two women bonded because of their mutual anger at being excluded. As a result of their exclusion, the two vowed to found their own movement and hold their own convention. Mott and Stanton were true to their word. Eight years later, in 1848, the first women's rights convention took place in Seneca Falls, New York. The Seneca Falls Convention is now considered the official starting point of a feminist movement that would forever change the social role of women in the United States and eventually give them the right to vote in 1920.

Implied Main Idea

a. The 1848 Seneca Falls Convention forever changed the role of women in the United States.

b. Thanks to Lucretia Mott, Elizabeth Cady Stanton was inspired to become a feminist, who spoke for an entire generation of women.

Copyright © Cengage Learning. All rights reserved.

c. Had Mott and Stanton not been excluded from the World Anti-Slavery Convention, the very influential Seneca Falls Convention might never have taken place.

d. Lucretia Mott profoundly influenced the life of Elizabeth Cady Stanton, who went on to become a leader of the nineteenth-century feminist revolution.

INTERNET FOLLOW-UP: Elizabeth Cady Stanton's Speech of a Lifetime

What is the title of the speech Elizabeth Cady Stanton gave when she retired from the National American Woman Suffrage Association in 1877?

_____

In the speech's opening lines, Stanton gives a very explicit reason why women needed equality with men. What is that reason?

_____

_____

_____

◆ **EXERCISE 4**   **Recognizing Implied Main Ideas**

DIRECTIONS   Read each passage. Then circle the letter of the implied main idea.

1. For many years, studies have suggested that being married is beneficial to a woman's health because married women tend to have lower rates of heart disease and stroke than unmarried women. However, researchers wanted to find out whether this is true for both happily and unhappily married women. In one study, psychologists followed 422 upper-middle-class women for twelve years, from their forties into their fifties. They checked the women's blood pressure, blood fats, glucose levels, and abdominal fat because all these factors indicate the risk for heart disease and stroke. They discovered that women who were either unhappily married or divorced by age fifty were twice as likely as single women to be at risk for heart attacks and

Copyright © Cengage Learning. All rights reserved.

strokes. Other studies, too, are producing similar results. (Source of study: Marilyn Elias, "Marriage Taken to Heart," *USA Today*, March 5, 2004, p. 8D.)

Implied Main Idea

a. Research has shown that married women are healthier than unmarried women.

b. Studies suggest that while a happy marriage may be good for a woman's health, an unhappy marriage does not produce the same benefit.

c. According to recent studies, single women are actually healthier than married women.

d. Studies indicate that women who marry in their forties tend to be healthier than women who marry in their twenties.

2. In 1822, James Forten responded to the American Colonization Society's proposal that free blacks like him "return" to Africa: "My great-grandfather was brought to this country a slave from Africa. My grandfather obtained his own freedom. My father never wore the yoke. He rendered valuable service to his country in the war of our Revolution; and I, though then a boy, was a drummer in that war. I have since lived and labored in useful employment, have acquired property, and have paid taxes....Yet some ingenious*gentlemen have recently discovered that I am still an African; that a continent three thousand miles away—and more—from the place where I was born is my native country." (Adapted from Conlin, *The American Past*, p. 302.)

Implied Main Idea

a. Many freed slaves followed the suggestion of the American Colonization Society and returned to Africa, but James Forten was not among them.

b. Many African Americans distinguished themselves during the Revolutionary War but none more so than James Forten.

c. James Forten was sarcastic about the American Colonization Society's idea that free African Americans like himself should "return" to Africa.

d. Like many other do-gooder groups throughout history, the members of the American Colonization Society had little real experience with the people they wanted to help.

---

*ingenious: clever, forward-thinking.

Copyright © Cengage Learning. All rights reserved.

Copyright © Cengage Learning. All rights reserved.

3. At this point, a convincing body of evidence suggests that the Wild West was never as wild as it is imagined by most Americans. Books like Richard Slotkin's immensely readable *Gunfighter Nation* have convincingly argued that while violence and lawlessness were present in the early days of the western states, there were actually many more attempts to cooperate and build primitive codes of law than there were gunfights. In fact, as Terry L. Anderson and Peter J. Hill, the authors of *The Not So Wild, Wild West: Property Rights on the Frontier*, point out, probably no more than a dozen bank robberies occurred in the heyday of the so-called Wild West, the years between 1869 and 1900. Yet Americans don't seem to care. Tourists still line up in droves to re-enact the gunfight at the O.K. Corral between Wyatt Earp and the Clanton boys. And those same tourists keep dude ranches and fake ghost towns booming. Tourists in pursuit of the Wild West are probably also the main reason why groups like the "Cheyenne Gunslingers Association," "Gunfighters for Hire," and "Cowboys of the Old West" continue to multiply.

Implied Main Idea

a. Writers of history textbooks are completely out of touch with the interests of the American people.

b. Americans' fascination with the Wild West continues despite convincing evidence that the West was not nearly as wild as people imagine.

c. The people who travel west to re-enact the adventures that supposedly took place in the heyday of the Wild West (1869–1900) are just wasting their money.

d. If historians didn't write just dry, dusty prose, perhaps more people would pay attention to books claiming to dispel the myth of the Wild West.

4. In 2010, the International Center for Media and the Public Agenda decided to explore the idea that many of today's students are addicted to social media. Titled "24 Hours Unplugged" and performed by researchers at the University of Maryland, the study asked 200 students what they would do if they had to spend a day without being hooked up to social media. Subjects in the study had to give up cell phones, Facebook, Twitter, etc., and then answer questions about their experience by blogging on a private website. Although the researchers had expected subjects to dislike not having access to social media, even they were surprised by their subjects' responses.

One student wrote that without access to texting or instant messaging, she felt "quite alone and secluded from my life." Those feelings were echoed by many of the other students in the study, who reported symptoms similar to addicts withdrawing from a drug: They were jittery, anxious, and miserable. As one student expressed it, "Although I started the day feeling good, I noticed my mood started to change around noon. I started to feel isolated and lonely." Susan D. Moeller, the project director, said that for many students in the study, "going without media meant, in their world, going without their friends and family." It was that feeling of being cut off from loved ones that made not using any social media, even for twenty-four hours, seem unbearable. (Source of quotations: Laster, "Students Denied Social Media Go Through Withdrawal," *The Chronicle of Higher Education,* April 29, 2010.)

Implied Main Idea

a. The suggestion that young people today are addicted to social media seems to be more than idle chatter; studies show that students denied access to social media are incapable of functioning.

b. Students today no longer have a personal connection to friends and family; they have replaced their family and friends with a variety of social media that act as substitutes for relationships the students don't have.

c. All the students in a study conducted by the International Center for Media and the Public Agenda behaved like addicts withdrawing from a drug after they were denied access to social media.

d. One 2010 study conducted by the International Center for Media and the Public Agenda suggests that some students, initially at least, may suffer addiction like symptoms of withdrawal if they have no access to social media.

TAKING A CLOSER LOOK

Who Said That?

In passage 4, who says that the lack of access to social media felt "unbearable" to the students participating?

_____

Does it matter who used the word?

_____

_____

_____

Copyright © Cengage Learning. All rights reserved.

◆ **EXERCISE 5**   **Inferring Main Ideas from Paragraphs**

DIRECTIONS   Read the paragraph. Then write a sentence that expresses the implied main idea.

EXAMPLE   The plant known as kudzu was introduced to the South in the 1920s. At the time, it promised to be a boon* to farmers who needed a cheap and abundant food crop for pigs, goats, and cattle. Because it grows like a weed, it was assumed that kudzu could provide an inexpensive and plentiful supply of food for agricultural animals. However, within half a century, kudzu had overrun seven million acres of land, and huge patches of the plant had developed root systems weighing up to three hundred pounds. Currently, no one really knows how to keep kudzu under control. It's creating problems for everyone from boaters to farmers.

Implied Main Idea   Intended to help farmers, kudzu has proven to be more harmful than beneficial.

EXPLANATION   The author starts off discussing the benefits kudzu was supposed to provide but ends by saying what a pest the plant has become. The implied main idea has to unite these two points of view.

1. According to the dictates of the Catholic Church, when a person reveals during confession that he or she has physically harmed another, priests are required to observe canon law† and withhold the information from law-enforcement authorities. Although the practice has come increasingly under attack, state law has generally acknowledged what is known as the priest-penitent privilege. Some states like New Hampshire and Kentucky, however, do not permit priests to offer confidentiality to child-abuse suspects. Others distinguish between conversations inside and outside the confession box. While many states still grant confidentiality to all priest-penitent conferences regardless of their setting, others are allowing courts to rule that conversations outside the confessional box do not always qualify as privileged communications. In Idaho, for example, a court ruled that an abusive father's confession to a hospital chaplain was not protected by canon law and could be used as evidence.

Implied Main Idea   _____

_____

_____

*boon: gift, benefit.
†canon law: rules and regulations governing Christian churches.

Copyright © Cengage Learning. All rights reserved.

2. Some spider webs contain drops of glue that hold their prey fast. Other webs contain a kind of natural Velcro that tangles and grabs the legs of insects innocently flying by. But spider webs don't always function simply as traps. Some webs also act as lures. Garden spiders use a special silk that makes their intricate decorations stand out because, as experiments have shown, the decorated parts attract more insects. Lured by the beauty of the web's design, the spider's prey moves in for a closer look. As soon as the web is touched, it snaps shut to enclose its prisoner and the spider's dinner. Other kinds of spiders, like the spitting spider, use webs as weapons. The spitting spider "spits" a sticky substance to form a web, which plasters its prey against a wall.

Implied Main Idea _____

_____

3. The day you learned of your acceptance to college was probably filled with great excitement. No doubt you shared the good news and your future plans with family and friends. Your thoughts may have turned to being on your own, making new friends, and developing new skills. Indeed, most people view college as a major pathway to fulfilling their highest aspirations.* However, getting accepted may have caused you to wonder: What will I study? How will I decide on a major? Will I do the amount of studying that college requires? Will I be able to earn acceptable grades? (Adapted from Williams and Long, *Manage Your Life*, p. 157.)

Implied Main Idea _____

_____

4. On the evening of January 24, 1848, a carpenter from New Jersey, James Marshall, took a walk along the American River where it tumbles through the foothills of the Sierra Nevada. Marshall was working for John Augustus Sutter, a colorful Swiss adventurer, who had turned a Mexican land grant into a feudal domain.† Marshall was building a sawmill for Sutter on the river. He was inspecting a ditch that returned water to the river when he noticed a curious metallic stone. "Boys," he told his crew, "I think I have found a gold mine." He had, and that was it for the sawmill. Sutter's employees

_____

*aspirations: hopes, dreams, desires.
†feudal domain: land that is completely under the control of the owner.

Copyright © Cengage Learning. All rights reserved.

dropped their hammers and set to shoveling gravel from the river, separating the sand and silt from what proved to be plenty of gold dust and nuggets. Marshall's discovery briefly ended the existence of San Francisco. A town of 500 on a huge harbor, it was depopulated when "everyone," including the recently arrived military garrison, headed for the hills. (Conlin, *The American Past*, p. 338.)

Implied Main Idea _____

_____

5. In the nineteenth century, when white settlers moved into territory inhabited by Navajo and other tribal peoples, the settlers took much more than they needed simply to survive. They cut open the earth to remove tons of minerals, cut down forests for lumber to build homes, dammed the rivers, and plowed the soil to grow crops to sell at distant markets. The Navajo did not understand why white people urged them to adopt these practices and improve their lives by creating material wealth. When told he must grow crops for profit, a member of the Comanche tribe (who, like the Navajo, believed in obeying rather than controlling the laws of nature) replied, "The Earth is my mother. Do you give me an iron plow to wound my mother's breast? Shall I take a scythe[†] to cut my mother's hair?" (Adapted from Norton et al., *A People and a Nation*, p. 499.)

Implied Main Idea _____

_____

TAKING A CLOSER LOOK

The Point of Comparison
The Comanche tribesman combines what two things?

_____

What is the point of his comparison?

_____

_____

———————
[†]scythe: large, curved knife.

Copyright © Cengage Learning. All rights reserved.

Copyright © Cengage Learning. All rights reserved.

> ## ✔ CHECK YOUR UNDERSTANDING
>
> Explain the difference between logical and illogical inferences.
>
> _____
>
> _____
>
> _____

◆ Drawing Inferences About Supporting Details

Even when the topic sentence is present in a paragraph, readers still need to draw bridging inferences. Readers draw these inferences to understand how supporting details relate to one another and contribute to the main idea. Bridging inferences answer questions like: What is the function of this sentence? Does it further explain the previous sentence, or does it refer to or revise a point made earlier in the paragraph?

Although **bridging inferences** are not essential to every supporting detail in a paragraph, they are necessary for a good many. Without them, it would be difficult for readers to follow the writer's train of thought. Here's an example:

¹In the nineteenth century, questions about natural resources caught Americans between the desire for progress and the fear of spoiling the land. ²By the late 1870s and early 1880s, people eager to protect the natural landscape began to coalesce* into a conservation* movement. ³Among them was the Western naturalist John Muir, who helped establish Yosemite National Park in 1890. ⁴The next year, under pressure from Muir and others, Congress authorized President Benjamin Harrison to create forest reserves—public land protected from cutting by private interests. ⁵Such policies met with strong objections. ⁶Lumber companies, lumber dealers, and railroads were joined in their opposition by householders accustomed to cutting timber freely for fuel and building materials. ⁷Public opinion on conservation also split along sectional lines. ⁸Most supporters of regulation came from the eastern states. ⁹In the East, resources had already become less plentiful. ¹⁰Not surprisingly opposition was loudest

*coalesce: combine, form around, connect.
*conservation: protecting and preserving nature's resources or other essential supplies; also preventing loss or change.

in the West, where people were still eager to take advantage of nature's enormous resources (Adapted from Norton et al., *A People and a Nation*, p. 509.)

In this paragraph, the topic sentence is the first sentence. It tells us that by the nineteenth century Americans were caught between a simultaneous desire for progress and a fear of destroying the land in pursuit of that progress. The paragraph then gives an account of both sides, describing the first conservationists as well as those who opposed them.

But if you look closely at sentences 1 and 2, you'll see that it's up to the reader to infer the appropriate relationship between the sentences. To correctly understand just those two sentences, readers need to add the following information:

1. The people mentioned in sentence 2 are no longer trapped between the desire for progress and the desire to protect the land; they have opted for protecting the land and its natural resources.

2. The people eager to protect the natural landscape in sentence 2 are also Americans like those referred to in sentence 1.

Now look at sentence 3, which reads, "Among them was the Western naturalist John Muir, who helped establish Yosemite National Park in 1890." Here again, it's up to readers to infer why the author follows sentence 2 with sentence 3. Readers supply the following information:

1. The antecedent for *them* is "people eager to protect the natural landscape" and therefore coalescing "into a conservation movement."

2. John Muir agrees with the conservationists that the land's natural resources cannot be sacrificed to progress.

3. Establishing a park is one method conservationists use to protect the land.

Sentence 4 continues with another example of the actions conservationists took to protect the landscape—pressuring the government for forest reserves. But at no point do the authors say, "Another action that conservationists took to protect the land was pressuring the government." It's readers who have to supply the chain of reasoning behind the sentence.

The same thing is true for sentence 5, "Such policies met with strong objections." The authors don't say, "such policies designed to protect the land." They rely on readers to infer and add that detail.

Copyright © Cengage Learning. All rights reserved.

The need for reader-supplied inferences persists throughout the passage. Look closely, for instance, at sentences 8 and 9: "Most supporters of regulation came from the eastern states. In the East, resources had already become less plentiful." The connection between these two sentences is implicit rather than explicit. The reader is the one who supplies the cause and effect relationship connecting the two. *Because* the eastern states were beginning to notice that resources were less plentiful, they were more inclined to be supporters of regulation.

CHECK YOUR UNDERSTANDING

What are *bridging inferences*?

_____

_____

CHECK YOUR UNDERSTANDING Through Writing

Write two sentences that require a bridging inference to communicate their meaning.

_____

_____

_____

◆ Writers and Readers Collaborate

You may be used to thinking that writers supply all of the text you read. But, in fact, the writer does only part of the job. Writers try to put enough information on the page to explain or prove their point. But if they put every word necessary to creating the meaning, the result would be so repetitive and long, no one would read it. Thus they are forced to rely on readers to supply some of the information necessary to their intended meaning.

No matter what you may have thought in the past, you need to think of reading as an act of collaboration in which you help create the text you read. If you don't make an effort to collaborate with the author, the text's meaning may well elude you.

Copyright © Cengage Learning. All rights reserved.

◆ **EXERCISE 6**   **Making Connections Between Sentences**

DIRECTIONS   Read each passage. Then circle the letter of the correct response or fill in the blanks.

EXAMPLE   [1]In the 1820s American politics was not just a matter of voting in periodic elections. [2]On the contrary, vast numbers of Americans participated directly in politics. [3]One gauge of this was the huge number of public meetings involving large audiences that attended for the purpose of discussing current political issues. [4]On occasion, audiences were so large that members of the elite even grew fearful that the meetings would get out of hand and democracy would take the form of "mobocracy." [5]The organizers, however, were overjoyed that the meetings included not only a cross section of the electorate but many others who lent valuable collective support, even though they could not vote. (Adapted from Gillon and Matson, *The American Experiment*, p. 379.)

1. What is the stated or implied main idea of this passage?
    a. In the early days of American independence, the wealthy were worried about democracy turning into mob rule.
    b. In the 1820s, organizers of large public meetings worked hard to make large numbers of people attend.
    (c.) In the 1820s, Americans made it a point to be actively involved in politics.

2. In sentence 3, the pronoun *this* refers to <u>Americans' participation in politics; Americans' direct political participation</u>.

3. What inference do readers need to make to understand the function of sentence 3 in the paragraph?
    a. Sentence 3 reverses the train of thought introduced in sentence 2.
    (b.) Sentence 3 offers an illustration of the claim made in sentence 2.
    c. Sentence 3 repeats for emphasis the point of sentence 2.

4. What inference do readers need to make to understand the function of sentence 4 in the paragraph?
    a. Sentence 4 offers proof of the claim made in sentence 3.
    (b.) Sentence 4 describes a consequence of the events mentioned in sentence 3.
    c. Sentence 4 repeats for emphasis the point made in sentence 3.

Copyright © Cengage Learning. All rights reserved.

5. What inference do readers need to make to understand the function of sentence 5 in the paragraph?

    a. Sentence 5 describes a criticism of events mentioned in sentence 4.

    (b.) Sentence 5 offers a contrasting opinion to the one expressed in sentence 4.

    c. Sentence 5 offers proof of the claim made in sentence 4.

EXPLANATION   In this passage, the authors return in every sentence to the same stated main idea: In the early days of the nineteenth century, "vast numbers of Americans participated regularly in politics." Then, sentence by sentence, the authors offer evidence for this point of view. They discuss the anxiety direct participation in politics evoked in some and the pride the organizers of such mass meetings took in their success.

1. ¹There is no denying the importance of the future. ²In the words of the scientist Charles F. Kettering, "We should be concerned about the future because we will have to spend the rest of our lives there." ³However, important or not, the future isn't easy to predict. ⁴In 1877, when Thomas Edison invented the phonograph, he thought of it as an office dictating machine and lost interest in it. ⁵Recorded music did not become popular until twenty-one years later. ⁶When the Wright brothers offered their invention to the U.S. government and the British Royal Navy, they were told airplanes had no future in the military. ⁷A 1900 Mercedes-Benz study estimated that worldwide demand for cars would not exceed 1 million, primarily because of the limited number of available chauffeurs. ⁸In 1899, Charles H. Duell, the Commissioner of the U.S. Patent and Trademark Office, said, "Everything that can be invented has been invented." (Beekman and Quinn, *Computer Confluence,* p. 62.)

1. What is the stated or implied main idea of this passage?

    a. People who predict the future are frequently mistaken.

    b. Although it's not easy, correctly predicting the future of technology can be done.

    c. "Expert" opinion about the future of new technology has often been wrong.

Copyright © Cengage Learning. All rights reserved.

2. What inference must readers make to understand the function of sentence 3 in the paragraph?

    a. Sentence 3 modifies and revises the point made in sentence 1.

    b. Sentence 3 repeats the point made in sentence 1.

    c. Sentence 3 illustrates the point made in sentence 1.

3. What inference do readers need to make to understand the function of sentence 4 in the paragraph?

    a. Sentence 4 offers a criticism of the point made in sentence 3.

    b. Sentence 4 further illustrates the point made in sentence 1.

    c. Sentence 4 illustrates the point made in sentence 3.

4. What inference must readers make to understand the function of sentence 6 in the paragraph?

    a. Sentence 6 offers a contrasting opinion to the point made in sentence 4.

    b. Sentence 6 illustrates the point made in sentence 4.

    c. Sentence 6 offers another illustration of the point made in sentence 3.

5. What inference do readers need to make to understand the function of sentence 8 in the paragraph?

    a. Sentence 8 continues a sequence of dates and events begun in sentence 4.

    b. Sentence 8 illustrates the point made in sentence 6.

    c. Sentence 8 further illustrates the point made in sentence 3.

2. [1]In thirty-nine states, voters select judges to sit on the bench, and they face elections like any other political candidate. [2]In theory, elections maximize the value of judicial accountability. [3]It's worth observing, however, that electing judges is virtually unknown in the rest of the world, where judges are appointed based on merit systems. [4]In the United States, voter turnout is very low in most judicial elections. [5]This fact is a major criticism of choosing judges by election. [6]The winners may not be truly accountable to the people, which is the principal advantage commonly associated with elections. [7]Yet low rates of voter interest and participation frequently combine with low-key, unexciting, and issueless campaigns to keep many judges

Copyright © Cengage Learning. All rights reserved.

on the bench as long as they run for re-election. [8]One study indicates that less than 10 percent of the judges who run are defeated. (Adapted from Bowman and Kearney, *State and Local Government*, p. 25.)

1. What is the stated or implied main idea of this passage?

    a. It's altogether appropriate that many state judges have to face regular elections if they are to rule in state courts.

    b. Electing judges seems like a sound democratic idea, but it has some serious drawbacks.

    c. Electing judges may sound like a good idea, but it doesn't really work because campaigning requires money, and that means people with money can have more say in the election of a judge than ordinary people do.

2. What phrase in sentence 2 suggests that the author is going to shift gears and move in another direction? _____

3. What inference do readers need to make to understand the function of sentence 3 in the paragraph?

    a. Sentence 3 brings the reader back to the point made in sentence 1.

    b. In different words, sentence 3 repeats the point made in sentence 2.

    c. Sentence 3 continues the shift in the train of thought begun in sentence 2.

4. Which phrase in sentence 5 refers to or stands in for the information presented in sentence 4? _____

5. Sentence 6 illustrates what phrase in sentence 5?

    _____

3. [1]Every year about 28 million Americans go to tanning salons, where exposure to ultraviolet (UV) radiation stimulates the skin to tan just as if it had been exposed to the sun. [2]According to the indoor tanning industry, those who use tanning salons are reaping a dual benefit. [3]Industry representatives claim that using UV light to tan in small increments, without reddening, prevents sunburn, and sunburn is a major cause of the skin cancer melanoma. [4]They also argue that exposure to UV light in tanning salons stimulates the body's

Copyright © Cengage Learning. All rights reserved.

production of vitamin D, believed to be helpful in preventing a variety of cancers. [5]While these arguments make spending money at a tanning booth seem like a good investment, medical experts might well disagree. [6]In 1994, a Swedish study found that 18- to 30-year-old women who went to tanning salons ten times or more a year were seven times more likely to develop melanoma than women who did not use tanning salons. [7]A 2002 study at Dartmouth Medical School found that people who used tanning beds had two-and-a-half times the risk of developing a type of skin cancer called squamous cell carcinoma. [8]They also had a greater chance of developing basal cell carcinoma, another kind of skin cancer. [9]As for the second indoor tanning benefit—an increased supply of vitamin D—nutritionists insist that the proper diet provides adequate amounts of the vitamin without the accompanying skin-cancer risks.

1. What's the stated or implied main idea of this passage?

   a. Medical research does not support claims made by the tanning industry concerning the benefits of indoor tanning.

   b. The tanning industry argues that there are two basic benefits from tanning indoors, but research indicates that at least one of these claims is false.

   c. Indoor tanning might be bad for people, but tanning outdoors is even more dangerous.

2. What inference do readers need to make to understand the function of sentence 3 in the paragraph?

   a. Sentence 3 provides research backing the point made in sentence 2.

   b. Sentence 3 illustrates part of the benefit mentioned in sentence 2.

   c. Sentence 3 reverses the train of thought begun in sentence 2.

3. What inference do readers need to make to understand the function of sentence 4 in the paragraph?

   a. Sentence 4 further describes the benefit mentioned in sentence 3.

   b. Sentence 4 challenges a point made in sentence 2.

   c. Sentence 4 further clarifies the point of sentence 2.

Copyright © Cengage Learning. All rights reserved.

4. In sentence 4, the pronoun *they* refers to _____.

5. What inference do readers need to draw to understand sentence 7?

   a. Sentence 7 further develops the sequence of dates and events begun in sentence 6.

   b. Sentence 7 compares a study at Dartmouth Medical School with the Swedish study mentioned in sentence 6.

   c. Sentence 7 introduces a study that further supports the point of sentence 5.

TAKING A CLOSER LOOK

Context

In paragraph 2, based on the context, what does *judicial accountability* (sentence 2) mean?

_____

_____

WORD CHECK I

The following words were introduced and defined in pages 344–64. See how well you can match the words with the meanings. When you finish, make sure to check the meanings of any words you missed because the same words will turn up in tests at the end of the chapter.

1. orientations _____
2. introspective _____
3. guru _____
4. irrationally _____
5. pun _____
6. ingenious _____
7. boon _____
8. aspirations _____
9. coalesce _____
10. conservation _____

a. teacher, wise person

b. play on words that are similar in sound or spelling yet have different meanings

c. protecting and preserving the environment and its resources; preventing change or loss

d. clever, original, forward-thinking

e. favor, benefit, blessing

f. combine, unite, gather around

g. hopes, desires, dreams

h. serious, inward-looking

i. lacking in reason or logic

j. leanings, tendencies

Copyright © Cengage Learning. All rights reserved.

◆ **EXERCISE 7**   **More About Form and Meaning**

DIRECTIONS   Use one of the words listed below to fill in the blanks.

orientations	irrational	puns	ingenious	coalesce
introspective	guru	aspirations	boon	conservation

1. Someone who tells you that he or she is interested in global warming because it is a very heated topic, probably has a weakness for _____.

2. Although Lady Gaga might be so in real life, no one who has ever seen her perform or heard her interviewed would imagine that she is _____.

3. Only a cynic would call steroids a(n) _____ to baseball.

4. When there is no rain for weeks, the _____ of water becomes essential.

5. Someone who studies yoga, meditates, and has the cash to spare might well consider traveling to India in search of a(n) _____.

6. Inventors come up with _____ solutions. That's why they are called inventors; they find a way of doing things that no one before them has thought of.

7. People readily _____ around an issue or get behind a cause that directly relates to their lives.

8. Our _____ keep us motivated and help us get out of bed in the morning.

Copyright © Cengage Learning. All rights reserved.

9. Sometimes political _____ can become so strong they can turn into prejudices.

10. Although it's common to ask someone to be reasonable, it's unusual to make the opposite request—that they be _____.

Implied Main Ideas in Longer Readings

Longer readings, particularly those in textbooks, generally include thesis statements expressing the main idea of the entire reading. However, even writers of textbooks occasionally imply a main idea instead of explicitly stating it. When this happens, you need to respond much as you did to paragraphs lacking topic sentences. Look at what the author explicitly says and ask what inference can be drawn from those statements. That inference is your implied main idea.

To illustrate, here's a reading that lacks a thesis statement, yet still suggests a main idea.

J. Edgar Hoover and the FBI

1   Established in 1908, the Federal Bureau of Investigation (FBI) was initially quite restricted in its ability to fight crime. It could investigate only a few offenses, such as bankruptcy fraud and antitrust violations, and it could not cross state lines in pursuit of felons. It was the passage of the Mann Act in 1910 that began the FBI's rise to real power. According to the Mann Act, the FBI could now cross state lines in pursuit of women being used for "immoral purposes," such as prostitution. Prior to the Mann Act, the FBI had been powerless once a felon crossed a state line; now at least the FBI could pursue those engaged in immoral activities.

2   It was, however, the appointment of J. Edgar Hoover in 1924 that truly transformed the FBI. Hoover insisted that all FBI agents had to have college degrees and undergo intensive training at a special school created just for agents. He also lobbied* long and hard for legislation that would allow the FBI to cross state lines in pursuit of all criminals. He got his wish in 1934 with the Fugitive Felon Act, which made it illegal for a felon to escape punishment for a crime by crossing state lines. Thanks to Hoover's intensive

---

*lobbied: worked to influence government officials.

Copyright © Cengage Learning. All rights reserved.

efforts, the way was now open for the FBI to become a crack crime-fighting force with real power.

3   And fight crime the agency did. Its agents played key roles in the investigation and capture of notorious criminals in the 1930s, among them John Dillinger, Clyde Barrow, Bonnie Parker, Baby Face Nelson, Pretty Boy Floyd, and the boss of all bosses—Al Capone.

4   In 1939, impressed by the FBI's performance under Hoover, President Franklin D. Roosevelt assigned the FBI full responsibility for investigating matters related to the possibility of espionage* by the German government. In effect, Roosevelt gave Hoover a mandate* to investigate any groups he considered suspicious. This new responsibility led to the investigation and arrest of several spies. Unfortunately, J. Edgar Hoover did not limit himself to wartime spying activities. Instead, he continued his investigations long after World War II had ended and Germany had been defeated.

5   Suspicious by nature, Hoover saw enemies of the United States everywhere, and his investigations cast a wide net. In secret, the agency went after the leaders of student and civil rights groups. Even esteemed* civil rights leader Martin Luther King Jr. was under constant surveillance by the FBI. Investigation techniques during this period included forging documents, burglarizing offices, opening private mail, conducting illegal wiretaps, and spreading false rumors about sexual or political misconduct. It wasn't until Hoover's death in 1972 that the FBI's secret files on America's supposed "enemies" were made public and these investigations shut down.
(Source of details about Hoover's career: Adler, *Criminal Justice*, pp. 146–47.)

If you look for a sentence or group of sentences that sum up this reading, you're not going to find it. There is no thesis statement summing up the positive and negative effects of J. Edgar Hoover on the FBI. It's up to the reader to infer a main idea like the following: "J. Edgar Hoover was a powerful influence on the FBI. Although he did some good, he also tarnished the agency's reputation and image."

This implied thesis statement neatly fits the contents of the reading without relying on any information *not* supplied by the author. It is also *not* contradicted by anything said in the reading itself. In short, it meets the criteria, or standards, of a logical inference.

---

*espionage: spying.
*mandate: legal right, authority; also used as a verb meaning to authorize or enact a law.
*esteemed: respected.

Copyright © Cengage Learning. All rights reserved.

◆ **EXERCISE 8**   **Recognizing Implied Main Ideas in Longer Readings**

DIRECTIONS   Read each selection. Circle the letter of the statement that most effectively sums up the implied main idea of the entire reading.

EXAMPLE

The Hermits of Harlem

1   On March 21, 1947, a man called the 122nd Street police station in New York City and claimed that there was a dead body at 2078 Fifth Avenue. The police were familiar with the house, a decaying three-story brownstone in a rundown part of Harlem. It was the home of Langley and Homer Collyer, two lonely recluses* famous in the neighborhood for their eccentric—the unkind called it crazy—ways.

2   Homer was blind and crippled by rheumatism. Distrustful of doctors, he wouldn't let anybody but Langley come near him. Using their dead father's medical books, Langley devised a number of odd cures for his brother's ailments, including massive doses of orange juice and peanut butter. When he wasn't dabbling in medicine, Langley liked to invent things, like machines to clean the inside of pianos or intricately wired burglar alarms.

3   When the police responded to the call by breaking into the Collyers' home, they were astonished and horrified. The room was filled from floor to ceiling with objects of every shape, size, and kind. It took them several hours to cross the few feet to where the dead body of Homer lay, shrouded in an ancient checkered bathrobe. There was no sign of Langley, so authorities began to search for him.

4   When they found him, he was wearing a strange collection of clothes that included an old jacket, a red flannel bathrobe, several pairs of trousers, and blue overalls. An onion sack was tied around his neck; another was draped over his shoulders. Langley had died some time before his brother. He had suffocated under a huge pile of garbage that had cascaded down upon him.

5   On several occasions, thieves had tried to break in to steal the fortune that was rumored to be kept in the house. Langley had responded by building booby traps, intricate systems of trip wires and ropes that would bring tons of rubbish crashing down on any unwary intruder. But in the dim light of his junk-filled home, he had sprung one of his own traps and died some days before his brother. Homer, blind, paralyzed, and totally dependent on Langley, had starved to death.

---

*recluses: people who want to be alone and shun the presence of others.

Copyright © Cengage Learning. All rights reserved.

Implied Main Idea   a. In the end, the Collyer brothers' eccentric and reclusive ways led to their deaths.

b. The Collyer brothers' deaths were probably suicides.

c. The Collyer brothers have become more famous in death than they ever were in life.

> **EXPLANATION**   In this case, *a* is the most appropriate inference because statements in the reading combine to suggest that the brothers' eccentricity contributed to their deaths. It was, for example, a trap of Langley's own devising that killed him. However, there is no evidence that either of the brothers chose to die and the only reference to the brothers' fame is to how well known they were in the neighborhood.

1. Frustration

1   External frustrations are based on conditions outside of the individual that impede progress toward a goal. All the following are external frustrations: getting stuck with a flat tire, having a marriage proposal rejected, finding the cupboard bare when you go to get your poor dog a bone, finding the refrigerator bare when you go to get your poor tummy a T-bone, finding the refrigerator gone when you return home, being chased out of the house by your starving dog. In other words, external frustrations are based on delay, failure, rejection, loss, or another direct blocking of motives.

2   Personal frustrations are based on personal characteristics. If you are four feet tall and aspire to be a professional basketball player, you very likely will be frustrated. If you want to go to medical school, but can earn only D grades, you will likewise be frustrated. In both examples, frustration is actually based on personal limitations. Yet failure may be perceived as externally caused.

3   Whatever the type of frustration, if it persists over time, it's likely to lead to aggression. The frustration–aggression link is so common, in fact, that experiments are hardly necessary to show it. A glance at almost any newspaper will provide examples such as the following:

Justifiable Autocide

BURIEN, Washington (AP)—Barbara Smith committed the assault, but police aren't likely to press charges. Her victim was a 1964 Oldsmobile that failed to start once too often.

When Officer Jim Fuda arrived at the scene, he found one beat-up car, a broken baseball bat, and a satisfied 23-year-old Seattle woman.

"I feel good," Ms. Smith reportedly told the officer. "That car's been giving me misery for years and I killed it." (As quoted in Coon, *Essentials of Psychology*, p. 419.)

Copyright © Cengage Learning. All rights reserved.

Implied Main Idea

a. External frustration is the more painful type of frustration, and it frequently leads to aggressive feelings and actions.

b. Although there are two different types of frustration, both can, if they persist, lead to aggressive behavior.

c. Experiencing personal frustration is more psychologically wounding than feeling the effects of external frustration.

2. The Stress of Valentine's Day

1 Every year on February 14, millions of Americans make it a point to show their affection. Mailboxes fill with cards. Florists wire roses around the country. Chocolate hearts show up on store shelves. Lovers spend millions of dollars showing their "one and only" just how much they are loved. Collectively, the country celebrates romance in the name of passion's patron saint, St. Valentine. Or so it seems if you don't look too closely.

2 In an attempt to explore the effect of Valentine's Day on relationships, researchers Katherine Morse and Steven Neuberg tracked the relationships of 245 undergraduate students (99 male and 146 female; mean age 19.5 years). The researchers were especially focused on how the couples under observation survived during the week before Valentine's Day and the week after.

3 Morse and Neuberg predicted that during the two-week period straddling Valentine's Day, there would be more breakups than during other holiday times of year, say one week before and after Christmas. As it turned out, their predictions were correct. The odds of a couple breaking up were five times greater pre- and post-Valentine's Day than during any other comparable pre- and post-holiday period. Overall, the couples who had been on solid ground to begin with survived Valentine's Day without difficulty, but the shakier relationships couldn't handle the stress of a holiday devoted to romantic love. (Source of study: Strong et al., *The Marriage and Family Experience*, p. 300.)

Implied Main Idea

a. Valentine's Day is supposed to be a holiday for lovers, but in reality it's more like a holiday for becoming ex-lovers.

b. Valentine's Day, like most other holidays, puts terrible stress on relationships.

c. One study of the effect of Valentine's Day suggests that the holiday encourages couples already in troubled relationships to give in and break up.

Copyright © Cengage Learning. All rights reserved.

TAKING A CLOSER LOOK

Pronoun and Antecedent

In paragraph 1 of the reading on Valentine's Day, what does the pronoun *it* refer to in the last sentence?

_____

◆ **EXERCISE 9** **Inferring Main Ideas in Longer Readings**

DIRECTIONS Read each selection. Then write the implied main idea in the blanks that follow.

1. ## Women and the Grange

1 The story of American agriculture after the Civil War is gloriously exciting mainly when looked at in the aggregate.* For the individuals who opened up the Great Plains, life was laborious, dirty, and lonely. Winters were marked by long stretches of subzero weather and ferocious blizzards when men and women had to find their way from house to barn via a rope they had strung between the buildings. Summers were blistering hot. The only shade was under a wagon.

Life on the Great Plains was not easy, especially for women.

Bettmann/Corbis

_____

*aggregate: as a whole, in combination with other elements; sum or total.

Copyright © Cengage Learning. All rights reserved.

2   Much of the era's writing about farm life dwells on its loneliness. This is especially true for women, who never forgot their early isolation. Even in middle age, many a farm matron told her granddaughters about the day she arrived at the new home her husband had selected in the great emptiness of the plains. If the men celebrated the arrival, the women sat down and wept.

3   But some of that loneliness was diminished when in 1867, a federal employee at the Department of Agriculture, Oliver Hudson Kelley, grew distressed over the lack of sound agricultural practices in the southwestern and western regions of the country. To educate farmers, Kelley formed the National Grange of the Patrons of Husbandry,† which was organized into local Granges, or farm associations. The goal of the group was to encourage sound farming practices. Yet in the early years, Grange lodges often served as social and cultural centers for isolated rural areas. For that reason, Grange meetings often included dances and dinners, an addition some disapproved of but many were grateful for.

4   By 1900, the Grange had a million members. Surprisingly for the time, women enjoyed equality with men in decision making and other grange activities. Visitors consistently observed the same phenomenon:* Farm wives, rather than husbands, held the associations together during the Grange's early days. The women planned and administered the activities and, of course, cleaned up after them. In many ways, it was the women who, initially at least, kept the Granges going. (Adapted from Conlin, *The American Past*, p. 520.)

Implied Main Idea   _____

_____

2. Will African Penguins Go the Way of the Passenger Pigeon?

1   One hundred years ago, a million and a half African penguins waddled and swam along the coasts of South Africa and Namibia. Today, only about 120,000 African penguins remain, and they are confined to a few

_____

†husbandry: a rather old-fashioned way of talking about agricultural practices.
*phenomenon: happening, event.

Copyright © Cengage Learning. All rights reserved.

small islands off the coast of South Africa. Fortunately for the penguins' future, they are adorable. Only two feet tall with big eyes and a black stripe around their bellies, the birds attract human visitors in droves. If they are lucky, their popularity with humans will keep them alive and help them survive.

2   African penguins feed on anchovies and sardines, which until recently could readily be found in nearby waters. But around 1997, the sardines began to disappear from waters near the penguins' habitat. Some of the fish were relocating because global warming had increased water temperature and sent the fish in pursuit of cooler temperatures. However, tons of sardines and anchovies were also swept up in the nets of commercial fishermen, who have been depleting the fish population along the coast of Africa. The disappearance of their usual food supply has left the penguins stranded and starving.

3   The islands where the penguins live are also home to feral, or wild, cats who have made a meal out of penguin chicks whenever they could find them. In addition to the cats, penguin parents have had to protect their chicks from the aggressive kelp gull, a tough predator that searches out unprotected nests in order to swoop down and devour vulnerable chicks. The penguins used to be able to dig their nests so deep they could escape the threat of gulls, but settlers have dug out so much penguin guano to use as fertilizer, the ground is not as soft as it used to be, and it is harder for the birds to dig deep nests. As if threats by land and air weren't enough, in 2000 an oil spill made the waters even more dangerous than the beach. A huge bird-rescue operation saved almost forty thousand penguins, but thousands more didn't make it.

4   Environmentalists are currently mounting a campaign to save the African penguin. While relocating the birds would be difficult, supporters of the campaign are raising money to build igloos, where the birds can be protected from the sun's heat and gulls' attacks. Environmentalists are also overseeing the removal of feral cats from the island in the hopes of increasing the penguins' slim chances for survival. (Source of figures: Michael Wines, "Dinner Disappears, and African Penguins Pay the Price," www.nytimes.com/2007/ 06/04/world/africa/04robben.html.)

Implied Main Idea   _____

_____

Copyright © Cengage Learning. All rights reserved.

INTERNET FOLLOW-UP: The Grange Movement and Victory in the Supreme Court

As a result of a severe economic depression that began in 1866, the Grange movement spread rapidly, moving beyond its early social stage. By the mid-1870s, it had become a powerful force in a number of agricultural states. With the help of friendly legislators, Grangers even got state laws passed that limited railroad rates. The railroads retaliated by challenging the laws in court. In 1877, the Grange won what was viewed as a huge Supreme Court victory over the railroads. What was the name of the case, and why was it a victory for the Grange?

_____

_____

_____

_____

_____

ALLUSION ALERT

A Man for All Seasons

A Man for All Seasons was a 1954 play by Robert Bolt. Bolt's drama focused on Sir Thomas More, an adviser to King Henry VIII. Although the play dramatizes More's refusal to support Henry in his demands that the church grant him a divorce—a refusal that cost More his life—the title comes from what a contemporary of More's, Robert Whittington, wrote about More. Citing More's ability to be both witty and serious, learned and plain-speaking, Whittington called him "a man for all seasons." It was the play, however, and the movie, which followed it, that made the phrase famous. It's now used to describe a man or a woman who has numerous and varied talents, along with an ability to fit into any situation or slot—for example, "A highly acclaimed actress and a much-admired member of the British parliament, Glenda Jackson can rightly be called a woman for all seasons."

Copyright © Cengage Learning. All rights reserved.

Making Connections Between Paragraphs

Inferring the connections that link paragraphs is essential to understanding multi-paragraph readings. Look, for example, at these two paragraphs from a reading discussing the reality and the myth of frontiersman Davy Crockett.

Davy Crockett: A Man for All Seasons

The Walt Disney version of Davy Crockett's life, *Davy Crockett: Indian Fighter*, became a runaway hit in 1954 when an unknown actor named Fess Parker donned Crockett's trademark coonskin cap and played him on television. The show spawned several movies—and millions of coonskin caps—among them the 1960 smash hit *The Alamo*, starring John Wayne. In an attempt to use the film's popularity to support his favored presidential candidate, Richard Nixon, Wayne even helped finance a movie ad that showed Crockett at the Alamo.[†] The caption for the ad—"There were no ghostwriters at the Alamo, only Men"—slyly alluded to rumors that John F. Kennedy, Richard Nixon's opponent in the presidential race, had used a ghostwriter for his Pulitzer Prize–winning book, *Profiles in Courage*. A long-time Republican, Wayne was no fan of Kennedy, a Democrat, and he was deeply disappointed when Nixon was defeated, despite Wayne's attempt to link him to the heroic Davy Crockett.

Wayne, who died of lung cancer in 1979, must have spun in his grave when Paul Andrew Hutton's 1989 essay, "Davy Crockett: An Exposition of Hero Worship," was published. Hutton argued that young men volunteering for the Vietnam War had been inspired by their twin heroes, John F. Kennedy and Davy Crockett. According to Hutton, when Kennedy "issued a clarion call to fight for freedom in a distant land," young men answered the call because "they knew full well what he was talking about, for they had been brought up on those same liberal values by Disney's Davy Crockett." (Source of quotation: Allen Barra, "American Idols," *Salon.com*, April 10, 2004.)

To move smoothly between these two paragraphs, readers are expected to infer a cause and effect relationship: John Wayne, a staunch

---

[†]Alamo: In the war to make Texas part of the United States, the battle of the Alamo was a decisive one; it was also the battle in which Crockett died.

Copyright © Cengage Learning. All rights reserved.

supporter of Republican Richard Nixon, would have spun in his grave *because* he would have hated the idea of Crockett being linked to Kennedy, the man who challenged and beat his political favorite. But here again, the author does not include that information in the supporting details. Readers have to draw the right inference. In other words, bridging inferences are essential not just to connecting sentences but to connecting paragraphs as well.

ALLUSION ALERT

Clarion Call

A clarion was a medieval horn that was often used to announce a military action. From the horn and in the context in which it was used, we now have the allusion "a clarion call," which refers to a loud and clear signal that an action must be taken before it's too late to act—for example, "The party's loss in the election was a clarion call to take a new direction."

TAKING A CLOSER LOOK

Allusions and Idioms

What does the title with its allusion to "A Man for All Seasons" suggest?

_____

_____

In paragraph 2, the phrase "spun in his grave" is an idiom. Idioms are expressions that acquire their meaning through usage in a specific language. Thus non-native speakers of a particular language don't always know what idioms mean. If a non-native speaker of English asked you to explain the sentence using that idiom, how would you paraphrase it?

_____

_____

◆ EXERCISE 10 Making Connections Between Paragraphs

DIRECTIONS Read the following selection. Then circle the appropriate letters to identify the implied main idea and the connections between paragraphs that readers need to infer.

Copyright © Cengage Learning. All rights reserved.

A Boy Soldier's Story

1 When Ishmael Beah was interviewed on Jon Stewart's *The Daily Show*, the normally wisecracking Stewart showed a serious side. Even he, whose gift for on-the-spot quips seems genetically inspired, couldn't find anything amusing to say about Beah's book, *A Long Way Gone: Memoirs of a Boy Soldier*. Beah, who now lives in Brooklyn, New York, grew up in Sierra Leone, Africa, and writes about being a twelve-year-old soldier in the civil war that tore his country apart throughout the 1990s until an uneasy peace was achieved in 2002. The book does not make for good bedtime reading, unless, of course, the reader is looking for nightmares.

2 Beah's journey into hell began when members of the rebel army, the Revolutionary United Front (RUF) led by Foday Sankoh, entered his village, intent on slaughtering everyone in it. Along with several other young boys, Beah ran away and ended up moving from village to village in search of shelter, food, and safety. When he finally found a safe haven, it was a government military base.

3 But Beah's new-found safety came at a price. He was given a choice: Become a soldier or leave the base and face the rebel army, notorious for amputating the arms of its victims. Seeing this as no choice at all, Beah accepted the AK-47 handed to him and became one of the government's child soldiers. Fueled by the mix of cocaine and gunpowder all the boys were given to keep them as mindless and conscience-free as possible, Beah and his cohorts were willing to do anything asked of them no matter how bloody or horrible. As Beah describes one incident, "We walked around the village and killed everyone who came out of the houses and huts."

4 Jon Stewart was right to skip the jokes during his interview with Beah. There are few bright moments in his largely tragic story, unless one counts the time where Beah escaped the anger of rebel supporters by having some rap cassettes with him when he was captured. Miming the lyrics and dancing to the sounds of LL Cool J and Naughty by Nature among others, Beah entertained the villagers intent on maiming or killing him. In exchange, they gave him his freedom.

5 Yet what is probably most astonishing about *A Long Way Gone* is the fact that its author seems to have survived "childhood" with his humanity intact. When his commander volunteers Beah and a few other very young boys for rehabilitation, it seems to prove the truth of his father's motto, "If you are alive, there is hope for a better day." Although he and the other

Copyright © Cengage Learning. All rights reserved.

boys initially fought all attempts to make them stop being bloodthirsty child soldiers, their resistance finally gave way. After awhile, they began to act like what they were, children.

6   After leaving the rehabilitation center, Beah lived for awhile with his uncle because the rebels who had driven him from his village had kept their word: They had burned the village and slaughtered Beah's parents, along with the rest of the inhabitants. At fifteen, Beah had no home to go to, so his relatives took him in. While living with his uncle, Beah was selected to speak at the United Nations because the international delegates wanted to better understand the fate of child soldiers. The UN appearance led to Beah's coming to the United States, where he graduated from high school and Oberlin College with a degree in political science.

7   Beah has grown up, but he hasn't forgotten his nightmarish past. Instead, through his memoir, he uses it to make a point: "I believe children have the resilience to outlive their sufferings if given a chance." His life is a testament to those words. (Source of quotation: www.npr.org/templates/story/storyid=7519542.)

1. What is the implied main idea of the reading?

    a. The civil war in Sierra Leone destroyed the lives of countless children.

    b. Ishmael Beah's life story illustrates how tragic war is, especially for children, who seldom recover from the psychological wounds of war even if they do get over the physical wounds.

    c. Tragic as Ishmael Beah's early years were, his story still suggests that his father was right: "If you are alive, there is hope for a better day."

    d. Although Ishmael Beah's horrifying time as a child soldier is over, he is still haunted by the experience.

2. To understand why paragraph 2 follows paragraph 1, the reader has to infer which connection?

    a. Paragraph 2 illustrates why the peace mentioned in paragraph 1 is considered "uneasy."

    b. Paragraph 2 explains why Beah decided to write his memoirs.

    c. Paragraph 2 illustrates why the book can cause the "nightmares" mentioned in paragraph 1.

Copyright © Cengage Learning. All rights reserved.

3. To understand why paragraph 3 follows paragraph 2, the reader must infer which connection?

   a. Paragraph 3 further explains why the book can cause nightmares.

   b. Paragraph 3 offers an exception to the book's description of a tragic time in Ishmael Beah's life.

   c. Paragraph 3 reverses the suggestion of a "safe haven" introduced in paragraph 2.

4. To understand why paragraphs 5, 6, and 7 follow paragraph 4, the reader has to infer which connection?

   a. Paragraphs 5, 6, and 7 continue the description of Beah's tragic childhood.

   b. Paragraphs 5, 6, and 7 move away from the boy's nightmarish childhood and introduce a positive outcome of his experience.

   c. Paragraphs 5, 6, and 7 describe the chain of events that led Beah to the UN.

◆ Drawing Logical Conclusions

Readers truly intent on mastering an author's message don't limit themselves to drawing just the inferences intended by the author. To deepen their understanding, readers frequently draw conclusions that follow from the reading but were not necessarily consciously intended by the author. This next passage and the two conclusions that follow provide an illustration.

Exit exams are tests that high school students in some states must take to successfully pass a course or earn a diploma. Although exit exams have numerous supporters, they have come under fire where diplomas are concerned. In Massachusetts, for instance, state officials had to quell a rebellion of school superintendents who wanted to award diplomas to 4,800 students who had failed the exam. In Florida, protesters demanded that the governor give diplomas to 14,000 seniors who had failed the exit exam. Given all this controversy, the question that has to be answered is, "What's wrong with exit exams?" After all, high school exit exams ensure that a diploma accurately indicates how much information students have actually absorbed from their courses. This is important because it's widely

Copyright © Cengage Learning. All rights reserved.

assumed that grade inflation is rampant in some schools. If this assumption is correct, the passing grades which allow students to get a diploma are not necessarily proof they have mastered the course material. However, if a diploma is backed up by an exit exam, we can be sure students have mastered the courses identified on their transcripts. By the same token, exit exams should help reassure prospective employers who have begun to lose faith in the diploma as proof of achievement. In short, the presence of an exit exam grade on a student's transcript increases the value of the diploma.

The implied main idea in the above passage is something like this: "Exit exams are a good idea and school administrators should not cave in to the pressure to abandon them." The author does not say this explicitly. Instead, she implies her main idea by offering reasons why exit exams are valuable for documenting achievement.

However, based on what the author says, you can also draw two conclusions that she does not address: (1) the author would probably agree with legislation that made high school exit exams mandatory throughout the nation, and (2) the author would probably be unwilling to sign a petition demanding that students who failed their exit exams be allowed to receive diplomas anyway. Based on what the author explicitly says, these are legitimate or logical conclusions. Both follow from what the author says about exit exams even though nothing in the paragraph directly addresses either conclusion.

Illustrating an Illogical Conclusion

Far less logical would be the following conclusion: "The author believes that the school superintendents should have been allowed to give diplomas to the 14,000 students who failed in Florida." Under some special conditions, the author might well agree. But given her concern that trust in the meaning of grades and diplomas is dwindling, it doesn't make sense to argue that she would favor giving out diplomas to failing students. On the contrary, she would probably oppose such a petition because she argues so forcefully in favor of exit exams as a way of bolstering the public's failing faith in the meaning of a diploma.

Copyright © Cengage Learning. All rights reserved.

CHECK YOUR UNDERSTANDING

How do the inferences in this section differ from those described in the preceding section?

_____

_____

◆ **EXERCISE 11   Drawing Logical Conclusions**

DIRECTIONS   Read each paragraph. Circle the letter of the conclusion that follows logically from what's said in the passage.

EXAMPLE   Some 6,000 languages are spoken in the world today, but about 2,400 of them are close to dying out because the number of speakers is rapidly declining. Around 500 languages are already spoken by fewer than 100 people. Even worse, experts estimate that over the next 100 years, fully 90 percent of all current languages will be either totally or virtually extinct, replaced by "mega-languages" such as English, Spanish, French, or Arabic. Just as we become alarmed when a species of plant or animal nears the brink of extinction, we should be equally concerned about languages becoming extinct. When a language dies, what dies with it is a very specific representation of a particular culture. It's also true that the few individuals left who still speak a nearly extinct language experience a loss of identity. As anthropologist Wade Davis expressed it, "When you strip away language and the culture it embodies, what you have left is alienation,* despair, and tremendous levels of anger." (Sources of statistics and quotation: Thomas Hayden, "Losing Our Voices," *U.S. News & World Report*, May 26, 2003, p. 42; Margit Waas, "Taking Note of Language Extinction," originally published in *Applied Linguistics* 18(1):101–3, 1997.)

Which conclusion follows from the reading?

a. In addition to English, the author probably speaks several other languages, speaking and writing all of them with a high level of skill.

b. The author probably opposes teaching English to citizens of other countries.

_____

*alienation: the feeling of being left out, of not belonging.

Copyright © Cengage Learning. All rights reserved.

(c.) The author would probably support efforts to create text and audio computer files of endangered languages.

EXPLANATION   Answer *a* won't do because nothing in the passage indicates how many other languages the author does or does not speak. Answer *b* has to be eliminated because the author says nothing about just English being taught to citizens of other countries. Answer *c* is the only conclusion that follows logically from the paragraph. A writer worried about what's being lost when a language dies out is very likely to conclude that preserving text on computer files is a good thing to do.

1. In his book *After Virtue*, philosopher Alasdair MacIntyre argues that virtue is the product of social training. From MacIntyre's point of view, virtue can be acquired only in a community where the young are consciously initiated into the reigning set of social values, including what it means to be a good person. MacIntyre interprets the word *community* in its broadest sense, making it refer to families, schools, religious institutions, political groups, and even avenues of entertainment. From his perspective, it's important that these aspects of the community be respected because it is their authority that persuades the child to accept their teachings and pursue the path of virtue. Far from simplistic in his thinking, MacIntyre recognizes that communities are historical entities that can change over time. It follows, then, that the virtuous life can also be redefined as the character of the community undergoes historical change.

   Which conclusion follows from the reading?
   a. MacIntyre is probably a modern-day disciple of Plato, who believed that virtue was inborn in special people who had a natural knowledge of perfection.

   b. MacIntyre is following in the footsteps of St. Augustine, who believed that virtue is a gift of God.

   c. MacIntyre would probably take the side of Aristotle, who believed that virtuous behavior is not inborn but can be learned.

2. Periodically, the price of gasoline soars and infuriated Americans blame Congress, the White House, and the Organization of the Petroleum Exporting Countries (OPEC). According to an editorial in the *Miami Herald*, however, if Americans want to know who

Copyright © Cengage Learning. All rights reserved.

to blame for high gas prices, they should look in the mirror. "The real cause of gas-pump sticker shock," says the *Herald*, "is American consumers' addiction to the automobile and the lifestyle it allows." The editorialist goes on to point out that far too many Americans act as if they are entitled to own big, gas-guzzling cars and oversized pickup trucks, which together account for a sizable portion of vehicles sold in this country. The result? America has an insatiable* appetite for oil, and OPEC simply takes advantage of our dependence on its product. Rather than demanding lower gas prices, says the *Herald*, Americans should be driving as little as possible and insisting that their leaders do more to make mass transportation available, reliable, and affordable.

Which conclusion follows from the reading?

a. The *Miami Herald* editorialist quoted in the passage would heartily agree with those who advocate drilling in the Arctic National Wildlife Refuge as a way of solving the oil shortage.

b. The *Miami Herald* editorialist is likely to endorse policies designed to force OPEC to lower its prices so that gas and oil will be available at cheaper prices.

c. The *Miami Herald* editorialist would be inclined to blame not just the oil company BP for the colossal 2010 oil spill in the Gulf but also the American public.

3. All segments of society have a great deal to gain by changing the health care system. The emphasis through the years has shifted from the "caring" to the "system," and the medical care industry has become the biggest business in the United States. In 1950, the cost of health care was $12 billion, but it was more than a trillion dollars by the end of the century, having risen faster than any other item in the cost of living. Despite the exorbitant bills, however, the system has failed for many citizens. About 43 billion people at the Census Bureau's last count are denied access to health care because they lack insurance. But even if people do have health insurance, their coverage may be limited because companies profit not by providing insurance but by trying to avoid paying for its use. The costs of the enormously complicated health care industry—the doctors, the health care workers,

*insatiable: never satisfied.

Copyright © Cengage Learning. All rights reserved.

the hospitals, the clinics, the nursing homes, the prescription drug industry—continue to increase. Although patients are referred to as health care consumers, they are not the ones to decide, as they may with other services and products, what and how much medical care to buy. Generally, they take what they can get. (Sloane, *Biology of Women*, p. 11.)

Which conclusion follows from the reading?

a. The author of this reading would agree that the United States should become more like other industrialized countries and make affordable health care the right of every citizen.

b. The author of this reading would not agree with the underlying assumption that guides health care throughout Europe: Health care is a citizen's right rather than a product with a price tag.

c. The author would be against any attempts to change the existing health care system by instituting a public option, which would allow the government to offer health insurance to people too young to qualify for Medicare.

4. In 2009, Facebook's founder, Mark Zuckerberg, announced that all information uploaded onto Facebook's pages would be considered open to the public unless the user implemented specific settings to keep the information private. The announcement shocked and angered some Facebook users but not as many as one might expect, given the way the very notion of privacy has been eroded by the intrusion of the Internet into our lives. But the question has to be asked, Is this what we really want; do we really want to have our past and present movements tracked and accounted for, not just by our friends and family, but by employers, the federal government, and complete strangers, who happen to have access to the Internet? If your answer to that question is "Yes, what's the problem?" you might want to read *Delete: The Virtue of Forgetting in the Digital Age* by Viktor Mayer-Schonberger. Schonberger effectively argues that the Internet, if not used with discretion,* can profoundly disrupt our lives. To illustrate his point, he describes the case of the sixty-six-year-old Canadian psychotherapist, Andrew Feldmar, who tried to cross the border into the United States in 2007. A border agent Googled Feldmar's name

---

*discretion: sound judgment.

Copyright © Cengage Learning. All rights reserved.

and found a link to an article in which Feldmar admitted that in the 1960s, more than forty years before, he had experimented with the drug LSD. As a result, Feldmar was barred from entering the United States because he had admitted the use of an illegal drug.

Which conclusion follows from the reading?

a. The author would agree with Facebook founder Mark Zuckerberg's claim that privacy is out of date.

b. The writer mentioned in the reading, Viktor Mayer-Schonberger, would probably support the idea that our lives should be an open e-book available on the Internet to everyone who takes an interest in us.

c. Viktor Mayer-Schonberger would probably support the idea that our laws protecting privacy will need to be rewritten given the technological changes over the last decade.

WORD CHECK II

The following words were introduced and defined in pages 374–92. See how well you can match the words with the meanings. When you finish, make sure to check the meanings of any words you missed because the same words will turn up in tests at the end of the chapter.

1. lobbied _____
2. espionage _____
3. mandate _____
4. esteemed _____
5. recluses _____
6. aggregate _____
7. phenomenon _____
8. alienation _____
9. insatiable _____
10. discretion _____

a. well known, trusted, respected
b. people who purposely live apart from society
c. event, happening, amazing talent
d. feeling of being left out, of not fitting in or being part of the larger group
e. attempted to influence actions of legislators or other public officials
f. in combined form, total, mass, authority
g. authorize, legal right, law
h. never satisfied
i. spying
j. care, sound judgment

Copyright © Cengage Learning. All rights reserved.

◆ **EXERCISE 12 More About Form and Meaning**

DIRECTIONS Use one of the words listed below to fill in the blanks.

> lobbyists   mandate   reclusive   phenomenon   insatiable
> espionage   esteemed   aggregate   alienation   discretion

1. You are unlikely to find _____ people attending a neighborhood block party.

2. Having a lot of money can make you envied, but it's much less likely to make you _____.

3. When people speak about the hive mind at work, they are talking about people in the _____ coming up with ideas.

4. You would expect to find a sense of _____ among people living in circumstances that offer no promise for the future.

5. Presidents who win a lot of votes in an election often talk about having a(n) _____ from the people to make decisions of national importance.

6. Even if they are completely full, people at a pie-eating contest have to pretend to be _____ and just keep eating.

7. Although the word normally applies to events, an individual who is really good at something is likely to be called a(n) _____.

8. Kids with concerned parents who monitor their comings and goings would probably like to accuse their parents of _____, but parents are supposed to keep an eye on their children; that's not an illegal activity.

Copyright © Cengage Learning. All rights reserved.

9. People who post photos of themselves on the Internet suffering the ill effects of too many beers could hardly be accused of having too much _____.

10. It's not especially reassuring to see elected officials lunching day after day with _____.

Copyright © Cengage Learning. All rights reserved.

DIGGING DEEPER   J. Robert Oppenheimer and the Manhattan Project

Looking Ahead In Chapter 7, you will read about one of the most controversial decisions in American history—to end World War II by dropping the atomic bomb on the Japanese cities of Hiroshima and Nagasaki. This reading will tell you more about the man who helped make the atomic bomb a reality.

1   [1]Initially at least J. Robert Oppenheimer (1904–1967) seemed destined to lead a charmed life. [2]Handsome, brilliant, and charming, Oppenheimer had been born into a well-to-do family that readily indulged his varied interests in everything from writing poetry to mineral collecting. [3]As a young man, Oppenheimer had whizzed through Harvard and earned his doctorate in physics by the age of twenty-three.

Roger Ressmeyer/Corbis

2   [1]Oppenheimer was just thirty-eight when what seemed to be the biggest plum of all fell into his lap. [2]In 1942, the Army engineer General Leslie Groves was looking for someone to head "The Manhattan Project."[†] [3]The project's top-secret goal was to develop an atomic bomb that would turn the United States into a military superpower. [4]Its success would require the work of many gifted scientists, ranging from chemists to mathematicians.

3   [1]While Groves was no scientist, he was also no fool. [2]He knew that geniuses often have egos to match their intellect. [3]Thus someone had to be found who could understand the complicated work of those participating in the project and simultaneously play peacemaker during those unavoidable moments when egos collided and the project was endangered. [4]Groves found the man he wanted in J. Robert Oppenheimer.

4   [1]Oppenheimer gathered together the cream of the scientific world and persuaded the group to live in almost total isolation, for some twenty-plus months, hidden away in New Mexico, having little or no contact with the outside world. [2]On December 2, 1942, the Italian physicist Enrico Fermi, one of the men working at Los Alamos, created the first self-sustaining, nuclear chain reaction, on Stagg Field in the University of Chicago football stadium. [3]At that point, the energy was available for the explosion of an atomic bomb. [4]On July 16, 1945, in Alamogordo, New Mexico, Groves and Oppenheimer watched as an enormous ball of fire followed by a mushroom cloud rose in the skies over the desert.

[†]The project got its name from the fact that much of the money raised to get it underway came from Columbia University in Manhattan.

Copyright © Cengage Learning. All rights reserved.

Copyright © Cengage Learning. All rights reserved.

5   [1]At the sight, Oppenheimer, who, had been hell-bent on building an atomic bomb, is said to have quoted a sentence from Hindu scripture: "I am become death, the shatterer of worlds." [2]The physicist's sense of doubt was apparently not momentary. [3]Shortly after, Oppenheimer wrote to his former high school teacher expressing his "misgivings" about the alleged accomplishment of The Manhattan Project: "You will believe that this undertaking has not been without its misgivings; they are heavy on us today, when the future which has so many elements of high promise, is yet only a stone's throw away from despair." [4]The bombing of Nagasaki and Hiroshima in August 1945 only intensified Oppenheimer's change in feeling from enthusiasm to shame.

6   [1]Hiroshima's streets were teeming with people when the first atomic bomb, nicknamed "Little Boy," struck, killing 100,000 people (by 1950, radiation deaths would swell the number to 200,000). [2]Nagasaki was hit three days later with an atomic bomb called "Fat Man." [3]The bomb obliterated 44 percent of the city and 54 percent of the people.

7   [1]Oppenheimer was devastated by his role in the destruction and never really accepted the government's explanation—that dropping the atomic bomb forced the Japanese to surrender and avoided even greater bloodshed. [2]He informed government officials that he and most other scientists involved in creating the atomic bomb would not continue working on the project, particularly if the government wished to pursue the even bigger and potentially deadlier hydrogen bomb. [3]Oppenheimer also expressed his guilt to Harry Truman, the president who had made the decision to drop the bombs on Hiroshima and Nagasaki. [4]Oppenheimer told Truman at a meeting, "I feel we have blood on our hands." [5]Truman was not especially sympathetic. [6]He responded bluntly, telling Oppenheimer the blood on his hands would "come out in the wash."

8   [1]If Truman was unsympathetic, Oppenheimer's fellow scientist Edward Teller was openly outraged by his colleague's comments. [2]Teller wanted Oppenheimer's help convincing government officials that they needed to build a fusion, or hydrogen, bomb, and he was convinced that Oppenheimer's public hand-wringing was seriously undermining support for what many called the super bomb, or simply "The Super." [3]By the time the Soviets had detonated an atomic bomb of their own in 1949, Teller was even more obsessed with the need to build The Super, but Oppenheimer was still, as were many other scientists, dead set against it.

9   [1]When the time came and he had his chance, Teller made sure that Oppenheimer suffered for what, in Teller's mind, was a personal and, even worse, a national betrayal. [2]In 1954, the country was at the height of its

hysteria over communists in the U.S. government, and Oppenheimer was called to Washington for a security clearance review. [3]Most of those called to testify gave Oppenheimer unqualified praise and approval. [4]Teller, however, said that he had serious doubts about Oppenheimer being given a security clearance that would allow him access to government secrets: "I would feel personally more secure if public matters would rest in other hands." [5]Because Lewis Strauss, the head of the Atomic Energy Commission, already detested Oppenheimer for what he considered the man's arrogance, Oppenheimer was denied security clearance. [6]From then on, he would never again play a role in how the government used the destructive weapons he, perhaps more than anyone else, had made possible.

10   [1]Oppenheimer continued to work as the director for the Institute for Advanced Study in Princeton, New Jersey, but he was never the same. [2]The review of his security clearance and its subsequent withdrawal had been a public humiliation for his proud spirit. [3]Oppenheimer's security clearance was reinstated in 1963 by Lyndon Baines Johnson, but it made little difference. [4]Four years later, J. Robert Oppenheimer was dead of throat cancer. (Sources of quotes and statistics: Evans, *The American Century*, pp. 323–27, 376, 448–49; Halberstam, *The Fifties*, pp. 24–40.)

Sharpening Your Skills

DIRECTIONS   Answer the following questions by circling the letter of the correct response or filling in the blanks.

1. Which of the following best expresses the implied main idea of the reading?
   a. The personal animosity Edward Teller felt for J. Robert Oppenheimer destroyed Oppenheimer's career, and Oppenheimer never forgave Teller for his betrayal.
   b. The Manhattan Project, which was initially considered a feather in Oppenheimer's cap, caused him much misery, both personally and professionally,
   c. J. Robert Oppenheimer's guilt over the success of The Manhattan Project is understandable and appropriate given what he let loose on the world.
   d. Harry Truman and J. Robert Oppenheimer were of very different minds when it came to evaluating the success of The Manhattan Project.

Copyright © Cengage Learning. All rights reserved.

2. What is a reader likely to predict based on the phrase "initially at least" in paragraph 1?

   a. Oppenheimer's life remained as charmed as it had seemed in his early years.

   b. Oppenheimer never really had a charmed life, even from the very beginning.

   c. Oppenheimer's life did not turn out to be so charmed as it had seemed at first.

3. The pronoun *its* opening sentence 4 in paragraph 2 refers to

   _____.

4. In sentence 3 of paragraph 3, the word *egos* is a substitute or stand in for

   _____.

5. What's the implied relationship between these two sentences: "On December 2, 1942, the Italian physicist Enrico Fermi, one of the men working at Los Alamos, created the first self-sustaining, nuclear chain reaction, on Stagg Field in the University of Chicago football stadium. At that point, the energy was available for the explosion of an atomic bomb."

   a. comparison and contrast

   b. cause and effect

   c. definition and illustration

   d. statement and reversal

6. What does the word *sight* refer to in the first sentence in paragraph 5?

   _____

7. To connect paragraphs 4 and 5, which inference does the reader need to draw?

   a. The reality of the explosion made Oppenheimer recognize for the first time just how destructive the bomb could be.

   b. Oppenheimer was the kind of man inclined to quote poetry at every opportunity.

   c. Oppenheimer felt proud because he had helped create such a destructive weapon.

Copyright © Cengage Learning. All rights reserved.

    d. Oppenheimer was a Buddhist and building the atomic bomb contradicted his beliefs.

8. To understand sentences 1 and 2 in paragraph 7, readers need to make what connection?

    a. Oppenheimer refused to do any more work on the atomic bomb because he didn't want to work alone.

    b. Oppenheimer refused to do any more work on the atomic bomb because the Japanese had surrendered, and there was no longer any reason for the bomb to be used.

    c. Oppenheimer refused to do any more work on the atomic bomb because he was horrified by his role in the destruction and death caused by the bombing of Hiroshima and Nagasaki.

    d. Oppenheimer refused to continue working on the atomic bomb because he hated Edward Teller.

9. To connect paragraphs 7 and 8, which inference does the reader need to draw?

    a. Teller believed that Oppenheimer worked to get all the credit for the hydrogen bomb.

    b. Teller was convinced that Oppenheimer hindered work on the hydrogen bomb because Oppenheimer personally disliked Teller.

    c. Teller believed that Oppenheimer didn't want the hydrogen bomb developed because that would make the atomic bomb less important.

    d. Teller did not share Oppenheimer's guilt about the detonation of the atomic bomb.

10. Based on the reading, what conclusion seems more likely?

    a. Harry Truman abandoned all work on the hydrogen bomb.

    b. Harry Truman eventually went along with Teller and gave the go-ahead for a project devoted to The Super.

Please explain your answer.

_____

_____

_____

Copyright © Cengage Learning. All rights reserved.

▶ **TEST 1**   **Reviewing New Vocabulary**

DIRECTIONS   Use one of the following words to fill in the blanks.

esteemed	recluse	alienation	introspective	aspiring
boon	ingenious	aggregate	phenomenally	guru

Loving Loneliness

1   In the age of Facebook—and the general zeal for sharing—the notion
of being a(n) _____ is probably unthinkable to many.
Yet some highly _____ people have chosen to livealone
rather than be part of the social _____. For such people,
being alone is a(n) _____, not a deficiency.

2   Disappearing from public view was the choice of cartoonist Bill
Watterson, _____ creator of the famous *Calvin and
Hobbes* comic strip. _____ by temperament, Watterson
just dropped from sight when the _____ popular cartoon
strip ended. The same is true of J. D. Salinger, creator of *Catcher in the
Rye's* perpetually depressed Holden Caulfield, who, until recently,[†] was
embraced by generations of teenagers _____
to be like him.

3   Apparently sharing Holden's constant feeling of _____,
Salinger refused all interviews and avoided the press and people in
general. Those who expected Salinger to play the role of cultural
_____, dispensing wisdom about how to lead a
satisfying life, were disappointed.

[†]In 2009, the *New York Times* ran an article saying that teenagers today thought Holden
was a whiner in need of antidepressants, see pages 671–73.

Copyright © Cengage Learning. All rights reserved.

▶ **TEST 2**   **Reviewing New Vocabulary**

DIRECTIONS   Fill in the blanks with the words listed below. *Note*: In the second excerpt, you will have to use the same word twice, changing the ending to fit one of the blanks.

insatiable	lobbied	discretion	coalesced	espionage
conservationists	mandated	irrationality	orientation	puns

1. Truman and the Loyalty Oath

1   In 1947, President Harry Truman was _____ by members of his party to do something that would prove the Democrats were *not* soft on communism. In response to political pressure, Truman _____ that everyone holding a federal appointment would have to sign a loyalty oath. In any realistic sense, the oath was worthless. Having government employees swear that they were loyal was not going to keep Russian spies intent on _____ out of government. A spy with even a minimal sense of _____ would just swear his or her loyalty and then go back to the business of snooping for the Soviet Union.

2   However, the _____ of the oath did not disturb those groups with a strong anti-communist _____. For these people, the loyalty oath was only a step in the right direction and a small step at that. Intent on ridding the country of any groups they perceived to be leaning toward the left, from civil rights activists to _____, they rejected Truman as too liberal and _____ around the political figure of Senator Joseph McCarthy, who built his entire career on hunting down Communists and destroying thousands of innocent lives in the process.

2. No Laughing Matter?

1   _____ treat homonyms, or words that sound alike, as synonyms. For fans, therein lies their humor. Writer Richard Lederer celebrates them in his essay "Get Thee to a _____ nery," claiming they reveal the richness of language.

2   Asked for a slogan appropriate to a legal firm, Lederer showed he was among the quickest of wits when it came to double meanings. Without

Copyright © Cengage Learning. All rights reserved.

hesitation, he replied, "Remember the Alimony," which associated the specialty of divorce lawyers—winning their clients alimony—with the battle cry of the doomed Texas fort, the Alamo.

3   While some, like the playwright Oscar Wilde[†] have an almost

_____ desire to use such word play, there are those who have exactly the opposite reaction. They consider it the lowest form of humor and aren't especially shy about openly sneering when someone engages in word-play wit. For these wet blankets, a line like Groucho Marx's[†] famous "Time wounds all heels" is more likely to produce a bored groan than a smile or a chuckle.

[†]Oscar Wilde: the nineteenth-century playwright's humor is heavy on word play.
[†]Groucho Marx: A member of the famed Marx brothers, whose movie comedies delighted audiences in the thirties, Groucho went on to television fame. His joke is based on the line "Time heals all wounds."

Copyright © Cengage Learning. All rights reserved.

▶ **TEST 3**　　　　**Drawing Inferences About Pronouns and Other Noun Substitutes**

DIRECTIONS　　Answer the following questions by circling the letter of the correct response or filling in the blanks.

1. ¹In the early 1800s, leading Republicans had hoped to end the nation's political divisions. ²*They* sought compromise among sectional interests and welcomed the remaining Federalists into their fold. ³*They* praised the one-party system. (Adapted from Gillon and Matson, *The American Experiment,* p. 379.)

   In sentences 2 and 3, to what does the pronoun *they* refer?
   a.　American citizens
   b.　political factions
   c.　leading Republicans
   d.　early 1800s

2. ¹As film-industry attorney Schuyler Moore has written, "The saving grace in the film industry is that when the rare blockbuster occurs, *it* can make up for the losses of a lot of other films." ²Moore compares movies to wildcat oil drilling—a lot of capital is required to make enough films to produce a rare blockbuster. ³This system naturally favors the big studios that take care of their own distribution. ⁴Independent filmmakers farm their distribution out to third parties, a costly but necessary operation. (Defleur and Dennis, *Understanding Mass Communication,* p. 144.)

   In sentence 1, to what does the pronoun *it* refer?
   a.　the film industry
   b.　the losses
   c.　the blockbuster
   d.　the saving grace

   In sentence 3, to what does the phrase "this system" refer?
   a.　the saving grace
   b.　blockbusters making up for losses
   c.　the movie industry
   d.　big studios underselling little ones

Copyright © Cengage Learning. All rights reserved.

3. [1]Before the bombing of Hiroshima and Nagasaki in 1945, the use of the atomic bomb did not raise profound moral issues for policy makers. [2]The weapon was conceived in a race with Germany, and *it* undoubtedly would have been used against Germany had the bomb been ready much sooner. (Adapted from McMahon and Paterson, *The Origins of the Cold War*, p. 96.)

In sentence 2, what's the first word that refers to the phrase *atomic bomb*? _____

In sentence 2, what does *it* refer to? _____

4. [1]After his father retired as the head of IBM, Thomas Watson Jr. took over and led IBM into the computer field with a vengeance, dwarfing all competitors in the decades to come. [2]After establishing its first microcomputer as the business computing standard in 1981, the conservative giant was slow to adjust to the rapid-fire changes of the 1980s and 1990s, *which* made it possible for more nimble companies to seize emerging markets. (Adapted from Beekman and Quinn, *Computer Confluence*, p. 72.)

What phrase in sentence 2 is used as a stand-in, or substitute, for *IBM*? _____

In sentence 2, to what does the pronoun *which* refer?
a. IBM's establishing of the first microcomputer
b. IBM's becoming the de facto business standard
c. IBM's slowness to adjust to rapid-fire changes
d. Thomas Watson's taking over for his father as head of the company

5. [1]In the late 1920s and early 1930s, the United States renounced its unpopular policy of military intervention and shifted to a new method to maintain its influence in Latin America, including support for strong local leaders, the training of national guards, economic and cultural penetration, export-import bank loans, financial supervision, and political subversion, or undermining from within. [2]Although *this general approach* predated his presidency, Franklin Roosevelt gave *it* a name in 1933, the "Good Neighbor Policy," *which*

Copyright © Cengage Learning. All rights reserved.

means that the United States would be less blatant or obvious in its domination—less willing to defend exploitative business practices, less eager to launch military expeditions, and less reluctant to consult with Latin American officials. (Berkin et al., *Making America*, p. 210.)

What does the phrase *this general approach* refer to in sentence 2?

a. support for strong local leaders

b. training of national guards

c. economic and cultural penetration

d. the U.S.'s new method for maintaining its influence

What does the pronoun *it* refer to in sentence 2?

a. presidency

b. the general approach

c. Roosevelt's presidency

d. financial supervision

What does the pronoun *which* refer to in sentence 2?

a. Roosevelt's presidency

b. predated

c. this general approach

d. the Good Neighbor policy

Copyright © Cengage Learning. All rights reserved.

Copyright © Cengage Learning. All rights reserved.

▶ **TEST 4**   **Recognizing the Implied Main Idea**

DIRECTIONS   Read each paragraph. Then circle the letter of the implied main idea.

1. Every year desperate cancer victims travel to the Philippines hoping to be cured by people who call themselves "psychic surgeons." These so-called surgeons claim to heal the sick without the use of a knife or anesthesia, and many victims of serious illness look to them for a cure. But curing the sick is not what these surgeons are about. When they operate, they conceal bits of chicken and goat hearts in their hands; then they pretend to pull a piece of disease-ridden tissue out of the patient's body. If a crowd is present, and it usually is, the surgeons briefly display the lump of animal tissue and pronounce the poor patient cured. Not surprisingly, psychic surgeons cannot point to many real cures.

Implied Main Idea
a. More people than ever before are flocking to psychic surgeons.
b. Psychic surgeons are complete frauds.
c. When people are desperate and all other cures have failed, they are inclined to put their faith in quacks, or frauds.
d. Psychic surgeons should be imprisoned for the harm they do to their poor patients.

2. In 1963, writer and feminist Gloria Steinem became a Playboy Bunny to give readers an inside look at what female employees of the Playboy clubs had to go through to please the boss as well as the customers. In 1982, the journalist Carol Lynn Mithers posed as a man to get a job on a sports magazine and published the results in a *Village Voice* article called "My Life as a Man." In the seventies, news anchor Walter Cronkite voted under false names twice in the same election to expose election fraud, while *Miami Herald* reporters went undercover to expose housing discrimination. In 1977, CBS's *60 Minutes* and the *Chicago Sun-Times* set up a bar called Mirage, staffed it with undercover journalists, and watched as various city officials walked in and demanded bribes for their services. The *Chicago Sun-Times* also sent female journalists into downtown Chicago clinics that performed costly abortions on women who were not pregnant. In 1992, ABC News's *PrimeTime Live* used undercover reporters and hidden cameras to document charges that some Food Lion grocery stores sold tainted meat and spoiled fish. In 1999, another *PrimeTime Live*

reporter posed as a telephone psychic to expose the fraudulent practices of the psychic hotline industry. (Source of examples: Saltzman, "A Chill Settles Over Investigative Journalism," *USA Today*, p. 29.)

Implied Main Idea

   a. In the past, investigative journalists have used deception to expose corruption.

   b. No ethical journalist would use deception to get a story.

   c. Food Lion sued and won its case against journalists who exposed some unsafe practices in Food Lion stores.

   d. Reporters who use deception to get a story should not be surprised when the result is a lawsuit against both the journalist and the paper that runs the story.

3. Social scientists have been studying the phenomena of both speed and online dating for a while now, with some interesting results. At the University of Pennsylvania, Robert Kurzban and Jaspon Weeden studied more than 10,000 clients of HurryDate—a company that gathers men and women together for a round robin of speed dates lasting about three minutes each. At the end of the "dates," those attending find out who was interested in dating whom. Kurzban and Weeden found that the women attending the group dating sessions were much pickier than the men. Women usually got a "yes, I'd like to see her again" from about half the men they chatted with. Men who participated got that response from only about one-third of the women they talked to. A similar German study found that the female subjects—attractive women in particular—were very choosy about whom they would see again. The men, in contrast, indicated that they wanted to get acquainted with most of the women they had encountered during the speed-dating sessions. In another study of more than 20,000 online daters, the results indicated that women were interested in more than looks. They wanted to know about the men's level of education and their profession. Although education didn't rate high with men, a woman's having blond hair appeared to be an advantage.

Implied Main Idea

   a. Studies of speed and online dating indicate that men are much pickier than women about whom they will date.

   b. Studies of speed and online dating indicate that women, unlike men, care more about a man's education and profession than they do about his looks.

Copyright © Cengage Learning. All rights reserved.

c. Studies of speed and online dating suggest that women tend to be more selective than men, and they prefer men who have high-powered careers.

d. Men engaged in speed dating do not tend to marry the women they meet, so they spend little time thinking about anything but appearance.

4. *Troll* is a term for an anonymous person who is abusive in an online environment. It would be nice to believe that there is only a minute troll population living among us. But in fact, a great many people have experienced being drawn into nasty exchanges online. Everyone who has experienced that has been introduced to his or her inner troll. I have tried to be aware of the troll within myself. I notice that I can suddenly become relieved when someone else in an online exchange is getting pounded or humiliated, because that means I'm safe for the moment. If someone else's video is being ridiculed on YouTube, mine is temporarily protected. But that also means I'm complicit in the mob dynamic. (Lanier, *You Are Not a Gadget*, p. 60.)

Implied Main Idea

a. Trolls can be particularly abusive about videos posted on YouTube.

b. Everyone can become a troll under the right circumstances.

c. The online troll population is a good deal larger than many of us like to think.

d. Participating in online anonymous discussions tends to bring out the worst in everyone.

5. In one 1970s experiment conducted by psychologist Leonard Bickman, a male who wore a suit and tie, a milk company uniform, or what appeared to be a security guard's uniform approached pedestrians on a Brooklyn street and asked them to pick up some litter, give some change to a man who needed it for a parking meter, or move to a different location. When the man was wearing a guard's uniform, 36 percent of the people he approached did as they were asked. When the man wore a suit and tie, 20 percent complied. However, when he was wearing the milk company uniform, only 14 percent did as they were told. Similarly, in a 1988 study, a female dressed in a dark blue uniform; a business suit; or stained T-shirt,

Copyright © Cengage Learning. All rights reserved.

pants, and tennis shoes approached pedestrians in a St. Louis shopping center. The woman would point at her accomplice and say, "This fellow is over-parked at the meter and doesn't have any change. Give him a nickel." When the woman was wearing a uniform, 72 percent of those asked complied with her request. When she was wearing the business suit, 48 percent of people did as they were asked. But when she was wearing the T-shirt and pants, only 32 percent did as they were told. In 1993, when communication researcher Chris Segrin analyzed nineteen similar experiments, he found that all had yielded similar results. (Adapted from Remland, *Nonverbal Communication in Everyday Life*, pp. 266–67.)

Implied Main Idea

a. The results of several studies suggest that people like, trust, and respect individuals who wear uniforms.

b. The results of several studies suggest that we are more likely to comply with the requests of people in official uniforms or business attire.

c. Several studies suggest that we respond positively to those who dress the way we do.

d. New studies about the effect of clothing on behavior suggest that most people are naturally obedient, no matter what the person giving the orders is wearing.

Copyright © Cengage Learning. All rights reserved.

Copyright © Cengage Learning. All rights reserved.

▶ **TEST 5**   **Drawing a Logical Inference**

DIRECTIONS   Write a sentence expressing the implied main idea of the passage.

1. When the Barbie doll first appeared in prefeminist 1959, she had large breasts, a tiny waist, rounded hips, shapely legs, and little feet shod in high-heeled shoes. Barbie wore heavy makeup, and her gaze was shy and downcast. She was available in only two career options: airline stewardess or nurse. In the early 1960s, though, when feminism reigned, Barbie had her own car and house. A "Barbie Goes to College" play set was also available. Then, in 1967, Barbie's face was updated to sport a more youthful, model-like appearance with a direct and fearless gaze. By the 1970s, Barbie's career options had expanded to include doctor and Olympic medalist. She also got another facelift, which left her with a softer, friendlier look. She now had a wide smile and bright eyes. During the 1980s and 1990s, when girls were encouraged to grow up to be independent wage earners, Barbie's options increased even more to include professions such as business executive, aerobics instructor, and firefighter. Today Barbie has a thicker waist, slimmer hips, and smaller breasts. More importantly, in response to the country's increasing diversity, she comes in black, Asian, and Latina versions.

Implied Main Idea   _____

_____

2. In 1984, Congress passed a law prohibiting anyone from selling his or her organs to a person needing a transplant. Since then, however, the number of people on waiting lists to receive an organ has risen steadily. Sadly about 6,000 individuals die every year because the need for organs greatly exceeds the number donated. As a possible solution, the American Medical Association has begun encouraging transplant centers and organ procurement organizations to study whether more people would donate organs if they or their loved ones received a small financial reward for doing so. But Dr. Gregory W. Rutecki of the Center for Bioethics and Human Dignity doesn't think a study is necessary. He argues that "introducing money into an enterprise that has until now been solely characterized by acts of selfless goodwill is crass and . . . can lead to abuse."

Dr. Rutecki believes that even modest financial incentives would lead to a black market, where human body parts got sold to the highest bidder. He is also concerned that the introduction of money could compromise the ethics of "informed consent," a decision to donate that is made with an understanding of the risks involved. Poor people, in particular, would be desperate enough to sell organs. Then there is the possibility of severe abuse within a system that permits financial compensation. Ruthless criminals might actually begin stealing body parts from living individuals to sell. (Source of quotations: www.bioethix.net/resources/healthcare/rutecki_2002_06_25.htm.)

Implied Main Idea _____

_____

3. Over billions of years, the human body has evolved to function and thrive in a gravity-controlled environment. Thus when astronauts spend extended periods of time in outer space, where there is no gravity, they lose muscle mass. That's because weightlessness in space lets many muscles in the body go unused. Lacking the constant pull of gravity to work against, the muscles become weak. Astronauts who spend months aboard a space station can barely stand when they first return to Earth. Even their heart muscles deteriorate. Living in an atmosphere lacking the weight of gravity also decreases bone mass, making the skeletal system weaker. Moreover, the redistribution of fluids in a zero-gravity environment also causes fluid loss, often causing dehydration. The human immune system also does not function as effectively in a gravity-free environment, so astronauts are more readily prey to viruses they might otherwise have fought off.

Implied Main Idea _____

_____

4. Based on simple observation, it's pretty clear that animals experience fear. Many mammals, for example, exhibit an anxious "fight or flight" response when confronted by a threatening predator. In addition to fear, many mammals seem to feel grief as well. Elephants, for instance, appear to mourn for days over dead or dying family members. Chimpanzees who lose a relative often exhibit signs of

Copyright © Cengage Learning. All rights reserved.

depression and even refuse to eat. Some animals also display obvious affection for their partners. Mating whales, for example, stroke each other with their flippers and swim slowly side by side while courting. In addition, many creatures are capable of expressing what looks to be playful happiness. Mammals such as dolphins frolic and chase each other, especially when they're young. Scientists claim that young dolphins are not just developing adult skills. They are displaying their joy at the fun they're having.

Implied Main Idea _____

_____

Copyright © Cengage Learning. All rights reserved.

▶ TEST 6   Inferring Main Ideas and Supporting Details

DIRECTIONS   Read each paragraph. Then answer the questions about the implied main idea and supporting details by filling in the blanks.

1. Next time you hear complaints about how long it takes the Food and Drug Administration to approve a new drug, you might want to remind the person complaining about the 1950s thalidomide scandal. Thalidomide was produced by a small German pharmaceutical firm called Chemie Grünenthal, and it appeared on the market around 1957. Sold as a tranquilizer as well as a treatment for morning sickness during pregnancy, thalidomide was inadequately tested. Yet assured by the drug's makers that it was safe, doctors prescribed it. On doctor's orders, thousands of patients, most of them pregnant women, dutifully ingested it. Then in the early 1960s, hospitals in Germany, the United States, Canada, Great Britain, and the Scandinavian countries began to report the births of babies with horrifying deformities. The infants had hands but no arms, feet but no legs. However, it wasn't until Dr. William McBride, a physician in Australia, made the connection between thalidomide and the babies' deformities that the drug was finally removed from the market. But that was in 1961. By that time, twelve thousand deformed infants had already been born. Astonishing as it might seem in the light of its tragic past, thalidomide actually made a comeback in the 1990s when it was discovered that the drug might be useful in the treatment of leprosy and AIDS.

Implied Main Idea   _____

_____

Implied Supporting Detail   The author does not say what caused twelve thousand infants to be born with deformities. Instead, she expects readers to infer what detail?

_____

_____

2. In May of 1963, Martin Luther King Jr. and other civil rights activists organized demonstrations to end segregation in Birmingham,

Copyright © Cengage Learning. All rights reserved.

Alabama. Although it may not have seemed so at the time, the protesters found the perfect enemy in Birmingham's police commissioner, Eugene "Bull" Connor. With his beefy features and snarling demeanor, Connor looked to be the living symbol of everything evil. Even worse for the cause of segregation, Connor and his police force used clubs, dogs, and fire hoses to chase and arrest the demonstrators. All the while, television cameras were filming what was happening. President John F. Kennedy, watching the televised brutality with the rest of the country, publicly confessed that what he saw made him sick. He later observed that "the civil rights movement should thank God for Bull Connor. He's helped it as much as Abraham Lincoln." As a result of the Birmingham demonstrations, the president sent the head of the Justice Department's civil rights division to the city to work out an arrangement that would permit desegregation of lunch counters, drinking fountains, and bathrooms. The president also made several calls to business leaders himself, all of whom agreed to his terms. (Adapted from Schaller, Schart, and Schulzinger, *Present Tense*, p. 235.)

Implied Main Idea

_____

_____

**Implied Supporting
Detail**

The authors never explain why President Kennedy thought Bull Connor actually helped the civil rights movement. Instead, they expect readers to infer what detail?

_____

_____

3. On Christmas Day 1859, the ship HMS *Lightning* arrived at Melbourne, Australia, with about a dozen wild European rabbits bound for an estate in western Victoria. Within three years, the rabbits had started to spread beyond western Victoria, after a bush fire destroyed the fences enclosing one colony. From a slow start, the spread of the rabbits picked up speed during the 1870s, and by 1900 the rabbit was the most serious agricultural pest ever known in Australia. The rabbits ate grass, the same grass used by sheep and cattle, so quickly the cry went up: "Get rid of the rabbit!" Millions of rabbits were poisoned and shot at great expense with absolutely

Copyright © Cengage Learning. All rights reserved.

no effect on their numbers. Nowhere else has the introduction of an exotic species had such an enormous impact. (Adapted from Krebs, *The Message of Ecology*, p. 8.)

Implied Main Idea

_____

_____

Implied Supporting Detail

Although the author does not specifically say how the rabbits got off the estate, he expects readers to infer what detail?

_____

4. Charter schools are publicly and privately funded elementary or secondary schools, which have been freed from some of the rules and regulations governing public schools. Charter schools can avoid many traditional rules and regulations because their charter, or statement of goals, says the schools can be held accountable for the specific objectives defined in the charter. Exactly how or what a school's charter has to achieve varies from state to state. The National Education Association (NEA), like many other individuals and groups, has high hopes for charter schools. As the NEA website expresses it, "NEA believes that charter schools and other nontraditional public school options have the potential to facilitate education reforms and develop new and creative teaching methods that can be replicated in traditional public schools for the benefit of all children." Yet, so far at least, the key word in that statement is "potential." In 2004, the National Assessment Governing Board (NAGB) released a report widely referred to as "The Nation's Report Card." The report found that, on average, charter school students were performing less well than students in public schools. A 2009 report showed similar results. Even more disturbing is the large number of charter school teachers who end up leaving. The Great Lakes Center for Education Research and Practice reported in 2007 that, over the course of a decade, as many as 40 percent of new charter school teachers left charter school positions for other jobs. The rate of teachers leaving charter schools was double that of public schools. Perhaps the NEA should rethink the idea that charter schools will be the source of successful educational reforms. (Source of studies: Diane Ravitch, *The Death and Life of the Great American School System*.)

Copyright © Cengage Learning. All rights reserved.

Implied Main Idea _____

_____

Implied Supporting
Details

Although the author does not explicitly say it, the quotation from the NEA appears in the paragraph in order to _____ _____, while the reports from the NAGB appear in order to _____.

Copyright © Cengage Learning. All rights reserved.

▶ **TEST 7**   **Drawing Your Own Conclusions**

DIRECTIONS   Answer the following questions by circling the letter of the correct response.

1. Research has shown that people are more likely to help others when they're in a good mood. Psychologists have named this tendency the *good mood effect*. In one experiment conducted over the course of a year, pedestrians in Minneapolis were stopped and asked to participate in a survey. When researchers examined the responses in the light of the weather conditions, they found that people answered more questions on sunny days than on cloudy ones. In another experiment, researchers found that the more the sun was shining, the larger the tips left by restaurant customers. Yet another experiment focused on pedestrians at a shopping mall, who were asked to change a dollar. Researchers discovered that when the request was made outside a bakery or coffee shop, where strong, pleasant odors from just baked chocolate chip cookies or freshly brewed coffee were in the air, people were more likely to help than they were if the request was made in a location devoid of any pleasant aromas.

(Source of experiments: Brehm and Kassim, *Social Psychology,* pp. 367–68.)

Which conclusion follows from the passage?

a. If you're trying to raise money for your favorite charity, you would be better off stationing yourself outside a doughnut shop than in front of your neighborhood cleaners.

b. Someone who tries to raise money for charity by standing in front of the local police station in hopes of donations will never collect a dime.

c. If you want to raise money for your local basketball team, you should probably go door to door accompanied by two of the team members.

2. Several states in America are converting one or more lanes on some of our nation's busiest highways into toll lanes. These pay-as-you-go routes allow drivers to buy their way out of traffic jams and sail past nonpaying motorists stuck in traffic. Some states are allowing private companies to build the new toll lanes in exchange for the revenue generated from them. Other states are simply designating existing lanes as toll lanes. However, many people consider this

Copyright © Cengage Learning. All rights reserved.

trend unfair. Several driver-advocacy groups claim that tolls amount to yet another tax on people who have no choice but to drive. As AAA spokesperson Mantill Williams put it, "Our overall philosophy is tolls are a... tax on motorists." Others have dubbed the new routes "Lexus Lanes." These people see the pay-as-you-go lanes as a luxury for those who can afford to pay. Advocates of whiz-through toll lanes, however, say that they are just like any other convenience that some people choose to pay for and some people don't. "It offers a model of personal choice for drivers," says John Horsley of the American Association of State Highway and Transportation Officials. "If you're willing to pay a bit more, you can get there faster." This position, however, ignores the fact that some of those "willing to pay" may not also be in the "can afford to pay" category. (Source of quotations: Bayles, "Toll Lanes: A Freer Ride, for a Price," *USA Today*, April 8, 2004, p. A3.)

Which conclusion follows from the passage?

a. John Horsley would probably support a transportation bill that allows states to add toll lanes with special privileges to portions of interstate highways.

b. Mantill Williams is likely to agree with those who think toll lanes are a great way of giving more flexibility and more options to state governments.

c. The author of this passage is firmly opposed to adding toll lanes to our nation's busy highways.

3. Is it ethical to keep animals in zoos? Some animal rights groups say no. They believe that animals have a right to be free. They conclude, therefore, that *all* zoos are wrong because they deprive wild creatures of their freedom. Those in favor of zoos, however, argue that the need for species conservation outweighs the cost to individual animals. They justify the existence of zoos because of the role they play in the preservation of animal populations, particularly through captive breeding programs. Furthermore, they maintain that the alternative to zoos—letting species simply dwindle or perish altogether in the wild—is the less ethical choice. However, Dr. Michael Hutchins of the Department of Conservation and Science for the American Zoo and Aquarium Association believes that even zoos that focus on conservation may not be doing enough to justify keeping animals in captivity. According to Dr. Hutchins,

Copyright © Cengage Learning. All rights reserved.

"A strong commitment to individual animal welfare is equally important." Many agree with Dr. Hutchins that zoos behave ethically *only* if they work toward the dual goals of conserving species while providing high-quality care in as natural an environment as possible. (Source of quotation: Kuehn, "Is It Ethical to Keep Animals in Zoos?" *Journal of the American Veterinary Medical Association*, December 1, 2002.)

Which conclusion follows from the passage?

a. Dr. Michael Hutchins probably agrees that it is perfectly acceptable for traveling circuses to include animals in their acts.

b. Dr. Michael Hutchins would be likely to defend researchers who keep animals in laboratories to conduct experiments on them.

c. In all likelihood, Dr. Michael Hutchins would be willing to donate or raise funds for zoo renovation projects devoted to re-creating an animal's natural habitat in the wild.

4. Controversial Dutch author and filmmaker Ayaan Hirsi Ali may have been named one of *Time* magazine's most influential people, but reactions to the story of how she came to reject Islam and advocate an end to what she calls its persecution of women have been mixed. Born in Somalia in 1969, she and her family eventually moved to Kenya, where she was raised in the religion of Islam. In 1992, according to her biography, Hirsi Ali balked at the idea of an arranged marriage to a distant cousin in Canada. To avoid the marriage, Hirsi Ali fled to the home of a female relative in the Netherlands. While living there, she earned a degree in political science and worked as a Somali-Dutch translator, often translating for battered Muslim women who sought refuge from abusive male relatives. Although she did not renounce her religion until 2002, it was at this point that Hirsi Ali's quarrels with Islam truly began. According to Hirsi Ali, the September 11, 2001, terrorist attacks on the United States led her to conclude that she could no longer believe in the God worshiped by the nineteen Muslim terrorists. Thus, in 2002, Hirsi Ali not only became an atheist, she also began to argue against what she called a "politically correct" approach to religious communities whose cultural values violated fundamental human rights along with the law. She was particularly outspoken about the role of women in the Muslim world, insisting that "the position of women is, in my view, nowhere as bad as it is in the Muslim world."

Copyright © Cengage Learning. All rights reserved.

While Hirsi Ali has won the admiration of many, she has her share of critics. Her challengers insist that she stereotypes all Muslim women as victims and fails to make distinctions between distortions of Islamic thought and authentic Islamic beliefs. Critics also say she persistently misrepresents her former faith, particularly in her reading of the Koran, which, they insist, does not justify the mistreatment of women as Ali claims. (Source of information: Anthony, "Taking the Fight to Islam," *The Observer*, February 4, 2007; Ali, *The Caged Virgin*, p. 18.)

Which conclusion follows from the passage?

a. Critics are correct to claim that Hirsi Ali's view of Islam stems from her own unhappy experience, not from her knowledge of Islamic thought and practice.

b. Despite her ideas about Islam, Hirsi Ali would probably agree that *madrasahs*, schools that include education in the religion of Islam, deserve public support.

c. Hirsi Ali would probably not send a child of hers to a school that included Islamic religious training in the curriculum.

Copyright © Cengage Learning. All rights reserved.

▶ TEST 8   Inferring Implied Main Ideas in Longer Readings

Copyright © Cengage Learning. All rights reserved.

DIRECTIONS   Read each selection and write the implied main idea in the blanks.

1. Explaining the Growth of Bureaucracies*

1   What accounts for the growth of bureaucracies and bureaucrats since the late 1800s? Was all this growth the result of bureaucratic incompetence and unresponsiveness? Many observers believe that the growth can be attributed directly to the expansion of the nation itself. There are a great many more of us and we are living closer together. Not only do the residents of cities and suburbs require many more services than did the predominantly rural dwellers of the early 1800s, but the challenges of urban and industrial life have intensified and outstripped the capacity of families or local and state governments to cope with them. Thus the American people have increasingly turned to their national government for help.

2   There is considerable evidence that the growth of bureaucracies is "of our own making." Public opinion polls indicate widespread public support for expanding federal involvement in a variety of areas. Even when public support for new programs is low, pollsters find Americans unwilling to eliminate or reduce existing programs. Furthermore, the public's expectations about the quality of service it should receive are constantly rising. The public wants government to be more responsive, responsible, and compassionate in administering public programs. Officials have reacted to these pressures by establishing new programs and maintaining and improving existing ones.

3   The federal bureaucracy has also expanded in response to sudden changes in economic, social, cultural, and political conditions. During the Great Depression and World War II, for example, the federal bureaucracy grew to meet the challenges these situations created. Washington became more and more involved in programs providing financial aid and employment to the poor. It increased its regulation of important industries and during the war imposed controls over much of the American economy. As part of the general war effort, the federal government also built roads and hospitals and mobilized the entire population. When these crises ended, the public was reluctant to give up many of the federal welfare and

———————
*bureaucracy: management through bureaus, or departments, staffed by nonelected officials.

economic programs implemented during the time of emergency. (Gitelson et al., *American Government*, p. 358.)

Implied Main Idea
_____

_____

2. Improving Your Memory

1   Do you, like just about everyone else, want to improve your memory? Well, the good news is that you can. All you have to do is put the following advice into practice, and you'll see immediate results.

2   For example, remembering when Christopher Columbus discovered America is easy enough if you use visualization. You could, for example, imagine Columbus standing on the beach with his ships in the harbor in the background. Fortunately, unrealistic images work just as well or better, and you could imagine Columbus's boat having the large numerals *1492* printed on its side or Columbus reviewing his account books after the trip and seeing in dismay that the trip cost him $1,492. You could even envisage something still more fanciful: Because 1492 sounds like the phrase "for tea, nightie two," you might imagine Columbus serving tea in his nightie to two Indians on the beach. A weird image like this is often easier to remember than a realistic one because its silliness makes it more distinct (Levin, 1985).

3   Visual imagery also works well for remembering single terms, such as unfamiliar words in a foreign language. The French word for snail, *l'escargot*, can be remembered easily if you form an image of what the word sounds like in English—"less cargo"—and picture an event related to this English equivalent, such as workers dumping snails overboard to achieve "less cargo" on a boat. The biological term *mitosis* (which refers to cell division) sounds like the phrase "my toes itch," so it is easier to remember if you picture a single cell dividing while scratching its imaginary toes.

4   Another device for memory improvement is called the *method of loci*, or *locations*. With this method, you purposely associate objects or terms with a highly familiar place or building. Suppose you have to remember the names of all the instruments in a standard symphony orchestra. Using the method of loci, choose a familiar place, such as the neighborhood in which you live, and imagine leaving one of the instruments at the doorstep of each house or business in the neighborhood. To remember the instruments, simply take an imaginary

Copyright © Cengage Learning. All rights reserved.

walk through the neighborhood, mentally picking up each instrument as you come to it.

5   The same loci, or locations, can work repeatedly on many sets of terms or objects without one set interfering with another. After memorizing the musical instruments in the previous example, you could still use your neighborhood to remember the names of exotic fruit, without fear of accidentally "seeing" a musical instrument by mistake. Loci can also help in recalling terms that are not physical objects, such as scientific concepts. Simply imagine the terms in some visual form, such as written on cards, or, better yet, visualize concrete objects that rhyme with each term and leave these around the mental neighborhood.

6   Imagery and visual loci work for two reasons (Pressley and McDaniel, 1988). First, they force you to organize new information, even if the organization is self-imposed. Second, they encourage you to elaborate mentally on new information. In "placing" musical instruments around the neighborhood, you have to think about what each instrument looks like and how it relates to the others in a symphony. These mental processes are essential for moving information into long-term memory. (Adapted from Seifert, *Educational Psychology*, pp. 199–201.)

Implied Main Idea   _____

_____

3. Remembrance of Things Past

1   A whiff of perfume, the top of a baby's head, freshly cut grass, a locker room, the musty odor of a basement, the floury aroma of a bakery, the smell of mothballs in the attic, and the leathery scent of a new car—each may trigger what Diane Ackerman (1990) has called "aromatic memories." Frank Schab (1990) tested this theory in a series of experiments. In one, subjects were given a list of adjectives and instructed to write an antonym, or word opposite in meaning, for each adjective. In half of the sessions, the sweet smell of chocolate was blown into the room. The next day, subjects were asked to list as many of the antonyms as they could—again, in the presence or absence of the chocolate aroma. As it turned out, the most words were recalled when the smell of chocolate was present at both the learning and the recall sessions. The reason? The smell was stored in the memory along with the words, so it later served as a retrieval cue.

Copyright © Cengage Learning. All rights reserved.

2   The retrieval of memories is influenced by factors other than smell. In an unusual study, researchers Duncan Godden and Alan Baddeley presented deep-sea divers with a list of words in one of two settings: fifteen feet underwater or on the beach. Then they tested the divers' recall in the same or another setting. Illustrating what is called *context-dependent memory*, the divers recalled 40 percent more words when the material was learned and retrieved in the same setting. The practical implications are intriguing. For example, recall may be improved if material is retrieved in the same room in which it was initially learned (Smith, 1979).

3   Indeed, context seems to activate memory even in three-month-old infants. In a series of studies, Carolyn Rovee-Collier and her colleagues (1992) trained infants to shake an overhead mobile equipped with colorful blocks and bells by kicking a leg that was attached to the mobile by a ribbon. The infants were later more likely to recall what they learned (in other words, to kick) when tested in the same crib and looking at the same visual cues than when there were differences. Apparently, it is possible to jog one's memory by reinstating the initial context of an experience. This explains why I will often march into my secretary's office for something, go blank, forget why I was there, return in defeat to my office, look around, and ZAP!, suddenly recall what it was I needed.

4   Studies also reveal that it is often easier to recall something when our state of mind is the same at testing as it was while we were learning. If information is acquired when you are happy, sad, drunk, sober, calm, or aroused, that information is more likely to be retrieved under the same conditions (Bower, 1981; Eich, 1980; Eich et al., 1994). The one key complicating factor is that the mood we're in leads us to evoke memories that fit our current mood. When we are happy, the good times are most easy to recall; but when we feel depressed or anxious, our minds become flooded with negative events of the past (Blaney, 1986; Ucros, 1989).

(Adapted from Brehm and Kassim, *Social Psychology*, p. 231.)

Implied Main Idea   _____

_____

Copyright © Cengage Learning. All rights reserved.

▶ **TEST 9**   **Taking Stock**

DIRECTIONS   Read each passage. Then answer the questions by filling in the blanks or circling the letter of the correct response.

1. **Are Hands-Free Models the Answer?**

1   [1]After a 1997 study published by the *New England Journal of Medicine* revealed that drivers are four times more likely to be involved in accidents while talking on cell phones, some states, such as New York, decided to ban handheld cell phones and permit motorists to use only hands-free models. [2]Do hands-free phones solve the problem of driver distraction? [3]Over the last several years, psychologist David Strayer and his colleagues at the University of Utah have conducted several experiments to study the consequences of talking on cell phones while driving. [4]In 2001, they found that people who were talking on both handheld and hands-free cell phones while reacting to traffic signals were likely to react slower than people who were not on the phone.

2   [5]In another study, published in 2003 in the *Journal of Experimental Psychology: Applied*, researchers placed 110 volunteers in a driver-training situation that mimicked the inside of a car and was enclosed by screens that displayed realistic-looking surroundings. [6]Some of the participants talked on hands-free cell phones to other students while they simulated driving on a highway and in heavy, city traffic. [7]The participants with the hands-free cell phones exhibited a slower reaction time than the students not talking on cell phones. [8]Those with the hands-free phones also took longer to brake and longer to accelerate, moved their eyes less, and paid less attention to their environment. [9]They also did not remember elements of their surroundings as accurately as participants without cell phones. [10]Three hands-free cell phone users even rear-ended a simulated car in front of them. (Sources of studies: Goodman, "The $64,000 Question: Just How Dangerous Is Car-Phoning?" *Boston Globe*, July 10, 2001, p. A9; University of Utah News and Public Relations, "Cell Phone Users Drive 'Blind,'" January 27, 2003.)

1. What is the implied main idea?

   _____

   _____

2. What kind of transition opens sentence 3 in paragraph 1?

   _____

Copyright © Cengage Learning. All rights reserved.

3. How would you define the word *simulated* in sentence 6?

_____

4. The author expects the reader to infer that New York's decision to ban handheld cell phones was a
   a. pure coincidence and not related to the 1997 study mentioned in sentence 1.
   b. result of the 1997 study mentioned in sentence 1.
   c. plan that had been in the making long before the 1997 study mentioned in sentence 1.

5. How might David Strayer respond to claims that the New York legislation had solved the problem of cell phones being a distraction while driving?

_____

_____

2. Deadly Epidemics

1 ¹In the Middle Ages sometime around 1347, a disastrous plague known as the Black Death swept through western Europe. ²Estimates suggest that the plague killed close to one-third of the population by the time it passed out of Europe. ³In France, the death rate was so high that Cardinal Clement VI had to bless the Rhone River so that corpses could be allowed to sink into its waters and disappear. ⁴France had neither time nor room to provide a proper burial. ⁵In the seventeenth century, a smallpox epidemic decimated the Native American tribes in the New World. ⁶The first major outbreak of the disease struck the Northeast Atlantic coast between 1616 and 1619, leaving the Massachusetts and Algonquin tribes reduced from 30,000 people to 300. ⁷In 1918, a deadly flu epidemic roamed the world, taking a terrifying toll wherever it appeared. ⁸In a single year, it killed more Americans than died in battle in World Wars I and II, the Korean War, and the Vietnam War. ⁹Although official estimates suggest that twenty million people died as a result, the true number can never be known because medical facilities were in such chaos, it was difficult to keep accurate records. (Sources of flu incidents: Surowiecki, "The High Cost of Illness," *New Yorker*, May 12, 2003; Gina Kolata, *Flu*.)

Copyright © Cengage Learning. All rights reserved.

1. What is the implied main idea?

   _____

   _____

2. How would you define *decimated* in sentence 5?

   _____

3. Sentences 5, 7, and 8 open with what kind of transition?

   _____

4. To make sense of sentence 4, readers have to infer what answer to this question: Why did France lack time and room?

   _____

   _____

5. In her book *Flu,* which describes the effects of the 1918 flu epidemic mentioned in the passage, Gina Kolata uses the word *obsessed* to describe researchers determined to track down the virus that caused that flu. Based on the passage, what do you think is the motive for their obsession?

   _____

   _____

Copyright © Cengage Learning. All rights reserved.

Synthesizing Sources

© Ed Bock/Corbis

IN THIS CHAPTER, YOU WILL LEARN

- how to read different writers on the same topic and infer a relationship that links them together.

- how to combine those similarities and/or differences into a synthesis statement that sums up the relationships or suggests your own point of view.

Get into the habit of analysis—analysis will in time enable synthesis to become your habit of mind.

—Frank Lloyd Wright, American architect

Chapter 7 builds on everything you have learned so far while taking you deeper into critical thinking territory, where readers apply, evaluate, and elaborate on what they've read. In this chapter, you'll learn how to synthesize, or find a way to link, different readings on the same topic so that you better understand each one and come up with your own original point of view, or position.

As you can probably guess, synthesizing similar or competing ideas on the same topic is a critical academic skill. Being able to synthesize various viewpoints can give you the ideas you'll need to answer essay questions and write good term papers.

Synthesizing Sources

Imagine you are assigned to read an account of President John Adams's[†] tenure in the White House and the reading emphasizes Adams's praiseworthy efforts to stop the country's undeclared war with the French. Now imagine as well that you are assigned an outside reading on the same topic. This reading, however, harshly criticizes Adams's role in bringing about passage of the Alien and Sedition Acts.[†] Having read about two different sides of the same subject, John Adams's tenure in the White House, how do you think you should proceed? Should you take notes on each reading separately? Or should you try to **synthesize**, or link, the two different positions into one unified statement that connects them together?

If you opted for the second choice, it may be because you already know the basic rule of remembering: The human mind is better at storing related pieces of information than isolated ideas, theories, or facts. Keep that principle in mind whenever you read different authors who discuss the same subject. It pays to see if you can synthesize the point each author makes into a broader statement that refers to or acknowledges the different points of view. If you can synthesize several ideas on the same topic, you have understood them thoroughly enough to write about them, whether it's for an exam or a term paper.

Consider the two readings about Adams just mentioned. Each one focuses on a different aspect, or side, of Adams's career. One reading

---

[†]John Adams (1735–1826): the second president of the United States (1797–1801).
[†]Alien and Sedition Acts: acts that discriminated against the foreign born and blurred the distinction between political dissension and attempts to overthrow the government.

Copyright © Cengage Learning. All rights reserved.

notes a positive accomplishment; the other focuses on a more negative achievement. A statement like the following synthesizes the two readings and acknowledges both perspectives, or points of view, on Adams's career. "Fans of John Adams like to point to his abilities as a peacemaker during the conflict with the French, but his critics can't forget that the Alien and Sedition Acts came into being during his presidency." Using that sentence as your thesis statement, you can write a term paper. You can also prepare for a test by trying to recall the supporting details from both readings as a method of review.

Taking the time to synthesize two, three, or even four different sources of information into a statement that links them together does more than encourage remembering. It also deepens your understanding of the individual viewpoints.

To synthesize different sources on the same subject, you have to determine the main idea for each one. Then you have to infer how those main ideas, along with the supporting details used to develop them, relate to one another. This prolonged processing of information improves both comprehension and remembering. It will also take the terror out of writing term papers because you will know how to make sense of your research.

Synthesizing to Inform or to Persuade

Synthesizing is particularly important when you write research papers. Keep in mind, however, that synthesis statements, like longer readings in general, can vary in their purpose. Sometimes they merely inform readers, while at other times they are clearly designed to persuade.

For example, imagine that you were assigned a paper on the USA Patriot Act, which came into being in response to the terrorist attacks on September 11, 2001. From your research, you might discover that there is much disagreement, some of it quite heated, on the effectiveness of the Patriot Act. There are people who say it is essential to protecting the country. Others, however, argue that it is ineffective.

If the goal of your synthesis is mainly to inform—and that may be a requirement of the assignment—then the synthesis statement[†] you use to guide the writing of your paper would connect what you've read

---

[†]If the term *synthesis statement* is starting to seem synonymous with *thesis statement*, that's because thesis statements for term papers are the result of synthesizing sources.

Copyright © Cengage Learning. All rights reserved.

on the topic without expressing your personal opinion—for example, "Since the moment it was formulated, the Patriot Act has been a source of controversy, with many people supporting it and probably an equal number challenging its existence."

However, if your paper is expected to persuade, then your final paper might synthesize your point of view with the ideas of others into a statement like the following: "While portions of the Patriot Act were certainly necessary given the threat that faced the country following September 11, 2001, in current and calmer times, some elements of the Act need to be modified. They need to be modified because they do more to undermine civil rights than they do to eliminate terrorism."

Or you might argue the opposite: "While it is easy to understand the widespread criticism of the Patriot Act because it does, in fact, intrude on civil rights, it's also clear that in times like the current ones, even the portions of the Act that intrude on civil liberties are necessary."

Step-by-Step Synthesizing
◆

Synthesizing two or more sources into one statement requires these steps:

1. Identify and paraphrase the main idea of each reading.

2. Determine what makes the readings similar or different (see the chart on pages 433–34 for questions that will help you analyze different readings on the same topic).

3. Write a sentence or two that identifies, in fairly specific terms, the relationship among different authors focused on the same topic. Look, for example, at the following synthesis statement, which connects the theories of three different psychologists:

   > For Sigmund Freud, unacknowledged sexual desires were the main source of neurotic behavior in adults, but Freud's pupils Carl Jung and Alfred Adler publicly refused to follow in his footsteps. While Jung emphasized the power of historical patterns to alter behavior, Adler focused on the way in which a sense of inferiority could motivate both positive and negative reactions to the world.

4. Include the names of the people taking each position if those names are (1) central to the opinion being expressed (e.g., almost no one else holds the opinion), or (2) the instructor wants the names included in the assignment.

Copyright © Cengage Learning. All rights reserved.

Keep Your Purpose in Mind

If you are synthesizing for a term paper, you might need a fifth step, depending on your purpose. The synthesis statement shown above to illustrate step 3 is fine as it is *if* the purpose of the paper is strictly informative. However, if part of your assignment is to argue for a particular point of view, then you need to indicate whether you (1) agree with the sources you've read, (2) disagree wholly or in part, or (3) hold a completely different point of view.

Here, for instance, is how the informative synthesis statement combining the ideas of Freud, Jung, and Adler could be re-written with a persuasive purpose:

> His disciples Carl Jung and Alfred Adler both rejected Sigmund Freud's theory that repressed sexual desires caused neurosis. Instead, they went on to formulate their own theories about the causes of psychic disturbance. However, of the two, it is Adler's theory of low self-esteem which has proven the most useful for therapeutic purposes. Jung's ideas about ancient mythic figures dominating our unconscious make interesting reading but don't allow for any practical application.

Ten Questions for Synthesizing Sources

Sometimes the connections among sources are obvious. This is particularly true when the writers all agree or disagree. But when the connections are not so obvious, the questions that follow will prove useful.

1. Do the authors generally agree but offer different examples or reasons to prove the same point?
2. Does one author offer an interpretation that is challenged by the others?
3. Do the authors express a similar point of view only in different forms, say poem and essay, fiction and nonfiction?
4. Do the authors completely disagree or only partially disagree?
5. Do the authors address the same topic or issue but from different time frames, for instance, past and present—or from different perspectives—the elderly and the young or the working person versus a corporation?

Copyright © Cengage Learning. All rights reserved.

6. Does one author focus on the cause or causes of a problem while the other looks more closely at solutions?

7. Does one author zero in on the causes of a historic event while the other concentrates on the aftermath or effect of the same event?

8. Do the authors come from different disciplines? Does one author focus on the psychological roots of an event while the other views it from an economic perspective?

9. Did the ideas of one author influence the work of another?

10. Does one author offer a personal account of events that the other describes in more impersonal or objective terms?

◆ **EXERCISE 1**   **Synthesizing Brief Passages**

DIRECTIONS   Read each group of passages. Then circle the number of the statement that most effectively synthesizes or connects all three. *Note*: Remember the synthesis statement should not contradict anything said in the original sources.

The movie made from John Steinbeck's novel *The Grapes of Wrath* has become a classic.

© John Springer Collection/Corbis

Copyright © Cengage Learning. All rights reserved.

EXAMPLE

Sources

a. John Steinbeck's *The Grapes of Wrath* movingly conveys the misery facing the migrant workers who, throughout the Depression, traveled Route 66 across the country searching for work. Steinbeck writes, "Route 66 is the path of a people in flight, refugees from dust and shrinking land, from the thunder of tractors and shrinking ownership, from the twisting winds that howl up out of Texas, from the floods that bring no richness to the land and steal what little richness is there."

b. Statistics suggest the magnitude of the Great Depression's effect on the business world. The stock market crash in October 1929 shocked investors and caused a financial panic. Between 1929 and 1933, 100,000 businesses failed; corporate profits fell from $10 billion to $1 billion; and the gross national product was cut in half. Banks failed by the thousands. (Adapted from Norton et al., *A People and a Nation*, p. 754.)

c. As unemployment soared during the Great Depression, both men and women suffered homelessness. In 1932, a squad of New York City police officers arrested twenty-five in "Hoover Valley," a village of tents and crates constructed in Central Park. All over the country, people were so poor they were forced to live in miserable little camps called "Hoovervilles," named in sarcastic honor of President Herbert Hoover, whose policy on the Depression was to pretend it wasn't happening.

Synthesis Statement

1. During the Great Depression, statistics show that no one suffered more than the men and women who earned their living as migrant workers.

2. Whether we look to the world of fiction or fact, it's clear that the Great Depression took a terrible toll on people in all walks of life, from bankers to migrant workers.

3. John Steinbeck's description of the hardships people faced during the Great Depression is enormously moving to this day, and Steinbeck's novel is more real than any statistic.

EXPLANATION Sources *a*, *b*, and *c* all describe specific groups that suffered as a result of the Great Depression. Thus statement 1 is not a good synthesis statement because it makes a claim about statistics not mentioned anywhere in the original source material. Sentence 2 is an effective synthesis statement because it combines the ideas in all three passages without inventing any facts that weren't there in the first place.

Copyright © Cengage Learning. All rights reserved.

Statement 3 is incorrect because it focuses solely on Steinbeck's novel and ignores the other sources. Note: All three are informative synthesis statements. But that is not necessarily the case with those that follow.

Sources

1. a. When World War II broke out in Europe on September 1, 1939, the United States was the only world power without a propaganda agency. Since World War I, Americans had been suspicious of the claim that propaganda could be used to good effect. Many believed that British propaganda had helped maneuver the United States into World War I. They also had not forgotten the bloody anti-German riots touched off by movies like America's own *Hitler, Beast of Berlin* (1919). To most Americans, *propaganda* was simply a dirty word, no matter what its purpose.

   b. In 1939, the president of the United States, Franklin Delano Roosevelt, applied pressure on Hollywood to make feature films that were little more than propaganda vehicles. Hollywood producers, however, were reluctant to give Roosevelt what he wanted. Committed to the doctrine* of pure entertainment, pure profit, and, above all, the need for America to stay out of the war, lest ticket sales decline, most balked at making films that reflected the horror engulfing Europe.

   c. The Japanese bombed Pearl Harbor on December 7, 1941. Astonished and outraged, the United States entered World War II. On December 17 of the same year, President Roosevelt appointed Lowell Mellett as head of the Hollywood propaganda office. Mellett's job was to make sure that Hollywood films aided the war effort. In the aftermath of Pearl Harbor, Hollywood producers were happy to cooperate by making films that celebrated the war effort and castigated* America's enemies by exploiting common and often vicious stereotypes.

Synthesis Statement

1. Until the bombing of Pearl Harbor, the United States did not have an official propaganda office, a terrible mistake that produced unexpected and horrifying consequences.

*doctrine: principle, theory.
*castigated: harshly criticized or punished.

Copyright © Cengage Learning. All rights reserved.

2. Before the bombing of Pearl Harbor, Hollywood, like most of America, mistrusted propaganda. But after the attack, propaganda became an acceptable part of the war effort and Hollywood embraced it with a vengeance using the worst stereotypes to describe America's enemies, which may be one reason why the internment of Japanese Americans aroused hardly a ripple of protest.

3. During wartime, it is very likely that propaganda is a necessity; unfortunately, the effects of propaganda sometimes live on after the war ends, when those vilified* as our enemies have once again become allies.

Sources **2.** **a.** The Egyptians revered Ma'at as the goddess of justice. She was depicted weighing the hearts of the dead on a scale, with an ostrich feather on one side and a heart on the other. A balance between the two guaranteed a happy afterlife because an almost weightless heart showed an absence of evil deeds. An imbalance of the scale, however, promised torment for the deceased.

b. The ancient Greeks worshipped Dike as the goddess of justice. When the Romans inherited her, they renamed her Justitia and represented her with a blindfold around her eyes to symbolize her lack of bias, or prejudice in favor of one side or the other.

© Christophe Boisvieux/Corbis

c. With the arrival of Christianity and the rejection of the ancient gods, the goddess of justice was turned into a saint called Santa Justitia. However, images of Santa Justitia suggested that people were suspicious of her ability to fairly deal out justice. Santa Justitia was often depicted holding an unevenly balanced scale. The implication was that the rich got different justice than the poor.

Synthesis Statement **1.** While the ancient Egyptians, Greeks, and Romans held the goddess of justice in great respect, the early Christians were more suspicious of how justice was meted out,* and the image of Santa Justitia reflected their skepticism concerning the nature of justice.

---

*vilified: viciously insulted or criticized, using abusive language to destroy a reputation.
*meted out: distributed, given.

Copyright © Cengage Learning. All rights reserved.

2. The Christians refused to accept all of the ancient gods and goddesses, including Justitia, the goddess of justice. This is not surprising given that there was no justice in ancient society.

3. When one country conquers another, the conquerors usually try to wipe out the religion of the occupied population. It follows, then, that the Christians wanted little or nothing to do with the gods and goddesses associated with earlier civilizations.

Sources 3. a. In the 1992 presidential election, political action committees (PACs) contributed more than $50 million to the various campaigns. The 1996, 2000, and 2008 elections saw even greater amounts of PAC money pour into campaign coffers. This sort of funding of the presidency puts a price tag on democracy: Whoever contributes the most money has the most access to the president and the most influence over our society.

b. In the name of campaign reform, some people would increasingly restrict the contributions of political action committees (PACs). Yet these contributions, no matter how high the sums, are nothing more than a legitimate form of free speech. Any group who wants to contribute to a political campaign as a show of support should have the right to do so. Ultimately, it is up to people to accept or reject what the political action committees have to say, and the guarantee of free speech to such groups, even if it is in the form of campaign contributions, does not necessarily mean that their speech will have a profound effect on our society.

c. In 2010, the Supreme Court of the United States reversed a long-standing right of corporations and unions to promote political candidates. It's now legal for corporations and unions to use monies from their treasuries to underwrite ads for the candidate of their choice. Long-time watchdogs of campaign financing are dismayed, believing that candidates in need of funding will be inclined to curry favor with those giving them the most money. Those backing the Supreme Court decision insist that giving money to candidates is just another form of free speech, which cannot be denied to corporations or unions. From their perspective, the decision was a fair one.

Copyright © Cengage Learning. All rights reserved.

Synthesis Statement

1. When it comes to the campaign contributions of political action committees, or PACs, there's a good deal of disagreement as to how much money is appropriate to contribute to campaigns before it looks like outright bribery. But on one point, no one disagrees: PACs have contributed huge sums to the presidential campaigns, and their contributions have earned them too much influence over government policy.

2. Political action committees (PACs) and their contributions to political campaigns have been much discussed over the past decade However, no one has ever proven that PAC contributions affect the political decisions of those on the receiving end of PAC generosity, and it's unlikely that anyone ever will.

3. Although a 2010 Supreme Court decision lent support to those who believe campaign contributions by corporations are a form of free speech guaranteed by the Constitution, the debate over the effect PAC money has on our government is not likely to die down anytime soon.

Sources

4. a. In 2003, when millions of people around the world objected to President George W. Bush's decision to wage war on Iraq, critics of the war used the Internet extensively to organize antiwar demonstrations.

   b. In the campaign for the elimination of land mines[†] around the world, the Internet played a key role. Those who supported the elimination of the mines kept in touch and up to date via email.

   c. President Barack Obama's prodigiously successful use of the Internet to raise money for his 2008 presidential campaign was a lesson in modern-day fundraising.

Synthesis Statement

1. Because of the Internet, people are staying in touch with friends and family more than ever before.

2. Thanks to the Internet, it's become easier for political activists around the world to challenge repressive governments that limit both civil rights and freedom of speech.

[†]land mines: explosive devices buried in the earth.

Copyright © Cengage Learning. All rights reserved.

3. The Internet has forever changed both political activism and political fund-raising.

Sources 5. a. With its brilliant and innovative techniques, D. W. Griffith's *The Birth of a Nation* dramatically changed the face of American movies forever. Before Griffith, movies contained neither close-ups nor fade-outs. It was Griffith who brought those two techniques to the screen. With the exception of Orson Welles and the film *Citizen Kane*, no other director and no other film have been as influential as Griffith and *The Birth of a Nation*.

b. By 1910, motion pictures had become an art form, thanks to creative directors like D. W. Griffith. Griffith's most famous work, *The Birth of a Nation* (1915), an epic film about the Civil War and Reconstruction, used innovative techniques—close-ups, fade-outs, and battle scenes—that gave viewers heightened drama and excitement. Unfortunately, the film fanned racial prejudice by depicting African Americans as a threat to white moral values. An organized black protest against it was led by the infant National Association for the Advancement of Colored People (NAACP). (Norton et al., *A People and a Nation*, p. 583.)

c. Despite the film's famed innovations, it's nearly impossible for moviegoers to take pleasure in D. W. Griffith's *The Birth of a Nation*. Powered by racism, the film enrages more than it entertains, and it's no wonder that African-American groups picketed the film when it first appeared, fearing, correctly as it turned out, that Griffith's film would revitalize the Ku Klux Klan.

Synthesis Statement 1. D. W. Griffith was a famous film director who dramatically influenced the American film industry; in fact, Griffith changed the face of American film.

2. Despite the contributions that D. W. Griffith's *The Birth of a Nation* made to filmmaking, many people are appalled by the film's racism.

3. No one before or after has influenced movie-making as profoundly as D. W. Griffith.

Copyright © Cengage Learning. All rights reserved.

INTERNET FOLLOW-UP: *The Birth of a Nation* and the Ku Klux Klan

What was the original title of D. W. Griffith's movie *The Birth of a Nation*?

_____

What effect did the movie have on membership in the Ku Klux Klan?

_____

_____

_____

◆ **EXERCISE 2**   **Writing Synthesis Statements**

DIRECTIONS   Read each group of passages. Then write a synthesis statement that links them together.

EXAMPLE

a. Even before the war, Nazi officials had targeted Jews throughout Europe for extermination. By war's end, about six million Jews had been forced into concentration camps and had been systematically killed by firing squads, unspeakable tortures, and gas chambers. (Norton et al., *A People and a Nation*, p. 843.)

b. To protest Hitler's treatment of the Jews during World War II, the philosopher Simone Weil went on a prolonged hunger strike. In the end, Weil starved to death rather than take food while the prisoners of concentration camps were being reduced to walking skeletons.

c. Born to a wealthy Swedish family, Raoul Wallenberg could easily have ignored the horror Adolf Hitler unleashed on the world. But he chose not to. Using his considerable daring, charm, and brains, Wallenberg saved the lives of thousands of Jewish refugees who would have died a horrible death without his help.

Synthesis Statement   During World War II, the tragic plight of the Jews stirred people like Simone

Weil and Raoul Wallenberg to extraordinary acts of heroism.

Copyright © Cengage Learning. All rights reserved.

EXPLANATION   The first source explains the plight of the Jews during World War II. The other two sources identify individuals who tried to stop or hinder what was happening. As you can see, the synthesis statement links together the information in all three passages, connecting both the tragic situation and individual responses to it.

Sources   1. a. Every society is concerned with the socialization of its children— that is, with making sure that children learn early on what is considered socially correct and morally ethical behavior.

b. In Asian societies, the family is considered the most important agent of socialization. Thus if children misbehave, it's a great source of shame to the family. It follows, then, that worry about the family's reputation is one reason Japanese children raised in the traditional fashion are likely to be very well behaved. They do not want to dishonor their families.

c. In the last decade, a number of studies have suggested that in the United States a child's peer group may be overtaking the family as the most powerful agent of socialization. Values and attitudes that the family has patiently tried to teach children are often profoundly challenged by their interaction with their peers. Children who want to fit in are inclined to behave and think like their peers, even when that behavior and those thoughts go against what's been learned at home.

Synthesis Statement

_____

_____

Sources   2. a. Dan Tapscott, the author of books such as *Growing Up Digital* and *Grown Up Digital* believes that the Internet and the search engine Google are ushering in a new age of learning when students no longer need to be taught anything. In Tapscott's view, they will be their own teachers, turning to the Internet to find out everything they want or need to know about the world. In his enthusiastic vision of the future, this is "an extraordinary period in human history . . . for the first time the next generation can teach us how to ready our world for the future." Tapscott wants parents, in particular, to recognize that "digital immersion is a good thing for their kids." (Tapscott, *Grown Up Digital*, p. 8.)

Copyright © Cengage Learning. All rights reserved.

b. In his book *The Dumbest Generation: How the Digital Age Stupefies Young Americans and Jeopardizes Our Future,* English professor Mark Bauerlein voices his concerns about the effects of technology on the brains of the next generation. The word *concerns* is an understatement since Bauerlein is a prophet of doom, who believes that young people today are losing the ability to focus on and analyze the information they are bombarded with when they log on to the World Wide Web. Although Bauerlein cites a number of reasons for a decline in analytical reasoning ability, his major target is the huge amount of time kids spend on computerized gadgetry.

c. In his book *The Shallows* Nicholas Carr makes it clear that he uses the Internet all the time for research. He relies on it, in fact. But the author, who also penned the controversial article "Is Google Making Us Stupid," has some concerns about what our newfound access to multiple sources of information that can be accessed simultaneously is doing to our brains. Carr believes that the brain, which is highly plastic—i.e., capable of changing in response to experience—is getting into a mental rut capable of only one response to new information. As he puts it, "Because there is so much information at our fingertips, we can get stuck just constantly uncovering new relevant information and never stopping and actually reading and thinking deeply about any one piece of information."

Synthesis Statement

_____

_____

Sources 3. a. In 2008, McAfee Security researchers announced the detection of a coordinated effort by hackers attempting to steal passwords used in online games such as *Lord of the Rings Online.* According to McAfee, the hackers, operating out of China, had managed to infiltrate over 10,000 Web pages. The infected websites don't look any different, but they are capable of installing a password-stealing program on the victim's computers. The hackers' goal seems to be the theft of passwords, which can give them access to online source codes and Web designs, all of which can be extremely lucrative when resold.

Copyright © Cengage Learning. All rights reserved.

b. In 2004, programming analyst Shawn Carpenter at Sandia National Laboratories uncovered a well-organized cyber-espionage ring operating out of Guandong Province in China. While under investigation by the FBI, the hackers had managed to steal massive amounts of information from military and space labs, and the World Bank. However, Carpenter, instead of being rewarded, was fired and investigated after telling the FBI what he had uncovered. Carpenter had been terminated because hacking foreign computers is a crime in the United States. He later sued, arguing that he had been protecting the country's security. Carpenter was awarded three million dollars in damages.

c. In 2009, members of Students for a Free Tibet, a group that publicly criticizes China's control of Tibet, discovered that their gmail accounts, provided by Google, had been hacked. Google eventually traced the hackers back to China and announced in 2010 that the sabotage* was not an isolated event but was part of a pattern of cyber-attacks on those who criticize China's policies. Larry Clinton, president of the Internet Security Alliance, was quoted as saying that the cyber-attacks on China's critics were likely conducted by "people who have a loose affiliation with the Chinese government." (Source of quotation: http://bit.ly/8TXhpl.)

Synthesis Statement

_____

_____

TAKING A CLOSER LOOK

Repetition and Reference

In item c above, the word *sabotage* is used as a substitute or stand in for what activity introduced in the previous sentences?

_____

_____

---

*sabotage: destructive actions used to hinder or defeat the activity of others.

Copyright © Cengage Learning. All rights reserved.

Synthesizing Longer Readings

The following readings are a good deal longer than any you have worked with so far. However, the same principle applies. The first step in synthesizing sources is to identify the overall main idea of each one. The examples shown here are no exception.

Read this first selection. When you finish, write what you believe is the main idea in the blanks. Once you have the main idea of each reading, we can talk about the various ways to synthesize them.

Reading 1: Reexamining Truman's Motives

1   What motivated President Harry Truman to order the dropping of the atomic bomb? Truman explained that he did it for only one reason: to end the war as soon as possible and thus prevent the loss of one million American lives in an invasion of Japan. An earlier generation of historians, writing in the aftermath of the war, echoed President Truman's explanation. But more recently historians have revised this interpretation: They argue that Japan might have surrendered even if the atomic bombs had not been dropped, and they dispute Truman's high estimate of casualties as being pure fiction and several times the likely figure. These revisionists have studied the Potsdam Conference of July 1945[†] attended by Truman, Joseph Stalin, and Winston Churchill. In their research, they have demonstrated the value of diaries as historical evidence by consulting those kept by certain participants, notably Secretary of War Henry Stimson and Truman himself.

2   Scholars cite Stimson's diary as evidence that Truman's chief motivations included not only ending the war but also impressing the Russians with America's military might and minimizing the USSR's[†] participation in the final defeat and postwar occupation of Japan. On July 21, Stimson reported to Truman that the army had successfully tested an atomic device in New Mexico. Clearly emboldened by the news, Truman said that possession of the bomb "gave him an entirely new feeling of confidence. . . ." The next day, Stimson discussed the news with British prime minister Churchill. "Now I know what happened to Truman," Churchill responded. "When he

---

[†]The Potsdam Conference was called to decide the fate of Japan.
[†]USSR: Union of Soviet Socialist Republics. After World War II, this was the name used to designate all the countries controlled by the Russian Communist Party.

Copyright © Cengage Learning. All rights reserved.

got to the meeting after having read this report he was a changed man. He told the Russians just where they got off and generally bossed the whole meeting."

3   A few historians contend that the decision to drop the atomic bomb was partly racist. For proof, they point to Truman's handwritten diary entry in which he discussed using the bomb against "the Japs," whom he denounced as "savages, ruthless, merciless and fanatic." Others cite these same words, claiming that Truman desired to avenge the Japanese attack at Pearl Harbor. It is clear that while personal diaries can help to settle some historical disagreements, they can also generate new disputes.

4   The deeply emotional question about the necessity for dropping the atomic bomb has stirred debates among the public as well as among historians. In 1995, for example, the Smithsonian Institution provoked a furor with its plan for an exhibit prompted by the fiftieth anniversary of the bomb's explosion. Rather than incur the wrath of politicians, veterans' groups, and other Americans outraged by what they perceived to be an anti-American interpretation of events, the Smithsonian shelved most of the exhibit. (Adapted from Norton et al., *A People and a Nation*, p. 766.)

Main Idea _____

_____

Determining the Main Idea

In this reading, the authors open with a question: What motivated Truman to drop the atomic bomb? But the first answer—he wanted to end the war with Japan as soon as possible to avoid further casualties—is *not* the answer the authors develop. The answer they are really interested in exploring can be summed up like this: "Due in large degree to their having access to personal diaries, many of today's historians have revised their opinion about Truman's motivation for dropping the atomic bomb." The rest of the reading then explains why some historians no longer accept the explanation that Truman dropped the bomb in order to avoid huge numbers of casualties.

The next excerpt is taken from a textbook published in 1965. As you read it, consider how this author's perspective compares with the one expressed in the first reading.

Copyright © Cengage Learning. All rights reserved.

Reading 2: Truman's Choice

Although many Americans have expressed contrition over exploding the first atomic bombs, it is difficult to see how the Pacific war could otherwise have been concluded, except by a long and bitter invasion of Japan. . . . The explosion over Hiroshima caused fewer civilian casualties than the repeated B-29 bombings of Tokyo, and those big bombers would have had to wipe out one city after another if the war had not ended in August. Japan had enough military capability—more than 5,000 planes with kamikaze[†]-trained pilots and at least two million ground troops—to have made our planned invasion of the Japanese home islands in the fall of 1945 an exceedingly bloody affair for both sides. And that would have been followed by a series of bitterly protracted battles on Japanese soil, the effects of which even time could hardly have healed. Moreover, as Russia would have been a full partner in these campaigns, the end result would have been partition of Japan, as happened in Germany. (Morison, *The Oxford History of the American People*, pp. 1044–45.)

Main Idea _____

_____

Determining the Main Idea

The opening sentence of this reading makes a concession to those who believe dropping the atomic bomb on Hiroshima was a terrible mistake. But as is so often the case, the author only makes the concession in order to pose a challenge. He then lists the reasons why Truman had to make the decision he did in order to stop the war and save lives.

To get a sense of how much people differ on this subject, look now at reading 3 from writer Harold Evans, author of *The American Century*.

Reading 3: The Myth of the Atomic Bomb

1 Research over five decades has confirmed that Truman and his civilian advisers knew enough and knew it early enough to appreciate that a siege strategy of sea blockade and non-atomic bombing had a prospect, though not a certainty, of ending the war before the November date set for Operation Olympic, the invasion of Kyushu.[†]

2 The state of knowledge was summarized in a review in *Diplomatic History* (Spring 1995) by J. Samuel Walker: "The consensus among scholars

---

[†]kamikaze: pilots trained to fly what were suicidal crash-attacks.
[†]"Operation Olympic" and "invasion of Kyushu" both refer to an invasion of Japan.

Copyright © Cengage Learning. All rights reserved.

is that the bomb was not needed to avoid an invasion of Japan and to end the war within a relatively short time. It is clear that alternatives to the bomb existed and that Truman and his advisers knew it." It is clear, too, that this last fact is the one there has been the most effort to fudge. The myth of Hiroshima the unavoidable seems to have embedded itself in the American psyche in a remarkable manner. It has survived for five decades in high school and college textbooks and in popular journalism. In the publications and television programs on the fiftieth anniversary of Hiroshima and Nagasaki there was an emotional aversion to acknowledging the summation of research. Critical historians were denounced as "diabolical* revisionists" as if history were not a continual process of discovery and revision.

3   The most dramatic manifestation of the attitude was the response to an exhibition planned for the Smithsonian National Air and Space Museum in Washington, [D.C.,] in 1995. The exhibit, focused on the Enola Gay B-29, intended to highlight all aspects of the bombing, including pictures of the victims. It was canceled because of a hue and cry, led by the American Legion[†] and then taken up by sections of Congress, that to discuss the bombing was unpatriotic, pro-Japanese and a dishonor to American servicemen. This is curious. It is not as if the servicemen had anything to do with the decision to drop the bombs. The Smithsonian's mistake may have been to confuse a simple commemoration of the sacrifices made by American servicemen with an attempt at dramatizing a complex history, to offer a seminar instead of a salute. But what was striking about the responses was the eruption of hostility to presenting any fact—anywhere at any time—that does not conform with the official version of the events of 1945. (Adapted from Evans, *The American Century*, p. 324.)

Main Idea   _____

_____

Determining the Main Idea

If the authors of the first reading suggested that Truman's explanation might not be fully backed by evidence, the author of the third reading makes an even stronger claim: He says bluntly that Truman had

---

*diabolical: tricky like the devil, evil.
[†]American Legion: a veterans organization.

Copyright © Cengage Learning. All rights reserved.

an alternative to dropping the atomic bomb, and there is "research" proving that claim.

As the opening sentence signals he will, the author then identifies some of that research. He also says that explanations about Hiroshima are a "myth." Despite evidence to the contrary, Americans are unwilling to acknowledge the "fact" that Truman had other alternatives besides dropping the atomic bomb. Having made that claim, the author then provides some incidents that he believes illustrate his main idea, which goes something like this: "Given what we now know, it's ridiculous to say that dropping the atomic bomb on Hiroshima was a necessity."

TAKING A CLOSER LOOK

Point of View
In paragraph 2 of reading 3, what two sentence orienters, or openings, explicitly tell readers how they should view what's being said?

_____

In paragraph 3, what sentence does the author use to tell readers how they should view the upcoming information?

_____

TAKING A CLOSER LOOK

The Function of Supporting Details
The authors of readings 1 and 3 both cite the Smithsonian exhibit. Do they use the exhibit to make a similar or different point? Please explain.

_____

_____

_____

Creating a Synthesis

Here's a list of the main ideas from each of the readings. Look them over to see how they might be synthesized into a statement that accurately reflects or comments on all three viewpoints.

Copyright © Cengage Learning. All rights reserved.

1. Although earlier historians accepted the idea that President Truman had no choice but to drop the atomic bomb on Hiroshima, later ones have challenged that idea based on the evidence of personal documents.

2. Truman had no choice but to drop the bomb on Hiroshima; in fact, dropping it saved many lives.

3. Americans may not want to admit it, but Truman had an alternative to bombing Hiroshima and Nagasaki.

The first and most general connection to be made is that the authors of readings 1 and 3 tend to be in agreement while the author of reading 2 disagrees with their position. Another connection that can be inferred between readings 1 and 3 is that both authors cite "new" evidence to support their claims.

Also, readings 1 and 3 both come from a later time frame while reading 2 belongs to a much earlier era. Thus one possible synthesis statement might read like this: "In the decades immediately following Truman's detonation of the atomic bomb, it was possible to argue, as Samuel Eliot Morison does in the *Oxford History of America*, that Harry Truman had no choice but to bomb Hiroshima and Nagasaki. But as new evidence emerged, it became harder to make that argument, and current historians are less likely to defend Truman's decision."

Synthesis Statements Aren't Created with a Cookie Cutter

Here are three more synthesis statements, all of which illustrate additional ways to combine these three points of view into one synthesis statement that takes them all into account. Keep in mind while reading them that there is no one way to write a synthesis statement. The end result depends on two things: (1) the purpose of your synthesis, whether it's to inform or to persuade, and (2) the element of similarity or difference you choose to emphasize.

All of the following are possible synthesis statements. There could be more, particularly if the author has a persuasive purpose in mind. An informative purpose leads to a synthesis statement that generally sums up the different points of view. A persuasive purpose leads to a synthesis statement that encourages readers to take sides and share a particular opinion.

Copyright © Cengage Learning. All rights reserved.

1. While an earlier generation of historians was far too quick to accept the idea that the bombing of Hiroshima was necessary to end the war, some current historians have publicly voiced their skepticism, and the evidence they cite lends a good deal of weight to their claim that Truman had far more leeway than he maintained.

2. Until the 1960s, many historians argued that the bombing of Hiroshima was necessary to end the war, which is what the Truman administration had claimed. By the 1990s, however, doubt had crept into the discussion. In fact, some, like Harold Evans, the author of *The American Century*, bluntly call Truman's explanation a "myth."

3. In the 1960 textbook *The Oxford History of the American People*, Samuel Eliot Morison, like so many other historians of the time, insisted that Harry Truman had no other choice but to bomb Hiroshima. However, more than four decades later, the authors of the textbook *A People and a Nation* are not completely sure that Truman's explanation holds up in the light of new evidence, while Harold Evans, the author of *The American Century*, insists that there is no doubt: All the evidence indicates that Truman's explanation was false.

4. Modern historians, relying on both personal journals and historical analysis, tend to doubt Truman's claim that dropping the atomic bomb on Hiroshima and Nagasaki was unavoidable. But earlier ones who were closer to the actual events show no such doubts. Interestingly enough, it is the earlier historians who seem more in touch with the public perception of Truman's decision.

Note the differences in emphasis among these four statements. Fueled by a persuasive purpose, statement 1 sides with the more current interpretation. Statement 2 also notes how time has affected the evaluation of Truman's actions. However, the focus of statement 2 is on the work of Harold Evans.

Statement 3 focuses on present-day evaluations of Truman's decision but indicates that modern historians aren't all equally sure Truman had choices. Statement 4 highlights an element of the readings unmentioned by the other synthesis statements: the public's tendency to side with Truman no matter what historians may say.

Copyright © Cengage Learning. All rights reserved.

INTERNET FOLLOW-UP: Oppenheimer and the Bhagavad Gita
J. Robert Oppenheimer wrote that when he first saw the atomic bomb explosion he was reminded of a line from the Bhagavad Gita, a Hindu holy text. What was that line?

_____

ALLUSION ALERT

Hedonism
Among the ancient Greeks, Hedonism referred to a school of philosophy that claimed pleasure was the highest good. But nowadays, the philosophical associations have pretty much disappeared. To call someone a hedonist or speak of hedonism is to suggest that some person or group is interested solely in personal pleasure or gain, often of a sexual nature—for example, "Unlike the male stars of rock or rap, male country-and-western singers don't portray themselves as hedonists."

CHECK YOUR UNDERSTANDING

If different people synthesize the same sources, should the resulting statements all resemble one another? Please explain your answer.

_____

_____

♦ **EXERCISE 3** **Recognizing Effective Synthesis Statements**

DIRECTIONS Read the selections and identify the main idea for each one. Then choose a synthesis statement that best expresses the relationship among the three.

Copyright © Cengage Learning. All rights reserved.

1. Reading 1: Television Still Wins Out in Prime Time

1 With all the attention the media gives to the digital revolution, you might well be thinking no one except the very elderly watch television anymore. That perception is understandable. It's also wrong.

2   Families are not curling up together in front of a laptop, nor are family members all going their separate ways in order to download a new phone application or check out their tweets. Instead, polls show that four out of five Americans still watch around ten hours of television per week, and most prefer to watch their favorite programs on a TV screen rather than a computer monitor.

3   If anything, in the harsh economic times that began in 2008, television viewing increased as most Americans were forced to cut back on spending for entertainment. As one entertainment analyst expressed it, "consumers are choosing to invest in the enhancement of their TV experience." In other words, with money being tight, consumers are buying flat-screen TVs because they don't know when they can afford to go to the movies again.

(Source of quotation: www.homemediamagazine.com/research/npd-america-a-nation-couch-potatoes-17868.)

What's the main idea of this reading?

_____

_____

Reading 2: Less Television, More Computer Games Not Such a Bad Idea

1 In 2008, researchers in the United States and Spain studied 111 children ages 3–8. Throughout the study, the children were monitored so that researchers could tell how much time the children spent in inactive pursuits. Overall the children spent about five hours each day in inactive, or minimal movement, pursuits such as playing computer games or watching television.

2   When researchers further analyzed those periods of inactivity, they made a surprising discovery: When it comes to children's health, watching television is definitely the bigger threat. Children who watched more television than played computer games tended to be overweight and had higher blood pressure. In part that's due to television's being such a completely passive activity as opposed to computer games, where some movement is involved.

Copyright © Cengage Learning. All rights reserved.

3   But it's also caused by, or at least the study's authors suggest, children's snacking habits while watching television. They tend to eat fast food while watching TV, and they eat a lot of it. Bags of chips or plates of fries are likely to be consumed without children realizing how much they are eating. They are too involved in their television program to notice.

4   Parents worried about their kids being too involved with social media or too addicted to computer games might want to re-think their concern. Computers seem to be better for children than their other, once steady companion, the TV. As David Ludwig, director of the Optimal Weight for Life program at Children's Hospital, Boston, expresses it, "TV-viewing really is the worst of all sedentary activities." (Source of quotation: Park, "Watching TV: Even Worse for Kids Than You Think," *Time*, August 4, 2009.)

What's the main idea of this reading?

_____

_____

Reading 3: Kids Looking More at Monitors Than Television Screens

1   The results of a 2010 study by the Kaiser Family Foundation seemed to confirm the worst fears of television media executives. According to the study, the amount of time kids spend in front of a television set is declining. Between 2004 and 2008, the time kids ages 8–18 spent watching live television dropped by 25 minutes. The study titled "Generation M^2: Media in the Lives of 8- to 18-Year-Olds" indicated that kids were using other kinds of media for both television viewing and other forms of entertainment. Hulu and iTunes were two ways kids were still viewing television content without sitting in front of a television screen. The study also suggested, however, that kids were finding other forms of amusement, with social networking taking up a good portion of their time.

2   Quick to respond to the report was Nielsen Media Research, a firm that surveys and rates television programming. Nielsen says the Kaiser Foundation report is wrong and that, in fact, live-television viewing among kids has actually increased. Unlike Kaiser, which used viewer diaries of what was watched in the course of a week, Nielsen based their study on digital meters, and the meters show that kids 8–18 currently watch seven more minutes of television than kids the same age did five years ago.

Copyright © Cengage Learning. All rights reserved.

What's the main idea of this reading?

_____

_____

Synthesis Statement Which synthesis statement does the best job of combining all three readings into a new main idea?

a. Although journalists like to portray television and computers in a battle to the death, there is no hard evidence that the computer monitor has replaced the television screen for providing entertainment and news.

b. Television revenues from advertising are going to plummet dramatically as more viewers watch television programming on their laptops.

c. It's still not clear how much effect the digital revolution has had on television viewing, but at least one study suggests it would be good for kids to play more computer games and watch less television.

2. Reading 1: Photographs of a Tragedy: Compassion or Exploitation

1   When an earthquake crumbled Haiti in 2010, photographs of the destruction and death were front-page news. The *New York Times*, in particular, displayed photos that were both heartbreaking and harrowing.* One such photo showed a woman walking along a street, her eyes glazed with shock. In the background, corpses lying in the street were clearly visible. Other pictures were even more distressing, so much so that the *Times* received numerous letters protesting the photos as a gross exploitation* of human suffering.

2   Some readers were so offended that Clark Hoyt, the *Times* public editor, acting as the liaison* between the paper and the public, ran a column titled "Face to Face with Tragedy." In it, he quoted the sentiments of people like Christa Robbins of Chicago who said, "I feel that the people who have suffered the most are being spectacularized

---

*harrowing: agonizing, painful.
*exploitation: using others to benefit oneself.
*liaison: contact who maintains communication between two different groups; also a close relationship.

Copyright © Cengage Learning. All rights reserved.

by your blood-and-gore photographs. . . ." Hoyt's response was to publish the statements of others who supported the paper's publication of the photos. In a letter to the *Times* defending the photos, Mary Claire Carroll asked, "How else can you motivate or inspire someone like me to donate money?" Hoyt also quoted several photographers who insisted that victims of the quake had implored them to come into their homes to photograph what the quake had done to their lives.

What's the main idea of this reading?

_____

_____

Reading 2: A Picture Tells the Story

1   One of the most famous photos ever taken shows a young Vietnamese girl,[†] naked and burned by napalm, running toward the camera. She is screaming. Her face is twisted in pain. The photo won the photographer who took it, Nick Ut, a Pulitzer prize and probably did more than any editorial could do to turn the American public against the U.S. involvement in Vietnam's civil war.[†] Another Pulitzer prize-winning photograph, by photojournalist Eddie Adams, was also taken during the Vietnam War. It shows a Viet Cong[†] officer at the moment of his execution by a South Vietnamese officer, who holds a gun to the man's head. Then there are the tragic photos showing President Kennedy's motorcade racing away from Dealey Plaza, while the life of the mortally wounded president ebbed away.

2   Robert H. Jackson of the *Dallas Times-Herald* won a Pulitzer for his photo capturing the murder of Lee Oswald by Jack Ruby in the basement of the Dallas police station. In 2000, photographer George Kochaniec earned a Pulitzer for his photograph of schoolchildren in anguish over the murders they had just witnessed at their school, when two classmates opened fire and killed thirteen people. These photographs all bear witness to human tragedies. They all tell important, heartbreaking stories.

[†]The little girl in the photo survived the burns; she was nine at the time of the photo.
[†]South Vietnam in Southeast Asia was the scene of civil war, and the United States took the side of the existing government.
[†]The Viet Cong were soldiers fighting on the side of North Vietnam's communists.

Copyright © Cengage Learning. All rights reserved.

3   To keep the public informed, newspaper editors have to run such photographs. These are the photos that make readers pay attention to what's happening in parts of the world they will never see. They put a human face on tragedies that might otherwise leave readers untouched and unmoved. Referring to photographs of the twin towers that came crashing down in flames on September 11, 2001, Jim Fisher, a former photojournalist and war photographer, now a professor at the University of Utah, identified the purpose of photos that capture horrific tragedy: "Being aware of the truth of the day's events sometimes takes extra effort—not to search for it but to face it." (Source of quotation: Connie Coyne, "Disturbing News Pictures Tell Important Stories," *Salt Lake Tribune*, September 14, 2002.)

What's the main idea of this reading?

_____

_____

Reading 3: Catastrophes Are News

1 Violence and tragedy are staples of American journalism because readers are attracted to gruesome stories and photographs. "If it bleeds, it leads" is an undesirable rule of thumb. Judges of contests also have a fatal attraction. Pulitzer prizes are most often awarded to photographers who make pictures of gruesome, dramatic moments. *Milwaukee Journal* editor Sig Gissler summed up the newspaper profession's sometimes hedonistic philosophy when he admitted, "We have a commercial interest in catastrophe."

2   Ethical problems arise for photographers and editors because readers are also repulsed by such events. It is as if readers want to know that tragic circumstances take place but do not want to face the uncomfortable details. After the publication of a controversial picture that shows, for example, either dead or grieving victims of violence, readers, in telephone calls and in letters to the editor, often attack the photographer as being tasteless and adding to the anguish of those involved. As one writer noted, "The American public has a morbid* fascination with violence and tragedy, yet this same public accuses journalists of being insensitive and cynical and of exploiting victims of tragedy" (Brown, 1987, p. 80). (Excerpted from Lester, "Photojournalism: An Ethical Approach.")

_____

*morbid: psychologically unhealthy.

Copyright © Cengage Learning. All rights reserved.

What is the main idea of this reading?

_____

_____

Synthesis Statement Which synthesis statement does the best job of combining all three readings into a new main idea?

a. When tragedy strikes, photographers are always among the first to arrive on the scene. Some say that's because catastrophes draw viewers and sell papers. Photojournalists, however, insist that the pictures they take serve the public good and make people more deeply aware of what's happening in the world because pictures can touch the emotions in a way words cannot.

b. Those who make and publish photos of human misery in times of catastrophe offer a convincing argument for what they do: Photographs give viewers and readers a deeper insight into a human tragedy than words can ever do. Yet some people don't accept that argument, seeing in the photos a lack of both compassion and respect for tragedy's victims.

c. Readers and viewers may complain that photographs of people suffering the effects of a tragedy increase the victims' pain, but these are the photographs that people remember. They are also the photographs that win Pulitzer prizes, which suggests that those who are horrified by photographs of people in the throes of suffering are very much in the minority.

TAKING A
CLOSER LOOK

Understanding Allusions
What connection does the author of reading 3 expect readers to make between the philosophy of the hedonists and the journalist who says, "We have a commercial interest in catastrophe."

_____

_____

_____

Copyright © Cengage Learning. All rights reserved.

WORD CHECK

The following words were introduced and defined in pages 436–55. See how well you can match the words with the meanings. When you finish, make sure to check the meanings of any words you missed because the same words will turn up in tests at the end of the chapter.

1. doctrine	_____	a.	distributed
2. castigated	_____	b.	agonizing, painful to experience
3. vilified	_____	c.	psychologically unhealthy, unwholesome
4. meted out	_____	d.	tricky like the devil, evil
5. sabotage	_____	e.	destructive actions used to hinder or defeat the activity of others
6. diabolical	_____		
7. harrowing	_____	f.	contact who maintains communication between two groups; a relationship or connection
8. exploitation	_____		
9. liaison	_____	g.	using people or a situation to benefit one's own interests
10. morbid	_____		
		h.	theory, policy, set of guiding principles
		i.	verbally insulted or criticized
		j.	viciously criticized, using abusive language to ruin someone's reputation

◆ **EXERCISE 4**   **More About Form and Meaning**

DIRECTIONS   Fill in the blanks with one of the words listed below.

liaison	castigated	harrowing	vilify	morbid
doctrine	sabotage	exploitation	meted out	diabolical

1. Even as a young child, the author showed a(n) _____ fascination with death.

Copyright © Cengage Learning. All rights reserved.

2. It's certainly true that misplacing one's car keys is an annoying experience, but it would be silly to call it _____.

3. A courtroom is a likely place for people to be _____.

4. Except for horror movies like *The Exorcist* and *Saw*, it's unusual for children to be described as _____.

5. Anyone who wants to work as a(n) _____ between the police and the community better have good people skills and a lot of patience.

6. We frequently say that justice can be _____ but rarely fruit or toys.

7. "Sticks and stones will break my bones, but names will never hurt me" is one way to respond to someone who tries to _____ your reputation.

8. The rules for playing poker would not be called a(n) _____, but the principles that guide governments would.

9. In the movie, *The Bridge over the River Kwai,* prisoners of war attempt to blow up a bridge to defeat the plans of their Japanese captors. The prisoners were engaged in an act of _____.

10. No matter what their children think, parents who expect their children to do some chores around the house cannot be accused of _____. That word is more appropriate for people who employ illegal aliens to work for them so that they can pay very low wages and threaten deportation if the employee complains.

Copyright © Cengage Learning. All rights reserved.

DIGGING DEEPER Practice with Synthesizing

Looking Ahead The exercise on pages 443–44 introduced the topic of Web security. The two readings shown here focus on the same topic. First answer the questions about the readings. Then find a way to synthesize what you read on these pages with what you learned on pages 443–44.

Reading 1: If Your Password Is 123456, Just Make It Hack Me

1 Back in the dawn of the Web, the most popular account password was "12345." Today it's one digit longer but hardly safer: "123456." Despite all the reports of Internet security breaches over the years, many people have reacted to the break-ins with a shrug.

2 According to a new analysis, one out of five Web users still decides to leave the digital equivalent of a key under the doormat: they choose a simple, easily guessed password like "abc123," "iloveyou," or even "password" to protect their data. "I guess it's just a genetic flaw in humans," said Amichai Shulman, the chief technology officer at Imperva, which makes software for blocking hackers. "We've been following the same patterns since the 1990s."

3 Mr. Shulman and his company examined a list of 32 million passwords that an unknown hacker stole last month from RockYou, a company that makes software for users of social networking sites like Facebook and MySpace. The list was briefly posted on the Web, and hackers and security researchers downloaded it. (RockYou, which has already been widely criticized for lax privacy practices, has advised its customers to change their passwords, as the hacker gained information about their e-mail accounts as well.) The trove provided an unusually detailed window into computer users' password habits. Typically only government agencies like the FBI or the National Security Agency have had access to such a large password list.

4 Imperva found that nearly 1 percent of the 32 million people it studied had used "123456" as a password. The second-most-popular password was "12345." Others in the top 20 included "qwerty," "abc123" and "princess." More disturbing, said Mr. Shulman, was that about 20 percent of people on the RockYou list picked from the same, relatively small pool of 5,000 passwords. This suggests that hackers could easily break into many accounts just by trying the most common passwords. Because

Copyright © Cengage Learning. All rights reserved.

of the prevalence of fast computers and speedy networks, hackers can fire off thousands of password guesses per minute. "We tend to think of password guessing as a very time-consuming attack in which I take each account and try a large number of name-and-password combinations," Mr. Shulman said. "The reality is that you can be very effective by choosing a small number of common passwords." (Vance, *New York Times*, January 11, 2010.)

1. What does the author imply in the title?

   _____

   _____

2. What is the overall main idea of the reading?

   _____

   _____

3. What would be a good synonym for *prevalence* in the following sentence: "Because of the prevalence of fast computers and speedy networks, hackers can fire off thousands of password guesses per minute" (paragraph 4)?

   _____

4. In paragraph 3, what does the word *trove* refer to in this sentence: "The trove provided an unusually detailed window into computer

   users' password habits"? _____
   What is a trove? If you don't know for sure, what does the context

   suggest it is? _____

5. What conclusion can you draw from the reading?
   a. People aren't more careful about passwords because they are too lazy to think of unusual ones.
   b. Most people don't realize how rapidly hackers can go through an assortment of common passwords until they hit the right one.
   c. Most people who use common passwords are very trusting of others and get taken advantage of in all walks of life.

Copyright © Cengage Learning. All rights reserved.

Reading 2: Information Security

1   Information security means protecting data, whether data stored on your computer's hard disk or data being transmitted across a network. Security can be breached at many different levels, and therefore many different types of precautions need to be taken.

2   In the early days of computing when big mainframes were the only option and the Internet did not exist, physical security was enforced by means of securing the rooms housing the computers. Only authorized persons had access. Now that there is a machine on virtually every desk and files and email are routinely sent over the Internet, that kind of physical security is all but impossible to maintain. However, you can take some obvious steps: Don't leave your laptop lying around; never leave your workstation running when you are not in the room; and do not share your password with anyone or leave it on a sticky note attached to your monitor!

3   Make sure, too, that you use a log-on password to access your computer's operating system. The operating system uses the log-on password as an *authentication device*, which identifies a particular user. (Hackers breaking into a computer system look for a file of passwords as the "Open, Sesame" for all locked doors.) Once on the system, the authenticated user (remember this simply means a person with knowledge of the password) automatically has certain file accesses and privileges that the operating system enforces. . . .

4   If, despite password precautions, files on a hard disk or passing along a network connection are illegally accessed and fall into the wrong hands, we can still protect the contents of those files through *encryption*, or encoding, which makes the files meaningless if they are accessed. Without a key to decrypt them, they would be of little use to anyone who managed to read them. Thus the two main thrusts of information security are authentication (don't let the bad guys get at the stuff) and encryption (make the stuff meaningless if they do get it). (Adapted from Schneider and Gersting, *Invitation to Computer Science*, pp. 606–7.)

1. The title of this reading identifies

    a. the topic.

    b. the main idea.

    c. neither the topic nor the main idea.

Copyright © Cengage Learning. All rights reserved.

2. What is the overall main idea of the reading?

_____

_____

3. Based on the context, what you do you think would be a good definition for *virtually* in the following sentence: "Now that there is a machine on virtually every desk . . . , that kind of physical activity is harder to obtain" (paragraph 2)?

_____

4. In your own words, what is an authentication device?

_____

5. Which of the following statements best synthesizes the readings on pages 443–44, along with the two readings you've just completed?

a. For all of our current sophistication about information technology, early computers were probably better protected from hackers than our current ones are. Even the savvy hackers operating out of China could not penetrate a locked door from a distance.

b. Authentication, encryption, and using common sense to choose passwords are three ways to protect information on your computer. Unfortunately, some hackers, particularly those operating out of China, seem unstoppable.

c. In our modern, technologically sophisticated society, it is amazing to think that anyone would be silly enough to choose obvious passwords such as 123 and ABC. But that is precisely what many people do, says Amichai Shulman, a security expert. As a result, even the most inexperienced hackers have an easy time getting into systems holding critical information about military and government secrets.

Copyright © Cengage Learning. All rights reserved.

▶ **TEST 1**   **Reviewing New Vocabulary**

DIRECTIONS   Use one of the following words to fill in the blanks.

castigated	liaison	morbid	meted out	sabotage
doctrine	vilified	harrowing	diabolical	exploit

1. Seeing Red

1   In the aftermath of World War II, the Russian and Chinese

Communists were seen as dangerous, _____ forces that
had to be controlled. Certainly, the threat of communism's spread was
one of the reasons why President Harry Truman, in 1947, gave a speech

on what came to be known as the Truman _____.

2   Worried that the Communists were going to _____

postwar chaos in an effort to _____ democratic
governments, Truman made it clear that a severe penalty would be

_____ by the United States if any group interfered
with a country's attempt to follow a democratic route. He also said that
countries rejecting communism would receive economic aid from the

United States. _____ by some and celebrated by others,
Truman's new foreign policy made it clear that postwar America was now a
superpower ready to flex its muscle if its interests were threatened.

2. Nancy Wake: The Spy Who Lived to Tell the Tale

1   New Zealand–born Nancy Wake was an independent and imaginative
child, but it was precisely those qualities that got her repeatedly

_____ by her strict and religious mother. Fed up with

her mother's harsh scoldings and _____ focus on evil,
young Nancy left home at sixteen. She traveled to Europe after an
aunt gave her the money for the trip. While in Europe, Wake watched
as Hitler's forces grew in power and was horrified by their brutality. It
wasn't long before she decided to become a spy for the Allied forces.[†]

――――――――――

[†]Allied forces: refers to the military forces of those countries that fought the Nazis.

Copyright © Cengage Learning. All rights reserved.

2   To her surprise, Nancy Wake had a gift for espionage. She was so good at it, she ended up on the Germans'"Most-Wanted" list, thanks to her successful work as a(n) _____ between the Allied military forces and the various citizen groups fighting the German occupation. Adept at handling guns, explosives, and radio communications, Wake always managed to be just a step ahead of the Germans, making one _____ escape after another. Because of the way she repeatedly slipped through their fingers, the Germans nicknamed her "The White Mouse." When the war ended, Wake had become the Allies' most decorated servicewoman.

Copyright © Cengage Learning. All rights reserved.

▶ **TEST 2**   **Recognizing Effective Synthesis Statements**

DIRECTIONS   Read the following selection. Then re-read passages a, b, and c on page 441. When you finish, select the synthesis statement that best combines the main idea of this reading with the points made in those three passages.

The White Rose Remembered

1   In 1941, a group of students in Munich decided to do what many others—allegedly older and wiser than they—were not doing: They decided to resist the terrifying power of Adolf Hitler and the Nazi Party. Because the brutality of the Nazi regime was well known, many other Germans just put their heads down and hoped the government's iron hand would leave them untouched.

2   That self-serving approach to survival, however, was not acceptable to the group of young people who called themselves "The White Rose.†" Hans, Sophie, and Inge Scholl, along with Christoph Probst, Alexander Schmorell, Willi Graf, and Jurgen Wittenstein, the founding members of the group, chose to fight back, engaging in acts of passive resistance that eventually got all but one of them executed for sedition, or crimes against state authority.

3   Inspired by a sermon given by a pastor openly critical of Hitler's government, the young members of The White Rose started out painting anti-Nazi slogans like "Down with Hitler" on building walls. But with the help of their philosophy instructor, Kurt Huber, they were able to print thousands of leaflets, which they distributed throughout the city. The leaflets made their position on the government and their resistance to it dangerously clear.

> We want to try to show them that everyone is in a position to contribute to the overthrow of the system. It can be done only by the cooperation of many convinced, energetic people—people who are agreed as to the means they must use. . . . The meaning and goal of passive resistance is to topple National Socialism, and in this struggle, we must not recoil from our course, any action, whatever its nature.

4   Not surprisingly, the Nazis were outraged at the open resistance, and the hunt was on for the authors of the pamphlets. On February 18, the group's two leaders, Hans and Sophie Scholl, were distributing leaflets at the university when Jakob Schmidt, a member of the Nazi Party

---

†The origin of the name is unclear. One theory is that the name was picked because a white rose symbolized purity, another that the group named themselves after a poem titled "The White Rose" written by Clemens Brentano.

Copyright © Cengage Learning. All rights reserved.

spotted them. Schmidt immediately reported their names to the police. Within hours, the brother and sister were arrested. When their house was searched, the police discovered a handwritten note from Christoph Probst. He too was taken into custody.

5   Two days later, the three young people appeared in court, where the judge delivered a furious lecture on their vile and unpatriotic behavior. However, even he was shocked by Sophie Scholl's cool response as she explained, "Somebody, after all, had to make a start. What we wrote and said is also believed by many others. They just don't dare express themselves as we did." Not surprisingly, nothing the accused said made a difference to the verdict. The three were found guilty of sedition. Only a few hours later, they were executed by guillotine. Their comrades Schmorell, Graf, and Huber met a similar fate in the same year.

6   Although reviled by the government in their lifetime, members of The White Rose are now considered heroes in Germany. They are celebrated as examples of "good Germans," who did not turn away when they saw others brutalized, imprisoned, and killed. Instead, they stood up to be counted and paid with their lives. A square next to the university in Munich is named for the Scholls, while streets, squares, and schools all over Germany bear the names of the other founding members.

Related Readings   Re-read the passages on page 441 and decide which of the following synthesis statements does the best job of combining the main ideas of all four readings.

Synthesis Statement   a. When the German people came under the diabolical rule of Adolf Hitler, the population, in general, refused to acknowledge what was happening around them as Jews, Communists, gypsies, homosexuals, and anyone who did not meet the Nazi idea of perfection lost their lives. Sadly, the few voices that spoke out in protest at Nazi brutality were foreigners like Simone Weil and Raoul Wallenberg, whose lives could have remained untouched by the dark shadow of Nazism had they been willing to just look the other way. The question is, What motivates the kind of altruism that made Wallenberg and Weil take action?

b. The phrase "good Germans" is often used in its negative sense, to refer to Germans who took orders under Hitler's rule without asking

Copyright © Cengage Learning. All rights reserved.

the questions that needed to be asked. But in the case of The White Rose, the term is a form of praise rather than criticism.

c. History has rightly praised people like French philosopher Simone Weil and the Swedish diplomat Raoul Wallenberg for refusing to look the other way when those less fortunate than they were suffering a harrowing and deadly fate. However, it shouldn't be forgotten that it wasn't just foreigners who were courageous. The Germans had their homegrown heroes as well. They had, for instance, the extraordinary group of students known as The White Rose, who gave their lives fighting to free their country from Hitler's iron grip.

Copyright © Cengage Learning. All rights reserved.

▶ **TEST 3**   **Recognizing Effective Synthesis Statements**

> **DIRECTIONS**   Read each set of passages. Then identify the synthesis statement that effectively links them together.

1. **a. Eleanor Roosevelt Did Not Stand on Ceremony**

1   Eleanor Roosevelt (1884–1962) shattered the traditional, ceremonial role of the first lady and used her position and talents to make her own positive contributions to American society. Initially, she assisted her husband, Franklin D. Roosevelt, by acting as in informal liaison between the White House and the American public. While touring the country, she gathered information about the needs and desires of the American people and reported her findings directly to him.

2   Over time, though, Eleanor took up her own causes. She aggressively promoted civil rights for African Americans, and it was she who convinced her husband to sign a series of executive orders that prevented discrimination in the creation and administration of his New Deal† projects. She also devoted her considerable energies to numerous organizations focused on social reforms. In particular, she argued for equal rights and equal opportunities for women. She publicly advocated women's right to work outside the home and even secured government funding to build child-care centers. The first lady also used her gifts as a speaker and writer to publicize the abuses associated with child labor.

3   More than any first lady before her, Eleanor Roosevelt challenged society's stereotypical view of presidential wives as pleasant, well-spoken White House decorations, who echoed the sentiments espoused by their husbands. A tireless fighter for social justice, she had a powerful impact on social justice in America.

b. Hillary Clinton, an Activist First Lady

1   As first lady, Hillary Rodham Clinton (1947–) used her intelligence and talent to improve the lives of people across the United States and all over the world. While in the White House, she published a book, *It Takes a Village*, in which she argued that people from all parts of society must work together to improve the lives of American children. During her husband's two-term presidency, she also headed a task force devoted to improving the health care system. In this position, she traveled the country, talking to

---

†The New Deal was the collective name for the various projects Roosevelt implemented to get the country out of a deep financial depression.

Copyright © Cengage Learning. All rights reserved.

health care professionals and ordinary citizens about how the government could provide access to high-quality, affordable medical care.

2   In addition, she traveled the world, serving as a goodwill ambassador for the United States and speaking out for human rights, women's rights, and better health care for the world's poor. At the end of her term as first lady, she managed to do what none of her predecessors had done before: She established an independent political organization and successfully ran for the U.S. Senate in New York State. By 2007, to no one's surprise, she was campaigning for the presidency, and Hillary Clinton came close to beating Barack Obama as the Democratic candidate for president of the United States. When Obama was elected, he made her his secretary of state.

c. Bess Was No Activist

1   On April 12, 1945, after serving a mere eighty-two days as vice president, Harry Truman became the president of the United States and his wife, Bess, became the first lady. It wasn't long before Bess Truman became known as one of the busiest and hardest-working hostesses in Washington.

2   What she wasn't known for, though, was holding press conferences. She abolished the custom—established by her predecessor Eleanor Roosevelt—of holding regular meetings with reporters. Unused to being in the spotlight, Bess Truman was more interested in public service roles traditionally associated with presidential wives. She served as honorary president of the Girl Scouts and the Washington Animal Rescue League.

3   She also held honorary memberships in the Daughters of the Colonial Wars and the Women's National Farm and Garden Association. Known for her ability to remember the names of everyone she met at state affairs, Bess also made it a habit to personally answer the letters she received as the president's wife. Like her husband, Bess Truman was considered extremely down-to-earth. Proud of her frugal ways, her habits and routines did not change with her status. During her time in the White House, Bess never spent more than three dollars on a manicure. Instead of having an in-house hairdresser, she made it a point to have her hair styled off the premises. It was cheaper that way.

Synthesis Statement   a. As first ladies go, Bess Truman was probably the nicest and most frugal woman to ever live in the White House.

b. In their political ambitions, Eleanor Roosevelt and Hillary Clinton were very similar first ladies. They did not assume it was a man's job to change the world and a woman's job to tend family affairs.

Copyright © Cengage Learning. All rights reserved.

   c. As first ladies, Eleanor Roosevelt and Hillary Clinton were very active politically; Bess Truman, however, kept her distance from politics, preferring a more traditional role.

   d. Bess Truman carefully dismantled the political organization Eleanor Roosevelt had established while her husband was in office, and it wasn't until Hillary Clinton's term as first lady that a president's wife, once again, displayed a desire for political power.

2. a. The Warren Report

1   When President John F. Kennedy was assassinated in Dallas, Texas, on November 22, 1963, a traumatized American public wanted to know who was responsible. Police promptly captured ex-Marine Lee Harvey Oswald and charged him with the murder. But when he too was gunned down one day later by local nightclub owner Jack Ruby in the police department's basement, new questions quickly arose. Had Oswald acted alone, or had he and Ruby been involved in a conspiracy to murder America's leader? Had Ruby been sent to silence Oswald and prevent him from exposing his co-conspirators?

2   In an attempt to answer these and other questions, Kennedy's successor, President Lyndon Johnson, quickly appointed a group that included two senators, two members of Congress, and two attorneys. It was headed by Supreme Court Justice Earl Warren. Known as the Warren Commission, this group was instructed to "evaluate all the facts and circumstances surrounding [the] assassination, including the subsequent violent death of the man charged with the assassination."

3   Over the next ten months, the commission attempted to reconstruct the sequence of events surrounding Kennedy's and Oswald's murders by reviewing the investigative reports of the Dallas police department, the Federal Bureau of Investigation, the Secret Service, the Central Intelligence Agency, and other federal agencies. Members of the commission heard the testimony of 552 witnesses and visited Dallas to see the crime scene.

4   The result of this investigation was an 888-page report presented to President Johnson on September 24, 1964. The Warren Commission's report concluded that Oswald was psychologically disturbed and not politically motivated. The commission also concluded that he acted alone to kill President Kennedy and wound Texas governor John Connally. In addition, the commission endorsed the theory that one bullet had missed while the other two bullets had caused all of the injuries.

Copyright © Cengage Learning. All rights reserved.

5   The first of those two bullets had struck President Kennedy in the upper back, passed through him, and then hit Governor Connally, who had been sitting directly in front of the president in an open limousine. The second of those two bullets fatally wounded Kennedy in the head.

6   Although the Warren Commission did not completely rule out the possibility of a domestic or foreign plot to kill the president, it found no evidence of one. Unable to uncover any connection between Oswald and Ruby, the commission found Ruby innocent of conspiracy. It also concluded that he was motivated by rage. Ruby had simply decided to appoint himself Oswald's judge and executioner.

7   To most Americans, these conclusions seemed then and seem now perfectly sound. The Warren Commission, they believe, fulfilled its mission. It thoroughly investigated the assassination of their president and provided much-needed reassurance during an anxious and terrifying time.

b. Doubts About the Warren Commission

1   In the wake of President John F. Kennedy's murder in Dallas, Texas, on November 22, 1963, a seven-member panel headed by Supreme Court Chief Justice Earl Warren undertook the task of investigating the assassination. The goal of the investigation was to determine whether the alleged assassin Lee Harvey Oswald had acted alone. After examining all of the evidence related to the events, the Warren Commission published a report concluding that neither Lee Harvey Oswald nor Jack Ruby, the man who shot and killed Oswald the day after he was arrested, had been involved in a conspiracy to murder Kennedy. According to the commission, both men had been mentally unstable, lone gunmen.

2   But almost before the ink on the Warren Commission's report was dry, people began to criticize its findings. Books such as the influential *Inquest* by Edward Jay Epstein and *Rush to Judgment* by Mark Lane, both published in 1966, argued that the commission's investigation had not been thorough enough to be conclusive. Others vilified the commission's conclusions as a "whitewash" and castigated its methods.

3   Although two more U.S. government investigations—in 1968 and 1975—agreed with the Warren Commission's conclusions, President Johnson himself and even four of the seven members of the commission were said to have privately expressed doubts about the group's findings. In 1967, New Orleans district attorney Jim Garrison fueled suspicions about the existence of a conspiracy by trying businessman Clay Shaw

Copyright © Cengage Learning. All rights reserved.

for participating in a plot to kill the president, but Shaw was acquitted because of lack of evidence.

4   In 1978–1979, a special committee of the House of Representatives reexamined all of the evidence. The committee declared that Oswald had indeed fired the fatal shots but had probably been part of a conspiracy. This conclusion was based on evidence that a fourth bullet, which missed, had been fired by a second assassin on the ground. Yet, so far no one has been able to disprove the Warren Commission's conclusions. The facts about the Kennedy assassination remain the subject of ongoing debate.

c. Bullets Don't Lie

1   By conducting a new type of bullet analysis, a research team has undermined the theory that a lone gunman assassinated President John F. Kennedy in 1963. The team, which included a top former FBI laboratory expert and two Texas A&M University scientists, obtained boxes from two of the four total lots of Mannlicher-Carcano bullets manufactured in 1954. The ammunition used by assassin Lee Harvey Oswald to kill the president came from one of these lots.

2   Selecting 30 bullets, ten from each of three different boxes, and using techniques not available in the 1960s, the researchers then analyzed the bullets' chemical composition. They found that many bullets within the same box have a similar composition. This means that bullet fragments having the same chemical makeup don't necessarily come from the same bullet. Researchers also discovered that one of their test bullets, which was not even in the same box of ammunition used by Oswald, matched one of the five bullet fragments found at the assassination scene.

3   These findings are significant because they call into question the number of bullets that were fired when Kennedy was shot. Scientists who first analyzed the lead in the bullet fragments found at the scene of the crime claimed that each of the bullets in a box of ammunition had a unique chemical composition. This suggested that the recovered fragments, which were similar in chemical composition, had to have come from just the two bullets traced to the batch in Oswald's possession.

4   This conclusion supported the theory that Oswald was the lone assassin. As it turns out, though, this conclusion was based on the technology of the time. Newer methods of analysis suggest that more than two bullets may well have been fired.

Copyright © Cengage Learning. All rights reserved.

5   Only two of Oswald's bullets struck President Kennedy. Therefore, if the fragments found actually came from *three or more* bullets, then at least one other bullet might have been fired by a second shooter. Although the researchers did not go so far as to say that their study supports theories that Oswald was involved in a conspiracy, they did point out that their analysis of the ammunition does not conclusively rule out the possibility of a second assassin. They also urged authorities to reexamine the five bullet fragments recovered after the assassination. (Sources of findings: Solomon, "Scientists Cast Doubt on Kennedy Bullet Analysis," *Washington Post*, May 17, 2007, p. A03; "Bullet Evidence Challenges Findings in JFK Assassination," *Science Daily*, May 17, 2007.)

Synthesis Statement
a. While some accept the Warren Commission report as accurate, the controversy about its findings continues to the present day.

b. New research has now conclusively proven what was once considered a ridiculous and unfounded rumor—that Lee Harvey Oswald did not assassinate John F. Kennedy.

c. Current research supports the findings of the 1964 Warren Report, yet doubts about the report's accuracy continue to surface.

d. Despite all evidence to the contrary, conspiracy theorists refuse to believe that the assassination of John F. Kennedy was the act of one lone gunman.

Copyright © Cengage Learning. All rights reserved.

▶ **TEST 4**   **Taking Stock**

DIRECTIONS   Read each of the following selections. Then answer the questions by circling the letter of the correct response or filling in the blanks.

1. Dogs at War

1   Bounding along a dusty road in Afghanistan, the young Labrador could be any dog out for a run. It's only when the Lab, named Crush, stops short and turns motionless that something becomes obvious. Crush isn't at play. He's at work. The dog is out with four other marines looking for bombs. When he finds one, he freezes. Then he lies down with his head on his paws to signal mission accomplished. He's just found one.

2   Dogs like Crush are trained by the U.S. government under a program run by the Defense Department. After the training, which begins when they are puppies, the dogs are shipped to locations like Iraq and Afghanistan, where bomb detection is essential for military missions. Labs, rather than guard dogs like German shepherds, are the preferred animals for bomb-squad training. Labs are fast learners and less aggressive than breeds bred to be guard dogs. Possessed of a more tranquil temperament, the Labs are easier to train. Raised to be hunting dogs, they can pick up a scent from as much as 500 yards away.

3   Schooling bomb-sniffing dogs is extremely expensive, but the results seem worth the time, money, and effort. According to dog handler Corporal Andrew Guzman, the dogs "are 98 percent accurate" at detecting bombs. In Guzman's opinion, they are better than "metal detectors and mine sweepers." The dogs also help psychologically as well. Wherever they go, there are plenty of soldiers who miss their pets at home. Playing with the Labs during off-duty hours helps the soldiers—many away from home for the first time—fight homesickness.

4   By 2010, there were at least seventy dogs in Afghanistan alone and, given their success rate at detecting bombs, plans were afoot to send more. (Source of quotations: Gutierrez, "Dogs of War Saving Lives in Afghanistan," *Yahoo News*, January 28, 2010.)

1. What's the overall main idea of the reading?

_____

_____

2. In paragraph 2, the detail about Labradors being preferred for bomb detection is

    a. a major detail in terms of the paragraph.

    b. a minor detail in terms of the paragraph.

Copyright © Cengage Learning. All rights reserved.

In terms of the reading as a whole, that fact is

a. major.

b. minor.

3. In paragraph 2, the claim that the dogs are 98 percent accurate at detecting bombs is

a. a major detail in terms of the paragraph.

b. a minor detail in terms of the paragraph.

In terms of the reading as a whole, that claim is

a. a major detail.

b. a minor detail.

4. What meaning fits the word *tranquil* in the following sentence: "Possessed of a more *tranquil* temperament, Labs are easier to train" (paragraph 2)?

_____

5. The opening paragraph

a. provides background.

b. introduces the thesis statement.

2. Dogs in Armor

1 K9 Storm of Winnipeg, Canada, earns a tidy profit making armor for dogs used by the U.S. Army, Navy, Marines, Special Forces, police departments, and security firms. A small firm, it has done well for itself. However, the big test may still be ahead. In 2010, the company launched K9 Storm intruder, a specially designed bulletproof dog vest with a built-in wireless camera, speaker, and microphone, which will allow the handler to see and hear what the dog does. According to the company's owner, Glori Slater, the new vest will dramatically "change the way dogs are managed in emergencies" and "extend the range of the handler to 300 yards."

2   The inspiration for the company came when Slater's husband, a former dog handler for the Winnipeg police department, subdued a prison riot with the help of his German shepherd guard dog Olaf. The prisoners were armed with screw drivers and other makeshift weapons. Understandably, Slater was worried about his dog being attacked. After the riot ended, he decided to create a makeshift flak jacket that gave the dog some padded protection. Other canine handlers were soon asking him where he got the jacket, and K9 Storm was born.

Copyright © Cengage Learning. All rights reserved.

3   For the Slaters, the K9 Storm Intruder is another step forward in canine protection. Extremely lightweight, it allows the dog to have mobility without leaving the watchful eye of the handler. Although the newly designed vests aren't cheap—starting at $20,000 per vest—the Slaters say they have dozens of orders, especially from the military, which spends as much as $50,000 purchasing and training a dog for military duty. However, even nonmilitary sources have been able to order the vests, thanks to the generosity of donors like football player Ben Roethlisberger. Roethlisberger donated $250,000 to the Pittsburgh police and fire departments, earmarking the money for canine armor. (Source of quotations: Blum, "Armor to Guard $50,000 Dogs," November 30, 2009, CNNMoney.com.)

1. What's the overall main idea of the reading?

    _____

    _____

2. In paragraph 2, the opening sentence is
   a. the topic sentence.
   b. an introductory sentence.

   In terms of the reading as a whole, that opening sentence is
   a. a major detail.
   b. a minor detail.

3. In paragraph 3, the detail about the money being earmarked is
   a. a major detail in terms of the paragraph.
   b. a minor detail in terms of the paragraph.

   In terms of the reading as a whole, that statement is
   a. a major detail.
   b. a minor detail.

4. How would you define the word *earmarking* in the last sentence?

    _____

5. The purpose of the reading is to
   a. inform readers that the K9 Storm Intruder exists.
   b. persuade readers that the K9 Storm Intruder is a terrific new product.

Copyright © Cengage Learning. All rights reserved.

3. Dogs and Humans: How It All Got Started

1   We will probably never have conclusive evidence to tell us how dogs and humans first formed their personal and working relationship with each other, but it is most likely the case that man did not initially choose dogs; rather dogs chose man. Dogs were likely attracted to human campsites because humans, like dogs, were hunters, and animal remains, such as bones, bits of skin, and other scraps of offal[†] from recent victims, were likely to be scattered around human campsites. The ancestors of today's dogs (being ever food conscious) learned that by hanging around man's habitations, they could grab a quick bite to eat now and then, without all the exertion involved in actual hunting.

2   Although primitive man may not have been very concerned with cleanliness, health issues, or sanitation, it is still true that rotting food stuff does smell, and attracts insects that will make humans uncomfortable. Thus it is likely that dogs were initially tolerated around the perimeter of camps simply because they would dispose of the garbage. This waste disposal function continued for countless centuries. It's still being fulfilled by the pariah dogs[†] in many less developed regions of the world.

3   Anthropologists studying primitive tribes in the South Pacific have noticed that on those islands where people keep dogs, the villages and settlements are much more permanent. Villages without dogs have to move every year or so simply to escape the environmental contamination caused by rotting refuse. This has even led to the suggestion that dogs may have been a vital element in the establishment of permanent cities in that bygone era before we learned the importance of public sanitation.

4   Once the wild canines that would eventually become dogs were attracted to human settlements, our ancestors noticed an added benefit. Remember that early humans lived in dangerous times. There were large animals around, which looked on humans as potential sources of fresh meat. There were also other bands of humans with hostile intentions. Since the canines around the village began to look upon the area as their territory, whenever a strange human or wild beast approached, the dogs would sound the alarm. This would alert the residents in time to rally some sort of defense. As long as dogs were present, the human guards did not need to be as vigilant, thus allowing for more rest and a better lifestyle. It takes only a short journey to get from dogs guarding the village to a personal house dog. (Coren, *The Intelligence of Dogs*, www.stanleycoren.com/index.htm.)

[†]offal: guts of dead animals.
[†]pariah dogs: wild dogs that live near human communities and survive by eating what humans throw away.

Copyright © Cengage Learning. All rights reserved.

1. What's the main idea of the reading?

   _____

   _____

   _____

2. In paragraph 2, which sentence is the topic sentence?
   a. sentence 1
   b. sentence 2
   c. sentence 3

3. What's the implied main idea of paragraph 4?

   _____

   _____

4. What is the meaning of *perimeter* in the following sentence: "Thus it is likely that dogs were initially tolerated around the perimeter of camps simply because they would dispose of the garbage" (paragraph 2)?

   _____

5. Which of the following most effectively synthesizes all three readings?

   a. Humans and dogs have been bonding quite literally for centuries. But one thing is clear: The bond has benefited humans a good deal more than it has dogs. Dogs who sniff out bombs and patrol prison corridors are likely to die for the risks they take in their service to humans.

   b. Centuries ago, humans let dogs stay close because there were practical benefits to their presence. But those ancient humans could never have known how close the relationship would become between humans and animals, as the dogs became not just guardians and protectors but also companions.

   c. Given their history together, it's hard to understand how humans can engage in something as disgustingly brutal as dogfights. In times past and present, dogs have been protectors and companions, yet there are those who would make these devoted animals fight and maim one another for sport.

Copyright © Cengage Learning. All rights reserved.

8

Understanding the Difference Between *Fact* and *Opinion*

© William Manning/Corbis

IN THIS CHAPTER, YOU WILL LEARN

- how to tell the difference between *fact* and *opinion*.
- how to recognize statements that mix opinion with fact.
- how to distinguish between *informed* and *uninformed* opinions.
- how to recognize *irrelevant facts* and *reasons*.
- how textbooks often include opinions as well as facts.
- how to evaluate opinions on the Web.

*"In all matters of opinion,
it's a fact that our adversaries are insane."*

—Oscar Wilde, nineteenth-century playwright

The goal of this chapter is to provide a clear set of criteria, or standards, for deciding if a statement is a fact or an opinion. Once you know exactly what kinds of statements the two terms refer to, you'll be in a better position to evaluate how well or how poorly writers present their facts and share their opinions. You'll also be alert to the way many writers, often without realizing it, mix opinions into what at first glance seem to be purely factual descriptions.

 ## Facts Versus Opinions

Statements of **fact** provide information about people, places, events, and ideas that can be **verified**, or checked, for accuracy. Facts do not reveal the author's personal perspective, or point of view. The following are all statements of fact:

- Twitter was the creation of software engineer Jack Dorsey.
- The Spanish-American War began and ended in 1898.
- Sonia Sotomayor is the first Hispanic justice to serve on the Supreme Court.
- John Wilkes Booth assassinated Abraham Lincoln on April 14, 1865.
- In February 1903, more than 1,200 Mexican and Japanese farm workers organized the Japanese-Mexican Labor Association.

These facts can be checked in print or Web encyclopedias as well as other reference works, and they will always be the same. Facts do not vary with place or person. Whether you live in Dayton, Ohio, or Fairbanks, Alaska, if you look up Barack Obama's date of birth, it remains the same: August 4, 1961.

Obscure Facts

Because facts can be checked, they are generally not subject to question or argument. However, statements of fact can be questioned if they are obscure, or not widely known. For example, it's a fact that Muhammad, the Arab prophet who founded Islam, preached several sermons devoted to the rights of women. But since that fact is not well known, it's likely to be questioned.

Copyright © Cengage Learning. All rights reserved.

Changing Facts

Then, too, facts can and do change over time as new discoveries come to light or methods of research improve. This is especially true in fields like science, history, and medicine, where information is considered factual only insofar as it is based on existing knowledge. As scientists and historians gain more precise knowledge of the world, the facts on which they base their theories sometimes undergo dramatic change.

For example, it was once considered a fact that the sun revolved around the earth. But in the sixteenth century, a Polish astronomer named Nicolaus Copernicus used the laws of planetary motion to challenge that "fact." Copernicus proved that, *in fact*, the earth revolves around the sun.

Generally speaking, though, facts are unchanging pieces of information. They often include dates, events, names, and numbers that cannot be affected by the writer's background or training. Facts can be verified and *proved* accurate or inaccurate, true or false, to the satisfaction of most people. Unless they are newly discovered, facts are not often the subject of disagreement.

Statements of Fact ◆	• can be checked for accuracy or correctness.
	• can be proven true or false.
	• are not affected by the writer's background or training.
	• rely heavily on names and events, along with dates, numbers, and other units of measurement.
	• are not usually the subject of disagreement unless they are not widely known.
	• rely mainly on **denotative** language, or words that evoke no emotion in the reader.

Calling It a Fact Doesn't Necessarily Make It One

Because people tend to accept facts without giving them too much thought, some writers and speakers preface their opinions with phrases like "the fact is," as in the following sentence: "*The fact is* that Sarah Palin was totally unprepared to be John McCain's running mate in 2008." Despite the opening phrase, this statement is an opinion. Many people

Copyright © Cengage Learning. All rights reserved.

would not agree with it. What the author tries to do with that beginning phrase is bully readers into agreeing that the statement is an indisputable, or unquestionable, fact when it's anything but.

Generally speaking, beware of expressions like "it's a well-known fact that . . . ," "in point of fact," "without a doubt," "obviously," and "without question." Writers sometimes use this kind of confident language to discourage readers from actually thinking about and evaluating opinions disguised as facts.

Subjective and Objective

Statements that reflect the author's personal experiences and background are called *subjective* while those that avoid giving any hint of the author's feelings are called *objective*. Thus the word *subjective* is often linked to the word *opinion* while the word *objective* is frequently tied to *facts*.

But like labeling their opinions facts, writers sometimes use both of these terms to bully readers into accepting a point of view without asking any questions, for instance: "Objectively speaking, this movie reviewer is completely ignorant of film history."[†] "If this kind of government spending continues, we are headed for an economic disaster, and that's not a subjective opinion."

In both of these examples, we are dealing with opinions. But the writers use the words *subjective* and *objective* to avoid having readers look too closely at their claims. Their hope is that readers will be inattentive and consider the statements as facts. Critical readers, however, know better. If an author announces that a statement is objective or absolutely not subjective, critical readers take the time to figure out if the author's assessment is accurate.

Finding Facts on the World Wide Web

If you are using a search engine like Google to locate facts via the World Wide Web, always double-check your search results. This advice is doubly important if the website addresses you explore don't end in the

---

[†]For illustrations of the tendency to use the words *subjective* and *objective* to turn opinions into facts, try logging onto a site that reviews movies and scroll through the comments. You'll be amazed at how many people call the reviewer a genius or an idiot and yet claim that they are "speaking objectively" or that their statements of opinion are untainted by subjectivity.

Copyright © Cengage Learning. All rights reserved.

letters *edu*, *gov*, or *org*, endings that indicate large (and generally reliable) institutions.

One of the wonderful things about the Internet is that it allows ordinary people to share their knowledge or expertise with others. However, many of these amateur experts, while knowledgeable, don't necessarily have a team of editors to verify their information. Thus they can and occasionally do misinform.

One Web search, performed by the author of this text, revealed—to the author's amazement—that Frances Hodgson Burnett, the creator of a famous children's book, *The Secret Garden*, had amazing longevity. According to one website, Burnett was born in 1849 and died in 1974, making her 125 years old at the time of death. Now this "fact" is impressive. It's also incorrect. Burnett was born in 1849. But she died in 1924, a fact confirmed by a quick search of *several sites* related to Burnett's life and work. Someone managing the website had missed the error.

Where the Web is concerned, this kind of factual error is not all that unusual. Books, particularly reference and textbooks, have usually been double-checked by teams of people. Many websites,[†] however, are maintained by a single person or a few overworked souls, who don't always have the time or staff to double-check all their facts or proofread carefully. Thus errors remain until some sharp-eyed reader spots them and notifies the website manager. When using websites maintained by a single person or small group, always confirm the accuracy of their facts by checking to see if two or more websites agree on the facts in question.

✔ CHECK YOUR UNDERSTANDING Through Writing

Give three examples of factual statements.

_____

_____

_____

[†]Where factual errors are concerned, this statement is less true of websites based on print products, like the website based on the print version of the *New York Times*.

Copyright © Cengage Learning. All rights reserved.

Opinions

Shaped by an author's personal experience, training, and background, **opinions** about the same subject can vary from person to person, group to group, and place to place. For an illustration, ask a group of teenagers how they feel about high school dress codes. Then ask their parents. Don't be shocked if you uncover a marked difference of opinion.

You Can't Verify Opinions

Unlike facts, opinions cannot be verified by using outside sources. They are too subjective—too personal—to be checked in reference books or historical records. The following are all statements of opinion:

- If Facebook administrators continue to infringe on users' right to privacy, they will see a decline in their consumer base.

- Thanks to acclaimed cellist Yo-Yo Ma, the glorious music of Argentinean Astor Piazzolla is now more widely known.

- Pet owners deserve to be held legally accountable if their animals do someone harm.

- For up-to-date news about current events, Twitter is simply unbeatable.

- Feminists of different generations are inclined to disagree on the meaning and goals of the feminist movement.

Because opinions are so heavily influenced by individual training, knowledge, and experience, it's impossible to talk about them as accurate or inaccurate, right or wrong. For example, if you own a dog and firmly believe that dogs make more desirable pets than cats, no cat lover can *prove* you wrong. That's because you're expressing an opinion, not stating a fact.

Copyright © Cengage Learning. All rights reserved.

Statements of Opinion ◆	• can be evaluated but cannot be verified for accuracy or correctness.
	• cannot be proven true or false, right or wrong (although they can be termed ethical or unethical, informed or uninformed).
	• are shaped by the writer's knowledge, background, or training.
	• often communicate value judgments, indicating that the author thinks something is right or wrong, good or bad.
	• use language that expresses or arouses personal feelings—for example, *effective, ineffective, slender, skinny, delightful, disgusting.*

In addition to the characteristics listed in the preceding box, the language a writer uses is another important clue to the presence of opinions.

The Language of Opinions ◆	• often includes verbs or adverbs like *suggests, appears, seems, might, could* or *should be, possibly, probably, likely, apparently, presumably, arguably, allegedly, supposedly.*
	• frequently makes comparisons using words such as *more, most, better, best, greatest, finest.*
	• is likely to include words that make value judgments, e.g., *beautiful, perfect, significant, interesting, critical, key, crucial.*
	• is often laced with words and phrases such as *one interpretation of, another possibility is, this study suggests, in all likelihood, it would seem, arguably, supposedly.*
	• sometimes challenges preexisting beliefs or traditions using phrases like *Although it's often said that, While in the past we have, Even though for years now.*

CHECK YOUR UNDERSTANDING Through Writing

Give three examples of opinion statements.

_____

_____

_____

Copyright © Cengage Learning. All rights reserved.

✔ **CHECK YOUR UNDERSTANDING**

What's the essential difference between facts and opinions?

_____

_____

◆ **EXERCISE 1** **Identifying Facts and Opinions**

DIRECTIONS Label each statement *F* for fact or *O* for opinion.

_____ 1. All this uproar about animal rights is nonsense. Animals don't have rights.

_____ 2. In 1909, Ernest Rutherford showed that atoms were mostly space.

_____ 3. When it was under Spanish control, the city of Los Angeles was called *El Pueblo de Nuestra Señora la Reina de los Angeles del Río de Porciúncula*, which means "The Town of Our Lady the Queen of the Angels by the Little Portion River."[†]

_____ 4. Using Craigslist to find romance is a dumb idea.

_____ 5. Martin Luther King Jr.'s "Letter from Birmingham Jail" was published in 1963 by the American Friends Service Committee, a Quaker organization.

_____ 6. Pop singer Michael Jackson died on June 25, 2009.

_____ 7. Jaron Lanier, the author of *You Are Not a Gadget*, is correct to argue that Web anonymity encourages people to say things they would never dare say if their real identity were known.

_____ 8. Although the singer Selena has been given most of the credit, it was the band La Mafia that made *tejano* music popular in the United States.

_____

[†]Bill Bryson, *Made in America*, p. 106.

Copyright © Cengage Learning. All rights reserved.

_____ 9. Dionysus was the Greek god of wine and fertility.

_____ 10. Queen Victoria of England died on January 22, 1901; at her death, she had been queen for almost sixty-four years.

ALLUSION ALERT

Dionysus, Greek God of Wine
The Greek god Dionysus was associated with wild, drunken rituals, called the Dionysian rites. Allusions to Dionysus, which usually take the form of a modifier, now suggest events associated with or fueled by alcohol and marked by a lack of all restraint or inhibition—for instance, "Few parents can acknowledge to themselves the kind of Dionysian revels their children are exposed to at school parties."

Be Alert to Opinions Mixed in with Facts

Reading critically would probably be a good deal easier if authors kept statements of fact and opinion neatly divided. But they don't. Whether consciously or unconsciously, writers—and textbook authors are no exception—can't always avoid coloring a fact with an opinion.

Your job as a critical reader is to make sure you recognize when and where fact and opinion blend together. Then you won't mistakenly accept as fact an opinion you haven't consciously thought through or considered. Take, for example, the following sentence:

> At least thirty-eight states have sensibly decided to give terminally ill patients the right to refuse medical treatment.

At a quick glance, this sentence might appear to be a statement of fact. It's easy enough to verify how many states have given terminally ill patients the right to reject medical treatment.

But think again about the author's use of the word *sensibly*. This word has positive **connotations**, or associations. Use it to describe someone, and chances are he or she would be pleased. What the author has done in the above sentence is to include her opinion of the action taken by those thirty-eight states. She uses the word *sensibly* to suggest they did the right thing. That makes the statement a blend of both fact and opinion.

Copyright © Cengage Learning. All rights reserved.

Connotative Language Is the Language of Personal Evaluation

Writers dealing in pure fact tend to rely heavily on denotative language that suggests little more than dictionary definitions of words—for example, "The flying fox is a bat with a wingspan that can extend to five feet."

However, writers who express opinions are likely to use connotative language that implies a value judgment. Think here of words like *effective, intelligent, hard-working,* and *determined.* All of these words have positive connotations, and all of them reveal the writer's point of view. For an illustration, compare these two descriptions of the same event:

> *Hard-working* and *determined,* the new liaison between the Indians' tribal organizations and the federal government was *committed to finding out* if all the royalties on mineral rights had been paid into the appropriate account.

> The new liaison between the Indians' tribal organizations and the federal government checked to see if all the royalties on mineral rights had been paid into the appropriate account.

In the first sentence, the language suggests a writer who supports or is impressed by the efforts of the liaison to get the job done, especially since the phrase "committed to finding out" implies the job is not all that easy. The second sentence is more purely descriptive, with the writer telling readers what the liaison between the two groups is responsible for. It's no longer clear if the writer approves or disapproves of the behavior.

As you know from the box on page 487, words that make value judgments are a strong sign that an opinion is present. But many of the words that make those value judgments are more subtle than you might realize. Words like *good* and *bad* or *moral* and *immoral* obviously express a value judgment. In contrast words like *effective, convincing, pointedly, clearly,* and *surprising* don't scream out value judgment. Yet that's precisely what they all are.

 CHECK YOUR UNDERSTANDING Through Writing

Here is a largely denotative description of two people having dinner. Rewrite it to make the language more connotative than denotative. Revise it so that the language tells the reader more about what is going on between the two people.

Copyright © Cengage Learning. All rights reserved.

The man and woman sat across from one another. The man's head was tilted to the side while the woman spoke, and he was drumming his fingers. He shook his head twice while she gestured with her hands. He appeared to be in his mid-thirties, while his dinner companion looked to be in her late fifties. She had short, red hair and was wearing a suit. She also wore heels and carried a large black bag. He was dressed in slacks and a tee shirt with a brand name on the front. He wore leather sandals. After the appetizers arrived, they ate without speaking. When they finished eating, she paid the check and left.

◆ **EXERCISE 2**   **Recognizing When Fact and Opinion Come Together**

DIRECTIONS   Read each sentence and look carefully at the italicized word or words. Then label each statement *F* for fact, *O* for opinion, or *B* for a blend of both.

F   **EXAMPLE**   *Twentieth-century author* Gertrude Stein spent most of her life in France.

EXPLANATION   The phrase *twentieth-century author* does not carry with it any positive or negative associations. It simply identifies the time in which Stein lived. The amount of time Stein actually spent in France can also be verified.

_____ 1. In his 2010 book *True Enough*, Farhad Manjoo describes how Photoshop has changed the way we think about photographs, and he *convincingly* argues that this change has undermined the use of photographs as evidence.

_____ 2. "Zulu" is a *general name* for some 2.5 million Bantu-speaking peoples who live in South Africa.

_____ 3. The Amazon River is the *second-longest river* after the Nile.

_____ 4. Nuclear weapons are the *major plague of this century*.

_____ 5. In the nineteenth century, Marshal James "Wild Bill" Hickok was *fearless* in his daring pursuit of outlaws.

Copyright © Cengage Learning. All rights reserved.

_____ 6. *Famed revolutionary hero* Emiliano Zapata was *worshipped* by the poor of Mexico.

_____ 7. Gospel music is *intense, joyful music* that *makes the spirit sing*.

_____ 8. Francisco Goya was a Spanish painter of the *late eighteenth and early nineteenth centuries*.

_____ 9. The nineteenth-century naturalist* John James Audubon was a painter *of surprising skill*.

_____ 10. *Astonishing as it may seem*, John D. Rockefeller, founder of the Standard Oil Company, was famous for his charity work.

◆ EXERCISE 3   **Recognizing When Fact and Opinion Combine**

DIRECTIONS   Some of the following statements are purely factual. Others blend fact and opinion. Label the statements that are pure fact with an *F*. Label the statements that blend fact and opinion with a *B*. For those sentences you mark with a *B*, underline the word or words that led you to your conclusion.

_B_   **EXAMPLE**   Singer Ednita Nazario's <u>splendid</u> album *Corazón* was produced by Dolores del Infante, an alias for Latin singer Robi Rosa.

EXPLANATION   In this statement, the author provides factual information about the album, but the word *splendid* announces the author's opinion of the music.

_____ 1. According to the Television Bureau of Advertising, an extraordinary 98.2 percent of all American households have a television set.

_____ 2. Psychiatrist Bruno Bettelheim spent decades meticulously studying fairy tales and their effect on children.

_____ 3. An astounding number of people have tattoos covering 98 percent of their body.

───────────
*naturalist: person who studies and writes about the plants and animals in nature.

Copyright © Cengage Learning. All rights reserved.

_____ 4. Amazingly, Diane Nash was only twenty-two years old when she led the campaign to desegregate the lunch counters in Nashville, Tennessee.

_____ 5. Jerry Garcia, the long-time lead singer for the Grateful Dead, died on August 9, 1995.

_____ 6. Juan Rodríguez Cabrillo explored the coast of California in 1542.

_____ 7. At the end of World War I, victorious Britain and France greedily divided up the Turkish Empire.

_____ 8. Highly acclaimed for her book about textbook censorship, _The Language Police_, Diane Ravitch returned to the subject of education in her 2010 book _The Death and Life of the Great American School System_, proving once again her commitment to educating our young people.

_____ 9. After World War II, Great Britain turned Palestine over to the United Nations, which in November 1947 voted to create the State of Israel.

_____ 10. In 1908, the phenomenal Jack Johnson became the first African American to win the world heavyweight championship.

Changing the Connotation with the Context

Change the **context**, or setting, of a word and it can become more connotative than denotative. For example, the word _stories_ in the following sentence evokes little more than its denotation.

Aesop's Fables is a collection of _stories_ written by a Greek storyteller.

However, look what happens when the context of the word _stories_ changes:

In an effort to deny Jean a promotion, a jealous co-worker spread _stories_ about her character.

With this change in context, the word _stories_ no longer refers to "an account of events"; instead, it becomes a synonym for _lies_ and takes on

Copyright © Cengage Learning. All rights reserved.

a negative connotation. This example illustrates a key point about labeling language connotative or denotative: *Context is crucial.* Don't assume a word denotative in one sentence is always lacking an emotional charge. A word can be connotative or denotative, depending on the setting in which it appears.

CHECK YOUR UNDERSTANDING Through Writing

Use each word in two different contexts. One sentence should use the word in its denotative sense. The other should make it assume connotations. If you need to, you can change the word ending to make it more connotative or denotative. For instance, "They decided on tile for the *floor* because it would be easier to clean" and "The instructor was *floored* when the student defied the rule and used his cell phone in class."

1. home

_____

_____

_____

2. crack

_____

_____

_____

Informed Versus Uninformed Opinions

You probably know the expression, "Everybody has a right to an opinion." That's certainly true. It doesn't follow, though, that every opinion deserves the same degree of attention or respect.

Imagine, for example, that a friend saw you taking an aspirin for a headache and told you that chewing a garlic clove was a better remedy. When you asked why, he shrugged and said: "I don't know. I heard it someplace." Given this lack of explanation, argument, or evidence, it's unlikely that you would start chewing garlic cloves to cure your headaches. **Uninformed opinions**—opinions lacking

Copyright © Cengage Learning. All rights reserved.

sufficient or appropriate support—usually do (as well they should) fail to persuade.

More likely to convince are **informed opinions** backed by facts and reasons. For an example, look at this paragraph, which opens by expressing an opinion about the Internet's darker side.

> Although the Internet provides us with a convenient way to conduct research and to shop, it also has a darker side. Every day, hundreds of people report that they are victims of online stalking. In 2000, police arrested John Edward Robinson, the first Internet serial killer, who murdered at least five women he met and corresponded with online. In 1999, the FBI investigated 1,500 online child solicitation* cases, a number more than double that of the previous year. Criminals are also using the Internet to steal credit card numbers, thereby costing cardholders and issuers hundreds of millions of dollars per year. Still other criminals are using the Internet for adoption fraud. For example, Internet adoption broker Tina Johnson caused much heartache and created an international dispute in 2001 when she took money from two couples in two different countries for the adoption of the same infant twin girls. Internet crimes have also involved the distribution of illegal drugs such as anabolic steroids. In September 2007, the FBI made a number of arrests involving men distributing steroids through MySpace.com profiles. Then, too, in 2010, four men were indicted for illegally earning over 25 million dollars by hacking into sites like Ticketmaster.com and reselling tickets to the hottest concerts and shows. (Source of dates and events: www.cybercrime.gov/porterindict.htm.)

This passage starts with the author's opinion—the Internet, whatever its advantages, also has a "darker side." Aware, however, that not everyone might agree, she adds a number of facts and reasons designed to convince readers that the opening opinion is informed and thus worth sharing.

Among other things, we learn that on a daily basis hundreds of people report they are the victims of online stalkers. We also hear about an Internet serial killer and about criminals' use of the Internet to rig up phony adoptions, steal concert tickets, and market illegal drugs. Most of these supporting details are factual. One way or another, they can be verified, and that's important.

---

*solicitation: the act of approaching someone for sexual or monetary purposes, also to persuasively ask for something other than money or sex—for instance, votes or information.

Copyright © Cengage Learning. All rights reserved.

But equally important, all the supporting details are **relevant**, or related, to the opinion expressed. They all illustrate dangers associated with the Internet. Thus they help prove the author's claim that the Internet has a dark side. What about this paragraph, though? Are we again dealing with an informed opinion?

> Given that at least thirty thousand patients per year die from bloodstream infections, health care workers need to take better precautions with washing their hands before handling patients. When patients enter a hospital for treatment, they expect to be cured of their illness or injury; they don't expect to acquire another problem, particularly not a deadly one. Yet that's precisely what happened to Carol Bradley when she entered a hospital to be treated for stomach cancer. As a result of a bloodstream infection, Bradley spent three weeks in intensive care and more than a year on antibiotics. Some hospitals that have taken precautions to prevent infections have virtually eliminated them altogether. *Consumer Reports* lists 105 hospitals reporting zero incidents of bloodstream infection. (Source of Carol Bradley's story: http://ab-clocal.go.com/wabc/story?section=news/consumer&id=7253884)

The opinion expressed in the paragraph is strongly stated. But does that make it an informed opinion? Not quite. What's not completely clear is how the case of Carol Bradley is relevant or connected to the author's insistence that health care workers need to do more hand washing.

Nor do readers know why the list from *Consumer Reports* is in the passage since it isn't directly tied to the central opinion. Put another way, the author hasn't related the supporting details to the main idea. What we have is an opinion seemingly lacking in relevant support.

To make readers take this opinion seriously, the author needs to make tighter connections for readers. She needs to show them how the details provided are relevant, for example:

> Given that at least thirty thousand patients per year die from bloodstream infections, health care workers need to spend more time washing their hands before handling patients. In intensive-care units, long flexible catheters,† called "central lines," can quickly deliver desperately

---

†catheter: a hollow flexible tube that can be inserted into the body to allow the passage of fluids.

Copyright © Cengage Learning. All rights reserved.

needed fluids, nutrition, and medication. However, if those central lines are inserted by caretakers who have not properly washed their hands, the lines can also deliver deadly bacteria. That's what happened to Carol Bradley when she was treated in a hospital for stomach cancer. It wasn't the cancer that almost killed her, it was the bloodstream infection that kept her in intensive care for three weeks and taking antibiotics for over a year. Bradley now says that if she "went into the hospital again, I would try to make sure I had my family available around the clock to make sure everyone did . . . good handwashing." Her sentiments are very much in line with the findings published in the December 2006 issue of the *New England Journal of Medicine*, which showed a 66 percent decrease in central-line infections after hospitals instituted simple precautions such as washing hands before and after handling a patient.

✔ CHECK YOUR UNDERSTANDING

Explain the difference between relevant and irrelevant details.

_____

_____

_____

TAKING A CLOSER LOOK

Sentence Connections

What does the phrase "that's what happened" refer to in the following sentence from the paragraph about bloodstream infections: "That's what happened to Carol Bradley when she was treated in a hospital for stomach cancer"?

_____

_____

What function does that sentence serve in the paragraph?

_____

_____

Copyright © Cengage Learning. All rights reserved.

◆ **EXERCISE 4** **Evaluating Opinions**

DIRECTIONS Read each passage. Then write *I* in the blank if you think the writer expresses an informed opinion supported by relevant details. Put *U* in the blank if you think the author is uninformed and has not provided enough relevant support.

© William Manning/Corbis

1. When Barack Obama tapped Solicitor General Elena Kagan to replace retiring Supreme Court Justice John Paul Stevens, several pundits* worried that Kagan was, like Sonia Sotomayor, a woman with no children. Others wondered if the Court didn't need a Protestant judge since, with Stevens's retirement, the Supreme Court would be without a single Protestant. But for some reason far fewer news analysts highlighted what is a much more worrisome omission on the Supreme Court: diversity of academic background. Look over the résumés of our Supreme Court justices and you'll think that the Ivy League is apparently the only place to find qualified judges. This is the impression despite the fact that law schools at Notre Dame University, George Washington University, and the University of Texas are ranked among the nation's top twenty-five schools of law. Yet diversity in academic training is important because the Supreme Court justices are, due to their professional position, somewhat detached from the concerns of ordinary life to begin with. That tendency to detachment is only encouraged by presidents who repeatedly choose justices with the same or very similar academic backgrounds. As legal scholar and law professor Johnathan Turley succinctly expresses it, "The high court is a cloistered† enough institution as it is—so why risk making it even more detached from the rest of us by turning it into a Harvard-Yale Law Review† reunion." (Source of quotation: Tim Padgett. "Is the Supreme Court Too Packed with Ivy Leaguers?" Time.com.)

———

———————

*pundits: public sources of opinion, people who give an opinion through the mass media and who, allegedly, are knowledgeable about the topic discussed.
†cloistered: A cloister is a monastery or convent, but in this case the word is used figuratively, or in a comparative way, to mean the judges are isolated or set apart from the public in the way a cloister is in real life.
†Law Review: This is a scholarly journal published by law school students. To be selected to be on the Law Review is a huge honor.

Copyright © Cengage Learning. All rights reserved.

2. Every American should seriously consider buying a hybrid gasoline-electric car. Thousands of people have already bought a Honda Insight or a Toyota Prius, both of which cost under $25,000. The demand for these cars, which combine a small gasoline engine with an electric motor, already exceeds production. Within the next few years, various auto manufacturers plan to introduce a hybrid sport utility vehicle, a hybrid minivan, and a hybrid truck. It's clear that hybrid vehicles are a growing trend, and one day in the near future, there should be one in every American garage. Fortunately, there are signs that hybrid autos are catching on and becoming trendy among celebrities. Anxious to imitate their idols, ordinary Americans will probably follow suit, which makes good sense.

   _____

3. Whenever there is a tragedy, grief counselors rush to the scene to offer their services. Generally, this is considered a public service. We take on faith the idea that grief counseling is helpful, especially when death is sudden and unexpected. We also assume that grief counselors can help people who have experienced the loss of a loved one in ordinary circumstances. But is grief counseling in either context really necessary? Probably not. The truth is, grief counseling does more harm than good. Think about it. When people experienced the death of family, friends, or colleagues fifty years ago, grief counselors did not exist. Yet their absence did not mean that everyone affected by the loss of a friend, loved one, or co-worker was condemned to continuous mourning. Grief does abate* with time after all, so what is the matter with letting nature take its course? Grieving is a normal process. It's about adjusting to the loss of a loved one. Although it's a cliché to say it, time does heal all wounds. Time can heal the misery of grief without the help of special counselors.

   _____

4. The career of legendary queen of salsa Celia Cruz (1925–2003) was both long and influential. During her half-century career, Cruz recorded more than seventy albums and traveled all over

---

*abate: cease, stop.

Copyright © Cengage Learning. All rights reserved.

the world, entertaining four generations of fans with her extraordinary voice and flamboyant performances. More than anything else, she helped define salsa, an Afro-Cuban musical style characterized by Latin rhythms. Cruz also received numerous awards and honors—including the prestigious National Medal of Arts, a Grammy Award, and an honorary doctorate degree from Yale University—all in recognition of her contributions. Perhaps most important, Cruz is credited with breaking down racial and cultural barriers by winning a mainstream audience over to Latin music. Twenty of her albums went gold, selling more than 500,000 copies each. Because her music appealed to a wide range of people and because she took such pride and joy in her Cuban heritage, she served as a passionate ambassador of Hispanic culture. Proud of her accomplishments, Cruz always credited them to her father, saying, "In a sense, I have fulfilled my father's wish to be a teacher; as through my music, I teach generations of people about my culture."

———

5. Although the so-called Mozart effect has been widely accepted by many educators, parents, legislators, and music marketers, evidence indicates that it may not exist. In 1993, researchers at the University of Wisconsin claimed that college students who listened to ten minutes of a Mozart sonata prior to taking a spatial*-reasoning test significantly improved their ability to perform tasks such as cutting and folding paper. This study gave birth to the belief that listening to Mozart's music helps increase intelligence. However, researchers have not been able to duplicate the results of this first experiment. As a matter of fact, a Harvard University graduate analyzed the conclusions of sixteen similar studies and found no scientific proof that music increased IQ or improved academic performance. Researchers at Appalachian State University and two Canadian universities have come to the same conclusion.

———

*spatial: related to location in space.

Copyright © Cengage Learning. All rights reserved.

TAKING A CLOSER LOOK

Support for Opinions

In paragraph 4, the author says "Cruz is credited with breaking down racial and cultural barriers by winning a mainstream audience over to Latin music." Is that an opinion or a fact? Please explain.

_____

_____

How could winning a mainstream audience over to her music do anything to "[break] down racial and cultural barriers"?

_____

_____

_____

Forming Your Own Opinion
◆

Do you share the author's view of music's power to break down cultural barriers? Why or why not?

_____

_____

Checking for Relevance in Longer Readings

As readings get longer, readers have to become even more vigilant. Sometimes writers start with relevant facts and reasons that support their position. But they end up drifting off and piling up details that add little more than length to the reading. Is that what happens in this example?

Walter Hickel's Transformation

1   In the early days of his political career in Washington, Walter Hickel, the former Alaska governor and Secretary of the Interior, who died in 2010, was considered a foe of environmentalists. Environmental activists were furious when Richard Nixon selected Hickel to be the Secretary of the Interior in 1968. They fought hard to defeat his confirmation. Prior to becoming Nixon's choice for Secretary, Hickel had aroused

Copyright © Cengage Learning. All rights reserved.

conservationists' ire by suggesting that they were mindlessly protecting every plant and creature in nature while at the same time ignoring human concerns. He was, as he put it, opposed to those who believed in "conservation for conservation's sake."

2   But when a Chevron Oil platform caught fire in the Gulf of Mexico in 1970, pouring more than 40,000 barrels of oil into the the gulf, perceptions of Hickel changed, and he became an environmentalist hero. Outraged by the company's failure to have a response plan ready for such an event, Hickel demanded an investigation. He also insisted that the Justice Department charge Chevron with 900 violations of the Outer Continental Shelf Lands Act of 1953. Disgusted by the environmental disaster Chevron had created, Hickel wrote regulations designed to control offshore drilling and make the oil industry financially responsible for any blowouts or spills that occurred.

3   During his 22-month tenure as the Secretary of the Interior, Hickel also led a successful campaign to stop the construction of a jetport in the Everglades, wrote legislation protecting endangered alligators and whales, and published the names of companies that were polluting the country's rivers and lakes with mercury. In addition, he proposed banning billboards on federal lands and enthusiastically supported making Earth Day a national holiday.

4   Hickel was also admired because he bluntly told his boss, President Richard M. Nixon, that he was badly mismanaging youthful opposition to the Vietnam War. Nixon did not appreciate the advice. Shortly after voicing his criticism of presidential policy, Hickel was dismissed as Secretary of the Interior.

5   Those opposed to the war loved Hickel for his stand-up attitude. The president of the United States, however, did not share the public's affection for the governor from Alaska. Nixon sent him back home, where Hickel ran for governor four times before finally winning in 1990.

If you answered "yes" to the question posed at the beginning of the reading, you were correct. Initially the facts and reasons offered are relevant. They do support the claim that the perception of Hickel as a foe of the environmentalists changed. The positions Hickel eventually took certainly sound like the behavior of a man open to environmental concerns. It's believable, therefore, that he would be perceived differently as a result.

However, by paragraph 4, the writer has gotten off target. The details supplied in paragraphs 4 and 5 suggest a man who spoke his mind. But Hickel's outspokenness about Nixon's handling of the anti-war movement does nothing to prove the author's opening point about Hickel and

Copyright © Cengage Learning. All rights reserved.

the environmentalists. The details in paragraphs 4 and 5 are not really relevant to the opinion expressed in the reading.

If it turns out that a writer does include some irrelevant details in a reading, that doesn't mean you should dismiss the author's opinion as uninformed. It does mean, though, that you should double-check how opinion and support match up throughout the selection. If the author included one irrelevant detail, there might be more.

✔ CHECK YOUR UNDERSTANDING Through Writing

In a sentence or two, explain what John F. Kennedy meant when he said, "I hope that no American will . . . throw away his vote by voting either for or against me solely on account of my religious affiliation. It is not relevant."

_____

_____

TAKING A CLOSER LOOK

Titles and Predictions
To give your reading a focus, what questions should you ask based on the title of the passage about Walter Hickel?

_____

As the basis for making predictions, how useful is the title of the reading on Hickel? Please explain your answer.

_____

_____

www

INTERNET FOLLOW-UP: The Two Governors from Alaska
Sarah Palin is another famous governor from Alaska. How did she and Walter Hickel get along?

_____

_____

Copyright © Cengage Learning. All rights reserved.

◆ **EXERCISE 5** **Checking for Relevance in Longer Readings**

DIRECTIONS Read each selection. Then write *R* or *I* in the blank at the end. *R* indicates that all the facts and reasons are relevant. *I* indicates that you spotted one or more irrelevant facts or reasons. If you write *I* in the first blank, indicate in the second blank which paragraph includes irrelevant information. Leave that blank empty if all the details are relevant.

1. Hold the Salt or Pay the Price

1   If State Assemblyman Felix Ortiz had had his way, New Yorkers might well be eating out a good deal less. In 2010, Ortiz tried to ban the use of salt in New York City restaurants. To motivate the reduction in salt use, he insisted that violators of the no-salt rule should be fined $1,000 for every salted dish on the menu.

2   Not surprisingly, the ordinance* did not gain much traction in the New York Assembly. Nor was it especially popular with the public. With some modification, however, Mr. Ortiz's idea is worthy of serious consideration and shouldn't be so readily dismissed. It has merit.

3   As Sonia Angell, the director of the cardiovascular disease and prevention program for the Health Department of New York, correctly said, "You can live with salt in your diet. The problem in our society is excess salt." Excess salt is a problem because study after study has shown a direct connection between excessive salt consumption and high blood pressure, heart problems, and kidney disease. It's that connection that has made Angell get behind the New York mayor's push to make food producers and restaurants cut the salt, or sodium, content of food by 25 percent.

4   New York City's mayor, Michael R. Bloomberg, announced his plans to cut salt consumption in January 2010. Not surprisingly, he had the backing of health officials throughout the city. Unlike Mr. Ortiz's plan, Bloomberg's much more moderate proposal was voluntary and did not involve any new legislation. The hope is that restaurants and food producers will comply voluntarily because they don't want to be seen as making or producing food that is injurious to public health.

5   Those who are skeptical that Mr. Bloomberg's proposal will have an effect should remember that he also started his campaign to cut trans fat in food by first requesting voluntary compliance. When that didn't work, he passed a law forcing restaurants to eliminate trans fat from the menu. Where salt is concerned, Mayor Bloomberg may need to take a similar step. In terms of lives saved, such a move might be worth the

———————

*ordinance: rule or regulation.

Copyright © Cengage Learning. All rights reserved.

controversy it will surely arouse. (Source of quotation: www.nydailynews.com/nylocal/2010/03/11/2010-03-11_assault_on_salt_an_insult_chefs.html.)

———

The information in paragraph _____ is not relevant to the author's opinion.

2. Getting Smart

1 For decades now, there have been numerous, much-publicized claims that intelligence is inherited, with books like Arthur Jensen's *The g Factor* (1998) and Charles Murray and Richard Herrnstein's *The Bell Curve* (1994) fueling debate over which contributes more to intelligence, genetic inheritance or environmental training and experience. Both books suggest, and in some chapters insist, that nature, or genetic inheritance, plays an overwhelming role in the development of human intelligence, at least as it is measured by IQ tests.

2 In his 2009 book *Intelligence and How to Get It: Why Schools and Cultures Count*, the esteemed cognitive psychologist Richard E. Nisbett begs to differ. Nisbett has looked closely at the research used in support of the heritability claims, and he doesn't find it all that convincing. Nisbett is far more enthusiastic about studies suggesting that a child's environment and personality are the more decisive influences on the development of intelligence. For Nisbett, genes are less important than the context in which a child is raised. That is the carefully argued and altogether convincing thesis of his book.

3 Nisbett is not especially impressed, for instance, by studies of identical twins which show that twins, after being separated and raised miles apart, often have similar IQ levels. Historically, such studies seemed to prove the role of genetic inheritance in intelligence. But Nisbett points out that the twins participating in such studies are almost always raised by parents of the exact same social class. Thus each twin was usually given similar intellectual and cultural advantages or, for that matter, disadvantages, which could just as easily account for the similarity in IQ scores.

4 Unfortunately, people are all too readily beguiled* by the subject of twins, largely because there is so much popular folklore* surrounding their existence. There are stories of twins who felt one another's physical pain when one of them fell ill or was injured and even more tales of twins who lived in different cities yet somehow managed to buy the exact same

———

*beguiled: fascinated.
*folklore: beliefs, traditions, and customs associated with a culture and informally learned or acquired.

Copyright © Cengage Learning. All rights reserved.

dress or suit. This common lore about the mystical* connection between twins may be one reason why identical-twin studies have made such an impression on the public's mind.

5   In making his point about the way environment shapes intelligence as much as or more than genes, Nisbett moves away from twin studies in order to talk about the relationship between personal traits and intellectual achievement. As he sees it, parents who raise their children to have the right mindset about learning—i.e., to be self-disciplined and exert impulse control—are doing their kids a huge favor. In support of this belief, Nisbett cites the work of psychologists Martin Seligman and Angela Duckworth.

6   Duckworth and Seligman studied student achievement in an effort to determine which factor was a bigger predictor of success, a child's IQ score or an ability to be focused and self-disciplined about completing tasks. What they found was that IQ was not nearly as good a predictor of academic success as the presence of what Nisbett calls "strong self-discipline."

7   As he puts it, "If you had to choose for your child a high IQ or strong self-discipline, you might be wise to pick the latter." Self-discipline, of course, is not a characteristic that's inherited; it's something we learn by example and experience. Thus studies like the ones performed by Duckworth and Seligman go a long way toward proving Nisbett's claim that our environment—that is, how we are raised and what we experience—is the main ticket to getting smart. (Source of quotation: Nisbett, *Intelligence and How to Get It: Why Schools and Cultures Count*, p. 17.)

———

The information in paragraph _____ is not relevant to the author's opinion.

TAKING A CLOSER LOOK	**Clues to Meaning in Titles** Why do you think Richard Nisbett subtitled his book "Why Schools and Cultures Count"? _____ _____ _____ _____

———

*mystical: spiritual, mysterious.

Copyright © Cengage Learning. All rights reserved.

ALLUSION ALERT

Tweedledee and Tweedledum

Numerous allusions revolve around twins. Perhaps the most famous of them is the allusion to the twins Tweedledee and Tweedledum. The twins first appeared in an eighteenth-century English rhyme comparing two musicians. They later turned up in a collection of rhymes for kids, *Original Ditties*[†] *for the Nursery*.

But their real claim to fame comes from their appearance in Lewis Carroll's *Through the Looking Glass and What Alice Found There*, which tells the story of Alice in Wonderland. The twins also appeared in the Walt Disney and Tim Burton movies about Alice's adventures in Wonderland.

Tweedledee and Tweedledum are almost always portrayed as identical, even mimicking one another's speech. Thus allusions to them suggest that the people under discussion, despite any outward signs of difference, are exactly the same—for instance, "Consumer activist Ralph Nader was widely quoted when he referred to the Democratic and Republican parties as Tweedledee and Tweedledum."

INTERNET FOLLOW-UP: Another Twin Allusion

Use the Internet to find answers to these questions: According to Roman mythology, the founders of Rome were twins. What were their names? Who was nursing them when they were discovered? Who was alleged to be their father?

_____

_____

◆ Recognize Fact and Opinion in Textbooks

Many students assume that textbook writers restrict themselves to reporting facts and avoid presenting their opinions. Although that may be true for some science texts, it's not true for textbooks in general,

_____

[†]ditties: comical rhyming songs and poems.

Copyright © Cengage Learning. All rights reserved.

particularly in the areas of psychology, history, and government. Look, for example, at the following passage. Do you detect the presence of an opinion?

> Presidents are not just celebrities, they are the American version of royalty. Lacking a royal family, Americans look to the president to symbolize the uniqueness of their government. (Gitelson et al., *American Government*, p. 311.)

If you said the entire passage was an opinion, you'd be right. There's no way to verify how *all* Americans feel about the role of the president. A good many may have no interest in royalty at all. Why, then, would they look for a substitute?

Opinions in Textbook Writing Aren't Always Knowingly Included

Here's another textbook excerpt; see any opinions among the facts?

> Few people work constantly at their jobs. Most of us take breaks, and, at least once in awhile, goof off. We meet fellow workers at the coffee machine and we talk in the hallway. Much of this interaction is good for the company, for it bonds us to fellow workers and ties us to our jobs. (Henslin, *Sociology*, p. 197.)

This excerpt describing what most people do at their jobs is also almost all opinion. The world of work described here has little or nothing to do with the working conditions of someone on an assembly line, where one of the most common worker complaints is the absence of enough bathroom breaks, never mind having time for a hallway chat.

However, that does not mean the author is trying to trick you. He's just doing what most people do: He's assuming that the world he knows applies to almost everyone else as well. That's one reason why opinions turn up so often in textbooks, because just about everything we do, say, or write is shaped to some degree by our own background and experience.

As long as readers are aware of the opinions tucked into their textbooks, those opinions are not a problem. It's unknowingly absorbing them, right along with the facts, that could be a problem for those who don't read with a critical, or careful, eye.

Copyright © Cengage Learning. All rights reserved.

Check for Supporting Details

But textbook authors don't always include opinions they themselves are not conscious of sharing with readers. They also knowingly offer their opinions. Most facts in any situation, past or present, have to be interpreted to be meaningful to readers, so you shouldn't be surprised when the author of a textbook offers an opinion of the events described.

Here, for example, is another textbook excerpt. The authors open with an opinion about the American military's attempt to manage news during the first Gulf War. The word *spin* in the first sentence of the paragraph is a dead giveaway. It's doubtful that the military would consider their handling of the news to be an example of spin, which is a way of describing unpleasant events so that the events appear more positive or beneficial.

Note, however, that the opinion is not left unsupported. On the contrary, a specific example follows right on its heels. The presence of an illustration is important. Textbook authors should give readers the basis for their evaluations of events. It's a way of saying to readers, "Here's why I believe this."

Opinion

Support

Part of the strategy [during the first Gulf War] was to "spin" the news so that U.S. successes were emphasized and losses minimized. When announcing that eleven marines had been killed in action, for example, the military first showed twenty minutes of footage on Iraqi bridges and buildings being blown up, and the American deaths were treated virtually* as an afterthought. The strategy, which worked, was to force nightly news programs to divide their attention between the bad news—eleven killed at the outset of a potentially difficult ground war—and the good news—visually spectacular footage of a truck traveling across a bridge seconds before the bridge blew up. (Johnson et al., *American Government*, p. 354.)

The excerpts shown here and on page 508 should make it clear that opinions are not limited to the editorial pages of newspapers. They also turn up in textbooks. Therefore, you need to be alert to the ways an author can mix a personal point of view with factual discussions or descriptions.

When an author interprets, or offers an opinion on, the events or experiences described, you need to look for support of that interpretation.

*virtually: practically, nearly, almost.

Copyright © Cengage Learning. All rights reserved.

Most authors will provide it. If an author doesn't, it may be because the author is convinced that the interpretation requires no support.

Unfortunately, that's not an author whose ideas you want to unthinkingly accept. It may be that the author is letting a personal **bias**, or the preference for one point of view over another, artificially limit the number of ways a situation can be understood. That leaves you, the reader, only partially informed. If an author doesn't offer some support for an interpretation, or explanation of events, you shouldn't consider the author's explanation the final word on the subject.

◆ **EXERCISE 6**   **Detecting Textbook Opinions**

> **DIRECTIONS**   Read each textbook passage. Fill in the blank at the end with an *F* to indicate that the passage is purely factual or a *B* to indicate that opinions are blended in with the facts. Underline as well any words that you think give away the presence of opinions.

1. While well over 80 percent of the people vote in many European elections, only about half of the people vote in American presidential elections (and a much smaller percentage vote in congressional elections). Many observers blame this low turnout on voter apathy, or lack of interest, and urge the government and private groups to mount campaigns to get out the vote. But . . . voting is only one way of participating in politics. It is important (we could hardly call ourselves a democracy if nobody voted), but it is not all-important. Joining civic associations, supporting social movements, writing to legislators, fighting city hall—all of these and other activities are ways of participating in politics. It is possible that, by these measures, Americans participate in politics *more* than most Europeans—or anybody else for that matter. Moreover, it is possible that low rates of voter registration indicate that people are reasonably satisfied with how the country is governed. If 100 percent of all adult Americans registered and voted, . . . it could mean that people are deeply upset about how things are run. (Adapted from Wilson and DiIulio, *American Government*, pp. 145–46.)

———

2. Methaqualone was first synthesized in 1951 in India, where it was introduced as an antimalarial drug but found to be ineffective. At the same time, its sedating effects resulted in its introduction

Copyright © Cengage Learning. All rights reserved.

in Great Britain as a safe . . . sleeping pill. The substance subsequently found its way into street abuse; a similar sequence of events occurred in Germany and Japan. In 1965, methaqualone was introduced into the United States as the prescription drugs Sopors and Quaalude. It was not listed as a scheduled (controlled) drug. By the early 1970s, "ludes" and "sopors" were part of the drug culture. Physicians prescribed the drug for anxiety and insomnia, believing that it was safer than barbiturates. Thus the supplies for street sales came primarily from legitimate sources. (Adapted from Abadinksy, *Organized Crime*, p. 383.)

––––––

3. Author and pastor Charles Swindoll is credited with saying, "The longer I live, the more I realize the impact of attitude on life." Swindoll is convinced that attitude is more important than appearance, giftedness, or skill. For example, people who go through life with a positive mental attitude see daily obstacles as opportunities rather than roadblocks and are therefore more likely to achieve their personal and professional goals. People who filter daily experiences through a negative attitude tend to focus on what is going wrong and find it difficult to achieve contentment or satisfaction in any aspect of their lives. It makes no difference how attractive, intelligent, or skilled they are; their attitude holds them back. (Reece and Brandt, *Effective Human Relations in Organizations*, p. 149.)

––––––

4. Filipinos began settling in the Yakima River Valley around 1918–1920. The majority of those who settled there became agricultural laborers. By the late 1920s, there were many who worked on truck farms, in orchards, and in packinghouses. Some leased plots for independent farming. . . . If Filipinos were going to settle in the Yakima River Valley, they had to secure work within agriculture; Yakima was a single-economy region. By 1927, Filipinos had engendered the resentment of many whites who viewed them as competitive sources of labor. So deep was the anti-Filipino animosity that mob attacks took place the same year. Filipinos were attacked wherever vigilante groups encountered them. Some Filipinos were

Copyright © Cengage Learning. All rights reserved.

even assaulted in their homes, while others were forcibly rounded up and placed on outbound trains. (Chan et al., *Peoples of Color in the American West*, p. 243.)

———

 5. Most authorities agree that there is room for improvement in business ethics. A more problematic question is: Can business be made more ethical in the real world? The majority opinion on this issue suggests that government, trade associations, and individual firms indeed can establish acceptable levels of ethical behavior. The government can encourage ethical behavior by legislating more stringent regulations. For example, the landmark Sarbanes-Oxley Act of 2002 provides sweeping new legal protection for those who report corporate misconduct. . . . Among other things, the law deals with corporate responsibility, conflict of interest, and corporate accountability. However, rules require enforcement, and the unethical businessperson frequently seems to "slip something by" without getting caught. Increased regulation may help, but it surely cannot solve the entire ethics problem. (Pride, Hughes, and Kapoor, *Business*, p. 41.)

———

Opinions on the Web

As you know from pages 484–85, you should double-check any facts you locate on the Web. For different reasons, the same is true for opinions. After all, anyone can put an opinion on the Web. Just think of the many *Web logs*, or *blogs*, personal websites where people express their opinions on any range of topics from politics to movies.

Opinions on the Web aren't necessarily evaluated by anyone except the person holding them. This means that those opinions don't have to be informed by logic or research. On the Web, you will find people willing to express an opinion without even pretending to cite evidence or outline their logic. They feel they don't have to. Convinced of their own rightness, they often don't even acknowledge that someone else might hold a different opinion.

Copyright © Cengage Learning. All rights reserved.

How Expert Is an Amateur Web Expert?

Sadly, it's not just crackpots you should be worried about on the Web. Sometimes really knowledgeable and thoughtful people use the Web to express opinions that are not grounded in the latest or best evidence. To people who know even less than they do, their opinions might appear to be informed. But the truth is becoming an expert about a subject doesn't happen in a few days or a few months, it takes years of training, reading, and thought. Collecting information on the Web for six months or a year doesn't necessarily create trustworthy experts.

One of the best examples of how amateur Web experts—as opposed to people who have studied a subject in and out of school for years—can be completely wrong is recounted by Farhad Manjoo in his book *True Enough*. Manjoo describes a website that appeared to prove what had long been a rumor—that John Kerry, not George W. Bush, had actually won the state of Ohio in 2003. Much of the evidence provided for the claim was based on the fact that exit polls had showed Kerry winning by a large margin. How was it possible then that he had lost to George Bush? To people not especially knowledgeable about polling methods and records, this opinion seemed to have a solid basis in fact.

But when trained polling experts were consulted about this alleged fraud, it turned out that, as Manjoo states, "exit polls in the United States do not have a perfect record. They've been off before." According to one pair of long-time poll analysts, the Democratic vote had been overstated in Senate and gubernatorial races in 1990, 1994, and 1998. The experts Manjoo consulted knew this because they had been studying polling results for most of their professional lives. They hadn't become "experts" by collecting data from the Web for a year.

For information junkies, the Web is a perfect treasure trove of information. It can teach us a lot. But for getting informed opinions about topics that profoundly affect our lives, total reliance on the Web as opposed to all other sources might not be the best strategy for anyone to rely on, at least not yet.

If you find a controversial opinion on the Web that you think makes good sense, make sure it's coming from a long-time expert on the subject. Or at the very least, check the opinion with someone, on or off the Web, who has spent years, rather than months, studying the same subject.

Copyright © Cengage Learning. All rights reserved.

WORD CHECK

The following words were introduced and defined in pages 492–509. See how well you can match the words with the meanings. When you finish, make sure to check the meanings of any words you missed because the same words will turn up in tests at the end of the chapter.

1. naturalist _____
2. solicitation _____
3. pundits _____
4. abate _____
5. spatial _____
6. ordinance _____
7. beguiled _____
8. folklore _____
9. mystical _____
10. virtually _____

a. related to location in space

b. rule or regulation

c. fascinated, enchanted

d. beliefs, facts, traditions, knowledge, often with the implication of being informally learned or acquired

e. spiritual, mysterious

f. practically, nearly, very close to, almost

g. person who studies plants and animals in nature

h. the act of approaching someone for sexual or monetary purposes; also to persuasively ask for something other than money or sex, for instance votes or information

i. public sources of opinion, people who give an opinion through the mass media and who, allegedly, are knowledgeable about the topic discussed

j. cease, stop

◆ **EXERCISE 7**   **More About Form and Meaning**

DIRECTIONS   Fill in the blanks with one of the words listed below.

pundits	mystical	naturalist	beguiled	folklore
soliciting	abate	ordinances	virtually	spatial

Copyright © Cengage Learning. All rights reserved.

1. People newly in love find it easy to be _____ by one another; the trick is to have the same ability after twenty years together.

2. We don't want people whom we depend on for our safety, like firefighters and police officers, to be _____ competent; we want them to be completely competent.

3. You don't need to be a(n) _____ to know you should avoid sitting in poison ivy.

4. Architects have to be especially good at imagining different _____ relations among a variety of forms.

5. It seems that the more a town needs to raise money, the more _____ there are with financial penalties attached for not following or observing them.

6. How is it that so many political _____ can consistently get everything wrong yet still be seen on television every week being asked to give their opinion?

7. According to herbal _____, echinacea can reduce the length of the common cold.

8. Anyone with a toothache prays for it to _____.

9. The owners of the house received a letter _____ information about the former tenants.

10. People expect to have _____ feelings in places of worship, but similar feelings can also occur out of doors in the midst of nature.

Copyright © Cengage Learning. All rights reserved.

DIGGING DEEPER   Encouraging Ethical Behavior in the Corporate World

Looking Ahead   Here's the entire excerpt on how to encourage ethical behavior in business (p. 512). As you read, consider how many of the statements are fact, opinion, or a blend of both.

1   Most authorities agree that there is room for improvement in business ethics. A more problematic question is: Can business be made more ethical in the real world? The majority opinion on this issue suggests that government, trade associations, and individual firms indeed can establish acceptable levels of ethical behavior.

The Government's Role in Encouraging Ethics

2   The government can encourage ethical behavior by legislating more stringent regulations. For example, the landmark Sarbanes-Oxley Act of 2002 provides sweeping new legal protection for those who report corporate misconduct. At the signing ceremony, President George W. Bush stated, "The act adopts tough new provisions to deter and punish corporate and accounting fraud and corruption, ensure justice for wrongdoers, and protect the interests of workers and shareholders." Among other things, the law deals with corporate responsibility, conflicts of interest, and corporate accountability. However, rules require enforcement, and the unethical businessperson frequently seems to "slip something by" without getting caught. Increased regulation may help, but it surely cannot solve the entire ethics problem.

3   Trade associations can and often do provide ethical guidelines for their members. These organizations, which operate within particular industries, are in an excellent position to exert pressure on members who stoop to questionable business practices. For example, recently, a pharmaceutical trade group adopted a new set of guidelines to halt the extravagant dinners and other gifts sales representatives often give to physicians. However, enforcement and authority vary from association to association.

Individual Companies' Role in Encouraging Ethics

4   Codes of ethics that companies provide to their employees are perhaps the most effective way to encourage ethical behavior. A **code of ethics** is a written guide to acceptable and ethical behavior as defined by an organization. It outlines uniform policies, standards, and punishments for violations. Because employees know what is expected of them and

Copyright © Cengage Learning. All rights reserved.

what will happen if they violate the rules, a code of ethics goes a long way toward encouraging ethical behavior.

5   However, codes cannot possibly cover every situation. Companies also must create an environment in which employees recognize the importance of complying with the written code. Managers must provide direction by fostering communication, actively modeling and encouraging ethical decision making, and training employees to make ethical decisions.

6   During the 1980s, an increasing number of organizations created and implemented ethics codes. In a recent survey of Fortune 1000 firms, 93 percent of the companies that responded reported having a formal code of ethics. Some companies are now even taking steps to strengthen their codes. For example, to strengthen its accountability the Healthcare Financial Management Association recently revised its code to designate a contact person who handles reports of ethics violations, to clarify how its board of directors should deal with violations of business ethics, and to guarantee a fair hearing process. S.C. Johnson and Son, makers of Pledge, Drano, Windex, and many other household products, is another firm that recognizes that it must behave in ways the public perceives as ethical; its code includes expectations for employees and its commitment to consumers, the community, and society in general. (Pride, Hughes, and Kapoor, *Business*, pp. 41–42.)

Sharpening Your Skills

DIRECTIONS   Answer the following questions by circling the letter of the correct response or filling in the blanks.

1. Based on how it is used in this sentence, what do you think is a good approximate definition for the word *stringent*: "The government can encourage ethical behavior by legislating more stringent regulations" (paragraph 2)?

    _____

2. Why do the authors use the phrase "real world" in the second sentence of paragraph 1?

    _____

    _____

Copyright © Cengage Learning. All rights reserved.

3. What word do the authors use to implicitly evaluate the 2002 Sarbanes-Oxley Act?

_____

4. In your own words, what did the Sarbanes-Oxley Act accomplish?

_____

5. How might Walter Hickel (pp. 501–2) answer the question the authors pose in the opening paragraph of this reading: "Can business be made more ethical in the real world?"

_____

_____

6. Is the following statement a fact or an opinion: "Because employees know what is expected of them and what will happen if they violate the rules, a code of ethics goes a long way toward encouraging ethical behavior" (paragraph 4)? Please explain.

_____

_____

_____

7. Which of the following paragraphs better summarizes the reading?

a. There are three different ways that business ethics can be improved. The government can apply more stringent regulations. However, regulations need to be enforced, and some violators manage to never get caught. Trade associations can control the behavior of members. But if the control measures are too tough, they defeat the purpose of the trade association. Firms can also effectively police themselves through ethics codes, but it's not possible to have the company ethics code fit every situation, much as some companies may try to create one that does.

b. Government regulation and codes of ethics are the best ways to improve business ethics. Government regulations need to be strictly applied, and every effort must be made to catch and punish companies that violate the regulations. Ethics codes created and enforced by the company are probably the most effective way

Copyright © Cengage Learning. All rights reserved.

to improve business ethics. S.C. Johnson is a company that can serve as a model for others. It has a very detailed code that identifies what's expected of employees as well as what consumers expect of the company.

8. The following opinions appear in the reading. Which one is supported?

   a. Increased regulation may help, but it surely cannot solve the entire ethics problem.

   b. Because trade associations exist for the benefit of their members, harsh measures may be self-defeating.

   c. Some companies are now even taking steps to strengthen their codes.

9. Why do the authors mention Healthcare Financial Management Association in paragraph 6?

   _____

   _____

10. The authors are

    a. biased in favor of a particular method for improving business ethics.

    b. not biased in favor of any one method for improving business ethics.

    Please explain the basis for your answer.

    _____

    _____

    _____

Forming Your Own Opinion ◆

What do you think about the value of corporate codes of ethics? Do they offer an effective way of controlling corporate wrongdoing?

Copyright © Cengage Learning. All rights reserved.

▶ **TEST 1**　　　　**Reviewing New Vocabulary**

DIRECTIONS　　Fill in the blanks with one of the words listed below.

| naturalist | solicit | ordinances | beguiled | virtually |
| mystical | abate | pundits | lore | spatial |

1. In 2009 when a resident of Wishek, North Dakota, erected a 39-foot wind

   turbine[†] in his backyard, he was fined for violating city _____
   about structures erected in residential zones. The zoning laws said

   _____ restrictions needed to be carefully observed and
   the owner of the turbine had not done so. When the story broke,

   _____ on the right and left had a field day interpreting
   the events in Wishek. Those on the liberal left praised the man for "going
   green" and preserving the environment. Those on the conservative right
   insisted he was correct to assume he should be allowed to do whatever
   he wanted with his own property.

2. The American psychologist Abraham Maslow coined the term *peak*

   experiences to describe _____ moments in life when
   a person, for no apparent reason, feels an intense sense of happiness.

   Although peak experiences are quick to _____, Maslow
   thought that some individuals could learn to induce and control the
   sensation to make it longer lasting. These longer-lasting sensations
   of being deeply happy and in tune with the world he called "plateau

   experiences." Certainly a good deal of _____ from different
   cultures, myths, fairy tales, legends, and the like, suggests that Maslow was
   correct in assuming that such spiritual moments do not have to be fleeting.

3. **In Darwin's Shadow**

   Already as a young boy, the future _____ Alfred Wallace

   was _____ by the world of plants and animals. As a young
   man, he decided to travel to faraway places to gather plants, animals, and
   insects for wealthy collectors. Collecting specimens for those with the

   _____

   †turbine: a machine powered by wind and capable of generating electricity.

Copyright © Cengage Learning. All rights reserved.

money to pay his way was Wallace's only chance to do what he loved and still avoid ending up in one of England's notorious poorhouses.

While he was on his travels, Wallace thought at length about the variety in the related plants and creatures he collected. It didn't take

long before he came up with what was _____ the same theory Charles Darwin[†] had developed to explain how plants and animals evolved, or changed over time. Darwin, however, was in constant contact with the most famous scholars of his time, and he relied on their expertise and support. Wallace was working totally on his own. The one man he

did _____ for help was Darwin.

But that request only had the effect of making Darwin go forward with finally publishing his own theory and, in effect, laying claim to the discovery of *natural selection*, the mechanism which induced evolutionary change. That left Wallace to become the man who *almost* discovered the principle of evolution.

[†]Charles Darwin (1809–1882): the man credited with discovering the mechanism which propelled evolutionary change in everything from plants to humans.

Copyright © Cengage Learning. All rights reserved.

▶ **TEST 2**   **Distinguishing Between Fact and Opinion**

DIRECTIONS   Label each of the following statements *F* for fact, *O* for opinion, or *B* for a blend of both.

_____ 1. As George Orwell so correctly said, "The great enemy of clear language is insincerity."

_____ 2. Among people suffering from depression, one portion of the brain is significantly smaller than the other.

_____ 3. The planet Neptune was discovered in 1846 by the German astronomer Johann G. Galle.

_____ 4. The devastating flooding that overwhelmed parts of Tennessee in May 2010 did not get nearly the media attention such a disaster deserved.

_____ 5. The Mexican revolutionary Emiliano Zapata (1879–1919) had a profound influence on modern Mexico.

_____ 6. Louise Brown, the world's first test-tube baby, was born on July 25, 1978.

_____ 7. We should return to the days when films were made in black and white rather than color.

_____ 8. Iraq has the world's second-largest reserves of crude oil.

_____ 9. People who walk along the street with cell phones pressed to their ears are just trying to prove they have friends who want to talk to them.

_____ 10. According to the Centers for Disease Control and Prevention in Atlanta, Georgia, food-borne diseases cause approximately 325,000 hospitalizations and 5,000 deaths per year.

Copyright © Cengage Learning. All rights reserved.

Copyright © Cengage Learning. All rights reserved.

▶ **TEST 3**   **Checking for Relevance**

DIRECTIONS   Read each passage. Write *R* or *I* in the blank at the end. *R* indicates that all the facts and reasons are relevant. *I* indicates that you spotted one or more irrelevant facts or reasons.

1. Even though Elvis Presley died on August 16, 1977, he is certainly not forgotten. On the contrary, the legend of Elvis lives on. To honor the twentieth anniversary of his death, RCA released a four-volume CD set, *Elvis Presley Platinum: A Life in Music.* It was so popular that record stores couldn't keep it on the shelves. In honor of that same anniversary, more than fifty thousand fans descended on Graceland, Elvis's Tennessee home. In 1997 and 1998, the San José Ballet toured the country performing a ballet in the singer's honor, calling it *Blue Suede Shoes* after one of Presley's earliest and biggest hits. Sightings of Elvis continue to be reported to this day; in fact, an up-to-date list can be found at www.elvissightingbulletinboard .com. Anyone who needs further proof that for many "The King" lives on in memory need only type his name into a search engine and sit back to watch the results pile up to somewhere well over a million.

____

2. The label *organic* doesn't necessarily mean that food has been grown or raised without pesticides and human-made fertilizers. Currently, what's considered organic in one state may not be in another. Some states' certification programs allow organic produce to be grown with certain fertilizers and insecticides that other states specifically prohibit. Moreover, twenty states have no rules whatsoever governing organic food. "As it now stands, in an unregulated state there's nothing to stop some farmers from just sticking an organic label on their tomatoes, say, and putting them out for sale without ever having followed any organic principles," observes Katherine DiMatteo, executive director of the national Organic Trade Association. (Quotation from Jennifer Reid Holman, "Can You Trust Organic?" *Self*, November 1997, p. 163.)

____

3. Like Susan B. Anthony, Lucretia Mott, and Elizabeth Cady Stanton, Ernestine Rose was one of the founding members of American feminism; yet her name has barely made it into the history books. One reason for this omission may be that Rose was an outsider who fit none of the nineteenth-century patterns of American womanhood. Like Stanton, Rose was an eloquent speaker whose gift for words drew praise even from those who disagreed with her. After listening to Rose speak, the editor of the *Albany Express* in 1854 wrote, "Though we dissented much—very much—from what she said, yet we did admire her eloquence, her pathos,* her elocution. She spoke wonderfully well." Fellow abolitionists William Lloyd Garrison and Lucretia Mott admired her as well and paid no attention to the many attacks on her character made by those who despised her political beliefs. Susan B. Anthony kept a picture of Rose in her study. In an 1869 volume titled *Eminent Women of the Age*, no mention of Rose appears. (Source of information: Jacoby, *Freethinkers*, p. 102.)

4. Autism is a brain disorder that is generally diagnosed when a child is between the ages of one and three. As the disease takes its toll, victims have difficulties with speech, imaginative play, and interaction with others. Despite many claims to the contrary, the disease has become an epidemic. In a landmark 2007 case, some 4,800 petitioners sued the federal government, claiming that ordinary vaccinations against childhood diseases had caused their children to develop autism. As Roy Richard Grinker points out in his book, *Unstrange Minds: Remapping the World of Autism*, psychiatrists have broadened the definition of autism so that the term now applies to more people. Because more people have been included in the definition of the disease, it is also more widely known, making more child psychiatrists prepared to diagnose it. A 2004 study by the Institute of Medicine found no compelling evidence linking autism to childhood vaccines, but there are undoubtedly other environmental factors contributing to the epidemic that is claiming more and more victims. (Source of information: Monastersky, "Making Autism Familiar," *Chronicle of Higher Education*, May 11, 2007, pp. A-24–27.)

*pathos: sad or tragic feeling.

Copyright © Cengage Learning. All rights reserved.

▶ TEST 4   **Checking for Relevance**

DIRECTIONS   Read each passage. Write *R* or *I* in the blank at the end. *R* indicates that all the facts and reasons are relevant. *I* indicates that you spotted one or more irrelevant facts or reasons.

1. The penny still plays several necessary roles, so Americans should not eliminate this coin. First, rendering the penny obsolete would hurt those who have the least. Merchants would round up to the nearest nickel on cash purchases. Thus lower-income Americans, who conduct most of their business using cash, would wind up paying more. According to the nonprofit organization "Americans for Common Cents," rounding up to the nearest nickel will cost consumers an additional $600 million a year. Those who advocate keeping the penny also say that eliminating it would hurt charities because they collect millions of dollars in donated pennies. Finally, the penny should remain in circulation because Americans are fond of it. According to Americans for Common Cents, polls consistently show that up to 65 percent of Americans oppose getting rid of this coin.

    _____

2. Local, state, and federal governments violate citizens' right to privacy when they post public records on the Internet. Easy access to the personal information contained in voter-registration records, property-tax rolls, and court records should alarm every American. Putting such data online makes public records *too* public and it's much too easy to obtain personal information that should be kept private. Look how much trouble people have gotten into by putting photos and comments on Facebook. Some people have failed to get jobs because their prospective employers invaded their privacy and looked at their personal photos posted on Facebook. Some people have even lost their jobs because they used their Facebook page to insult their employers. That's why local and state governments should not improve the public's access to sensitive records by putting them online.

    _____

Copyright © Cengage Learning. All rights reserved.

3. In the United States, the ability to speak Spanish in addition to English offers numerous professional advantages. Currently over 45 million Hispanics reside in this country, and over the last decade, the number of Hispanic residents has doubled. In some states, Kansas, Texas, and California, for instance, Hispanics now account for almost half the population. Not surprisingly, then, the Spanish language has found a home in pop culture, turning up in music, films, and television and giving writers for the entertainment industry a leg up if they can speak Spanish and English. Speaking Spanish is also a tremendous asset in the workplace as increasing numbers of businesses seek to hire bilingual employees who can communicate with their Hispanic clients. Professionals who interact with the public on a daily basis—such as teachers, law-enforcement officers, firefighters, and medical personnel—are also in great demand if they are fluent in both English and Spanish.

───────

4. **Ex-Felons and the Right to Vote**

The laws that prohibit convicted felons who have served out their sentences from voting are both inconsistent and unfair. As the *New York Times* has pointed out, the laws vary significantly from state to state. In some states, for instance, felons on parole can't vote, but those on probation can. In other states, felons can apply to have their voting rights restored. However, local governments can, without giving a reason, deny the application. Unfortunately, the states that do restore felons' voting rights once their time has been served are not particularly efficient when it comes to notifying the men and women leaving prison about their rights.

Some supporters of Al Gore insist that the removal of former and alleged felons from the voter rolls in Florida tipped the 2000 election scales in the direction of George W. Bush. It's not surprising that several courts of appeals have ruled that taking away voting rights from those who have served time for a felony may well violate the Voting Rights Act of 1965.[†]

───────────────

[†]On August 6, 1965, President Lyndon Johnson signed into law legislation designed to protect voters from discrimination by state governments that placed restrictions, conditions, or limitations on voting rights.

Copyright © Cengage Learning. All rights reserved.

The courts of appeals are correct. Released prisoners have served their time. They have paid their debt to society. Disenfranchising them is not only undemocratic, it also completely undermines the notion that people who have committed a serious crime can be rehabilitated. In effect, the refusal to return the vote to those who have committed yet paid for a crime suggests that there is no such thing as an ex-felon. On the contrary, it suggests the opposite: Once a felon, always a felon. This is hardly the message we should be sending to those men and women struggling to once again become productive citizens.

———

5. Video bloggers, or vloggers, regularly record video diaries of their most intimate thoughts and feelings and put them on the Internet so that they can share them with the world. This is just one more example of what Professor Jean Twenge of San Diego State University has suggested in her study of today's college students: They belong to the most narcissistic generation in all of academic history. While college students of a decade ago were obsessing about whether all the good jobs were disappearing, these kids are obsessing about how many hits their video got on YouTube, the highly popular video-sharing site. Michael L. Wesch, an assistant professor of cultural anthropology at Kansas State University, has written a paper about social networking on the Web and, to test some of his ideas, he made a video and put it on YouTube. Within a few weeks, Wesch's video had had more than two million hits and was a testament to the way the Internet is changing how we communicate. Unfortunately, the Internet seems to be changing our notion of privacy as well, and more and more people are using it to discuss their childhood traumas along with their sexual triumphs and inadequacies. (Source of information about study concerning social networking and the Web: Jeffrey R. Young, "An Anthropologist Explores the Culture of Video Blogging," *Chronicle of Higher Education,* May 11, 2007, p. A42.)

———

Copyright © Cengage Learning. All rights reserved.

▶ **TEST 5**   **Taking Stock**

DIRECTIONS   Read the passage. Then answer the questions by filling in the blanks or circling the letter of the correct response.

Controversy Surrounding Saving the Manatees

1   Since 1967, the manatee, a gentle marine mammal that lives mainly in Florida waters, has been on the federal government's endangered species list. Yet between 1974 and 2002, biologists still counted as many as 4,673 manatee deaths. During that time, predictions that the manatee would soon become extinct prompted animal advocates, like members of the Save the Manatee Club and the Sierra Club, to insist on greater protections. Beginning in 1978, the Florida legislature responded by passing laws establishing areas where boating is banned or restricted, lowering boat speed limits in areas populated by manatees, and limiting permits for waterfront development. While these laws seem to have helped the manatees, they have also created conflict between environmentalists and some Florida residents who feel that their lifestyles and livelihoods have been adversely affected.

2   Initially, laws designed to protect manatees seem to have reduced the number of deaths. Manatees swim from the ocean into warmer rivers during the winter months. Therefore, many of them are injured or killed in collisions with boats. Limiting boaters' speeds and prohibiting them from entering areas where manatees tend to congregate appear to have lowered the mortality rate. In 1972, the first aerial population survey indicated that there might be only 600 to 800 manatees; several censuses in the 1990s, though, indicated that their numbers were somewhere between 1,500 and 2,500. In January 2001, a survey conducted by the Florida Fish and Wildlife Conservation Commission (FWCC) counted 3,300 manatees, far more than expected. In 2004, the FWCC counted 2,505 manatees and in 2006, 3,111.[†] By 2010, the count had climbed to 5,000.

3   But statistics like these, as it turns out, have only served as ammunition for those who advocated removing the manatee from the endangered species list and re-evaluating manatee protections. In 2006, for instance, despite vocal and widespread public opposition, the Florida Fish and Wildlife Conservation Commission voted to downgrade manatees

---

[†]The FWCC does not claim that the surveys provide an accurate picture of the manatee population or its chances of survival.

Copyright © Cengage Learning. All rights reserved.

from *Endangered* to *Threatened*. For groups like those represented on Savethemanatee.org, the decision amounted to a death warrant for the gentle creatures because "Threatened" status does not provide the same number of protections as "Endangered" does. The feeling was that the board was siding with those hoping to exploit the manatees' habitat for shoreline development and high-speed recreation.

4   That feeling was apparently shared by many Floridians, and a lot of them wrote letters to Florida's governor Charlie Crist. In response to the public outcry, Governor Crist stepped in and asked the FWCC board to postpone implementing the decision until new board members had had a chance to study the issue. When the board met again in December of 2007, it voted down the manatees' change in status.

5   But no one involved in the controversy over the manatees' status expects the issue to go away anytime soon. There are still those who see protection of the manatees as a hindrance to their personal freedom and financial well-being. In numbers at least, they are more than matched by those determined to make sure the manatees thrive and multiply, thanks to protections provided by their *Endangered* status. (Sources of quotations and statistics: Craig Pittman, "Fury Over a Gentle Giant," *Smithsonian*, February 2004, pp. 54–60; "Synoptic Surveys: 1991–2004," Save the Manatee Club, www.savethemanatee.org/population4a.htm.)

1. What question or questions based on the title could help you focus your reading?

   _____

   _____

2. In your own words, what is the main idea of the entire reading?

   _____

   _____

3. Based on the context, the word *hindrance* in paragraph 5 means
   a. help.
   b. obstacle.
   c. guarantee.
   d. erase.

Copyright © Cengage Learning. All rights reserved.

4. Which pattern(s) organize the details in the reading?
   a. definition
   b. sequence of dates and events
   c. comparison and contrast
   d. simple listing
   e. cause and effect

5. The first sentence in paragraph 1 is
   a. a fact.
   b. an opinion.
   c. a blend of fact and opinion.

6. The last sentence in paragraph 1 is
   a. a fact.
   b. an opinion.
   c. a blend of fact and opinion.

7. In the first sentence of paragraph 2, the word *seem* suggests
   a. a fact.
   b. an opinion.

8. The word *ammunition* in paragraph 3 suggests that the controversy over protecting the manatees
   a. is not emotionally charged.
   b. involves people who are generally friends with one another.
   c. has a degree of hostility.

9. In sentence 1 of paragraph 4, what does the phrase "that feeling" refer to?

   _____

   _____

   _____

Copyright © Cengage Learning. All rights reserved.

10. What do you think is the author's purpose?

    a. To describe the controversy surrounding legislation protecting the manatees.

    b. To persuade readers that the manatees need to be listed as *Endangered*.

    c. To persuade readers that developers and high-speed boaters should not be hindered in their pursuits by unnecessary legislation protecting the manatees.

Forming Your Own Opinion
◆

What do you think? Should Florida continue to protect the manatees or eliminate the protections that have increased their numbers?

Copyright © Cengage Learning. All rights reserved.

Focusing More on Purpose and Tone

9

© John E. Marriott/All Canada Photos/Corbis

IN THIS CHAPTER, YOU WILL LEARN

- why discovering the author's purpose is essential to critical reading.
- how the title and the source of a reading help you predict the writer's purpose.
- how thesis statements help you confirm or revise your prediction.
- how tone is linked to purpose.
- how to recognize an ironic tone.
- how to recognize the evidence of bias in informative writing.

Writers, whether they want most to be wealthy or wise, have specific purposes they hope to achieve by any piece or work. If they are skilled writers—that is, in control of what they write—they design each aspect of what they are writing to achieve their purpose.

—Charles Bazerman, *The Informed Writer*

Deciding if a piece of writing is meant primarily to inform or to persuade[†] is an essential part of critical reading. Sometimes an essay or article that starts with a seemingly informative purpose changes intention midway. That's because it's very common for writers intent on persuasion to provide background about an issue *before* mounting an argument.

A reader not attuned to signs of a mid-point change in purpose might well miss the shift, failing to notice how much opinion had gotten mixed into a supposedly informative explanation. It's also possible for a writer who intends mainly to inform to unthinkingly include some language or content that carries with it a point of view. When this happens, the purpose becomes more persuasive no matter what the author's original intent.

There's nothing wrong with that as long as readers are attuned to the author's occasional shift in purpose. Being attuned to the author's purpose will help you avoid making other people's opinions yours, without even realizing that you are doing it.

This chapter will give you several pointers on how to determine an author's purpose no matter how subtle or shifting it might be.

Make a Prediction About Purpose

The only way to truly identify an author's purpose is to read what he or she has to say from beginning to end. Still, even at the survey stage of reading, it's a good idea to try to determine what the author's **primary**, or central, purpose seems to be. That way you'll be quicker to notice when the writer's words either confirm or contradict the purpose you had initially predicted based on, for instance, the title. To get an idea of an author's purpose in the preliminary stages of reading, keep in mind the following.

The Source Is a Clue to Purpose

The source, or location, of a reading is often a good clue to purpose. Technical manuals, guidebooks, science texts and journals, reference books, dictionaries, reports of scientific experiments, and newspaper

---

[†]Most writing falls into three categories: (1) writing meant to inform, (2) writing designed to persuade, and (3) writing intended purely to entertain. Because this textbook focuses on critical reading issues, such as evaluating evidence and separating fact from opinion, it's solely concerned with the two purposes already introduced, informative and persuasive.

Copyright © Cengage Learning. All rights reserved.

accounts of current events are usually written to inform. Writing drawn from these sources generally does not promote any one particular point of view. It's more likely to offer an objective, or impersonal, account of both people and events.

However, writers are only human. Sometimes their feelings intrude, no matter what their intention. When this happens, a piece of writing, in, say, a reference work, may turn out to have some emotionally charged language or revealing details that suggest a persuasive intent. Skilled critical readers are quick to notice when elements of persuasion turn up in unexpected places.

Unlike the sources mentioned above, editorials, opinion pieces, and letters to the editor; as well as book, movie, and theater reviews in newspapers and magazines are all written to promote one particular point of view over other, competing points of view. The same applies to pamphlets published by political parties or special-interest groups, books and articles challenging or revising commonly held beliefs or theories, biographies of famous people, and journals promoting particular causes. All these sources are likely to feature persuasive writing.

The Author's Background Is Significant

Information about the author's background is not always available to you. But when it is, it can be a useful clue to purpose. For example, a government official who represents the U.S. Department of Health and Human Services and reports on the use of antibiotics in poultry raising is less likely to have a persuasive intent than the president of the New England Poultry Association. If a writer represents a group that could benefit from what he or she claims, then be prepared for a persuasive purpose and closely examine the author's reasoning as you read.

Titles Supply Clues to Purpose

Titles that simply describe a state of affairs—"Teamwork Used to Teach Math"—usually signal that the writer wants to inform readers without necessarily persuading them. Titles that express an opinion are quite a different matter. A title like "Teamwork and Mathematics Don't Mix" should immediately suggest to you that the author's primary purpose is persuasion.

Copyright © Cengage Learning. All rights reserved.

Sometimes, of course, the title is no help in determining the author's purpose. Titles like "A Look at the Nation" or "Family Affairs," for instance, reveal little about the author's purpose.

Emphasis on the Word *Primary*

There's a reason why the term *purpose* in this text is consistently modified by the word *primary*. As you already know, a writer who wants to persuade almost always has to inform as well.

Say, for instance, the writer of a newspaper editorial wants to persuade readers that giving money to failing auto companies on the verge of bankruptcy is a good idea. To make his point, he may start by informing readers about the contributions auto companies made to the middle-class standard of living during the 1950s before introducing his opinion.

Although it's not unusual for a writer to begin with what seems to be an informative purpose that blends into a persuasive one, the *primary purpose is the one writers end with*, not the one that guides the introduction. This is an important point. If a writer starts out offering pure information but then begins arguing an opinion, the *primary* purpose is persuasive, not informative.

Point of View Often Peeks Out of Informative Writing

Much as writers might want or need to abandon their personal point of view when doing informative writing, it's not always possible. Sometimes a point of view slips into their writing in single words, whole sentences, or even entire passages. There is nothing wrong with that as long as you are aware of it and don't absorb the point of view along with the information. (More on point of view in textbooks follows on pages 558–60.)

◆ **EXERCISE 1**   **Predicting the Author's Primary Purpose**

DIRECTIONS   What follows is a list of possible sources for written material. Next to each item on the list is a blank. Put a *P* in the blank if you think the source is likely to contain persuasive writing. Put an *I* in the blank if you think it's likely to contain informative writing.

Copyright © Cengage Learning. All rights reserved.

EXAMPLE

___P___ A blog about new technology written by a writer who also works for Apple Inc.

___I___ An explanation of cloud computing posted on Answers.com.

EXPLANATION Blogs used to be personal Web diaries, but they have expanded in number over the past five years and many companies promoting products have hired bloggers to encourage the growth of an online audience. Although it happens, it would be unlikely for a blog financed by a company to have a purely informative intent.

Answers.com is an online reference site drawn from many different sources. Because it answers questions posed by readers and draws its responses from numerous sources, it would be unlikely to have a persuasive purpose. Too many people contribute to the responses for that to be possible.

_____ 1. An article about Cuban leader Fidel Castro appearing on Biography.com

_____ 2. An article about Fidel Castro appearing on the front page of the *New York Times*

_____ 3. A biography of Fidel Castro published by *Cuba Socialista*, a magazine founded by Fidel Castro's supporters

_____ 4. A book titled *An Encyclopedia of American Architecture*

_____ 5. A government pamphlet titled *Historic Buildings in the Southern States*

_____ 6. A book review of a work titled *The Triumph of American Architecture*

_____ 7. A state manual explaining the rules of the road

_____ 8. A newsletter put out by Mothers Against Drunk Driving

_____ 9. A book titled *The Field Guide to North American Birds*

_____ 10. An article about the disappearance of songbirds appearing in a journal titled *Save the Earth Now*

Copyright © Cengage Learning. All rights reserved.

◆ **EXERCISE 2**   **Understanding the Relationship Between Title and Purpose**

DIRECTIONS   Read each pair of titles. If the title suggests the writer wants mainly to inform, put an *I* in the blank. If it suggests that the author wants mainly to persuade, put a *P* in the blank.

EXAMPLE

a. The Number of Charter Schools Has Doubled __I__

b. Charter Schools Are a Bad Answer to Declining Test Scores __P__

EXPLANATION   The first title simply describes a state of affairs without passing any judgment. The second title takes a stand. It indicates that the writer wants readers to share or at least consider an opinion.

1. a. Making a Case Against Assisted Death _____
    b. Assisted Death in the Netherlands _____

2. a. Support for Same-Sex Schools Is Increasing _____
    b. It Will Take More Than Same-Sex Schools to Get Rid of Gender Bias _____

3. a. Women Rise to the Challenge of Military Life _____
    b. Women in the Military _____

4. a. Astrology: The Science of Crackpots _____
    b. The History of Astrology _____

5. a. The American Classroom and Bilingual Education _____
    b. It's Time to Imitate the Swiss† _____

◆ **EXERCISE 3**   **Make the Title Reveal the Purpose**

DIRECTIONS   Try creating titles that express your intent. Make title *a* a statement that suggests an informative purpose. Make title *b* a statement that reveals your intention to persuade. The topic is provided for you.

Copyright © Cengage Learning. All rights reserved.

†The Swiss learn to speak four national languages.

EXAMPLE

Topic   Animal Rights

a. The History of the Animal Rights Movement in America

b. Animals Don't Have Rights; People Do

EXPLANATION   Title *a* suggests that the writer is describing the animal rights movement. Title *b* sounds as if the author wants to discourage support for the movement.

1. **Topic**   Women's Sports

    a. _____

    b. _____

2. **Topic**   School Prayer

    a. _____

    b. _____

3. **Topic**   Online Dating

    a. _____

    b. _____

4. **Topic**   Divorce

    a. _____

    b. _____

5. **Topic**   Cloning

    a. _____

    b. _____

The Main Idea Is Usually the Clincher

The title, source, and any available information about the author's background can frequently help you predict his or her purpose. But once you start reading, identifying the thesis statement or inferring the

Copyright © Cengage Learning. All rights reserved.

controlling main idea will tell you whether your initial prediction about purpose was accurate or in need of revision.

Main Ideas in Informative Writing

In informative writing, main ideas describe but do not judge or evaluate events, people, or ideas. In the following thesis statement, for instance, the writer describes the results of magnetic resonance imaging (MRI) studies. No attempt is made to link the studies to a value judgment.

> MRI studies have revealed huge spurts in brain growth in children between the ages of six and thirteen. These growth spurts appear in regions of the brain connected to language and spatial relationships.

Based on this thesis statement, which does not in any way interpret or evaluate the studies, experienced critical readers would assume the author intends to describe in more detail when the MRI studies took place, who conducted them, what they revealed, and what researchers think the studies suggest. In other words, the author's purpose is mainly informative.

Main Ideas in Persuasive Writing

Writers intent on persuasion will usually state or imply a main idea that identifies some action that needs to be taken, some belief that should be held, or some value judgment that should be shared. The following thesis statement is no exception:

> Recent research using magnetic resonance imaging (MRI) to study the growth and workings of the brain strongly suggests that the adolescent brain is *incapable* of exerting the same impulse control exhibited by adults. This means that adolescents who commit crimes are not receiving anything resembling justice if they are tried and sentenced as adults.

In this example, the author is using the MRI research to convince readers that they should share her view of what that research means for adolescents who go through the justice system. Her insistence that a particular point of view is the correct one makes the author's purpose persuasive.

Copyright © Cengage Learning. All rights reserved.

Look now at the next two thesis statements. Which one do you think suggests that the author's goal is to persuade? Put a *P* in the blank next to that statement.

_____ 1. Not one but a number of factors cause children to become obese, or seriously overweight.

_____ 2. Because obesity is a serious health problem, parents need to monitor their children's diet.

If you filled in the blank next to statement 2, you correctly recognized that the first statement did not encourage readers to pass any judgment or take any action. Statement 2, in contrast, suggests that readers should share the author's feelings about obesity in children—it's a serious health problem. It also encourages parents to act on those feelings by keeping a close watch on their children's diet. This kind of thesis statement is an important signal: It tells readers to look for and evaluate the author's evidence for such a claim.

CHECK YOUR UNDERSTANDING

What's the central difference between informative and persuasive main ideas, both stated and implied?

_____

_____

_____

Forming Your Own Opinion
◆

Do you believe that adolescents who commit violent crimes should be tried as adults? Please explain the basis for your opinion.

◆ **EXERCISE 4**   **Recognizing Informative and Persuasive Thesis Statements**

DIRECTIONS   Read each pair of thesis statements. Write an *I* in the blank if the writer intends mainly to inform. Write a *P* in the blank if the writer intends mainly to persuade.

Copyright © Cengage Learning. All rights reserved.

EXAMPLE

a. In the 1990s, lawsuits involving bias in the workplace tripled after the government enacted new antidiscrimination legislation.

    ___I___

b. In the United States, too many lawsuits are filed for frivolous reasons.

    ___P___

EXPLANATION   Statement *a* simply identifies an existing state of affairs, while statement *b* suggests a change is needed in the current state of affairs.

1. a. In spring, wildlife organizations often get calls to rescue abandoned fawns that someone has found huddled among bushes. Well-intentioned as these attempts at rescue are, they often do more harm than good and people should learn more about wildlife behavior before rushing to the rescue.

    _____

   b. Spring is the birthing season for deer, but once the fawns are born, the adults must leave them temporarily to forage for food. Thus what looks like maternal abandonment is actually a form of maternal caretaking.

© John E Marriott/All Canada Photos/Corbis

    _____

2. a. The Tuskegee Study of Untreated Syphilis in the Negro Male was begun in 1932, when the U.S. Public Health Service began tracking 399 black men with syphilis. The study's stated purpose was to chart the natural history of the disease without recourse* to any treatment, but the men recruited for the study were never told its true purpose.

    _____

   b. In May 1997, President Clinton apologized on behalf of the nation to the survivors of the Tuskegee Study of Untreated Syphilis in the Negro Male. But his apology can never erase the horrible stain the Tuskegee experiment left on America's history.

    _____

_____

*recourse: access to protection or aid; also the person or action providing help or aid.

Copyright © Cengage Learning. All rights reserved.

3. a. The study of working-class women by sociologists Elaine Wethington and Ronald Kessler has been widely discussed and highly publicized. However, when closely examined, it's clear that their work brings little or nothing new to the debate about women and work.

_____

   b. Sociologists Elaine Wethington and Ronald Kessler found that women who worked at low-wage, part-time jobs experienced more stress than women who worked full time.

_____

4. a. Radon, particularly combined with smoking, poses an important public health risk and should be recognized as such.

_____

   b. According to the Environmental Protection Agency, radon, a naturally occurring radioactive gas, which collects in many homes, is linked to more than 20,000 deaths annually from lung cancer.

_____

5. a. Now that scientists have found the hormone that triggers hunger, they should take the next step and discover how this hormone can be controlled. Such a discovery would be an enormous advance in the war against obesity.

_____

   b. Based on research at the University of Texas Southwestern Medical Center, scientists believe they have found the hormone that triggers feelings of hunger.

_____

INTERNET FOLLOW-UP: The Tragedy of Tuskegee
How long did the Tuskegee Syphilis Study last? Who was Peter Buxton?

www

_____

_____

_____

Copyright © Cengage Learning. All rights reserved.

Purpose and Figurative Language

Figurative language encourages the comparison of two seemingly unlike people, things, events, or ideas, which, when examined more closely, share an underlying similarity. The presence of figurative language in writing is a tip-off to purpose. The more figurative language present, the clearer it becomes that a writer's purpose is persuasive. Similes and metaphors are the most common kinds of figurative language used in persuasive writing.

Similes

A writer who uses a simile makes an overt comparison by using the word *like* or *as*. President Ronald Reagan's speechwriters were very good at creating easy-to-grasp similes that clarified concepts. This is precisely what a simile is supposed to do in an article or essay.[†] Here, for instance is how Reagan used a simile to clarify his theory of education:

> Education is like a diamond with many facets: It includes the basic mastery of numbers and letters that give us access to the treasury of human knowledge, accumulated and refined through the ages; it includes technical and vocational training as well as instruction in science.

For the president, comparing education to a diamond helped express his idea of education as training in many different subjects.

Similes were also a part of what made mystery writer Raymond Chandler such a terrific stylist. In one famous simile, he said that a character was "as crazy as two waltzing mice." In another well-known comparison, he said the character was about as "inconspicuous* as a tarantula on an angel food cake."

Metaphors

Like similes, metaphors make comparisons. They aren't, however, quite as easy to spot because they don't use the words *like* or *as*. In the following

---

[†]The use of similes is more complicated in poetry. Fortunately, this book is dealing with prose, where the simile is used to explain an idea that might otherwise remain unclear.
*inconspicuous: not readily noticeable.

Copyright © Cengage Learning. All rights reserved.

passage, writer and scholar Charles Bazerman tries to convince writers to take care in how they form their sentences. To make his point, he uses a metaphor. Can you identify the metaphor?

> If your sentences are carelessly formed, not only will the summary be unreadable, you will also lose the connection among the pieces of information in the summary. You could simply wind up with a tossed word salad. (Bazerman, *The Informed Writer*, p. 79.)

If you picked out the phrase "tossed word salad," you are correct. Bazerman is implying that writers who don't pay close attention to their sentences can end up with a summary that has no unity. Instead, the sentences in the summary will seem thrown or tossed together like the leaves of lettuce in a salad. They won't combine into a unified whole.

CHECK YOUR UNDERSTANDING

What does figurative language in persuasive writing do?

_____

_____

What's the central difference between a simile and a metaphor?

_____

_____

Explain the point of the simile in the following sentence: "Many parents complain that bringing home a first baby is like walking around with a dozen eggs on their head."

_____

What two things was Thomas Jefferson comparing in the following metaphor and what does the metaphor imply? "Slavery is a wolf America holds by the ears."

_____

_____

Copyright © Cengage Learning. All rights reserved.

TAKING A CLOSER LOOK

Figurative Language

In item 2(b) of Exercise 4 (p. 541), the author implicitly compares the Tuskegee experiments to what? _____ Is that a simile or a metaphor? _____ What point is the author making through this figure of speech?

_____

_____

_____

Pros *and* Cons

If you know the main idea and still have some doubt about the author's purpose, the attention the author gives to opposing points of view should be the deciding factor. Writers who want primarily to inform will usually describe the arguments for *and* against the main idea developed in the reading, and they won't evaluate either side.

Informative Writing
◆

- is found in textbooks, newspapers, lab reports, research findings, case studies, and reference works.

- uses a title that simply names or describes a topic or issue.

- includes a main idea that describes a situation, an event, a person, a concept, or an experience without making a judgment or offering an evaluation.

- relies more on denotative than connotative language.

- relies mainly on facts and gives opinions largely to illustrate what others think.

- takes an emotionally neutral tone.

- remains objective and reveals little or nothing about the author's personal feelings.

- includes pros and cons of the same issue.

Copyright © Cengage Learning. All rights reserved.

Writers intent on persuasion may well give you both sides. But they will usually tell you why the opposition's opinion is not quite as sound as it might seem at first glance. As soon as that happens, you know for sure that the writer's goal is persuasive.

Persuasive Writing ◆	• is found in newspaper editorials, political pamphlets, opinion pieces, and articles or books written to explain an author's position or theory about current or past events.
	• uses a title that suggests a point of view.
	• states or suggests a main idea identifying an action that needs to be taken or a belief that should be held—or, at the very least, considered.
	• often relies heavily on connotative language.
	• relies a good deal on opinion and uses facts mainly to serve opinions.
	• frequently employs a tone that conveys an emotion or attitude.
	• reveals the author's personal feelings and encourages a specific response from the audience (see pages 551–52).
	• often includes reasons for taking an action.
	• explains why arguments against the author's position are not sound.
	• often employs irony, or suggests the opposite of what is actually said (see pages 563–64).
	• uses rhetorical questions,† which expect no answers because the answer is obvious.
	• frequently uses figurative language.

---

†For example, What kind of person would harm an innocent child? Do you really want to see your property taken over by the town and your house torn down?

Copyright © Cengage Learning. All rights reserved.

✔ CHECK YOUR UNDERSTANDING Through Writing

What follows is a series of topics. Pick one and write two thesis statements on the same topic. One should suggest to readers the intention to inform. The other should suggest the intention to persuade. Feel free to come up with your own topics.

1. high heels

   _____

   _____

2. rescuing stray animals

   _____

   _____

3. privacy settings on Facebook

   _____

   _____

   _____

   _____

4. cyberbullying

   _____

   _____

ALLUSION ALERT

Holding the Trump Card
In the card game called bridge, the trump card outranks all the other cards. Thus anyone who holds the trump card has a winning hand. The allusion to someone holding the trump card is now used outside the context of bridge to describe someone who has an advantage, as in the following sentence, "Because she now held her husband's shares and her own, the president's widow was holding the trump card, and her expression said that she was enjoying every minute of her triumph."

Copyright © Cengage Learning. All rights reserved.

◆ EXERCISE 5 Identifying the Author's Purpose

> **DIRECTIONS** Read each selection. Then identify the purpose by writing an *I* or a *P* in the blank at the end.

1. Baby Preferences

1 In 1958, Robert Fantz placed babies on their backs in an enclosed, criblike chamber. Through a peephole, he and his colleagues observed how long the babies gazed at different visual stimuli inserted in the top of the brightly illuminated* chamber. Observers were able to determine where the infants were looking because the reflection of the stimulus could be seen on the cornea, the outer surface of the babies' eyes, as they looked at objects. Using this method, Fantz found that infants attended to some things longer than others. For example, babies one to six months old looked at disks decorated with bull's eyes, stripes, newsprint, or face-like figures far longer than at solid-colored circles.

2 The simple methodology encouraged many researchers to study the visual capacities of infants by observing their *preferential looking*, the tendency to look at some things more than others. The procedure has some limitations, however. What can we conclude, for example, when the infant attends to both members of a pair of stimuli for the same length of time? Is the infant unable to discriminate between the two, or does she prefer to look at one just as much as the other? Nor can we be certain what features the baby is processing when gazing at a stimulus.

3 Despite the limitations, babies often show preferences in what they attend to, and this simple procedure has proven enormously useful in assessing their visual capacities. . . . Such procedures have revealed, for example, which features of a human face infants are most likely to focus on. (Adapted from Bukatko and Daehler, *Child Development*, p. 198.)

———

2. Was the Bomb Necessary?

1 At first, there was only wonder that one bomb could destroy a city. Within a year, when, in *Hiroshima*, novelist John Hersey detailed the horrors the people of that city suffered, some Americans began openly to question if dropping the atomic bombs had been necessary. President Truman insisted that it had been, to avoid a million American

---

*illuminated: lit, shining, made understandable, clarified.

Copyright © Cengage Learning. All rights reserved.

casualties (and several million Japanese casualties) that the invasion of Japan would have meant.

2   Could not the Japanese have been persuaded to surrender, critics asked, by demonstrating the power of the bomb on an uninhabited island as Secretary of War [Henry L.] Stimson suggested? Truman's defenders replied that no one was sure that the bombs would work. An announced demonstration that fizzled would have encouraged diehards to hold on.

3   Decades later, historians known as revisionists said that "Little Boy" and "Fat Man" were dropped not primarily to end the war with Japan but to inaugurate* the Cold War with the Soviet Union. Truman cynically slaughtered the people of Nagasaki and Hiroshima as a way to put the Russians on notice that the United States held the trump card in any armed conflict between them. Their critics responded that there was no hard evidence that Truman's anti-Soviet sentiments, which were strong enough, had anything to do with his decision to use the atomic bombs. The simplest explanation of the event—he did it to end the war quickly—was the correct explanation.

4   The debate has not ended. (Conlin, *The American Past*, p. 716.)

---

3. Is There a Male and a Female Style?

1   In the summer of 2003, . . . three Israeli computer scientists fed 604 current texts—half written by men, half by women—into a computer. When they crunched the numbers, they emerged with an algorithm† that, they claimed, could predict the gender of any text's author with 80 percent accuracy. The formula is based on word use. Certain words seem to come more frequently to men and women, respectively. The biggest single difference is that women use personal pronouns far more often than men, who in turn are partial to determiners (*a*, *the*, *that*, and *these*), numbers, and quantifiers such as *more* and *some*. *With*, *if*, and *not* are heavily female words; *around*, *what*, and *are* are male.

2   It seems a little kooky, but it seems to work. I know that because a website (www.bookblog.net/gender/genie.html) allows anyone to type or paste in any text of 500 words or more, indicate whether it is fiction, nonfiction, or a blog entry, and have it instantly analyzed according to the algorithm, including a numerical account of the usage of the key words. Then you are asked to indicate if the computer was right or wrong, allowing it to keep a running tab of the results.

---

*inaugurate: start, begin, open.
†algorithm: a mathematical formula or procedure that can be used to solve a problem.

Copyright © Cengage Learning. All rights reserved.

3 When I last checked, more than 110,000 samples had been submitted, and the correct answer had been given 75.67 percent of the time. I'm not surprised by the 110,000 figure because this is seriously addictive. I started entering texts that I pulled from the Web at random—the first chapters of Willa Cather's *O Pioneers!*, Herman Melville's *Moby-Dick*, George Eliot's *Middlemarch*, and an F. Scott Fitzgerald short story called "The Baby Party." The only one the computer got wrong was the Fitzgerald story, evidently because of the author's frequent use of the "feminine" words *with* and *and*.[†]

(Adapted from Yagoda, *The Sound on the Page,* 76.)

Tone and Purpose

Once you have begun reading and can confirm or revise the purpose you first predicted, you should also try to determine the author's tone. **Tone** in writing, like tone of voice in speech, is the emotion, attitude, or feeling evoked by the author's words, style, and selection of detail.

The easier it is to detect a tone in writing, the clearer it is that the writer's purpose is persuasive. Writers who have an informative purpose, generally speaking, use a limited range of tones, from completely **neutral**, or devoid of all personal opinion and connotative language, to relaxed and friendly. But informative writing will not convey a passionate, cynical, or worried tone. If it does, then the writer's intention is to persuade, not inform.

Tone, Persuasion, and Bias

If identifying tone doesn't play an enormous role in reading informative writing, the opposite is true for persuasive writing, where tone can help readers evaluate how much of a role **bias**, or personal preference, plays in the author's presentation of information. Specifically, tone can indicate how trustworthy the writer is when it comes to citing facts, describing opposing points of view, or paraphrasing experts and events accurately. It can also indicate when bias has become so excessive that it is no longer a preference. Tone can often tell you when a preference has turned into a prejudice that prevents the writer from fairly evaluating opposing points of view.

[†]The site still exists. It's called "The Gender Genie." In my case, it wasn't much of a genie though. It tagged me as male. See if it correctly guesses your gender from your writing.

Copyright © Cengage Learning. All rights reserved.

If the author's tone is bossy or overbearing, you probably need to hold off agreeing until you have double-checked the writer's factual evidence, statements about opposing points of view, and claims about what the experts say. A bossy, how-could-anyone-think-otherwise tone suggests that the writer may be too prejudiced to be fair. The author of the following excerpt, for instance, could use some extra scrutiny, or double-checking, on the reader's part.

> No one who knows anything about horses could think otherwise; horse racing is not a barbaric sport. Horses love to run. Those who say that horse racing is animal cruelty are speaking theoretically and have no experience with the animals themselves. What they know about horses probably came from watching old-fashioned westerns on television.

While double-checking what an author says never hurts, you can probably relax your vigilance a bit with a writer whose tone suggests an openness to opposing points of view:

> I take seriously the worries expressed by those who believe that censoring individual speech harms free speech in general. Nevertheless, I am uncomfortable guaranteeing the right to spew hate and bigotry. True, such language might not provoke any immediate threat, but it probably paves the way for future ones, and that concerns me.

Some writers may well earn your trust from the way they employ tone to persuade, but others should arouse your skepticism.

Thinking About Tone from the Writer's Perspective

From the writer's perspective, tone is a device used to shape or influence audience response.[†] For instance, a writer who wants you to share his or her opinion may consciously assume a folksy, we-share-the-same-values tone, for example:

> We all know what it's like to feel that we have been left in the lurch by those we think we can trust. All you have to do, then, to understand the feelings of people standing knee to neck deep in water during

---

[†]I'm limiting the function of tone here because we are dealing with writing meant to inform or to persuade. In personal essays, there is another dimension of tone: It is a way of consciously revealing the author's internal state.

Copyright © Cengage Learning. All rights reserved.

Hurricane Katrina is to multiply that feeling by a hundred, because that's how the inhabitants of New Orleans felt when local and federal officials were slow to pitch in and save not just their city but the lives and property of the people in it.

Then again, a writer who wants mainly to inform but who knows she is addressing a controversial topic about which people feel passionate may consciously take on a neutral tone. Not only does a neutral tone betray absolutely no sense of the writer's point of view, or personal perspective, it also avoids any connotative language that might affect the reader emotionally. The goal of the neutral tone is to keep the reader receptive to information but totally unprejudiced by an emotional reaction; for example,

> A financial instrument called credit default swaps (CDS) played a large role in the financial problems that emerged in the United States during 2008. A credit default swap is a form of insurance in which the seller of the swap insures the bond or loan of the buyer. Should the bond or loan default or lose money, the seller will pay the buyer the value of the insurance. CDSs have existed since the 1990s, but their popularity increased greatly starting in 2003. Because credit default swaps were, until 2010, largely unregulated, there was no way to ensure that the seller of the swap could repay a buyer who lost money on a loan or bond. When many mortgage loans failed in 2008, buyers who owned CDSs on mortgage-based funds turned to the seller for the money owed them, based on their original agreement. But in some cases the sellers of the CDSs did not have the funds on hand to make the payment. This had a huge, negative effect on the economy.

Starting in 2008, the U.S. economy went into a tailspin, and many people lost homes and jobs. The causes of that tailspin are bound to evoke an emotional reaction. But here you see the author trying to avoid the emotional response by keeping the tone as denotative or neutral as possible.

A Writer's Tone Consists of Many Different Elements

Tone is the result of many different choices made by the writer. Decisions about sentence length, word choice, references to the audience, expressions of personal preferences, type of grammar (formal or informal),

Copyright © Cengage Learning. All rights reserved.

selection of detail, use of figurative language, and choice of imagery, among other things, all contribute to a writer's tone.

These ingredients can be mixed and matched in numerous ways to create any number of tones, some of which are listed here.

A Range of Tones Writers Can Use ◆		
admiring	humorous
amused	insulted
angry	insulting
annoyed	ironic
anxious	joyful
appalled	mistrustful
astonished	neutral
awed (filled with wonder)	nostalgic (looking fondly toward the past)
bullying	
cautious	outraged
confident	passionate
contemptuous	playful
critical	puzzled
cynical	regretful
disgusted	sad
disrespectful	sarcastic
dumbfounded (very surprised)	shocked
	solemn
embarrassed	soothing
engaged (deeply involved)	sorrowful
enthusiastic	sure
generous	surprised
horrified	trusting

Copyright © Cengage Learning. All rights reserved.

CHECK YOUR UNDERSTANDING Through Writing

The writer of the following passage employs a neutral tone. Please rewrite it using a different tone.

> In April 2010, a German shepherd dog was found locked in a garage after a passerby who knew of his existence saw the dog and brought him to an emergency veterinary clinic. The adult dog, named Bosco, weighed only thirty-seven pounds. He was weak from hunger and could neither walk nor lift his head. When alerted of his condition, the German Shepherd Rescue of Orange County, California (GSROC), offered to care for the dog, who was renamed Courage. Courage required emergency care, which included blood and plasma transfusions, along with antibiotics and a complete flushing of his intestinal tract. The dog survived and gained thirty pounds. By May he was behaving like a normal dog, and a member of the GSROC had adopted him. The dog's owner was arrested for animal cruelty.

◆ **EXERCISE 6**   **Recognizing Tone**

DIRECTIONS   After reading each selection, circle the letter of the word or phrase that best fits the author's tone.

EXAMPLE   Jazz singer Ella Fitzgerald was a quiet and humble woman who experienced little of the love she sang about so exquisitely for more than fifty years. Her voice, even in later years when she suffered from crippling arthritis, was always filled with a clear, light energy that could set the toes of even the stodgiest* listeners tapping. Although Fitzgerald, an African American, came of age in an era when racism was rampant, whatever bitterness she felt never spilled over into her music. She sang the lyrics of a white Cole Porter or a black Duke Ellington with the same impossible-to-imitate ease and grace, earning every one of the awards heaped on her in her later years. When she performed with Duke Ellington at Carnegie Hall in 1958, critics called Fitzgerald "The First Lady of Song." Although she died in 1996, no one

---

*stodgiest: most overly proper, stuffy, lacking in life or energy.

Copyright © Cengage Learning. All rights reserved.

has come along to challenge her title, and Ella Fitzgerald is still jazz's first lady.

Tone   a. coolly annoyed
        (b.) enthusiastic and admiring
        c. neutral

> **EXPLANATION**   Throughout the passage, the author describes Ella Fitzgerald in strong, positively charged language, creating an enthusiastic and admiring tone that encourages readers to share the admiration. The purpose, therefore, is persuasive.

1. There is something happening here. The Net Generation has come of age. Growing up digital has had a profound impact on the way this generation thinks, even changing the way their brains are wired. And although this digital immersion* presents significant challenges for young people—such as dealing with a vast amount of incoming information or ensuring balance between the digital and physical worlds—their immersion has not hurt them overall. It has been positive. The generation is more tolerant of racial diversity and is smarter and quicker than their predecessors. These young people are remaking every institution of modern life, from the workplace to the marketplace, from politics to education, and down to the basic structure of the family. (Tapscott, *Grown Up Digital*, p. 10.)

Tone   a. neutral
        b. heated
        c. enthusiastic

2. In January 2002, I was asked to give an opening talk and performance for the National Association of Music Merchants, the annual trade show for makers and sellers of musical instruments. What I did was create a rhythmic beat by making the most extreme funny faces I could in quick succession. A computer was watching my face through a digital camera and generating varied . . . percussive† sounds according to which funny face it recognized each moment. . . . This is the sort of deceptively silly event that should be taken seriously as

---

*immersion: deep involvement, concentration, also the physical act of sinking into water.
†percussive: related to sound vibrations created by two objects hitting one another.

Copyright © Cengage Learning. All rights reserved.

an indicator of technological change. In the coming years, pattern recognition tasks like facial tracking will become commonplace. On one level, this means we will have to rethink public policy related to privacy, since hypothetically* a network of security cameras could automatically determine where everyone is and what faces they are making, but there are many other extraordinary possibilities. (Lanier, *You Are Not a Gadget*, pp. 158–59.)

Tone
   a. confident

   b. concerned

   c. neutral

3. As a mail carrier for more than twenty years, I can tell you firsthand that we are much maligned members of the population. Customers see only the flaws in mail delivery. They never appreciate the huge effort that makes service both speedy and efficient. For an absurdly small price, you can send mail anywhere in the country, from Hawaii to Alaska. You'd think this would impress most people, but no. Instead of thanking us for services rendered, they whine and complain about the few times mail gets lost. And just because a few members of the postal service have engaged in violent behavior, people now use the rude expression *going postal* to refer to unexpected outbreaks of violence brought on by stress. This phrase unfairly insults the rest of us hardworking employees who do our jobs without complaint day in and day out.

Tone
   a. comical

   b. insulted

   c. neutral

4. In his book *An Anthropologist on Mars*, the renowned neurologist† Dr. Oliver Sacks gives readers an important and insightful perspective on injuries and disorders of the brain. According to Dr. Sacks, some injuries and disorders result in greater creativity and achievement. Dr. Sacks describes, for example, a painter who becomes color blind through a car accident. Initially in despair, the painter eventually starts painting stunning black-and-white canvases that win him more critical acclaim than he had received before his mishap. As

---

*hypothetically: in theory, theoretically.
†neurologist: a doctor who specializes in the workings and diseases of the nervous system.

Copyright © Cengage Learning. All rights reserved.

in his previous works, Dr. Sacks offers readers an unexpected and unusual perspective on disease and injury. In *An Anthropologist on Mars*, he once again makes us rethink and reconsider our most cherished beliefs about health and illness. His book should be required reading for anyone interested in the power of human beings to adapt to and ultimately overcome loss.

Tone
    a. admiring
    b. neutral
    c. cautious

5. In 1999, the world champion of chess, Garry Kasparov, agreed to play against the entire world. The game was played on the Internet, with the World Team's decision coming as a result of majority or plurality vote. Four young chess experts were asked to suggest possible moves, but the world was entitled to do as it wished. To promote extended thinking, moves were slowed down to permit one move every two days. Before the game began, it was widely expected that Kasparov would win easily. How could the majority or plurality view of the world's players, almost none of them anywhere near Kasparov's level, hope to compete with the world's champion? But the game turned out to be exceptionally close. After four gruelling months, Kasparov ultimately prevailed. But he acknowledged that he had never expended as much effort on any game in his life. (Sunstein, *Infotopia*, p. 22.)

Tone
    a. cautious
    b. sad
    c. neutral

TAKING A CLOSER LOOK

Balancing Fact and Opinion

There are seven sentences in the first paragraph of Exercise 6 on page 555. How many of those sentences are opinion and how many are fact?

_____

Do you think the author makes his case convincingly?

_____

_____

Copyright © Cengage Learning. All rights reserved.

Considering Textbook Neutrality

The following passage is from a textbook, where many of us expect an informative purpose and a completely neutral tone. This passage fits both expectations.

> Two factors in the development of obesity in children are beyond human control. These two factors are heredity and age. Like it or not, thinness and fatness do run in families. Overweight children tend to have overweight parents. Underweight children tend to have underweight parents (LeBow, 1994). In addition, most people inevitably* put on more fat during certain periods of life than during others. Late childhood and early puberty form one of these periods. At this time, most children gain fat tissue out of proportion to increases in other tissues, such as muscle and bone. (Seifert and Hoffnung, *Child and Adolescent Development*, p. 390.)

In this passage, the authors describe two factors in obesity that are beyond human control. Nothing in their choice of language, imagery, or details suggests any preference of prejudice in favor of a particular theory, opinion, or point of view. Their tone is completely neutral with no suggestion of any bias.

Complete Neutrality Is Hard to Come By

But maintaining an absolutely neutral tone is more difficult than you might think. Leaf through different textbooks covering the same material and you'll realize that informative writing is not always accompanied by a tone as purely neutral as the one shown above.

Even textbook authors who mainly want to inform you of events rather than convince you to share any specific point of view sometimes use language that is more connotative than denotative. Or else they choose details that encourage one point of view over another. In other words, their tone reveals a bias, despite their informative purpose.

True, textbook bias doesn't ever reach the level of a blind prejudice. But without realizing it, textbook authors do frequently imply a personal preference for one interpretation over another. Compare, for instance, these two excerpts on the Taft-Hartley Act and Truman's response to it.

---

*inevitably: unavoidably.

Copyright © Cengage Learning. All rights reserved.

Each comes from a different textbook. Each one has a slightly different slant on both the legislation and the president.

[In the late forties], the growing muscle of organized labor deeply annoyed many conservatives. They had their revenge against labor's New Deal gains in 1947, when a Republican-controlled Congress (the first in fourteen years) passed the Taft-Hartley Act over President Truman's vigorous veto. Labor leaders condemned the Taft-Hartley Act as a "slave-labor law." It outlawed, the "closed"† (all union) shop, made unions liable for damages that resulted from jurisdictional disputes among themselves, and required union leaders to take a non-communist oath. Taft-Hartley was only one of several obstacles that slowed the growth of organized labor in the years after World War II. (Kennedy, Cohen, and Bailey, *The American Pageant*, pp. 910–11.)

Among the most critical vetoes cast by Truman and overridden by Congress was the Taft-Hartley Act. The Taft-Hartley Act, passed in June 1947, was a clear victory for management over labor. It banned the closed shop, prevented industry-wide collective bargaining, and legalized state-sponsored right-to-work laws that hindered union organizing. It also required that union officials sign affidavits* that they were not Communists. Echoing Truman's actions in the coal strike, the law also empowered the president to use a court injunction to force striking workers back to work for an eighty-day cooling-off period. Privately Truman supported much of the bill and cast his veto knowing it would be overridden. He also knew his veto would help "hold labor support" for his 1948 run for the presidency. (Berkin et al., *Making America*, p. 800.)

Paragraph 1 supplies more context for the Taft-Hartley Act—it was a vengeful backlash against the increasing power of the labor movement. Paragraph 2 makes the act a straightforward victory of management over labor. There's no indication that the authors think it was an attempt to diminish the gains of the labor movement.

Note as well how the author of paragraph 1 cites Truman's "vigorous veto," which suggests the authors believe Truman was strongly against the legislation. The authors of paragraph 2, however, include a detail that suggests Truman actually supported the legislation. According to

---

†closed shop: When a company employs a union that insists on a closed shop, non-union people cannot be employed there.
*affidavits: written statements of fact, made under oath, and signed by the author.

Copyright © Cengage Learning. All rights reserved.

this paragraph, he only cast the veto to win the support of labor in the next presidential election.

Textbooks, reference works, and newspaper reports might well pass on value judgments embedded in the writer's choice of language and detail. There's nothing wrong with that as long as you are attuned to the language and content that suggests a critical or an admiring point of view, mixed into what is, for the most part, informative writing.

ALLUSION ALERT

The Magna Carta
In 1215, King John of England signed a document widely viewed as one of the most important in the history of democracy. The Magna Carta bound the king and his heirs to grant certain civil rights and liberties to all free men. When the Magna Carta is used as an allusion, it signifies a great advance in democratic freedom—for instance, "For the feminists meeting at the Seneca Falls convention in 1848, the Declaration of Sentiments read at the meeting was as important to feminism as the Magna Carta was to democracy."

◆ **EXERCISE 7**   **Evaluating Neutrality in Textbook Writing**

DIRECTIONS   For each pair of selections, decide if the passage is neutral in tone or reveals a point of view. Then write *N* or *P* in the blank at the end. *Note*: Both passages might be neutral or both might reveal a personal point of view or bias. Don't automatically assume that one is neutral and the other not.

1. a. [During World War II, the Navajo language] was an attractive choice for code use because few people outside the Navajo nation had ever learned to speak the language. Virtually no books in Navajo had ever been published. Outside of the language itself, the Navajo spoken code was not very complex by cryptographic† standards and would likely have been broken if a native speaker and trained cryptographers worked together effectively. The Japanese had an opportunity to attempt this when they captured

---

†cryptographic: related to coded writing.

Copyright © Cengage Learning. All rights reserved.

Joe Kieyoomia in the Philippines in 1942 during the Bataan Death March. Kieyoomia, a Navajo Sergeant in the U.S. Army, but not a code talker, was ordered to interpret the radio messages later in the war. However, since Kieyoomia had not participated in the code training, the messages made no sense to him. When he reported that he could not understand the messages, his captors tortured him. Given the simplicity of the alphabet code involved, it is probable that the code could have been broken easily if Kieyoomia's knowledge of the language had been exploited more effectively by Japanese cryptographers. The Japanese Imperial Army and Navy never cracked the spoken code. (Excerpted from Wikipedia.)

———

b. About 420 Navajo Indians served with the Marines in a unique capacity. In the heat of combat, the code talkers handled radio communications between units by speaking in Navajo in code. They could transmit in twenty seconds a message that, by machine code, took a half hour. The Marines selected Navajo because it was unwritten and extremely difficult. In 1942, there were only thirty non-Navajos who could converse in it. The code talkers made their messages unintelligible to other Navajos, which proved to be a good thing: The Japanese deduced that they were dealing with a Native American language and among their Indian prisoners of war was a Navajo who had been captured on Bataan. He, however, could make no sense of it. (Conlin, *The American Past*, p. 716.)

———

2. a. When the Supreme Court axed the blue eagle,[†] a Congress sympathetic to labor unions undertook to fill the vacuum. The fruit of its deliberations[*] was the National Labor Relations Act of 1935, more commonly known as the Wagner Act, after its Congressional sponsor New York Senator Robert F. Wagner. This trailblazing law created a powerful new National Labor Relations Board for administrative purposes and reasserted the right of

———

[†]The blue eagle was the symbol of the National Industrial Recovery Act. Companies that were complying with it displayed the blue eagle on their products. The Supreme Court abolished the compulsory coding system.
[*]deliberations: acts of careful and concentrated thinking.

Copyright © Cengage Learning. All rights reserved.

labor to engage in self-organization and to bargain collectively through representatives of its own choice. Considered the Magna Carta of American labor, the Wagner Act proved to be a major milestone for American workers. (Kennedy, Cohen, and Bailey, *The American Pageant*, p. 841.)

———

b. The Second Hundred Days [of the Roosevelt Administration] also responded to organized labor with the passage of the National Labor Relations Act (NLRA) in 1935. Largely the work of Senator Robert Wagner, and called the Wagner Act, it strengthened unions by putting the power of government behind workers' right to organize and to bargain with employers for wages and benefits. It created the National Labor Relations Board to ensure workers' rights—including their right to conduct elections to determine union representation—and to prevent unfair labor practices such as firing or blacklisting workers for union activities. The act had its limitations. It excluded many non-unionized workers as well as those in agriculture and service industries. Despite its limitations, the NLRA altered the relationships between business, labor, and the government and created a source of support for workers within the executive branch. (Berkin et al., *Making America*, p. 735.)

———

INTERNET FOLLOW-UP: Joe Kieyoomia's Ordeal
What did his Japanese captors do to try to make Joe Kieyoomia break the code for them?

www

_____

_____

_____

_____

Copyright © Cengage Learning. All rights reserved.

Irony and Persuasion

No discussion of tone or persuasion would be complete without some mention of **irony**—the practice of saying one thing while implying exactly the opposite. This might sound confusing at first, but, like most of us, you've probably used irony more than once in your life. Haven't you ever had a really horrible day and said to someone, "Boy, what a great day this was!" Or, seeing a friend wearing a sad expression, maybe you said, "Gee, you look happy."

If either of these examples sounds familiar, then you know more about irony than you think. Thus you're well prepared for writers who assume an ironic tone like the one used in the following passage.

> The school board has decided to reduce the school budget once again. But why take half measures? Why not eliminate the budget altogether and close our schools? After all, a little learning is a dangerous thing. Better to keep our children totally ignorant and out of harm's way.

The author of this paragraph doesn't want his readers to take what he says *literally*, or at face value. After all, who would seriously suggest that keeping children ignorant is a good idea? The author's point is just the opposite of what he actually says. He doesn't want the school budget further reduced. But instead of saying that directly, he makes an outrageous suggestion that draws attention to where the cuts could lead.

When writers present what seems to be an outrageous or impossible opinion as if it were obvious common sense, critical readers assume the writer is being ironic, and they respond by inferring a message directly opposed to the author's actual words. As you might expect, *an ironic tone is a good indicator of a persuasive purpose.*

Copyright © Cengage Learning. All rights reserved.

✔ CHECK YOUR UNDERSTANDING

What is irony?

_____

_____

_____

_____

◆ **EXERCISE 8** **Identifying Tone in Persuasive Writing**

DIRECTIONS Read each passage and circle the letter that best identifies the author's tone.

1. According to the American Association of Furriers, wearing fur coats is once again back in fashion. Now that's good news for the thousands of mink, rabbits, foxes, and raccoons that are brutally slaughtered so that fashionable men and women can sport a trendy fur coat or hat. No doubt these animals are honored to suffer and die for the sake of humans' vanity.

Tone   a. anxious

          b. comical

          c. neutral

          d. ironic

2. When the voters of Michigan sent Charles Diggs Jr. to the U.S. House of Representatives in 1954, he became the first black congressman in the state's history. He was not, however, the first black congressman in the United States. During the period of Reconstruction, from 1865 to 1877, the U.S. government tried to rebuild the South after the political and economic destruction caused by the Civil War. Black citizens held prominent government positions throughout the

Copyright © Cengage Learning. All rights reserved.

nation, including the posts of mayor, governor, lieutenant governor, state Supreme Court justice, U.S. senator, and U.S. congressman. (Williams, *Eyes on the Prize*, p. 49.)

Tone

a. outraged

b. lighthearted

c. neutral

d. ironic

3. It is refreshing to note that many right-thinking citizens are calling for a ban on the celebration of Halloween because the holiday encourages devil worship. Hallelujah? It doesn't take the intellect of a TV evangelist to see that the wearing of "Casper the Friendly Ghost" costumes leads children to the wanton embrace of Beelzebub.† And it is a fact that candy corn is the first step toward addiction. Only the devil (or an underemployed dentist) would knowingly offer popcorn balls to innocent children. But why stop at Halloween? Many other holidays conceal wickedness behind a vicious veil of greeting cards and Bob Hope TV specials. (Steve Ruebal, "Toss Out Halloween? Let's Not Stop There," *USA Today*, October 29, 1991, p. 11A.)

Tone

a. confident

b. ironic

c. neutral

d. friendly

4. According to one of your readers, insufficient attention has been paid to the possibility that men are also victims of domestic violence. It is his opinion that men are, in fact, just as likely to be victimized by women as women are by men. The difference is that men, for fear of looking unmasculine, fail to report it. Well, I'm just all broken up at the thought of this new social problem. I can imagine how horrible it is for a 220-pound male to be terrorized by a 120-pound female. The poor thing must live in terror at the thought of her menacing approach. A man like that is certainly as much in

---

†Beelzebub: another name for the devil.

Copyright © Cengage Learning. All rights reserved.

need of our sympathy as are the women who end up hospitalized or worse in the wake of a domestic dispute.

Tone   a. ironic

           b. friendly

           c. neutral

           d. sympathetic

5. On December 1, 1955, Rosa Parks left the Montgomery Fair department store late in the afternoon for her regular bus ride home. All thirty-six seats of the bus she boarded were soon filled, with twenty-two Negroes seated from the rear and fourteen whites from the front. Driver J. P. Blake, seeing a white man standing in the front of the bus, called out for the four passengers on the row just behind the whites to stand up and move to the back. Nothing happened. Blake finally had to get out of the driver's seat to speak more firmly to the four Negroes. "You better make it light on yourselves and let me have those seats," he said. At this, three of the Negroes moved to stand in the back of the bus, but Parks responded that she was not in the white section and didn't think she ought to move. She was in no-man's-land. Blake said that the white section was where he said it was, and he was telling Parks that she was in it. As he saw the law, the whole idea of no-man's-land was to give the driver some discretion to keep the races out of each other's way. He was doing just that. When Parks refused again, he advised her that the same city law that allowed him to regulate no-man's-land also gave him emergency police power to enforce the segregation codes. He would arrest Parks himself if he had to. Parks replied that he should do what he had to do; she was not moving. She spoke so softly that Blake would not have been able to hear her above the drone of normal bus noise. But the bus was silent. Blake notified Parks that she was officially under arrest. (Branch, *Parting the Waters*, p. 128.)

Tone   a. ironic

           b. admiring

           c. neutral

           d. irritable

Copyright © Cengage Learning. All rights reserved.

WORD CHECK

The following words were introduced and defined in pages 541–62. See how well you can match the words with the meanings. When you finish, make sure to check the meanings of any words you missed because the same words will turn up in tests at the end of the chapter.

1. recourse _____
2. inconspicuous _____
3. illuminated _____
4. inaugurate _____
5. stodgiest _____
6. immersion _____
7. hypothetically _____
8. inevitably _____
9. affidavits _____
10. deliberations _____

a. in theory, theoretically

b. deep involvement, concentration, physical act of sinking into water

c. access to protection or aid; also the person or action providing help or aid

d. start, begin, open

e. unavoidably

f. written statements of fact, made under oath and signed by the author

g. acts of careful and concentrated thought

h. not easily noticed, easy to overlook

i. lit, shining, made understandable, clarified

j. most boring, old fashioned and tired

◆ EXERCISE 9   More About Form and Meaning

DIRECTIONS   Use one of the words listed below to fill in the blanks.

illuminated	recourse	inaugural	stodgy	immerse
affidavit	inconspicuous	hypothetically	inevitable	deliberations

1. In the early days of the American republic, new presidents did not make a(n) _____ speech.

2. Except for death and taxes, little in life is _____.

3. The best way to learn a language is to totally _____ yourself in it so that the new language is all you hear or speak.

Copyright © Cengage Learning. All rights reserved.

4. Pumpkins are often turned into brightly _____ jack-o-lanterns around Halloween.

5. The antiques dealer was perfectly agreeable to everything the buyer wanted until she asked the dealer for a(n) _____ saying the signature on the portrait had been evaluated by experts.

6. Jurors on a murder trial should be prepared for some long and intense _____.

7. You can't claim to be speaking _____ if you are describing events that have already happened.

8. Writing, like some people, can be _____ and slow.

9. Believing that he had been treated unjustly, the employee's only _____ was to file a complaint against his supervisor.

10. The actress claimed she hated the attentions of the press but she didn't exactly dress to be _____. She was wearing a minidress with a plunging neckline and heels so high she had trouble walking.

Copyright © Cengage Learning. All rights reserved.

DIGGING DEEPER Baseball Invades Japan

Looking Ahead
Baseball became America's national pastime in the second half of the nineteenth century. American teams then took baseball to Japan, expecting to encourage American values along with an appreciation of the game. But that's not how things turned out.

1 Baseball, the "American pastime," was one of the new leisure-time pursuits that Americans took with them into different parts of the world. The Shanghai Baseball Club was founded by Americans in China in 1863, but few Chinese paid much attention to the sport, largely because the Imperial Court renounced the game as spiritually corrupting. However, when Horace Wilson, an American teacher, taught the rules of baseball to his Japanese students some time around 1870, the game received enthusiastic welcome as a reinforcement of traditional virtues. In fact baseball quickly became so much a part of Japanese culture that one Japanese writer commented, "Baseball is perfect for us. If the Americans hadn't invented it, we probably would have."

2   During the 1870s, Japanese high schools and colleges organized baseball games, and in 1883 Hiroshi Hiraoka, a railroad engineer who had studied in Boston, founded the first official local team, the Shimbashi Athletic Club Athletics. Fans displayed wild devotion to this and similar teams as they developed over the next several years.

Replete with bats, gloves, and uniforms, this Japanese baseball team of 1890 very much resembles its American counterpart of that era. The Japanese adopted baseball soon after Americans became involved in their country, but also added their cultural qualities to the game.

© Albert Harlingue / Roger-Viollet / The Image Works

Copyright © Cengage Learning. All rights reserved.

3   Before Americans introduced baseball to Japan, the Japanese had no team sports and no concept of recreational athletics. When they learned about baseball, they found that the idea of a team sport fit into their culture very well. But the Japanese had difficulty applying the American concept of leisure to the game. For them, baseball was serious business, involving hard and often brutal training. Baseball drills of the Ichiko nine, one of Japan's two great high school baseball teams in the late nineteenth century, were dubbed "Bloody Urine" because many players passed blood after a day of drilling.

4   There was a spiritual quality as well, linked to Buddhist values. According to one Japanese coach, "The purpose of [baseball] training is not health but the forging of the soul, and a strong soul is only born from strong practice. . . . Student baseball must be the baseball of self-discipline, or trying to attain the truth, just as in Zen Buddhism." This attitude prompted Japanese to consider baseball as a new method to pursue the spirit of Bushido, the way of the samurai.[†]

5   When Americans played baseball in Japan, the Japanese thought them to be strong and talented but lacking in discipline and respect. Americans insulted the Japanese by refusing to remove their hats and bow when they stepped up to bat. An international dispute occurred in 1891 when William Imbrie, an American professor at Meijo University in Tokyo, arrived late for a local game. Finding the gate locked, he climbed over the fence to watch the game. The fence, however, had sacred meaning and some Japanese fans attacked Imbrie for his sacrilege. Imbrie suffered facial injuries, prompting the American embassy to lodge a formal complaint. Americans assumed that their game would encourage Japanese to become like westerners to some extent, but the Japanese transformed the American pastime into an expression of team spirit, discipline, and nationalism that was uniquely Japanese. (Adapted from Norton et al., *A People and a Nation*, p. 535.)

Sharpening Your Skills

DIRECTIONS   Answer the following questions by circling the letter of the correct response or filling in the blanks.

1. In paragraph 1, what two more general words do the authors use to refer to *baseball* in order not to repeat the word over and over?

_____

_____
[†]samurai: professional warrior.

Copyright © Cengage Learning. All rights reserved.

2. In paragraph 3, what is the antecedent for *they* in the second sentence?

_____

3. Read this pair of sentences from paragraph 3. Then circle the letter of the relationship readers have to infer in order to understand why the authors followed one with the other: "For them, baseball was serious business, involving hard and often brutal training. Baseball drills of the Ichiko nine, one of Japan's two great high school baseball teams in the late nineteenth century, were dubbed 'Bloody Urine' because many players passed blood after a day of drilling."

   a. The second sentence challenges the idea that baseball was a serious business.

   b. The second sentence explains what made the Japanese serious about baseball.

   c. The second sentence illustrates just how serious baseball was for the Japanese.

4. Which statement best expresses the main idea of the entire reading?

   a. Although Japan enthusiastically embraced American baseball, the Japanese were never able to rival the speed and skill of American players.

   b. Given their long tradition of team sports, the Japanese quickly embraced baseball and ended up being better at the game than the Americans, who lack the discipline shown by the Japanese players.

   c. Unlike the Americans who thought of baseball as a leisure-time sport, the Japanese treated the game as a chance to prove their physical strength and spiritual endurance.

   d. Baseball was a popular sport in Japan long before it became the national pastime in the United States.

5. What definition do the authors provide for the word *Bushido*, introduced in paragraph 4?

_____

Copyright © Cengage Learning. All rights reserved.

6. In paragraph 4, why is there a quotation from a Japanese coach? What purpose does the quote serve?

   _____

   _____

7. The topic sentence of paragraph 4 is
   a. the first.
   b. the second.
   c. the third.
   d. the fourth.

8. Overall, which three patterns organize this reading?
   a. comparison and contrast; cause and effect; sequence of dates and events
   b. definition; process; classification
   c. sequence of dates and events; definition; simple listing
   d. simple listing; definition; classification

9. What is the authors' purpose?
   a. The authors want to tell readers how the Japanese modified American baseball to suit their culture.
   b. The authors want to persuade readers that it's not healthy to play baseball the way the Japanese did in the nineteenth century.

   What word or words would you use to describe the tone?

   _____

10. Based on paragraph 4, what conclusion could you draw?
    a. The Americans purposely tried to insult the Japanese because they disliked the changes made to what they thought of as "their game."
    b. The Japanese expected the Americans to know and follow their traditions when playing baseball in Japan.
    c. Like soccer audiences today, Japanese baseball fans in the nineteenth century were always spoiling for a fight.

Copyright © Cengage Learning. All rights reserved.

▶ TEST 1   **Reviewing New Vocabulary**

> **DIRECTIONS**   Fill in the blanks with one of the words listed below.

> | inaugural | immersed | inevitably | illuminate | deliberations |
> |-----------|----------|------------|------------|---------------|
> | stodgy | affidavits | hypothetically | inconspicuous | recourse |

1. The Verdict Isn't Always the End

1 Jury verdicts usually bring a trial to a close but not _____ as it turns out. In a case tried in Tennessee against a gastroenterologist,[†] the jury awarded damages amounting to $6 million to a woman who suffered brain damage following a colonoscopy.[†] The verdict, however, just fueled more accusations and controversy.

2   When the verdict was appealed, jurors were asked to submit _____ in which they described how they arrived at their multimillion dollar award during jury _____.

_____, the documents were meant to _____ a process normally kept under wraps. But, as usual, theory and reality were not a perfect match. While some jurors said they felt bullied into awarding damages, others insisted no pressure was applied.

3   The whole process of having jurors recount how they arrived at their decision has been heavily criticized as a waste of time, largely because twelve different jurors are inclined to describe twelve different versions of what took place. But the lawyer in charge of the appeal claimed his client had no other _____ except to demand written accounts of how the jurors came to believe that his client was at fault.

2. Remembering the Good Old Days

1 Because we are so accustomed to finding ourselves _____ in those grand but often tedious and _____ affairs that surround a new president's oath of office, it's hard to believe that presidents once took office with little _____ ceremony. Yet, treasonous as it might seem to say aloud, there are those of us who would willingly do without the presidential festivities. We'd prefer to

---

[†]gastroenterologist: a physician who specializes in diseases affecting the stomach and intestines.
[†]colonoscopy: an exam of the colon.

Copyright © Cengage Learning. All rights reserved.

return to an earlier era when, believe it or not, the first lady—who wasn't even called that until 1877— tried to be as _____ as possible. Initially, she didn't even show up to see her husband take office.[†] For that matter, several of our early presidents didn't bother preparing speeches.

2   If only we, too, could celebrate our presidents' arrival in office without all the speeches, balls, and interviews. Even more desirable would be a celebration without the media's making trivia, like every detail of the first lady's wardrobe, a matter of national significance.

_____

[†]James Madison's wife, Dolley, was the first wife, in 1809, to attend her husband's inaugural.

Copyright © Cengage Learning. All rights reserved.

▶ TEST 2   **Identifying Purpose**

DIRECTIONS   Circle the appropriate letter to identify the author's purpose.

1. Women Mayors

1   More women are running for and winning local elective offices. The data from cities with populations of 30,000 or more are instructive. In 1973, fewer than 2 percent of the cities in that population range had female mayors. A quarter-century later, the number of women mayors had increased to 202, or 21 percent, a level around which it has fluctuated. (In 2009, 17 percent of cities of 30,000 or more were governed by women.) Eleven women are at the helm of large U.S. cities (populations of 200,000 or more).

2   The number of female mayors of major cities nearly increased by one in 2004 when Donna Frye, a member of San Diego's city council, ran against the incumbent mayor. Frye, competing as a write-in candidate, lost in a hotly disputed election. At issue were 5,547 ballots in which voters had written in Frye's name but neglected to fill in the small oval next to the write-in line. Election officials did not count these ballots because state law requires that the ovals be filled in for a write-in vote to count. Frye's supporters contended that regardless of the ovals, voter intent was clear: a vote for Frye. Had those ballots been counted, Frye would have won by 3,439 votes.

3   Studies of female mayors have dispelled several electoral myths. For example, women do not appear to experience greater difficulty in raising money or gaining newspaper endorsements than men do. Women mayors, however, do tend to be political novices. Few female mayors in Florida, for instance, had held elective office before their mayoral election: If they had, it was usually a city council seat. Other research indicates that mayors, regardless of gender, see their political environments similarly, which makes sense. Successful local politicians know their communities. (Bowman and Kearney, *State and Local Government*, pp. 312–13.)

Purpose   a. The reading is meant to persuade readers that the country needs to increase its number of women mayors.

b. The reading is meant to inform readers about the current status of female mayors.

2. Making Google a More Efficient Search Tool

1   If you are like most people who use the Web, you probably also use the search engine Google numerous times throughout the day. The question

Copyright © Cengage Learning. All rights reserved.

is, though, do you know how to create search terms that get you precisely the information you want? For that matter, are you aware of the many different kinds of information Google can provide to the savvy user?

2   Now, according to Google's CEO Eric Schmidt, there will come a day when you won't even need search terms. Google will anticipate and find what you want based on your previous search patterns and website visits.

3   But who knows if that day will ever come or if its arrival is particularly desirable. For now, you still have to use search terms to get the information you want. The following five tips for making efficient use of Google's many and various search capabilities should be helpful.

1. Searching Specific Sites for Key Terms

4   Let's say you want to search a website for a specific word or phrase. The site itself, however, has no built-in search feature. Google can come to the rescue if you know how to use it. Here's what to do: type into Google's search box the term you're looking for followed by the word *site*, a colon, and the URL of the website.

5   For instance, if you wanted to search for the term "main idea" on a website devoted to reading, you would put the following into the search box: **main idea site:laflemm.com**. Within seconds, you would have all the references to "main idea" appearing on that particular website.

6   You can also search specific sites for the types of files they include, such as Word documents, PowerPoints, or pdfs.[†] For example, if you wanted to find out if the same website you searched for "main idea" also included pdf files, you would use this search term: **site:www.laflemm.com filetype:pdf** and discover that yes, indeed, it does.

2. Finding Information for a Particular Time Frame

7   Imagine you are doing a paper on Supreme Court Judge Sonia Sotomayor. The focus of your paper is on the work she did while in private practice between 1984 and 1991. If you type just her name into the search box, up will come a host of websites, many of them dealing with events not related to your paper. You will find some websites that discuss Sotomayor's years as a corporate lawyer, but you will have to sift those sites out from many others. Translation: You will waste precious time.

8   What you really want is a list of websites focused on the judge's years in private practice. To get that list, all you need to do is add the years 1984

---

†pdfs: Portable Document Formats are files that allow for the exchange of documents across all types of hardware or operating systems without altering the appearance of the page.

Copyright © Cengage Learning. All rights reserved.

and 1991 to Sonia Sotomayor's name and separate the years with two dots. The resulting search term would look like this: **Sonia Sotomayor 1984..1991**. Google will then give you a long list of websites focused on that specific period of time in Sotomayor's career.

3. Using Quotation Marks to Restrict the Topic

9 Should you want to do a highly focused search that gets you specific information about a sub-topic related to a much larger issue, try enclosing your search term in quotations. In other words, say you want to find websites that identify the symptoms of cyberbullying. At the same time, you want to avoid calling up a long list of websites that discuss any number of issues related to cyberbullying, such as attempts by schools to control it or its relationship to social media.

10   If that's your goal, then enclose the phrase in quotation marks, "symptoms of cyberbullying." Type that phrase, complete with quotes, into your search box and Google will produce only sites describing the symptoms of cyberbullying.

4. Searching for One Term While Specifically Excluding Another

11 As you know, some words have a wide range of meanings. Thus using them in a search term can bring up websites devoted to wildly different topics. Use the search term "varieties of bass," for instance, and you will get some websites devoted to fish and some devoted to guitars. Anytime you know that your search term has divergent meanings, make sure you exclude the one you don't want by putting a minus sign in front of it. If what you are researching is the fish, then your search term should look like this: **varieties of bass –guitars** or even **varieties of bass –music**.

5. Finding the Names Attached to Phone Numbers

12 Let's say someone calls you and you don't know who it is. Type the number into Google's search box and the name and address of the person will be at the top of the list that comes on the screen. Right now, this search strategy will only work if the person calling you was on a land line. But given how Google has evolved in a very brief span of time, it probably won't be long before searching by phone number works for cell phones, too.

Purpose   a. The reading is meant to show readers how the right search term can get them different kinds of information.

b. The reading is meant to encourage the use of Google as a search engine.

Copyright © Cengage Learning. All rights reserved.

▶ **TEST 3**   **Recognizing Tone**

DIRECTIONS   Circle the appropriate letter to identify the author's tone.

1. In areas with a large Mexican population, politicians running for office are likely to talk about amnesty for the millions of illegal immigrants currently living in the United States. However, it's time that they did more than talk, because the number of Mexican men and women living here illegally is growing at a rapid rate. The majority are productive, law-abiding people who simply want to earn a better standard of living for themselves and their families. In many cases, they have already endured great hardship just to get to this country. Once here, they are often forced by unscrupulous employers to accept low wages and poor working conditions because they fear being deported. Granting them amnesty would give illegal immigrants the right to complain and the right to demand fair working conditions. It is the compassionate and humane thing to do. The idea should not be abandoned once the campaign speeches are over and the votes have been counted.

The author's tone is

a. neutral.

b. casual.

c. arrogant.

d. sympathetic.

2. From 1972 through 1996, the South was more Republican than the nation as a whole. The proportion of white southerners describing themselves to pollsters as "strongly Democratic" fell from more than one-third in 1952 to about one-seventh in 1984. There has been a corresponding increase in "independents." As it turns out, southern white independents have voted overwhelmingly Republican in recent presidential elections. If you lump independents together with the parties for which they actually vote, the party alignment among white southerners has gone from six-to-one Democratic in 1952 to about fifty-fifty Democrats and Republicans. If this continues, it will constitute a major realignment in a region of the

Copyright © Cengage Learning. All rights reserved.

country that is rapidly growing in population and political clout. (Wilson and DiIulio, *American Government*, p. 161.)

The author's tone is

a. neutral.

b. critical.

c. solemn.

d. surprised.

3. Oregon[†] and Washington have proven that voting by mail is far superior to the old method of voting in a polling place. First, state surveys clearly show that voting by mail is an option people want. Among those surveyed, seventy percent of Oregonians and 65 percent of Washingtonians said they prefer voting by mail. What they like is the convenience. A mail-in ballot allows them to integrate voting more easily into busy lives. Voters also feel that voting by mail helps them make more informed choices. Residents in both states say they make better decisions because they can take more time studying their ballot at home. They don't have to rush to complete it in a voting booth. Not surprisingly, voting by mail encourages a big voter turnout during elections. In Oregon, for instance, 86.5 percent of registered voters submitted ballots in the 2004 elections. Compare that figure to a nationwide average of 51 percent voter turnout. Other states should follow the example set by Washington and Oregon.

The author's tone is

a. anxious.

b. neutral.

c. enthusiastic.

d. sarcastic.

4. The Apollo space program of the 1960s and 1970s was responsible for a series of moon landings. In 1967, the project got off to a tragic start when fire killed three astronauts during a pre-flight test on the launch pad. The tragedy, however, did not put an end to the space program. In 1968 and 1969, a series of successful missions took

---

[†]Oregonians vote entirely by mail.

Copyright © Cengage Learning. All rights reserved.

astronauts into space for six to ten days at a time. Apollo missions 7, 8, 9, and 10 tested the equipment and operations necessary for placing men on the moon's surface. On July 20, 1969, the *Apollo 11* mission fulfilled its purpose when astronauts Neil Armstrong and Buzz Aldrin did what had once seemed impossible: They walked on the moon while people all over the world stayed glued to their television sets and watched in awe. A second lunar landing occurred that same year as part of the *Apollo 12* mission. In 1970, *Apollo 13* was supposed to result in a third landing. However, damage to the spacecraft caused the mission to be aborted, and the astronauts barely made it safely back to Earth. Near tragedy, however, did not prove a permanent obstacle. In 1971 and 1972, four more Apollo flights produced four more lunar landings. *Apollo 14, 15, 16,* and *17* astronauts walked on the moon.

The author's tone is

a. neutral.

b. skeptical.

c. critical.

d. admiring.

5. For more than four decades, ecologists and environmentalists have revered Rachel Carson, author of the 1962 book *Silent Spring,* for alerting the world to the dangers of chemical pesticides. Arguing that pesticides such as DDT upset the balance of nature, kill wildlife, and cause cancer in humans, Carson created widespread "chemophobia" that culminated in a ban on DDT's use. Unfortunately, though, Carson's impassioned and vividly written plea for protecting nature and human health has left generations of readers with a skewed view of pesticides.

As Dr. I. L. Baldwin, a professor of bacteriology who reviewed *Silent Spring* in a 1962 issue of *Science* pointed out, early on, Carson greatly exaggerated the risks. Using questionable statistics and anecdotes, such as the doubtful tale of a woman who immediately developed cancer after spraying her basement with DDT, Carson pronounced this pesticide to be a human carcinogen[†] even though most scientists disagreed.

[†]carcinogen: cause of cancer.

Copyright © Cengage Learning. All rights reserved.

Carson was also irresponsible in her refusal to acknowledge the pesticides' benefits, which far outweighed their potential for harm. As Dr. Baldwin pointed out, pesticides have dramatically improved human health and welfare by getting rid of insects and parasites that destroy crops and transmit deadly diseases. Today, mosquito-borne malaria is still a leading cause of death and illness worldwide because Carson's devotees won't allow DDT to be restored as a weapon in the battle against this disease. (Source of information: Tierney, "Fateful Voice of a Generation Still Drowns Out Real Science," *New York Times*, June 5, 2007.)

The author's tone is

a. amused.

b. objective.

c. sad.

d. critical.

Copyright © Cengage Learning. All rights reserved.

▶ **TEST 4**   **Taking Stock**

DIRECTIONS   Read the following selection. Then answer the questions by circling the letter of the correct response(s) or filling in the blanks.

Our Roads Need Fixing Now!

1 Despite the road improvements that resulted from President Obama's economic stimulus package, many of the country's roads and bridges are still in dangerous disrepair. Crumbling and marred by potholes, often too narrow or too damaged for the amount of traffic they bear, many of our roadways are inadequate to support the huge number of vehicles that travel them every day. While it's true that driver error accounts for the thousands of traffic deaths that occur annually, cracked and rutted, poorly maintained roads and bridges encourage accidents and create an additional threat to our safety.

2   In 2005, a highway ramp in Albany, New York, separated from the bridge to which it connected. In 2006, an oil truck in Portland, Oregon, fell into a sinkhole that suddenly appeared after the pipes under the street collapsed. But those were minor incidents compared to the 2007 collapse of the I-35W Mississippi River Bridge in Minnesota. The bridge collapsed during rush hour, killing 13 people and injuring 145. Make no mistake, incidents like these will continue if more money is not devoted to roadway repair. According to a new report from the U.S. Public Interest Research Group (PIRG) 150,000 miles of road, 71,000 bridges, and 12 percent of all highway spans are in poor to bad condition.

3   Those who balk at spending federal or state money on road and bridge repair need to consider the financial and emotional cost of continued neglect. Damaged and congested roads and bridges exact a heavy price on all of us. The deaths and injuries related to aging roads and bridges consume about $230 billion a year in medical expenses, lost wages, and travel delays. The highway accidents to which bad roads contribute are also a major source of legal and insurance bills. Two- and three-lane highways built in the fifties before Americans went everywhere in cars create traffic jams that slow the delivery of goods and services. They also prevent people from getting to work on time. It's been estimated that breakdowns and delays due to aging, poorly maintained roadways rob the U.S. economy of $70 billion per year.

4   In addition to being the source of tragedy, our aging roadways also reduce the quality of life. Congested roads and highways increase commute times, thus shortening time spent at home. Bumper-to-bumper traffic slows us down on our way to work and increases our anxiety,

Copyright © Cengage Learning. All rights reserved.

contributing to tension and stress-related diseases. And one thing Americans do not need these days is more stress. So next time some politician starts promoting new roads, which are a flashier way to impress voters, tell him or her to fix the old ones first. (Source of statistics: Bond, "Roads Are a Good Investment," *USA Today*, February 18, 2004, p. A1; www.thetransportpolitic.com; www.oregonlive.com/politics/index.ssf/2008/06/part_one_america_is_falling_ap.html.)

1. Which statement best sums up the main idea?
   a. America's roads and highways are ancient.
   b. America's highways and bridges were badly constructed in the first place, and we are now seeing the results of that initial error.
   c. We cannot afford to wait any longer to spend money repairing America's roadways and bridges.
   d. America's roads, bridges, and highways are in worse repair than those in other countries, a fact that frequently astonishes American tourists.

2. To understand the relationship between paragraphs 1 and 2, readers have to infer which relationship?
   a. Paragraph 2 offers an exception to the point made in paragraph 1.
   b. Paragraph 1 provides background for the point made in paragraph 2.
   c. Paragraph 2 contradicts the point introduced in paragraph 1.
   d. Paragraph 2 offers specific illustrations of the claim made in paragraph 1.

3. The author's primary purpose is
   a. to inform.
   b. to persuade.

4. Which type of transition opens paragraph 2?
   a. time order
   b. cause and effect
   c. comparison
   d. contrast

5. How would you paraphrase the topic sentence in paragraph 3?

   _____

   _____

Copyright © Cengage Learning. All rights reserved.

6. Which of the following sentences is a major detail?
   a. "And one thing Americans do not need these days is more stress" (paragraph 4).
   b. "The deaths and injuries related to aging roads and bridges consume about $230 billion a year in medical expenses, lost wages, and travel delays" (paragraph 3).

7. Paraphrase the cycle of causes and effects the author expects you to infer from the following sentence: "Bumper-to-bumper traffic slows us down on our way to work and increases our anxiety, contributing to tension and stress-related diseases" (paragraph 4).

   _____

   _____

   _____

8. Which pattern or patterns organize this reading?
   a. definition
   b. simple listing
   c. comparison and contrast
   d. cause and effect

9. How would you describe the author's tone?
   a. optimistic
   b. sad
   c. warning
   d. neutral

10. Which of these conclusions follows from the reading?
    a. The author would applaud a heavily funded federal program dedicated to roadway repair.
    b. The author believes that America's highways were poorly constructed when first built.
    c. The author believes that America's highways cannot be repaired; they must be replaced.
    d. The author would not support any federally funded program, even if it was devoted to improving the roadways.

Copyright © Cengage Learning. All rights reserved.

© Galen Rowell/Corbis

IN THIS CHAPTER, YOU WILL LEARN

- why arguments and persuasion go hand in hand.

- how to recognize common introductions to the point of an argument.

- how to analyze an argument.

- how to recognize faulty reasoning.

- how to spot excessive bias.

Fear not those who argue, but those who dodge.

—Dale Carnegie, author and lecturer on the subject of
personal success

Where persuasive writing is involved, expect an argument. That doesn't mean a fight. It means be prepared for the author to put forward an opinion along with convincing support or evidence.

Once you identify the opinion and the support, your next step is to check how the author handles opposing points of view. Does the author treat them with respect while pointing out that they don't really undermine his position? Or does she describe opposing points of view with contempt, as if they weren't worth mentioning except for the sake of pointing out how stupid they are?

If it's the former, you might seriously think about whether or not you share the author's opinion. If it's the latter, you need to read what other people have to say on the subject before spending any time pondering the author's opinion or claim. A writer who takes a bullying tone with the reader while insulting the opposition is not a writer you can trust.

Opinions Are the Foundations of Arguments

You can't really have an argument without an opinion. People don't argue over statements of fact, such as William Jefferson Clinton served as president of the United States for two terms. With this statement, there is nothing to dispute, or disagree over. Any reference work will confirm its factual accuracy. What would be the point of mounting an argument to defend it?

But if you tell someone that Bill Clinton was a great president, be prepared to argue your claim. In other words, you'll need to offer evidence, that is, reasons, facts, or statistics, that might convince someone who disagrees with you.

Clinton is a controversial figure. Some people love him. Others despise him. Some have mixed emotions about both the man and his presidency. While you could probably not convince those who despise him no matter what you said, a good argument might win over those in the middle. Who knows? It might even raise a doubt or two in the minds of those who think Clinton was a complete failure as president.

What this discussion about Bill Clinton illustrates is that all arguments begin with an opinion, point of view, or belief that the writer wants known and shared. Thus the first thing skilled readers do is scan the opening paragraphs of an article or essay, looking for the thesis statement or implied main idea expressing the writer's opinion. In pursuit

Copyright © Cengage Learning. All rights reserved.

of that thesis statement, experienced readers are especially alert to the kinds of sentences that typically introduce the central argument of a persuasive reading. The following list identifies six of the most common methods authors use to introduce the point they intend to argue.

When looking for the opinion that's being argued, look for opening statements that

1. **contrast one opinion with another:** "What's clear to most of us in teaching is that the Internet is a powerful educational tool; it is, however, not a magic bullet."

2. **challenge an existing tradition or belief:** "For years, we've been told that vigorous exercise was a boon to the body, yet now it appears that vigorous exercise involving long periods of cardio can also harm the body."

3. **insist some action must be taken:** "If incidents of bullying in the schools continue to increase, we need to put into place penalties that make the price of bullying behavior too high to pay."

4. **cite new research as evidence for a new perspective**: "The assumption has long been that humans must be taught how to dance. However, a new study from Stanford University suggests we may have to revise that hypothesis since researchers have discovered that their infant subjects were bouncing to the beat at less than five months old. The desire to dance may very well be part of the human condition."

5. **predict some event (often a bad one) will occur:** "I want to dust off my crystal ball and make a prediction: In the future, the biggest land animals will be smaller than they are now. Here's why I think so. . . ." (Olivia Judson, "Opinionator," *New York Times*.)

6. **evaluate an idea, a person, or a group:**
   a. "The author of *You Are Not a Gadget*, Jaron Lanier, makes a valid* point when he says that we should beware of the idea that only good can come out of emphasizing the 'hive mind' over individual achievement. He is correct to argue that where the group is concerned, there is always the danger of positive group dynamics* turning into a more dangerous mob psychology."

---

*valid: justified, just, well grounded in reason or proof, up to date.
*dynamics: interactions, patterns of behavior.

Copyright © Cengage Learning. All rights reserved.

b. "Some cognitive scientists are claiming that the virtues of hypertext reading have been, pardon the pun, over-hyped, because of limitations on the processing abilities of the human brain. However, the very fact that our brains have become so exquisitely adapted for reading letters instead of shapes suggests that our brains can evolve to meet this new challenge." (Adapted from Alison Gopnik, "Mind Reading," *New York Times*, January 3, 2010, p. 15.)

Are there additional ways to introduce the opinions that anchor an argument? Absolutely. But the six methods described above are among the most common.

CHECK YOUR UNDERSTANDING Through Writing

Flip through the pages of this chapter to find a topic you think you could write about. Maybe privacy settings on Facebook or becoming an organ donor? Once you have a topic (you can also just make up your own topic), write a thesis statement expressing an opinion you think you could defend. Introduce the thesis statement using one of the methods described on pages 587–88—for example, compare it to an existing belief or opinion.

◆ **EXERCISE 1** **Identifying the Point of the Argument**

DIRECTIONS Read each passage and in the blanks paraphrase the opinion the writer wants readers to share.

1. In a post-feminist world, some consider high heels a symbol of male dominance. They don't recognize that high heels can also be a sign of female power. Viewed in the right light, wearing high heels is, in fact, a way of flaunting feminine power. Well, at least it can be. High heels only act as a powerful arsenal if worn correctly. From the way that they are modeled to the clothing with which they are paired, high heels can appear unattractive if used incorrectly. For this reason, I address the dos and don'ts of wearing high heels. (Adapted from www.voice.sbc.edu/archives/v5n6/wntw.php.)

_____

_____

Copyright © Cengage Learning. All rights reserved.

2. Anytime you think *you* are not catching a break in life, remind yourself of what happened to "Shoeless"[†] Joe Jackson and you might feel just a bit better. If anyone ever got a raw deal, it was "Shoeless" Joe. Jackson's 356 batting average is the third best of all time. In 1917, his fielding percentage (.984) was near the top of the league, He also led the American League in almost every category.

   Based on the statistics, there is no serious debate about Jackson's right to be in Baseball's Hall of Fame. Thus the current Commissioner of Baseball needs to right the wrong that has been done and let Jackson into Baseball's Hall of Fame. What's keeping Shoeless Joe Jackson out of the Hall of Fame is the fact that he was banned from baseball for life. But the truth is, justice was not served when Jackson was banned.

   _____

   _____

3. So you think that your brain is sleeping soundly when you are? Well, think again. New brain scanning technology suggests that the brain is more active during sleep than it is during its waking hours. And it's active for a reason. What the research shows is that the brain uses the hours of sleep to process and reorganize new information received during the day.

   That's one reason why brain scans made during the hours of REM sleep are often strikingly similar to the patterns of activity revealed during the day. During sleep, the brain seems to rehearse new skills acquired during its waking hours. In effect, it's re-enacting what it did earlier in the day.

   _____

   _____

4. For close to a decade now, those of us capable of managing just one task at a time have been hanging our heads in shame when confronted by the almost superhuman powers of our multitasking

---

[†]Early in his career, Jackson is said to have had blisters from shoes that were too tight. Thus he would take his shoes off when he ran the bases. At one point, a fan of the opposing team called him a "Shoeless Son of a Gun," and the "shoeless" part stuck.

Copyright © Cengage Learning. All rights reserved.

friends. Thankfully, we no longer need feel ashamed. A growing body of research compiled since 2001 suggests that multitasking and superior performance do *not* go hand in hand. In fact, multitaskers are downright mediocre when it comes to focusing their attention and storing or organizing information in long-term memory.

_____

_____

5. In the 1990s, an antitrust lawyer named Gary Reback went after what he believed was Microsoft's monopoly of the technology market. Now Reback has set his sights on a new target. He is demanding that the government exert greater regulatory control over the search engine giant Google. According to Reback, Google has become the "arbiter of every single thing on the Web." And while there may be some exaggeration in that claim, it is hard to understand how so many people can be complacent about Google's increasing Web dominance. The figures, after all, don't lie: Microsoft's search engine Bing controls 11.8 percent of the market, Yahoo! controls 17.7 percent, and Google controls a whopping 64.4 percent.

Also, given Google's growing dominance in every aspect of information technology, from its plans to put all the books in the world online to its increasing share of the mobile phone market, it's time to find out, before it's too late, just how well the company is holding to its famous motto: "You can make money without doing evil."

_____

_____

TAKING A CLOSER LOOK

Metaphors

In paragraph 1 of the previous exercise, the author describes the conditions under which high heels can act as a "powerful arsenal." The word *arsenal* refers to a store of weapons. Explain this metaphor. How can high heels be compared to an arsenal?

_____

_____

_____

Copyright © Cengage Learning. All rights reserved.

Five Common Types of Support

Writers who want their arguments to be taken seriously know they have to do more than state their opinion. To be persuasive, they also have to provide their readers with support. In response, critical readers need to recognize and evaluate that support, deciding if it is both relevant and up to date. Although people argue their position in many different ways—compare, for instance, Ann Coulter with Paul Krugman[†]—five common types of support are particularly likely to be used in an argument: personal experience, reasons, examples and illustrations, the opinions of experts, and research results.

Personal Experience

Authors who want to persuade their readers to share an opinion are unlikely to rely solely on personal experience. However, they will use personal experience to set the stage for their point of view. Opening with a personal experience is the author's way of getting readers on their side. Here's one example.

Becoming an Organ Donor

I've never thought much about being an organ donor. Since I've never fully accepted that I might die one day, registering as one didn't seem really necessary. But then my husband's kidneys started to fail due to complications from diabetes and everything changed. I found myself desperately searching for a donor—I'm not a match—while simultaneously trying to figure out the tangle of rules and regulations that govern organ donation. The experience has changed me, and I have become obsessed by my quest to make everyone become an organ donor.

And yes I am looking at you. Close to 100,000 people a year die from renal disease because they can't get a donor to help them. We need to do something about this, and we need to do it now. People who don't need to be are dying. This will continue unless we help by becoming organ donors, a procedure so simple it's hard to understand why more people don't do it.

[†]If you are not familiar with the work of either, check online to see the *enormou*s difference in how they argue their point of view.

Copyright © Cengage Learning. All rights reserved.

Discussions of arguments tend to focus on how they should be guided by sound reasoning and solid use of evidence. That's certainly true. But readers often skip an article or essay that opens with reasons and statistics because the numbers and reasons seem too dry and uninteresting. Writers who want to persuade know that happens. Therefore, they often open with or include personal experiences to encourage readers to get involved. They believe, and they are probably correct, that a reader sympathetic to the writer will be more open to sharing the writer's point of view.

Reasons

Reasons are probably the main method of support used by authors who want to persuade readers to share their opinion. In the following passage, the author hopes to convince readers that cockfighting is a bloody and dangerous sport:

They Call This a Sport?

Cockfighting, the pitting of two roosters in a ring to fight one another, often to the death, is illegal in all fifty states. Unfortunately, the so-called "sport" of cockfighting continues despite laws forbidding it. Thus efforts to discourage participation must continue. Those who consider themselves fans of the fights must begin to see what a violent, inhumane, and dangerous pastime it truly is.

Cockfighting is one of the worst forms of animal cruelty. Participants strap razor-sharp spurs to two roosters' legs and feed them stimulants. Then they toss the birds into a pit, where the birds tear each other apart until one dies a bloody and painful death.

Besides being cruel to animals, cockfights encourage illegal and violent behavior. They are notorious arenas of illegal gambling and drug trafficking, firearms dealing, and fighting. Shootings have sometimes occurred when the violence in the pit spills over into the crowd. What's particularly vile* about cockfights is that they reinforce the notion that cruelty and violence are sources of amusement. Perhaps worst of all, they send the same message to children whose parents have allowed them to witness the fights. These parents apparently consider cockfighting to be nothing more than good, clean fun, the perfect way to spend an afternoon or evening with the kids.

---

*vile: disgusting, despicable.

Copyright © Cengage Learning. All rights reserved.

To persuade readers to share her point of view—that efforts to stop cock fights from occurring must continue because outlawing them hasn't worked—the author of this passage provides four specific reasons: (1) cockfighting is cruel to animals, (2) it encourages illegal and even violent behavior, (3) it reinforces the idea that violence is a source of amusement, and (4) it sends a terrible message to children. By listing these four reasons, the author hopes that readers will begin to share, or at least to seriously consider, her point of view.

Examples and Illustrations

Writers who want readers to share an opinion are also likely to cite specific examples and illustrations that prove their point. Look at how the following author uses examples to persuade readers that plastic litter is not just unsightly but also deadly.

> As litter, plastic is unsightly and deadly. Birds and small animals die after getting stuck in plastic six-pack beverage rings. Pelicans accidentally hang themselves with discarded plastic fishing line. Turtles choke on plastic bags or starve when their stomachs become clogged with hard-to-excrete crumbled plastic. Sea lions poke their heads into plastic rings and have their jaws locked permanently shut. Authorities estimate that plastic refuse annually kills up to two million birds and at least 100,000 mammals. (Turbak, "Plastic: 60 Billion Pounds of Trouble," *American Legion Magazine.*[†])

Here's a case where the author piles example on example in an effort to convince readers that plastic can be lethal.

Statistics as Examples

Notice how the author of the above reading uses examples. On the one hand, the passage contains vividly described examples, the pelicans which "accidentally hang themselves" and the turtles that "choke on plastic bags." But, on the other, the author also uses statistics to cite large numbers of examples. Where persuasion is concerned, this is a knock-out combination.

The vividly described examples compel readers' sympathy (or outrage, or admiration, depending on the context), while the statistics

---

[†]Also used in Rosen and Behrens, *The Allyn & Bacon Handbook.*

Copyright © Cengage Learning. All rights reserved.

indicate the magnitude of the problem. With this double-whammy approach, the writer avoids two obstacles examples can pose: (1) the reader responds to the specific examples but thinks they aren't all that common or typical, and (2) the reader notes the statistics, but the numbers carry so little emotional impact the reader doesn't care. By citing both examples and statistics, that is, going through the heart and the head, the writer has a better chance of persuading his audience to share his concerns.

Expert Opinions

In order to persuade, writers often call on one or more experts for support. In the following passage, for instance, the author suggests that cloning geniuses may not be a good idea. To make her point, she gives a reason *and* cites an expert.

Cloning Is No Guarantee of Greatness

After the birth of Dolly, the first successfully cloned sheep, in 1996, it was often suggested that we could now consider the human gene pool a natural resource. We could, if we wished, clone a Nobel Prize–winning writer like Junot Díaz or a star athlete like LeBron James and thereby create a population of gifted and talented people. What could be wrong with that? Well, in the long run, probably a lot.

There's simply no guarantee that the clones would be everything the originals were. Genes don't tell the whole story, and the clone of a prize-winning scientist, if neglected as a child, might well end up a disturbed genius, no matter what the original gene pool. As John Paris, professor of bioethics[†] at Boston College, so correctly says on the subject of cloning, "Choosing personal characteristics as if they were the options on a car is an invitation to misadventure." (Source of quotation: Kluger, "Will We Follow the Sheep?" *Time*, March 10, 1997, p. 71.)

In this case, the author doesn't just let her argument rest solely on her own reasoning. She also makes it clear that at least one knowledgeable expert is very much on her side.

[†]bioethics: using ethical and moral standards to evaluate practices in science and medicine.

Copyright © Cengage Learning. All rights reserved.

Research Results

In the same way they use experts, writers who want to persuade are likely to use the results of research—studies, polls, questionnaires, and surveys—to argue a point. In the following passage, for example, the author uses an expert *and* a study to make his point.

> In a tiny shop built on the side of a farmhouse in Pennsylvania's Lancaster County, Katie Stoltzfus sells Amish† dolls, wooden toys, and quilts. Does she ever. Her shop had "a couple of hundred thousand" dollars in sales last year, says the forty-four-year-old Amish entrepreneur and mother of nine. Mrs. Stoltzfus's success underscores a quiet revolution taking place among the Amish. Amish women, despite their image as shy farm wives, now run about 20 percent of the one thousand businesses in Lancaster County, according to a study by Donald B. Kraybill, a professor of sociology at Elizabethtown College in Elizabethtown, Pennsylvania. "These women are interacting more with outsiders, assuming managerial functions they never had before, and gaining more power within their community because of their access to money," says Professor Kraybill, who recently wrote a book about Amish enterprises. (Aeppel, "More Amish Women Are Tending to Business," *Wall Street Journal.*)

To make sure that readers seriously consider his position, the author cites a study and identifies the person who conducted the study, making it clear that his opinion is grounded in solid research.

CHECK YOUR UNDERSTANDING

Name the five ways writers support their opinions when using arguments intended to persuade:

_____

_____

---

†Amish: a religious group that generally avoids contact with the modern world and its modern machinery.

Copyright © Cengage Learning. All rights reserved.

✔ **CHECK YOUR UNDERSTANDING Through Writing**

Take the thesis statement you created for your "Check Your Understanding Through Writing" assignment on page 588. Make a very rough draft of how you think you can argue it. When you are finished drafting the support, introduce the thesis statement by describing a personal experience (yours or someone else's) which might grab your readers' interest.

◆ **EXERCISE 2** **Identifying Support for Opinions**

DIRECTIONS Each group of statements opens with an opinion or a claim that needs to be argued. Circle the letters of the two sentences that help argue that point.

EXAMPLE Eyewitness testimony is much less reliable than most people think.

ⓐ The testimony of eyewitnesses can often be influenced by the desire to please those in authority.

ⓑ Studies of eyewitness testimony conducted by the researcher and psychologist Elizabeth Loftus reveal an astonishingly high number of errors.

c. Eyewitness testimony carries a great deal of weight with most juries.

EXPLANATION Statements *a* and *b* both undermine the reliability of eyewitnesses and thereby provide reasons why eyewitness testimony cannot always be considered trustworthy. Statement *c*, however, is not relevant, or related, to the claim made about eyewitness testimony.

1. Uniforms should be mandatory* for all high school students.
   a. Most students hate the idea of wearing a uniform.
   b. Parents on a strict budget would no longer have to worry about being able to provide expensive back-to-school wardrobes.
   c. If uniforms were mandatory in high school, students would not waste precious time worrying about something as trivial as fashionable, brand name clothing.

---

*mandatory: required or commanded by law or some other authority.

Copyright © Cengage Learning. All rights reserved.

2. All zoos should be abolished due to the cruelty they inflict on their imprisoned inhabitants.

   a. Zoos encourage the notion that animals are on earth for the amusement of humans and discourage the idea that they have needs separate from those of humans.

   b. If all zoos were closed, no one has any idea what would happen to the animals now living in them.

   c. Although many zoos have improved the living conditions for the animals they possess, those animals still lack the freedom they have in the wild.

3. Because the deer population is sky high, hunters should be allowed to shoot more deer per season.

   a. Desperate for food, deer are foraging by the roadside, where many are hit by cars, another indication that their population has to be reduced.

   b. With the exception of hunting, there doesn't seem to be any practical way to slow down growth in the deer population.

   c. Most hunters have a great respect for the animals they kill.

4. Migraine headaches are much more painful and debilitating* than people who do not have them realize, and the government needs to fund research to find a cure.

   a. Hemiplegic migraine, although rare, is devastating: It can cause a paralysis that lasts for several days.

   b. Thomas Jefferson, Virginia Woolf, and Winston Churchill are just a few of the famous people who suffered from migraines.

   c. The onset of a migraine can bring with it reduced vision, making it impossible for the sufferer to carry on with ordinary daily activities.

◆ **EXERCISE 3**   **Identifying Opinion and Support**

DIRECTIONS   Read each passage. Then answer the questions that follow.

EXAMPLE   Unfortunately, some people still believe that African Americans endured slavery without protest. But nothing could be further from the truth. In 1800, for example, Gabriel Prosser organized

----

*debilitating: weakening, causing a lack of energy.

Copyright © Cengage Learning. All rights reserved.

an army of a thousand slaves to march on Richmond. However, a state militia† had been alerted by a spy, and the rebellion was put down. Prosser was ultimately executed for refusing to give evidence against his co-conspirators. In 1822, Denmark Vesey plotted to march on Charleston. However, he, too, was betrayed by an informer. The most serious and widely reported revolt occurred in 1831 under Nat Turner. Believing he was following god's instructions, Turner and his followers attacked and killed about fifty people. Turner had hoped to set off a chain of rebellions, but he and his followers, around seventy-five total, were overwhelmed by a two-thousand-men-strong state militia. Turner escaped. However, he was caught and executed. So too were more than a hundred black men and women, most of whom had had nothing to do with the original uprising.

a. What is the point of the author's argument?

It's simply not true that African Americans endured slavery without protest.

b. Paraphrase the examples used to support that point.

1. In 1800, Gabriel Prosser organized an army of slaves to march on Richmond.

2. In 1822, Denmark Vesey plotted to take over Charleston.

3. In 1831, Nat Turner and more than 75 rebels revolted.

EXPLANATION   In this case, the author uses three examples to convince her readers that African Americans did not endure slavery without protest.

1. The fact that more women are lawfully arming themselves should be good news for everyone concerned with violence against women. Ever since the publication of Betty Friedan's *The Feminine Mystique*, feminists have been urging women to be independent and self-sufficient. What better evidence that women have "arrived" than that they no longer have to rely exclusively on the police (still mostly male) for protection? Feminists should applaud every woman who is skilled in handgun use. (Talk about controlling your own body.) Liberation from fear when walking on a dark street, driving

---

†militia: group of civilians trained to be soldiers but not belonging to any formal military group.

Copyright © Cengage Learning. All rights reserved.

on a country road late at night, or withdrawing cash from a bank machine is more important on a daily basis to most women than smashing any glass ceiling in the workplace. (Adapted from Ingraham, "Armed and Empowered," *Pittsburgh Post-Gazette*.)

a. What is the point of the author's argument?

_____

_____

_____

b. Paraphrase the reasons used to support that point.

_____

_____

_____

_____

2. We've all read about those horrific cases in which a mother either abandons or kills her newborn child. Such acts seem so vicious and so heartless we are quick to condemn the mothers involved as monsters worthy of the severest punishment. That instinctive reaction is understandable. Yet a convincing case can be made for a different response, one based more on compassion than fury, because women who commit such crimes are extremely ill and not conscious of what they are doing. As Michael Delcroix, a former gynecologist and trial expert on the subject points out, the women who murder their children following pregnancy are in a "psychotic[†] state and no more responsible for their actions than a schizophrenic[†] who kills" under the delusion that he or she is being attacked. Those sentiments are echoed by Felix Navarro, president of the French Association for the Recognition of Pregnancy Denial. According to Navarro, "The judgment of the women is altered; they're not aware of what they're doing. Legally, they should not be tried. They are in a sort of state of

---

[†]psychotic: related to psychosis, a mental disorder characterized by a loss of contact with reality.
[†]schizophrenia: a form of psychosis that is often characterized by delusions, or false ideas about the nature of reality.

Copyright © Cengage Learning. All rights reserved.

temporary insanity." (Source of quotations: Tracy Clark-Flory. "Defending Mothers Who Kill," Salon.com, July 30, 2010.)

a. What is the point of the author's argument?

_____

_____

_____

b. Paraphrase the experts used to support that point.

_____

_____

_____

_____

_____

_____

3. It's never too late to get physically fit. A 2009 study published in the *New England Journal of Medicine* showed that taking up weight training can reverse some of the effects of aging. In the experiment, nursing home residents ranging in age from eighty-six to ninety-five participated in a supervised, eight-week weight-training program. All of these elderly people increased their strength and improved their balance. Another more recent study conducted by the University of Pennsylvania Medical School has shown that elderly people who take up weight training can improve their bone density and reduce arthritic pain.

a. What is the point of the author's argument?

_____

_____

_____

b. Paraphrase the results of the studies used to support that point.

_____

_____

Copyright © Cengage Learning. All rights reserved.

_____

_____

4. Almost every college student has experienced pre-finals terror—the horrible anxiety that puts your stomach on a roller coaster and your brain in a blender. Few escape those final-exam jitters because everyone knows just how much is riding on that one exam, often more than half of the course grade. Yet therein lies the crux* of the problem. Infrequent high-stakes exams don't encourage students to do their best work. More frequent tests—given, say, every two or three weeks—would be a much more effective method of discovering how well students are or are not mastering course concepts. With more frequent testing, students would be less anxious when they take exams; thus anxiety would no longer interfere with exam performance. More frequent testing also encourages students to review on a regular basis something that a one-shot final exam does not do. Lots of tests also mean more feedback, and students would know early in the course what terms or concepts required additional explanation and review. They wouldn't have to wait until the end of the semester to find out that they had misunderstood, or missed altogether, a critical idea or fact.

a. What is the point of the author's argument?

_____

_____

_____

b. Paraphrase the reasons used to support that point.

_____

_____

_____

_____

_____

*crux: core, heart, key point.

Copyright © Cengage Learning. All rights reserved.

Copyright © Cengage Learning. All rights reserved.

ALLUSION ALERT

The Great Gatsby
The Great Gatsby by F. Scott Fitzgerald is one of the most famous American novels ever written. The novel tells the story of Jay Gatsby, a man who amasses great wealth to win Daisy Buchanan, the woman he adores. It also describes how the very rich sometimes make their own rules while destroying the lives of others in the process. Allusions to the book have come to suggest the pursuit of wealth, excessive spending, and a longing for the American dream, defined as financial success—for example, "Except for Fitzgerald's Gatsby, few people have gone to so much effort to display their wealth."

Flawed Arguments

The preceding section introduced five common ways to support an argument. In this section, you'll learn about some of the most common mistakes writers can make in their attempts to build an argument. Familiarize yourself with these errors in reasoning so that you can readily spot them when they appear in writing.

Irrelevant Reasons

As you know from Chapter 8, authors sometimes include reasons that aren't really relevant to their opinion or claim. Here, for example, is an argument that does not quite work because the author includes an irrelevant reason:

© Galen Rowell/Corbis

The 1996 tragedy on Mount Everest in which eight people died in a single day is proof enough that amateurs should not be scaling the world's highest mountain. Even with the most skillful and reliable guides, amateurs with little or no mountaineering experience cannot possibly know how to respond to the sudden storms that strike the mountain without warning. Dependent on their guides for every move they make, amateur climbers can easily lose sight of the guides when a heavy storm hits. Left to their own devices, they are more than likely to make a mistake, one that will harm themselves or others. Besides, rich people—the climb can cost anywhere from $30,000 to $60,000—shouldn't be encouraged to think that money buys everything. As F. Scott Fitzgerald so powerfully illustrated in *The Great Gatsby*, it's precisely that attitude that often leads to tragedy and death.

The point of this passage is clear: Amateurs should not be climbing Mount Everest. To support that opinion, the author does offer a relevant reason: Mount Everest can be the scene of sudden storms that leave amateur climbers stranded, separated from their guides, and likely to harm themselves or others because they don't have the experience to handle the situation.

But tucked away in the passage is a less relevant reason: Rich people should not be allowed to think money buys everything. Well, maybe they shouldn't. Yet that particular reason, along with the allusion to *The Great Gatsby*, is not related to the author's claim. Neither one clarifies why amateurs and the world's tallest mountain don't mix. This is the point that needs to be argued with relevant reasons.

Circular Reasoning

Writers convinced of their own rightness sometimes engage in **circular reasoning**. They offer an opinion and follow it with a reason that says the same thing in different words. Circular reasoning is, unfortunately, not unusual. If a writer is hopelessly biased and believes that no other opinion is worth holding, he or she may not bother to support the opinion, believing that its rightness is self-evident.

In the following passage, for example, the writer believes that the U.S. system of food inspection needs to be seriously overhauled. The author is so convinced he is right he has forgotten to give us reasons why this change should occur. Yet to consider sharing this opinion, we need to know more about the problems with the current system and why a different one would be better. But, instead of offering reasons for his opinion, the author merely repeats it in different words.

Currently, our food supply is in danger of being contaminated from many different sources. When the very food we put into our mouths endangers our health, it is clear that we need to institute strict and

Copyright © Cengage Learning. All rights reserved.

regular inspections of food raised or grown in the United States. These inspections should also apply to food imported from other countries. People should be able to sit down to a meal and not worry that the food they eat will make them sick. However, we won't have that sense of security about our food supply unless we improve our current system of inspections.

Hasty Generalizations

Generalizations are broad statements that summarize a number of different but related events. The following are all examples of generalizations:

> 1. Americans have finally learned to love soccer.
>
> 2. The work of Mexican painter Diego Rivera (1886–1957) constantly invited controversy.
>
> 3. Media sensationalism has become the norm and objectivity the exception.

Because generalizations cover a lot of territory, the rule of thumb for using them effectively is this: The broader and more wide-ranging the generalization, the more examples writers need to supply in order to convince. If an author generalizes about a large group on the basis of one or even two examples, critical readers think twice before making the author's opinion their own.

In the following passage, the author makes a general statement about all HMOs. Unfortunately, that statement is based on one lone example. That makes it a **hasty generalization**, or a generalization based on too few examples to be meaningful. For critical readers, hasty generalizations are a sign of sloppy thinking. Their presence in an argument works against acceptance of the author's opinion.

> HMOs are not giving consumers adequate health care. Instead, budget considerations are consistently allowed to outweigh the patients' need for treatment. In one case, a child with a severely deformed cleft palate was denied cosmetic surgery because the child's HMO considered the surgery unnecessary, yet the child had trouble eating and drinking.

Copyright © Cengage Learning. All rights reserved.

Unidentified Experts

In the passage about cloning on page 594, it makes sense for the author to quote a bioethicist in support of her opinion. After all, a bioethicist specializes in the study of moral and ethical issues that result from or apply to medical and biological discoveries and procedures. However, critical readers are rightly suspicious of references to unidentified experts, who may or may not be qualified to offer an opinion. Consider, for example, the "expert" cited in the following passage:

> Despite the doom-and-gloom sayers who constantly worry about the state of the environment, the Earth is actually in pretty good shape. As Dr. Paul Benjamin recently pointed out, "Nature is perfectly capable of taking care of herself; she's been doing it for hundreds of years."

The author uses Dr. Paul Benjamin to support her claim that environmentalists anxious about the Earth's future are dead wrong. Yet for all we know, Dr. Benjamin might be a dentist. A dental degree does not qualify him as an environmental expert. Without some knowledge of Dr. Benjamin's credentials, or qualifications, we shouldn't be swayed by his opinion. It also would help to know more about Dr. Benjamin's personal background and biases. If, for example, he's worked for a company cited for abuses to the environment, his ability to stay objective is suspect.

Inappropriate Experts

Occasionally, a writer might also attempt to support an argument by citing a famous person who doesn't truly qualify as an expert in the area under discussion.

> We should never intervene in the affairs of other countries. After all, didn't George Washington tell us to avoid entangling ourselves in the affairs of other nations? Even today, we should let his wisdom be our guide and steer clear of foreign involvements that drain our energy and our resources.

During the eighteenth century, George Washington may well have qualified as an expert in foreign affairs. But to cite him as an authority on modern problems is inappropriate. It is doubtful that Washington

Copyright © Cengage Learning. All rights reserved.

could have imagined America's current status as an international power. Thus his opinion could not be considered adequately informed. Critical readers would not be impressed by references to his name and authority.

Unidentified Research

In the following passage, the author relies on some "studies" to convince readers that pornography should be more strictly censored. But to be convincing as support, scientific research needs **attribution**. In short, readers need to know who conducted the research. Unnamed studies like those referred to in this passage should arouse readers' skepticism.

> Because pornography puts women's lives in danger, it must be more strictly censored. Studies have shown again and again that pornography is directly related to rapes and assaults on women. As if that weren't enough, by repeatedly presenting women as sexual objects, pornography encourages men to think of women as lesser beings, a cause and effect relationship noted by several prominent researchers.

Authors may identify a study in the text itself or in a footnote that refers readers to a list of sources at the back of the book. Where a study is identified doesn't matter so much. What matters is that the author provides readers with enough information to check the study or studies being used to support the writer's opinion.

Dated Research

It also helps to know *when* the study was conducted; a writer who uses out-of-date studies rightfully risks losing readers' confidence. Take, for example, the following passage:

> The threat of radon gas is not as serious as we have been led to believe. In 1954, a team of government researchers studying the effects of radon in the home found no relationship between high levels of the gas in private dwellings and the incidence of lung cancer.

Here we have an author trying to prove a point about radon gas with a more than half-century-old study. To be considered effective evidence for an opinion, scientific research should be considerably more up to date.

Copyright © Cengage Learning. All rights reserved.

CHECK YOUR UNDERSTANDING

Complete the following chart by describing the types of errors that can occur in arguments.

Type of Support	Possible Error	Definition of Error
Reasons	Irrelevant reasons	
	Circular reasoning	
Examples and illustrations	Hasty generalizations	
Expert opinion	Unidentified experts	
	Inappropriate experts	
Research results	Unidentified research	
	Dated research	

◆ EXERCISE 4   **Recognizing Errors in Reasoning**

DIRECTIONS   Identify the error in reasoning by circling the appropriate letter.

EXAMPLE

Fast Food and Obesity

These days it's difficult to avoid the fact that the United States is in the grip of a serious health problem: More than 60 percent of the population is overweight. As a result, many men and women are at increased risk of serious diseases, ranging from colon cancer to diabetes. But if you count up the calories in, say, an oversized cheeseburger or a slice of double-cheese pizza, is it any wonder that obesity is a growing problem?

Copyright © Cengage Learning. All rights reserved.

Fast-food companies arose to meet a real need: Americans were pressed for time and often needed to eat their meals on the run. But instead of making those meals healthy as well as profitable, the fast-food industry decided it was better if they used cooking methods that shortened preparation time and, not incidentally, increased profits. Thus Americans were consuming, without their knowledge, high-calorie meals that didn't cost all that much in dollars but were very expensive in terms of health risks. No wonder people are suing fast-food companies for obesity-related health problems. As Professor James Darwin has pointed out, when it comes to America's health problems, the fast-food industry has a lot to answer for.

a. irrelevant reason

b. circular reasoning

c. hasty generalization

d. unidentified or inappropriate expert

e. unidentified or dated research

EXPLANATION   In this case, *d* is the correct answer because the author uses the words of Professor James Darwin to support his case. However, we know nothing about Professor Darwin's background. Thus we cannot tell if he is qualified to decide what the fast-food industry does or does not have to answer for.

1. If you have a grass lawn surrounding your house, you are probably contributing to this country's environmental problems. For one thing, you could be using fertilizers and pesticides that can damage the soil structure, pollute wells, and kill wildlife. Homeowners with lawns actually use more fertilizers annually than the entire country of India puts on its crops. They also apply up to ten times more pesticides than U.S. farmers do. Unfortunately, research has proven that these chemicals wash off and pollute water supplies, thus contaminating the food chain. Lawn mowers cause another environmental problem. Studies show that they produce as much air pollution in one hour as a car produces in a 350-mile drive. In addition, grass clippings are choking already overflowing landfills. Yard waste, most of which is cut grass, is the second-largest component of the 160 million tons of solid waste we dump into landfills every year. If that weren't enough, your lawn may be contributing to the destruction of plant and animal species. When developers building new houses bulldoze complex habitats and

Copyright © Cengage Learning. All rights reserved.

replace them with houses and grass, many plants and animals are killed or starved out.

a. irrelevant reason

b. circular reasoning

c. hasty generalization

d. unidentified or inappropriate expert

e. unidentified or dated research

2. The U.S. government needs to invest more money to improve and expand this country's rail service. In particular, Congress should commit to developing a national intercity network of high-speed trains. An intermodal transportation system (one that includes rail along with highways and airlines) is essential to keeping Americans moving in the event of a crisis. During a national emergency, if one mode of transportation is disrupted, the others should be able to absorb the traffic and allow travel to continue. For example, when airplanes were grounded for several days following terrorist attacks in September 2001, people relied on Amtrak passenger trains to get them where they needed to go. Without the trains, our nation would have been paralyzed. Furthermore, countries such as France and Germany have high-speed rail systems. Railroad transportation is an important public service, and it needs to be kept efficient and up to date.

a. irrelevant reason

b. circular reasoning

c. hasty generalization

d. unidentified or inappropriate expert

e. unidentified or dated research

3. Thousands of people who need organ transplants die every year because too few people agree to donate organs. Consequently, some people have begun to argue for tempting donors or their families with financial incentives in the form of either cash payments or tax credits. This is a terrible idea. Under no circumstances should we institute a system that permits the exchange of money for organs. Individuals or their families should not be allowed to gain financially from helping people who need transplants. Indeed, putting price tags on human organs is an appalling solution to the problem

Copyright © Cengage Learning. All rights reserved.

of an inadequate organ supply. We may need more donors to solve this crisis, but buying organs is just not the right way to address the shortage.

a. irrelevant reason

b. circular reasoning

c. hasty generalization

d. unidentified or inappropriate expert

e. unidentified or dated research

4. It just may be nature itself—not humans burning fossil fuels—that is causing global warming. Naturally occurring gases, such as water vapor, methane, nitrous oxide, and ozone, contribute to the so-called greenhouse effect that has raised Earth's temperature 30 degrees since the "Little Ice Age" of the seventeenth and eighteenth centuries. The oceans, too, seem to be partly responsible for the overall increase in our planet's temperature. From 1998 to 2008, Dane Chang and his colleagues carefully studied the correlation between ocean temperatures and levels of carbon dioxide, the gas that causes global warming. These researchers found that increases in ocean temperature follow a rise in the atmosphere's carbon dioxide level. Such studies would seem to indicate that natural factors are producing our warmer climate.

a. irrelevant reason

b. circular reasoning

c. hasty generalization

d. unidentified or inappropriate expert

e. unidentified or dated research

5. A growing number of school districts are banning the childhood game of dodge ball from physical education classes, and rightly so. The game is simply too aggressive and can cause serious harm. In one California incident, a child playing dodge ball was knocked to the ground by the ball's impact. The child suffered a broken arm due to the fall. Dodge ball is also not especially good exercise, particularly for those who are overweight. The slowest and heaviest children usually get knocked out of the game quickly. They then spend the rest of the game on the sidelines while the more athletic kids keep playing. It doesn't take a highly trained psychologist to

Copyright © Cengage Learning. All rights reserved.

realize that this experience cannot be good for an overweight child's self-esteem or self-image.

a. irrelevant reason

b. circular reasoning

c. hasty generalization

d. unidentified or inappropriate expert

e. unidentified or dated research

Identifying the Opposing Point of View

Any argument worthy of the name has to include an opinion along with relevant and up-to-date support. Arguments, however, also frequently include the author's response to opposing points of view. Shown below is an article on home schooling. In which paragraph does the author start responding to the opposition?

The Benefits of Home Schooling

1 Although it has been harshly criticized by many—often by those who have a vested interest* in supporting the status quo*—home schooling just may be the answer to our current educational crisis. In state after state, scores in reading, science, and mathematics continue to decline in comparison to other countries. Our children are not facing the future with the skills they need to keep our country strong and competitive.

2 At home, children can learn one-on-one or in small groups. If they need some additional explanation or instruction, the home tutor can readily supply it. In public schools, in contrast, children often sit in classrooms with twenty or thirty other students. Even in charter schools, where class size is smaller, teachers often find it difficult to give students the individual attention they need. There are so many competing voices and questions, a teacher can't always respond to all of them. Some students go consciously unattended or unconsciously ignored.

3 Home schooling also allows children to learn in a familiar environment, one lacking distractions. Any parent who has delivered a weeping child to the door of his or her classroom knows full well how terrifying some children find the classroom atmosphere with its noisy hubbub. Even when

---

*vested interest: having a special reason to promote or protect that which gives one a personal advantage.
*status quo: existing state of affairs.

Copyright © Cengage Learning. All rights reserved.

children become used to the school environment, their ability to learn can be inhibited by other children who unthinkingly laugh at their mistakes or set a poor example by chatting or texting on cell phones.

4   Critics who claim that home schooling can't provide children with the breadth of knowledge they need always assume that the parents doing the teaching don't have the necessary qualifications. Yet of the parents I know personally who teach their children at home, two have a master's degree in physics, another has a doctorate in psychology, and still another is a former elementary teacher with ten years of teaching experience. Besides, who says that it's only the parents who play the role of teachers. Many home schoolers make it a point to seek out neighbors and friends who have expertise in particular subject areas. Then they invite them to teach a class.

5   Parents who take on the responsibility of home schooling do not do so lightly. They know that they must provide their children with an education that prepares them for the world they will eventually enter. Thus they make sure that they themselves or the people who come into their homes to tutor are well-prepared to teach their children what they need to know.

In this reading, the author introduces the opinion she wants readers to share in the very first paragraph: Home schooling may be the answer to what she considers an "educational crisis." The next two paragraphs then offer reasons that support this claim:

1. Children will get the attention they need when they need it; they won't be ignored.

2. They will be in a familiar environment, free of distractions and kids who provide a bad example.

By paragraph 4, though, the author feels she has to answer criticism of home schooling. She does it by insisting that parents who home school are informed about the subjects they teach, and if they are not, the tutors they employ are. Her evidence for this claim is based purely on personal experience.

In writing meant to persuade, writers frequently do address objections to their position. That means critical readers often need to go beyond evaluating the clarity of an author's opinion and the soundness of the support supplied. Sometimes, they also need to evaluate how fair and open-minded writers are in describing opposing beliefs.

Actually, it's in describing the opposition that writers are most likely to reveal a bias that limits their ability to think clearly or fairly. But more about that after Exercise 5.

Copyright © Cengage Learning. All rights reserved.

Copyright © Cengage Learning. All rights reserved.

TAKING A CLOSER LOOK

🔍

Evaluating Supporting Details
What would strengthen the author's response to critics of home schooling?

_____

_____

_____

_____

_____

_____

www

↖

INTERNET FOLLOW-UP: Making Comparisons in Education
Particularly these days as the battle over who should teach our children, public or private schools, heats up, the claim is constantly made that American kids are woefully undereducated in relation to other countries. Use the Web to evaluate that claim. Are today's children really falling so far behind the rest of the world when it comes to learning?

_____

_____

_____

_____

_____

_____

Forming Your Own Opinion
◆

If you had children, would you teach them at home as opposed to sending them to a public or a charter school? Please explain your reasoning.

◆ **EXERCISE 5**   **Identifying the Writer's Response to Opposition**

DIRECTIONS   Read each of the following selections and answer the questions that follow. Check to see how the writer responds to opposition. *Note*: If there is no response to an opposing point of view, then leave the lines for that question blank.

EXAMPLE

Home Schooling Isn't Really School

1 As a public school teacher, I have to admit I cringe every time I hear the phrase "home schooling." I know that many parents believe they are helping their children by teaching them at home. But in my experience, home schooling may do more harm than good.

2   Children who enter my class after a long period of home schooling usually have huge gaps in their education. True, they often read and write better than the average fifth grader, and their spelling is good. But they know very little about the social sciences, and science itself seems to be a foreign word.

3   In addition, children who have been schooled at home frequently have difficulty working with other children. Unused to the give-and-take of group interactions, they quickly show their discomfort or displeasure. Their response is understandable since they have spent years at home in a class of one or two at most.

4   I know that many parents believe that home schooling protects their children from dangerous or corrupting ideas and experiences. To some degree, they are probably correct in that assumption. Unfortunately, the protection home schooling provides may come at too heavy an intellectual price. Parents just do not have the necessary training or background to give their children the wide-ranging and up-to-date education they need. And certainly parents cannot provide the kind of peer socialization found in schools outside the home.

1. What is the point of the author's argument?

Home schooling may do more harm than good.

2. What two reasons does the author give in support of that point?

a. Children can end up with big gaps in their education.

b. Children schooled at home usually have difficulty working in groups.

3. Identify the opposing point of view mentioned in the reading.

Parents believe that they are protecting their children from bad experiences and

inappropriate ideas.

Copyright © Cengage Learning. All rights reserved.

4. Paraphrase the author's response.

The protection costs too much socially and intellectually.

EXPLANATION　　As is often the case, the author states the point of the argument at the beginning of the reading—home schooling can do more harm than good—and then follows with two reasons for that position. Although the answer to a possible objection appears at the end, this is not necessarily standard. Answers to objections can just as easily be sprinkled throughout.

1. Teacher Performance Linked to Pay

1　In January 2004, The Teaching Commission, a blue-ribbon panel of nineteen leaders in government, business, philanthropy, and education that was chaired by former IBM chairman Louis V. Gerstner Jr., released its report on improving education in America's schools. Among the commission's conclusions was the controversial recommendation that each teacher's pay be determined by student performance on standardized tests. Although immediately opposed by many teachers and teachers' organizations, this suggestion is increasingly being implemented in our schools and that is all to the good. Teachers should get bonuses if their students get high scores on tests of what they have learned.

2　Compensating teachers based on test results would replace an ancient system that pays a good teacher the same as a poor one. Currently, teachers' salaries are based only on years of experience, so an ineffective teacher who has taught for twenty years earns far more than a newer but far more effective one. According to The Teaching Commission, this system "does nothing to reward excellence." In other words, it would be fairer to the hardest-working teachers to reward them with bigger paychecks.

3　Opponents of performance-based pay argue that such a plan ignores the many factors affecting student performance, such as poverty or family background, that are outside teacher control. The commission, however, has recommended that teacher evaluations be designed to take such factors into account. What's more, commission members argue that many other professions use performance-based pay plans. Gerstner said, "Lawyers do it, engineers do it, business people do it. All professional people ultimately come up with methodology to judge the difference between great performance and mediocre performance. Just because it's hard doesn't mean we can't do it."

Copyright © Cengage Learning. All rights reserved.

4   In fact, The Teaching Commission believes that tying teachers' salaries to performance will help raise their overall professional status. Unfortunately, teaching is often viewed as a second-rate occupation. The commission believes, though, that if teachers were compensated like professionals in other fields and were less limited by antiquated, experience-based pay scales, the highest-performing teachers would garner more respect for their efforts. Plus, bright and more talented individuals might be attracted to the profession.

5   The end result would be an increase in student achievement. Incentives could make teachers' work more difficult, but they would be rewarded for achieving better results. They would be more inclined to do whatever it takes to help their students learn; therefore, students stand to benefit the most. (Source of dates and quotations: The Teaching Commission, "Teaching at Risk: Blue-Ribbon Panel Calls for Overhaul of Teacher Education and Compensation to Recruit and Retain Talent in America's Public Schools," Press Release, January 14, 2004.)

1. What is the point of the author's argument?

_____

_____

2. Identify the four reasons used to support that point.

a. _____

_____

b. _____

_____

c. _____

_____

d. _____

_____

3. Identify the opposing point of view mentioned in the reading.

_____

_____

Copyright © Cengage Learning. All rights reserved.

4. Paraphrase the author's response.

_____

_____

_____

2. Time to Regulate the Baby Business

1   The American Bar Association (ABA) believes that the various state laws governing the practice of surrogacy—the process in which a woman carries a child for an individual or a couple who cannot give birth—need to be standardized while the procedure in general needs more and better regulation. Given the current chaotic state of affairs, with some surrogacy agreements causing a good deal more misery than joy, it's hard to imagine how anyone could argue with this position. Probably the only people who might disagree with the ABA are those who are making huge sums of money from surrogacy arrangements.

2   Although many surrogacy arrangements work out well with minimal trauma, others become a source of misery for everyone concerned. That applies with special intensity to the babies involved in a surrogate arrangement. When the parties to what is officially titled "third-party reproduction" start quarreling, the infant or infants being fought over can end up spending a huge amount of time in foster homes. It can take months for the courts to decide who has the legal right to custody, the surrogate mother or the individuals who paid her to have what they consider to be "their" child.

3   Part of the problem haunting surrogacy arrangements is the amount of money involved. To put it bluntly, surrogacy is big business. Once all the medical expenses and fees are paid, the cost of a successful surrogacy is somewhere between $80,000 and $120,000. One agency advertising on the Web claims it can arrange for a surrogate mother to give birth for under $50,000. In other words, they offer bargain babies.

4   Not surprisingly, given sums of money that can soar into six figures, the surrogacy business has attracted some unscrupulous characters, who engage in criminal activities in order to cash in on the desperation of would-be parents. The Central American country of Guatemala has been particularly hard hit by illegal baby rings, which either coerce women into having children that can be sold or kidnap children outright. Guatemala is an impoverished country, and the women who are targeted for this treatment have little recourse when their children are taken from them. Uniform state laws that make it impossible to adopt children born to

Copyright © Cengage Learning. All rights reserved.

anonymous mothers living in foreign countries would go a long way toward curbing these horrific practices.

5   Yet heartbreaking problems can arise even when the surrogacy agreements are arranged and carried out completely within the United States. As the *New York Times* reported in a 2010 article titled "Building a Baby, with Few Ground Rules," Amy and Scott Kehoe thought they did everything right. Using the Web, Amy Kehoe found a pre-med student at the University of Michigan to donate her eggs. She found an anonymous sperm donor the same way. Using the website surromomsonline.com, the couple also found Laschell Baker of Ypsilanti, Michigan. Mrs. Baker had four children of her own and had previous experience acting as a surrogate. Once Mrs. Kehoe had hired a fertility clinic, also located online, everything seemed to be in order.

6   Initially things did go smoothly, with Mrs. Baker giving birth to twins, Bridget and Ethan, and the Kehoes taking home what they believed were their babies. One month later, though, police arrived at the Kehoes' home to take the twins away. Mrs. Baker had discovered that Mrs. Kehoe was under the treatment of a psychiatrist and had to take medication to keep her illness under control. Even the testimony of the psychiatrist, who said Mrs. Kehoe would be a good mother, could not calm her anxiety: "I couldn't see living the rest of my life worrying and wondering what had happened, or what if she hadn't taken her medicine or what if she relapsed."

7   Laschell Baker demanded and got the babies back. Had the surrogacy arrangement been carried out in California, it's likely the Kehoes would have kept the children. California has legislation friendly to surrogacy agreements. Michigan does not. The state holds that such agreements are unenforceable. Mrs. Baker was, therefore, within her rights to change her mind and assume care of the children.

8   It is precisely this kind of crazy quilt of legislation that the American Bar Association thinks should be addressed. While making the legislation uniform would not completely eliminate the heartbreak that can accompany surrogacy arrangements, it would at least ensure that both parties knew exactly what they might be getting into when they set out to engage in third-party reproduction.

1. What is the point of the author's argument?

_____

_____

Copyright © Cengage Learning. All rights reserved.

2. Identify the three reasons used to support that point.

a. _____

_____

b. _____

_____

c. _____

_____

3. Identify the opposing point of view mentioned in the reading.

_____

_____

4. Paraphrase the author's response.

_____

_____

_____

CHECK YOUR UNDERSTANDING

Add to the original draft you wrote for the Check Your Understanding Through Writing assignment on page 588 by (1) explaining how someone might challenge your opinion and (2) responding to the challenge.

TAKING A CLOSER LOOK

Clues to Meaning and Bias
In the second reading, the last sentence in paragraph 5 (p. 618) signals what to the reader?

_____

_____

Copyright © Cengage Learning. All rights reserved.

What do you think the title suggests about the author's attitude toward the existing surrogacy procedures?

_____

_____

Does anything in the reading confirm or deny your prediction based on the title? Please explain.

_____

_____

Forming Your Own Opinion
◆

Explain your position on surrogacy agreements. Would you be willing to engage in a third-party reproduction arrangement?

More About Recognizing When Bias Becomes Excessive

When writers argue an opinion, we expect them to indicate point of view, to tell us where they stand on the idea, event, or issue. We even expect them to express a bias and tell us why the side or perspective they favor is really more informed, better researched, more carefully analyzed, or easier to implement than the other ideas proposed.

What we don't expect or, more to the point, don't want is for writers presenting their opinions to be so imprisoned or blinded by their own biases they can't even imagine another point of view. While writers intending to persuade can certainly acknowledge whom or what they favor, they should respond to opposing points of view fairly and respectfully.

In the following examples, the authors seem incapable of either fairness or respect. Instead, they launch character attacks, use slippery slope reasoning, or just flat out insult the opposition.

Distracting with Personal Character Attacks

Be wary of writers who respond to opposing points of view by attacking the actions or past behavior of those they disagree with. In the following

Copyright © Cengage Learning. All rights reserved.

passage, note how the author attacks her opponent's past actions rather than his point of view.

> Once again, David DeGrecco, columnist for the *New Jersey Sun*, has presented his tired old case for gun control. DeGrecco serves up the argument that gun-control laws can help eliminate some of the violence plaguing city streets across the country. Outspoken as usual, DeGrecco is curiously silent about his recent bout with criminal behavior. Less than two weeks ago, he and his daughter were arrested at a demonstration against off-shore drilling in the Arctic. For one so determined to bring law and order to our streets, DeGrecco does not seem to mind breaking a few laws himself. Nor does he mind raising his children to do the same.

The author is opposed to the gun-control laws championed by David DeGrecco. That's certainly her right. Still, to be persuasive, she needs to challenge what the columnist claims—that gun-control laws can help eliminate violence.

But instead of doing that, she attacks the man personally, pointing out that he was recently jailed for being involved in a protest totally unrelated to gun control. Yet, DeGrecco's position on or response to off-shore oil drilling has nothing to do with the issue at hand—gun control. This is a clear instance of using a character attack to avoid addressing an opposing point of view. It's also an indication of excessive bias clouding the writer's ability to react effectively to an opposing point of view.

Sliding Down the Slippery Slope

Writers whose bias has gotten out of hand are also inclined to engage in **slippery slope** thinking. Using this approach, the writer insists that taking even one step in a particular direction will *invariably* lead to a series of steps ending in disaster. Here's an example:

> If we ban handguns, the next step will be the banning of rifles, and then people who hunt for food will no longer be able to feed their families.

Writers who use the slippery slope approach are using scare tactics rather than reason. They want you to believe that if the action, position, or behavior they don't like is allowed to occur, then a train of disasters will follow. They ignore the fact that events usually arise in response to or as a result of particular circumstances. In other words, two events being similar doesn't make them produce the same results.

Copyright © Cengage Learning. All rights reserved.

For example, many people want to ban handguns because they believe there is a connection between handguns in the home and violent crime, both inside and outside the home. However, they don't necessarily make the same connection between hunting rifles and crime. Thus it makes no sense to claim that banning handguns will *automatically* lead to banning rifles. Handguns and rifles are similar kinds of weapons, but they are used for very different purposes and under very different circumstances.

However, writers who are excessively biased in favor of their own opinion don't want to encourage any such analysis. They just want to scare you into agreeing with them. Don't let them do it.

If Reason Fails, Try Insults

Insults are a close relative of personal attacks. The author who uses insults doesn't go after the behavior or past experience of the opposition. Instead, the writer labels the opposing point of view as ridiculous, stupid, outrageous, and so on. Take your pick of nasty adjectives as long as it's negative.

Here's an example of someone who has given up on analyzing and responding to opposition. This writer's answer is to simply insult anyone who doesn't agree that social media in the classroom are a disaster.

Social Media Needs to Stay Outside the Classroom

1 It appears that a growing number of instructors are trying to make social media like Twitter, Facebook, and Flickr part of their courses. Flip through the contents of highly esteemed journals on education and instruction, and you can find articles describing how teachers can make tweets a part of class discussions or use Facebook to discuss homework assignments.

2 As a veteran instructor of more than two decades, I have seen numerous, silly educational fads come and go. But this one just takes the cake for sheer idiocy. As Mark Bauerlein, the author of *The Dumbest Generation,* has eloquently pointed out, "the fonts of knowledge are everywhere, but the rising generation is camped in the desert passing stories, pictures, tunes, and texts back and forth."

3 So what should instructors do in response to the fact that our students couldn't care less about their cultural inheritance when the thrill of being connected to their peers beckons? Why, what else, just capitulate totally to standards established by the students they are allegedly teaching. After all, not to capitulate might actually require some serious planning and effort

Copyright © Cengage Learning. All rights reserved.

on their part. That takes time, and time is what these teachers don't have, given all the texting and tweeting they have to do to "teach" their classes.

The author of this passage expresses a very strong bias against bringing social media into the classroom. There's nothing wrong with that opinion. Many people share it. What the writer fails to do, however, is to address, in any way, the reasons put forth by people who believe that social media like Facebook and Twitter can play a significant role in education. To adopt the author's tone, that might take "some serious planning and effort." She would rather insult the opposing point of view than seriously examine it.

◆ EXERCISE 6   Looking for Evidence of Excessive Bias

DIRECTIONS   Each of the following selections expresses a strong bias for or against a particular position. But in several instances, the author is so heavily biased, he or she gets careless and makes some errors in reasoning. Circle the appropriate letter to indicate an error. *Note*: Even the readings with errors may have some sound logic, so examine each paragraph in the readings individually.

1. No Sexual Harassment Equals No Soldiers

1   Over the years, there's been a good deal of attention focused on sexual harassment in the military, and rightly so. No one wants to see officers in charge of young female recruits abuse their power by sexually harassing those in their care. However, supporters of women in the military are making a crucial mistake when they try to eliminate sexism in the military and at the same time insist that women should go into combat alongside men.

2   To be a warrior means that a soldier has to revert to a more primitive mode of behavior and thought. It means that one has to assume a kill-or-be-killed mentality that allows little room for compassion or sensitivity. It is very difficult, perhaps impossible, to encourage this mindset in men and at the same time expect them to fight side by side with women without reverting to a more primitive mode of behavior. As Fred C. Iklé, an undersecretary of defense in the Reagan administration, expressed it, "You can't cultivate the necessary commitment to physical violence and fully protect against the risk of harassment. Military life may . . . foster the attitudes that tend toward rape, such as aggression and single-minded assertion."[†]

[†]This line of reasoning was used by Richard Rayner, "The Warrior Besieged," *New York Times*, June 22, 1997, p. 29.

Copyright © Cengage Learning. All rights reserved.

3   Viewed from this perspective, efforts to eliminate sexual harassment could have disastrous consequences during wartime combat. Committed to being respectful toward women, male soldiers will also feel they have to rein in their aggression. Consequently, they will hold back during combat training. In the end, they will even hold back during combat itself. Our country will lose its military strength and its position as a world power.

a.   The author insults the opposing point of view.

b.   The author uses slippery slope reasoning.

c.   The author engages in a character attack.

d.   The author does not display excessive bias.

2. Egg Donation May Not Be Such a Miracle for Donors

1   Because so many couples desperately want a child and can't have one, the search for women willing to donate their eggs for in vitro fertilization[†] has become a big business. Although many people consider in vitro fertilization a wondrous miracle, I must admit to being skeptical about the use of egg donors. The couple who gains a child, thanks to a donor, may be rightly jubilant. The donor, however, may be taking more risks than she realizes.

2   For starters, the egg-donation process is not particularly pleasant. To prepare for it, women take daily hormone injections which force the maturation of ten to twenty eggs instead of the normal one or two. As a result of the injections, donors often suffer cramping and mood swings. Sometimes their ovaries become dangerously enlarged. At this time, there have been no signs of long-term side effects on donors, but it is possible that the injections may increase the risk of ovarian cancer. No one really knows for sure what the long-term effects are mainly because in vitro fertilization hasn't been around for very long.

3   Those who favor the use of egg donors argue that the women are being well paid for the risks they take. Unfortunately, the issue of payment only points to another objection. Some clinics pay donors as much as $8,000 for their eggs. In the face of such a sum, women who are young or poor—or, in many cases, both—can be lured by the money into ignoring the risks. Diane Aronson, the executive director of Resolve, the national support group for infertile couples, has pointed out that large sums of money offered donors can lead to "inappropriate assessment of risk. If you're a

---

[†]in vitro fertilization: *in vitro* literally means "in glass"; the term refers to the process of creating life in an artificial setting outside the human body.

Copyright © Cengage Learning. All rights reserved.

college student, four cycles at $5,000 each may pay for . . . college" and if you're a poor, unmarried mother, $5,000 will pay the rent for months.

4   Yes, egg donation may well provide infertile couples with the baby they so desperately desire, but someone else may be paying a terrible price for their joy. Couples considering egg donation should ask themselves whether they are willing to let another woman take serious health risks so that they can become parents.

a. The author insults the opposing point of view.
b. The author uses slippery slope reasoning.
c. The author engages in a character attack.
d. The author does not display excessive bias.

3. Dress Codes Should Go Out of Fashion

1   Unlike teenagers of a generation ago, many of today's kids have a more relaxed attitude about gender identity. In contrast to their parents, they don't feel compelled to follow the unspoken rules of their gender. This is particularly true concerning their appearance, and teenagers all over the country are challenging the boundaries of appropriate male or female dress and demeanor.*

2   In Houston, Texas, a cross-dressing senior was sent home when his wig violated school rules about hair length for males. A similar fate met a teenager in Cobb County, Georgia, after he arrived at school in full make-up and skinny jeans. A Mississippi teen found her photo eliminated from her yearbook because she had posed in a man's tux instead of the girls' traditional black drape around the shoulders.

3   However, not all high schools are so inflexible and rigid about student attire. The gold standard for a school where administrators show both compassion and common sense is probably Rincon High School in Tucson, Arizona. At Rincon High, the population is extremely diverse—students come from more than thirty countries—which may be one reason why rigid standards of dress are not observed. As school counselor Brenda Kazen expressed it, "Gender expression is very fluid here. . . . Our kids are just used to seeing different things, and they're O.K. with it."

4   So, too, apparently are school administrators, who don't try to uphold old-fashioned standards about what's appropriate dress for teenage girls and boys. If they want to, boys at Rincon can wear make-up. If they choose to accessorize with frilly scarves and wigs, that's fine, too. Girls have the same freedom of choice, and wearing male attire is not going to get them booted out of school. The wonder is why more high schools don't follow in Rincon's footsteps,

*demeanor: behavior in relation to others.

Copyright © Cengage Learning. All rights reserved.

because telling kids not to dress in the way they choose is like telling a puppy not to play or a mother grizzly not to protect her young. It's pointless.

5   For teenagers, dress is a form of self-expression and social experimentation. It's a way of trying on and testing personal and sexual identity in order to determine the right fit, even if that fit doesn't follow traditional patterns of behavior. If kids can't try out different modes of being in high school, when can they do it? They certainly can't do it when their job might be at stake.

6   Also interacting on a daily basis with those who don't necessarily fulfill society's norms concerning appropriate gender behavior teaches kids an important lesson about accepting people whose sexual orientation may differ from theirs. Administrators who are obsessed with appearing normal and insist on applying dress codes that suspend students for cross dressing are only encouraging harassment and discrimination.

7   Even more oblivious to the changing times are those so out of touch they think uniforms are the answer to cross dressing in the schools. This response is so dim-witted, it's hard to know what to say to parents and administrators who propose it. Perhaps the kindest response is to point out that the age of Victoria ended more than a century ago, and anyone living or working with kids today needs to mentally move into the twenty-first century or risk being regarded in much the way fossils are, as relics of a bygone age.

a. The author insults the opposing point of view.
b. The author uses slippery slope reasoning.
c. The author engages in a character attack.
d. The author does not display excessive bias.

4. Of Power and Prosecutors

1   In April 2007, the attorney general of North Carolina, Roy A. Cooper III, announced that he was dismissing all charges against three Duke University lacrosse players. The three young men had been accused of raping a young woman who performed at one of their parties. At the same time that he announced the dismissal of the charges, Cooper also rebuked Michael B. Nifong, the district attorney of Durham County, for rushing to accuse the young men while failing to thoroughly investigate the woman's allegations.

2   Cooper's public rebuke highlights a point made by Angela J. Davis in her 2008 book, *Arbitrary Justice: The Power of the American Prosecutor*. Davis, a professor of law at American University Washington College of Law, argues that prosecutors all over the country have the power to direct and control the outcome of criminal cases, often with serious, even disastrous, consequences.

Copyright © Cengage Learning. All rights reserved.

3   According to Professor Davis, Nifong, who has been accused of withholding evidence favorable to the defense, is the rule rather than the exception. She insists that prosecutors intent on winning withhold evidence all the time, without oversight or penalty for their actions, and that our current judicial system, with its lack of transparency,* has no system in place for checking prosecutorial power. If anything, Davis argues, state legislatures have routinely passed laws that increase the power of prosecutors without worrying about the possibility that prosecutors might, unconsciously or intentionally, be corrupted by the extent of their authority. Victims of prosecutorial excess, she insists, are usually poor people who do not have the resources to mount a defense against prosecutorial injustice. Her hope is that the Duke case will shine a much-needed light on this problem in the American justice system and force a change.

4   Despite Professor Davis's detailed and often eloquent analysis of the failings inherent in the current judicial system, those ready to agree with her and demand a change in our justice system should remember that Professor Davis herself was once intimately acquainted with the criminal justice system. Angela Davis first came to the public's attention when she was linked to the murder of Judge Harold Haley during an attempt to free a Black Panther defendant in a courtroom in 1970. Davis went underground, becoming the subject of an intense manhunt. After eighteen months as a fugitive, she was captured, arrested, tried, and eventually acquitted in one of the most famous trials in recent U.S. history. Is it any wonder that she doesn't like prosecutors? (Source of information on Professor Davis's book: Evan R. Goldstein, "The Power of the Prosecutor," *Chronicle of Higher Education*, May 11, 2007, p. B2.)

    a. The author uses circular reasoning.

    b. The author uses slippery slope reasoning.

    c. The author engages in a character attack.

    d. The author does not display excessive bias.

✔ CHECK YOUR UNDERSTANDING

Explain slippery slope reasoning and personal character attacks.

_____

_____

_____

Copyright © Cengage Learning. All rights reserved.

*transparency: openness, ease of visibility.

WORD CHECK

The following words were introduced and defined in pages 587–627. See how well you can match the words with the meanings. When you finish, make sure to check the meanings of any words you missed because the same words will turn up in tests at the end of the chapter.

1. valid	_____	a.	core, heart, key point
2. dynamics	_____	b.	behavior in relation to others
3. vile	_____	c.	weakening, causing loss or lack of energy
4. mandatory	_____	d.	disgusting, despicable
5. debilitating	_____	e.	openness, ease of visibility
6. crux	_____	f.	existing or given state of affairs
7. vested interest	_____	g.	having a special reason to promote or protect that which gives one a personal advantage
8. status quo	_____		
9. demeanor	_____	h.	justified, just, well grounded in reason or proof, also up to date
10. transparency	_____		
		i.	required or commanded by law or another authority
		j.	interactions, patterns of behavior

◆ **EXERCISE 7**   **More About Form and Meaning**

DIRECTIONS   Fill in the blanks with one of the words listed below.

dynamics	crux	valid	vile	vested interest
debilitating	mandatory	demeanor	status quo	transparency

1. Among many other things, social psychologists explore the _____ of personal relationships.

2. Telling someone to get to the point is a less formal way of asking for the _____ of an issue.

Copyright © Cengage Learning. All rights reserved.

3. Writers have a _____ in encouraging a passion for language.

4. Helmets should be _____ for everyone who rides a motorcycle.

5. To enter the country, you will need a _____ passport and proof of recent immunization against cholera and typhoid.

6. More _____ is needed in the government's negotiations, or the public will mistrust the resulting agreement.

7. It's not exactly surprising when people who have all their needs and wants met are happy with the _____; why would they want anything to change?

8. Making fun of people with disabilities, abusing one's pets, and profiting from the misfortune of others are all good examples of absolutely _____ behavior.

9. Her son was trying to seem natural as if nothing unusual had occurred, but his _____ was telling another story, and she knew he was anxious about something.

10. Professional athletes suffer so many _____ injuries in the course of their careers, their bodies never quite recover.

Copyright © Cengage Learning. All rights reserved.

DIGGING DEEPER What Exactly Is a Frivolous Lawsuit?

Looking Ahead Close to twenty years ago, Stella Liebeck spilled a cup of McDonald's coffee on her skin and as a result of her injuries, she sued the company and won over $2 million in damages.[†] That lawsuit, however, became grist for a nationwide movement pushing for "tort reform."[†] The claim was that frivolous lawsuits were hurting the country economically and socially. Tort reform remains a hot-button issue to this day.

1   The lawsuit seventy-nine-year-old Stella Liebeck launched against McDonald's in 1994 after spilling hot coffee on herself as she went through the drive-through lane immediately become the stuff of comedy. A *Seinfeld*[†] episode even used it, making one of the characters sue for damages after he spilled coffee on himself. But the general attitude toward the suit, on television and off, was summed up in the response of another *Seinfeld* character, Elaine, who expressed puzzlement at the very idea of a lawsuit involving hot coffee being spilled and McDonald's being somehow liable, "Who ever heard of this anyway? Suing a company because their coffee is too hot? Coffee is supposed to be hot." In other words, the suit was a ridiculous joke.

2   What got left out of all the jokes, though, were the actual details of the case. Liebeck suffered third-degree burns. Third-degree burns are the most serious kind, especially for a woman her age. Plus, there had been at least 700 previous cases of people being scalded by McDonald's coffee before Liebeck went to court. McDonald's had settled other claims but did not want to give Liebeck the $20,000 compensation she had requested. So she sued and the case went to court.

3   What Liebeck's lawyers proved was that McDonald's was making its coffee 30 to 50 degrees hotter than other restaurants. In fact, the Shriner Burn Institute had already warned McDonald's not to serve coffee above 130 degrees. Yet the liquid that burned Liebeck was the usual temperature for McDonald's brew—about 190 degrees. As a result of Liebeck's suit, McDonald's coffee is now sold at the same temperature as most other restaurants.

4   Yes, there probably are trivial lawsuits filed on a regular basis. But Liebeck's wasn't one of them. It's actually ironic that the "hot coffee"

[†]The judge reduced the amount to half a million.
[†]tort reform: refers to a movement to revise or create legislation that would put limits on damages paid out in lawsuits.
[†]*Seinfeld* was a popular sitcom that aired between 1989 and 1998.

Copyright © Cengage Learning. All rights reserved.

lawsuit, as it's come to be called, is often cited as an illustration of why the country desperately needs tort reform. Yet a closer examination of this issue suggests that citizens might want to think twice before joining in the chorus of calls to enact tort reform.

5   Tort reform legislation, in place or pending, differs from state to state. Thus one of the questions involved in the debate is how tort reform should go forward. Should it be on a state or federal level?

6   In general, though, the tort reform movement focuses on three goals: (1) the need to limit the circumstances under which injured people may file a lawsuit after being injured by a product or procedure, (2) the goal of making it more difficult for people injured by a product or procedure to obtain a trial by jury, and (3) the desire to place limits on the amount of money injured parties may be awarded.

7   In the eyes of some, like political activist and organizer Jon Greenbaum, the idea that the country is desperately in need of tort reform is a myth. From his perspective, the right to sue corporations or companies if their products were defective or their procedures badly managed or fraudulent was a consumer victory won in the 1950s. In his eyes, *now* is not the time to abandon that right. He thinks implementing tort reform would be a step backward for consumers, not a step forward: "It will limit our ability to hold corporations accountable for their misdeeds. Corporate America has succeeded to a great extent in buying up our legislators and capturing regulatory bodies. We must not let them wrest control of the judicial system as well."

8   That, however, would not be the position of Court Koenning, the president of Citizens Against Lawsuit Abuse of Houston. For him, lawsuits demanding compensation for injury due to defective products or procedures reveal a growing canker on American society—the abdication of personal responsibility. As he writes, "The somebody's gotta pay attitude is pervasive and that does not bode well for future generations. We need to reacquaint ourselves with personal responsibility and stop playing the blame game. We need to realize that every dilemma or personal disappointment is not fodder for a lawsuit and does not warrant a treasure trove of cash."

9   These are all stirring sentiments. But they need to be viewed in the light of what consumers "playing the blame game" in court have actually tried to accomplish. In Los Angeles, California, consumers have gone to court to stop health insurers from cancelling policies of people newly diagnosed with a serious illness. The insurance cancellations, usually based on technicalities, seem to target people who will require long-term and expensive care, for which the insurance companies would have to pay if the policies weren't cancelled.

Copyright © Cengage Learning. All rights reserved.

10   In Harrisburg, Pennsylvania, consumers turned to the courts to take action against "mortgage rescue" companies who, for a fee, claimed they could help those falling behind on their payments. But after the fee was paid, no help was forthcoming. In Hartford, Connecticut, consumers also went to court against a pharmaceutical company that was blocking generic alternatives to the high-priced drugs on which the company's profits were based.

11   This is not to say that all personal injury complaints taken to court are worthy of respect. Did anyone really want to see the woman who sued a cosmetics company for changing the shade of her hair become a millionaire? But many of the personal injury lawsuits brought by consumers do real good, helping not just the litigant but the public in general. We might want to consider that fact next time we hear or read another argument in favor of tort reform because what we might be reforming is our own right to seek justice by legal means. (Source of quotes: www.setexasrecord.com/ arguments/226869-starbucks-hot-tea-lawsuit-highlights-a-void-in-personal-responsibility; Jon Greenbaum, "McDonald's Hot Coffee Lawsuit and Beyond: The Tort Reform Myth Machine," CommonDreams.org.)

Sharpening Your Skills

DIRECTIONS   Answer the following questions by circling the letter of the correct response or filling in the blanks.

1. Which of the following statements accurately paraphrases the main idea of the reading?
   a. The movement for tort reform is spreading throughout the country, thanks to the frivolous lawsuits that have been waged over the last few decades; they are clogging the system and something needs to be done to put an end to them.
   b. Consumers who take their concerns to court should be praised rather than criticized for their efforts; personal injury lawsuits have never done anything but good.
   c. While some personal injury claims may be worthless, many are necessary in order to hold corporations and companies accountable for their actions, and we should think twice about supporting tort reform.
   d. The tort reform movement is controlled by the country's big corporations, and it is yet another way to deny citizens their right to social justice.

Copyright © Cengage Learning. All rights reserved.

2. The author's purpose is
   a. to tell readers about the tort reform movement's history and goals.
   b. to convince readers that the tort reform movement has some serious drawbacks.

3. The author is
   a. biased in favor of tort reform.
   b. biased against tort reform.

   Please explain your answer.

   _____

   _____

   _____

   _____

   _____

4. Would you label the author's bias excessive? _____
   Please explain your answer.

   _____

   _____

5. The author opens with a description of an episode from *Seinfeld*. What is the purpose of that detail?

   _____

   _____

   The detail is
   a. major.
   b. minor.

6. Paraphrase the three goals of the tort reform movement.

   1. _____

   _____

Copyright © Cengage Learning. All rights reserved.

2. _____

3. _____

7. Based on how it's used in this sentence, what do you think a *canker* is? "For him, lawsuits demanding compensation for injury due to defective products or procedures reveal a growing canker on American society—the abdication of personal responsibility."_____

   Is this an example of figurative language? _____ Please explain your answer.

   _____

   _____

   _____

8. In paragraph 11, the author says at the end of the paragraph, "We might want to consider that fact. . . ." In your own words, what does the word *fact* refer to?

   _____

   _____

   Does the word *fact* actually refer to a fact? _____ Please explain your answer.

   _____

   _____

9. How does the author respond in paragraph 9 to Court Koenning, the person quoted in paragraph 8?

   _____

   _____

   _____

Copyright © Cengage Learning. All rights reserved.

10. How would you describe the author's tone?

    a. neutral

    b. skeptical

    c. disgusted

    d. hopeful

---

www

INTERNET FOLLOW-UP: Grist for the Mill

The "looking ahead" section of the previous reading uses the word *grist*, which is a shorthand version of the idiom† "grist for the mill." What is grist?

_____

How can a lawsuit be compared to grist?

_____

_____

Can this idiom be considered figurative language? _____

Forming Your Own Opinion ♦

What do you think about tort reform? Do you support it? Are you against it? Are you somewhere in between? Please explain the basis for your opinion.

ALLUSION ALERT

Rip Van Winkle

Rip Van Winkle is a character in a story by the nineteenth-century writer Washington Irving. After drinking a mysterious liquor given to him by some strange people he meets in the woods, Rip fell asleep for twenty years. When he returned home, life was very different and the country was in the middle of the Revolutionary War. When allusions are made to Rip Van Winkle, they are meant to suggest that someone has missed out on events that the rest of the world is altogether familiar with. "Returning to school after twenty years as a corporate executive, Karen felt like Rip Van Winkle returning to a village and a home she no longer recognized."

---

†idiom: an expression specific to a particular language, which makes no sense when translated. It only makes sense to native speakers, who have heard or seen it used numerous times and understand the meaning from the context.

Copyright © Cengage Learning. All rights reserved.

▶ **TEST 1**   **Reviewing New Vocabulary**

DIRECTIONS   Fill in the blanks with one of the words listed below.

debilitating	dynamics	crux	valid	vested interest
transparency	mandatory	demeanor	vile	status quo

1. **Understanding Mob Psychology**

In one of his most famous books, *Group Psychology and the Analysis of the Ego*, Sigmund Freud tried to explain the _____ of what happens when a group of seemingly independent individuals turns into an unthinking, uninhibited, and often dangerous mob. For Freud, people in groups were inclined to give over their free will to a powerful leader, who they thought could provide safety from harm in exchange for their complete obedience.

Freud's theory may be _____ because people in groups do seem to lose their independence and defer to the person who is most outspoken and aggressive. The more strong-willed and determined the speech and _____ of the leader, the less inclined group members are to speak out and insert their individuality or disagreement. They are also less willing to question the _____ because to do so might get them thrown out of the group providing them with safety.

2. _____ drug testing for certain professions, like police, pilots, and firefighters, arouses understandable controversy. At the _____ of the controversy is, to a large degree, the method of testing. After all, it does seem _____ for an employer to ask employees to submit urine samples. But employers and the public at large have a _____ in being sure that those responsible for the public's safety are not under the influence of _____ drugs that might interfere with performance. The public might also be more willing to trust organizations whose rules and regulations suggest a desire for complete _____.

Copyright © Cengage Learning. All rights reserved.

♦ **TEST 2**   **Analyzing Arguments**

DIRECTIONS   Read each argument and answer the questions that follow by filling in the blanks or circling the letter (or letters) of the correct response. *Note*: The author may or may not respond to opposition. The argument may or may not include an error. Then again, it may include more than one error.

1. Kids and Sports

1   For many parents, competitive team sports like Little League Baseball and Peewee Football are an essential part of childhood. Thus parents are anxious for their kids to try out for and "make the team." Supposedly, competitive sports build physical strength. Even more important—or so the argument goes—playing competitive sports early on in childhood builds character. Still, parents intent on making sure their kids learn how to compete might want to rethink the notion that sports in which somebody has to win or lose are important to a young child's development. Competitive sports for preteens have some important disadvantages; these disadvantages need to be considered before parents push kids onto a playing field where the winner takes all.

2   Here's one thing that should be considered: Competitive sports can unduly stress a child's still-developing body. Football, basketball, baseball, and even tennis are physically very demanding. They put a heavy strain on the body. This is particularly true when muscles and bones are still developing. Now, a ten-year-old who is just playing for the fun of it will probably not repeat a movement or motion that hurts, but what if that same child is playing for a trophy? Is he or she going to stop throwing that tough-to-hit curve ball just because there is a little pain involved? It's not likely.

3   Unfortunately, the end result can be lifelong damage to a shoulder or an arm. Thomas Tutko, author of *Winning Is Everything and Other American Myths*, argues that kids should not be playing physically demanding sports before the age of fourteen. From Tutko's perspective, playing competitive sports before that age is simply too "traumatic," both physically and psychologically.

4   In his book *No Contest: The Case Against Competition*, author and researcher Alfie Kohn emphasizes that the psychological effects of competitive sports on those still too young to play them may be worse than the physical injuries that can ensue. Kohn's book summarizes the results of several hundred studies focusing on the effects of competition both on and off the playing field. Whether in the context of sports or the classroom, Kohn contends that competition "undermines self-esteem, poisons our relationships, and holds

Copyright © Cengage Learning. All rights reserved.

us back from doing our best." Clearly, Kohn would not support the notion of competition as a character builder for children. If anything, he sees it as a character destroyer, even if those competing are grown-ups.

5   To be fair to those who insist there's no point to playing basketball, football, or baseball unless you keep score, these are games where the score counts. However, the position argued here is not that competitive sports should be abandoned; rather, they should be postponed until the child is ready to be not just a winner but a loser as well. A fifteen-year-old is probably able to accept the simple fact that, at some time in life, everyone loses at something. But does a nine-year-old have to learn this lesson? In their early years, kids should concentrate on achieving their personal best. Are they running faster, jumping higher, or throwing faster than they did the last time around? Those are the questions they should be asking themselves, not who won and who lost.

1. What is the author's point?

_____

_____

2. Identify the two reasons used to support that point.

a. _____

_____

b. _____

_____

3. Does the author respond to any opposing point of view? _____ If so, fill in the blanks that follow.

Opposition   _____

Response   _____

_____

4. In responding to the opposition, does the author reveal excessive bias? _____ Please explain your answer.

_____

_____

Copyright © Cengage Learning. All rights reserved.

5. Circle the appropriate letter or letters to indicate any errors in the author's argument.

a. irrelevant reason

b. circular reasoning

c. hasty generalization

d. unidentified or inappropriate expert

e. unidentified or dated research

f. no errors

2. Banning Peanuts from Our Schools

1 There was a time when the peanut butter and jelly sandwich was a staple of the school lunchbox. It was often the one food that fussy children would willingly eat. Parents were grateful it existed, even if they personally found the combination distasteful. The popularity of peanut butter and jelly sandwiches, however, is a thing of the past as schools from New York to California have stopped serving them in the cafeteria. Many school officials have even asked parents not to put peanut products of any kind into their kids' lunches.

2 If the ban on peanuts sounds silly to you, then you may not know an important fact: Based on 2000 U.S. Census data, the Food Allergy and Anaphylaxis[†] Network (FAAN) estimates that 1 in every 125 children is affected by peanut allergy. Other studies also strongly indicate that the number of children with allergies is increasing at alarming rates. Dr. Paula Prentiss suggests that the current figures are even higher than those indicated by the 2000 census data. The need for a ban on peanuts in the schools is not a trivial issue. It's a matter of life or death.

3 In May 2010, seventeen-year-old Mia Aquino of California died after she unknowingly ate peanut butter at her senior prom. She is not the first young person to die as a result of ingesting the nuts her body could not tolerate. The volunteer group Washington Feast, which disseminates information about food allergies, formed after ten-year-old Kristine Kastner of Mercer Island, Washington, died from anaphylactic shock. Kastner went into shock after eating a chocolate chip cookie that had finely minced peanuts in it. The reality is that children can and do die if they unwittingly ingest peanut products. It's also true that allergies to peanuts are among the most dangerous and deadly. That's because the allergic reaction almost

---

[†]anaphylaxis: hypersensitivity to a foreign substance that, in some cases, can result in death.

Copyright © Cengage Learning. All rights reserved.

always involves breathing problems. Neither parents nor educators can afford to take the chance that a child might unknowingly ingest peanuts at school.

4   Critics of the ban, among them some members of FAAN, worry that the peanut ban pits parent against parent, especially when desperate parents reduce the issue to "Which is more important, my kid's life or your kid's peanut butter and jelly sandwich." Opponents of the ban argue that there are other ways to handle the problem. They focus on studies suggesting that self-management on the part of the child—along with separate lunch zones for kids with allergies—can effectively protect children with allergies.

5   Such suggestions, however, overlook a crucial point. Kids don't always do what they are told. While the 2006 Food and Allergy Labeling Consumer Protection Act (FALCPA) makes it possible for a seven-year-old to read labels identifying allergens in products, not all kids are going to bother, despite parental warnings.

6   Likewise, tell kids to stay in one area of the cafeteria while avoiding another, and there's a good chance they will do the exact opposite. Thus if peanuts in any form are allowed in school, there's always the possibility that a child with an allergy will ingest a snack that might prove deadly. Naturally, a child allergic to peanuts is not going to bite into a peanut butter and jelly sandwich. However that same child might well munch on a chocolate chip cookie containing peanuts, not realizing nuts are in the cookie.

7   Parents of children allergic to peanuts are aware that many people do not want peanut products banned from schools. One of those parents is Mark LoPresti of Grand Island, New York. LoPresti's son is severely allergic to peanuts, and the father is fiercely determined that peanuts must be banned from his son's school. As LoPresti puts it, "I'm not going to sacrifice my son's life for the right to have a peanut butter sandwich." It's hard not to sympathize with that point of view. When it comes to the ban on peanut products in schools, an old adage seems to apply: "It's better to be safe than sorry."

1. What is the author's point?

_____

_____

Copyright © Cengage Learning. All rights reserved.

2. Identify the reason used to support that point.

_____

_____

3. Does the author respond to any opposing point of view? _____ If so, fill in the blanks that follow.

Opposition _____

_____

Response _____

_____

4. In responding to the opposition, does the author reveal excessive bias? _____ Please explain your answer.

_____

_____

5. Circle the appropriate letter or letters to indicate any errors in the author's argument.

a. irrelevant reason

b. circular reasoning

c. hasty generalization

d. unidentified or inappropriate expert

e. unidentified or dated research

f. no errors

Copyright © Cengage Learning. All rights reserved.

▶ **TEST 3**   **Analyzing Arguments**

DIRECTIONS   Read each argument and answer the questions that follow by filling in the blanks or circling the letter of the correct response. *Note*: The author may or may not respond to opposition and the argument may or may not include an error.

1. ## Plagiarism Should Not Be the Wave of the Future

1   Only a modern-day Rip Van Winkle could have missed the fact that digital technology has made it a whole lot easier to plagiarize. As a 2010 *New York Times* article expressed it in the title of an article on the subject, "Plagiarism Lines Blur for Students in Digital Age." The article goes on to say what many instructors on college campuses have noted: A disturbing number of students seem to think it is acceptable to "write" a paper by pulling up several websites on the same topic and then cutting and pasting together sentences or entire paragraphs drawn from the different sites. Even worse, there are signs that this trend is on the rise. According to surveys taken by the Center for Academic Integrity, the number of students who think cutting and pasting from sites on the Web is serious cheating has declined markedly in only a few short years. A few years ago, 34 percent considered it serious. Now only 29 percent do.

2   Perhaps what's even more disturbing about the article than the report of those declining numbers is the empathic understanding some educators have exhibited toward plagiarizing. A University of Notre Dame anthropologist, Susan D. Blum, makes it sound as if students' tendency to lift other people's work and call it their own was a natural outgrowth of the new technology. She writes, "Today's students stand at the crossroads of a new way of conceiving texts and the people who create them and who quote them." From her perspective, "our notion of authorship and originality was born, it flourished, and it may be waning."

3   Professor Blum's words have a nice ring to them. Viewed from this perspective stealing someone else's words and ideas can almost be labeled "progress." We are, it seems, moving away from individualism into some new state of mind, where everything is shared and no one is seen to be making any original contributions. But as my grandmother liked to say, sometimes a lot of schooling just makes people dumber.

4   Professor Blum's ridiculously charitable point of view completely ignores the fact that most people who write—and I mean really write, not just cut and paste what other people have written—expend enormous amounts of time, energy, and anguish trying to find the right words to express their

Copyright © Cengage Learning. All rights reserved.

thoughts. For someone to come along and use those same words to express the same ideas, *without* sharing any of the time, energy, and anguish seems like intellectual exploitation. It flouts a basic rule of fairness, which goes something like this: If you didn't do the work, you don't get the reward.

5   Fortunately, there's at least one student out there (undoubtedly, there are many more) who recognizes that the source from which you plagiarize doesn't change a basic truth: If you copy words from a book or the Web, it's still intellectual theft. Writing in her school newspaper, the *Indiana Daily Student*, senior Sarah Wilensky perfectly expressed what many people feel about the increasingly popular notion that there is no such thing as originality, that everyone is free to copy the words and ideas of others without any attribution. In an editorial titled "Generation Plagiarism," Wilensky wrote that "technology hasn't changed one relatively, non-controversial societally held moral: stealing the words and ideas of others is wrong and cannot be permitted." She then goes on to say that instructors and teaching assistants would do well to give a "big old F" every time they wondered about the source of a paragraph or passage.

6   While a failing grade for just the suspicion of plagiarism seems unduly harsh, it's probably true that students would get the message rather quickly if their cut and paste papers were repeatedly challenged. Instructors could follow up on their suspicions by quizzing students about passages that sound like they came from a source other than the person whose name appears on the paper. Instructors should also consider using plagiarism-detecting software from online firms like Turnitin, which studies show has a good track record when it comes to identifying plagiarized passages. They could give students who plagiarized once a chance to rewrite the paper. But if they got caught a second time, they would get the "big old F" Ms. Wilensky rightly recommends.

1. What is the author's point?

_____

_____

2. Identify the two reasons used to support that point.

a. _____

_____

b. _____

_____

Copyright © Cengage Learning. All rights reserved.

3. Does the author respond to any opposing point of view? _____ If so, fill in the blanks that follow.

Opposition _____

_____

Response _____

_____

4. In responding to the opposition, does the author reveal excessive bias? _____ Please explain your answer.

_____

_____

_____

5. Circle the appropriate letter or letters to indicate the presence or absence of errors in the author's argument.

a. irrelevant reason

b. circular reasoning

c. hasty generalization

d. unidentified or inappropriate expert

e. unidentified or dated research

f. no errors

2. Protecting Our Children from Pornography

1 The Children's Internet Protection Act (CIPA) requires schools and libraries to have in place software filters that block computer access to sites featuring obscenity or pornography and considered harmful to minors. Libraries or schools that do not have such filters in place cannot participate in the federal E-rate program, which offers affordable technology for schools and libraries.

2 This legislation appears so eminently sensible. It seems almost impossible that anyone would quarrel with it. Yet, in fact, when CIPA was first proposed there was immediate opposition from the American Civil Liberties Union and, in particular, the American Library Association. Stranger still, a lower court actually sided with the American Library Association in a suit challenging the constitutionality of applying CIPA to libraries.

Copyright © Cengage Learning. All rights reserved.

3   Fortunately, on June 23, 2003, the Supreme Court struck down the lower court's ruling. But even though the issue has come to a legal resolution, and CIPA is now the law of the land, the question remains: How is it that sensible people in the past, and in the present, can challenge legislation that does nothing more than protect innocent children?

4   Practically all of our nation's public libraries now offer Internet access. Thanks to that access, any twelve-year-old—unless filters are in place—can reach sites featuring hardcore sex scenes. Even worse, kids can access chatrooms where they could make contact with sex offenders or child molesters. Children should not be exposed to such websites or chatrooms. As Dr. Melanie Powers has pointed out, even one experience with a pornographic site can irreparably damage a child's psyche. As proof of her claim, she cites a ten-year-old boy who became addicted to pornography after one experience viewing Internet porn. Isn't this evidence enough to prove the dangers of letting children have unfettered Internet access?

5   Opponents of the filters on library computers argue that they also block access to constitutionally protected free speech and unfairly infringe on the right of adults to access information not considered illegal in any way. But this complaint is sheer nonsense. Adults who want access to sites filtered out by the software can ask that it be temporarily dismantled. This is a right that is actually guaranteed by the CIPA legislation.

6   Libraries routinely act the role of censor when they refuse to stock their shelves with pornographic books, magazines, or videos, and you won't find copies of *Hustler* or *Penthouse* tucked away in the magazine rack of your local library. Nor for that matter will you find a copy of *Deep Throat* in the video department. Yet no one claims that this act of censorship infringes on the right to free speech. Why shouldn't the same principle apply to the Internet? Libraries don't stock pornography; therefore, why shouldn't they exclude pornographic sites from their offerings to the public?

7   Our libraries need to be open to everyone. But by allowing children access to any website available on the Internet, we are turning our libraries into adult bookstores and doing what real adult bookstores cannot do for fear of legal retribution. Libraries that don't use software filters are exposing vulnerable children to pornographic material that might well do them terrible, even deadly, harm. (Sources of information: www.net/services/cipa; www.cnn.com/2003/law/06/24/scotus.internetporn.library.)

1. What is the author's point?

_____

_____

Copyright © Cengage Learning. All rights reserved.

2. Identify the two reasons used to support that point.

   a. _____

   _____

   b. _____

   _____

3. Does the author respond to any opposing point of view? _____ If so, fill in the blanks that follow.

   Opposition _____

   _____

   Response _____

   _____

4. In responding to the opposition, does the author reveal excessive bias? _____ Please explain your answer.

   _____

   _____

5. Circle the appropriate letter or letters to indicate the presence or absence of errors in the author's argument.

   a. irrelevant reason

   b. circular reasoning

   c. hasty generalization

   d. unidentified or inappropriate expert

   e. unidentified or dated research

   f. no errors

Copyright © Cengage Learning. All rights reserved.

Copyright © Cengage Learning. All rights reserved.

▶ **TEST 4**   **Recognizing Excessive Bias**

> **DIRECTIONS**   Circle the appropriate letter to indicate how an author reveals excessive bias.

1. Every five to ten years, it seems that someone decides that the Food and Drug Administration (FDA) is not doing its job, and currently there are, once again, calls for reform. This time, three former secretaries of the Department of Health and Human Services have created what they call the Coalition for a Stronger FDA, an organization demanding agency reform. The goal of the group is to spend more taxpayers' money to increase food inspections and give the agency more regulatory authority. One of the group's spokespeople, Dr. David A. Kessler, a former FDA commissioner, bluntly says, "Our food safety system is broken." The question that has to be asked, though, is this: If the food safety system was so bad, why didn't Dr. Kessler fix it when he was commissioner? All too often, political officials, once they are out of the limelight, look for causes that will help them recover the public's attention, and that's what David Kessler is doing. Besides, why would anyone listen to a man famous for his lack of self-control? David Kessler's binge eating has made his weight fluctuate wildly from 160 to 230 pounds. He should reform himself before he starts trying to fix our food system.

   The author reveals excessive bias by
   a. hurling insults.
   b. using slippery slope thinking.
   c. launching a character attack.

2. **Who Goes Free Next, Charles Manson?†**

   1   In May 2007, Jack Kevorkian, the advocate for assisted suicide, was released from prison after serving eight years of his ten- to twenty-five-year sentence for second-degree murder. While it is true that Dr. Kevorkian is seventy-nine years old and in poor health, it is also true that releasing him from prison sets a very bad example for all those who believe that assisted suicide is not murder. Currently, Oregon is the only state in the country that allows terminally ill patients to ask for and get what are, in fact, lethal amounts of medication. Most other states have rejected such legislation because they

   ---

   †The title is an allusion to Charles Manson: a convicted killer, who slaughtered innocent people for the thrill of it.

do not want to encourage assisted suicide. Yet in letting Dr. Kevorkian leave prison early, the state of Michigan, where Dr. Kevorkian was incarcerated, suggests precisely that, that helping people commit suicide is not a crime deserving the severest possible penalty. What the shortening of Dr. Kevorkian's prison term does is open the door for more people to follow in his footsteps, as indeed they will. After all, what is eight years to a fanatic committed to the belief that people have the right to choose the moment in which they die?

2   Given the reduction of Dr. Kevorkian's sentence, it would not be surprising to find more states allowing physician-assisted suicide. Once the idea of helping the terminally ill end their lives seems an acceptable and penalty-free practice, the time will quickly come when it's easier to argue that those on life support should be taken off, even if they have not, prior to being hospitalized, indicated that they refuse all attempts to keep them alive by artificial means.

The author reveals excessive bias by

a. hurling insults.

b. using slippery slope thinking.

c. launching a character attack.

3. Comparing Apples and Oranges

1   Race-car driver Danica Patrick is often compared to Janet Guthrie, the first woman to ever race in the Indianapolis 500. Both women, we are told, shattered conventional notions about women not having enough nerve or determination to make it in the world of racing. Yet such silly, uninformed comparisons are both misguided and misleading. More to the point, they do Guthrie a terrible disservice. What Patrick, a spoiled diva with a vulgar strain of exhibitionism, faces in the world of racing is nothing compared to the prejudice and discrimination that confronted Guthrie at every turn.

2   Guthrie came to racing in the 1970s when male drivers didn't even bother to hide their disdain for women. Racing legend Bobby Unser publicly proclaimed his contempt, saying, "I could take a hitchhiker, give him a Corvette from the showroom, and teach him to drive faster than Janet Guthrie."

3   In addition to insults from other drivers, Guthrie also had to contend with organized protests against her very presence in the lineup. But

Copyright © Cengage Learning. All rights reserved.

she didn't give up; she just kept on coming until her presence was accepted and her ability acknowledged. And she never used her sexuality to get herself accepted or noticed. That's something no one in his or her right mind would say about Patrick, who first got the public's attention by posing in a bikini.

The author reveals excessive bias by
a. hurling insults.
b. using slippery slope thinking.
c. launching a character attack.

Copyright © Cengage Learning. All rights reserved.

▶ **TEST 5**   **Taking Stock**

> **DIRECTIONS**   Read the passage. Then answer the questions by filling in the blanks or circling the letter of the correct response.

Identity Theft

1   In the spring of 2010, I decided to clean out piles of old files that had been building up in my office and collecting dust. For once I actually acted on the decision to get rid of old papers, notes, and letters that I hadn't look at in years. Everything that had been piling up for a decade, maybe more, got dumped into the trash. I was enormously pleased with myself. Unfortunately, I was a good deal less pleased eight weeks later when the calls started coming in about unpaid cell phone and credit card bills. Thanks to my dumping of documents without shredding them first, I had become the victim of a crime that increases with each passing year— identity theft. This is a problem that needs to be addressed at both federal and state levels, but the potential victims also have to take steps to protect themselves.

2   Stealing someone's identity is not all that difficult. Thieves just need to get their hands on an individual's name, Social Security number, and date of birth—the required information for getting credit. While increasingly criminals get this information off the Internet, they also rely heavily on low-tech methods like searching through trash deposited outside for pickup.

3   The trash is a gold mine for documents containing personal information, and many identity thieves go "dumpster-diving" in search of discarded tax forms, legal documents, and hospital records. (That's how my identity got stolen.) Others rob postal drop boxes to get information from correspondence. Some set up bogus websites that lure victims into providing personal data. Still others pay company employees to steal customers' records. As one identity thief put it, "All you need is some idiot, some young kid working at a hospital, or bank, who's not happy with his job, who's not making enough money. He'll sell you Social Security numbers." After gathering the necessary details, an identity thief can apply for a credit card. He or she can even list his or her own name as an additional cardholder on the account. When the cards arrive, the thief goes on a spending spree.

4   The growing number of identity theft crimes is having severe consequences for both businesses and individuals. The Federal Trade

Copyright © Cengage Learning. All rights reserved.

Commission (FTC) estimates that identity theft costs *billions of dollars* annually. Because federal law protects them, consumers are usually not responsible for thieves' purchases. However, even if cardholders' liability is only $50, they may still be forced to spend thousands more to undo the damage to their credit histories. Most victims of identity theft have to devote countless hours sorting out the various fraudulent bills, dealing with angry creditors, and restoring their reputations as trustworthy consumers.

5   Businesses and government agencies have tried to combat this problem in a number of ways. Congress has made identity theft a separate crime. The FTC created and maintains an identity theft database that provides information to law-enforcement agencies about perpetrators, victims, and potential witnesses. The three major credit-reporting companies—Equifax, Experian, and TransUnion—have begun sharing fraud notifications with each other. In addition, some state legislators are trying to pass new laws to limit the appearance of Social Security numbers on identification cards and other public documents. They are also seeking to double the maximum prison time, from ten to twenty years, for identity theft.

6   However, almost everyone involved agrees that not enough is being done. Individuals and businesses criticize law-enforcement agencies for letting jurisdiction issues hamper investigations and for focusing only on the larger cases while letting the smaller ones languish. As security issues analyst Avivah Litan points out, fewer than 1 in 700 instances of identity theft ends with the offender's conviction. Therefore, says Litan, many thieves have learned that identity theft is a "lucrative, low-risk crime."

7   Others, in contrast, blame organizations for not doing more to safeguard the information they collect when consumers pay with credit cards. Hospitals and universities, for example, aren't required by federal law—as financial services and insurance companies are—to protect information. Still others blame credit card companies for their lax security practices. According to Ed Mierzwinski of the U.S. Public Interest Research Group, "There's so much money to be made that [credit card] companies don't care if they lose some money to identity theft." As a result, says Mierzwinski, "They don't have passwords that are changed often enough. They don't have audit trails,[†] . . . and they make credit too easy to get."

[†]audit trails: lists of documents that would allow the company to trace illegal credit back to the thief.

Copyright © Cengage Learning. All rights reserved.

He also criticizes the U.S. Congress, which "has made identity theft a crime for the criminal, but it hasn't gone after the companies who aid and abet identity theft."

8 Then, too, consumers themselves contribute to the problem. The average American uses several cards and carries an average of $8,000 in credit card debt from month to month. According to the American Bankruptcy Institute, over 1 million people filed for bankruptcy in just the first nine months of 2009. Heavy credit card debt contributed to the bankruptcies in the majority of cases. Clearly, people are living well beyond their means. Many of them are teetering on the brink of financial disaster.

9 Still, consumers can take a few steps to protect themselves. For instance, if your Social Security number appears on your driver's license, have the state issue an alternate number. Also, don't print your Social Security number on checks, and do not share it with anyone unless absolutely necessary.

10 Rip up the credit card solicitations you receive in the mail so that no one can get them from the trash and fill them out. Before throwing them away, shred all documents that contain vital personal information. Obtain a copy of your credit report at least once a year to check for suspicious activity. Don't leave mail in your mailbox with the red flag up. As FTC Identity Theft Program manager Joanna Crane says, "To prevent [identity theft] from ever happening at all, you have to be extremely vigilant." (Sources of quotations and statistics: Stephen Mihm, "Dumpster-Diving for Your Identity," *New York Times Magazine*; www .consumeraffairs.com/news04/2009/10/one_million_bankruptcies.html.)

1. In your own words, what is the main idea of the entire reading?

_____

_____

2. Which statement best sums up the main idea of paragraph 2?

   a. Dumpsters contain all the information an identity thief needs to commit crimes.

   b. It is relatively easy to steal identities.

   c. People can protect themselves from identity thieves in a number of ways.

   d. Credit cards are much too easy to obtain.

Copyright © Cengage Learning. All rights reserved.

3. The following statement illustrates what phrase from paragraph 2? "The trash is a gold mine for documents containing personal information, and many identity thieves go 'dumpster-diving' in search of discarded tax forms, legal documents, and hospital records."

_____

4. Dumpster-diving is an example of a(n)
   a. simile.
   b. metaphor.
   c. allusion.

5. In paragraph 5, the phrase "this problem" in sentence 1 is a stand-in for what phrase? _____

6. Which pattern or patterns organize the details in paragraph 4?
   a. definition
   b. simple listing
   c. comparison and contrast
   d. cause and effect
   e. classification

7. What conclusion follows from the reading?
   a. The author considers identity theft a difficult problem that has no solution.
   b. The author was once a victim of identity theft.
   c. Currently, the best hope for avoiding identity theft is in the hands of the consumer rather than with the government or legal system.

8. In paragraph 8, the author suggests that American consumers are part of the problem because they are so deeply in debt. This criticism reflects what error in logic?
   a. circular reasoning
   b. slippery slope thinking
   c. irrelevant evidence

Copyright © Cengage Learning. All rights reserved.

9. From the information in paragraph 10, a reader might logically draw the conclusion that Joanna Crane

   a. believes very little can be done to stop identity theft.

   b. would support laws that make credit much harder to get.

   c. would probably agree that every business and household should have a paper shredder.

10. The author's purpose is

   a. to inform.

   b. to persuade.

   The author's tone is

   a. neutral.

   b. concerned.

   c. disgusted.

   d. optimistic.

Copyright © Cengage Learning. All rights reserved.

Putting It All Together

The readings that follow give you a chance to review everything you have learned in Chapters 1 through 10. However, even more than in the previous readings (pp. 312–38), the emphasis here is on drawing conclusions and developing your own point of view.

© Ulrich Flemming

◆ **READING 1**   Are Today's Students Lacking in Empathy?

Laraine Flemming

Looking Ahead   Labeling and analyzing young adults in their teens and twenties is something of a spectator sport among members of the media. Every generation seems to get a nickname, from Bobby Soxers[†] to Generation X to the Me Generation—along with a few characteristics that supposedly typify behavior and attitudes. Now there's even a study that allegedly proves what the label Me Generation implies: Today's young people have little interest in anyone except themselves.

Getting Focused   Any time the title is a question, reading for the answer is absolutely essential.

1   According to a study presented at the 2010 meeting of the Association for Psychological Science, today's college students are not as empathetic as college students of the 1980s and 1990s. The lead researcher on the study, Dr. Sara Konrath, who specializes in issues related to self-esteem and narcissism, says that "college kids today are about 40 percent lower in empathy than their counterparts of twenty or thirty years ago, as measured by standard tests of the personality trait."

2   Konrath and two University of Michigan students, graduate student Edward O'Brien and undergraduate Courtney Hsing, conducted what is called a *meta-analysis*—that is, they looked at 72 different studies of 14,000 American college students carried out between 1979 and 2009. The trio also looked at representative samples of the population queried about their views concerning young people of college age. Their goal in this separate but related study was to determine how others viewed today's young people. The results of the group's analysis were not especially heartening from either perspective.

3   In contrast to students in the late 1970s, today's college students were much less likely to agree with statements like the following: "I sometimes try to understand my friends better by imagining how things look from their perspective"; "I often have tender, concerned feelings for people less fortunate than I"; and "I try to look at everybody's side of a disagreement before I make a decision." Based on negative responses to these and similar statements, Konrath concluded that empathy among college-age kids was on the decline: "We found the biggest drop in empathy after the year 2000. College kids

---

[†]Bobby Soxers was the nickname for teenagers in the 1940s.

Copyright © Cengage Learning. All rights reserved.

today are about 40 percent lower in empathy than their counterparts twenty or thirty years ago, as measured by standard tests of this personal trait."

4   The researchers had multiple theories as to why this apparent drop in empathy might be occurring. One researcher, Edward O'Brien, pointed to the possibility that social media might be having an effect. "The ease of having friends online might make people more likely to just tune out when they don't feel like responding to others' problems, a behavior that could carry over online." O'Brien also suggested that "college students today may be so busy worrying about themselves and their own issues, they don't have time to spend empathizing with others."

5   Another culprit from O'Brien's point of view was students' "over-inflated expectations of success, borne of celebrity 'reality shows.'" College students who see themselves engaged in a no-holds-barred fight for the most exciting jobs available—which is the theme of numerous reality shows—are unlikely to spend much time thinking about others, except to figure out how they can beat out those others in their pursuit of success.

6   Like O'Brien, Dr. Konrath also posited a reason. But she didn't finger social media or reality shows as much as video games, with their emphasis on murder and mayhem. As she expressed it, "This generation grew up with video games, and a growing body of research, including work done by my colleagues at Michigan, is establishing that exposure to violent media numbs people to the pain of others."

7   As for how the current crop of college students [is] seen by others, the results of the researchers' analysis complemented the studies of the students themselves. Konrath explained that people in general did not consider today's college students to be members of the helpful generation: "Many people see the current group of college students—sometimes called Generation Me—as one of the most self-centered, narcissistic, competitive, confident, and individualistic in recent history." Exactly how people arrived at this determination of youthful character was not clear from accounts of the study results.

8   What was clear, though, was that the media response to the empathy study resembled trout spotting bait: They swallowed it whole. Just about every account treated the study as empirical proof, or hard evidence, of kids' selfishness. In fact, when the study first came out, no one in the traditional media raised any critical questions about its methodology. For instance, might kids who grew up watching the ironic humor of *Seinfeld* be less inclined to say yes to questions that so obviously patted themselves on the back, questions like "I often have tender, concerned feelings for people less fortunate than I"?

Copyright © Cengage Learning. All rights reserved.

9   Might the results have been different if today's students were asked, "In the last week, have you posted on your Facebook page any websites that offer help for people being confronted by tragedy?" or "Have you tweeted any articles that describe social causes you think others should know about?" More specifically, did it occur to anyone at all to question the language of the twenty-year-old questions rather than the character of the twenty-year-old kids?

10   Then there is the larger question of how easy it is to study empathy through questionnaires. Unfortunately, the people who posed this question were not among those working for mainstream publications. The mainstream news outlets generally quoted one another and uniformly portrayed today's young people as navel-gazing narcissists.

11   Bloggers, however, were less inclined to accept the study's findings as fact. One critic on the blog Perverse Egalitarianism made a point it would have been nice to find in, say, a report of the study by MSNBC News: Measuring empathy is not quite so easy as the study suggests. As the post on Perverse Egalitarianism cleverly expressed it, "These efforts to study empathy as though it was a chemical element are quite comical to me. I wonder if someone is working on a precise instrument to measure it—*empathometer*—and whether this technology could be used to assess, for example, full-of-himself-ness?"

12   Yes, social media, video games, and reality shows may well have had an effect on young people's ability to empathize with others. But as of yet, I'm not convinced. I see too many people on Twitter, Digg, and Facebook posting websites and videos about social causes they care about and want to discuss or contribute to. Now, don't tell me they were all born before 1979. (Source of quotations and study description: http://health.usnews.com/health-news/family-health/brain-and-behavior/articles/2010/05/28/todays-college-students-more-likely-to-lack-empathy.html; www.sciencecentric.com/news/10052932-empathy-college.)

Comprehension: Reviewing Concepts and Skills   **DIRECTIONS**   Answer the following questions by circling the letter of the correct response or filling in the blanks.

Main Idea   1. What is the main idea of the reading?

   a. A new study suggesting that today's college students may be less empathetic than college students of an earlier generation has been too easily accepted by the mainstream media.

   b. Today's college students are much less empathetic than they were two decades ago and the rise of social media is to blame.

Copyright © Cengage Learning. All rights reserved.

c. A new study has provided scientific proof for what everyone knows: Today's college students are completely focused on themselves and their own concerns.

d. The media like studies that encourage the tendency to label entire generations.

Using Context and Paraphrasing

2. Based on the context and the definition in the reading, what, in your own words, is a meta-analysis (paragraph 2)?

_____

_____

Repetition and Reference

3. In sentence 2 of paragraph 2, what word or phrase stands in for the names of the researchers? _____

Patterns of Organization

4. The topic sentence in paragraph 4 suggests what pattern of development?

_____

Allusions and Supporting Details

5. The allusion to the comedy *Seinfeld* (paragraph 8) is used to make what point?

_____

_____

www

INTERNET FOLLOW-UP: Is There a Connection Between Video Violence and Lack of Empathy?

Skim at least two or three websites that address the research on whether video violence encourages a lack of sensitivity to others. Then answer this question: Has it been proven that kids who grow up playing video games are likely to show less empathy than kids of previous generations who did not?

_____

_____

_____

_____

_____

_____

Copyright © Cengage Learning. All rights reserved.

Critical Reading: Reviewing Concepts and Skills

Copyright © Cengage Learning. All rights reserved.

DIRECTIONS Answer the following questions by filling in the blanks or circling the letter of the correct response.

Purpose 1. How would you describe the author's purpose?

    a. The author wants to report on a new study of empathy among college students.

    b. The author wants to convince readers not to take the study of declining empathy among college students too seriously.

Drawing Conclusions 2. Based on the quotation that follows, should readers assume that there is definitely a cause and effect relationship between watching a lot of video-game violence and developing emotional numbness to the suffering of others? "This generation grew up with video games, and a growing body of research, including work done by my colleagues at Michigan, is establishing that exposure to violent media numbs people to the pain of others" (paragraph 6). _____

    Please explain your answer.

    _____

    _____

    _____

    _____

   3. For this statement and the study itself to be considered as evidence, what word or phrase should be clearly defined: "College kids today are about 40 percent lower in empathy than their counterparts of twenty or thirty years ago, as measured by standard tests of the personality trait" (paragraph 1)?

    _____

Figurative Language 4. What figure of speech do you see at work in the following sentence: "What was clear, though, was that the media response to the empathy study resembled trout spotting bait: They swallowed it whole" (paragraph 8)? _____

    What point does the figure of speech make?

    _____

    _____

5. What figure of speech do you see at work in the following sentence: "These efforts to study empathy as though it was a chemical element are quite comical to me" (paragraph 11)? _____

What point does the author make with that figure of speech?

_____

Identifying Bias   6. Which statement best describes the author's bias?

a. The author is inclined to strongly agree with the study results about students' lack of empathy.

b. The author is inclined to be suspicious of the study results.

c. It's impossible to find any evidence of bias in either direction.

7. Which statement more accurately describes the author's point of view in this reading?

a. The author favors bloggers over mainstream media as a source of news.

b. When it comes to how the empathy study was reported, the author favors bloggers over mainstream media.

c. The author reveals no preference.

Errors in Reasoning   8. In paragraph 11, the author says, "Bloggers, however, were less inclined to accept the study's findings as fact." What evidence does the author offer to support that generalization? _____

Is the support adequate?_____
Please explain your answer.

_____

_____

_____

Tone   9. How would you describe the author's tone?

a. puzzled

b. neutral

c. cautious

d. skeptical

Copyright © Cengage Learning. All rights reserved.

The author's tone

a. remains the same throughout the reading.

b. shifts from neutral to skeptical.

c. shifts from neutral to puzzled.

Synthesizing
Information

10. What follows is a reading on the attitudes of recent college graduates toward work. Read it and then decide which synthesis statement most effectively combines the points of both readings into a synthesis statement with a persuasive purpose.

Finding the Perfect Job

1   Jeffrey Jensen Arnett is a psychology professor from Clark University who's working on a book entitled *Emerging Adulthood: The Winding Road from the Late Teens Through the Twenties.* Part of Arnett's work on the book involves interviewing hundreds of college students who have graduated or are getting ready to graduate. In those interviews, Arnett discovered that college students are supremely confident about what the future holds for them despite entering a job market in the worst economic downturn since the 1930s. Arnett says that today's graduates believe they are going to get "not just a job but an expression of their identity, a form of self-fulfillment" and they are not about to settle for anything less. From Arnett's perspective, college students are "extraordinarily optimistic" that "bright days are ahead and eventually they will find that terrific job."

2   So convinced are college graduates that their professional future is bright, they are willing to turn down jobs that don't suit their desires. According to the National Association of Colleges and Employers, which annually surveys thousands of college students about their work attitudes and prospects, 41 percent of the job seekers interviewing in 2010 turned down jobs they felt didn't suit them. Instead of taking a job they didn't like, they moved back home with their parents, where they could wait for the right job offer to come along.

3   To their critics, these supremely confident young people are a textbook case of overconfidence, and that may be what will get them into trouble in the long run. Jean Twenge, a professor of psychology at San Diego College and the author of *Generation Me*, argues that such overconfidence is bound to come smack up against life's hard knocks and falter, at which point the confident generation will slide straight into a well of depression and lack the emotional resources to climb out again.

Copyright © Cengage Learning. All rights reserved.

4   Judith Warner, the author of the best-selling book *Perfect Madness: Motherhood in the Age of Anxiety*, has a different take. She believes that the current generation of young people has an emotional resilience that may armor them against the anxiety and fear that dogged other generations faced with life's difficult realities and choices. As she expressed it in an article for *The New York Times Magazine*, today's college students are "not maladapted. . . . On the contrary with their seemingly inexhaustible well of positive self-regard, their refusal to have their horizons be defined by the limitations of our era, they just may bear witness to the precise sort of resilience that all parents, educators and pop psychologists now say they view as proof of a successful upbringing." Could be, and then again maybe not. Only time will tell how this generation fares in the years ahead. (Source of quotations: Judith Warner, "The Why-Worry Generation," *The New York Times Magazine*, May 30, 2010, pp. 11–12.)

Synthesis Statements

a. What "Finding the Perfect Job" and "Are Today's Students Lacking in Empathy?" both suggest is that today's college students consider themselves to be at the center of the universe. It's precisely this attitude that makes them unable to consider the feelings of others and equally unable to develop financial independence from their parents.

b. In contrast to "Finding the Perfect Job," which paints a depressing portrait of how college students view their future, "Are Today's Students Lacking in Empathy?" suggests that young adults today do not necessarily deserve the labels bestowed on them by the media.

c. The readings "Finding the Perfect Job" and "Are Today's Students Lacking in Empathy?" suggest that the attitudes of today's college students cannot be easily pigeonholed as right or wrong, good and bad. How those attitudes or behaviors are viewed depends on who's doing the viewing.

Forming Your Own Opinion

What do you think? Is empathy among the young declining?

Thinking Through Writing

Write a few paragraphs in which you explain why young adults *should* leave home after college and make their own way rather than burdening their parents. Or argue the opposite, that young people who move back in with parents after graduating to wait for the right job to come along are doing the right thing. You can also come up with your own point of view on this topic. Just make sure you mount an argument for it.

Copyright © Cengage Learning. All rights reserved.

◆ **READING 2**   Down with Taxes!

Ann O'M. Bowman and Richard C. Kearney

Looking Ahead   Several readings in this book have addressed the topic of government and how it affects, or can affect, your life. That the form of government we live under has a powerful effect on how we live is never more apparent than when tax time rolls around in April. According to the authors of this reading, taxes are inclined to make many of us irrational. Read what they have to say and see if you agree.

Getting Focused   The preview for this reading says that taxes make people irrational. Read to identify the examples the authors use to prove that point.

1   One of the most difficult decisions for an elected official is to go on record in favor of raising taxes. The political heat can scorch even the coolest incumbent. But when revenues do not equal service costs and citizens do not want to cut services, raising taxes may be the only answer. However, most people do not want higher taxes. This is the familiar **tax-service paradox:**[†] People demand new, improved, or at least the same level of government services but do not want to pay for them through higher taxes.

2   For instance, the people of Washington in their collective wisdom voted in a 1999 constitutional initiative[†] to slice taxes. But the very next year, they passed another initiative to reduce class sizes and boost teacher pay—without, of course, providing any new money. Voters in other states have taken similar actions. As a former legislator put it, "I wouldn't say voters are stupid. But the voter who wants unlimited services also does not want to pay for it. There is a disconnect." Is it any wonder that user charges have become a popular option?

3   The tax-service paradox reflects a growing alienation between government and its citizens. The widespread belief that government at all levels has become too big and wasteful undoubtedly has some basis in fact. The size and responsibility of state and local governments have grown dramatically and waste and inefficiency have sometimes accompanied this growth. But the unwillingness of citizens to accept the inevitable reductions in services that follow tax cuts borders on mass schizophrenia.

[†]paradox: an apparent contradiction that, with thought, reveals an underlying truth, for instance, "Being in prison had made him feel free in a way he had never before experienced." In the reading, a paradox refers to a straightforward contradiction.
[†]The initiative process involves citizens circulating petitions to get new legislation on the ballot so that voters can decide if they want it or not. It is an example of direct democracy, where every vote counts the same. Use of the initiative process originally evolved from an attempt to limit the influence of special-interest groups in state politics.

Copyright © Cengage Learning. All rights reserved.

4   Helping promote the tax-service paradox are the news media, which "commonly paint government with the broad brush of incompetence." Prime-time television news capsules on "how government wastes your money" and typical reporting on actions of states and localities search for and emphasize the negative while ignoring the positive. Government-bashing is a popular talk-radio sport. Meanwhile, state and local government functions have become much more complex and technical, tending to make government more difficult to understand, interact with, and communicate with.

5   State and local governments are responding to this near impasse with outreach efforts designed to educate citizens about what their governments are doing for them and where their tax dollars are going. New York City's website provides personalized tax receipts showing what each citizen's tax dollars paid for. Local governments everywhere are striving to write their annual budgets in reader-friendly formats. . . .

Tax Revolt

6   Tax-payer resentment of property taxes and changes in assessment practices, and the general perception that government is too big, too costly, and too wasteful, first took on a tangible form in 1978 with the passage of Proposition 13 in California.† Today, twenty-seven states have enacted limitations on taxing and spending by slashing personal or corporate income taxes, indexing their income taxes to the cost of living, and cutting the sales tax.

7   In some instances, citizens have taken tax matters into their own hands through the initiative process. In other cases, state legislators jump in front of the parade and cut taxes and spending themselves. The taxpayer revolt continues at a slower pace today. Its legacy, however, remains enormously important. Watchdog organizations such as the Americans for Tax Reform, led by famous taxophobe Grover Norquist, insist that candidates for elective office sign a no-tax pledge. Public officials must work hard to justify tax increases; otherwise, they risk a citizen uprising and perhaps political death.

8   Indeed, the stirrings of new tax revolts are constantly in evidence. The prairie fire of tax revolt is never dead—only smoldering. Responding to citizen pressure, the Florida legislature rolled back property taxes in 2007. Oregon voters fanned the tax-revolt flames in 2003 by soundly defeating a proposal to raise personal and corporate income taxes, choosing instead to accept prisoner releases, layoffs of state troopers, a shortened school year, and other serious budget-balancing measures. In desperation, the state legislature passed a plan to impose a three-year income tax surcharge. At least Beaver State voters acted civilly. Angry protesters in Tennessee once stormed the capitol building, screaming insults and hurling rocks at legislators. . . .

---

†Proposition 13 reduced and placed limits on property taxes.

Copyright © Cengage Learning. All rights reserved.

9   Political and economic consequences of the tax revolt have been much
studied. In many cases, taxation and expenditure limitations (TELS) have made
state and local finance an extraordinarily difficult undertaking: Voters insist on
passing spending mandates for education, law enforcement, or other popular
programs while at the same time tying the hands of legislators with restrictions
on new revenue-raising. This, in turn, can spawn the imposition of new fees
in attempts to gather sufficient funds to pay for essential services. So far, TELS
have not significantly reduced the size and cost of government as had been
advertised. However, TELS have led local governments to depend more on
the states and to greater recognition by public officials of the continuing need
to measure the taxpaying public's pulse on tax issues. (Adapted from Bowman and
Kearney, *State and Local Government*, p. 368.)

Comprehension: Reviewing Concepts and Skills

DIRECTIONS   Answer the following questions by circling the letter of
the correct response or filling in the blanks.

Main Idea   **1.** What is the main idea of the reading?

   a. Tax revolts have a long history in the United States.

   b. Because people don't understand that important public services
   are provided through tax revenues, they keep cutting taxes.

   c. If people would think rationally about what happens when taxes
   are severely reduced or eliminated, they might be less inclined to
   complain about taxes, let alone try to eliminate them completely.

   d. The rebellion against taxes is just another example of America's
   willingness to embrace all kinds of people, including those who
   have no common sense.

Supporting Details   **2.** The state of Washington is mentioned in paragraph 2 in order to
illustrate what main idea?

_____

_____

Repetition and Reference   **3.** In paragraph 5, New York's "personalized tax receipts" are used to
illustrate which phrase?

   a. near impasse

   b. their tax dollars

   c. outreach efforts

   d. annual budgets

Copyright © Cengage Learning. All rights reserved.

4. In paragraph 7, the watchdog group Americans for Tax Reform illustrates what word from the previous sentence?

_____

5. In paragraph 8, what word or phrase stands in for Oregon?

_____

Critical Reading: Reviewing Concepts and Skills

DIRECTIONS Answer the following questions by filling in the blanks or circling the letter of the correct response.

Purpose   1. The purpose of this reading is to
    a. describe the tax-revolt movement.
    b. make readers see the lack of logic behind many acts of tax rebellion.

Fact and Opinion   2. In paragraph 1, when the authors describe the "tax-service paradox" as "familiar," they are conveying
    a. a fact.
    b. an opinion.

Tone   3. What's the tone of this sentence from paragraph 2: "For instance, the people of Washington in their collective wisdom voted in a 1999 constitutional initiative to slice taxes"?
    a. neutral
    b. friendly
    c. sarcastic
    d. angry

4. How would you describe the tone of the entire reading?
    a. neutral
    b. friendly
    c. ironic
    d. critical

Copyright © Cengage Learning. All rights reserved.

Copyright © Cengage Learning. All rights reserved.

Paraphrasing and Figurative Language

5. Please paraphrase this sentence without using any figurative language: "The political heat can scorch even the coolest incumbent" (paragraph 1).

_____

_____

The sentence relies heavily on

a. similes.

b. metaphors.

c. allusions.

6. In what sentence from the reading do the authors again use figurative language that links taxes to heat?

_____

Please paraphrase this sentence without using any figurative language.

_____

_____

_____

7. In paragraph 7, the authors say that sometimes legislators "jump in front of the parade" and lower taxes. What figure of speech is the author using? _____

What point do they make with that figure of speech?

_____

_____

Recognizing Bias

8. How would you describe the author's level of bias?

a. The authors reveal no personal bias.

b. The authors are highly critical of how citizens respond to taxes and tax increases.

c. The authors are sympathetic to the feelings many citizens have about tax increases.

9. Identify one sentence in the first three paragraphs that you think most clearly reveals the authors' bias.

_____

_____

Copyright © Cengage Learning. All rights reserved.

Synthesis Statements

10. What follows below is another reading on the subject of tax revolts in American history. Once you finish the reading, identify the synthesis statement that makes the best connection between the two readings on the subject.

a. Those modern-day rebels who wish to throw off the burden of taxes do so because they are aware that tax rebellions have a long and proud tradition in the United States.

b. Although the authors of "Down with Taxes!" don't spend much time discussing the more rational reasons behind tax rebellions, "America's Early Tax Revolts" suggests that there have been times in the country's history when tax rebellions were not quite so illogical as the authors believe the current ones to be.

c. "America's Early Tax Revolts" illustrates what "Down with Taxes!" never even hints at: Tax rebels of both the past and present have been outraged because it was unclear to them where their money was going. Government spending seemed to offer them few if any benefits.

America's Early Tax Revolts

1 After the American Revolution ended, the country was in debt to those at home and overseas who had helped finance the war. To make good the monies owed, city governments introduced new taxes, most of which fell heavily on the shoulders of poor farmers, many of them veterans who had fought in the Revolutionary War. If the farmers couldn't pay their taxes, their land, crops, and farm animals were seized and sold to raise the money. Infuriated by what they saw as a profound injustice, farmers began to rebel against being taxed. While some tax rebels set fire to courthouses, others sent petitions to the authorities or used the threat of force to prevent trials from getting under way.

2 One major tax revolt was led by Daniel Shays, an ex-soldier who had fought in the battles of Lexington, Bunker Hill, and Saratoga and survived being wounded in action. When Shays couldn't pay his taxes, he was threatened with debtor's prison. Then the Supreme Judicial Court of

Massachusetts met and indicted him and other leaders of the movement for being disorderly and seditious.[†] Shays's response was to organize 1,700 men, who marched to the courthouse with pitchforks and shovels in hand. Shays and his men were not alone in his rebellion, and the newly independent union of colonies began splintering over taxes. In the end, state militias, funded by wealthy merchants, were formed, and the rebellion was crushed. Some tax-revolt leaders were executed but not Shays. He lived out the rest of his days in abject poverty.

3   When two of the country's most famous founding fathers heard of the tax rebellions, they had very different reactions. Thomas Jefferson said, "A little rebellion now and then is a good thing. It is a medicine necessary for the sound health of government. God forbid that we should ever be twenty years without such a rebellion." Samuel Adams's response was not so forgiving: "Rebellion against a king may be pardoned or lightly punished, but the man who dares to rebel against the laws of a republic ought to suffer death."

INTERNET FOLLOW-UP: Whiskey Rebellion
What was the Whiskey Rebellion? How did it get started and how did it end?

www

_____

_____

_____

_____

_____

_____

_____

_____

Thinking Through Writing Write a paragraph in which you explain why people who rebel against paying taxes do (or do not) have your respect.

_____

[†]seditious: inclined to incite rebellion against the state.

Copyright © Cengage Learning. All rights reserved.

◆ **READING 3** Holden Who?

Jennifer Schuessler

Looking Ahead For close to forty years, Holden Caulfield, the unhappy teenage hero of J. D. Salinger's novel *Catcher in the Rye*, was an idol of American teenagers. Kids identified with Holden's status as a lonely outsider disgusted by the money-obsessed culture around him. Holden craved more spiritual satisfactions and kids loved him for that. Or at least they did before the era of Facebook.

Getting Focused The preview of this reading suggests that the character of Holden Caulfield, once widely admired, is losing favor with teenagers today. Read to understand and paraphrase what it is about Holden that an earlier generation admired and the current generation rejects.

1   On Wednesday [June 2009], a federal judge granted a temporary restraining order forbidding publication in the United States of *60 Years Later: Coming Through the Rye*, a takeoff on—J. D. Salinger's† lawyers say rip-off of—*The Catcher in the Rye*, written by a young Swedish writer styling himself J. D. California. Until the judge makes her final ruling, Mr. Salinger's fans will be spared the prospect of encountering Holden Caulfield, the ultimate alienated teenager, as a lonely old codger who escapes from a retirement home and his beloved younger sister, Phoebe, as a drug addict sinking into dementia.

2   But Holden may have bigger problems than the insults of irreverent* parodists and other "phonies," as Holden would put it. Even as Mr. Salinger, who is 90 and in ailing health, seeks to keep control of his most famous creation, there are signs that Holden may be losing his grip on the kids. *The Catcher in the Rye*, published in 1951, is still a staple of the high school curriculum, beloved by many teachers who read and reread it in their own youth. The trouble is today's teenagers. Teachers say young readers just don't like Holden as much as they used to. What once seemed like courageous truth-telling now strikes many of them as "weird," "whiny" and "immature."

3   The alienated teenager has lost much of his novelty, said Ariel Levenson, an English teacher at the Dalton School on Manhattan's Upper East Side, Holden's home turf. She added that even the students who liked the book tend to find the language—"phony," "her hands were lousy with rocks," the

---

†J. D. Salinger died in June 2010.
*irreverent: not respectful.

Copyright © Cengage Learning. All rights reserved.

relentless "goddams"—grating and dated. "Holden Caulfield is supposed to be this paradigmatic* teenager we can all relate to, but we don't really speak this way or talk about these things," Ms. Levenson said, summarizing a typical response. At the public charter school where she used to teach, she said, "I had a lot of students comment, 'I can't really feel bad for this rich kid with a weekend free in New York City.'"

4   Julie Johnson, who taught Mr. Salinger's novel over three decades at New Trier High School in Winnetka, Ill., cited similar reactions. "Holden's passivity is especially galling and perplexing to many present-day students," she wrote in an e-mail message. "In general, they do not have much sympathy for alienated antiheroes; they are more focused on distinguishing themselves in society as it is presently constituted than in trying to change it."

5   Of course, Holden has always had his detractors. Harcourt Brace, the publishing house that originally solicited *The Catcher in the Rye*, turned it down, saying it wasn't clear whether Holden was supposed to be crazy. Later, highbrow critics like Joan Didion and George Steiner mocked his moral shallowness. . . .

6   But Holden won over the young, especially the 1960s generation who saw themselves in the disaffected preppy, according to the cultural critic Morris Dickstein. "The skepticism, the belief in the purity of the soul against the tawdry, trashy culture plays very well in the counterculture and post-counterculture generation," said Mr. Dickstein, who teaches at the Graduate Center of the University of the City of New York. Today, "I wouldn't say we have a more gullible youth culture, but it may be more of a joining or togetherness culture. . . ."

7   Young people, with their compulsive text-messaging and hyperactive pop culture metabolism, are more enchanted by wide-eyed, quidditch-playing Harry Potter of Hogwarts than by the smirking manager of Pencey's fencing team† (who was lame enough to lose the team's equipment on the subway, after all). Today's pop culture heroes, it seems, are the nerds who conquer the world—like Harry—not the beautiful losers who reject it.

8   Perhaps Holden would not have felt quite so alone if he were growing up today. After all, Mr. Salinger was writing long before the rise of a multibillion-dollar cultural-entertainment complex largely catering to the

---

*paradigmatic: representative, suggesting the pattern for.
†Holden was the manager of the fencing team; Pencey is the prep school he attends in the novel.

Copyright © Cengage Learning. All rights reserved.

taste of teenage boys. These days, adults may lament the slasher movies and dumb sex comedies that have taken over the multiplex, but back then teenagers found themselves stranded between adult things and childish pleasures. As Stephanie Savage, an executive producer of the *Gossip Girl* television series, told National Public Radio last year, in Holden's world "you can either go to the carousel in Central Park, or you can choose the Wicker Bar. You can have a skating date, or you can have a prostitute come up to your hotel room. There's really not that sense of teen culture that there is now."

9   Some critics say that if Holden is less popular these days, the fault lies with our own impatience with the idea of a lifelong quest for identity and meaning that Holden represents. Barbara Feinberg, an expert on children's literature who has observed numerous class discussions of *Catcher*, pointed to a story about a Holden-loving loser in the Onion headlined "Search for Self Called Off After 38 Years." "Holden is somewhat a victim of the current trend in applying ever more mechanistic approaches to understanding human behavior," Ms. Feinberg wrote in an e-mail message. "Compared to the early 1950s, there is not as much room for the adolescent search, for intuition, for empathy, for the mystery of the unconscious and the deliverance made possible through talking to another person."

10   Ms. Feinberg recalled one fifteen-year-old boy from Long Island who told her: "Oh, we all hated Holden in my class. We just wanted to tell him, 'Shut up and take your Prozac.' " (Jennifer Schuessler, "Get a Life, Holden," *New York Times*, June 20, 2009, p, 19.)

INTERNET FOLLOW-UP: Does Holden Have Any Fans Left Under Fifty?

Use the Web to get a sense of whether Holden Caulfield and Salinger's *Catcher in the Rye* have been consigned to the dust bin of literary history by everyone except maybe your parents.

_____

_____

_____

_____

Copyright © Cengage Learning. All rights reserved.

Comprehension: **DIRECTIONS**   Answer the following questions by filling in the blanks
Reviewing or circling the letter of the correct response.
Concepts and Skills

Main Idea   1. What is the connection between the title and the main idea of the
reading?

_____

_____

_____

Context Clues   2. Based on the context, the word *codger* in paragraph 1 refers to
a. a man on the run.
b. an elderly person.
c. a nurse's aid.
d. an ex-soldier.

3. Based on the description of Holden Caulfield as he appears in
60 Years Later: Coming Through the Rye versus the description of
him based on Salinger's book, what would be the best definition for
parodist in the following sentence: "But Holden may have bigger
problems than the insults of irreverent parodists and other 'phonies,'
as Holden would put it" (paragraph 2)?
a. someone who steals the work of others
b. someone who consistently writes sad stories with depressing endings
c. someone who exaggerates a writer's style for comic effect
d. someone who writes comic fiction for adolescents

Supporting Details   4. Why is there a reference to Harry Potter in paragraph 7? What does
the reference contribute to the reading?

_____

_____

_____

Sentence Analysis   5. In paragraph 2, the first sentence is
a. an introductory sentence.
b. a transitional sentence.
c. a topic sentence.

Copyright © Cengage Learning. All rights reserved.

Critical Reading: Reviewing Concepts and Skills

DIRECTIONS Answer the following questions by filling in the blanks or circling the letter of the correct response.

Purpose 1. In this article, the author wants to
   a. tell readers about a shift in the reading tastes of teenagers.
   b. convince readers that teenagers who don't read *Catcher in the Rye* are missing out on a truly great novel.

Evaluating Support 2. Given what you know about using expert opinion, how would you rate the author's use of expert opinion where Julie Johnson (paragraph 4) is concerned?
   a. good
   b. fair
   c. poor

   Please explain your answer.

   _____

   _____

   _____

3. How would you rate the author's use of expert opinion where Barbara Feinberg (paragraph 9) is concerned?
   a. good
   b. fair
   c. poor

   Please explain your answer.

   _____

   _____

   _____

Tone 4. How would you describe the author's tone?
   a. sad
   b. comic
   c. neutral
   d. sarcastic

Copyright © Cengage Learning. All rights reserved.

5. Does the author's tone match her purpose? _____

   Please explain your answer.

   _____

   _____

6. Which statement best describes the author's personal feelings about the change in Holden's popularity?

   a. The author shares the feelings voiced by many of the teenagers quoted and thinks it's about time Holden disappeared from high school curricula.

   b. The author doesn't really understand how today's teenagers could not idolize Holden Caulfield.

   c. It's impossible to determine how the author feels about Holden's failing popularity.

Drawing Inferences and Conclusions

7. In paragraph 9, children's literature expert Barbara Feinberg says that the current response of teenagers to Holden may result from society's tendency to take more "mechanistic approaches" to problems. A mechanistic approach is used in various areas of study to describe responses that are automatic and impersonal. For instance, if your best friend has a cold, you don't give him sympathy, you hand him a bottle of Nyquil. Based on that definition, what specific example of a mechanistic approach to problem solving appears in the reading?

   _____

8. Based on her quote in paragraph 9, how do you think Barbara Feinberg would respond to the study described in Reading 1?

   _____

   _____

   _____

   _____

   _____

Copyright © Cengage Learning. All rights reserved.

9. Based on what the writer tells you, Barbara Feinberg finds modern teenagers' lack of interest in Holden Caulfield to be a

a. positive social change.

b. negative social change.

c. temporary fad that will reverse itself in a few years.

Please explain your answer.

_____

_____

_____

Synthesizing Sources 10. Look over the reading about Nancy Drew on pages 276–78. Then select the statement that best synthesizes ideas in that reading with the one you just completed.

a. Holden Caulfield and Nancy Drew both illustrate how hard it is for a fictional hero or heroine popular among one generation of young people to survive and stay popular with generations that follow.

b. Unlike Nancy Drew, Holden Caulfield's popularity with teenagers did not depend on the historical moment. His popularity survived for generations while hers did not.

c. While Nancy Drew still thrives after more than eighty years on the literary scene, Holden Caulfield may not survive the digital revolution.

Thinking Through Writing Write a paragraph or two in which you describe your favorite fictional hero. He or she can be from a book (comic books count) or a movie. The important thing is for you to explain why you like this fictional character.

Copyright © Cengage Learning. All rights reserved.

◆ **READING 4** Dating Violence

Bryan Strong, Christine De Vault, and Theodore F. Cohen

Looking Ahead Dating couples are expected to show one another mutual affection. What's less expected is that violence would enter the relationship. Tragically, though, violence rears its ugly head much more frequently than one might expect.

Getting Focused The authors suggest that dating violence is a bigger problem than most people realize. Pay close attention every time they offer hard evidence for that claim and highlight the study or statistic mentioned.

 1 The incidence of physical violence and emotional or verbal abuse in dating relationships, including those of teenagers, is alarming. Evidence suggests that it even exceeds the level of marital violence (Lloyd, 1995). One study of relationships among college students found that of the sample of 572, 21% had engaged in "physically aggressive" behavior, acts that included throwing something; pushing, grabbing, or hitting; slapping, kicking, biting, or punching; beating up; choking and threatening to or using a gun or a knife on a partner.

2 Verbal abuse was even more common: 80% acknowledged having been verbally abusive toward a dating partner in the previous twelve months. Verbal abuse consisted of insulting or swearing at a partner, sulking or refusing to talk with a partner, stomping out of the house or room, and saying or doing something to spite a partner (Shook et al., 2000). For both the females and the males, the two variables most strongly associated with verbal aggressiveness were alcohol use three hours before the incident and a childhood history of parent-child aggression.

3 In two studies of undergraduate couples (eighteen through twenty-five years old) in ongoing relationships, Jennifer Katz and colleagues found that one-third to nearly one-half of the students were in relationships in which their partners had acted violently toward them. In both studies, rates at which men and women were victimized were similar, although men experienced higher levels of moderate violence.

4 Dating relationships among high school students are also prone to violence. Reviewing research from the 1980s and 1990s, Susan Jackson, Fiona Dram, and Fred Seymour found that rates of reported violence range from 12% to 59%. A 1997 observational study of high school couples reported that 51% of participating couples displayed some form of aggression, such as shoving or grabbing. In this same study, males were unilaterally violent in 4% of the cases, and females were unilaterally violent in 17%. Both were mutually violent in the remaining 30%.

Copyright © Cengage Learning. All rights reserved.

5   Although some patterns are similar, the issues involved in dating violence appear to be different from those generally involved in spousal violence. Whereas marital violence may erupt over domestic issues such as housekeeping and childrearing (Hotaling and Sugarman, 1990), dating violence is far more likely to be precipitated by jealousy or rejection (Lloyd and Emery, 1990; Makepeace, 1989). For example, one young woman recounted the following incident of her boyfriend's furious treatment after seeing her chat with a group of male friends in front of the school. He was silent until they were home, then:

> He caught me on the jaw, and hit me up against the wall. . . . He picked me up and threw me against the wall and then started yelling and screaming at me that he didn't want me talking to other guys.

6   Although women and men may sustain dating violence at comparable levels, they do not appear to react similarly to it. As in the case of marital violence, women react with more distress than men do to relationship violence, even within mutually violent relationships (Latz, Kuffel, and Coblentz, 2002). They also sustain more physical injuries from dating violence. More surprising is the finding that "partner violence generally is unrelated to decreased relationship satisfaction." One study cited by Katz and colleagues found that more than 90% of adolescents in violent relationships described those relationships as "good" or "very good."

7   Many women leave a dating relationship after one violent incident: others stay through repeated episodes. Women who have "romantic" attitudes about jealousy and possessiveness and who have witnessed physical violence between their own parents may be more likely to stay in such relationships. Women with more "modern" gender-role attitudes are more likely to leave than those with traditional attitudes. Women who leave violent partners cite the following factors in making the decision to break up: a series of broken promises that the man will end the violence, an improved self-image ("I deserve better"), escalation of the violence, and physical and emotional help from family and friends. Apparently, counselors, physicians, and law-enforcement agencies are not widely used by victims of dating violence.

(Adapted from Strong, De Vault, and Cohen, *The Marriage and Family Experience*, pp. 467–68.)

Comprehension: Reviewing Concepts and Skills   **DIRECTIONS**   Answer the following questions by filling in the blanks or circling the letter of the correct response.

Main Idea   1. How would you paraphrase the main idea of this reading?

_____

_____

Copyright © Cengage Learning. All rights reserved.

Supporting Details **2.** The following sentence ends paragraph 3: "In both studies, rates at which men and women were victimized were similar, although men experienced higher levels of moderate violence." The sentence would benefit from a minor detail that clarified what word or phrase in the sentence? _____

Context Clues **3.** Based on the context, what do you think *precipitated* means in the following sentence: "Whereas marital violence may erupt over domestic issues such as housekeeping and childrearing (Hotaling and Sugarman, 1990), dating violence is far more likely to be *precipitated* by jealousy or rejection" (paragraph 5)?

_____

Patterns of Organization **4.** What primary pattern do you see at work in paragraph 5?

_____

5. What primary pattern do you see at work in paragraphs 6 and 7?

_____

Critical Reading: Reviewing Concepts and Skills **DIRECTIONS** Answer the following questions by filling in the blanks or circling the letter of the correct response.

Purpose **1.** What would you say is the authors' purpose?
  a. The authors want to tell readers that dating violence occurs at an alarming rate.
  b. The authors want to persuade readers that dating violence has a number of causes and requires a number of different individual and societal responses if it is to be eliminated in the near future.

Analyzing Evidence **2.** According to the authors, "Evidence suggests that [dating violence] even exceeds the level of marital violence" (paragraph 1). What evidence is provided in the paragraph? _____

Do you consider the evidence adequate? _____
Please explain your answer.

_____

_____

Copyright © Cengage Learning. All rights reserved.

Fact and Opinion **3.** The following statement from paragraph 6: "Although women and men may sustain dating violence at comparable levels, they do not appear to react similarly to it" is

a. a fact.

b. an opinion.

c. a blend of fact and opinion.

Please explain your answer.

_____

_____

_____

Drawing Inferences and Conclusions **4.** In paragraph 6, the authors say that women react to dating violence with more "distress" than men do. What information in the paragraph gives readers a strong clue as to what might well be the implicit cause of women's greater distress?

_____

Analyzing Evidence **5.** In paragraph 6, the authors tell us about a surprising finding: "Partner violence generally is unrelated to decreased relationship satisfaction." What basis for the finding does the paragraph provide? _____ Based on the evidence provided, should you be ready to accept that this finding has a wide or general application? _____

Please explain your answer.

_____

_____

_____

6. Based on what you know about using studies as evidence, how would you rate the authors' use of statistical evidence?

a. good

b. fair

c. poor

Copyright © Cengage Learning. All rights reserved.

Please explain your answer.

_____

_____

_____

_____

_____

Tone   **7.** How would you describe the tone of the authors' writing?

_____

Drawing Inferences   **8.** What makes paragraph 7 different from all the other paragraphs in
and Conclusions   this reading?

_____

_____

_____

9. In paragraph 7, the authors say that women with "romantic" attitudes toward possessiveness and jealousy are more inclined to stay
in abusive relationships. What do they mean by _romantic_ attitudes?

_____

_____

_____

Synthesizing   **10.** The passage that follows, "The Tragedy of Yeardley Love," is excerpted
Sources   from a website called DoSomething.org. The passage discusses the
prevalence of dating violence. However, there is a specific difference
between the authors' discussion in "Dating Violence" and the website
discussion. Identify that difference when you finish reading the passage.

What's the difference in how the writers approach the same topic?

_____

_____

Copyright © Cengage Learning. All rights reserved.

The Tragedy of Yeardley Love

Yeardley Love was an accomplished University of Virginia lacrosse player, and she was a victim of dating abuse [2010]. While her untimely death has gained a lot of attention, she is among many young people who are abused every year in relationships. Women sixteen to twenty-four years old experience the highest percentage of relationship-linked violence. Yeardley's university alone has received reports of over 100 cases of dating abuse in the last decade (and that doesn't include those that stayed silent). The university has responded with a warning—dating abuse can happen to anyone, regardless of status or culture. "The perception often among students is that such violence exists only for unhappy married couples," warned Claire Kaplan, the director of Sexual and Domestic Violence Services at the university. "In reality, [this] affects all types of relationships and all backgrounds and personalities of people." Yeardley's story has shown people that dating abuse can happen anywhere, and you and your peers have the chance to take action against it. (www.dosomething.org/news /victim-sparks-dating-abuse-awareness.)

INTERNET FOLLOW-UP: The Victims of Dating Violence
Use the Web to answer this question: Is violence among dating couples an equal problem for both men and women? Please list some of the websites you checked to find your answer.

_____

_____

_____

_____

Thinking Through Writing The authors of reading 4, "Dating Violence," point out that many of the people in a violent relationship also call the relationship "good." Write a paragraph or two explaining how it's possible that someone in an abusive dating relationship might still call it a "good" relationship.

Copyright © Cengage Learning. All rights reserved.

Acknowledgments

This page constitutes an extension of the copyright page. We have made every effort to trace the ownership of all copyrighted material and to secure permission from copyright holders. In the event of any question arising as to the use of any material, we will be pleased to make the necessary corrections in future printings. Thanks are due to the following authors, publishers, and agents for permission to use the material indicated.

Ronald Bailey: "The Pursuit of Happiness" from *Reason* magazine, December 2000 print edition. Reprinted by permission of *Reason*.

Carol Berkin et al.: *Making America*, 5/E. © 2011 Wadsworth, a part of Cengage Learning, Inc. Reproduced by permission. www.cengage.com/permissions.

Douglas A. Bernstein and Peggy W. Nash: *Essentials of Psychology*, 5E. © 2011 Wadsworth, a part of Cengage Learning, Inc. Reproduced by permission. www.cengage.com/permissions.

Douglas A. Bernstein, Louis A. Penner, Alison Clarke-Stewart, and Edward Roy: *Psychology*, 6E. © 2003 Wadsworth, a part of Cengage Learning, Inc. Reproduced by permission. www.cengage.com/permissions.

Ann O'M. Bowman and Richard C. Kearney: *State and Local Government*, 5E. © 2012 Wadsworth, a part of Cengage Learning, Inc. Reproduced by permission. www.cengage.com/permissions.

Paul S. Boyer et al.: *The Enduring Vision*, pp. 779a–b. Copyright © 2010 Wadsworth, a part of Cengage, Learning, Inc. Reprinted by permission. www.cengage.com/permissions.

Joseph Robert Conlin: *The American Past*, 9E. © 2010 Wadsworth, a part of Cengage Learning, Inc. Reproduced by permission. www.cengage.com/permissions.

Stanley Coren: "Dogs and Humans: How It All Got Started." Reprinted with the permission of The Free Press, a Division of Simon & Schuster, Inc., from *The Intelligence of Dogs: Canine Consciousness and Capabilities* by Stanley Coren. Copyright © 1994 by Stanley Coren. All rights reserved.

Joseph DeVito: From *The Interpersonal Communication Book* 10E. Published by Allyn and Bacon, Boston, MA. Copyright 2004 by Pearson Education. Reprinted by Permission of the publisher.

Harold Evans: From *The American Century* by Harold Evans, copyright © 1998 by Harold Evans. Used by permission of Alfred A. Knopf, a division of Random House, Inc.

Anthony G. Flude: "Internet: 'Pioneers in New Zealand,'" www.ihug.co.nz. Reprinted by permission of Anthony G. Flude.

Tom Garrison: *Essentials of Oceanography*, 5E. © 2009 Brooks/Cole, a part of Cengage Learning, Inc. Reproduced by permission. www.cengage.com/permissions.

Adam Gorlick: "Media multitaskers pay mental price, Stanford study shows," Stanford Report (online). (August 24, 2009). Available at http://news.stanford.edu/news/2009/august24/multitask-research-study-082409.html. Used by permission.

James M. Henslin: *Sociology: Down to Earth Approach*, pp. 48, 197. Copyright © 2008 James M. Henslin. Reproduced by permission of Pearson Education, Inc.

Janet Shibley Hyde: *Understanding Human Sexuality*, p. 524. Copyright © 1994, McGraw-Hill. Reproduced by permission.

Paul Martin Lester: "Photojournalism: An Ethical Approach" by Paul Martin Lester, Cal State University, Fullerton. Reprinted by permission.

G. Tyler Miller: *Living in the Environment*, 16E. © 2009 Brooks/Cole, a part of Cengage Learning, Inc. Reproduced by permission. www.cengage.com/permissions.

G. Tyler Miller and Scott E. Spoolman: *Sustaining the Earth*. Copyright © 2008 Brooks/Cole, a part of Cengage Learning, Inc. Reproduced by permission. www.cengage.com/permissions.

Jeffrey S. Nevid: *Psychology*, 3E. © 2009 Wadsworth, a part of Cengage Learning, Inc. Reproduced by permission. www.cengage.com/permissions.

Mary Beth Norton et al.: *A People and a Nation*. Copyright © 2008. Wadsworth, a part of Cengage Learning, Inc. Reproduced by permission. www.cengage.com/permissions.

William M. Pride, Robert J. Hughes, and Jack R. Kapoor: *Business*, 10E. © 2010 South-Western, a part of Cengage Learning, Inc. Reproduced by permission. www.cengage.com/permissions.

Martin S. Remland: *Nonverbal Communication in Everyday Life*, pp. 255–256. Copyright © 2008. Allyn & Bacon. Reproduced by permission.

Jack Rosenthal: Adapted from "No Docs," *The New York Times Magazine*, August 8, 17, 2008, p. 18. Copyright © 2008 The New York Times Co. All rights reserved. Used by permission.

G. Michael Schenider and Judith Gersting: *Invitation to Computer Science*, 4E, pp. 606–607. Copyright © 2006 Course Technology. Reproduced by permission. www.cengage.com/permissions.

Jennifer Schuessler: "Get a Life, Holden Caulfield" by Jennifer Schuessler from *The New York Times*, June 20, 2009. Copyright © 2009 by The New York Times Co. All rights reserved. Used by permission.

Kelvin Seifert: Adapted from *Lifespan Development*, 2E, pp. 494–495 by Kelvin Seifert. Reprinted by permission of the author.

Bryon Strong and Christine DeVault: *Cengage Advantage Books: The Marriage & Family Experience*, 10E © 2008 Wadsworth, a part of Cengage Learning, inc. Reproduced by permission. www.cengage.com/permissions.

Ashlee Vance: "If Your Password is 123456, Just Make It Hack Me" by Ashlee Vance from *The New York Times*, Technology Section, January 20, 2010. Copyright © 2010 The New York Times Co. Reprinted by permission.

Copyright © Cengage Learning. All rights reserved.

Index

Copyright © Cengage Learning. All rights reserved.

Copyright © Cengage Learning. All rights reserved.

Copyright © Cengage Learning. All rights reserved.

Copyright © Cengage Learning. All rights reserved.